The night was filled with the roar of tank cannon and the hectic rattle of machine gun fire. Grenades exploded and bursts of Russian machine gun fire sprayed the grenadiers who were struggling to recover their former positions. They were able to drive behind the Soviet troops, who had been robbed of their covering armor.

Suddenly three more T-34s appeared. Three hits in rapid succession shook the Tiger. None penetrated, however.

Richter rammed the next round into the chamber of the "eighty-eight." Groschl fired, and a direct hit smashed the closest enemy tank. The others turned away and fled at high speed.

"After them, Holzl!" ordered Bölter.

When the armored duel was over, Bölter had destroyed seven enemy tanks in this one action. . . .

PANZER ACES

Franz Kurowski
Translated by David Johnston

BALLANTINE BOOKS • NEW YORK

A Ballantine Book
Published by The Ballantine Publishing Group
Copyright © 1992 by J. J. Fedorowicz Publishing, Inc.

All rights reserved under International and Pan-American Copyright Conventions. Published in the United States by The Ballantine Publishing Group, a division of Random House, Inc., New York, and distributed in Canada by Random House of Canada Limited, Toronto. Originally published in English in Canada in slightly different form by J. J. Fedorowicz Publishing, Inc.

Ballantine is a registered trademark and the Ballantine colophon is a trademark of Random House, Inc.

www.ballantinebooks.com

ISBN 0-345-44884-7

This edition published by arrangement with J. J. Fedorowicz Publishing, Inc. (www.jjfpub.mb.ca).

Manufactured in the United States of America

First American Edition: February 2002

10 9 8 7 6 5 4 3 2 1

Contents

Introduction

The tracked armored fighting vehicle, or tank, was first used in action by the British army during the Battle of the Somme in July 1916. The British hoped that the new weapon would enable them to break the stalemate of the trench warfare. From the time of their introduction, however, there raged a heated debate as to how tanks should be used—as weapons to escort the infantry, or as independent weapons capable of breaking through the enemy's fixed defenses. For the Germans the appearance of the tank came as a tremendous shock and, despite their best efforts, they lagged well behind the Allies in tank development for the remainder of the war. The tank hadn't played a particularly large role in Germany's defeat, but German soldiers who had experienced a tank attack were convinced otherwise. The Treaty of Versailles denied Germany the right to build or buy tanks, but the leaders of Germany's postwar army, the *Reichswehr*, were determined to pursue the development of the new weapon; in their view, the lack of tanks had been one of the shortcomings of the Imperial Army during the First World War.

1

Generalmajor
Dr. Franz Bäke

**With the 6th Panzer Division in the East and West;
Company Commander during the French Campaign**

On 30 January 1940 the 6th Panzer Division, which had been
formed from the 1st Light Division, left its garrisons in Germany. The division was commanded by *Generalmajor* Kempf,
one of the pioneers of Germany's panzer arm. By 2 February
the division had assembled in the Euskirchen area. The division
headquarters was established in Münstereifel.

In the west, German and French forces still faced each other
across the frontier. The French promise of help to the Poles,
which was to see French forces attack Germany no later than
the beginning of the second week after a German attack on
Poland, had proved to be a pipe dream.

France missed its opportunity to simply overrun Germany's
weakly defended western frontier and end the war in 1939.
When Britain and France declared war, Germany did not have
a single panzer division in the west. With the return of Germany's six panzer divisions from Poland, any chance of a quick
Allied victory disappeared for good.

The core of the new 6th Panzer Division was provided by the
65th Panzer Battalion, commanded by Major Thomas. This
battalion, which had been part of the 1st Light Division, was
joined by the two battalions of the 11th Panzer Regiment,
which was commanded by *Oberst Dipl. Ing.* Wilhelm Phillips.
The two battalions were commanded by Major Stephan and
Major Koll. The period of quiet on the Western Front allowed
the newly formed division to carry out regimental exercises
commencing 18 October 1939.

On 1 March 1940 the 6th Panzer Division was moved into

the Westerwald, where one week later it was incorporated into XXXXI Army Corps under *General der Panzertruppe* Hans-Georg Reinhardt. Also included in XXXXI Corps were the 8th Panzer Division and the 29th Motorized Infantry Division. The corps was one of three assigned to Operation *Sichelschnitt* (Sickle Cut), the German armored thrust through the Ardennes.

XXXXI Corps, together with XIX Army Corps under General Guderian and XIV Army Corps under Gen. Gustav von Wietersheim, made up *Panzergruppe* Kleist. Under the command of *General der Kavallerie* Ewald von Kleist, it was to drive through to the River Meuse. The *Panzergruppe*'s vehicles all wore a large "K."

The *Panzergruppe* faced the difficult task of moving 41,140 vehicles of all types through the Ardennes over only four advance roads, which were also being used by the infantry units.

On 9 May the 6th Panzer Division's 11th Panzer Regiment was moved forward into the Mayen area; the main body of the division was still in the Westerwald, east of the Rhine.

The French campaign began on the morning of 10 May. The 6th Panzer Division moved westwards in four march groups, led by *Oberst* Freiherr von Esebeck, commander of the 6th Rifle Brigade, *Oberst* von Ravenstein, commander of the 4th Rifle Regiment, and *Oberstleutnant* von Seckendorff, commander of the 6th Motorcycle Battalion. The light columns and the combat train were under the command of Major Dr. Topf.

A general halt was ordered when the division came upon units of the 2nd Panzer Division, which were still waiting in their readiness positions. The division was held up for one day and crossed the Luxembourg frontier on 12 May, reaching the Belgian border at 1600.

The division's objective was the Meuse crossing at Monthermé. The battle group commanded by *Oberst* von Esebeck led the way. The division Ia, Maj. Helmut Staedtke, requested "strong air support."

The requested air support arrived, but a unit of HE-111s dropped some of its bombs on the 76th Artillery Regiment's 4th and 8th Batteries, commanded by Major Aschoff and Major Graf respectively. This error resulted in twenty dead and twenty-six wounded, the division's first casualties of the French campaign.

The briefings for the Meuse crossing were conducted by

General Kempf himself. Standing on a hill from which he and his staff could view the approaches to the Meuse and the river itself, he issued the attack orders to his unit leaders and battle group commanders. The assembled officers had a good view of the barbed wire entanglements and rifle pits as well as French artillery positions and bunker installations. Also visible were four armored cupolas on an island in the river.

The first attack went forward that afternoon. The crossing attempt failed, even though the infantry of the 3rd Battalion, 4th Rifle Regiment, received support from the tanks of 1st Company, 11th Panzer Regiment, which had been instructed to eliminate the enemy bunkers with direct fire. Nevertheless, part of the battalion did succeed in crossing the river, thanks to the efforts of its commander, *Oberstleutnant* Höfer.

After darkness fell on 12 May, General Kempf personally committed 1st Battalion, 4th Rifle Regiment, and part of the 65th Panzer Battalion to force a crossing for the remaining units.

"First Company to me!" ordered Kempf. *Oblt.* Dr. Franz Bäke, a still-youthful officer who had seen combat in the First World War, rolled forward in his Czech-built (Skoda) tank and reported to the division commander, who informed him, "We're driving to the Meuse! And as quickly as possible. One of your platoons will lead the way, the rest will follow close behind the infantry. We'll be driving with full lights!"

Dr. Bäke saluted and ordered his 1st Platoon into the lead position. Then the division's second attack force rolled toward the Meuse. On the far side of the river near Monthermé the French defenders suddenly saw a long column of lights moving at high speed toward the position where the River Semois emptied into the Meuse. General Potzert, who was commanding the 102nd French Fortress Division, called out in surprise: "It's a regular torchlight parade. If we had some bombers we could wipe out these attackers completely!"

The same thought had occurred to Dr. Franz Bäke, who was enjoying his first opportunity to lead an armored company into action. During the Polish campaign he had seen the war from the sidelines as battalion adjutant and executive officer. Now he was commanding 1st Company. He was determined to put all he had learned into practice and justify the confidence placed in him by his superiors.

After the war General Kempf wrote that he, too, had been concerned about the possibility of French bomber attacks on his division. As he related to the author: "At the same time I saw in this rapid forward movement the possibility of achieving a crossing with the minimum possible casualties."

Fortunately, the general's concerns were unfounded. As dawn was breaking on 13 May, the *Leutnant* leading the forward platoon of Bäke's company reported: "Before us is the Meuse, *Herr Oberleutnant!*"

Dr. Bäke passed the report on to the general.

"Forward, Bäke! Tanks to the front. Pioneer battalion likewise move forward through the gaps and ready the assault boats."

The mass of PzKfw.35(t) tanks rolled forward. Close behind the 1st Platoon was the general's command vehicle, and behind it the radio vehicle which kept the general in contact with the individual battle groups.

As the sun came up Dr. Bäke could see before him the silvery, shimmering ribbon of the Meuse. The first French guns opened fire from the far side.

"Tanks and assault guns move forward to take out the artillery positions, bunkers, and machine gun positions!"

Close behind the tanks were the mounted pioneers, who were to take the infantry across the river under the covering fire and help capture the village of Monthermé.

The tanks, armed with 3.7cm guns, rolled up the riverbank with the assault guns, which carried a short-barreled 7.5cm gun.

The first burst of machine gun fire smacked into the riverbank below the tanks. "Open fire on the machine gun nest at twelve o'clock!" ordered Dr. Bäke.

Bäke's gunner had already spotted the target. He made a slight correction and fired. The first shell flitted across the stream and struck just below the machine gun position. The second shot was a direct hit, which silenced the enemy gun.

Lined up along the bank, the tanks of Bäke's company opened fire. The assault guns concentrated their fire on the French bunkers, aiming for the embrasures.

While this was going on, the pioneers and infantry were moving down to the edge of the river, carrying their inflatable boats above their heads. The boats splashed into the water and their outboard motors roared to life, driving them toward the center of the stream.

The French shifted their fire onto the boats. One of them took a burst of fire and collapsed. The men inside jumped into the water and swam for the other side.

"Rapid fire on the machine guns!" Dr. Bäke instructed his tank commanders.

The eighteen tanks the company had on hand (four had been left behind with mechanical breakdowns) directed their fire at the French machine guns. Their high-explosive shells blasted away the French camouflage.

The assault guns drove to one side and opened fire on the French bunkers. The crash of gunfire merged with the sound of shells exploding on the far bank.

The assault by the German infantry struck the 42nd *Demi-Brigade* of the 102nd Colonial Division. Isolated French machine guns were still firing from Monthermé. Now that the crossing had succeeded, the tanks and assault guns shifted their fire onto these.

Monthermé was on fire. A short time later signal flares rose into the sky from the edge of the city, indicating to the panzer crews: "We are here!"

The tanks turned their fire once again to the far bank of the Meuse while the infantry moved into Monthermé and occupied the city.

"Everyone across the river through the ford!" ordered General Kempf. The panzers rolled to the shallow crossing point which had been discovered earlier. One strayed from the prescribed route and sunk up to its turret. It was later recovered by a heavy tractor.

General Kempf, who had crossed the river with his troops, placed himself at the head of his division just behind the fast advance detachment and ordered the advance to begin at once. The armored elements quickly won ground toward the west.

The objective was the Mon Idée. Patrols and aerial reconnaissance had determined that the French were preparing to make a stand there. They hoped to employ their artillery and tanks to stop this raid by the 6th Panzer Division, one of the first German armored divisions to enter France.

General Kempf used his panzers to break through the French defenses. The Mon Idée line of defense was broken on the evening of 13 May. The 6th Panzer Division was now sixty-five kilometers west of the Meuse, deep in the enemy rear.

For this daring advance, on 3 June, Werner Kempf was awarded the Knight's Cross. With his division he had success-fully translated the concept of the armored thrust, which he had been advocating for more than fifteen years, into reality.

The rest of the division's tanks, those which were unable to ford the Meuse, had to wait for the bridging of the river to be completed. Once across, they quickly caught up with the ad-vance elements, engaging French forces that opposed the division.

The 1st Company of the 65th Panzer Battalion under *Oblt.* Dr. Bäke was heavily involved in the battles of pursuit over the next three days, overcoming pockets of resistance that held up the advance. The company accounted for seven French tanks, two of which were credited to Dr. Bäke.

On the evening of 15 May, XXXXI Army Corps issued or-ders for the continued pursuit of the shattered enemy on the six-teenth. The 6th Panzer Division was to set out at 0600, its objective Hirson. The troops were hoping for another quick breakthrough. However, this was not to be the case. During the night *Panzergruppe* Kleist received orders to halt and advance no farther. The order was partially withdrawn following a heated exchange between General Guderian and General Kleist. Nevertheless, the *Panzergruppe* remained inactive for at least twenty-four hours.

On 16 May, General Reinhardt ordered the "further pursuit of the beaten enemy." The 6th Panzer Division was to advance as quickly as possible to the River Oise and reach the crossings at Etreaupont and Marly.

General Kempf summoned *Oberst* von Esebeck and *Ober-leutnant* Dr. Bäke. His instructions to von Esebeck's battle group were: "Fastest possible advance toward Guise! Bäke, you will form the battle group's breakthrough force, in case the enemy should offer resistance."

The attack was scheduled to begin at 1530. When his watch showed it was time, Bäke raised his right arm and gave the order: "Panzers forward!"

The idling engines roared to life, and the eighteen tanks rolled forward. After driving for an hour, during which Bäke scanned the terrain ahead while standing in his open turret hatch, the leading armored group suddenly came under machine gun fire from a wood to the right. Dr. Bäke ducked inside his tank and closed the hatch cover.

"Combat readiness!" he ordered.

"Weapons loaded and secured!" reported his gunner. The other tank commanders also reported ready.

"Leutnant Möbbs, take two tanks, veer off to the right, and circle around behind the wood. Signal when you are in position."

Leutnant Möbbs read back the order and Dr. Bäke watched as the two panzers drove off to the right and disappeared around the end of the wood.

"Open fire!" ordered the commanders when they were in range.

Bäke's gunner targeted a machine gun. Two shots were sufficient to silence it. The remaining tanks deployed into a wedge and advanced by platoons, alternately halting and firing. A few moments later a flare rose from the far side of the wood. Bäke ordered his tanks to advance as rapidly as possible.

While the two tanks positioned in the enemy's rear engaged the remaining machine guns, the rest of the company charged forward and broke all resistance.

Battle Group von Esebeck followed quickly. As darkness fell, von Esebeck gave orders for the tanks to close up and use only those lights absolutely necessary.

Dr. Bäke drove at the head of his company. The tanks rolled past fleeing French troops, who cleared the road as soon as they heard the rattle of tracks and the roaring tank engines. They were beaten and offered no resistance. Von Esebeck's battle group had no time to take prisoners and left the French for the following infantry units.

The night march became dangerous, however, when the battle group approached Falvigny, a suburb of Guise. The motorcycles of the advance detachment suddenly came under machine gun and cannon fire from the village.

"Antitank guns to the front!" ordered von Esebeck. The 3.7cm antitanks guns of the 41st Antitank Battalion were brought forward. As soon as the antitank guns opened up, French heavy tanks began to fire from well-camouflaged positions. The first antitank gun was hit and knocked out of action. The 3.7cm guns soon demonstrated their ineffectiveness against the heavily armored thirty-two-ton French tanks.

"Panzers forward!"

Dr. Bäke gave the order to attack. The tanks moved into favorable positions from which they could "charge past the enemy's heavy artillery" to Guise once the other forces were in place.

Dr. Bäke, a First World War officer experienced in battles against an enemy in fortified positions, sent patrols ahead to scout the objective. He himself drove forward to select the best route for his panzers. Leaving his tank and continuing on foot with his adjutant, he walked right into a French outpost. The French were so surprised, they surrendered to the two German officers. They were sent to the rear with two slightly wounded antitank gunners.

Following a final conference with *Oberst* von Esebeck, the attack on Guise began at first light on 17 May. As the panzers rumbled forward, French heavy tanks opened fire from positions at the edge of town.

"Tanks 114 and 115 go to the right, around the house on the corner. Try to take the enemy from the flank!" ordered Bäke. He was quite sure that the 3.7cm guns of the Skoda tanks would not be able to penetrate the frontal armor of the French tanks.

The dismounted motorcycle troops worked their way forward from cover to cover. The few still operational antitank guns fired on the enemy tanks, whose muzzle flashes betrayed their positions.

Bäke spotted an enemy tank next to a wall ahead and to the left. It was firing at the two panzers Bäke had sent ahead. He instructed his driver to move forward into a flanking position. The gunner already had the French tank in his sights when Bäke ordered a firing halt. The first shot struck the enemy tank's frontal armor and bounced off.

"Maximum speed!" ordered Bäke. "Veer off to the left!"

No sooner had the driver done as instructed when the French tank opened fire. The shell whizzed two meters past the rear of the company commander's tank.

Bäke's tank rolled forward seventy meters before halting and turned on one track to face the enemy. The loader had already rammed the next round into the chamber. Bäke's gunner made a slight correction and fired. The shell struck the gap between the French tank's turret and hull, jamming the turret.

The empty shell casing clattered off the guard and tumbled into the canvas bag below. Two more shots were required to finish off the enemy tank. Two members of its crew tried to scramble to safety, but the tank blew up before they could escape.

The two tanks Bäke had sent ahead now opened fire, drawing the enemy toward them. "Forward, maximum speed!" called Bäke. The tanks rumbled forward until they came upon an antitank gun position. In the battle against the stationary antitank guns the panzers took advantage of their maneuverability to emerge victorious.

In the meantime, the German motorcycle troops had fought their way past the enemy positions at the edge of town and were now engaged in house-to-house fighting in Guise. It required several hours of fighting, with Bäke's tanks providing supporting fire, before the enemy troops in Guise surrendered.

Dr. Bäke's company had achieved its first major success of the French campaign, destroying or putting out of action three heavy tanks, four antitank guns, and a large number of trucks.

The advance was resumed immediately. Von Esebeck's forces moved quickly and captured the bridges at Hauteville and Marquigny intact.

Von Ravenstein's battle group, which was accompanied by the division commander, was also successful, advancing as far as Grigny. On the evening of that eventful 17 May the forces of the 6th Panzer Division in the Hauteville-Neuvillette bridgehead had to face an attack by French tanks. The division's panzers took part in the defense, and Dr. Bäke was able to add another enemy tank to his total. He also damaged one French tank, which turned away smoking.

The German antitank guns, however, had a hard time of it trying to cope with the attacking French tanks. One 3.7cm Pak of the 41st Antitank Battalion's 3rd Company under *Oberleutnant* Neckenauer fired no less than twenty-six(!) shots at an attacking French tank before hitting both its tracks and immobilizing it. General Kempf immediately demanded 8.8cm antiaircraft guns, which had been used with success as antitank weapons in the first days of the campaign.

Battle Group von Ravenstein achieved a major success on 18 May when it stormed into La Catelet and captured the entire staff of the French 9th Army in a hotel in the center of town. Had it arrived in La Catelet a half hour earlier, it might have scored an even greater coup by nabbing Marshal Pétain and the commander in chief of the 9th Army, General Corap. Both had been at the headquarters of the 9th Army and left just thirty minutes before the Germans arrived. General Corap's successor, General Giraud, also escaped capture, as he was still en route to La Catelet. Many valuable documents were captured, among them the war diary of the 9th Army.

The 65th Panzer Battalion drove on toward the Schelde bridge.

Earlier Dr. Bäke had discussed the advance with the battalion commander, and they agreed that the battalion should push through to the objective, ignoring whatever was taking place to the sides of the advance road.

The panzers advanced at high speed. They overtook retreating columns of beaten French soldiers but met no resistance. The French 9th Army was in a state of disintegration following the loss of its command apparatus.

Later, the enemy made an attempt to interrupt the 6th Panzer Division's advance. Dr. Bäke engaged the French force, prompting Major Schenk, commander of the 65th Panzer Battallion, to come forward to the lead company to see what was going on.

The enemy was put to flight following a brief exchange of fire, and the advance was resumed behind the withdrawing French army. Several motorcycles had already reached and secured the bridge, removing the demolition charges that were in place.

By the time Bäke's panzers reached the bridge, the issue had been decided. The 11th Panzer Regiment's 5th Company also arrived, and the bridgehead was firmly in German hands. There was little cause for concern, however, as the French had no thoughts of launching a counterattack, or indeed of mounting any resistance at all. They had been completely demoralized by the loss of their headquarters staff and the rapid German advance.

Continuing the advance at the head of Battle Group von Esebeck, the 65th Panzer Battalion's 1st Company reached the important fork in the road ten kilometers from Cambrai and established another bridgehead near Banteux.

The rapid advance had bypassed many French units, and as night fell enemy forces appeared in the rear of the 6th Panzer Division. The 6th Motorcycle Battalion ran into a group of French armored cars withdrawing from La Catelet, suffering some casualties. *Oberstleutnant* Polzer, commander of the 76th Artillery Regiment's 1st Battalion, was killed in this action.

The 6th Panzer Division received further orders from corps on the evening of 19 May, which read: "In continuing the advance the division will reach the Canal du Nord and take possession of the crossings there." During this day's fighting the small number of Panzer IVs which had reached the division by 10 May suffered a large number of mechanical breakdowns.

The 6th Panzer Division's rapid advance and outflanking of the French 9th Army enabled it to capture another senior French commander, General Giraud. Giraud was cut off while en route to his army and sought cover in a barn, which, unfortunately for him, had been selected as the site of a field kitchen belonging to the 11th Panzer Regiment's 7th Company. The latter found him and delivered Giraud and his entourage to the division.

The 20th of May saw the first exchange of blows with British troops, with the enemy forces being pushed back by both battle groups. Dr. Bäke and his company engaged British tanks, also for the first time, destroying five. One of the enemy tanks was accounted for by Dr. Bäke.

By evening of that day the advancing forces had passed Cambrai, site of the first major tank battle of the First World War. The 6th Panzer Division under General Kempf was now only thirty kilometers from the sea. However, the division was inexplicably turned northward. The new objective was to encircle the British Expeditionary Force as well as the French 1st Army and the remaining Belgian troops.

Near Montreuil-sur-Mer, the 57th Armored Reconnaissance Battalion became the first of the division's units to reach the sea. The attack on Calais began on 22 May. The Aa was reached in the face of negligible opposition and the St. Omer–Calais rail line was cut near Setques.

The establishment of bridgeheads across the d'Aire Canal

just east of Arques and St. Omer was ordered for 23 May. The orders did not reach the 6th Panzer Division until 0620 on the morning of the twenty-third, however, when Battle Group von Esebeck was already advancing on Calais. Dr. Bäke and *Oberst* von Esebeck talked over the senseless order, which meant recalling the 57th Armored Reconnaissance Battalion and turning away from the most important objective.

"We could still reach Calais this afternoon, Bäke. What do you think of this order?"

"It might be certain that we could reach the objective, Herr *Oberst,* but that would mean disobeying an order, and you would be placed in a most difficult situation. Especially since all of the other units might possibly, even certainly, follow the new orders and we would be left on our own. I fear that you will have to order our spearhead to turn in the new direction, even though we're convinced that Calais is the most important objective, because that's the only place we can prevent the Tommies from getting back to their island."

"You're right, Bäke. I'll have to issue the appropriate orders."

At 1000 the 57th Armored Reconnaissance Battalion changed direction. Battle Group von Esebeck reached its new objective without incident.

The units of the 65th Panzer Battalion also played a decisive role in the advance by Battle Group Ravenstein. For example, the platoon commanded by *Leutnant* Horst Scheibert drove into the village of Eggingheim and captured two trains loaded with war materiel, which were standing there under steam. *Leutnant* Ritgen's platoon, which had been placed under the command of the 4th Rifle Regiment's 3rd Company commanded by *Oberleutnant* Sültmann, was able to put a battery of French 15cm artillery out of action near Fort Rouge and capture the gun crews.

Leading Battle Group von Esebeck, the 65th Panzer Battalion's 1st Company under *Oberleutnant* Dr. Bäke reached and captured the day's objective of St. Omer. Several French armored cars and light tanks were engaged. Three were destroyed by the company, one of these being credited to Dr. Bäke. Thanks to the panzer company's energetic assault, all enemy resistance was quickly broken. The 6th Panzer Division had advanced ten kilometers and eliminated the last armored

obstacle on the flank of Lord Gort's British Expeditionary
Force.

The German forces were now only ten kilometers from
Dunkirk, the second major port from which the British could
escape. Reconnaissance revealed that the way to Dunkirk was
guarded only by weak security forces, which could have been
easily overcome.

"We could take Dunkirk in a coup de main, *Herr Oberst!*"
suggested Dr. Bäke during a briefing by the battle group commander on the next day's orders. "If we have the English in the
bag no one will ask about other orders."

Hans Karl von Esebeck agreed. He sent a message to division: "Request approval for a breakthrough to Dunkirk. Enemy
in front of the battle group very weak. Quick and decisive success is certain!"

In the meantime, however, the 6th Panzer Division had
received orders which ran contrary to the suggestion by the
commander of Battle Group von Esebeck: "The division
can anticipate resuming its attack on the morning of 25
May, with its left wing through Cassel, main effort on the right.
The 8th Panzer Division has been deployed on the division's
right."

A further corps order arrived after midnight for 24 May,
which foresaw the division holding the existing bridgeheads
against an expected strong enemy attack.

The division saw this order as misguided and completely out
of touch with the situation at the front. Nevertheless, the division command was forced to submit "even though the enemy
had not been able to establish a defensive front on the canal in
the face of the 6th Panzer Division's surprise attack."

A message arrived from Führer headquarters on 24 May. It
read: "The Führer has ordered that the canal is not to be
crossed. XXXXI Army Corps is to commit sufficient forces to
the bridgeheads to ensure that the crossings can be held against
enemy counterattacks. The movement of further flak batteries
to the east bank of the canal is to be halted."

The resulting confusion was complete. Orders had been issued and countermanded. Subsequently, completely impossible
orders were issued, which "could have originated directly from
the enemy." The answer to this puzzle is contained in the war
diary of the chief of the Army General Staff, *Generaloberst*

Halder: "The fast left wing [including 6th Panzer Division], which had no enemy forces in front of it, was halted at the express wish of the Führer. The *Luftwaffe* was to decide the fate of the surrounded enemy armies."

This move by Hitler gave the final impetus to the escape of the 350,000-man British Expeditionary Force. These were the troops that would have defended England if the island had come under attack, and which later returned to France in the Allied invasion of 1944. Without these 350,000 men it is quite likely that Great Britain would have accepted Hitler's peace offer in July 1940, following the fall of France.

Finally, on 27 May, the 6th Panzer Division received orders to leave the bridgeheads and advance eastward to the Belgian frontier and destroy the enemy forces there. Thus the next objective was in the area of Cassel(!). This was the same objective the division could have reached on 24 May without fighting. In the meantime, the British had selected Cassel as the cornerstone of the defenses that were to cover their withdrawal to Dunkirk.

The initial attack by Battle Group von Esebeck failed to break through. Battle Group von Ravenstein, advancing on the right, and elements of the 4th Rifle Regiment, the 65th Panzer Regiment, 2nd Battalion, 76th Artillery Regiment, the 605th Artillery Battalion, and a company each of antitank guns and armored *Pioniers* were now committed.

The attack force bypassed the village of Hondeghm, detaching a rifle company to deal with it. In spite of strong armored support the company suffered heavy casualties. *Oberleutnant* Sültmann, the company commander, and *Leutnant* Winkelsträter were killed. The British forces defending Hondeghm held out until nightfall.

The next morning Dr. Bäke's company drove toward the French fortifications on the Belgian border as part of Battle Group von Ravenstein. The rear positions, which were virtually unmanned, were passed with little fighting. Then the panzers of the 65th Panzer Battalion's 1st Company reached the line of bunkers. *Oberleutnant* Bäke had his tanks engage the bunkers with direct fire. Eleven were destroyed. Twenty-five others fell victim to the remaining tanks of the division or to the *Pioniers*. Just as Bäke gave the order to resume the advance, an enemy tank rolled out from behind one of the bunkers and opened fire.

"To the right by the bunker!" shouted Bäke to his gunner. "Open fire!"

"Target in sight!"

The panzer's gun swung toward the enemy tank. The first shot was a direct hit. When the enemy tank tried to turn away it was hit again, this time in the flank. Smoke poured from the stricken vehicle. After a third hit it began to burn.

Three more enemy tanks were knocked out by the Skoda tanks of the 65th Battalion. The engagement once again demonstrated that none of the German tanks possessed a gun that could knock out an enemy tank with one shot.

The frontier fortifications fell. A divisional order of the day praised the division's accomplishments: "This great success is a new page in the victorious record of the 6th Panzer Division. It was achieved through a masterly joint effort between infantry, tanks, artillery, antitank guns and *Pioniers*. The organization of the attack was a masterpiece by *Oberst* von Ravenstein."

On 29 May, Battle Group von Ravenstein cut the road from Poperinge to Proven. It was there that the first contact was made with the infantry of Army Group B, a motorized patrol from 1st Company, 17th Infantry Regiment.

On 30 May, under cover of dense fog, the defenders of Cassel broke out in an attempt to reach Dunkirk. Battle Groups Koll and von Esebeck attempted to stop the breakout. The British had strong tank support and there was heavy fighting.

Oberleutnant Bäke led his panzers through the thickening fog in the direction of the British tanks, which were moving from Cassel in the direction of the village of Watten.

"To everyone: prepare to fire!"

"Weapons loaded and secured!" reported the gunners to their commanders. Shells had been loaded, and the machine guns were ready to fire.

Dr. Bäke could hear the enemy tanks firing. He wanted to approach from the south and take them from the flank, relieving Battle Group Koll, which was heavily engaged.

"Igel to chief: enemy in sight! Ten o'clock, range two thousand!" reported the tank on the far left flank.

"Open fire on recognized targets!" ordered Dr. Bäke.

As Bäke issued the order, the first enemy tank rolled past in

front of the company. Sixteen guns fired almost as one. The
enemy tank was hit at least eight times and went up in flames.

Bäke's loader and gunner worked swiftly and surely. The
second shot struck the right side of an enemy tank; seconds
later it was ablaze. An internal explosion blew open the turret
hatch. A jet of flame shot upwards, followed almost immediately by a terrific explosion that blew the tank to pieces.

Bäke's panzers maintained a high rate of fire. Soon eight
enemy tanks lay blazing or smoldering on the battlefield. A
shell struck close to the company commander's tank, throwing
up a fountain of earth. The tank that had fired the shot moved
toward Bäke's panzer.

Bäke's gunner tracked the tank until it halted to fire once
more, barely three hundred meters away, and pressed the firing
button. Almost at once the shell struck the enemy tank and dislodged its turret, preventing it from firing again. The second
shot finished it for good.

"Advance by platoons!" ordered Dr. Bäke when he saw the
enemy forces veer off toward the northeast. The panzers drove
forward and soon caught up to a smoking enemy tank that was
trying to escape. The panzer's gun swung around and the
enemy tank grew larger in the gunner's sight. There was a crash
as he fired, and the shell struck the flank of the enemy tank. It
ground to a halt. Figures emerged and dashed for cover.

"Onward, after the fleeing enemy!" called Dr. Bäke to his
commanders.

The tank battle raged along the entire front. Everywhere one
looked there were flashes of gunfire, exploding shells, and blazing tanks. The rattle of tank tracks drowned out all other
sounds.

The panzers approached the birch grove that Dr. Bäke had
given as their objective. When they were about 150 meters
away, a British tank emerged from the trees. Flames spat from
the muzzle of its gun. The shell hissed past the turret of Bäke's
panzer. His gunner took aim and fired. The first shot struck
near the enemy tank's right track. The loader rammed the next
round into the chamber. Bäke's gunner pressed the firing
button. This time it was a direct hit. The enemy tank began
to burn. The British crew scrambled from their blazing steel
coffin.

Dr. Bäke assembled his company and led it forward. He received instructions from *Oberst* Koll to catch and halt the leading enemy elements.

The Bäke company, now reduced to fourteen tanks, rolled onward at top speed. Bäke led his panzers to a position in front of the enemy. The tank-versus-tank duel resumed. One of Bäke's panzers took a direct hit and began to burn. The crew bailed out. Bäke sent two vehicles to the location of the knocked-out tank to provide covering fire for the crew.

Constantly moving, halting and firing, and frequently changing position to evade enemy fire, Bäke and his panzers stopped the enemy and allowed the following German tanks to engage.

When the fight against the British armored brigade was over, fifty enemy tanks lay smashed and burning on the battlefield. The brigade commander and forty of his officers—all of them wounded—went into German captivity. In addition to several hundred dead, a total of about two thousand of the brigade's soldiers were captured. The division's medical unit, the 46th Medical Battalion under *Oberfeldarzt* Dr. Spiegelberg, worked with British medical personnel to care for the wounded enemy soldiers.

The 6th Panzer Division had scored a great success while suffering only light casualties—and this against an enemy that had fought with bravery and determination.

Following this action the division received a corps order to go over to the defensive and hold the territory already won, as the enemy facing XXXXI Corps was in retreat toward the north. On the afternoon of that eventful day the division was pulled out of the line.

The day's booty consisted of sixty tanks and five armored cars, ten artillery pieces, eleven antitank guns, thirty-four cars, and 233 trucks.

The first part of the French campaign had come to an end.

The French Campaign, Part 2

The 65th Panzer Battalion in Battle

The 6th Panzer Division together with the rest of XXXXI Corps was now placed under the direct command of *Generaloberst* Guderian. The white "K" on the division's vehicles was replaced by a "G."

Panzergruppe Guderian assembled in the Charleville area in preparation for the second part of the French campaign. The 6th Panzer Division occupied quarters in the Monthermé-Rozoy area, which had been a battlefield before the move across the Meuse.

In addition to the XXXXI Corps, *Generaloberst* Guderian also had the XXXIX Corps under his command, placing a total of four panzer and two motorized infantry divisions at his disposal.

The *Panzergruppe*'s chief of staff was General Staff *Oberst* Walther K. Nehring; General Staff Major Fritz Bayerlein was Ia. Many of the commanders in the ranks of the 6th Panzer Division and *Panzergruppe* Guderian would later distinguish themselves on the battlefields of North Africa.

As a part of the 12th Army under *Generaloberst* List, which was a component of Army Group von Rundstedt, Guderian's panzers were given the task of advancing southward from the Chateau Porcien and Attigny areas across the Aisne River and the Aisne Canal.

On 3 June, *Generalleutnant* Werner Kempf and *Oberst* Johannes von Ravenstein received the Knight's Cross of the Iron Cross. The war diary of the 6th Panzer Division said: "Seldom before has the award of such a decoration produced such unqualified, sincere and enthusiastic joy and approval among officers and men."

Army Group Rundstedt was scheduled to attack on 9 June; however, the 6th Panzer Division remained at alert readiness. The division in front, the 86th Infantry Division, had failed in its attempt to cross the Aisne and was therefore unable to establish a crossing site for the 6th Panzer Division. As a result, Guderian was forced to move XXXXI Corps behind his XIX Corps west of Rethel where the Aisne had been successfully crossed. On the first day of the attack the 3rd Panzer Division had established a bridgehead on the far side of the Aisne, from which the 1st and 2nd Panzer Divisions of XIX Corps were attacking toward the south. Now the 6th and 8th Panzer Divisions were to follow.

Battle Group von Ravenstein crossed the Aisne over a bridge built by the *Pioniers*. Near Machault it ran into a strong enemy defensive position that contained a strong force of artillery. Battle Group von Esebeck encountered an equally strong enemy force near Semide and was forced to go over to the defensive.

Oberst von Ravenstein summoned the commanders of both the division's panzer units for a briefing. He ordered *Oberstleutnant* Koll to lead a tank attack against the enemy positions. The 4th Rifle Regiment's 2nd Battalion was to accompany the tanks in its armored personnel carriers, dismount near the point of penetration, and continue the attack on foot. All of the combat-ready elements of the 65th Panzer Battalion were involved, as well as 2nd Battalion, 11th Panzer Regiment.

General Kempf accompanied the attack, riding in his command car in the midst of the armored personnel carriers behind the first group of panzers. The general wanted to be on hand to intervene personally if the situation required.

The 65th Panzer Battalion's 1st Company under *Oberleutnant* Bäke was positioned roughly in the middle of the wave of tanks. Standing in his open turret hatch, Dr. Bäke saw the commander of the 11th Panzer Regiment to his right. All of the tank engines were idling. *Oberstleutnant* Koll gave the order to advance and the panzer unit set itself in motion. The tanks rolled toward the enemy positions. Artillery shells burst all over the landscape in front of the advancing armor without, however, inflicting any damage. When the tanks were about one hundred meters from the impacting shells, Dr. Bäke ordered, "Hatches closed! Come to battle readiness!"

Bäke dropped down into the turret, slammed the hatch shut, and locked it tight.

"Weapons loaded and secured!" reported the gunner.

The tanks drove onward. Shells burst to the right and left. The mounted infantry ducked lower in their armored personnel carriers. Then the armored battle group disappeared into a long, shallow valley and were out of sight of the enemy.

When the tanks reemerged on the far side of the valley, the French artillery fire intensified. However, the shells now passed over the tanks and struck the ground behind them.

The attack force had passed through the previously scouted valley in good order. On the right and left of the wave the first panzers were engaging the forward enemy positions. Machine guns rattled as the infantry dismounted. The tank gunners zeroed in on the enemy machine guns. There was a crash of gunfire and the French machine guns were silenced abruptly by the bursting shells. However, enemy artillery had now found the range. The tanks weaved and turned to escape the enemy fire, all the while drawing nearer to the French artillery position.

All of a sudden Bäke spotted an antitank gun ahead and alerted his gunner. The company's 1st Platoon halted and seconds later the antitank gun was in the gunner's sight. The other two platoons had driven on and by the time the 3rd Platoon stopped to fire, the 1st was already moving again.

Dr. Bäke issued target information to his gunner as he led the platoon forward: "Ahead, one o'clock, five hundred meters, enemy battery!"

"Target in sight!"

Three seconds later there was a crash as the Skoda tank's 5cm gun fired. The high-explosive shell was on target. Steel and pieces of equipment whirled through the air. Then the gun's ammunition went up in several thunderous explosions.

"Forward! Maximum speed!" ordered Bäke.

Once again the tank engines roared. A shell whizzed past over the turret. The next round was already in the chamber. The tank halted abruptly and fired. Another antitank gun was silenced.

Two antitank guns and an artillery piece that had been firing salvoes at the command vehicle now shifted their fire onto Bäke's company. Bäke's driver steered the tank out of the line of fire, then halted. Gunner and loader fired off five rounds in quick succession.

The noise within the tank was becoming unbearable. However, the barrage from Bäke's tank brought some relief to the 11th Panzer Regiment, which now moved forward quickly on the left flank.

A shot from an antitank gun hammered against the turret and bounced off. Then they were upon the French field position and drove over the first gun. Men fled for cover. Bäke's panzer tilted dangerously before falling back onto both tracks with a crash. The surviving French personnel fled toward the rear.

St. Etienne came in sight. There the enemy had built an even stronger defensive position. A shell fired from this second line threw up a fountain of dirt close to the right track of Bäke's panzer. Then another burst in almost the same spot. There was a terrible crash and the tank spun around in a semicircle. Bäke's driver swung the tank back to face the enemy fire.

"Track shot up!" reported the driver.

"Get out! Driver remain in the tank!" ordered Bäke.

While the other tanks roared past to the left and right, halting only to fire on the French position, Bäke's crew set about repairing the damaged track. Dr. Bäke stopped one of the trailing tanks. *Oberfeldwebel* Knoll got out and Dr. Bäke took over the platoon leader's vehicle.

He drove forward at top speed while his crew completed the repair in record time. Bäke soon caught up with his company and assumed command from *Leutnant* Möbbs, who had taken over in Bäke's absence.

The last enemy resistance was broken, or at least so it seemed. Then heavy guns opened fire on the tanks. General Kempf ordered the attack halted and instructed his forces to go over to the defensive in their present favorable location. The tanks rolled behind a wood and disappeared from the enemy's sight. *Oberleutnant* Bäke reported back to the battalion commander by radio and was given new orders for 1st Company.

The 11th Panzer Regiment's adjutant, *Oberleutnant* Schoeller, had been killed by the French artillery fire. Several panzers were so badly damaged, they had to be written off. The artillery fire which had halted 6th Panzer Division's attack finally ceased an hour after midnight.

That evening *Generaloberst* Guderian appeared at the command post of the 6th Panzer Division. General Kempf made his report, and Guderian declared himself in complete agreement with the decisions taken by his friend.

"I would have done the same thing, Kempf. To continue in this situation would have meant unnecessary losses."

Generaloberst Guderian noted in his war diary: "The XXXXI Corps, which was moving up on the left of XIX Corps, had to repel attacks against its left wing from the Argonne by the French 3rd Mechanized and 3rd Armored Divisions before resuming its move toward the south."

The enemy forces withdrew undetected during the night. As a result, when the attack was resumed on the morning of 12 June there was no opposition at first. Two hours later the day's objective of Somme-Pys was reached. The town itself was free of enemy forces.

At noon Kempf reorganized his division. Spearheading the

attack was Battle Group von Esebeck. The 11th Panzer Regiment's 2nd Battalion formed the steel tip of the attack force.

The battle group set out at 1800. After advancing three thousand meters it came upon a strong defensive position at the edge of the Châlons-sur-Marne troop training grounds. The advance ground to a halt.

The next attack, launched on the morning of 13 June, broke through. The German forces moved quickly through the wooded terrain of the Châlons camp.

On 14 June, while German troops moved into Paris, the 6th Panzer Division was fighting in a densely-wooded area near St. Mard, which General Kempf described to the author as "completely unsuited to the operation of tanks." He went on to say that, "Fortunately for us the 17th Infantry Division arrived quickly and was able to relieve us and free us for the next battles of attack."

In a several-hour night march on 16 June, the 6th Panzer Division drove forward through Langres to Jussey, where the 57th Reconnaissance Battalion had established a bridgehead.

Rainecourt was captured by the 6th Motorcycle Battalion and the 65th Panzer Battalion's 1st Company. Two thousand French soldiers were taken prisoner. *Oberfeldwebel* Seewald, a member of Dr. Bäke's company, described the action:

> As the leading group, our 1st was to drive up to the edge of Rainecourt, lay down effective fire on the enemy force suspected there, and open a way into the city for the motorcycle troops.
>
> When Dr. Bäke saw the first muzzle flash from an antitank gun concealed behind a low wall, he ordered us to spread out and open fire on the enemy position.
>
> We drove on about 100 meters and watched as Dr. Bäke and the commander of the 1st Platoon destroyed the two antitank guns and opened fire on a machine gun, which was firing on the two tanks. The first shell silenced the machine gun. Other machine guns concentrated their fire on the motorcycle troops. All of the company's panzers now joined the battle. Gunfire was heard from every direction. Thunderous explosions and the roaring engines of the advancing platoons turned the world into a madhouse.
>
> *Oberleutnant* Kreis's men stormed past us toward the edge of the city. Suddenly a half-dozen machine guns opened up on the

motorcycle troops. We were taking aim at the machine guns when the voice of our company commander rang out: "2nd Platoon, silence the machine guns!—1st Platoon, close up and advance. We'll place ourselves in front of the infantry!"

The 2nd Platoon opened fire. The eight panzers fired three brief salvoes and silenced the enemy guns. The tanks of the 1st Platoon rolled at high speed diagonally across the terrain. They screened the infantry and led them forward, sparing them further heavy losses.

The French fire became weaker. The panzers of the 1st Platoon now blocked our field of fire directly ahead.

"Bäke to the 1st: go past us on the left, move ahead as far as the stand of trees, and lay down flanking fire on the enemy from there!"

We roared off. One of our vehicles suddenly halted. We heard the voice of its commander:

"To chief. Have transmission failure!"

"Lay down fire on the enemy with all weapons. I'll send a recovery vehicle!"

This action by our chief saved the 1st Motorcycle Company, whose ranks had already been thinned considerably by the heavy enemy fire.

We later learned that *Oberleutnant* Kreis, commander of the motorcycle company, had been wounded and that *Leutnant* Hans-Joachim Wissemann had taken over command of the company. He had led the last attack, with the covering fire and support of our company commander.

Quickly assessing the situation, Dr. Bäke had drawn the enemy fire on himself and given cover to the motorcycle troops. It was then that *Leutnant* Wissemann came to the fore: "I'm taking command of the company!" he shouted through the din. He then ran through the hail of fire to Bäke's tank and discussed the final assault into the heart of the enemy position. The conversation was a brief one: "If you support us and advance on both flanks, *Herr Oberleutnant,* we can do it!"

"All right, Wissemann! We'll roll up to the city in two attack columns. Stay close behind and cover the area behind us until you're close enough for your assault."

"Company forward in two spearheads. Objective is the outskirts of the city. Stay together and clear a path for our motorcycle troops!" ordered Bäke by radio.

The panzers moved off. Anything that appeared in their path was fired on. The inverted "V" made good progress. While one wing halted, the other drove on, and the center followed slowly and supported the flank, which had halted to fire. The tanks fired in the direction of the muzzle flashes and rolled into the gardens, smashing down a low wall and crushing fences. Three small garden sheds were knocked down to provide a better field of fire.

The heavy machine gun fire being directed at the motorcycle troops slackened. *Leutnant* Wissemann followed the panzers on the right flank of the "V." After the machine guns firing from the windows had been silenced, he led his men forward and cleared the first two houses. Dr. Bäke rolled into the city with the 1st Platoon. An antitank gun firing down a city street struck the panzer with a grazing shot, then was blown up by a direct hit.

Dr. Bäke summoned all of the tanks forward. They rolled into the city, turned down the side streets, and flushed out the desperately defending enemy.

Rainecourt was in German hands. The history of the 6th Panzer Division described the action: *"Leutnant* Wissemann, who had taken over command of the company from the wounded *Oberleutnant* Kreis at the beginning of the battle, distinguished himself in the fighting. The battle in and around Rainecourt received particularly effective support from *Oberleutnant* Bäke's company of the 65th Panzer Battalion. Once again *Oberleutnant* Bäke distinguished himself in action."

Leutnant Wissemann and *Oberleutnant* Bäke were awarded the Iron Cross, First Class for their exploits. (On 8 February 1943, Hans-Joachim Wissemann, by then holding the rank of *Hauptmann* and commander of 2nd Company, 6th Motorcycle Battalion, was awarded the Knight's Cross for his actions in the Stalingrad battle zone. He did not live to receive the decoration, as he was killed in action in the pocket on 30 December 1942.)

At 2330 on that eventful day, *Generalleutnant* Kempf issued the division's orders for the coming day: "The 6th Panzer Division will take possession of the fortress of Epinal. Also taking part in this action will be the 20th Motorized Infantry

Division, which will advance to the right of 6th Panzer Division. The division staff and command echelon will accompany *Kampfgruppe* von Esebeck."

Generaloberst Guderian had deployed XXXXI Corps toward Epinal on his own initiative, even though *Generaloberst* von Leeb's 1st Army had also set out toward the same objective.

The first attempt to take Epinal in a coup de main had failed. This time the panzers of 2nd Battalion, 11th Panzer Regiment led Battle Group von Esebeck toward the fortress. The 660th Assault Gun Battery went along to provide supporting fire. The battery, formed in Jüterbog in April, had demonstrated its effectiveness in the early stages of the campaign. While attached to the 3rd Infantry Division during the Meuse crossing and later in operations with the 8th Panzer Division, the battery had been an outstanding success, helping to prove Erich von Manstein's plan a stroke of genius. Now, during the assault across the Aisne in the second phase of the campaign against France, it was attached to the 6th Panzer Division. The battery was again to prove a success while taking part in the action near Epinal.

1st Battalion of the 4th Rifle Regiment under Major Zollenkopf received orders to push through Epinal and take possession of the fortress. The assault guns were assigned to provide support. They advanced ahead of the infantry, shooting up nests of resistance. Epinal fell to Battle Group von Esebeck, but the citadel held out.

Once again the 65th Panzer Battalion was sent into action. The task fell to 1st Company, commanded by *Oberleutnant* Bäke, to silence the citadel's armored cupolas. Bäke directed his company into position and gave the order to open fire. Two of the cupolas were put out of action, but the defenders held on with the courage of desperation.

When the call for a French-speaking *parlementaire* reached Dr. Bäke, he sent "his Alsatian, a hard-drinking genius, but otherwise very useful," with *Hauptmann* Schemmel and *Oberleutnant* Hauschildt to act as interpreter. Following several negotiations it was agreed that the fort would be surrendered at noon the next day with full military honors. The garrison of Fort Longchamps marched out past an honor guard of the 6th

Panzer Division. The French flag was hauled down and the Reich war flag was raised over the fortress.

That same evening, 22 June 1940, a cease-fire was signed in the forest of Compiègne, and at 0135 on 25 June the following signal was sent to all German armed forces from the Channel coast to Switzerland: "Stand down!"

On 26 June the 6th Panzer Division held a large field parade. That evening, as the bugler sounded taps, *Oberleutnant* Erich Oeckel, commander of 5th Company, 4th Rifle Regiment, received the Knight's Cross that had been awarded him on 24 June. (Oeckel was killed on 13 July 1943, at which time he was a battalion commander holding the rank of *Hauptmann.*)

Casualties suffered by the 6th Panzer Division during the French campaign totalled 2,140 soldiers killed, wounded, or lost through illness. Included in this total were 108 officers. Considering these heavy losses, the fighting in France could scarcely be considered an "easy campaign." On 3 July the division moved into its peacetime garrison. *Oberst* von Ravenstein received an enthusiastic reception in Iserlohn.

The Russian Campaign

Reorganization and Re-formation

The reorganization of the 6th Panzer Division began on 1 August 1940. Associated with this was the release of a substantial number of troops to the 16th Motorized Infantry Division, which was to be re-formed as the 16th Panzer Division. The 11th Panzer Regiment and the 65th Panzer Battalion remained with the 6th Panzer Division, however.

In September 1940 the 6th Panzer Division was transferred to West Prussia, where it became part of the XVI Army Corps of the 18th Army. *Generalmajor* Landgraf became the division's new commanding officer. Landgraf had commanded the 4th Panzer Division in the French campaign and been awarded the Knight's Cross on 16 June for his exploits.

The 6th Panzer Division carried out its first unit exercises on the troop training grounds with its newly delivered panzers. In the place of *Oberst* von Ravenstein, *Oberst* Edward Raus now led the 4th Rifle Regiment. The 6th Panzer Division's list of panzer unit commanders had also changed significantly. *Oberst*

Koll continued to lead the 11th Panzer Regiment. The regiment's 1st Battalion was commanded by Major Löwe, while *Oberstleutnant* Sieber became the commander of 2nd Battalion. The 65th Panzer Battalion was now commanded by Major Schenk.

The division was still equipped with the obsolescent Czech-built PzKfw. 38(t) tank, whose 2.5cm frontal armor was incapable of withstanding the fire of a heavy tank, particularly the very heavy Soviet KV tanks and the T-34, which appeared later. It was planned to reequip the division with the heavier Panzer IV. The lighter Skoda tank did possess one advantage over the next generation of German panzer. It was light enough to cross the few available bridges in the planned northern sector of the Russian front without collapsing them.

One of the officers leading the training of the division's new soldiers was Dr. Bäke, since promoted to *Hauptmann*.

The Attack Begins!

On the morning of 22 June 1941 the 6th Panzer Division set out in the general direction of Leningrad in two battle groups. The division overcame several well-defended trench positions to reach the day's objective.

On the afternoon of the following day the leading elements of the division reached Rossienie. Major Schliemann, commander of the 6th Motorcycle Battalion, was killed in the attack on the city.

On the evening of 23 June the Dubyssa bridgehead, which was being held by Battle Group von Seckendorff, was attacked by powerful Soviet tank forces. The bridgehead was lost and the battle group suffered heavy casualties.

It was here that the first of the new Soviet heavy tanks appeared, whose frontal armor was impervious to the shells of the German 5cm antitank gun. The Kliment Voroshilov (KV) tanks weighed between fifty and sixty-two tons. Their frontal armor was 85 millimeters thick. Seven of these monsters rolled through the antitank positions of the 6th Panzer Division into the division's rear, where the tanks of the 11th Panzer Regiment were positioned. The shells fired by the division's panzers were unable to penetrate the armor of the Soviet tanks. *Leutnant* Eckhardt, commander of the 114th Rifle Regiment's 6th Company, succeeded in destroying one with a demolition charge fashioned from several Teller mines. The division commander called for 8.8cm flak and these arrived on the battlefield in time to destroy another of the Soviet giants, averting a very dangerous situation.

Hauptmann Dr. Bäke took little part in the first phase of the Russian campaign. No longer in command of his panzer company, he was now in charge of the tank recovery detachment. The few times Bäke saw action during this period was when his recovery teams were forced to defend themselves against Soviet troops. His job was to recover damaged tanks, tow them back to the repair shops, and see to it that the necessary repairs were carried out. Bäke carried out this assignment with great success.

Oberst Koll, commander of the 11th Panzer Regiment, soon took this knowledgeable and circumspect officer into his staff as an executive officer. In this capacity *Hauptmann* Bäke experienced armored warfare from the command level. Bäke's chance to return to action came on 1 December 1941 when Major Löwe, who was commanding the 11th Panzer Regiment's 1st Company, left temporarily to take command of the regiment.

Hauptmann Dr. Bäke led the last operational company of the 11th Panzer Regiment into action in the bitter cold of December, when temperatures fell to twenty degrees below zero. On 2 December the last of the company's Skoda tanks and Panzer IVs were put out of action. The division was halted only sixty kilometers from Moscow.

With the few panzers that could be put back into service, *Hauptmann* Bäke managed to reach the area of Kolovo. The 6th Panzer Division—or better, what was left of it—was serving as rearguard for the 3rd Panzer Army. The rifle companies were down to about thirty men each. On 9 December, Dr. Bäke lost his last panzer. The tank was unserviceable and had to be destroyed when Elisorovo was abandoned. The division was scheduled to return to Germany to refit.

Transport to Germany—Reorganization

On 15 January 1942 the 6th Panzer Division was forced to report to the LVI Panzer Corps: "The division is no longer capable of action. Re-formation, not refitting, is required. However, this is not possible in the present area."

On 12 February 1942 the OKH ordered the disbanding of the

65th Panzer Battalion. Its remaining elements joined the 11th Panzer Regiment, ensuring adequate personnel for two battalions. Thus this famous battalion, in which Dr. Franz Bäke had played a decisive role, disappeared forever.

It was to be several more weeks before the rest of the 6th "Foot Division"—with a touch of bitter gallows humor, the men had so dubbed their panzer division on account of its total lack of tanks—received travel orders to move west.

In the meantime Dr. Bäke had returned to the division and assumed command of a small force consisting of a repaired Panzer IV, three Panzer 38(t) tanks, and several armored personnel carriers. With this small "fire-brigade" Dr. Bäke was able to destroy the attacking T-34s in the battle for Cholminka. Two of these were accounted for by Dr. Bäke, who led the force in the sole Panzer IV.

That same evening Battle Groups Bäke and Römhild were released by Army Group Center for transport to Germany.

By 23 April 1942 all of the first eight transport trains carrying the 6th Panzer Division had arrived in France. The ninth and last train did not leave Novo Dugino until 2 May 1942, however. The 6th Panzer Division, now commanded by *Generalmajor* Raus, was to be re-formed by 31 July.

In France, Dr. Bäke initially took over a foot company from each of the 1st and 2nd Battalions of the 11th Panzer Regiment and the remaining regimental units, while Major Löwe, now recovered from his wounds, temporarily took command of the 11th Panzer Regiment in place of *Oberst* Koll, who had gone on leave. At first the only tanks available to the regiment were captured French models; its total complement was two Somua tanks and three platoons with six Hotchkiss tanks each.

On 22 June the two battalions of the 11th Panzer Regiment received the first of their new panzers: fifteen Panzer IIs and twenty-six Panzer IIIs armed with the long 5cm gun. On 2 July, *Oberst* Walther von Hünersdorff took command of the 11th Panzer Regiment. *Oberst* Koll was transferred to the Führer Reserve. (In January 1945 he was promoted to *Generalleutnant* in the inspectorate of artillery.)

Second Battalion, 11th Panzer Regiment conducted large-scale tank maneuvers on 10 September. Its new commanding officer was Major Dr. Franz Bäke. While leading this battalion he was to become one of the greatest armor commanders and tacticians. The demonstration of an "encounter with an in-depth antitank barricade by an armored spearhead" was carried out by Dr. Bäke with great skill and élan.

With the arrival of the last of its panzers on 14 September, the division was once again fully equipped. It now possessed more than 150 Panzer IIIs, armed with either the long 5cm gun or the short 7.5cm weapon. In addition, it also had a number of the more powerful Panzer IV tanks with the long 7.5cm gun, which made them a match for any of the Soviet tanks.

On 3 November 1942, Hitler ordered the 6th Panzer Division and two infantry divisions transferred to the East, where they were to assemble to the rear of Army Group B's front behind the 3rd Rumanian and 8th Italian Armies. There the three divisions were to be held in reserve.

The first trains carrying the 6th Panzer Division left France on 14 November 1942, bound for the southern sector of the Eastern Front. It was planned to detrain the division in Belgorod on 25 November. There, however, the division was sent onward to the south. A battle was raging in the 6th Army's area of operations near Stalingrad. That was the division's destination.

Operation Winter Storm

The 6th Panzer Division was now called upon to take part in a decisive action which would demand its utmost. It was to be part of a force whose objective was to free the 6th Army under *Generaloberst* Paulus, which was surrounded in the Stalingrad area. A total of twelve divisions was to be committed to the relief effort. Considering the situation, it is quite likely that such a force could have fought its way into the pocket; however, the reality was to be quite different. On arriving in the assembly area the 6th Panzer Division found itself quite alone. Operation Winter Storm, which was to be commanded by *Generaloberst* Hoth, a raid across one hundred kilometers of enemy-held territory to the edge of the Stalingrad pocket, became a makeshift battle in which all three divisions that eventually took part were bloodied.

Within LVII Panzer Corps, the 6th Panzer Division and the 17th and 23rd Panzer Divisions were supposed to take part in the operation. Elements of the 23rd Panzer Division were the first to arrive. The 17th Panzer Division was farther away, and in any case was halted on orders of the Führer. On the morning of 24 November the first of the 6th Panzer Division's units, the 4th Panzer Grenadier Regiment, arrived in Kotelnikovo. The regiment came under fire from Soviet tanks while it was still detraining. The guns of the 8th (Heavy) Company were unloaded under fire and engaged the enemy. The result of all this was that all following trains had to be unloaded at a station farther down the line.

On the morning of 29 November, *Generalmajor* Raus took command of the division. On 1 December the 6th Panzer Division was placed under the command of LVII Panzer Corps under *General der Panzertruppe* Kirchner. That same day saw the arrival of the 11th Panzer Regiment's 1st and 5th Companies. Properly speaking, at that time *Generalfeldmarschall* von Manstein should have had twelve divisions at his disposal to carry out the relief attack.

Two days later the 6th Panzer Division saw its first major action with Army Group Don under *Generalfeldmarschall* von Manstein. A force of enemy tanks had set out toward Kudinoff. Under cover of heavy blowing snow they reached Pochlebin. A platoon of antitank guns positioned there destroyed seven, but 3rd Company, 114th Rifle Regiment was forced to pull back toward Safranoff.

Major Dr. Bäke now received instructions to send his 5th Company to 1st Company. Both companies were then to drive to Kotelnikovo with 2nd Battalion, 114th Rifle Regiment of Battle Group Küper and assemble there for an attack.

When about twenty enemy tanks were spotted advancing toward Kotelnikovo along both sides of the road from Pochlebin, *Generalmajor* Raus dispatched 1st Company, 41st Antitank Battalion to deal with the threat. The antitank guns shot up the Soviet armored spearhead, but were then forced to pull back.

"All attack companies forward!" *Generalmajor* Raus ordered the 11th Panzer Regiment. "Battle Group Küper has been stopped by the enemy. The enemy forces near Pochlebin must be destroyed!"

Oberst von Hünersdorff now suggested sending Dr. Bäke's battalion to Maiorski. There it would be placed under the command of *Oberst* Zollenkopf, the CO of the 114th Panzer Grenadier Regiment, for the attack on Pochlebin.

During the night, patrols reported that the enemy was reinforcing his units near Pochlebin in preparation for an attack against Kotelnikovo.

General Raus assembled all his tanks for the attack. *Oberst* von Hünersdorff had more than ninety panzers at his disposal. He summoned the battalion commanders and briefed them on the plan of attack.

When the attack began, 2nd Battalion, 11th Panzer Regiment under Dr. Bäke rolled directly toward the hills at Pochlebin. When the tanks were in range, well-camouflaged Soviet tanks and antitank guns opened fire. One after another, three of 8th Company's tanks were hit and disabled. One took several more hits and blew up. Several panzers of 1st and 2nd Battalions, which had mounted fuel tanks on their rear decks to increase their range, were hit and went up in flames. The crews managed to scramble to safety, but the tanks were total losses. One tank lost in this way was that of *Hauptmann* Hagemeister, the company commander of 2./PR 11. He and his crew were forced to abandon their tank and the *Hauptmann* was seriously wounded.

First Company, 11th Panzer Regiment, which had been ordered to set out toward Pochlebin from the northwest, became involved in a battle with enemy forces, during the course of which it was forced farther and farther to the north.

Oberst von Hünersdorff issued orders by radio for the panzers to immediately turn and proceed straight toward Pochlebin. This was the only way to provide relief for Dr. Bäke's battalion, which was heavily engaged.

The tanks of 1st Company, 11th Panzer Regiment now rolled toward Pochlebin from the north. This sudden change in direction confused the enemy. He was forced to divide his forces, which noticeably reduced the pressure on Dr. Bäke's battalion.

Dr. Bäke acted at once. He instructed his heavy company and the entire battalion: "Attack, we have to break through now!"

The tanks rumbled toward Pochlebin at high speed. The heavy company led the way, with the remaining companies widely spaced behind. The Panzer IVs drove in the center, striking devastating blows at the enemy with their 7.5cm guns. Four Soviet tanks came out to face the panzers; all were destroyed. Soviet cavalry units appeared on the flank. They were halted by high-explosive shells. Dr. Bäke's panzer accounted for two Soviet tanks.

Franz Bäke breathed a sigh of relief as the panzers rolled into Pochlebin. Unfortunately, there was still a wide gap between his 2nd Battalion and 1st Battalion, through which the enemy, some on horseback, escaped.

Nevertheless, victory had been achieved, and that evening ten enemy tanks were counted that had been destroyed by 2nd Battalion, 11th Panzer Regiment. In addition, fourteen guns had been captured and 2,000 prisoners taken. Among the booty taken the next day were 800 horses and camels. The 6th Panzer Division's war diary stated: "The 2nd Battalion of the 11th Panzer Regiment under Major Dr. Bäke played a major role in the success. Especially deserving of recognition is *Oberleutnant* Ranzinger, the commander of 8th Company."

Statements by prisoners revealed that the Soviet units involved had been the 81st Cavalry Division and the 85th Tank Brigade of the Red Army. The Soviet buildup for an attack on the important jumping-off point of Kotelnikovo had been smashed. *Generaloberst* Hoth voiced his appreciation in a radio message: "Bravo 6th Panzer Division!"

On 5 December, LVII Panzer Corps released Corps Order No. 1, "Preparation for Operation Winter Storm."

In the meantime, near Werchne Kumsky (Verkhue-Kumsky), patrols from the 6th Panzer Division had discovered the approach of powerful enemy tank forces. Statements from prisoners indicated that these were the three hundred tanks of the 4th and 13th Soviet Tank Corps. These units would have to be smashed before the breakthrough to Stalingrad could begin.

During a conference of unit commanders, *Oberst* von Hünersdorff suggested that "this encounter of armored forces will be the decisive battle in the freeing of the Stalingrad pocket. All of the tanks available to the corps will be thrown into the battle. We can open the way to Stalingrad and save the 6th Army only if we succeed in striking a devastating blow against the enemy armor."

In a discussion between *Generaloberst* Hoth and *General der Panzertruppe* Kirchner in Simwoniki on December 7, Hermann Hoth argued that the operation "should not be a battle in open terrain, but a concentrated breakthrough to the 6th Army's Stalingrad Front."

In the meantime it had become clear that LVII Panzer Corps would have to undertake the attack alone, because the other corps assigned to the attack, XXXXVIII Panzer Corps under *General der Panzertruppe* von Knobelsdorff, was being forced to defend its own bridgehead at Chirskaya, which was under attack by powerful Soviet forces. Meanwhile, the first elements of the 23rd Panzer Division had arrived.

The attack by LVII Panzer Corps began on the morning of 12 December 1942. General Kirchner's force consisted of the 6th Panzer Division with 134 tanks, including 63 Panzer IIIs and 23 Panzer IVs, and seven command vehicles, and elements of the 23rd Panzer Division with 46 Panzer IIIs and 11 Panzer IVs.

This force amounted to the strength of exactly one and a half panzer divisions. This was all that was left of the promised twelve divisions. The only chance of saving the 6th Army had been squandered. Such a task was too great for the weak forces which began the operation, despite the bravery and self-sacrifice demonstrated by the troops.

IV *Fliegerkorps* was to provide 179 combat aircraft to give air support to the attack force. But these, too, were not to remain with the attack force, as the course of events will show.

Horst Scheibert, a participant in the desperate struggle, gave the following initial overview in his well-respected book, *48 Kilometers to Stalingrad.* "The 6th Panzer Division has assembled in four battle groups: three weaker panzer-grenadier groups, led by *Oberst* Zollenkopf, *Oberst* Unrein and Major Quentin, and the stronger panzer group under *Oberst* von Hünersdorff."

The attack began. The war diary of the 11th Panzer Regiment contains the following entry: "The most powerful wedge rolled forward, with 1st Battalion right, 2nd Battalion left, and between them the tank destroyers and self-propelled guns. Behind them on a wide front came 2nd Battalion, 114th Panzer Grenadier Regiment in armored personnel carriers. The day's objective, to cross the Aksai, could not be reached, as crossing two icy ravines delayed the advance considerably.

"The advance was resumed on the morning of 13 December and the crossing was made at 0800."

First Battalion rolled across the bridge unopposed. Afterward, as *Oberst* von Hünersdorff's command vehicle was driving across, a section of the bridge gave way and the vehicle blocked the crossing.

Oberst von Hünersdorff now requested Stukas. The dive bombers arrived and began to bomb enemy-held Werchne Kumsky. Von Hünersdorff ordered 1st Battalion, 11th Panzer Regiment to attack. As soon as the last bomb had fallen, the battalion rolled straight into Werchne Kumsky. The village was taken. The 23rd Panzer Division, which was supposed to join the battle at this point, had not yet arrived.

When large-scale tank movements were reported from Nishne Jablotschnij, General Raus once again requested Stuka support. The Stuka attacks continued until darkness fell, destroying some of the enemy tanks concentrating in the town. *Generaloberst* Hoth expressed his "full appreciation to commanders and troops alike."

On 14 December the 11th Panzer Regiment, together with all of its attached armored units, drove to Werchne Kumsky. In doing so it was moving out to face the enemy's armored forces instead of drawing them toward itself.

A tank battle began which was to last until 17 December. The battle cost Battle Group von Hünersdorff no less than 90 of its 120 tanks and tank destroyers.

This was the decisive error of Operation Winter Storm. To use *Generaloberst* Hoth's expression, it had "battled instead of breaking through."

The battle on 14 December was likewise successful and General Raus ordered the "destruction of the enemy" for 15 December.

On 15 December the entire 11th Panzer Regiment was standing around Werchne Kumsky. When enemy tank forces were reported, *Oberst* von Hünersdorff ordered Major Dr. Bäke to drive around Werchne Kumsky to the south and destroy the enemy forces between the village and Sagotskot.

Major Bäke set out at once. A low ridge was crossed, and here the battalion commander was presented with a sight that he could not have imagined in his wildest dreams. About a thousand meters away was a group of about forty tanks, all painted white, as were the German panzers.

"Get closer!—Come to battle readiness. Don't fire until we're sure they're enemy tanks."

Franz Bäke still thought it might be the tanks of the 23rd Panzer Division, which had been reported from this direction. In the tanks the gunners selected their targets. Slowly, the battalion's panzers rolled toward the dense mass of tanks. When they were six hundred meters away, two tanks separated from the main body in the shallow valley. Bäke realized that they were the enemy.

"Attention, everyone! The Russians!—Open fire!" he ordered.

Bäke's gunner fired at the tank driving on the right. At least six other panzers had taken aim at the same tank and all fired virtually at once. The two Soviet tanks were struck by a series of direct hits, blown apart, and left as burning hulks.

Dr. Bäke led the attack against the thirty-eight remaining tanks. He assigned each of his companies a sector to attack. In the staccato of tank gunfire and the few answering shots from the enemy, more and more Soviet tanks were put out of action. Several turned on shot-up tracks and fired wildly in all directions until they, too, were destroyed.

Dr. Bäke's gunner scored two more direct hits. One of the enemy tanks was left burning. When the last of the Soviet tanks had escaped beyond the range of the long 7.5cm guns of the Panzer IVs, thirty-two enemy tanks lay shot up and burning on the battlefield. The Bäke Battalion had scored a dramatic success. The Soviets were no longer in a position to destroy the German armored forces.

"Assemble!—Further advance to the north!" ordered the battalion commander, after reports indicated that his battalion still had sufficient fuel and armor-piercing ammunition to continue the battle.

The battalion's panzers moved off in the direction of Sagotskot. The unit's light platoon, which had been sent ahead to reconnoiter, was in trouble there and fighting for its survival.

Bäke's panzers were met by fire from Sagotskot, where the Soviet tanks had fled.

"Attack!—Move in!" ordered Bäke.

Following a brief exchange of fire, during which three or four more Soviet tanks were destroyed, the enemy pulled out of Sagotskot.

On their own initiative, *Oberst* von Hünersdorff and Major Dr. Bäke continued to pursue the Soviet tanks that day. When the battalion commander's command panzer was hit and disabled, he climbed into a Panzer IV whose commander had been wounded. Bäke destroyed two more Soviet tanks during an attack against a small enemy armored unit that was driving toward Werchne Kumsky. Several of his battalion's tanks were knocked out and had to be abandoned. The surviving crew members squeezed into other of the battalion's panzers.

When darkness fell, 2nd Battalion was guided to Werchne Kumsky by flares fired by 1st Battalion, where the regiment's commander was located. That day the 6th Panzer Division destroyed a total of forty-two enemy tanks. This was the highest total of the campaign so far.

Only two companies had been left behind in Werchne Kumsky that day, under the command of Major Löwe, commander of 1st Battalion, 11th Panzer Regiment. That afternoon, when three hundred enemy tanks appeared in the vicinity of the village and 2nd Battalion's previously described battle took place, a large number of Soviet tanks turned toward Werchne Kumsky. Major Dr. Bäke noticed this movement and reported to the regimental commander: "The Russians are moving toward Werchne Kumsky, *Herr Oberst!*"

Peering through his field glasses, he saw dense masses of tanks stream past his position, but was unable to do anything about it as his mission was not yet complete. He saw tanks and antitank guns in "enormous quantities."

A short time later a radio message from Major Löwe reached the regimental commander: "About thirty tanks just outside Werchne Kumsky. Our armor-piercing ammunition is almost gone. Request relief!"

Oberst von Hünersdorff radioed back: "Hold on, we're coming!"

The next message from Werchne Kumsky came in half an hour later: "Situation extremely serious!—Enemy in the village! When is Bäke coming?"

Oberst von Hünersdorff spoke with Major Bäke. Then Bäke instructed his tank commanders: "Into Werchne Kumsky at maximum speed! Save our comrades without regard to our own losses!"

Major Dr. Bäke led the mass of tanks toward Werchne

Kumsky. Two companies that still had adequate quantities of armor-piercing ammunition led the way, with three others behind.

The panzers raced wildly into Werchne Kumsky. Three enemy tanks that turned to face them were shattered by a dozen shells. Several Soviet tanks pulled back. Firing on the move, or halting briefly and firing, the panzers shot up the Soviet tanks, which began to flee. Bäke's gunner hit an enemy tank, which rolled away burning to one side, rammed the wall of a house, and sat immobile beneath the rubble.

Bäke's panzers reached the center of the village. The headquarters staff of 1st Battalion appeared and waved the panzers in. All of the officers had been wounded. Burning tanks indicated the bitterness of the fighting these men had been through. *Hauptmann* Wils, commander of 4th Company, and the rest of 6th Company drove to the village limits and recovered the wounded. Three Soviet tanks still there were destroyed.

Afterward the panzers, led by *Oberst* von Hünersdorff, drove south from Werchne Kumsky and reached Salivsky. Nineteen German tanks had been knocked out by the enemy. Five others had broken down with mechanical problems. The enemy lost twenty-three tanks in this battle.

Finally, on 17 December, the first elements of the 17th Panzer Division arrived. The division had reached the battlefield ten (!) days too late. (It turned out that it had been absent in order to force the successful tank battle and the breakthrough to its surrounded comrades.) Now, together with the 6th and 23rd Panzer Divisions, it was to recapture Werchne Kumsky.

The attack was supposed to begin at 0850 on 17 December. Working day and night, the field workshop had managed to have sixty unserviceable tanks ready for action again by the evening of 16 December. This was an outstanding feat, which was acknowledged by the division commander.

Panzergruppe von Hünersdorff, consisting of the operational tanks of the 6th Panzer Division, the 23rd Panzer Division's 201st Panzer Regiment, and 1st (armored personnel carrier) Battalion of the 126th Panzer Grenadier Regiment, was to take the Shestakov bridgehead as well as Werchne Kumsky.

The battle for Shestakov took a dramatic form. Twelve enemy tanks were destroyed in a very quick tank battle. However, the ice-covered Neklinska gorge proved impassable.

"Eleventh Panzer Regiment turn toward Werchne Kumsky as soon as the Stuka attack ends!" *Oberst* von Hünersdorff ordered his two battalion commanders.

The Stukas appeared overhead and flew directly toward Werchne Kumsky. Sirens howling, they plunged down through a curtain of antiaircraft fire toward the village where Major Löwe and his men had fought their heroic battle.

Standing in their open turrets, the tank commanders watched as the dive bombers pulled up sharply. Seconds later the sound of exploding bombs rang out through the day. Thick clouds of smoke rose from Werchne Kumsky.

"Attack! Move in!" Dr. Bäke ordered his company. The panzers set themselves in motion and rolled toward the south entrance to the village. There they were stopped by a Soviet antitank front. Three panzers were hit and disabled. The rest continued to move forward, firing on visible targets, but then were forced to pull back. The enemy was too strong here.

Once again Stukas were called in. They arrived and dived almost vertically toward the ground. Again bombs fell and explosions rocked the area. But this second attack from the east also failed to break through. First Battalion, 11th Panzer Regiment, which had made up the first wave, suffered heavy losses. *Oberst* von Hünersdorff canceled the attack altogether to avoid the destruction of the entire regiment.

At 2100, division ordered the 11th Panzer Regiment recalled to its jumping off positions. On the evening of that 17 December the 4th Panzer Army, commanded by *Generaloberst* Hoth, ordered the 6th Panzer Division to take the Mishkova River sector near Gromoslavka. From there to the edge of the Stalingrad pocket was exactly forty-eight kilometers. If the 6th Army could cover that distance, then the breakthrough and breakout would succeed.

In the battles the following day the 6th Panzer Division lost more tanks. By the evening of 18 December it had fifty-one panzers left as well as six command panzers, which lacked heavy weapons.

The 6th Panzer Division, led by the 11th Panzer Regiment, set out at 1320 on 19 December. Vasilevska, the first objective, was taken in a wild race. But, as Wolfgang Paul stated, this was "no longer the beginning of the decisive attack against the encircling ring, but the last gasp of the completely exhausted

XVII Panzer Corps" (see also: Kehrig, Manfred: *Stalingrad, Analyse und Dokumentation einer Schlacht).*

Following this last act, *Panzergruppe* von Hünersdorff had only twenty tanks left. Nevertheless, the night drive across thirty kilometers of terrain, some of it enemy-held, was one of the bright spots of Operation Winter Storm, even though it no longer made any contribution toward achieving the operation's objective.

The objective was reached at about midnight. The enemy's surprise was great when the German panzers, which they had imagined were far away, suddenly rolled across the bridge spanning the Mishkova and secured it.

From there it was only forty-eight kilometers to Stalingrad, but the 23rd Panzer Division was twenty kilometers farther behind and the forces were exhausted.

At 1800 hours on the nineteenth of December, *Generalfeldmarschall* von Manstein requested that the 6th Army begin its breakout toward the 4th Army, and therefore toward the 6th Panzer Division. Battle Groups von Hünersdorff and Zollenkopf continued to hold Vasilevska in order to meet the forces breaking out of the pocket.

Hitler forbade *Generaloberst* Paulus to break out, and Paulus was not the general to defy an order from the Führer, even if it was for the good of his army.

The Soviets launched powerful attacks on Vasilevska. On 21 December the Soviet 3rd Guards Rifle Division attempted to reduce the German bridgehead. The enemy struck the northeast corner with about thirty tanks in an effort to open a path for the infantry. Major Dr. Bäke's forces repelled the attack. Bäke destroyed one of the attacking Soviet tanks himself, while his battalion knocked out seven before the enemy withdrew.

Early on the morning of 22 December, another powerful Soviet attack was beaten off by Battle Groups Zollenkopf and Unrein, the latter having just arrived to reinforce the bridgehead. Everyone was waiting for the 6th Army. When would they come? Didn't they know in Stalingrad that the situation here was becoming perilous? The night before, Soviet tanks had got to within fifteen meters of *Oberst* von Hünersdorff's command post.

On the morning of 22 December the Soviets launched an attack against 2nd Company, 11th Panzer Regiment with fifteen tanks. It was 0600 when the report reached Dr. Bäke. He immediately jumped into the nearest tank and led his battalion's 8th Company in a counterattack.

When the panzers came upon the enemy, the Soviet tanks were about to overrun the forward German machine gun positions.

"To everyone: open fire!"

Bäke's gunner targeted the first enemy tank, which was turning over a German trench, trying to collapse the walls with its grinding tracks and bury the soldiers inside.

The first shot, fired from a range of six hundred meters, was a direct hit that penetrated the armor of the Russian tank. It stopped in mid-turn and soon began to burn. The Soviet crew scrambled clear, but were cut down by machine gun fire from the panzer grenadiers. This time there was no quarter.

In the further course of the brief but violent engagement, the battalion commander's tank destroyed another Soviet tank, while the remaining panzers knocked out four more T-34s. Only a handful of the attacking Soviet tanks managed to withdraw, and one of these was hit by the long-ranging 7.5cm gun of a Panzer IV from a distance of 1,400 meters. The enemy tank was not destroyed, but it disappeared trailing smoke.

In this situation, in the midst of a counteroffensive by the 2nd Guards Army under Marshal Vassilevski, General Kirchner ordered the 6th Panzer Division to reach the Werchne Zarinsky sector, even though it was already known that Hitler was going to leave the 6th Army in Stalingrad.

This met with unanimous opposition from *Oberst* von Hünersdorff and his two battalion commanders. The regimental commander radioed corps: "A further attack is impossible! The corps headquarters should come and see for themselves."

Instead of General Kirchner, General Raus arrived on the morning of 23 December with his Ia. However, General Kirchner did arrive soon afterward, as he wished to see the situation for himself.

After listening to *Oberst* von Hünersdorff's report and seeing that the 6th Panzer Division was down to about two dozen tanks, while the enemy had positioned an entire Guards army between the division and the 6th Army, General Kirchner also became convinced that there could be no further attacks here. The only result of this would be to destroy the 6th Panzer Division for no gain in return.

General Kirchner gave in: "You are right, Hünersdorff! It's all over here."

Ninety minutes later, after General Kirchner had spoken with the division commander, General Raus gave his regimental commander, who had assumed command in the Vasilevska bridgehead, orders to abandon the bridgehead.

In the meantime, the situation on the Donets and in the great Don Basin had so deteriorated that the entire southern front was threatening to collapse. *Generaloberst* Hermann Hoth later said, "I had to make the most difficult decision in my career as a soldier." On orders from *Generalfeldmarschall* von Manstein, the chief of staff of the 4th Panzer Army had a panzer division pulled out of the line that night. The affected division was the 6th Panzer. Operation Winter Storm was over. The 6th Panzer Division was withdrawn. Thanks to the efforts of the repair shops, it now had forty-one operational tanks.

When the last of 2nd Battalion's panzers left the battlefield, every tank crewman knew that the 6th Army was lost. All their efforts, the heavy losses, the deaths of so many good comrades: all of this had been in vain. The 6th Army stayed in Stalingrad. The last survivors of those taken prisoner there did not return to Germany until 1955.

The tanks of 2nd Battalion were ready to move out. Dr. Bäke stood in his open turret hatch gazing toward the north, where only forty-eight kilometers away lay Stalingrad. Silently, he raised his hand and saluted. Afterward he ducked inside. The hatch was slammed shut and he ordered: "Panzers forward!"

The Battle of Morosovskaya

On the evening of 25 December the fast units of the 6th Panzer Division reached Morosovskaya (Morozovsk). The job at hand now was to halt the enemy forces charging toward Rostov. The Soviets had pierced the front held by the 3rd Rumanian and 8th Italian Armies and were now attempting to cut off the entire Army Group Don.

The day before the Red Army had taken the airfield at Tatsinskaya, one of the two main bases for the aerial supply of Stalingrad, and destroyed some of the seventy serviceable Ju-

52 transports on the ground there. Now this corps (the 25th Tank Corps of the 1st Guards Army) wanted to take the second supply base, Morosovskaya, in order to starve the 6th Army to death or force it to surrender.

On 24 December the 11th Panzer Division had thrown itself against this avalanche of tanks, recaptured Skossyrskaja, and established a bridgehead. In addition, by 24 December the battered units of the 306th Infantry Division had withdrawn into the Morosovskaya area, permitting the establishment of a weak line of security.

When 6th Panzer Division arrived in Morosovskaya the leading elements of the 1st Guards Army were within ten kilometers of the base.

The first of the division's units sent into action was the 6th Armored Reconnaissance Battalion. Its assignment was to secure the supply road and rail line to Morosovskaya. Panzer grenadiers secured the Chikov area.

The forty-eight tanks of the 11th Panzer Regiment arrived in Morosovskaya at dawn on 26 December, following a march of 150 kilometers. *Oberst* von Hünersdorff assembled his tactical operations staff in Romanov. Almost immediately, Dr. Bäke had to take his 5th Company into the area east of Morosovskaya to bolster the base's defenses.

The 228th Assault Gun Battalion, which had made its way to the division, together with the core of the 4th Panzer Grenadier Regiment, was sent to strengthen Battle Group Unrein.

On 27 December, Battle Group von Hünersdorff attacked Tatsinskaya. The Soviets held, although the 228th Assault Gun Battalion managed to destroy twelve enemy tanks as well as three Soviet 7.62cm all-purpose guns, the so-called *Ratschbums*.

Under the command of XXXXVIII Panzer Corps, *Gruppe* von Hünersdorff, now supported by panzer grenadiers, antitank units, and elements of the 76th Artillery Regiment as well as attached units of the 23rd Panzer Division, attacked early on the morning of 29 December after assembling in Werchne Verbovka. First Battalion, 11th Panzer Regiment suffered heavy losses in the attack. *Oberleutnant* Ranzinger, in temporary command of the battalion, was killed at the outset. Among the others who fell were *Oberleutnant* Sander and *Oberleutnant* Beuth, both company commanders.

During the night of 27/28 December, *Oberst* Martin Unrein's forces entered Tatsinskaya. Once again the assault guns led the way. A letter from Unrein to the author following the war described the horrible scene that greeted him and his soldiers in Tatsinskaya: "When I received a report that the bodies of a large number of German soldiers, who had obviously been tortured, were in a trench at the Russian position at the edge of the village, I set out at once to investigate. There were about thirty German soldiers there, who had been shot by the Russians and simply thrown into the trench. Some had been shot through the back of the neck. Others were riddled with bullets, and some showed signs of mistreatment."

In the town Battle Group Unrein found a huge supply dump belonging to the Soviet 25th Tank Corps.

On 29 December, *Oberst* von Hünersdorff led an attack with only ten tanks in the direction of Chernykov-Sswiwoloboff, in an effort to relieve the pressure. Four Soviet tanks and five antitank guns were destroyed, six very heavy mortars run over, and a number of prisoners taken.

The enemy attacks in the Urjupin area, which continued until year's end, were repulsed by the 6th Panzer Division.

On New Year's Eve night a strong enemy force with tanks and infantry broke through the weak German defenses under cover of dense fog and entered Novo Marjevka at dawn on 1 January 1943.

This was a challenge to the 11th Panzer Regiment's 2nd Battalion, because this was where Major Bäke had set up the battalion command post, positioning his companies for all-round defense. Thirty Soviet tanks raced into Novo Marjevka with supporting infantry, some riding on the tanks and others following on foot.

The Soviet tanks rammed the train vehicles and rumbled, apparently irresistibly, in the direction of Dr. Bäke's command post. Bäke had got up with the first alarm call and rushed outside, where he alerted his few panzers.

"Form battle groups. All train personnel and the *Pionier* platoon to me!" he ordered.

When the Soviet tanks appeared, they were greeted by a barrage from Bäke's nine panzers. Three T-34s went up in flames. Dr. Bäke then led four panzers into the mass of enemy tanks. Combat took place at ranges of a hundred meters and less. Bäke quickly destroyed two more enemy tanks.

Two Soviet battalions pushed past the tanks into the town to the left and right. They took cover in some houses, but were soon driven out again by a force of train personnel, who charged the Soviet positions with loud shouts of "hurray!"

Bäke's panzers supported the *Pioniers,* who blasted the Soviets out of the houses with Teller mines.

"It was as if we were drunk, although we had had nothing to drink," *Feldwebel* Günther Holtz told the author. "When we saw how our old man, the panzer doctor, opened up, how he joined in the first shout and took part in all the others, then everything went like clockwork.

"Tanks fired to our left and right, and behind us as well, while shells burst all around."

Dr. Bäke called his tank commanders: "All vehicles advance in the direction of the western part of the town!"

The German panzers continued to pound the enemy. The Soviets backed up toward the west, not stopping until they reached the edge of town. Dr. Bäke alerted his gunner to the presence of an enemy tank, which he had spotted through a house window. "He's going to show up at eleven o'clock behind that shot-up house, Brümmer!"

The gunner aimed at a position three meters beyond the left corner of the house. The long gun barrel appeared first, then the tank's nose, and finally the whole length of the T-34 was exposed in front of the German panzer. The T-34's turret began to turn, but before it could rotate the required 80 to 90 degrees, Bäke's gunner fired. The impact dislodged the tank's turret from its turret ring. The Soviet driver engaged reverse and began to back up, but before it had gone more a few meters it was hit again. The T-34's turret hatch flipped open and a jet of flame shot up into the night sky. Then the tank's ammunition supply went up, completely destroying the T-34.

Dr. Bäke ordered his forces to withdraw into the center of town and establish a defensive position. The battalion adjutant had already sent a radio message to the regiment and reported to Dr. Bäke that *Oberst* Hünersdorff was going to launch a flanking attack from the south as soon as the division gave the go-ahead.

Bäke called his commanding officer: "Hopefully they won't decide too late, *Herr Oberst.* There are strong enemy tank forces in the west and northwest ready to attack."

"We'll take care of them, Bäke!"

"Hopefully, *Herr Oberst!*" said Bäke with a smile. "But you must send me two or three panzers and break through from the south along the main road."

"That will be no problem, Bäke!"

An hour after daybreak *Oberst* von Hünersdorff received approval from division for the proposed attack. He dispatched the 2nd Company of the 6th Armored Reconnaissance Battalion from the south toward Novo Marjevka in a flanking move, and sent a company of the 114th Panzer Grenadier Regiment along the main road toward the small attacking unit.

By the time the attacking forces reached the eastern end of Marjevka, it had become clear that a new Soviet threat from the flank would not allow a further attack.

Nevertheless, that morning the Bäke Battalion continued to hold on, destroying another seven tanks and raising its total to twenty-seven. Had the Soviets managed to break through the German defensive position there, it would have had dire consequences for the entire front.

The important thing now was to beat back the approaching enemy to create some breathing room and hinder the Soviet attack.

"Bäke, set out at about noon with everything you have. The spearhead which is driving between 2./PGR 114 in Werchne Obliwiskij and yourself in Novo Marjevka must be destroyed at all costs, otherwise the situation tonight will be desperate."

"I will attack, *Herr Oberst!*" replied Dr. Bäke. He spoke with the confidence of a seasoned veteran.

It was 1230 when Bäke's armored battle group went to the attack once more. Moving in a sweeping arc from the south, the companies rolled toward the enemy in wedge formation. The 11th Panzer Regiment's 5th Company was the first to make contact with the enemy. Everyone was ordered to battle readiness. The panzers were ready to fire. A minute later 5th Company engaged the enemy. Dr. Bäke saw a line of enemy tanks roll past the 5th Company, which was embroiled in a firefight, and turn toward its flank. He immediately led 7th Company forward to counter the threat. Ignoring the shells bursting all around them, the panzers raced forward until they were on the left flank of the enemy formation.

"Open fire!"

Six panzers fired as one. Five direct hits were registered. After the second salvo, three enemy tanks were on fire. Another turned helplessly with one track shot away until it, too, was destroyed.

"Eighth Company advance on the left flank, turn in behind Werchne Obliwiskij, and attack the enemy from the rear. Fire signal flares as soon as attack position is reached."

The 8th Company pulled out to the right and rolled toward the designated position at high speed, while Dr. Bäke led the rest of the flanks onward.

The tank battle raged along the entire width of the attack sector. There were frequent flashes from direct hits. Concealed antitank guns knocked out two German panzers. Dr. Bäke's tank was disabled with track damage. He summoned one of the heavy tanks and took command of it while the tank's commander oversaw the track repairs to Bäke's panzer.

In the next thirty minutes the battle increased greatly in intensity. Dr. Bäke led his shrunken groups of tanks into one action after another. Three times Dr. Bäke raced forward in a rapid advance toward the enemy tanks before halting at a range of eight hundred meters and firing. Three Soviet tanks were destroyed in this manner.

The wave of Soviet tanks was attempting to withdraw when the 8th Company reached its assigned position. The expected signal flare rose into the sky.

"To everyone! Attack the turning enemy!"

The panzers rolled forward. Far ahead they saw 7.5cm shells fired by 8th Company plowing into the mass of enemy tanks. Then they, too, opened fire. The Soviets were trapped. In a two-hour running battle the group of enemy tanks was completely destroyed.

By the time darkness fell, the wave of Soviet tanks had been smashed. Again acting on his own initiative, Bäke ordered his tanks to pursue the fleeing enemy in order to destroy the damaged tanks, which could be easily repaired, and strike at the Soviet infantry. Expending the last of their ammunition, the panzers destroyed another three tanks, two heavy antitank guns, and a number of vehicles.

Not only had the attack by the Soviet 25th Tank Corps toward Novo Marjevka failed, but the entire corps had been completely destroyed. This defensive success removed the danger of another Soviet breakthrough toward the important rail line west of Morosovskaya, which brought in the supplies for air delivery to the Stalingrad pocket.

At 1600, when the results of the day's fighting were tallied, it was revealed that against German losses of eight tanks, with seventeen killed and forty-one wounded, the Soviets lost thirty-two tanks, including twenty T-34s. In addition, seven 7.62cm antitank guns had been destroyed, as well as a large number of infantry weapons.

Oberst von Hünersdorff reported to division that Dr. Bäke had been assigned no command responsibilities relative to the attack, and that he had carried out the counterattack that had smashed the Soviet 25th Tank Corps on his own initiative.

As a result of this information General Raus recommended Major Bäke for the Knight's Cross, the second time he had been recommended for this high decoration. Bäke received the Knight's Cross on 11 January 1943.

In the meantime the division was involved in further heavy fighting. On 2 January 1943 the Soviets began a bombardment of the German positions with artillery, mortars, and multiple rocket launchers—the so-called "Stalin organs." This was followed by an attack by a force that included several companies of T-34 tanks (each Soviet tank company was issued ten of these tanks, while the third company of each tank regiment was equipped with T-70 tanks). A Soviet breakthrough seemed certain, but once again the decimated companies and battle groups of the 6th Panzer Division held firm. Once again Dr. Bäke was on the scene when the call went out: "Panzers forward to repel enemy attack!"

Bäke led two companies of his battalion against the attacking Soviet tanks. Committing both companies, Bäke rolled straight into a group of enemy infantry, escaping a salvo from a "Stalin organ" by a hair's breadth. He rolled to one side at high speed and blasted a path through the Soviet infantry. When the battle was over, twenty knocked-out enemy tanks littered the battlefield, two of which had been destroyed by Bäke's panzer.

Since 28 December, Tatsinskaya had again been the main departure point for supply flights into the Stalingrad pocket. The 6th Panzer Division had successfully completed its assignment of recapturing the village and its airfield and securing the vital Tatsinskaya-Morosovskaya rail line. The air units under *Oberst* Kühl had been able to resume their flights. However, on 3 January 1943, in an effort to minimize losses to his transport fleet, *Oberst* Kühl ordered his units back to Novocherkassk in the face of a threatening buildup of Soviet forces. It seemed likely that the Soviets were about to make another attempt to capture Tatsinskaya. The first surprise attack on the airfield and its capture by the Red Army had resulted in the loss of seventy transport aircraft on the ground as well as a large amount of ground equipment (see: Kurowski, Franz: *Luftbrücke Stalingrad*).

On the afternoon of 6 January the 6th Panzer Division received orders for Operation *Schneeball* (Snowball). The objective was to prevent an enemy breakthrough in the Bystraya-Kalitovo area. Just prior to this, however, the Bäke Battalion was once again forced to intervene, when 2nd Battalion, 114th Panzer Grenadier Regiment in Werchne Obliwiskij was attacked by strong Soviet forces. During the night the battalion was attacked from all sides. Surplus vehicles were set on fire to illuminate the scene. When the battalion's call for help reached the division, the von Hünersdorff Regiment was ordered to go to the aid of the surrounded unit.

Hünersdorff asked Dr. Bäke, who was billeted in a neighboring village, to carry out the attack. Bäke set out at once. Just outside the village Bäke's unit ran into Soviet tanks and antitank guns. In the subsequent engagement two of Bäke's panzers were knocked out. The gunner of one of the tanks was killed, but the rest of the two crews were picked up by other vehicles.

The attempt to drive the Soviet forces out of the village failed. Nevertheless, Bäke's tanks fought their way through to the surrounded panzer grenadiers, who were able to break through and reach friendly territory.

Reports reached division headquarters that the unit on its left had begun to pull back slowly, as the Soviets had discovered the gap in the front there. On receipt of this news, corps ordered the division to send the last of its tanks to Masloff. The next morning a call for help was sent out from Bystraya-Kalitovo by the Eberswalde Personnel Replacement Battalion, which was under attack.

Oberst von Hünersdorff led thirteen Panzer IIIs against the attackers. In the replacement battalion's sector he came upon Soviet heavy tanks, which had already broken through the front. Three of Hünersdorff's panzers were knocked out by the giants, which seemed invulnerable to damage. Two 5cm anti-tank guns that were moved forward suffered the same fate after firing several shots at the approaching tanks without any visible effect.

Von Hünersdorff's force withdrew to Karlovo-Obrywskij. There it received thirteen Panzer IVs armed with the long 7.5cm gun, which had just been unloaded at the Tatsinskaya station. They were intended for the 11th Panzer Regiment, but now they provided welcome reinforcement to von Hünersdorff's battle group.

Further tanks were unloaded on the evening of 9 January 1943. Designated Panzer Company Walzer, these drove out to join Battle Group von Hünersdorff. Dr. Bäke's armored group, which was down to fourteen tanks, was held in reserve as a mobile strike force. Under its commander, the Bäke group intervened wherever the situation became threatening. Two more enemy tanks were added to Bäke's score during the fighting. Bäke insisted that the kills were achieved "with little input on my part," and that the credit was due his gunner and driver, in short, his entire crew.

On 17 January the 6th Panzer Division was moved behind the Donets River as part of a mobile defense, occupying the Puzelujev-Kamensk sector. On 18 January a report reached the 11th Panzer Regiment in Werchne Jassenovski that Major Bäke had been awarded the Knight's Cross on the evening of 11 January. There was great joy at the news, and all of Bäke's friends and comrades who could do so came for the great celebration prepared by General Raus.

At the same time, it was announced that *Hauptmann* Metzler, who was in Münster, was to take over 1st Battalion in place of the wounded Major Löwe.

In its new positions on the far side of the Donets the 11th Panzer Regiment had available thirty-nine panzers. In the days that followed, another thirty tanks arrived, some of them repaired machines returning from the shops.

Early on the morning of 20 January, forward outposts on the

bank of the Donets reported an enemy attack across an ice bridge.

Dr. Bäke was soon on the scene. He led a dozen of his panzers against the enemy force, and destroyed three T-70 light tanks that were leading the attack. Close behind the tanks came trucks towing antitank guns. Five were destroyed from close range as they tried to move into position to fire on the panzers. Bäke's tanks then shot up troop-carrying trucks as they rolled across the ice. Fires blazed and there were loud explosions as the trucks' fuel tanks went up. The enemy was thrown back across the river and made no further attempts to cross here.

Once again Dr. Bäke had arrived on the scene just in time and had "ironed out" a dangerous situation.

On 22 January 1943 the 11th Panzer Division submitted a report on the state of the tank situation: "The Panzer III is in no way equal to the demands of the war in the East. Its armor is too thin, and the caliber of its gun is inadequate. In contrast, the assault gun has proved an outstanding success in the steppe war, even though it lacks a movable turret. The reason for this success lays in its considerably stronger armor and more powerful gun."

As a result of this report the 6th Panzer Division was sent a number of assault guns, which were employed by the individual battle groups of the panzer regiment. Major Dr. Bäke's 2nd Battalion received an assault gun company and a platoon of armored *Pioniers*.

Acting in the role of a mobile fire brigade, on 31 January 1943 the battle group was sent to the attack against Kamenev as part of *Panzergruppe* von Hünersdorff.

The powerful Soviet antitank defenses on the opposite bank of the Donets destroyed or disabled ten German tanks. Fortunately, all were recovered by the tank recovery platoons or drove back under their own power following repairs.

While the division command was informed on 1 February that it was to become the army group reserve, *Panzergruppe* von Hünersdorff still had combat responsibilities to fulfill north of Krassnodon, as did Battle Group Bäke in the Donets sector.

On 9 February 1943, *Oberst* von Hünersdorff was given command of the 6th Panzer Division. General Raus had received orders to take over XI Army Corps. (While commanding this corps, in the meantime promoted to the rank of *General der Panzertruppe,* he became the 280th member of the German armed forces to receive the Oak Leaves to the Knight's Cross.)

The division was now under the command of XXXXVIII Panzer Corps. The corps' assignment was to safeguard Army Group A as it withdrew from the Caucasus.

On 19 February 1943, Hitler, who had arrived at the headquarters of Army Group Don in Zaporozhye on the seventeenth, issued the following order:

> Soldiers of Army Group South!
> Fliers of *Luftflotte* 4:
> The outcome of a battle of decisive importance depends on you. Germany's fate, present and future, will be decided a thousand kilometers from the borders of the Reich.
> The entire German homeland has therefore been mobilized. Everyone, to the last man and the last woman, is being called into service to support your battle.
> The country's youth is defending German cities and workplaces in the flak arm. New divisions are being raised.
> New, innovative weapons are on their way to your front.
> I have therefore flown to you in order to employ all means to ease your defensive battle and in the end transform it into victory. If every one of you helps me, we will—as before—succeed, with the help of the almighty.

From the headquarters in Stalino, *Oberst* von Hünersdorff directed the division as it went into action on 21 February in heavy blowing snow. Orders had been given to retake Kharkov. German forces were on the march again.

Battle Group Zollenkopf was already in action. The 11th Panzer Regiment, now under the command of *Oberst* Hermann von Oppeln-Bronikowski, had orders to start out somewhat later.

The 6th Panzer Division's advance went quickly. The German operation between the Don and Dniepr Rivers was a success, and the danger facing Army Group Don (now renamed Army Group South) of being cut off was averted.

When the 6th Panzer Division linked up with the southern part of Army Group Lanz, the Soviet Army Group Popov was completely cut off.

The group of armored forces under von Oppeln-Bronikowski, of which 11th Panzer Regiment was the core, reached the western part of Bereka on 1 March, completing the encirclement of Popov's army group. When *Waffen-SS* divisions reached the outskirts of Kharkov, the XXXXVIII Panzer Corps was turned about toward the west and sent toward Kharkov from the west and southwest.

The Battle of Kharkov was a German success. While XXXXVIII Panzer Corps, including the 6th Panzer Division, tied down the enemy forces and foiled his attempts to break out, on 11 March the divisions of II SS-Panzer Corps entered Kharkov. By 14 March the city was in German hands.

It was at this time, much to the joy of all the panzer soldiers, that new tanks arrived. The division received fifteen flame-thrower tanks and several of the latest Panzer IV models with the long 7.5cm gun. New, larger caliber antitank guns also arrived, including twenty-four self-propelled models.

The 6th Panzer Division now had ninety panzers on strength. Soon two more arrived from the workshops. *Oberst* von Hünersdorff notified 1st Battalion that it was to be transported back to Germany to serve as a replacement training battalion. However, he categorically rejected the release of surplus personnel, as there was a shortage of fully trained panzer commanders in Germany.

Following the capture of Kharkov, the II SS-Panzer Corps under *SS-Gruppenführer* Hausser pressed on and captured Belgorod on 18 March. The way to Kursk was open.

Contact was reestablished between Army Group South and Army Group Center. German industry again had access to the Donets coal mining district. The 6th Panzer Division had played a significant role in the German success.

On 30 March the 6th Panzer Division was pulled out of the line prior to taking over a sector on the Donets east of Kharkov. Based in Tarnovaya, the 11th Panzer Regiment was designated corps mobile reserve. Its strength was now down to thirty-seven panzers.

On 8 April 1943, 1st Battalion, 11th Panzer Regiment entrained in Kharkov for transport back to Germany. All of the unit's tanks and other vehicles were handed over to 2nd Battalion under Major Bäke. This brought the battalion up to strength and made it 100 percent combat ready, especially since many of its tanks were the heavier Panzer IV variety with the long 7.5cm gun. First Battalion was not to return to the 11th Panzer Regiment until December 1944. By then the division was to have faced some of the heaviest fighting of the entire eastern campaign.

On 20 April it was announced that *Oberst* von Hünersdorff had been promoted to the rank of *Generalmajor.*

Major Dr. Bäke instructed his company commanders to submit reports to division on their experiences in the second phase of the Russian campaign. One of the reports discussed the battle for Werchne Kumsky, before which *Generaloberst* Hoth had warned against "battling" the Soviets. The officer who submitted the report, *Leutnant* Bonke, wrote: "During the tank battle near Werchne Kumsky we noticed a previously unknown tactic by the Russians. There they lured us out with several tanks, which withdrew before our attacking panzers after a few shots. We chased after them and ran into a strong prepared antitank front. Individual companies were deployed to outflank this antitank front, but the attempt failed.

"The Russians had simply placed a mobile tank force at each end of the stationary antitank front, which countered each outflanking attempt.

"I also saw how they pulled antitank guns out of the line with fast American Jeeps and moved them to the threatened flank."

On 12 May 1943 the 6th Panzer Division was placed under the command of the III Panzer Corps under *General der Panzertruppe* Breith. The division headquarters moved to Kharkov. On 22 May *Generalmajor* von Hünersdorff convened a briefing of his commanders in an army recreation center in Kharkov administered by his wife, Oda von Hünersdorff.

The division commander stated plainly that the upcoming Operation *Zitadelle* (Citadel) contravened all the basic principles of strategic command. The offensive was planned for the precise areas where the Soviets were massing their forces. The enemy would be awaiting the attack. He had laid down heavily fortified positions to a depth of fifty kilometers or more. "Our forces will not be sufficient to break the enemy's resistance and force a breakthrough. But if we do break through this in-depth front with our attack forces, we will be too weak to extend the breakthrough and cut off and surround the enemy. He, however, will still be in a position to throw his unused strategic reserve into the battle."

When Operation *Zitadelle* began, the 6th Panzer Division possessed a combat strength of 16,261 soldiers of all ranks. The 11th Panzer Regiment numbered forty-eight officers and 1,601 other ranks.

This new area of operations was to see Major Dr. Bäke achieve further success in a battle whose drama was unsurpassed, culminating in the greatest armored engagement in history near Prokhorovka.

Unternehmen Zitadelle (Operation Citadel): Oberst von Oppeln-Bronikowski Reports

At the beginning of Operation Citadel, the 6th Panzer Division was under the command of *General der Panzertruppe* Breith's III Panzer Corps. The corps itself was under the command of *Armeeabteilung* Kempf.

Part of the Citadel's southern pincer, *Armeeabteilung* Kempf, together with XI Army Corps, under *General der Panzertruppe* Raus, and III Panzer Corps, under *General der Panzertruppe* Breith, was to cover the 4th Panzer Army's flank on the right bank of the Korotscha.

The attack on the southern flank began on 5 July 1943. Together with XI Army Corps, the first units of *Armeeabteilung* Kempf crossed the Donets. III Panzer Corps was ordered to link up on the right wing of II SS-Panzer Corps under *General der Waffen-SS* Hausser.

Kempf's units faced the Voronezh Front, with the 5th Guards Tank Army under General Rotmistrov, and other powerful armored units. The first battles between major armored units resulted in heavy losses to both sides. These engagements would later lead to the great tank battle of Prokhorovka.

The 6th Panzer Division, under the command of *Generalmajor* von Hünersdorff, was at full strength, including the 11th Panzer Regiment. When the attack began, the division advanced to the southern part of Stary Gorod along a narrow lane through the kilometers-deep Soviet mine belt, which had been cleared by the *Pioniers*. The advance was slow, even after further tanks and assault guns were brought across the 19th Panzer Division's fifty-ton bridge.

The attack on Stary Gorod was called off and the units there were withdrawn during the night. The 6th Panzer Division was now to cross the Donets using 7th Panzer Division's bridge and assembled in the area of Krutoj Rog-Generalovka-Solomino.

The tanks of the 11th Panzer Regiment under *Oberst* Oppeln-Bronikowski were attached to the 7th Panzer Division to help ensure the success of the armored Schulz battle group (25th Panzer Regiment) and "advance as far as the area southeast of Jastrebovo" (Hasso von Manteuffel).

Battle Group Oppeln-Bronikowski, led by the attached Tiger company, rolled across the 7th Panzer Division's sixty-ton bridge, followed by 2nd Battalion, 11th Panzer Regiment. On the far side the tanks formed up and set out toward Generalovka.

Von Oppeln-Bronikowski described to the author the battles that followed: "When I drove onto the 19th Panzer Division's temporary bridge with the first of my panzers, it collapsed under the load. Any further advance at this point was stopped even before we made contact with the enemy. We were directed farther south and sent across the 7th Panzer Division's bridge over the Donets. There we were placed under the command of the 7th Panzer Division.

"Together with *Oberstleutnant* Adalbert Schulz, I led a tank attack on a broad front. It was the largest attack I had participated in to that time.

"With 240 tanks we broke through the two deep Russian positions before the Penna River. The guns of the panzers flashed like a tremendous lightning storm. This concentrated fire eliminated the Russian bunkers. Several quick salvoes destroyed the enemy antitank guns. Several of our tanks drove over mines and were disabled, while others were knocked out by antitank guns.

"Nevertheless, the enemy's deep defensive front was broken. Then, however, the Red Army threw in a large part of its strategic armored reserve: the 2nd Guards Tank Corps and the 3rd Mechanized Corps. In particular it was the 6th and 8th Companies of the 11th Panzer Regiment under the veteran Major Dr. Bäke, supported by the Tigers of the 503rd Heavy Panzer Battalion, which established contact with the 7th Panzer Regiment advancing on our right. Seven enemy tanks and ten antitank guns as well as a number of field guns were destroyed. I learned that Dr. Bäke had destroyed another T-34.

"The next morning my armored group set out again. Battle Group Unrein, with 2nd Battalion, 114th Panzer Grenadier Regiment, joined us and drove the enemy from the villages on the far side of the Rasumnaya, which had been crossed in the meantime."

The eighth of July saw the entire 6th Panzer Division move out at first light. Following a two-hour advance, the division's leading elements were halted by a Soviet antitank ditch. Behind this the enemy had laid a deep minefield, which was covered by artillery and antitank guns.

Generalmajor von Hünersdorff, now commanding the 6th Panzer Division, placed von Oppeln-Bronikowski's armored group under the command of the 19th Panzer Division, so that the two groups could set out toward Melichovo together.

The attack got under way, with Dr. Bäke's panzer battalion in the center. It encountered strong enemy infantry forces, which tried to halt the German armored wedge. These were wiped out by high-explosive shells. Then Soviet tanks approached.

Once again Dr. Bäke led his battalion into battle with great skill. He and three other panzers led the way in the center of the tank formation. The battle began and soon the enemy began to fall back. Bäke's panzer destroyed two Soviet tanks. In total, the two armored wedges of the 6th and 19th Panzer Divisions destroyed twenty-six Soviet tanks. The objective for that day was reached.

The advance by Bäke's battalion had opened the way for the 19th Panzer Division. It crossed the antitank ditches that had halted its progress and by the evening of 8 July reached Melichovo.

The 6th Panzer Division's tank situation early on the morning of 10 July was as follows: five Panzer IIs, seventeen Panzer IIIs long, five Panzer IIIs short, ten Panzer IVs, two command tanks, three flamethrower tanks, and four captured T-34s.

The regrouping of 10 July, with the objective of deploying the main forces toward Prokhorovka in order to overrun the Soviet forces there, brought, in the words of Marshal of the Soviet Union Zhukov, "a dangerous crisis for the sector of the Veronezh Front."

This crisis arose because the armored spearheads of III Panzer Corps had advanced twenty kilometers. The attack had been directed toward Olkhovatka. The attack hesitated at first due to the unfavorable weather situation. The 503rd Heavy Panzer Battalion under *Hauptmann* Clemens Graf Kageneck was attached to Battle Group Oppeln-Bronikowski. Major Dr. Bäke had divided his 2nd Battalion into two companies, commanded by *Oberleutnant* Spiekermann and *Oberleutnant* Reutemann.

Leading the attack, which began at 0330 on 11 July, were the nineteen Tigers of sPzAbt. 503, followed by the two companies (7th and 8th Companies) of the 11th Panzer Regiment.

The attack began to gain momentum. "Eighth Company go into Schlachowoje!" ordered Dr. Bäke, while he led the 7th Company in the direction of Olkhovatka. The advance continued toward Kasatschje and the Soviet antitank ditches there. On the way Dr. Bäke learned by radio that his 8th Company had taken Schlachowoje and was advancing toward Werchne Oljchanez.

After reaching the antitank ditches, *Oberst* von Oppeln-Bronikowski received orders to take Rshvets in a surprise night attack and establish a bridgehead across the Ssewernyi-Donets.

Hermann von Oppeln-Bronikowski described the raid in his personal diary: "I greeted the commanders as they arrived at a provisional command post outside Kasatschje: 'Gentlemen, we will carry out our mission by night. The terrain lends itself to such an attack. Bäke, you and 2nd Battalion take the lead, I will join you in my command vehicle.' "

Major Dr. Bäke nodded in agreement and noted something on his map board. The battle group commander continued: "We shall try to pass the Russian truck columns driving the same road in the same direction unrecognized."

The nocturnal advance began. Now and then the panzers and the Soviet truck columns were only meters apart. Everything appeared to be going as planned. Leading the way were two captured T-34 tanks under *Leutnant* Huchtmann. It was hoped that these would fool the enemy into believing that this was a Soviet column.

Suddenly, however, a Soviet armored column with mounted

infantry was spotted coming the other way. The Germans kept their nerve and tried to pass unnoticed, but then one of the captured T-34s developed a mechanical problem and pulled off to the side. There was momentary confusion among the approaching group of Soviet T-34s, but then they opened fire, having recognized the German ruse.

This action has been reconstructed from entries in Dr. Bäke's war diary:

> Leading the way was a captured T-34. I had ordered radio silence and no firing. Silently we passed the first enemy barricade, driving by the deadly antitank guns which remained silent, believing us to be one of their own units.
>
> When the T-34 broke down with engine trouble, a Panzer IV was forced to assume the lead. Rshvets appeared before us. At the edge of town stood a row of T-34s, which readily made way for what they obviously believed to be their own tanks returning from battle. Then a column of tanks appeared heading in the opposite direction.
>
> *Leutnant* Huchtmann in the lead tank reported twenty-two T-34s. These passed my unit, almost track to track. But then six or seven pulled out of the column, turned, rolled back, and pulled in behind us.
>
> I ordered the rest to continue and placed my command tank, which was equipped only with a dummy gun, across the road in order to force the enemy tanks to halt. Seven T-34s rolled up and formed a semicircle around me.
>
> I called my operations officer and ordered him to break out the hollow charges. Then the two of us left the tank. We slid out of the field of view of the T-34 standing to our right. Reaching the tanks, we placed the hollow charges on two T-34s and jumped into cover.
>
> The detonations rang through the night. Two T-34s were put out of action. We fetched two more hollow charges and put them in place. Two more T-34s were blown up.
>
> The fifth T-34 was destroyed by one of my panzers.

Oberst von Oppeln-Bronikowski drove into the rest of the Soviet tank column. The enemy tanks finally withdrew across the bridge and blew it up behind them.

As the bridge was no longer passable, the grenadiers of 2nd Battalion, 114th Panzer Grenadier Regiment waded across the river and established the first bridgehead, which was secured by machine gun positions.

III Panzer Corps now had a chance to drive to Prokhorovka, link up with the II SS-Panzer Corps there, and continue the attack.

On the morning of 12 July, Soviet Marshal Zhukov was forced to throw the entire 5th Guards Tank Army and the 5th Guards Army into the battle in an effort to stop this dangerous advance. The 5th Guards Tank Army possessed eight hundred T-34s and heavy self-propelled guns. The tank battle of Prokhorovka could begin.

Marshal Zhukov: "Stalin called me that day and ordered me to fly at once into the Prokhorovka area, in order to take the necessary measures to bring the Voronezh and Steppe Fronts into line."

On that same 12 July the Red Army opened the counteroffensive for which it had long been preparing, with the initial objective of retaking Orel. The same day *Generaloberst* Model, commander of the northern pincer, received directions from Führer headquarters to pull back from the territory already won and intervene in the battle for Orel, which had just broken out. This ended the German 9th Army's participation in Operation *Zitadelle*.

Early on the morning of 13 July, III Panzer Corps received a report that *Generalmajor* von Hünersdorff had been slightly wounded by shell fragments.

The German Air Attack on the 6th Panzer Division

Soon after, German bombers and Stukas attacked the Soviet troop concentrations in the Rshvets area. The 6th Panzer Division's headquarters staff hurried outside to watch the attack. The Stukas bombed the forward Russian lines while the following He-111 bombers dropped heavy bombs on the troop concentrations in the rear. At the end of the attack one He-111 approached the area, straggling far behind the rest. It dropped its bombs when directly over the headquarters of the 6th Panzer Division. All of the officers and commanders standing in the open were either killed or wounded.

Those who died were: Major Rogalla von Bieberstein, commander of the 114th Panzer Grenadier Regiment, who had been recommended for the Knight's Cross (awarded posthumously on 27 July 1943); *Hauptmann* Erich Oeckel, commander of 1st

Battalion, 114th Panzer Grenadier Regiment; *Oberleutnant* Wagemann, battery commander in the 228th Assault Gun Battalion, which was attached to the division; *Oberleutnant* Engel, and *Leutnant* Rauscher.

Wounded were *Oberst* von Oppeln-Bronikowski, Major Dr. Bäke, *Hauptmann* Meckauer, *Hauptmann* Jahn, *Oberleutnant* Guckel, *Oberleutnant* Forwick, *Oberleutnant* Schröder, and *Oberleutnant* Eberlein.

A large portion of the division's command staff had been put out of action. Total casualties from the disaster were fifteen dead and forty-nine wounded. This was more than the division could bear. Nevertheless, the battle had to go on.

Major Dr. Bäke had his wounds dressed on the spot and took over command of PR 11, as von Oppeln-Bronikowski's wounds were of a more serious nature. He handed over 2nd Battalion to *Hauptmann* Scheibert, one of the most dependable of the younger generation of tank commanders.

Dr. Bäke's battle group was to have attacked at 1800 that evening, but the other participating unit, the 7th Panzer Division, did not show up in time because its attack toward Krasnoye Anamja had been turned back by the Soviets.

Finally, on 14 July, the 7th Panzer Division managed to take the village after destroying a number of Soviet tanks and was able to cover the 6th Panzer Division's left flank.

At 0700, following a brief artillery bombardment, Major Dr. Bäke attacked Alexandrovka. A number of assault guns and Tiger tanks had been assigned to his battle group. All of his tanks were concentrated in a single company, enabling him to maintain strict control of the operation.

Armored Battle Group Bäke (as his unit was designated that day) shot up Alexandrovka and enabled 2nd Battalion, 114th Panzer Grenadier Regiment to take the village.

The battle group then stormed three hills. A tank-versus-tank battle ensued, in which Bäke's forces destroyed twenty-five tanks, thirty-one antitank guns, and twelve artillery pieces. Two tanks and one gun were accounted for by Dr. Bäke.

The victory was not without a high cost, however. *Generalmajor* von Hünersdorff, the division commander, accompanied Dr. Bäke as he led the attack. Von Hünersdorff was hit in the head by sniper fire. Pieces of the steel helmet he was wearing were driven into his brain.

The German brain specialist *Oberstarzt* Professor Tönnis was flown in at once. The doctor operated on the general, but it was already too late.

"Only an immediate operation, right after he suffered the wound, could have saved him. Nevertheless, I tried the impossible, because there was a slim chance."

Generalmajor von Hünersdorff died on 17 July 1943. On 14 July he had become the 259th German soldier to be awarded the Oak Leaves to the Knight's Cross. *Generaloberst* Hoth delivered the eulogy. *Generalfeldmarschall* von Manstein and Generals Raus and Kempf paid their final respects to their dead comrade. Also at the graveside was Hünersdorff's wife, nursing sister Oda von Hünersdorff. Her final words to the men assembled there were: "Hold the name of Hünersdorff in respect!"

Heavy Armored Battle Group Bäke Forward!

On the evening of 14 July, Army Group South informed the commanding general of III Panzer Corps that the corps was to advance northward the next morning to link up with II SS-Panzer Corps. The entire corps had only sixty-nine tanks left, including six (!) Tigers and twelve assault guns.

On 15 July, *Oberst* Martin Unrein, who was in temporary command of the 6th Panzer Division, ordered Bäke's armored battle group to assemble for an eventual counterattack as III Panzer Corps' reserve unit.

When the newly appointed division commander, *Oberst* Crisolli, arrived on the evening of 16 July, he found that the division had only six (!) tanks. Dr. Bäke was sent to accelerate the repair of the damaged tanks. He handed over command of the armored battle group to *Hauptmann* Scheibert. When III Panzer Corps pulled back to a new main line of resistance on 20 July, the 6th Panzer Division, thanks to the tireless efforts of Dr. Bäke, had available thirty-one tanks and three flamethrower tanks.

Along this sector of the front the initiative had passed to the Red Army. Operation *Zitadelle* had bogged down in the deep Soviet defensive zones. The 6th Panzer Division's ordeal was about to begin.

Under the command of Major Dr. Bäke, the armored battle group covered the withdrawal of the division, which was to relieve the 19th Panzer Division in the C-Line. There the division was again joined by the 503rd Heavy Panzer Battalion.

When a group of T-34s attacked, Bäke took command of six of the heavy tanks and attacked. Bursting out of a wooded area, the Tigers took the Soviets completely by surprise. Twenty-three T-34s were destroyed in this brief and one-sided battle, two of which were destroyed by Bäke's panzer.

On 23 July the Soviets attacked with an even larger armored force. Once again there was a large-scale armored engagement. Dr. Bäke led his forces with great skill, enabling his tanks to maintain the upper hand throughout. When the Soviets broke off the engagement, thirty-three T-34s lay burning and smoldering on the plain. Once again Dr. Bäke accounted for two of the enemy tanks.

The next day the Tiger unit left to assist the 19th Panzer Division. A large assembly of Soviet tanks was spotted in front of the 6th Panzer Division. A unit of Ju-87 and Ju-88 bombers managed to evade the Soviet fighter defenses and attacked. The dive bombers roared down on the enemy tanks and soon the assembly area was shrouded in smoke and flames.

On 25 July, Bäke's armored unit was made corps reserve. *Generaloberst* Hermann Hoth arrived and had a long talk with Dr. Bäke. The army commander in chief was very impressed with this officer. He said: "I decided to appoint this high quality officer first to a regiment, and then, following a division commander's course, to give him the opportunity to command a panzer division."

On 27 July, Armored Battle Group Bäke returned to the division. In a regimental order of 29 July 1943, the commander of the 11th Panzer Regiment stated: "You have destroyed 111 enemy tanks, 140 antitank guns, and other heavy weapons."

On 1 August 1943 the men of Armored Battle Group Bäke learned that their commander had become the 262nd German soldier to receive the Oak Leaves to the Knight's Cross.

"Second Battalion, 11th Panzer Regiment under *Hauptmann* Scheibert assembled in front of the commander of our armored battle group. Three volleys signified once again the entire regiment's great and sincere joy over this decoration."

Armored Battle Group Bäke continued to see action. Advancing out of the Gonki Forest on 3 August, the unit's panzers destroyed nine more T-34s.

The battle group's great success was due to the dashing and yet prudent manner in which Bäke commanded his unit. He knew the strengths and weaknesses of his tanks and those of the enemy, and was well versed in Soviet tactics. This assured his unit victory.

On 6 August, Dr. Bäke and *Oberst* Unrein managed to head off a potentially disastrous situation. A group of grenadiers had panicked and was falling back in disarray. The two officers went forward with only two tanks and two command vehicles and stopped the unchecked withdrawal, allowing that sector of the front to be held.

On 7 August, Bäke's small force of panzers blocked the main road and halted a rapid enemy advance, permitting the German forces to carry out an orderly withdrawal.

Bäke's panzers formed a steel barricade behind the 282nd Infantry Division, which had withdrawn from Kharkov as the result of a mistaken order, and halted the onrushing Soviet armor. Early the next morning forty enemy tanks attacked but were stopped by a sharp attack from the flank delivered by Bäke's armored battle group and several flak 88s. The former main line of resistance was recovered. The following night the 6th Panzer Division marched into Kharkov.

The order issued by XXXXII Army Corps on the evening of 13 August stated: "The Führer has ordered: 'Kharkov is to be held at all costs.'"

The battle for Kharkov continued until 17 August. The enemy's attempt to break through to the west had failed. However, on 23 August, Kharkov was again abandoned. The 6th Panzer Division formed the German rearguard outside the city.

The defensive battles raged on until 13 September. On that day the 6th Panzer Division destroyed its 1,500th enemy tank.

On 19 August, Major Bäke drove to 2nd Battalion's rear echelon, where he was to rest and oversee the training of new panzer crews. One platoon under *Oberleutnant* Reutemann remained behind with the division.

The 6th Panzer Division had fought on until it was almost destroyed. By the twenty-seventh of August, the day the 6th Panzer Division took over a new defensive sector in the Tarnovka area, several panzers had returned to the division. Bäke's panzers were employed as a mobile "fire brigade." Following a battle near the "Arrowhead Gorge" there were only two left. There, on 2 September, *Generalmajor* Freiherr von Waldenfels arrived to take command of the division, a position he would hold until the end of the war.

On 13 September the 6th Panzer Division pulled out of its positions near Tarnovka and Merefa and withdrew to the Udy. Once again Dr. Bäke covered the withdrawal. That day his small force of panzers destroyed no less than sixteen tanks from a large pursuing force of T-34s and prevented the division from being outflanked. Bäke and his crew accounted for three of the Soviet tanks.

On 23 September 1943, Dr. Bäke was forced to leave the division. His orders to report to Erlangen concerned the introduction into service of the new Panther tank.

First, however, he had to report to Hitler in the Führer headquarters. Hitler presented him with the Oak Leaves to the Knight's Cross, which was the usual practice with this decoration.

During the subsequent discussion, Hitler demonstrated that he was well informed about the events of the Battle of Kursk. He told the assembled Oak Leaves recipients that he had considered *Generalfeldmarschall* von Manstein's suggestion to continue fighting in the south, but that the events near Orel, and above all the Allied landings in Sicily, had led him to break off the battle.

Hitler was as active as ever. He showed no sign of resignation and wanted total victory, while *Generalfeldmarschall* von Manstein at this time was toying with the idea of a negotiated end to the war, which was certainly possible, as was indicated by the secret discussions with Molotov behind the front.

In November 1943, Dr. Bäke returned to his division as an *Oberstleutnant.* On the fourteenth, *Oberst* Oppeln-Bronikowski handed over command of the 11th Panzer Regiment to him. Bäke's successor as commander of the regiment's 2nd Battalion was Major Hermann Sachenbacher.

Sachenbacher was soon to be killed in action, however. On 27 November the 6th Panzer Division was ordered to fight its way through an enemy position outside Cherkassy, which was holding up an advance by the panzer grenadiers. Second Battalion 11th Panzer Regiment was given the job. Major Sachenbacher set a personal example by leading the attack, and was killed as the battalion broke into the Soviet position.

A short time later the Soviets entered Cherkassy. Dr. Bäke sent four Panzer IVs there. He was to retake Cherkassy.

"I was not given an opportunity to carry out the attack, which would have surely succeeded, because in Snamenka, the starting point for the attack, I received an order from 6th Panzer Division to return to the Glinki area. In my opinion this was a mistake which was to cost many thousands of German soldiers in Cherkassy their lives. But the order was unequivocal. As a result, in the following weeks the enemy was able to complete the encirclement of Cherkassy. I will not try and conceal the fact that naturally, the 6th Panzer Division was also needed in the new combat zone. On 20 December the division foiled a Russian breakthrough attempt into the rear of our front near Kirovograd."

Armored Battle Group Bäke saw more heavy fighting in support of the grenadiers until the end of December. On 31 December 1943 the 6th Panzer Division was withdrawn from the Fedwar area and sent by train into the area of Kirovograd.

Heavy Panzer Regiment Bäke in Action

At the beginning of January 1944, the 1st Ukrainian Front under General Vatutin split the 4th Panzer Army into several parts. The result of this was a series of major battles that placed great demands on the German army, particularly the panzer units. The 6th Panzer Division saw the developments as follows: "The 1st Panzer Army's rear was threatened as a result of the enemy breakthrough. The 6th Panzer Division was sent into action to eliminate this threat.

"*Panzergruppe* Bäke arrived in the new assembly area with twenty-six panzers on 2 January and took over the lead position. On the morning of 4 January began the attack toward Oratovka and Novo Shivotiv. The enemy holding there saw Bäke's panzers coming toward them. The panzers drove the enemy out of Oratovka and in the period that followed were repeatedly involved in a series of small engagements against a well-camouflaged enemy, who on several occasions was supported by tanks. Russian tanks were destroyed by tank-killing squads."

Dr. Bäke experienced an enemy attack at the regimental command post in Frantivka. The attacking Soviet battalion was wiped out by the German defensive fire. Marshal Zhukov wrote: "The enemy defended with tenacity against the 1st Ukrainian Front."

On 13 January the 6th Panzer Division was again attached to III Panzer Corps, and was therefore under the command of the 1st Panzer Army. Panzer grenadiers of the neighboring 16th Panzer Division and some of the division's own troops were surrounded by Soviet forces. On 21 January the 11th Panzer Regiment set out to relieve the encircled troops. *Oberstleutnant* Bäke now commanded two battle groups. Under Bäke's skillful leadership, both were completely successful. The enemy was driven back.

When Bäke returned to the command post following the successful mission, he found orders awaiting him for a special operation. In addition to the 11th Panzer Regiment, thirty-four Tigers (of sPzAbt. 503) and forty-seven Panthers (of 2./PR 23) had been placed under his command. These units combined to form Heavy Panzer Regiment Bäke. Also placed at his disposal was 1st Battalion, 88th Artillery Division, which was equipped with Hummel self-propelled artillery. *Oberstleutnant* Bäke now commanded a fighting force that would be able to stand up to any Soviet attack.

Bäke now had to carry out a tank attack that would have to be conducted without regard to its open flanks. The war diary of the 11th Panzer Regiment: "Through the fortunate composition of this heavy panzer regiment, and the readiness for action and drive of its commander, it succeeded—advancing irresistibly as ordered—in destroying the enemy."

This great triumph of leadership by *Oberstleutnant* Bäke was crowned by his panzer's destruction of three enemy tanks. "Once again Doctor Bäke demonstrated that he was an expert at achieving a major victory while keeping his own losses low." Following this the regiment was made XXXXVI Panzer Corps' (General Gollnick) mobile reserve.

An attack by the 3rd Soviet Tank Corps of General Bogdanov's 2nd Soviet Army was halted by *Oberstleutnant* Bäke and his heavy tank regiment. In a lengthy battle the Tigers and the fast and powerful Panthers destroyed 268 enemy tanks and assault guns. 156 guns were destroyed by gunfire or run over by the panzers. In his Panther, *Oberstleutnant* Bäke withstood seven Soviet attacks. Thanks to the speed and sureness of his crew he was able to parry attacks by two concealed antitank guns and destroy them. Six times Bäke emerged victorious from duels with Soviet tanks.

"If we had had this Panther in 1941, the army would have rolled straight to Moscow," declared Dr. Bäke when asked about the firepower, rate of fire, and speed of the new tank. "I prefer the Panther to the Tiger, although it, too, is an outstanding combat vehicle."

When a large armored force was assembled in the Proskurov area to counter a threatened Soviet breakthrough toward the west, the first unit to arrive was the 6th Panzer Regiment. There *Oberstleutnant* Bäke and his tank unit were ordered to carry out a relief attack with the 17th Panzer Regiment. The objective of the attack was to free the three German army corps surrounded in the Cherkassy (Korsun) Pocket.

Eleven Tigers and fourteen Panthers went into battle, attacking from the area northeast of Uman. Bäke's panzer group attacked from the fourth to the eighth of February, but was unable to break through the ring of Soviet forces.

Another attack from the Rubany-Most area, led by Bäke himself, was more successful. His heavy armored group encountered a powerful Soviet force of tanks and assault guns. Battle Group Bäke fought the engagement in three armored wedges. While the fast Panthers stormed forward to the left and right, the Tigers drove in the center, about three hundred meters behind. As soon as an enemy tank opened fire from long range, the Tigers fired on the targets assigned by Dr. Bäke and destroyed them.

While the Tigers engaged the enemy tanks, the faster Panthers outflanked the enemy's antitank front. The Tigers fired on the concealed antitank guns as soon as they were spotted.

This was further proof that a tank such as the Tiger, which could knock out the heaviest enemy tank from a range of two thousand meters, was a devastating weapon in the hands of a commander well versed in armored tactics.

No fewer than eighty enemy tanks and assault guns were destroyed or immobilized in this first attack. However, due to the enemy's tremendous numerical superiority, there was a high cost attached to this victory. When the battle ended in Chishintsy on 13 February, *Oberstleutnant* Bäke was left with only four Panthers and twelve support tanks.

On 15 January, Heavy Panzer Regiment Bäke, which had been brought back up to strength with panzers sent back by the repair shops, was turned toward Lysyanka. *Generalfeld-*

marschall von Manstein sent a teletype message congratulating Dr. Franz Bäke on his success: "Bravo! You have accomplished much, despite mud and Russians. Now you must take the last step! Grit your teeth and have at them! This, too, will succeed!"

Bäke's forces resumed the attack on 15 February, together with the 1st Panzer Division. This final effort brought the panzers to the boundary of the pocket. At 0330, early on the morning of 16 February, *Oberstleutnant* Bäke watched as the first surrounded units left the pocket. The commander of the heavy panzer regiment led the two battalions to Oktyabr, and personally asked their commanders to stay and help defend against the Russians and hold open the corridor for their comrades still in the pocket.

When the Soviets launched their expected attack, they were wiped out by the exhausted panzer soldiers. Unfortunately, the two battalions that had been freed by Bäke withdrew, even though they were still combat capable.

A total of 35,000 German soldiers were able to escape the Cherkassy Pocket. Much of the credit for regaining their freedom was due to Dr. Bäke's heavy panzer regiment.

In the Battle of Stary Konstantinov, which the division had ordered held, Bäke's armored battle group destroyed eleven T-34s and eight antitank guns. German losses were high, however: thirteen panzers were knocked out by the enemy. Fortunately, only a portion of them were total losses.

At the northern edge of Kamenka, west of Stary Konstantinov, *Oberfeldwebel* Bloos, a platoon leader in the 11th Panzer Regiment, took charge of the defense with the small number of tanks left to the regiment. When the Soviets attacked, the first T-34s were destroyed as they approached. The defenders then laid in wait for the following fifteen T-34s. These shot up the first rows of houses and set them on fire. Ludwig Bloos had positioned two of his panzers in ambush positions farther back while he waited for the enemy in his panzer behind a row of houses. When the enemy tanks came into sight, Bloos destroyed five T-34s in quick succession. A sixth was hit and turned away smoking. Now the Soviets moved forward a heavy antitank gun. The platoon leader's tank was hit and put out of action. Bloos was seriously wounded and had to be evacuated. On 6 April 1944 he received the Knight's Cross of the Iron Cross for this action.

Armored Group Bäke was formed on 6 March. It consisted of the 2nd Battalion, 11th Panzer Regiment, 1st and 2nd Battalions of the 1st Panzer Regiment, and the 509th Heavy Panzer Battalion. A battalion of grenadiers was attached to the battle group. The battle group's mission was to reopen the north-south road near Stary Konstantinov.

Bäke's Tigers and Panthers swept the area of enemy forces. Burning Soviet tanks marked Armored Group Bäke's rampage to Rosslowzy. The enemy advance from the west toward Stary Konstantinov collapsed.

The next major attack by Armored Group Bäke rolled westward across the main road from Proskurov. After smashing through several enemy positions and destroying fifteen tanks, two assault guns, and nineteen antitank guns and other heavy weapons, the battle group reached its objective.

The Soviet Offensive Southeast of Vinnitsa

On 4 March 1944 the 509th Heavy Panzer Battalion was placed under the command of the 6th Panzer Division. The division's armored elements—Armored Group Bäke—were to arrive in Stary Konstantinov that night. Dr. Bäke had been sent a fully equipped panzer company, the 6th Company of the 1st Panzer Division's 1st Panzer Regiment.

The Tiger battalion, under the command of *Hauptmann* König, arrived in Stary Konstantinov at 2300. Following several delays it set out at 1000 the next morning on the right wing of the 11th Panzer Regiment. Advancing southwestward, the battalion reached the village of Kusmin at about midday against opposition from enemy tanks. *Oberstleutnant* Bäke then ordered his unit to veer northward and advance through Lagodinzy. The Manewzy-Rosslowzy road was reached as darkness fell. Seventeen enemy tanks had been destroyed against two losses. Dr. Bäke's panzer played a role in the success, destroying two Soviet tanks.

Dr. Bäke's skillfully executed "horizon crawl" inflicted a heavy defeat on the enemy and enabled him to outflank the Soviet antitank front.

A local attack by the Soviets with T-34s near Kusmin on 6 March was successfully defeated.

The next day Armored Group Bäke was sent to Svinnaya to

defend against a threatened Soviet breakthrough east of Stary Konstantinov. Stary Konstantinov was abandoned and the three wooden bridges at the south end of the city were blown up by the 6th Panzer Division's *Pioniers* after the last tanks had crossed.

Svinnaya was secured on 8 March, and on the following day the 509th Heavy Panzer Battalion advanced through Lashava to the Ostropil-Babin-Pillava road. When heavy enemy column movements were reported there, Dr. Bäke ordered, "Move in at once and stop the traffic, and destroy as many vehicles as possible!"

The panzers fell on the enemy columns, firing as they came, and destroyed one hundred horse-drawn and motor vehicles. Also destroyed were two horse-drawn batteries. The armored battle group returned to its starting positions without loss.

When, on 10 March, the Red Army launched a major offensive at the junction between the 1st Panzer Army and the 8th Army southeast of Vinnitsa, the 509th Heavy Panzer Battalion was ordered to withdraw behind the Bozok River and hold there. The battalion was the last unit across the river, crossing on the evening of the twelfth and destroying two T-34s in the process. Still attached to the 6th Panzer Division, its assignment was to secure the major Proskurov-Vinnitsa road and the bridges over the River Bug near Sawniza-Triluchowzy.

Meantime, the Red Army—the 1st Guards Army and the 3rd Tank Army—had launched an attack at the junction between the German 1st and 4th Panzer Armies, and by the morning of 14 March had crossed the Ternopol-Proskurov rail line, which was the 1st Panzer Army's main supply line. Communications were broken between the 1st and 4th Panzer Armies.

The entire 1st Panzer Army was threatened with encirclement. On 16 March, Armored Group Bäke, now consisting of twelve Tiger I E tanks of the 509th Battalion, elements of the 11th Panzer Regiment, and 1st Company, 1st Panzer Regiment, was withdrawn from its positions and assembled at the eastern edge of Proskurov for an assault to the west. The assignment given Dr. Bäke was: "Reestablish contact with 4th Panzer Army!"

That evening the armored group was reinforced by the arrival of the entire 1st Battalion, 1st Panzer Regiment under *Hauptmann* Graf Wedel. *Oberstleutnant* Bäke now carried the hopes of two entire panzer armies.

Bäke's armored group, now once again bearing the title Heavy Panzer Regiment Bäke, received further deliveries of tanks in order to be equal to the difficult task it had been set.

Early on the morning of 17 March 1944, the armored group set out, led by the Tigers, to break through to the developing Kamenets-Podolsk pocket. Advancing rapidly, the panzers crashed through the first enemy resistance near Klimkovtsy. By midday Bäke's forces were already thirty kilometers west of Proskurov, and in the Vidva-Medvedovka area they came upon units of the 1st SS-Panzer Division *Leibstandarte*. Contact had been made with the 4th Panzer Army.

Following the arrival of further Tigers on 18 March, Bäke's armored group attacked Dselintsche and took the heavily defended village in spite of a determined Soviet defense.

Twelve assault guns and forty-four tanks, including four KV Is and KV 85s, thirty-three antitank guns, and a number of light artillery pieces were destroyed by the panzers. Dr. Bäke's Panther destroyed three enemy tanks and two antitank guns, the latter from close range.

Heavy Panzer Regiment Bäke's next attack began on 19 March. Four Tigers, seven Panthers, seven assault guns, and ten armored personnel carriers crossed Hill 340 and reached Hill 349. There they were met by heavy antitank fire. In the ensuing engagement all of the Tigers and three Panthers were put out of action. The attack had to be broken off. The entire regiment had been reduced to two Tigers, two Panthers, four assault guns, and four Panzer IVs as well as ten armored personnel carriers.

During an attack the following day the regimental commander's tank was hit and disabled. Dr. Bäke climbed into a fast armored personnel carrier and carried on. The last of his tanks were knocked out here in a duel against overwhelming numbers of Soviet armor, or were forced to withdraw with battle damage. The 11th Panzer Regiment had not a single operational panzer left, but the enemy's attempted breakthrough had been foiled.

On 19 March, *Oberleutnant* Dr. König received orders to tow all of his nonoperational tanks to Proskurov. Dr. Bäke remained in Dselintsche with those panzers that had been restored to service—a total of six, including two Tigers—to cover the withdrawal.

When the Soviets pursued rashly, they ran into a cleverly laid ambush by Bäke's small number of tanks. Four of the onrushing T-34s were destroyed and the entire Soviet armored front came to a halt. Bäke's panzers fired into the mass of enemy tanks that had become bunched up near the destroyed T-34s.

Firing from a concealed position behind a low rise, Dr. Bäke destroyed two T-34s that had managed to free themselves from the traffic jam. The Soviets attempted to advance no farther that day, allowing the main body of German forces to withdraw unmolested.

By 23 March the Tigers that had driven or been towed to the repair shops in Jaromolintsy had been overhauled. *Hauptmann* Burmester arrived to take command of the 509th Battalion from *Hauptmann* Radtke, who had been called away.

On 23 March, *Oberstleutnant* Dr. Franz Bäke said farewell to his comrades. He was flown out of the pocket to receive the Swords to the Knight's Cross with Oak Leaves from Hitler's hand in Führer headquarters. He had been awarded the decoration on 21 February for his action in freeing some of the troops surrounded in the Cherkassy Pocket.

The decoration was also recognition of this officer's outstanding career, during which he had been a comrade to every soldier and a father figure to his younger troops. Everyone knew that Dr. Franz Bäke was not going to return to the 6th Panzer Division, which had been his home for the entire war. It was a sure bet that this highly regarded panzer commander would be given a more senior appointment.

At the Führer headquarters, where Bäke described the fighting at the Cherkassy Pocket and his armored group's final actions, he learned from Hitler that, following completion of a division commander's course, he was to lead a panzer division.

The End of the War

Following his visit to Führer headquarters, Dr. Bäke was given a long home leave, and on 1 May 1944 was promoted to the rank of *Oberst*. Hitler had indicated that he had still another surprise in store. This was related to his promotion. Dr. Bäke was placed among the ranks of active line officers.

Part of the 1944 program to create thirteen modern panzer brigades was the formation of the 106th Heavy Panzer Brigade *Feldherrnhalle*. On 13 July 1944, *Oberst* Dr. Bäke became the brigade's first commanding officer. On 31 August he reported the brigade ready for action and was sent with his unit to the Western Front. The brigade's Panther battalion possessed four companies, each with eleven Panthers, while its headquarters company also had eleven. The brigade's total strength was 2,500 men.

From mid-September, Dr. Bäke and his brigade saw action in the area south of Metz under the command of XIII SS-Panzer Corps. Once again Bäke distinguished himself through the circumspect and yet decisive leadership of his armored unit. On 4 October the brigade was placed under the command of LXXXV Army Corps in the area west of Belfort.

During the course of the defensive battles in the west, Dr. Bäke and his Panthers were constantly in action under various commands. Once again Bäke demonstrated his skill in mastering the most difficult situations while fighting under the command of XIII Army Corps during the winter of 1944, and later with the 21st Panzer Division. His operations in the Mülhausen area of Alsace were classic examples of a commander getting the best from his men and equipment. Dr. Bäke accounted for further enemy tanks in his Panther, however, the exact number destroyed by him in this period is not known.

The 106th Panzer Brigade's heaviest fighting came in the defense of the Alsace bridgehead, beginning on 1 January 1945. The *Feldherrnhalle* Brigade was the heart of the German defense, which held the bridgehead until 7 February.

Dr. Bäke was relieved as commander of the brigade on 3 February. His successor was *Oberstleutnant* Dr. Drewes. Bäke had been summoned by the OKH to set up and take command of a panzer division.

The 18th Panzer Division, which had largely been destroyed in the battles to free Budapest, released its 4th Panzer Regiment to the new *Feldherrnhalle 2* Panzer Division. Creation of the new division was accelerated by detachments from other units, and soon afterward the division was sent to Slovakia.

It was clear to Dr. Bäke that his division's sole task was the safeguarding of the large numbers of German refugees fleeing the Red Army. Promoted to the rank of *Generalmajor* on 1 April, Dr. Bäke led his division in heavy fighting that saw it withdraw across the Carpathians to Mähren and eventually into the Budweis area. The division had achieved much, rescuing numerous columns of refugees and escorting them to the west.

At war's end, on 8 May 1945, Dr. Bäke attempted to surrender his division to the Americans to prevent it falling into Soviet hands. He was unable to convince the Americans, however, and his division, like many others, was delivered into the hands of the Soviets.

Generalmajor Bäke was forced to order his division to disband. He asked his officers to gather their men and try to slip through the American lines in small groups. Some of the small bands of soldiers managed to reach freedom in the west. One of them was led by Dr. Franz Bäke.

However, many members of the division fell into Soviet hands and were taken to the Soviet Union, where they were employed as slave labor in the mines for ten long years.

Generalmajor Dr. Franz Bäke

28 February 1898:	Born in Schwarzenfels, Franconia.
19 May 1915:	Joins the 53rd Infantry Regiment as a volunteer at the age of seventeen. First World War decorations: Iron Cross, First and Second Class.
November 1918:	Holds the rank of *Vizefeldwebel* and Officer Cadet in the 7th Foot Regiment.
January 1919:	Released from service.
1 December 1937:	Joins German *Wehrmacht* as a *Leutnant* of the Reserve. Participates in Polish campaign as platoon leader in 1st Light Division's 6th Reconnaissance Battalion.
1 November 1939:	Promoted to *Oberleutnant* of the Reserve.
1940:	Commander of 1st Company, 6th Reconnaissance Battalion in French campaign.

1 February 1941:	Appointed operations officer in 11th Panzer Regiment.
1 March 1941:	Appointed leader of 11th Panzer Regiment's *Panzerstaffel*.
1 May 1941:	Promoted to *Hauptmann* of the Reserve.
1 October 1941:	Operations officer in 11th Panzer Regiment.
1 December 1941:	Commander 1st Battalion, 11th Panzer Regiment.
1 April 1942:	Commander 2nd Battalion, 11th Panzer Regiment.
1 August 1942:	Promoted to major.
1 January 1943:	Awarded Knight's Cross of the Iron Cross as commander of 2./PR 11.
14 July 1943:	Named commander of 11th Panzer Regiment.
1 August 1943:	Becomes 262nd German soldier to receive Oak Leaves to Knight's Cross.
21 February 1944:	Becomes 49th German soldier to receive the Swords to the Knight's Cross with Oak Leaves.
13 July 1944:	Named commander of 106th Panzer Brigade *Feldherrnhalle*.
9 March 1945:	Commander of 13th Panzer Division and its successor *Feldherrnhalle 2* Panzer Division.
1 April 1945:	Promoted to rank of *Generalmajor*.
12 December 1978:	Died in Hagen, Westphalia, as the result of a traffic accident.

2

Hermann Bix

Alone Against an Enemy Battalion

It was raining on 6 September 1941 as the panzer grenadiers and tanks of the 4th Panzer Division assembled in Korop under the command of *Oberst* Eberbach. Battle Group Eberbach, consisting of elements of the 35th Panzer Regiment, the 34th Motorcycle Battalion, and elements of the 49th Antitank Battalion and the 103rd Artillery Regiment, had been given the assignment of advancing through Korylskoye and Attjuscha and forcing a crossing of the Ssejm River near Baturin. To the left of the battle group, the 33rd Rifle Regiment was to advance through Altynovka and support the river crossing.

The battle began with an artillery duel at a range of eight hundred meters. The first enemy positions on the low, extended heights near Korylskoye were taken by the motorcycle troops and the panzer grenadiers. First Battalion of the 35th Panzer Grenadier Regiment under Major von Lauchert pushed through this gap, advancing through Attjuscha toward Baturin. However, the motorcycle troops and panzer grenadiers were unable to follow the tanks because enemy resistance unexpectedly flared up again deep in the enemy positions. The tanks roared on alone. On the main road to Baturin they came upon a large enemy column consisting of wheeled and tracked vehicles. The battle began.

"Be careful, Schwartz," warned *Unteroffizier* Bix as the driver raced the tank uphill, its motor roaring, "the Russians might be in the village ahead of us." They reached the crest of the ridge at the same time as five other tanks. Before them lay the village. Suddenly there were flashes from huts, hedges, and behind fences. Armor-piercing shells howled toward the tanks. There were several hard crashes as the antitank rounds smashed into the tank on Bix's right. The *Unteroffizier* watched as the turret cupola was torn away, taking the tank's commander with it. Then a second and a third tank were hit. *Hauptmann* Lekschat's voice crackled over the radio: "Pull back to the back slope!" The tanks withdrew and reached safety. "What now, *Herr Unteroffizier?*" asked gunner *Obergefreiter* Krause. "We won't get through unless we get some air support," replied Bix. "As soon as we reach the top of the hill we're in their sights."

The Lekschat company was on the battalion's left wing; the Panzer III commanded by *Unteroffizier* Bix was on the extreme left. The fire from the village now shifted onto the tanks on the right wing. Muzzle flashes from the tanks showed that they were answering the Russian fire. Bix scrutinized the area around him. His gaze fell on a gully which extended to his left as far as the village gardens. After considering for a moment Bix said, "We're going to sneak into the village."

"That will just start more trouble, *Herr Unteroffizier*," warned radio operator *Gefreiter* Fink.

"Get going, Schwartz. Drive down the slope and turn left into the gully."

The driver backed up a short distance, turned, and reached the gully. The tank disappeared inside and rolled off in the direction of the village. Tensely, Bix waited for the enemy to open fire but nothing happened. Apparently the Russians in the village couldn't see them. Bix encouraged his driver as the tank emerged into the first garden of sunflowers: "Keep going, Schwartz!"

Suddenly a pair of Russian soldiers jumped up and ran back toward the village. The gunner and driver shouted almost simultaneously: "Enemy antitank gun ahead and to the left!"

"Straight toward it, drive through quickly, don't stop!"

With a glance Bix saw that he had no time to fire. A high wooden fence appeared ahead. With a mighty crash the tank drove through. Bix ducked instinctively. Then the Panzer III plowed sideways into a bank and stopped. The tank leaned dangerously to one side, threatening to tip over. Again the driver and gunner shouted as one: "There, on the road ahead!—A long column!"

Bix also saw the vehicles. "Straighten out the tank, Schwartz, and then down toward the road!"

The *Obergefreiter* succeeded in freeing the tank from the bank. The Panzer III reached the road which led through the center of the village. More than a kilometer to the rear, the rest of the battalion was trying in vain to break through the Russian antitank front. Theirs was the only tank that had got through. "We won't get any farther here," called Fink as he surveyed the enemy column through his sight. Hermann Bix knew that he couldn't go back, as the Russian antitank guns were behind them. The only chance lay ahead. When Bix turned around he saw that there were also enemy vehicles behind him. Fink kept up a steady flow of target information over the intercom. Russian troops jumped from their vehicles and fled, seeking cover in the village houses. A Soviet machine gun began to rattle. The burst of machine gun fire smacked into the thin metal of the baggage compartment on the rear of the turret.

"High explosive—open fire!" shouted Bix. There was a crash as the tank fired its first round. Shells smashed into the Soviet trucks, smashing them into debris. Seconds later they burst into flames. The commander and *Gefreiter* Fink opened fire on the column with the tank's two machine guns while the loader struggled to extinguish the burning "rag-bag," ducking whenever enemy fire smacked against the tank's armor. The straw roofs of the houses began to burn. Thick clouds of smoke obscured Bix's view, but at the same time also shrouded the tank, hiding it from view from behind. The sea of flames above the column grew ever larger. A munitions truck blew up with a tremendous explosion. The crash of the tank's cannon mingled with hectic bursts of machine gun fire. In between could be heard the sound of the heavy Maxim machine guns.

"Harpoon to chief. Stuck in the enemy column!"

In vain Bix tried to get through to the company to request help. But radio operator Fink had not yet turned off the intercom, so that communications with the company were impossible. Then Bix heard the voice of *Hauptmann* Lekschat: "Harpoon, what sort of nonsense are you up to? You're confusing the whole battalion!" Finally the radio operator realized that he had to switch over to external communications and *Unteroffizier* Bix was able to report: "I am located in the center of the village. Stuck in the Russian column, which is crammed with guns. Please follow me at once." Lekschat swore. "Who the hell sent you in there anyway?" But Bix had no time to answer because the members of his crew were calling him, drawing his attention to a gun that had opened fire on them. The gunner swung the turret in the direction of the muzzle flash. As the antitank gun fired its second shot, the tank's cannon roared in reply. The crew of the antitank gun was killed by the exploding shell.

Bix heard the voice of *Hauptmann* Lekschat: "Company forward!" They were coming! Their comrades were coming to free them from the spot they were in. The *Unteroffizier* breathed a sigh of relief. The lone German tank reached the far end of the extended village. A pair of horse-drawn wagons blocked the street. "Hang on!" warned Schwartz. There was a splintering and cracking noise as the Panzer III rolled over the first wagon, crushing it beneath its tracks. Ahead a *panje* wagon exploded in a ball of fire. "If we run over a cart like that and it's loaded with mines, then we'll see each other in heaven," shouted loader Petermann through the din of gunfire and bursting shells.

"Harpoon, Harpoon from chief. Where are you?" called *Hauptmann* Lekschat. "We can't find you. Fire a signal flare."

"Harpoon to chief. Will fire a green-white signal to mark my position."

Bix fired the two flares. Seconds later he again heard the voice of his chief: "What, that's where you are? On the other side of the village? That's impossible."

Bix replied, "I'll fire the green-white signal again," and fired two more flares.

Seconds later he again heard the voice of his chief, who had recognized the opportunity at hand: "This way men! Bix is up there all alone! Infantry forward!"

Bix's tank rolled down from the street into the gardens, firing only when he was recognized by the enemy. "When are the others going to get here?" asked gunner Krause. "It shouldn't have taken this long!" "Listen!" shouted Bix. There was a pause in the firing and they could hear the sound of tank cannon and the lighter crack of antitank guns. "They're fighting with the antitank guns we left behind." What Bix and his comrades didn't know was that the infantry and motorcycle troops were also advancing on the village. Finally the first tank approached. *Hauptmann* Lekschat drove up, and Bix, who had opened his hatch, made his report. The *Hauptmann* shook his head as he gazed at the shot-up trucks and burning houses. "Actually I wanted to give you a dressing down, Bix. But what I see here surpasses anything I had imagined."

The *Hauptmann* subsequently reported to battalion that all was well. The tanks rolled back the way they had come. At their next halt, Bix and his comrades learned that the infantry had taken eight hundred prisoners and captured sixty undamaged vehicles. Twelve antitank guns and sixteen heavy guns had been destroyed. Acting on its own, a single German tank had destroyed all of the vehicles and materiel of a Russian motorized battalion.

Major von Lauchert recommended *Unteroffizier* Bix for the Iron Cross, First Class. His entire crew was awarded the Iron Cross, Second Class. Bix received his decoration on 20 October 1941, twenty days after being promoted to *Feldwebel*.

On 1 October 1941, as Bix was putting the stars of a *Feldwebel* on his shoulder straps, Battle Group Eberbach was located just outside Dimitrovsk. Its objective was Orel. The Lekschat Company was driving in the lead and *Feldwebel* Bix's tank was the first of the entire battalion. "The enemy cannot be given any breathing space. We'll drive by night as well!" That was the order given by *Oberst* Eberbach.

It was beginning to get dark when Hermann Bix spotted enemy troops ahead. He had just reached one of the many wooden bridges, which were so narrow there was just room for a tank to get across. A Russian sentry stood on the bridge giving the tank directions so that it wouldn't go over the side. Bix sent back a message: "Don't fire on the sentry!" If no one fired, then no one would recognize the tanks as German. A little later *Hauptmann* Lekschat called: "Bix, I was just directed across the bridge by Ivan."

"When are they going to realize that we're coming?" asked Schwartz.

The first houses of Dimitrovsk appeared out of the darkness. Hermann Bix experienced the strange, oppressive feeling brought on by uncertainty. He saw the massive buildings and then, suddenly, the first Russian vehicles, which were dispersed and camouflaged. Most of the vehicles were trucks with trailers, but also some with limbered guns. Bix stuck his head just far enough out of the turret to get a good view.

"Bix, listen: hold your fire and gain as much ground as possible!"

Hauptmann Lekschat's order was unnecessary because the lead tank sneaked forward at half speed until it had reached the cobblestone marketplace. Finally Bix had a better view. The tank halted. Farther back, the company's vehicles rumbled through the night.

"Harpoon to chief: increase the interval so that if we open fire we won't run into each other or possibly hit one of our own."

A column of trucks came toward the *Feldwebel*. In the moonlight Bix could see mounted infantry holding their rifles vertically between their legs. The trucks drove slowly past the German tank. Bix saw Red Army troops running about excitedly at a building surrounded by a long wall; they had been spotted! Bix sent a message to the following vehicles: "The Russians are onto us, but please don't open fire yet."

It was an eerie, dangerous situation.

"Harpoon from chief. Push on ahead with two other tanks, I will secure around the marketplace with the company."

Bix then heard the chief summon a platoon of motorcycle troops, which moved forward to the marketplace and took over close protection of the tanks. Bix's tank rolled onward. The *Feldwebel* breathed a sigh of relief when he reached the exit from the city without being fired upon. The other two Panzer IIIs arrived and Bix secured the site with the three tanks.

All at once there was a crash behind them in the city. Within a matter of a few seconds the gunfire intensified greatly. Tracer ammunition flashed in flat trajectories through the night sky. Hand grenades exploded, followed by the crash of tank cannon. Detonations rang out as high explosive shells burst as they were fired into houses.

"What's that, *Herr Feldwebel*? Should we go back and see?" asked *Unteroffizier* Keibauer, commander of the second Panzer III who had just come over to Bix's tank on foot.

"There's nothing we can do. It looks like enough of a mixup over there without us," replied Bix. He could imagine all too well what might happen if they appeared suddenly from the direction of the enemy. Every tank in the battalion would open fire, and then God help them.

Several vehicles came driving from the east toward the city, undoubtedly Soviet reinforcements.

"Load high-explosive! Open fire!"

The three German tanks opened fire simultaneously. Shells smashed into the approaching trucks and set them on fire. Soviet soldiers ran about in the flickering light of the flames, seeking cover in ditches and behind bushes. Bursts of machine gun fire flitted among them.

Feldwebel Bix now called his CO: "Harpoon to chief. What is going on in the city?"

The *Hauptmann*'s sonorous voice came back: "Our infantry is here and is taking care of the enemy. Everything is in order."

"Should I help out? Our Panzers aren't much needed here anymore."

"Remain where you are, Bix!" ordered Lekschat.

"Everything is in order, men," Bix reassured his comrades. The three tanks sat in a semicircle in their security position. The exhausted crews, who had already spent the entire day in combat, now had to take turns standing watch. When Bix's turn came he found he had difficulty keeping his eyes open. But he didn't dare close them. If the Russians came during the instant he wasn't watching, it would be all over for them.

It was 0700 on 2 October when the three tanks were summoned back to the marketplace. Infantry took over the security role. A new assignment was awaiting Bix and his crew. He was to carry out a reconnaissance into no-man's-land in his Panzer III together with *Oberleutnant* von Kartell and his light tank. As dawn broke the two vehicles drove off in the direction of Orel. It was vital that they stay close on the enemy's heels.

Halfway to Kromy, Bix came upon a Russian fuel dump. There were five giant fuel tanks spaced at intervals on the ground. Suddenly the *Feldwebel* spotted a group of Russian soldiers. They were holding antitank rifles and firing at the fuel tanks in an apparent effort to set them on fire. The tank's gunner and loader, who until now had been sitting in the left and right turret hatches, dropped into their places. The tank's cannon roared and a high-explosive shell burst in the midst of the Red Army soldiers. The radio operator fired a few bursts of machine gun fire, whereupon the Russians abandoned their plans.

Oberleutnant von Kartell and an accompanying section of motorcycle troops stayed behind and guarded the vital fuel dump that would be so valuable to Battle Group Eberbach. *Feldwebel* Bix drove on alone. He advanced thirty-five kilometers past Dimitrovsk, then his fuel state forced him to turn back. Because he knew that the battalion was already on its way, he fired green and white recognition flares on the way back. Bix ran out of fuel just as he reached the battalion. *Oberleutnant* Wollschläger took over the lead position.

At about midday Wollschläger and his company reached Kromy and took the town by surprise. For this feat he was recommended for the Knight's Cross by *Oberst* Eberbach. Wollschläger received the decoration on 23 January 1942.

The next day's objective was Orel.

The First Appearance of the T-34

Battle Group Eberbach stormed into the Russian 13th Army and outflanked it. On the morning of 3 October, *Oberleutnant* Wollschläger took the lead. The tanks rolled forward at high speed. *Feldwebel* Bix found himself in one of the six tanks that was advancing on orders of the battle group's commander. The order had been a brief one: "To Orel!"

A bridge appeared ahead. Wollschläger knew, as did every other tank commander, that it would be here that the enemy placed his strongest defenses. Standing in the turret cupola, Bix watched as Wollschläger's tank disappeared behind a railway underpass. The first shots rang out. Two or three antitank guns opened fire and were immediately answered by the tank cannon.

"After him, Schwartz!"

The driver shifted into the next gear and the tank picked up speed. The underpass appeared. For a few seconds it was dark, then into the brightness again. But that was not all! Ahead blazed a dazzling muzzle flash, about four hundred meters away!

"Open fire!"

Krause fired the first round. Petermann was already loading the next one. The tank fired almost at the same time as the antitank gun. The Panzer III jerked backward from the recoil. The antitank round flitted smoking past the left side of the turret. The tank shell hit the antitank position. There was a crash and a cloud of thick smoke rose up, mixed with flashes of fire.

"Move on!"

As they drove off, the crew saw the remaining five tanks reach the gardens and crash through the fences. Wollschläger rolled straight down the center of the road toward Orel, and Bix followed. There were enemy columns in the city. Machine gun fire whipped toward the six German tanks. These six were mounting a frontal assault while *Oberst* Eberbach and the main body of the battalion tried to outflank the city. The tanks opened fire with their cannon and machine guns. Russian trucks were soon blazing. Escaping gasoline generated sizzling clouds of flame. Soviet troops appeared from behind the wall of smoke.

"There come some, *Herr Feldwebel!*" warned the gunner.

The radio operator's machine gun opened up and the group of Red Army soldiers that had been attempting to approach the tank from the flank disappeared behind the wall of a house.

As the *Feldwebel's* tank became involved in the fight with the enemy infantry, Wollschläger called over the radio, "Don't let yourself get separated, Bix!"

Schwartz stepped on the gas and set out after the other tanks at high speed. A *panje* wagon lay in their path. The Panzer III struck the wagon, pushed it ahead for a few meters, and then crushed it beneath its tracks. The tank came under fire from a house at the side of the road.

"Load high-explosive!"

The shell ripped open the wall of the house beneath the windowsill where the machine gun was positioned. The weapon was put out of action.

The drive to Orel went on. The tanks passed more vehicles. Whenever the trucks made a break for it and tried to escape down side streets, the tank cannon went into action. Soon they had pushed their way into Orel, but Wollschläger knew how dangerous a halt would be. What was more, there was still an enemy column fleeing toward the east to be pursued. The tanks rolled on at high speed for another six kilometers when they were forced to halt for lack of fuel.

"See to it that you siphon fuel from the Russian trucks, Bix," advised Wollschläger. "In case we have to move out again."

They soon found a truck with full tanks. Driver Schwartz took a siphon hose from his tool kit and sucked until the gasoline began to flow.

The tanks were then ordered to secure the eastern edge of Orel. The panzer grenadiers were already attacking. As they advanced they came under attack from enemy aircraft that strafed and dropped bombs. The grenadiers looked up as each new wave of aircraft approached. As soon as the machines came into sight it was into the ditches. Rifles, machine guns, and antiaircraft guns fired on the attackers.

It was not until nightfall that the regiment reached the assembly area for the attack on Orel. No one knew at that time that the advance detachment had already driven through the city. Throughout the night the tanks stood guard east of Orel. A group of Russians trying to sneak past the *Feldwebel*'s tank was taken prisoner. From the prisoners Bix learned that a freight train had just arrived at the Orel station carrying a load of heavy tanks.

A frustrated Bix said, "Confound it! And we don't have any radio communications!"

"Perhaps the Russians were lying, *Herr Feldwebel*," argued radio operator Krause.

"Possible, Krause, but we'd better halt here."

During the night they heard a freight train steam off in the direction of Mzensk.

"If the tanks were on that one, they'll be down on us soon, *Herr Feldwebel*," offered Petermann. He was soon to be proved wrong.

At dawn on 4 October the 12th Panzer Grenadier Regiment (at that time still the 12th Rifle Regiment) launched the attack against Orel. At the edge of the forest, on the city's flank, 1st Battalion captured five 3.7cm antiaircraft guns. The battalion commander had his men man the guns to provide a defense against air attack. Orel airfield was reached just as a Russian fighter was landing. The pilot was taken prisoner. At about 1000 the regiment crossed the airfield and reached the hangars and barracks on the far side. The troops subsequently combed the streets and houses as far as the train station. Straggling Soviet troops gave themselves up. Workers were caught by surprise in the tank and tractor works as they ate their lunch. Orel was captured. Battle Group Eberbach had reached the objective set for it by *Generaloberst* Guderian.

After getting a good night's sleep, on the morning of 5 October, Bix and his comrades set out once more in the direction of Mzensk. The long range objective was Tula.

Together with *Leutnant* Bökle, the platoon leader, Bix drove on the battalion's left wing. At first everything went well. The advance made rapid progress and the tanks reached Rokavaya Brook. Enemy machine guns raked the entire width of the advancing wedge, and Bix suddenly heard tank cannon firing. Shortly thereafter *Hauptmann* Lekschat reported: "Under heavy fire from Russian heavy tanks!"

Lekschat saw flame spurt from the muzzles of the long gun barrels of the Soviet tanks. He recognized two types. One was massive, one could almost say gigantic. The other was sleeker, but also carried a large-caliber gun.

"Watch out!" Lekschat radioed a warning to platoon leader *Leutnant* Küspert, who had rolled on a short distance. But it was already too late. Three Russian T-34s—making their first appearance at this part of the front—opened fire almost simultaneously on the platoon leader's tank. The armor-piercing shells from the T-34s struck the German tank with a crash. A terrific blow shook the platoon leader's Panzer III. Soon after came the report: "We have been hit, the turret will no longer move, *Herr Hauptmann.*"

"Pull back, Küspert!" ordered *Hauptmann* Lekschat while his gunner opened fire on the enemy.

"Damn it, the shells don't penetrate," shouted *Unteroffizier* Henrichs when he saw that his rounds were having no effect on the Russian giants. A heavy blow shook the company commander's tank. *Leutnant* Küspert called again: "Tank immobilized!"

"Bail out, Küspert, bail out!"

In the midst of the battle, the men of Küspert's crew climbed out of their stricken tank. Machine gun fire whipped toward them, but they were soon under cover behind their tank. The *Leutnant* watched as several shells struck the company commander's panzer. Damaged and unable to continue the battle, it was forced to pull back. A quick look around revealed to the *Leutnant* that there were approximately twenty enemy tanks, including several T-34s and others of the KV-I type. It was obvious that the short 7.5cm guns of the German tanks could not penetrate the thick armor of these giants.

The commander's tank rolled up. *Feldwebel* Rieger, *Oberst* Eberbach's driver, saw that the Lekschat Company had suffered losses. As they drove forward he saw several tank crews moving toward the rear.

"Artillery and flak forward!" ordered *Oberst* Eberbach. The *Oberst* scanned the battlefield through his scissors telescope. He saw the mass of enemy tanks, which was attempting to overrun the battalion.

Eberbach called a warning to the battalion commander: "Watch out, Lauchert, you're being outflanked!"

Major Lauchert ordered his tanks to pull back one hundred meters.

Meanwhile, the tanks on the left wing had not yet joined the battle. Bix heard over the radio that someone on the right flank was engaging the enemy. The tank commander involved called back: "I'm firing and firing but the armor-piercing isn't getting through! Use extreme caution!"

"Man, Bix, those are T-34s and KV-Is!" called *Leutnant* Bökle as the first enemy tanks came into sight. Suddenly Bix, too, saw the armored giants. They were about six hundred meters away, rolling toward him along the tracks of the Orel-Tula railway line.

Bix called back: "They don't look that big, and they can't be that dangerous, *Herr Leutnant*."

Bökle, a specialist in tank recognition, was of a different opinion. He warned the *Leutnant:* "Be careful Bix, those are T-34s!"

"Armor-piercing!" shouted the *Feldwebel*.

The T-34s came ever nearer. They were still three hundred meters away when, suddenly, they veered to the left. Their new course took them straight across in front of Bix.

"Open fire!"

Offering their broadsides to the German panzers, the T-34s were a good target for gunner Krause. He fired, and Bix saw the shell strike home.

"Well done, Krause!"

The second round struck the turret of the T-34 but did not penetrate.

"They're not paying any attention to us at all," cried

Schwartz. Indeed, it did seem as if the T-34s were ignoring the fly-bites from the cannon of the German tanks.

"Here comes our battalion, *Herr Feldwebel.*"

For the first time in the Russian campaign Bix saw German tanks in retreat. The panzers on the forward right flank pulled back, turned around, and—pursued by the shells from the T-34s and KV-Is—withdrew at high speed.

"Chief to everyone!" called *Hauptmann* Lekschat. "The battalion is pulling back. We can't handle these beasts, losses on the right flank are too high!"

At that moment Bix saw the tanks of 2nd Battalion under Major von Lauchert disappear. They had done all they could, but now were forced to withdraw to avoid being destroyed.

"Let's go, Bix!" ordered *Leutnant* Bökle. "Pull back and get out of here as fast as you can!" Bix followed the order and turned around. His tank rolled back along the highway at high speed. A lone tank was sitting at the right side of the road. Bix recognized *Oberst* Eberbach's command panzer. A 7.6cm round that had failed to penetrate was sticking out of its side armor. A little farther to the rear Bix came upon a tracked vehicle of the armored engineers. Flames licked from the vehicle. Next to it he saw a *Pionier* whose leg had been almost torn from his trunk. The flames were coming nearer and nearer to the wounded man.

"Halt!" shouted Bix.

Schwartz brought the tank to a halt. Bix jumped down and ran toward the injured *Pionier.* He felt the flames and the heat that was increasing by the minute. A thought went through the *Feldwebel:* what if the mines in the vehicle go up! Nevertheless, he kept running.

For a few seconds Bix stared into the wide eyes of the wounded man. Then he was beside him and dragged him into the ditch. They were not yet safe, however. He still had to pull him farther away from the flames. Just as Bix felt his strength leaving him, two men appeared who had likewise left their tank to help. In the flickering light from the burning vehicle Bix first recognized *Stabsarzt* Dr. Mühlkühner and then, hastening along behind him, *Oberst* Eberbach. Both men helped carry the wounded man out of the danger zone of the burning vehicle, which was loaded with mines. At that very moment the mines detonated. The earth seemed to open up with a terrific roar. The shock wave threw Bix on his face; he felt as if his lungs would burst.

Afterward Dr. Mühlkühner gave the wounded man an injection for his pain and dressed his wounds while the *Oberst* directed a flatbed trailer into position with which to evacuate the man and the other wounded. It was only then that Bix realized that the other panzers had already pulled back. Their pursuers were coming ever nearer and already lobbing shells in their direction.

Bix later said, "I will never forget this encounter with the battle group commander on the battlefield at Rokovaya Brook. The commander and the doctor remained on the battlefield until the last of the wounded had been recovered. After this tremendous example by my commander I never dared leave a wounded man on the battlefield during the later course of the war, because I had seen here how the commander fought to save the last of his soldiers."

The wounded *Pionier* survived. He lost a leg, but thanks to a pair of courageous men he still had his life.

A little later Bix and his men reached the spot where *Oberst* Eberbach had instructed the 8.8cm flak and 10.5cm field guns to establish a blocking position. These batteries now took up the fight with the onrushing tanks. The deadly "eighty-eights" did the job. The gunners fired round after round. One after another the T-34s and KV-Is were hit and caught fire. The armor-piercing shells of the 8.8cm flak could pierce the thickest armor plate. Ten KV-Is and seven T-34s were knocked out during the battle. The Russian breakthrough had been foiled.

This battle proved that the Russians were determined to defend the approaches to Mzensk. A surprise crossing of the Susha was therefore out of the question. It would require a time-consuming, planned attack.

For Hermann Bix and his fellow tank commanders the important thing was to find an effective way to deal with the T-34 and KV-I by using their small-caliber guns. They also had to find a way to recover from the shock the Russians had administered in this battle.

Cautiously the Germans resumed their advance. On 8 October the rain came down in torrents. It was on that day that the order arrived to attack Mzensk. The date specified for the attack was 9 October. While the bulk of the 4th Panzer Division—

with the 35th Panzer Regiment, Bridging Column 34, and the Rifle Regiment's 2nd Battalion—advanced to the right of the highway, the regimental headquarters and 1st Battalion, 12th Rifle Regiment, were to attack along the railway line.

On the morning of the ninth the roads were covered with thick mud. Progress by the panzers was slow. Night came and the men around Bix dug a sleeping trench between the tank's tracks, happy that the day's efforts were at an end. They had advanced to within ten kilometers of Mzensk.

Feldwebel Bix awoke on the morning of 10 October and threw back the tent square under which he had been sleeping. He rubbed his eyes in surprise, because, as far as the eye could see the landscape was completely covered with snow.

"Men, wake up! It has snowed. Get up for a snowball fight!" he shouted with a grim sense of humor.

Schwartz peeled himself out of his blankets. "First things first. Congratulations on your birthday, *Herr Feldwebel!*" he said with a grin.

"Thank you, Schwartz. I can't believe that I'm to celebrate my twenty-seventh birthday in Russia."

The rest of the crew came up and congratulated their commander.

Leutnant Küspert appeared beside panzer "Harpoon." "Let's go, Bix. You're driving reconnaissance with me!"

Five minutes later the two tanks rolled off in the direction of Mzensk. Bix reached the edge of the city just as it was becoming light. So far there had been no enemy fire. *Leutnant* Küspert's tank had broken down three kilometers from the city. He was now acting as a radio bridge, as his tank was equipped with a medium-wave transmitter. In this way he could pass *Feldwebel* Bix's observations back to the battle group.

"Russian field position ahead of us," reported Bix. "I'm driving toward it. It looks as if the Russians haven't spotted us yet."

Bix turned his cap around in order to make it more difficult for the enemy to recognize him as a German tank commander. This precaution was necessary as he had to expose his head to scan his surroundings. Several Russians, warmly wrapped, crawled out of their foxholes. They waved to Bix as if to say: It's good that we've received some tank support. It apparently never occurred to them that this might be a German tank.

Bix spotted signs of life at the edge of the city: "It looks as if they're awake here." He saw a pair of tanks projecting beyond the walls of some houses as well as some Russian soldiers. The soldiers crossed the street carrying steaming pots of coffee and disappeared into the houses.

"If only we had the whole battalion here," mused Krause.

"We can't do any more than observe," explained Bix. "As soon as we made a move the Russians would know where we were and give it to us on the nose."

It was an eerie situation, because the Russians could come over to the tank at any minute. Then all hell would break loose for sure. Bix continued passing along his observations. Once, when he looked back, he realized that there was a steep slope behind him. A little while ago they had driven down it quickly. But how could he—if it became necessary, and this was only a matter of time—get up the slope again in a hurry? What was more, Schwartz had shut off the engine. The moment of their discovery came sooner than Bix expected. A trumpet signal rang out and suddenly the Russians were running about wildly.

"The tanks are coming, *Herr Feldwebel*," warned the radio operator. Bix had already heard the noise of the Russian tanks firing up their engines. The T-34s rolled out of their well-camouflaged positions.

"Start up!" shouted Bix to his driver.

The panzer's motor roared to life. Carefully Schwartz rolled back up the slope. To Bix the maneuver seemed to take an eternity. Finally they made it.

"Turn around and get us out of here!" he ordered.

The driver swung the tank around, its tracks throwing snow and slush high into the air. Then he shifted into the next gear and rumbled toward the rear. The Russians fired a few shells after them but were unable to inflict any damage.

Moments later Bix reached *Leutnant* Küspert's tank. There he learned that the entire battalion had been committed in the meantime. *Oberleutnant* Wollschläger was driving in the lead and was about to attempt to take Mzensk from the north. Blowing snow now reduced visibility. A short while later the battalion's tanks appeared. Wollschläger swung his tank to the right and disappeared into the snowstorm.

"After them, Schwartz. We mustn't lose them!" called Bix to his driver. The *Obergefreiter* turned. Now and then through the snow he could see the red flames from the exhausts of the tanks ahead and thus was able to orient himself. They remained in contact and rolled behind Wollschläger toward the bridge at the northern entrance to Mzensk. As they approached, they could see the bridge now and then through the blowing snow. Aided by the swirling clouds of snowflakes, the tankers were able to overpower the Russian sentries and remove the demolition charges from the bridge.

The panzers rolled into Mzensk almost from the rear. The first antitank gun was overrun and several others put out of action as the tanks raced into the city. Salvoes of rockets from truck-mounted "Stalin organs" roared overhead toward the following infantry.

An antitank barricade held up the panzers of 2nd Battalion. Four were knocked out before *Oberleutnant* Wollschläger was able to attack the obstacle from the rear. As Bix came round a corner he saw an antitank gun not fifty meters ahead, which was firing down a side street. There was no need for him to issue any orders—Krause had targeted the antitank gun and his first shot was a direct hit. The gun's ammunition supply went up in a brilliant explosion. A machine gun turned its fire onto the tank. A shower of bullets spattered against the armor plate.

"Run over it!" shouted the *Feldwebel,* and the panzer lurched forward. It crashed through a fence, reached the enemy machine gun, and crushed it into the ground.

The machine gun's crew ran away to the left and right. A hand grenade landed on the rear deck of the tank. There was a dull thump as it exploded.

"Turn right, toward the Stalin organs!" ordered Bix.

The panzer rolled toward the din of the whizzing, howling rocket salvoes, reached the position of the four *katyushas* and opened fire with all guns. It was not long before all four rocket launchers had been destroyed.

Soon afterward the northwest section of Mzensk—the Podmonastyrskaya Sloboda district—was in the hands of the following infantry. The southeast quarter—the Streletskaya Sloboda district—was also captured. A short while later a rapid advance by tanks and mounted infantry resulted in the capture of the undamaged Susha road bridge. Only in the northern section of the city were a few T-34s still holding out. As darkness fell they were being pushed back across the railroad bridge.

The crews of the Russian tanks blew up the bridge. During the night the German infantry combed the city for stragglers and took the remaining groups of Russians prisoner.

Here in the Mzensk area, Battle Group Eberbach defended its bridgehead from 11 October to 22 October. How the unit had suffered during the advance and the battles of the past few weeks was described by *Generaloberst* Guderian in his book *Errinerungen eines Soldaten,* in which he wrote: "I met *Oberst* Eberbach, who described to me the course of the latest battles. For the first time during this strenuous campaign Eberbach gave the impression of exhaustion, and it was not only the physical, but the mental fatigue, which one noticed about him. It was startling to see that our best officers had been so seriously affected by these latest battles."

On 22 October the 6th Panzer Regiment and a battalion of the 18th Panzer Regiment were placed under *Oberst* Eberbach's command. With his newly formed panzer group he was to advance through Chern and capture the city of Tula.

Once again the utmost was demanded of every tank commander. Chern fell on 25 October and *Generaloberst* Guderian repeated his order: "Forward without delay and take Tula!"

Not far from Tula, *Feldwebel* Bix and *Leutnant* Bökle assembled an advance platoon from the panzers which still had full fuel tanks. They were to roll into Tula as the leading spearhead of the German attack.

At the periphery of the city they were met by German-speaking women.

"Hurry!" they called to Bix and Bökle. "Quick, the Russians in the city are in a state of panic!"

At that moment a bus appeared, driving directly toward Bix's panzer. It was filled with soldiers.

"Don't fire!" shouted Bix as he saw that there were also civilians on board. The driver stopped the bus and jumped out just as it pulled alongside the tank. As he did so he struck the left side of the tank and was flung to the ground.

Bökle issued an order and a warning to Bix at the same time: "Feel your way forward, Bix. But be careful!"

Bix was convinced that there would be no serious resistance in the city. He rolled through the suburbs at high speed. To his left Bix saw a motorized column driving into the city along a parallel street. The Russians recognized the Germans and opened fire with antiaircraft guns. The range was so great, however, that all of the shells exploded far ahead of the tanks of the Bökle platoon. Suddenly an order came through that neither Bix nor Bökle could understand: "Full halt!!"

Desperately Bix shouted, "That can't be true, *Herr Leutnant!*"

"We'll carry on on our own," said the *Leutnant,* as in his mind they were as good as in the city already. He was soon forced to change his mind, however, when he learned that the following tanks and other vehicles had no more fuel and that all of the battle group's supply vehicles were bogged down in the mud along the advance road. Some of the vehicles had even become frozen in the mud during the night.

When they attacked the next morning the panzers were halted by a powerful antitank barricade. Soviet T-34s launched a counterattack and in the ensuing tank-versus-tank fighting the German units suffered heavy losses. On 31 October, Battle Group Eberbach ws forced to go over to the defensive.

The Tank Battle at Venev

On 13 November, the Eberbach Brigade was called on by Gen. Freiherr Geyr von Schweppenburg for an attack in the direction of Venev. *Oberst* Eberbach had exactly fifty tanks left; at full strength he would have had three hundred.

The cold wave that had now set in was making life difficult for the panzer crews. By early morning on 13 November the temperature had fallen to twenty-two degrees below zero. Optics became misted and oil thickened. There was no winter clothing or antifreeze. Nevertheless, the Eberbach Brigade set out full of confidence.

The armored unit pushed past Tula on the right and drove— this time without infantry—toward the north. It rolled through Stalinogorsk unopposed. The next objective was Oslavaya.

"Filthy cold!" moaned Bix as he stared from the turret cupola. The wind, which was blowing out of the north, threatened to freeze his breath.

"If we only had some winter things," offered Schwartz.

"That's for sure!" murmured the *Feldwebel.*

Ahead, Bix saw a tank stop at the side of the road. The leading group rolled past and Bix realized that the figure standing in the commander's cupola in the black jacket was *Oberst* Eberbach.

"If the old man can stand it, then we can too," said Krause.

Knowing that their commander was in the same situation did not ease conditions, but did make them somewhat easier to bear.

The advance continued and next morning the panzers found themselves at the edge of a village not far from Oslavaya. Suddenly an entire regiment of Russian infantry appeared from out of the morning mist, advancing toward the tanks. The first bursts of machine gun fire were already whipping toward the waiting panzers.

"Lekschat Company, counterattack!" crackled through the headphones.

The motors of the tanks roared as they moved off toward the enemy in a broad wedge. Lances of flame spurted from cannon and machine guns. High-explosive shells exploded in the enemy formations. Many of the Red Army soldiers were run over by the tanks. It was a grisly scene: Russian infantry charging German tanks. But the situation was also dangerous enough for the panzer crews. As soon as a commander raised his head from the turret hatch to get a better view of the terrain, he immediately came under fire from machine guns or enemy snipers. Some of the shots whizzed close past their targets—others found the mark. Bix kept looking outside in an attempt to assist his driver. Once, a burst of machine gun fire whizzed just past his left ear. Bullets cracked against the steel of the armored cupola and ricocheted to the side. After the light snowfall the rather hilly terrain was so slippery that the tanks occasionally slid down the icy slopes like sleighs.

Bix's panzer slid to the side and toppled into a gully. It slid into an outcropping with a jolt.

"Hopefully we can get out of here again," sighed Bix.

Obergefreiter Schwartz, an auto mechanic by trade, just grinned. "We'll get out all right! Just hang on!"

Engaging first gear, he steered the tank diagonally up the towering slope, and it worked! Slowly the tank crawled higher, until it was again on level ground.

Once again the tanks fired high-explosive shells into the masses of Russians storming toward the gully. The Red Army soldiers dug into the snow and disappeared within a few seconds.

Lekschat radioed a warning: "Be careful, Bix. *Oberfeldwebel* Rieger has been killed by a sniper."

Rieger had been the commander's driver. Everyone in the unit knew him. Just recently *Oberst* Eberbach had granted his wish and made him a tank commander.

In the meantime a large part of the Russian regiment had been wiped out. Only a small number of soldiers escaped to the northeast.

The advance was resumed at about midday. Once again Hermann Bix drove in the lead position. The tank rolled forward almost unmolested. Bix had no idea where he was. He had no maps of the area, but since there was only one major road there, he assumed this must be the right way.

It was already early afternoon when the *Feldwebel* saw the first houses of Oslavaya before him. Bix was wearing a Russian fur-lined cap. This camouflage was so effective that the drivers of the Russian trucks that came toward him showed no inclination to flee. On the contrary, the Russian soldiers riding in the trucks even waved to him.

Bix radioed *Hauptmann* Lekschat: "Have passed some Russians; they haven't recognized me."

"Good, Bix! Carry on along the same road. The first vehicles are just arriving here now and are getting a polite reception. We won't fire unless absolutely necessary. Out."

The tank rolled slowly through the city until it came to the marketplace, where there was a fork in the road. Bix was uncertain for a few seconds.

He called back, "Which road should I take?"

"Take the one to the right, Bix," radioed his company commander. "According to my information it leads to the train station."

Bix had his driver swing the tank to the right. Soon afterward a Russian truck loaded with soldiers came toward them. The Russian crew recognized the tank as an enemy vehicle. Red Army soldiers jumped down and disappeared into the surrounding houses and gardens. A second, following truck likewise stopped.

"High-explosive!" ordered Bix.

The loader and gunner functioned like clockwork. The first shell crashed into the wall of a house. An antitank rifle appeared over the side of one of the trucks. The panzer's second shot was a direct hit. The effect was tremendous.

"Move farther forward, Bix!" The order crackled through the headphones. "The company will follow!"

The tank rolled past the burning truck and, turning behind a house, drove into a garden. Bix emerged cautiously from the turret hatch and scanned his surroundings. Now he could hear the noise of the following tanks as they advanced as far as the marketplace. *Hauptmann* Lekschat arranged each tank carefully so that it had a clear line of sight and an open field of fire.

At that moment Bix saw a KV-I fire its gun, but the shell was apparently not meant for him, as it whizzed past behind the corner of a house farther to the right.

"That shot was aimed at me!" reported *Leutnant* Bökle. "Enemy tank is sitting on the road facing in my direction. Take him in the flank!"

"Through that fence, Schwartz," bellowed Bix. The tank approached the fence and crashed through. When Bix's view was clear he recognized the outline of the mighty Russian tank about thirty meters away.

"That's a KV-I. He hasn't seen us yet. Load special round. Perhaps we'll be able to penetrate his turret with it!"

Petermann rammed the shell into the chamber just as the giant fired another shot at Bökle's panzer. Then the first shot left the barrel of their own cannon. The shell struck the turret of the enemy tank and glanced off. The second stuck in the KV-I's armor plate. The Russian tank showed no ill effects after the third direct hit and continued firing at the *Leutnant*'s panzer.

Bix realized that he would not be able to destroy this tank with gunfire. He called back, "My cannon has no effect on the KV-I! None of the shells are getting through, *Herr Leutnant!* Send some *Pioniers* with concentrated charges!"

Bökle's reply, passed along by the radio operator, was not long in coming. "Bix, if nothing else works, try to shoot his cannon in two, otherwise he'll knock you out as soon as he sees you!"

At first Bix thought the *Leutnant* must be pulling his leg.

"I'll try it," murmured the gunner, "but . . ."

"Well try then, Krause," shouted Bix, even though he considered the attempt to be hopeless. Something had to be done before they were spotted and knocked out.

Krause targeted the cannon of the enemy tank as near to the gun mantlet as possible. A normal armor-piercing round was loaded. The barrel of the KV-I's cannon was thickest at the mantlet. Perhaps he would be lucky.

"Open fire!" gasped Bix.

The armor-piercing round struck steel, but because of the short range the entire area between the German and Russian tanks was shrouded in thick smoke, so Bix could not see the results of the shot.

"The same again, Krause!"

The gunner fired a second and then a third shot. The KV-I now began to rotate its turret, and the long cannon swung in the direction of the German panzer. With a crunching sound the KV-I's gun barrel cracked against the trunk of a small tree. The tank's turret stopped and at that exact moment *Leutnant* Bökle opened fire on the giant.

"There, he's smoking!" shouted Schwartz. A dark cloud of smoke whorled out of the stricken KV-I's gun barrel and from within the body of the tank. Before that there had been a muffled explosion. On firing its cannon, the shell must have detonated inside the tank, as indicated by the smoke coming from within.

The radio operator reported: "His barrel has burst, *Herr Feldwebel!*"

Bix peered through his field glasses and saw with amazement that the gun barrel of the Russian tank had been pierced three times. It had been no burst barrel. The *Feldwebel* couldn't believe his eyes, but there it was: Krause had put all three shots through the gun barrel of the enemy tank and rendered it useless.

Suddenly the hatch of the Russian tank flipped open. The commander tried to climb out. A shot rang out and the Russian was left hanging in the opening.

This experience taught Bix that from short range, even with the small-caliber gun, he could engage and destroy the heaviest tank.

There were explosions all over the city as the *Pioniers'* concentrated charges went off. The armored engineers had moved forward and were blowing up the heavy enemy tanks one after another. Later the infantry and the *Pioniers* silenced the last remaining nests of resistance.

Oslavaya had fallen.

The panzers rolled onward in the evening hours. They drove on throughout the entire night. Venev was reached on the morning of 24 November. The battalion re-formed and rumbled toward the city in a broad wedge. The panzers came under fire from enemy tanks when they reached the railway line that ran south of the city. Once again the Lekschat Company was positioned on the right wing and "Harpoon" was on the extreme right flank.

"We can't get across here, *Herr Hauptmann*," radioed *Leutnant* Bökle. "We would most likely shed our tracks on the embankment and the railroad tracks. Then we'd be sitting ducks for the Russians. We must find another place."

Lekschat immediately agreed: "Good, Bökle, that would be best." Then he called "Harpoon."

"Harpoon from chief: go farther to the right and look for a favorable crossing. Report as soon as you find something, Bix!"

The *Feldwebel*'s panzer began to move. Schwartz turned it around and then, driving slowly, set off parallel to the railway embankment. After several hundred meters the embankment became lower, and Bix discovered a level crossing.

"Drive up to it cautiously, Schwartz!—Krause, load armor-piercing and stand ready!"

The panzer worked its way forward slowly. The nose of the tank was over the edge of the crossing and still there was no enemy fire.

"Across, Schwartz!" shouted the *Feldwebel*. The tank accelerated and rolled forward, reached a firm field road on the other side, and then drove on a few hundred meters more. Bix called in his report. At once Lekschat sent the company's tanks to follow. Not until the last was driving across the tracks did the Russians open fire.

"Move forward quickly, Bix!"

Bix was familiar with this order because he had heard it often enough during the past weeks. The tank drove on and when Bix looked around he saw that the rest of the company's tanks were lagging behind. The last Panzer III, which had come under fire from the Soviets, was stopped on the level crossing and was returning fire in an effort to keep the enemy's attention fixed to the front.

Left on his own, a little later Bix came to the northern arterial road from Venev. Here, too, the picture was one of enemy vehicles driving one behind the other. The lone German tank did not appear to be recognized as such. After receiving Bix's report, *Hauptmann* Lekschat ordered him to turn around and drive into the city.

"Just as at Mzensk, Bix. Into the city from behind, the last place they'd expect us from," added the chief.

A light antiaircraft gun appeared in front of the Panzer III. Tracks rattling, the tank rolled over the gun while its crew ran to the side. A heavy machine gun was also run over. The attack by the German tank had been too much of a surprise.

Right and to the front, Bix spotted a hill. Beneath it lay a frozen pond, along whose left side ran a road. It was covered with tank tracks, leading the *Feldwebel* to be cautious. It was therefore no surprise when a KV-I suddenly rolled out of a side street from behind one of the larger houses. Not realizing that the other tank was an enemy, the KV-I rolled straight past in front of Bix. The tank's commander even waved to the rear, urging Bix to follow. What should he do? Stop, fire, turn around?

While he was still deliberating, two Russian T-38 reconnaissance tanks came rattling down the hill.

"They've recognized us!" shouted the radio operator.

Just then the first tank began to slide on the icy slope. The driver of the following tank tried desperately to turn hard right and miss the ice, but it, too, slid straight down the slope and thundered against an outcropping, which straightened the tank out and sent it down the hill behind the first like a bobsled.

The first T-38 crashed through the ice at the foot of the hill. The second rumbled onto the ice and attempted to gain ground, but its tracks simply spun in place.

Schwartz immediately turned the Panzer III around. The gunner soon had the enemy in his sights. There was a flash as he fired and the shell hammered into the enemy tank between its turret and hull.

"Hit!" roared Schwartz as flames burst forth from the stricken tank.

Bix shouted to his gunner, "On to the second, quick, before he can fire!"

The second T-38 was now turning on the spot. Just as it came face-to-face with the Panzer III, it hesitated somewhat. Krause pressed the firing button and the shell struck the tank forward on the side. The force of the blow caused the T-38 to spin about its axis several times on the slippery ice. Both enemy tanks had been put out of action. Still ahead of them, however, was their "big brother." If it were to open fire, all hell would break loose. Bix was relieved to discover that the KV-I had meanwhile driven out of sight around a bend in the road.

"After him!" shouted the *Feldwebel*. As the tank moved off, Bix thought of the numbers he was likely to meet as soon as he entered the city. They passed the first houses. Then they were standing in a large square, probably a type of market-place. Russians ran in all directions when the German tank appeared.

"More heavy tanks, *Herr Feldwebel*," reported Schwartz, but Bix had already spotted the giants. Strangely, the tanks did not attack the lone German panzer, but disappeared at high speed down a side street.

"What's going on?" asked Bix, half to himself. This was un-usual for the Soviets. Their tanks usually attacked at once. Were these planning a trick of some sort? The Russian tank drivers were definitely not cowards; they had proved this more than once in the past weeks.

"We must find some good cover, *Herr Feldwebel*," warned Schwartz. "We're sitting ducks here. If they move up an anti-tank gun it will be able to fire on us as it pleases."

After a quick look around, Bix ordered: "Behind that wooden building, Schwartz!"

When they reached the building, Bix made sure they were out of sight to both sides. The company was coming from the rear and they had a good field of view to the front. Nothing came from there, however.

A little later the first of their own tanks appeared. The com-pany's leading tank stopped at the edge of the square and the rest held their positions in the street behind it. Apparently

Hauptmann Lekschat first wanted to hear what his reconnaissance tank had to tell him.

Bix emerged from his turret and listened. All at once he heard a tank motor being fired up about one hundred meters to his left. Then the sound of the motor came nearer.

"Move ahead as far as the end of the barrack!" he called to his driver.

Schwartz drove forward until the bow and forward edge of the turret came around and the commander could see. Bix at once spotted the heavy KV-I, which was heading straight for him. Bix tried to duck into the turret, but his jacket caught on something on the edge of the turret. He might be hit at any moment.

"Armor-piercing round at the mantlet!" he gasped.

Krause reacted at once. The first shot clouded the area between the two tanks with smoke. There was a crack as the second shot was fired and still there had been no movement from the KV-I. Then there was a flash from the muzzle of the long barrel of the Russian tank. The Russian gunner had fired blind, however, and the shell whipped by several meters from the German tank.

"Back up!" called Bix over the intercom. The Russian giant was going to ram them.

In his previous attempts to get into the turret, Bix had inadvertently ripped the communications cable from its connector and, amid the noise of the approaching enemy tank, none of the men in the fighting compartment could hear him. As he saw no other alternative, Bix now crawled all the way out the turret hatch and took cover behind the right side of the turret away from the direction of the approaching KV-I.

Voices rang out from the fighting compartment. The men inside now had no idea whatsoever what was going on. Without orders to do so, Schwartz had not backed the tank up. That left Bix only one choice.

The *Feldwebel* knew the dangerous situation he would be placing himself in by leaving the protection of the turret and crawling forward to signal the driver through his vision block to back up. There were only seconds left, because the enemy tank was now only a few dozen meters away. There was no longer any doubt: the KV-I intended to ram the side of the German panzer!

This maneuver had been tried often by the Russian heavy tanks lately, often with success. At this critical moment a thought occurred to the *Feldwebel:* why didn't he simply fire on them? At any moment he expected the shot that would end it all. Then he saw the driver's face through the bulletproof glass of the vision block and gave him the signal to back up. Schwartz reacted instantly. The tank abruptly jerked backward a few meters.

At the same instant the armored bow of the Russian tank flew past barely two meters in front of Bix and the corner of the barracks. The tank's tracks screeched and the air stank of diesel exhaust fumes. Seconds later the KV-I smashed into a massive stone wall. When the tank had rammed halfway through brick wall, the entire facade collapsed on top of it. There was a crashing, rumbling, and screeching, and the motor of the KV-I died. The dangerous foe had been immobilized. Bix had his gunner fire two armor-piercing rounds at the disabled KV-I's turret from barely ten meters. Both failed to penetrate. Panting, Bix forced himself back into the hatch. He saw how the driver of the KV-I was now attempting to back his way out of the rubble. Brickwork was already tumbling down.

Bix heard the *Hauptmann* call, "Harpoon from Chief, we're coming!"

The first shell from the approaching German tanks struck the turret of the KV-I. This, too, failed to penetrate the thick armor of the Russian tank. The KV-I's driver was gradually succeeding in freeing the big tank from the wall. Suddenly, Bix remembered the battle at Oslavaya, when they had put several shots through the cannon barrel of a Russian tank.

"Listen, Krause, aim as at Oslavaya!"

Krause had anticipated the order. He cranked the turret around until the thickest part of the KV-I's gun barrel was in his sight and fired the first armor-piercing round. The second followed soon afterward.

At the same time, armor-piercing shot from the other tanks began to strike the KV-I. Suddenly, glowing fragments of steel, which shot out in thin fountains from the armored sides of the Russian tank as the shells struck, were whizzing toward the *Feldwebel.* The armor-piercing shells, which bored into the thick armor plate and stuck there, had blasted out the glowing fragments.

After firing for the third time, Bix called to cease fire. Peering through his binoculars he could see that it had worked again. The gun barrel of the KV-I had been hit three times and definitely been rendered unusable.

"Now in the running gear!" he called to his gunner.

Krause fired four shots into the KV-I's running gear in short order. The giant was immobilized.

"The Russians are climbing out!" reported Schwartz.

Bix watched as the Russian crew climbed out of a hatch and then disappeared into the neighboring houses.

"Battalion thought that our company had been wiped out," called *Hauptmann* Lekschat after answering the battalion commander's anxious questions.

"It's no wonder, what with all the firing," responded the *Feldwebel*. Several more KV-I's had been abandoned by their crews and were captured undamaged by the battalion when it arrived on the scene. Bix and his crew would not soon forget the fighting in Venev. The combat there had been some of the most dangerous they had ever been involved in.

The advance by Panzer Brigade Eberbach continued. The tanks were now driving north. The first Moscow signposts appeared along the way.

On the last night of the advance the tanks drove toward Kashira in the freezing cold. Russian aircraft bombed the armored columns. That night the vehicles covered only ten kilometers, as the deep ruts left by Soviet tanks had frozen, creating a significant hindrance. Whenever one of the panzers drove into one of these ruts it was practically locked in. The track bolts, which had become as brittle as glass in the cold, sheared off on the walls of the ruts. When a track change was necessary, the men had to carry it out in minus forty degree temperatures. Attempts to drive in the bolts with hammers resulted in flying splinters of steel, which often inflicted painful injuries.

When the panzers reached their objective, a small market town, they were met by fire from Soviet antitank guns. Once again *Feldwebel* Bix's tank was involved in the attack. He put two antitank guns out of action and then they were in the town. The Russian soldiers still holding out in the houses were overcome by the following German infantry in house-to-house fighting. The Red Army soldiers defended desperately, because only in the houses was there shelter from the frightful cold. Whoever was driven outside faced death by freezing.

The tank crews and infantry had scarcely settled into the huts when there was another alert. "Everyone back to the jumping-off position at once!"

Hauptmann Lekschat had no idea what this meant. Moscow lay only sixty kilometers ahead of the panzers, and they were to pull back? For Bix and his men, for the Lekschat Company, and for the entire Eberbach Panzer Brigade the order was unfathomable.

"This is the end of our dream," said loader Petermann. "The blitzkrieg to Moscow has been called off."

Petermann was right. Never again did German tanks get so close to the Soviet capital as in the terrible winter of 1941.

Five Times over Enemy Mines

Feldwebel Bix survived the battles of retreat of December 1941, as one tank after another broke down. The crews fought shoulder to shoulder with the infantry in the trenches. There was bitter fighting and the cold punished everyone. Somehow they survived, although Petermann was killed during a night attack.

The 35th Panzer Regiment was reorganized in early 1942 and 1st Battalion became part of the 11th Panzer Division. The former Lekschat company became the 8th Company of the 15th Panzer Regiment. The company's new commander was *Oberleutnant* Schöpe. Schöpe had come from antitank guns, but he quickly caught on to the different conditions in this new branch of the service.

On 28 June 1942 the 8th Company once again rolled east. The objective of the attack was Voronezh, an important city on the east bank of the Don. Operation *Blau,* as the proposed battle of encirclement had been named, failed to materialize because Marshal Timoshenko refused to accept battle but instead withdrew quickly to the Don.

On 30 June, *Feldwebel* Bix was wounded by shrapnel in his upper and lower leg and upper arm. He remained with the unit's train and reappeared a few days later, ready for action (the attack on Voronezh had meanwhile been called off). The regiment then became involved in fighting in the Shisdra and Suchinitshi areas. Promoted to *Oberfeldwebel* on 1 August, Bix participated in the attack on Shisdra as a platoon leader.

The assault began on 17 August. The panzers rolled cautiously across the countryside. *Oberfeldwebel* Bix led the spearhead platoon. *Unteroffizier* Schwartz drove routinely and reacted instantly to every order. Bix stood in his turret and scanned the approaches to the town.

"I don't like that slope beyond the stream," he reported to his men inside the tank. "If I were a Russian, that's where I would set up my antitank guns."

Glancing to the side, Bix saw the battalion's tanks rolling forward in wedge formation. Behind them were the armored personnel carriers carrying the grenadiers. Seconds later several antitank guns opened fire from the slope, followed soon afterward by tanks. Within a matter of seconds the sector was alive with the sounds of battle. Shells crashed into the German panzers. An armored personnel carrier blew up with a harsh crack.

"Chief to everyone, withdraw to the back side of the slope!"

The armored vehicles rolled back 300 meters, where they were safe from the shells of the Russian antitank guns and tank cannon.

Oberleutnant Schöpe called his platoon leaders by radio: "Platoon leaders to me!"

When the three *Oberfeldwebel* arrived at the company commander's tank, Schöpe said, "All right, everyone listen: we will move out by darkness. Division wants a small bridgehead captured so the entire unit can cross the river in the morning."

"And we're the advance company, *Herr Oberleutnant?*" asked *Hauptfeldwebel* Hain.

"Correct, Hain! As soon as darkness falls the company will move out, cross the river and establish the bridgehead."

"It's a good two kilometers to the river, *Herr Oberleutnant,*" interjected the leader of 3rd Platoon.

"Yes, it's a critical situation, men," replied the company commander. He glanced briefly at the slope on the far side of the stream, which was just discernable in the evening twilight. Harsh muzzle flashes from the guns of Russian tanks flared up on the heights.

"The slope is studded with guns." Schöpe now turned

to *Oberfeldwebel* Bix, who had given rise to much comment in the past few days: "Do you want to lead the advance platoon?"

"Gladly, *Herr Oberleutnant!*" answered the platoon leader.

Hauptfeldwebel Hain had something on his mind. "Hermann, can you let me go along with your platoon this time?" he asked.

"You would be better off staying behind with your files, Ernst," replied Bix.

But the senior NCO was not going to be discouraged so easily. "I'd rather go with you."

"Come now!" replied Bix. "With you and me gone, I'd only have *Oberfeldwebel* Nowack and two *Feldwebels* to leave in charge. That's not exactly a star cast!"

The attack plan was discussed in great detail. The objective was to enable the division to cross the river with minimal casualties. Preparations were finally completed and Bix made his way back to his platoon to brief his men.

"The most important thing for us is to ensure that the bridge is kept passable for the wheeled vehicles. No one is to drive onto it. If you do you'll end up taking a bath with the bridge for sure!" he warned.

One of the men spoke up: "We've seen that often enough already, *Herr Oberfeldwebel*. It wouldn't be the first bridge that turned out to be a death trap for tanks."

Oberleutnant Schöpe came up.

"It's going to be a ticklish piece of work," he declared. "But if we pull it off, they'll certainly have to chalk up the success to us!"

Bix was rather unconcerned about that aspect of the operation. All that he knew for sure was that there would be no peace in the next few days. The whole thing stunk, that was for sure.

He turned once again to his company commander. *"Herr Oberleutnant,* I suggest that my platoon drive with a fixed interval of one hundred meters. Complete radio silence is very important, because experience has shown that radio communications can be heard over a great distance during the night."

The *Oberleutnant* agreed at once. "Good, Bix! You alone have permission to use your radio. All following tanks have a strict ban on radio communications."

In the meantime darkness had fallen. The crews were already

in their tanks, the commanders were standing in the turret hatches. Behind him, Bix, whose eyes had become accustomed to the low light, recognized the *Hauptfeldwebel*. He gave him a brief wave, then raised his arm three times. That was the signal to move out. The motors roared to life. When the leading tank had covered fifty meters the second moved off. This was necessary in the event that the first tank came under fire. By leaving an interval between vehicles, each was assured sufficient freedom of movement should evasive maneuvers become necessary.

The drivers drove at a low throttle setting. The sound of the tracks could scarcely be heard, as the tanks were driving along a sandy road.

From his position in the lead the *Oberfeldwebel* ordered: "No abrupt increases on the throttle!"

Schwartz steered the panzer forward, calling on all his skills as a driver. He was the only member of Bix's old crew still left. To Bix the whole thing felt rather strange. With every meter they were drawing nearer to the enemy-occupied village. Every track revolution might bring them over an enemy mine. Mines were a specialty of the Soviets. At any moment, too, antitank guns could open up from concealed positions.

But nothing like that took place. Unmolested, the tanks reached the edge of the village that lay before the small stream. They came to the road which turned off to the right just before the bridge and led into the village.

"Nowack, turn off at the fork to the right a few meters and secure toward the village!"

Turning round, Bix saw that the *Oberfeldwebel*'s panzer had already turned away. Now the Russians could come out of the village. Nowack would be in position to head them off.

The outline of the bridge emerged from the darkness, which was weakened somewhat by the moonlight. Bix recognized one of the four wooden bridges, none of which could support a tank. Under no circumstances could he permit any attempts to drive across the bridge, as it would certainly collapse.

"I'm going to look for a level spot in the stream," Bix advised his chief.

"Good luck, Bix!"

Bix worked his way along the stream bank. If only he had X-ray eyes to see where the Russians had laid their mines. He felt certain that the bank had been mined. Should he trust in luck and drive across? That was too risky. Moreover, the other side of the stream might be marshy. Was it not too steep here? It took only a few seconds for Bix to reach a decision.

His gaze fell upon a bomb crater close to the bank. There could be no mines there. What was more, the sides of the crater didn't appear to be too steep. He had driven across similar craters several times.

"Harpoon to chief! I'm standing before the bridge and I'm going to drive through a bomb crater into the river."

The *Hauptmann* called back: "Good, do that! I leave it to your judgment!"

"All right, Schwartz, in we go! Drive down as carefully as possible, no sudden movements. It would be best if you avoid any turns."

Bix knew that if the tank began to slide on the bank, it would all be over.

The tank rolled slowly headfirst down into the bomb crater. Soon it would reach the point of tipping over. But it reached the bottom safely, and Schwartz began pushing the tank literally by centimeters up the other side of the crater. The tracks ground deep into the mud, splashing and smacking.

"How does it look, Schwartz?" asked the *Oberfeldwebel*.

"We'll see," he murmured.

"Will we make it, or will we tip over backward?"

"We'll make it. The tracks are gripping well."

Bix breathed a sigh of relief. Seconds later the bow of the tank pushed its way above the lip of the crater, rose higher and higher, and then tipped forward. They had done it.

"Did you hear a pebble drop?" Bix asked his comrade of many battles.

"It seemed more like a boulder," croaked the driver, grinning.

"These must be the positions we ran into this morning," said Bix a little later. "Move over to the left and make room for the tanks behind us to follow."

The tank rolled slowly to the left.

The next orders came over the radio: "Hain, follow me. Then *Feldwebel* Reich and finally *Feldwebel* Gerlach. Once you reach the top, make way for the next. Nowack, remain at the fork and continue to secure there."

One after another the tanks rattled through the crater. Bix directed two to the right and the last to the left to join him.

"Hopefully the Ivans haven't seen us," remarked the driver.

"They can't see us, Schwartz. There's a tall stand of alders behind us with thick tops, which swallows us up so to speak."

A moment later Bix again called his commanders: "No Morse transmissions. Everyone stand by!"

Bix strained to hear or see something of the enemy, but all he could hear was the noise made by the rest of the company, which was following slowly under the command of the *Oberleutnant*.

Soon the *Oberleutnant*'s Panzer IV was rolling into the bomb crater. When he was halfway through, the night was torn by a multitude of brilliant muzzle flashes. *Oberfeldwebel* Bix suddenly found himself in the line of fire of at least ten guns. The crash of gunfire was ear-shattering. The flashes from the muzzles of the guns were blinding. The impacting shells nearly deafened the men in the tanks. Behind the tanks, treetops were severed as the shells smashed into them. The enemy guns were firing over the panzers on their side of the stream. Bix targeted the muzzle flashes.

His order went out to the other tanks: "Ready cannon and machine guns! Open fire only on my command. Aim at the muzzle flashes!"

The remaining three commanders reported that they had each targeted the muzzle flashes.

"To everyone: open fire!"

Four cannon and eight machine guns opened fire almost simultaneously. There was a terrific crash and Bix heard a pair of shells ricochet off something very near. They must have struck steel. Ricochets whistled about. The Russian fire ceased abruptly.

Bix reached for the flare pistol that hung beside him. He fired a white illumination flare toward the slope containing the enemy firing position. In the chalky light he could see the enemy guns twenty to thirty meters ahead and Russians running away. Bursts of yellow tracer from the German machine guns pursued the fleeing gun crews.

Another gun opened fire from farther back. Again shells crashed into the trees and several branches fell on *Oberleutnant* Schöpf's head. There was a resounding crash and the enemy's last gun was silenced.

Soon afterward the order came from behind: "Platoon move forward to make way for the others to cross!" The four tanks rolled forward as far as the enemy gun position and the tension of the last hour quickly fell away from the men. When the *Oberleutnant*'s tank had made its way through the crater and drove up to that of the *Oberfeldwebel*, Schöpf shouted, "Man, Bix, where did you get the nerve?"

"One has to be lucky," said Bix in reply.

The bridgehead had been established for the division. Bix and his platoon had played a vital role in overcoming the Russian antitank front. The day before the entire tank battalion had been unable to break through the antitank barricade. That night the four panzers of the Bix platoon had done it alone.

The following day Bix and his Panzer IV drove into the Shisdra forest. Several hundred meters into the wood the tank struck a mine. There was a tremendous crash and driver Schwartz reported that he could no longer steer the tank.

Everyone climbed out to repair the track. A half hour later the platoon leader's panzer set off again after the rest of the platoon, arriving just in time to help engage an enemy bunker position on the far side of the wood.

Bix's tank ran over more mines during the next two days. *Unteroffizier* Schwartz lost a foot in the explosion of the third mine. The radio operator was wounded in the arm but, miraculously, Bix was unhurt.

Bix's luck finally ran out on 22 August. One of the division's rifle battalions was pinned down in the Shisdra forest. Surrounded by Russian units, the battalion sent out a call for help.

The company commander said, "Bix, there's a job for your platoon."

Three tanks were still combat-ready. Led by *Oberfeldwebel* Bix, the three set off. They had not gone far when a pair of concealed T-34s opened fire. The three tanks split up and returned the enemy fire. The Panzer IVs were equipped with the new "long" 7.5cm gun that could penetrate the armor of any enemy tank. *Feldwebel* Reich destroyed two of the

T-34s while *Feldwebel* Gerlach disposed of a third. The way was clear.

"Through quickly!" ordered Bix.

They raced on, became stuck in a thicket, and then fought their way free. The panzers then reached a road which led through the forest. Fire from antitank rifles clattered against the armor.

"Load high-explosive!"

A group of Russian soldiers appeared. Shells exploded in the bushes, sending shattered branches whirling through the air. The tanks' machine guns hammered away and the enemy disappeared back into the forest.

A little later Bix spotted the clearing in which the battalion had been surrounded. Suddenly a mighty blow shook the tank. There was an immense pressure against his lungs and at the same instant Bix felt a stab of pain in his legs.

The panzer had stopped. A hole in the hull and torn tracks were the result of the fifth mine. His comrades recovered the severely wounded *Oberfeldwebel* and took him back to the main dressing station.

A few days later Bix took leave of his comrades, whom he was never to see again. Finally, Bix ended up in a military hospital in Germany. When he was released and went home on leave, he learned from his mother that his brother had been killed in Russia.

Some time later Bix received a teletype informing him that he had been awarded the German Cross in Gold on 5 November 1942. A medical examination revealed that it would be some time before he was fit to return to action at the front.

On these grounds Bix was sent to the Army Noncommissioned Officers School to become a platoon leader and instructor there. At the conclusion of his period of duty at the school he was sent to a training battalion in France, where he was retrained on the new Panther tank.

Because of its 7.5cm L/70 tank cannon and its great speed, the Panther was the best German tank at that time. Despite its good armor protection, it was faster than the Panzer IV that Bix had commanded earlier.

In June 1944, *Oberfeldwebel* Bix set out for the Eastern Front with his comrades and the new panzers. They disembarked in the Slutsk-Baranovichi area and made their way to

1st Battalion of the 35th Panzer Regiment, which was engaged in heavy defensive fighting in that sector.

Finally, Bix had returned to his old regiment.

Tank Battle near Warsaw

Shortly before the trains rolled into the small station, it had been attacked by Russian bombers and completely destroyed. There were no loading ramps available.

"We should make a right face at once and drive down from the cars," suggested *Oberfeldwebel* Bix to the young Bavarian officer.

"Damn!" The young officer scratched his neck. "All right! Turn to the right on the cars and then off through the center before the fire reaches us!"

Flames were already licking from the station buildings. The Panthers turned and rolled down from the flatcars. They formed up on the street and drove off into the countryside to get away from the station—which might be bombed again at any minute—as quickly as possible. It took exactly ten minutes for the tanks to form up into a column and roll off in the direction of their area of operations.

They reached 1st Battalion, which was soon to face a severe test. A few hours later Bix learned the extent of the threat. The Soviets had attacked the 34 German divisions that *Feldmarschall* Busch had available in this sector with 200 divisions and 6,000 tanks and assault guns. Five Soviet air armies had thrown thousands of aircraft of all types into the battle.

The 4th Panzer Division was fighting a delaying action west of Slutsk between Stolpce and Baranovichi; any more was no longer possible. To the north was the 12th Panzer Division and to the south the 28th Jäger Division. Bobruisk fell to the Soviets on 29 June. Of the 100,000 German soldiers there, only 30,000 could be saved. The area around Stolpce had to be held at all costs to keep open the crossings over the Beresina for the German Fourth Army, which was still on the east side of the river.

On 5 July 1944 General Völckers gave the order for the

Fourth Army to break through to the west. Slutsk had been in Soviet hands since 1 July. Their armored spearheads were 30 kilometers east of Baranovichi. The 4th Panzer Division was ordered to hold up the Soviets east of Baranovichi for as long as possible.

First Battalion rolled east in three wedge formations. The Goldhammer company led the way and *Oberfeldwebel* Bix and his company were in the front rank. As he turned in his open turret hatch, Bix saw the face of the diminutive *Leutnant* Görum. The *Leutnant* waved to him and motioned forward. The houses of the village now came into sight from behind several large trees.

"That's the village, Bix," said *Oberleutnant* Goldhammer over the radio.

"Hopefully our people are still there, *Herr Oberleutnant,*" replied the *Oberfeldwebel*.

They rolled through the village and came to a brook. The grenadiers had dug in on the near side of the stream. Several were still busy digging. About four hundred meters to the right Bix saw a single 7.5cm antitank gun.

"Where is the bridge I'm supposed to secure?" asked *Leutnant* Görum.

"Nothing here!" offered the chief.

An *Oberleutnant* of the grenadiers came running up to Bix's Panther.

"Where is the bridge?" asked the *Oberfeldwebel*.

"You're looking too far to the left. It's over there!" The *Oberleutnant* gestured in the direction they would have to take. Bix passed on the information to *Leutnant* Görum, using a pair of willows standing next to the bridge as points of reference.

"How are things here?" Bix asked the infantry officer.

"Damned poor! The Russians are on the other side of the stream and are keeping our positions under fire. I have heavy casualties from mortar and machine gun fire."

"Have you fixed their positions?" asked the panzer commander.

"Naturally! If you only had a few minutes you could make short work of them."

"I can arrange that, *Herr Oberleutnant,*" said Bix. "Fill me in."

The company commander was overjoyed: "Man, that would be great! Follow me to the command post!"

While *Gefreiter* Willrich steered the Panther along behind the infantry officer, Bix called his company commander.

"The bridge is ahead of me and slightly to my right. Görum is too far to the right."

"Görum reports fire, is engaging enemy antitank guns. You take the bridge, Bix!"

Meanwhile, the tank had reached the infantry command post. Mortar rounds were bursting on the west bank of the small stream. A pair of enemy machine guns was firing long bursts at the grenadiers. Bix observed the enemy through his field glasses.

The *Oberleutnant* called out the first target: "One thousand meters. The small gap to the left of the round bush. Enemy antitank gun!"

Bix scanned the described area through his glasses. Just then he spotted a muzzle flash.

"Do you have him, Hennemann?"

The gunner had already targeted the enemy. The shot cracked and the Panther rocked slightly from the recoil. The high-explosive round burst in the middle of the antitank gun position. Steel and wood whirled through the air.

"Got him!" shouted the *Oberleutnant* enthusiastically. "Now the heavy machine gun that's raking the right sector."

The next HE round smashed into the machine gun position, a direct hit. A wheel from the machine gun cart flew through the air. It took exactly six minutes for Bix to eliminate the entire enemy position in front of the village.

"Chief to Bix: proceed directly to the bridge!" came the order from *Oberleutnant* Goldhammer, who, with the company, was now engaged in battle.

"Let's go, Willrich. Turn half-right and then straight ahead."

After a hundred meters the bridge came into sight. Bix had to get out of the hatch to get a better look at the bridge. Would it support his Panther? It looked as if it would.

"Drive across carefully!" he ordered.

The planks sagged under the weight of the Panther, but held. Beyond the bridge the road made a slight turn. Wheat fields lay to the right and left.

Suddenly the *Oberleutnant* appeared behind the tank with a few grenadiers.

"Stay back a bit," Bix called to him. "You'll be in great danger if we're fired upon!"

He had scarcely spoken the words when antitank guns opened fire. There was a tremendous crash and seconds later Willrich reported that he could no longer steer the Panther. The antitank gun had presumably shot up both tracks. Soon afterward enemy mortars began to fire on them. Mortar rounds burst all around, leaving black smudges in the fields of wheat. As the infantry *Oberleutnant* leapt to the side, he ran straight into a bursting mortar round. When the smoke cleared Bix saw that the *Oberleutnant* had been killed.

"Fire!" Bix shouted to his gunner.

"Where, *Herr Oberfeldwebel?*" the gunner called back. "I don't see any muzzle flashes."

"It doesn't matter where. Just fire!"

Hit after hit now shook the stationary Panther. At any minute a direct hit might penetrate a vulnerable spot and then they would be lost.

Willrich attempted to move the tank forward. Not until then did it become apparent that it was not the tracks, but one of the tank's roadwheels that had been damaged. The Panther began to move. There was an ungodly crashing and cracking from the tracks, but they were moving.

A shell hammered against the turret. It rang like a tremendous bell stroke. The tank shook as if it were in terrible pain. Suddenly the crew could see again and they saw the muzzle flash of an antitank gun firing from a village approximately a thousand meters away. At almost the same instant Bix spotted an antitank gun about thirty meters farther to the left in a recently-mown wheat field and more guns behind it.

"High-explosive!" he shouted.

Hennemann and Krüger worked like mad. The first shell burst in the wheat field. The force of the exploding shells cleared away more and more of the Russian camouflage. Three, then four shells smashed into the enemy position. The Russian gunners abandoned their guns and ran for their lives. The shock of the panzer's assault had put them to flight. It was no small matter to stand up to such an armored giant at close range. The last figures vanished into a wheat field farther to the rear that extended as far as the village.

"Bix to chief: Am east of the bridge. Enemy antitank guns are out of action!"

"We're coming!" replied *Oberleutnant* Goldhammer.

Soon afterward the tanks of the company approached, rolled across the bridge, and stopped about fifty meters from the *Oberfeldwebel*'s Panther. Bix had his driver back the damaged tank into a ravine a few dozen meters to the rear.

"Climb out!" he ordered.

The crew now saw for the first time what their Panther had withstood. Hermann Bix counted no less than seventeen hits.

"Some mess!" murmured radio operator Dedekind in amazement. "Looks like it's done for."

"I'll have to get into another tank, *Herr Oberleutnant,*" reported Bix when the small Bavarian appeared.

"All right, take Cordes's vehicle."

After Bix and his crew had changed tanks, the order came from *Oberleutnant* Goldhammer they had all been expecting:

"We're going to drive into the village. If we're in the village it will be easier to hold the streambed."

The company's twelve tanks drove off and headed for the village at high speed. The first shots from enemy antitank guns showed that it was not going to be so simple.

Twelve tank cannon opened fire on the enemy. The first houses caught fire and then the Panthers roared down the main street, firing to both sides. All resistance soon collapsed. *Oberleutnant* Goldhammer reported this to battalion and was ordered to secure the village. The Panthers were stationed around the village and their crews had to take turns standing guard throughout the night. In the meantime, *Oberleutnant* Goldhammer had established contact with the battalion, which had driven up and gone into position behind the spearhead company.

At dawn heavy tank fire began on both sides of the Goldhammer company.

"There are the rest of our tanks," declared Hennemann.

"But they're a long way back," said Krüger, shaking his head with concern. "If the Ivans roar through, we'll really be stuck in it out here."

An hour later the *Obergefreiter*'s concerns became a reality. On making an inquiry, *Oberleutnant* Goldhammer received orders to pull back. The last sentence of the order was of special significance. It read: "Russian tanks have reached the west side of the stream, you are to break through their front."

A little later Goldhammer advised his platoon leaders: "We're caught in a trap."

Leutnant Görum began to curse in his Bavarian dialect. *Oberleutnant* Goldhammer was tempted to join him, but forced himself to remain calm.

"The bridge is in the pot, *Herr Oberleutnant*. How are we supposed to get across the damned brook?" interjected *Oberfeldwebel* Schratte.

Russian artillery now opened fire on the village. There was a hellish racket. Fresh fires began to blaze. Mortar shells burst among the houses. For a few minutes the men couldn't hear a word, then it became somewhat quieter.

Oberleutnant Goldhammer closed the situation briefing: "We're going to have to fight our way through the Russian line a few kilometers to the side. Everyone drive as fast as you can. Don't get involved in combat. Stay together no matter what and avoid breakdowns. This time the Görum platoon will drive in the lead."

The panzer company began to move. The tanks drove off with hatches closed. Bix saw shells bursting to the left and right. Earth, stones, and steel splinters cracked against the flanks of the Panther. The enemy fire intensified when *Oberleutnant* Görum reached the exit from the village.

The voice of *Oberleutnant* Goldhammer came over the radio: "Increase tempo! Stay together!"

The tanks picked up speed. *Gefreiter* Willrich shifted gears. The speedometer showed thirty kilometers per hour, then thirty-five, then forty.

Willrich spotted a trench running across their path. "Watch out!" he shouted. The men hung on for dear life. Every joint in the panzer creaked as it laid over hard to one side. The loader was thrown against the wall.

A Sherman tank opened fire from the right. American tanks, delivered by the Murmansk convoys, had been in action on the battlefields of the Eastern Front for some time. Bix saw *Leutnant* Görum pull out of the line and halt. Seconds later, after two tanks had passed by, the *Leutnant* opened fire. His first shot blew the turret off the Sherman. A few seconds later Görum's tank moved off and, driving along the side of the road at high speed, overtook the other tanks and regained its position at the head of the column.

A heavy blow shook Bix's Panther, but the shell failed to penetrate. Seconds later there was a renewed crashing and roaring. Russian infantry were firing machine guns and automatic rifles from the edge of the forest as the tanks roared past. It was a completely senseless undertaking, because the bullets were unlikely to cause any harm to the Panthers.

The tanks were now driving parallel to the front. A village appeared ahead. The order went out: "Through at full throttle! Maximum speed!"

The Panthers closed up and raced toward the village at fifty kilometers per hour. Russian soldiers fled the street seeking safety from the onrushing armor.

It was a wild ride. The panzers roared through the Russian positions like a ghost train. The Russians apparently had no idea that German tanks might still be in the area. They were so surprised by the appearance of the Panthers that they had no chance to effect any countermeasures.

Its motor thundering, the *Oberfeldwebel*'s tank raced along behind the Panther in front. Long flames flew from the exhausts and mighty clouds of dust whirled up from its tracks. The hot summer sun caused the temperature inside the tank to jump to over 120 degrees.

All at once lances of flame flashed from guns in the cornfields on both sides of the road close to the village.

Leutnant Goldhammer called his commanders: "Guns to three and nine o'clock respectively, fire on the move, no stopping!"

The armored turrets began to move. That of the tank ahead of Bix swung to the left, so the *Oberfeldwebel* ordered his gunner to rotate their Panther's turret to the right. The panzers opened fire with high-explosive shells. To halt would have been suicide.

Loader Krüger rammed shells into the chamber. Hennemann, the gunner, aimed and fired. He saw that the rounds were on target. An antitank gun's ammunition went up in the cornfield with a mighty blast.

The Soviets were returning the German fire. Hard blows shook the *Oberfeldwebel*'s Panther, but it rolled on. Striking the tank in flashes of flames, some of which were sucked into the fighting compartment, the armor-piercing shot glanced off and howled away to the side.

The Russian antitank guns were lined up practically wheel to wheel. There would be no getting through the front here. But the surprising dash by the German tanks parallel to the antitank front, sometimes only fifty or sixty meters in front of it, gave the Russians little time to fire accurately. The movement of the Panthers was so swift that they did not have time to fully comprehend what was going on.

For the Germans it was a hellish drive. Bix expected the end to come any minute. Shells whistled past his vision slit and crashed against the armor of the tank ahead. It looked as if a lightning storm were breaking over the panzers. Evasive maneuvers were impossible. They had to drive on. Finally, the long antitank front came to an end.

All other sounds were drowned out by the deafening roar of the battle and of the engines and tracks. The only interruption was the voice of *Oberleutnant* Goldhammer calling his commanders.

"Onward, onward! The last hundred meters!" joked Goldhammer with a touch of gallows humor.

The panzer grenadiers manning front-line positions a good three kilometers to the west heard the battle noise and asked themselves what was going on. The few who knew that a German panzer company was stuck out there gave the unit little chance of getting through. The cessation of the din of battle must mean that the German tanks were now no more than wreckage on the battlefield.

When the leading tank came to the turnoff to the west, Goldhammer ordered, "Left turn!"

The German tanks veered left and drove toward the German lines. War correspondent Robert Poensgen, who was with the grenadiers in the front lines, described the approach of the tanks:

Suddenly, in the distance, the men in the front lines saw a tank roll out of the enemy-occupied village trailing a giant cloud of dust. Then came a second, then a third and a fourth. There were more and more of them. One behind the other they approached the front at high speed.

The call went from foxhole to foxhole: "The Russians are

attacking with tanks!—Panzers to the front!—Assault guns forward!"

The close-range antitank weapons were readied. Suddenly, a *Leutnant* who had been observing the attack through his field-glasses roared: "Those are German Panthers." He jumped up, waving his fur cap. The first tank turned and drove directly toward him. It was an uncomfortable feeling for the *Leutnant*. Were there Russians in those tanks?

But then a signal flare was fired from the turret of the leading tank and then the black cap of a panzer commander appeared. The commanders of the remaining panzers also emerged.

The first tank halted. The others drove alongside. The hatches of the last tank flipped open. The tankers blinked in the bright sunlight. Exhausted, they climbed out of their stations, gasping for air. Then they lit cigarettes and, walking bow-legged like sailors, went round their vehicles and inspected the numerous gashes on the turret, flanks and rear. The panzer crews looked toward the village which was now burning fiercely. They were filled with a tremendous sense of happiness, the joy of having survived this great danger.

This brings Poensgen's report to an end. It remains to be said that the company lost not a single tank during the breakthrough. When Hermann Bix saw the hits on his Panther he was amazed that it could still be driven at all.

"Nothing can happen to us with this tank!" he said, and the four comrades who had shared the closed quarters of the steel box with him were in full agreement.

The 4th Panzer Division carried out a gradual withdrawal. The retreat gained momentum. In five weeks the Red Army covered seven hundred kilometers. Army Group Center was destroyed by this lightning advance made by Soviet forces possessing a tenfold superiority in numbers. Of the total of thirty-eight German divisions, twenty-eight had been smashed. The bravery of the individual soldier and the fighting spirit of the panzer units were of little use against the avalanche of war machines and men that the Soviets had mobilized.

The offensive rolled west like a steamroller. 350,000 German soldiers of Army Group Center disappeared from the battlefields. According to Soviet statements, German casualties included 200,000 killed and 85,000 captured. In response to the oft-repeated criticism of the "cowardly generals," it should be pointed out that of the forty-seven generals involved in the fighting as commanding generals or division commanders, no fewer than thirty-one were killed or taken prisoner.

In the suburbs of Warsaw the tanks of the 4th Panzer Division once again joined the battle. The crews of the Tigers and Panthers fought a tremendous tank battle. *Oberfeldwebel* Bix and his men faced a greatly superior force of Soviet armor. Many Russian tanks fell victim to the long-ranging panzer cannon. The 19th Panzer Division joined the battle and the Soviet force was smashed. However, fresh units were already advancing from the Russian rear areas. Nevertheless, the tanks of the 4th Panzer Division succeeded in capturing the bridge over the Bug near Wyschkow in a surprise attack. As a result of this advance the tanks were able to drive into the northern flank of a Soviet tank corps that was engaged in outflanking the forces of the German XXXIX Army Corps to the north.

A short time later XXXIX Army Corps *(Generalleutnant* von Sauken) was transferred to Army Group North *(Generaloberst* Schörner). Its assignment was to close the gap that had been created between Schörner and General Rauss. For *Oberfeldwebel* Bix, there now began a tank war such as he could never have dreamt of.

It was 18 August and the first serious fighting in the new area of operations already lay behind the battalion and its Panthers. The 4th Panzer Division had failed to reach its objective of Mitau and was located in Shagarev. On that day the 35th Panzer Regiment's 1st Battalion received orders to overrun and push back the Russian front line, which bulged westward at that point.

Oberfeldwebel Bix drove at the head of the company. As the most experienced tank commander, *Oberleutnant* Goldhammer had selected him to lead the company and find the best location to break into the Soviet lines.

Enemy guns opened fire.

"Hatches shut! Cannon and machine guns ready to fire!" ordered Bix.

The commanders disappeared into their turrets. The gunners reported weapons clear. Through his scissors telescope Bix saw the muzzle flash of a *Ratschbum.*

"Enemy gun position. Range eight hundred. Open fire!"

Hennemann fired the first round. A shell struck the turret at an angle and shot howling upward. Then a second shell smacked into the ground to the right of the Panther. Smoke and the harsh glare of flames were forced into the fighting compartment.

"Forward, Willrich!"

The driver shifted. The tank moved off, but suddenly there was a crashing and groaning from the reduction gears as teeth were sheared off. There was a grinding sound, a jolt went through the tank, and then the Panther stood still.

"Reduction gear is shot," called Willrich in dismay.

Bix's tank was now lying immobilized in front of the Russian main line of resistance. The remaining tanks rolled on, took up the battle, and tried to cover the disabled panzer.

"Fire, Hennemann!" ordered Bix.

The *Obergefreiter* targeted the *Ratschbum*. The second shot silenced the enemy gun. Others joined the battle. Two shells struck the Panther, jolting it backward. The noise of the impacting shells was tremendous, but fortunately they failed to penetrate the tank's armor.

The tank's machine guns now opened up on a group of Russians that was moving through the surrounding terrain toward the Panther.

Suddenly there was a tremendous crash. Everything happened in an instant. A chance hit had penetrated the hatch cover above the radio operator. The shot had ricocheted down off the gun mantlet, but still had enough force to pierce the hatch cover. A steel fragment torn from the hatch cover ripped off one of Dedekind's arms. It was a horrible sight.

"Bail out. Get moving, lend a hand."

Together they lifted the seriously wounded radio operator from his station. The seemingly impossible succeeded. Despite the enemy fire they all managed to get out of the tank and reach cover in a shellhole. While Hennemann and Krüger applied emergency dressings to stop the heavy bleeding, Bix tried to fetch help. He never left a comrade in the lurch, even when leaving comparatively safe cover was tantamount to suicide, as in this case.

The Russians had seen the crew abandon its tank, and ten or more of their mortars were now firing on its general location. The cough of the mortars, the bursting of shells, and the howling of dropping mortar rounds mingled with the fire of tank cannon and Soviet antitank guns in an infernal orgy of noise.

Hermann Bix got to his feet. He must find a medic. He had gone scarcely three meters when more mortar rounds came howling down. He threw himself to the ground, but as he fell he knew that it was too late. The mortar rounds landed only a few meters away. The crash of the exploding shells nearly deafened him. At the same instant he felt a stabbing pain in his hip and thigh.

His first thought was: now it's all over! But then his will to live took over. He could not and would not give up. His comrades fetched a medical unit. Fortunately, the attack by the German tanks was a success and the Soviets were pushed out of their projecting salient.

Bix and radio operator Dedekind were evacuated to the rear and taken to the main dressing station. The shell fragments were removed and the next day the two were on a hospital train for Germany. In the hospital Bix received the Wound Badge in Silver and the Panzer Assault Badge, Second Grade.

The weeks passed. Bix was happy to be home again, to be at peace, and not have to be ready to face battle—and death— every day and every hour.

Soon, however, he reported back to the front, even though the wound in his thigh had not completely healed. When he arrived in Obrin, near Libau, he immediately received a repaired Panther from the division repair shop there and a crew. With his four new comrades he rolled off in the direction of Schrunden-Prekuln, where his battalion was once again involved in heavy defensive fighting. He had arrived just in time to experience the beginning of the First Battle of the Courland.

Tanks!—Tanks!—Tanks!

The First Battle of the Courland began on 27 October 1944 with a Soviet artillery bombardment that started at about 0630. Two thousand guns of all calibers opened fire along the entire front between Prekuln and the Venta. A little later, under the protection of this mighty barrage that shifted slowly to the north, Soviet tank and infantry brigades went to the attack. The main blow was directed against the 30th Infantry Division, but soon the 4th and 14th Panzer Divisions were also under attack. This was the situation when Bix arrived in Obrin.

"Here's a mule for you that's just been made ready, Bix," said the *Waffenmeister,* pointing to a Panther that had just been loaded with a full supply of ammunition. The *Oberfeldwebel* nodded. He went around the tank, inspecting it closely.

"And the crew?" he asked finally.

"You can select them yourself, Bix," replied *Hauptmann* Völkmann, who was in command there. "Good, then I would like to get out of here in half an hour. If I could see the men now."

Soon Bix was surrounded by tank crews awaiting new assignments, and the *Oberfeldwebel* selected several men. A little later they climbed aboard the Panther and the tank rolled off in the direction of Schrunden-Prekuln. The battalion's area of operations was located somewhere near there. Bix asked his way. Then they could hear the sound of the battle. When Bix had almost reached his company he heard a comrade calling for help.

"Oberfeldwebel Borkmann is surrounded by Russian tanks," he informed his crew. "We're going in to get him out!"

"Where are you, Borkmann? Say something, we're coming!" The *Oberfeldwebel* replied: "We're in the middle of the forest near Valdoni. Two tanks are stuck in a deep ravine."

"Your exact location, Borkmann!" Bix called back. Finally he received the information.

Bix turned to his driver, an experienced tank crewman: "Exactly as on the map, Schädelbauer!"

They rolled on. The company still knew nothing of Bix's return even though he was already almost in their midst.

The Panther worked its way along field roads and through shallow valleys. Night fell but Bix didn't wait, because the increasing strength of the radio transmissions convinced him that they were very close to their trapped comrades.

"Drive on slowly!" he called to the *Obergefreiter.*

Schädelbauer drove the tank across an open field toward the edge of the forest, which stood dark like a brush mark before them.

They halted so Bix could listen: "They must be in there," he said. "That sounds like machine gun fire."

"Yes, the Ivans are shooting into the hole again for sure," confirmed gunner Kruck.

"Move on!" ordered Bix.

The Panther again rolled toward the forest, drove in along a field road and found the ravine where their comrades were trapped.

"Defensive fire on the enemy machine guns, we'll pull you out one at a time!"

A burst of machine gun fire caused Bix to duck quickly into his turret.

"Send a few bursts up there, Berghaus," he called to the radio operator.

Obergefreiter Berghaus took aim at the muzzle flashes on the far side of the gully and pressed the trigger. Tracers flitted through the darkness and disappeared into the far slope. The second burst coincided with the next salvo from the Russians' Maxim machine gun. Berghaus adjusted his aim slightly and fired again. A red, glowing rosette of flame sprang up from the enemy position and with the crash of the explosion the "Maxie" fell silent.

"Well done, Berghaus!"

Oberfeldwebel Borkmann and his gunner now attempted to attach a tow cable while his radio operator and that of the other tank added the weight of their fire to Berghaus's in an attempt to drive the Soviets from the edge of the ravine.

Schädelbauer backed the Panther up slowly. The cable tightened until it was taut, quivering like a violin string. But it held. Schädelbauer carefully stepped on the gas and towed the other tank up the slope meter by meter, assisted by its driver. It was more than a half an hour before *Oberfeldwebel* Borkmann's Panther reached the top. The second towing operation went somewhat faster.

The maneuver had taken a total of one hour. The three Panthers were now on the high ground on a field road. Bix and his tank were in the rear, facing the enemy. Suddenly Bix saw the glowing thread of a tracing round, and it was heading straight for him. He wanted to get to cover but there was no time. One of the Russian explosive rounds detonated. Harsh flames flashed in front of his face, half blinding him. Instinctively he closed his eyes. Miraculously Bix was unhurt. Furious, he thought to himself: that was slick work!

Bix called to his driver: "Forward, Schädelbauer! We must get out of this wood before the Russians knock us out with close-range weapons."

"I can't go any faster. The tank was damaged by going into the gully," replied the *Oberfeldwebel.*

Behind Bix, whose vision had by now improved somewhat, there appeared two Russians. He ordered his gunner to open fire. With the tank's cannon in the six o'clock position, he fired a couple of high-explosive rounds at the Russians, who disappeared into the woods and were not seen again. Dawn was already breaking by the time they reached the edge of the forest.

When they could breathe a little easier, *Oberfeldwebel* Borkmann said, "It's about time that I said thank you, Hermann."

"No need to. But it's time for me to report to the company chief."

Bix gave the signal to move on. He had no interest in being the center of attention and was slightly uncomfortable at the thought of having his praises sung.

Soon afterward Bix reported himself back from Germany. *Oberleutnant* Goldhammer was overjoyed to have such an experienced platoon leader and tank commander back with the company.

"Report to me right away, Bix," called the Bavarian *Oberleutnant* over the radio.

Just then gunner Kruck shouted excitedly: "The Ivans are coming out of the woods, *Herr Oberfeld!*"

After a quick look toward the edge of the forest, Bix reported: *"Herr Oberleutnant,* I must stay here until the Russians have been beaten back."

"Good, do that! Good luck, Bix!"

"Here come the tanks!" reported *Unteroffizier* Mündelein, who was commanding the third Panther.

To the right, about eight hundred meters distant, a group of T-34s emerged from the forest. Beside them and somewhat to the rear were several superheavy Joseph Stalin tanks. One of the giants turned directly toward Bix's Panther.

"The big one first, Kruck!" shouted Bix.

The gunner swung the long gun around. The shape of the Russian giant crept into his sight. Kruck pressed the firing button. The Panther rocked from the recoil as the armor-piercing shot whipped toward the enemy.

A thought flashed through Bix's mind: Just back and I'm going to get it again!

But then he realized that this crew, none of whom he knew, was working well together. Kruck's second shot struck the Stalin between its turret and hull. The heavy tank's cannon pointed downward. The next shot pierced the Stalin's armor. Flames shot out of the open turret hatch and then the Soviet tank blew up with a mighty explosion.

The other two Panthers had engaged the T-34s. Four were destroyed and the rest veered away and rolled parallel to the three Panthers for a few seconds. Kruck swung the turret around. The first T-34 came into his sight and he fired. A long tongue of flame shot up from the rear deck of the enemy tank. The T-34 halted. The crew was trying to get out, but then there was a mighty explosion as the tank's fuel went up. The Russian crew met a terrible end.

Bix, who had taken command, ordered: "Change position to the left!"

The three Panthers rolled around, reached a shallow depression, and drove into cover behind some bushes.

"We'll let them come to within five hundred meters. As soon as they're in the open we'll fire. But together!"

They waited. From the noise they could tell that the enemy tanks had regrouped.

"Here they come!" called Bix to his two comrades. They could not yet see the T-34s, as they were in a blind spot. Then he instructed his gunner: "Target the one farthest back on the right flank."

Kruck traversed the long gun toward the flanking T-34.

"I see them, Bix!" called Borkmann.

A few seconds later the *Unteroffizier* reported: "I have them in sight, too."

"Let them come closer!" warned Bix.

Now they could see the Soviet tanks clearly. When they were in the center of the open field the *Oberfeldwebel* cleared his throat. Then his voice resounded clearly through the other commanders' headphones: "Open fire!"

Kruck's first shot tore the forward right roadwheel off one of the enemy tanks. The T-34 turned suddenly on the spot and opened fire. It had no time to fire a second time, because within a few seconds Kruck's next shot had set it ablaze.

All of the T-34s had now stopped and were firing on the muzzle flashes, which were visible from behind the bushes in the shallow depression. Four of the Soviet tanks were already in flames.

"Move, Schädelbauer. Drive to the right and forward. The rest of you remain here!"

The driver shifted into gear and the Panther nosed its way rapidly out of the bushes. The big tank moved faster and faster, and before the T-34s had a clear view of it, the Panther had arrived on the flank of the mass of enemy tanks.

"Firing halt, Schädelbauer!"

The Panther halted and swung around. Kruck opened fire. The gunner fired several more times. Then the Panther again went into motion and rattled toward the forest whence the Russian tanks had come. Its motor howling, the tank rumbled over the young trees and crushed them into the earth.

"Remain parallel to the forest!" shouted Bix.

Schädelbauer drove around a thick, old birch trunk, skirted a shellhole, grazed an oak—sending all of the men flying from their seats—and came into another stand of young trees.

"Everything all right, Sattler?" Bix asked his loader. The *Obergefreiter* nodded, already holding the next shell ready.

"Ahead fifty meters and then halt!"

The Panther left the protection of the forest. With one look Bix saw the burning and crippled enemy tanks and also spotted the two T-34s that were trying to outflank the Germans on the right.

"Keep going. Don't fire yet!"

At high speed the Panther rolled farther into the rear of the shattered enemy tank formation. A shell from *Oberfeldwebel* Borkmann's tank hissed past the Panther's nose. Schädelbauer veered out of his line of fire. In the meantime, the silhouettes of the two T-34s were growing ever larger.

The Soviet tanks halted. The Panther did likewise. Just as the T-34s were about to engage the other two Panthers, Bix opened fire on the enemy from the rear. The first shot set one of the T-34s on fire. The next shot struck the second T-34 in the tracks, and after two more shots the Russian tankers gave up. What was left of the mass of Russian tanks turned and disappeared into the forest barely a kilometer from Bix's tank. The Panther fired several rounds after them without, however, scoring any hits.

Bix returned to the other tanks in the hollow.

Borkmann called: "You did it, Bix! Everything went well!"

Bix nodded and then said, "We must get out of here as quickly as possible. If I know Ivan, he'll soon be pouring fire in here!"

The German tanks pulled back several hundred meters and went into cover behind a line of pines. The Russian bombardment was not long in coming. Heavy mortars and Stalin organs began to pour fire into the hollow that the three German Panthers had just left. During the course of the day Bix's crew accounted for a sixth enemy tank.

When Bix reported to *Oberleutant* Goldhammer, the latter said, "You made quite an entrance, Bix. I hope it's a good omen for you and for us!"

The next day the Russians achieved a penetration into the German main line of resistance. The grenadiers were pushed out of their positions. By 29 October the Russians had advanced across the Priezukrogs-Dzelzgaleskrogs road and were storming northward.

"We're to counterattack with the 108th Grenadier Regiment," explained *Oberleutnant* Goldhammer to his platoon leaders. He had assembled the men at the company command post. "The entire battalion is to spearhead the attack. We are to force the enemy back toward the Letila Heights."

"When does it begin, *Herr Oberleutnant*?" asked one of the platoon leaders.

The company commander looked at his watch.

"It's time we got going. The grenadiers will already be waiting."

A short while later the tanks rumbled off. It was not long before they made contact with Soviet forces. Mixed tank units with T-34s and Stalins attempted to parry the German counterattack.

The battle began. The German panzers succeeded in forcing back the Soviet tanks during a seven-hour battle. *Oberfeldwebel* Bix's Panther was hit several times. The tank's armored skirts were torn to pieces, the luggage compartments were holed, and there was much damage to the tank's armor plates. Nevertheless the Panther remained in the battle.

In the first hour Bix and his crew destroyed three enemy tanks. He and his crew intervened when a wave of Russian armor seemed about to overrun the grenadiers. Bix knocked out three more tanks and forced the rest to withdraw.

During the course of a two-hour duel in the forest in front of the heights, it appeared as if the Russians would overwhelm the German Panthers. *Oberfeldwebel* Borkmann's crew was rescued practically at the last second.

As he drove forward, Bix came upon a T-34 that had backed into a wide trench. Well camouflaged, it lay there in ambush. Bix was not aware of the tank's presence until flame spurted from the T-34's gun. Fire flashed into the fighting compartment. Kruck fired as well. The shot was slightly high and whizzed over the T-34's turret. The Russian's next shot struck the turret of the Panther and bounced off, but the second round from the German tank blew off the T-34's turret.

The advance continued. Suddenly a heavy blow shook the Panther. The tank's right track had been hit. Before the second T-34 could finish off the Panther, Kruck took aim and fired. His first shot was a direct hit. The T-34 blew up with a terrific explosion.

The battle came to an end. *Oberfeldwebel* Bix had destroyed eight enemy tanks. His Panther had also been hit, but apart from the damage to the track, he had been lucky. The damage was repaired in an hour.

On 2 November the German defensive front ran just south of a line Svimpli-Dzelzgaleskrogs-Matraine-Vartaja. In the vicinity of Striki it veered ninety degrees in the direction of Prekuln.

Despite the destruction of both of the Dzelzda bridges, the Soviets had managed to reach the north bank of the river. Red Army soldiers defended bitterly near the Mazdzelda farm and in the village of Matraine against a counterattack by German units.

Bix and his Panther were in action again at the forest near Glaznieki and at the Dzelzgaleskrogs crossroads. It was to be a noteworthy day of fighting. In a life-or-death battle Bix destroyed twelve Soviet tanks. The battle was about as grim as could be imagined. Nevertheless, Bix was able to decide the outcome in his favor. His success in the face of such odds was assured by the speed of his Panther, his own quick reactions, and the readiness and ability of his crew.

Halting, firing, and moving again, Bix employed the most daring maneuvers in this battle. He was forced to call on all his experience in order to emerge victorious against the numerically far superior enemy forces.

When evening came the Soviets called off their attack, because the majority of their tanks were now lying shot up, burning, and smoldering on the battlefield. Hermann Bix and his crew were at the end of their strength. They crawled from their tank and threw themselves onto piles of straw in one of the peasant huts and despite their exhaustion could not sleep. Over and over again they saw the flickering fires, the Russian tankers shrouded in flames as they attempted to escape their burning tanks. Over and over again they heard the hard crashes of the enemy's armor-piercing shells as death knocked on their own steel box. There was still no end to this gigantic struggle in sight. Tomorrow would be another day and tomorrow they would have to set out again.

The fate of the Bix panzer crew was decided on 4 November. Near the major road crossing near Dzelzgaleskrogs the Soviets once again attacked with massive forces. Bix and his Panther rolled forward. Followed by the other two tanks of his platoon he reached the positions of the grenadiers. Russian tanks feeling their way forward there were stopped by several well-aimed shots. The Soviets then opened fire with multiple rocket launchers that they had hastily moved forward. Swarms of rockets roared through the air and exploded in the positions of the grenadiers. The ear-shattering din came closer and closer to the tanks. Then a sixteenfold blow hammered down on the platoon. Fire and smoke poured down and one of the fireballs fell directly on the platoon commander's Panther. There was a shattering crash and flames raced through the fighting compartment. Schädelbauer's cry rang out above the din and everyone in the tank was struck by the sound wave like a hammer-blow.

Half deaf and unable to hear his own voice, Bix shouted over the radio: "We have taken a direct hit from a Stalin organ!"

Red-hot metal seemed to be boring into his brain. It felt as if a terrible pressure was trying to burst his skull, and yet, he knew that he was uninjured. The survivors bailed out, taking Schädelbauer's body with them. He had apparently been killed immediately after the impact.

The Panther of *Feldwebel* Haase brought the men back. Their tank, whose tracks had been torn off, was towed away.

Following an examination of the *Oberfeldwebel,* the battalion medical officer said, "You must go to a hospital, Bix."

This was a chance to get out in one piece. Bix knew that he might never again get such a chance. However, the physically small tank commander, who had proved his elan and cleverness in so many battles, didn't want it that way. He stayed!

Once again he went not to a hospital, but to the battalion's rear echelon. Following a brief recovery period he was back in action leading counterattacks and relief attacks.

At the end of 1944 the 4th Panzer Division was transferred from the Courland to Danzig.

Sixteen Tanks Destroyed

The following days saw the 4th Panzer Division involved in heavy defensive fighting north of Dirschau (Tczew). The enemy attacked relentlessly with a tenfold superiority in tanks. From his defensive position Bix could often see the Russians massing their forces for another attack.

On the German side cohesive companies and battalions no longer existed. The nonstop nature of the battles no longer allowed the Germans the luxury of sending whole units into action. Tanks were needed everywhere to back up the hard-pressed grenadiers.

While one battalion of the 35th Panzer Regiment was in action on the Tucheler Heath, holding positions against superior enemy forces, the other panzer battalion, which included the company led by *Leutnant* Tautorus, had been split up into small battle groups and placed under the command of the various grenadier units in the areas of Dirschau and Prussian Stargard.

Almost all of the company's Panthers had been knocked out of action. Among the replacements were six new Jagdpanthers, which had been destined for an assault gun company.

"Bix, you will take over the Jagdpanthers for your platoon," ordered the battalion commander by radio.

The new tank destroyer was built on the chassis of the Panther and armed with an 8.8cm Pak L/71. The fact that the gun had only a limited range of vertical and horizontal movement in the fixed superstructure of the vehicle caused some difficulties at first. Nevertheless, the men of Bix's platoon, who had been assigned five of the Jagdpanthers, soon became accustomed to their new vehicles. Before long they would swear by the new tank destroyer and its powerful gun, which possessed great penetrative capability and was extremely accurate.

"Bix, the Russians have just taken Prussian Stargard. You and your five vehicles secure east of the village against a further advance. The infantry has been ordered to pull back. You are to cover their withdrawal. Any questions?"

"No questions, *Herr* Major!" replied the *Oberfeldwebel*.

Bix drove back to his tank. Even though he was now commanding tank destroyers, he still thought and spoke of them as tanks. Bix had taken up a position with his Jagdpanther at the edge of the village behind a steaming compost heap. From there he could see the field positions just abandoned by the grenadiers.

The infantry had been defending from behind the dark hillocks in the terrain in front of him. From there they had opened fire on the Soviets whenever their tanks and infantry tried to advance, but had been forced to withdraw to avoid being overrun.

"How does it look, Dehm?" Bix asked the *Oberfeldwebel*, whose vehicle was positioned to the left of and behind his own.

Oberfeldwebel Dehm cleared his throat before answering: "I'm almost out of ammunition. Only six HE and four armor-piercings left."

"And you, Poller?" Bix asked the commander of the other tank destroyer in position there.

"It's the same with me," replied the *Feldwebel*. "Nine HE and three armor-piercing rounds."

"Very well! Poller and Dehm, pull back and intervene only in an extreme emergency."

Poller began to argue: "But we can . . ."

"Pull back one kilometer and observe. Don't intervene until I call you."

Bix knew that with so little ammunition the two tanks would be a liability if the Soviets attacked. He watched the two tank destroyers roll back. Then he concentrated all his attention on the low hills over which the Soviets must come. The flat roof of the Jagdpanther projected only slightly above the frozen compost heap.

It became lighter and suddenly, through his glasses, Bix saw two enemy tanks appear cautiously at the top of the hill.

"Those are not T-34s or KV-Is, they appear to be American tanks," Bix reported to his comrades. "They are about twelve hundred meters away. We'll take them. Do you have them both in sight, Rollmann?"

The gunner nodded.

"The best, *Herr Oberfeld!*"

"Then open fire!"

The first round struck the tracks of the right tank, which immediately stopped. The second round set the tank on fire. Bright flames shot from the hatches and within a few seconds the vehicle was enveloped in a red, molten cloud.

The second tank halted and fired. An armor-piercing shell raced by two meters above the compost heap. Then the Soviet tank was struck by the first shot from the "eighty-eight." Loader Schulz loaded a fresh armor-piercing round and Rollmann adjusted his aim a little. The second tank was also in flames.

"That took care of them," observed driver Becker laconically.

Bix nodded, then came a message.

"Herr Oberfeld, we'll give you close cover so the Russians don't get at you with Molotov cocktails," reported *Unteroffizier* Wegener, a tank commander whose vehicle had been destroyed the night before. He had assembled around him ten tank crewmen who were without vehicles. They now established a defensive perimeter around Bix's Jagdpanther.

Bix called back to the *Unteroffizier,* "Good, Wegener, thank you!" Wegener crawled back to the cover of the houses.

"Now we can't be taken by surprise," Bix informed his crew.

A half hour had passed since the destruction of the two enemy tanks when Bix again heard tanks approaching. He scanned the terrain through his field glasses and suddenly saw two Russian tanks about one hundred meters away attempting to outflank the village.

"Achtung, Rollmann!"

"Turn to the right, Becker!"

The driver swerved the Jagdpanther around.

"Good, I've got them," called Rollmann as both tanks appeared in his sight. From this range it would be nearly impossible to miss.

The first shot pierced the flank of one of the tanks, which had not yet spotted the tank destroyer lurking behind the compost heap. It began to burn at once. The second Soviet tank turned on the spot. Its gun swung toward the deadly enemy, but before it could fire, the 8.8cm gun crashed again. There was a hard, dry crash. The second enemy tank caught fire and stopped. Machine guns began to rattle as the covering force opened fire on the fleeing Russian tank crews.

Bix reported back to company: "The Russians are seeking a weak spot!"

"Be especially careful, Bix!" warned *Leutnant* Tautorus.

"Will do, *Herr Leutnant!*" Then he turned to his crew.

"How is our ammunition, Schulz?"

The loader counted the remaining rounds.

"Five HE and twenty armor-piercing left, *Herr Oberfeld!*" he reported a moment later.

"Not counting the one that's in the chamber," added Rollmann with a grimace.

Another enemy tank attempted to break through but fled into a valley after the first shot from the Jagdpanther.

"I have twenty armor-piercing rounds left, *Herr Leutnant,* and am being attacked repeatedly by enemy tanks," reported Bix.

"What about Dehm and Poller?" came the reply from the *Leutnant,* who was tied down in another sector.

"Dehm is out of ammunition. Poller has engine damage and is trying to get his mule back."

"You have to hold, Bix," replied the *Leutnant* after a brief pause. "The infantry hasn't pulled back far enough yet."

Bix closed the conversation: "We'll hold until our ammunition is gone, *Herr Leutnant."*

Meanwhile, the covering force also had been forced to

withdraw as Russian patrols had pushed into the village from several sides. Now Bix could no longer know what was going on in the village next to him on the right. The Russians could do what they wanted there without hindrance.

Suddenly Bix spotted movement on the facing slope. He raised his binoculars and saw that the Russians had placed two antitank guns there, apparently in an effort to smoke him out.

"Attention, Rollmann! Antitank guns on the front slope next to the two round bushes."

"Target in sight!" reported the gunner.

"Load high-explosive!—Open fire!"

With the first shot, fragments of wood and other material flew through the air near the position of the antitank guns.

"Stop!" shouted Bix. "The bastards have tricked us!"

The Russians had placed dummy guns on the slope so as to draw the German fire and reveal the position of the tank destroyer. Apparently, however, the Russians had failed to spot the hiding place behind the compost heap, because they now moved two more dummy guns into position.

"We're not falling for it this time," said Bix, grinning. "We'll save our ammunition for a better target."

To be on the safe side he ordered the driver to back up a few meters. The Jagdpanther rumbled backward. Now the enemy wouldn't be able to spot the tank hunter until they were in the village, but Bix could still see across to the low hill.

Soon the Russians came rolling toward the village at full speed. They appeared on the hill in a long column about twelve hundred meters away. In front were tanks, followed by supply trucks and radio vehicles. There were also several personnel carriers. In the meantime, Bix had taken the range of prominent features in the area of terrain in front of him.

"Armor-piercing at the lead tank!" he ordered. "But not until he's within eight hundred meters, Rollmann."

The *Obergefreiter* waited. He tracked the leading T-34. When it had approached to eight hundred meters he pressed the firing button. The tank destroyer's cannon gave a dull crack. The Jagdpanther jerked backward and the armor-piercing shot whistled toward the enemy tank. It missed, however, and instead sawed off the top of a tree just in front of the leading

T-34. The crown of the tree crashed down on top of the Russian tank. To Bix, it looked as if the T-34 had taken the treetop like a bull on its horns.

"He's been blinded by the tree, Rollmann. Target the others!" called the commander to his gunner.

At that moment the leading Russian tank rolled into a ditch. It plunged nose-first down the bank and was stuck fast. The following tanks were close behind. Their guns were trained not to the left toward the tank destroyer's position, but to the right, where the mounds of earth from the grenadiers' positions projected dark against the sky. The first Russian tank cannon roared. The shell flitted into the abandoned German positions.

"Let's go, Rollmann, first the tank in the middle. Aim between the turret and hull."

They now had the Russian broadside in their sights. Nothing could go wrong. The first shot from the "eighty-eight" struck the enemy tank, which was in the middle of the column firing the other way, and set it on fire.

"Now the one on the end!" shouted Bix.

The Jagdpanther turned slightly. Rollmann corrected his aim and fired. The second tank also went up in flames.

This was the signal for the beginning of a wild mixup among the Soviet tank commanders. Several tried to traverse their turrets to engage their attacker. Others attempted to leave the road, but the tanks were too close together in the column and there was no room to maneuver. Still others drove into the ditches and became stuck there.

"Make every shot count!" warned Bix.

Rollmann fired and Schulz reloaded. The noise of battle raged like a hurricane. The Soviets, taken completely by surprise, still didn't see the lone tank destroyer.

Rollman fired round after round at the Soviet tanks, which had now turned their turrets toward him. The scene was one of fires, explosions, running tankers, and the repeated flashes of flame as the Jagdpanther's "eighty-eight" fired.

A Russian shell struck the sloped bow of the Jagdpanther and howled skyward. Rollmann fired and the shot smashed the Russian tank's tracks. He then aimed a little higher and the next shot blew off the tank's turret.

For ten minutes the "eighty-eight" roared; soon the road

was enveloped in flames. The tanks that were wedged tight in the column were also caught by the flames. Eleven enemy tanks lay shot-up and burning on the road. Four others had been knocked out earlier. The lone Jagdpanther had destroyed a total of fifteen Russian tanks without receiving a scratch.

"Now the trucks with HE rounds!" ordered Bix, while the men leaned against the steel walls of the tank destroyer, drenched in sweat.

"We have only two shells!" shouted the gunner. And after a brief pause: "The machine gun ammunition is also gone!"

That was the alarm signal to get out fast. Bix knew as well as the others that without ammunition they were in trouble.

"Head back, Becker!" he ordered.

As the Jagdpanther drove back, Bix suddenly saw an enemy tank in the village to his right. It must have been scouting ahead of the others. Not finding the German tank, the commander of the T-34 had apparently sent back an "all clear" message. The rest of the column had come driving toward the village right into an ambush. This was the only explanation Bix could think of for the unguarded and careless advance by the Russian tank and truck column.

Bix's next order rang out above the roar of the motor: "Toward the tank!"

The Jagdpanther drove ahead a short distance and turned on the spot; the T-34 appeared in the gunner's sight. From a range of eighty meters the T-34 was struck by an armor-piercing round and began to burn. This T-34 raised Bix's total for the day to sixteen enemy tanks destroyed.

When he finally returned to the company, Bix was surrounded by his comrades. On this day he had become the most successful tank destroyer in the entire battalion.

While the Jagdpanther was refueled and rearmed, Bix reported to the battalion commander. *Leutnant* Tautorus was also present. He, too, had destroyed a number of Russian tanks.

The Knight's Cross for *Oberfeldwebel* Bix

"Kleschkau has fallen, comrades. It's our job to prevent any further advance by the Russians and support a counterattack on Kleschkau by the grenadiers this afternoon."

Leutnant Tautorus looked down the line of tank commanders. Then he continued: "We must form small battle groups, each of two or three tanks under a platoon leader. We no longer have platoons."

A little later *Oberfeldwebel* Bix and his three tank hunters took their leave of the company commander. The *Leutnant* bade the three tank commanders farewell: "Good luck, Bix! You, too, Igel and Schwafferts!"

Then they set off toward the enemy. Bix knew the terrain from which the enemy must come, because he had driven back over the same route. He therefore knew where the enemy tank column would appear.

Bix deployed his crews accordingly. During the course of the afternoon they turned back the leading Soviet tanks that were hesitantly feeling their way forward.

"We have a good field of fire and we know where they're coming from, Schwafferts. That should give us a slight advantage."

"Yes, *Herr Oberfeld,* if we stay alert, we'll stop them," confirmed *Unteroffizier* Schwafferts who, together with Igel, had gone forward to the commander's tank for a discussion of the situation. Soon afterward they went back to their tanks. Then the grenadiers arrived. The commander of the assault battalion came over to Hermann Bix.

"Can't you give us support until my grenadiers and I reach the edge of the village?" he asked the *Oberfeldwebel.*

"I'm supposed to remain here and see to it that no enemy tanks roll through, *Herr* Major," replied Bix.

The major's mouth tightened into a thin line. Bix saw the surprised expression on his face, which had been marked by stress and responsibility. To hell with orders, thought Bix.

"Wait, *Herr* Major!" he called to the officer, who had already turned to go.

The major stopped. His expression suddenly changed. "You mean you'll really . . . ?"

Instead of an answer, Bix said, "Assemble your men and follow close behind me, *Herr* Major!"

The grenadiers assembled. When Bix saw that they were all ready and waiting on both sides in the ditches and bushes, he had his driver move off.

They moved forward quickly. The village appeared before

the grenadiers. Machine guns and rifles opened fire on the advancing infantry from houses and behind hedges.

"The heavy machine gun to the right of the house!" Bix warned his gunner.

"Target in sight," confirmed Rollmann. There was a crash as the big gun fired. The high-explosive shell hammered into the wall of the house, shattering all the windows. Firing from the heavy machine gun ceased abruptly.

"Onward, Becker, onward!"

They reached the village and behind the Jagdpanther, which kept nests of enemy resistance under fire, the grenadiers cleared the houses of the enemy.

A round from an antitank rifle struck the side armor of the tank hunter.

"Antitank rifle, *Herr Oberfeld!*" shouted the radio operator as he opened fire on the Russians with his machine gun. Again there was an impact, this time close to the gun mantlet. The flash of the impact was a warning signal for Bix, because antitank rifles were damned accurate and represented a danger, even for the tank destroyer.

"We're driving through!" ordered Bix. "Advance as far as the center of the village!"

He had to blast a path clear for the grenadiers. The Jagdpanther rattled forward and ran over a machine gun position. An antitank rifleman fell under the right track. A wall collapsed as the nose of the tank pushed through. A shot from the "eighty-eight" silenced another nest of resistance and then they were at the center of the village.

At that moment a message came from battalion: "Bix platoon. Have special assignment for you! Report to company commander."

Bix called in and heard the voice of *Leutnant* Tautorus.

"Chief to Bix platoon: return immediately. Enemy is attacking the main road to Danzig with tanks. We must stop them or Danzig is lost."

"*Herr Leutnant,* we have to stay here a few minutes longer. The grenadiers have just cleared the village. If we withdraw now . . ."

"You must withdraw, Bix. Twenty enemy tanks are advancing on Danzig. There are no other antitank weapons in their

path. Regardless of your present situation you must turn around
and return! Out!'"

There was a crack. Bix called twice but contact had been
broken.

"Back up, Becker!" ordered Bix. When they turned and left
the village along the main street, Bix saw that the grenadiers
were withdrawing with them. An *Oberleutnant* came running
toward the Jagdpanther in long strides.

"What's going on up front? Are the Ivans coming with
tanks?" he cried.

"I have orders to head back. Everything is in order up front!"
he shouted to the *Oberleutnant*. From the latter's disbelieving
expression, Bix realized that he thought he was making
excuses.

He swore bitterly to himself as he saw the grenadiers hanging onto his tank like grapes in their haste to escape the supposed danger zone. But exactly the opposite was true. By
hanging on to the outside of the tank they were actually placing themselves in danger.

Mortars opened up on the Jagdpanther as it backed
up slowly. The exploding mortar shells knocked the grenadiers off the tank, throwing them dead or wounded to the
ground.

"Faster, Becker. Damn it, faster!"

"But then we'll leave them behind and . . ."

"Faster!" roared Bix.

Becker obeyed and the grenadiers were left behind. In this
situation they realized that they would find better cover in the
houses and gardens than out in the open on a tank driving along
the road.

"Damn, damn!" swore Becker. Bix's conscience also bothered him after having to leave his comrades to their fate in
order to carry out an order.

Leutnant Tautorus was rather excited when he received Bix.

"Take your three tanks in the direction of the 'Death's
Head,' " he said. "Below the hill is a large estate which must be
held."

The Death's Head was a cone-shaped piece of high ground
projecting from an area of otherwise flat terrain.

"What are we to do there, *Herr Leutnant?*"

Leutnant Tautorus looked at the *Oberfeldwebel*. The small officer had calmed down somewhat and this in turn had a calming effect on Bix.

"The Russians have surrounded a *Volksgrenadier* battalion on the estate. They are attacking with tanks and if they've eliminated the *Volksgrenadiers* then they'll drive on toward Danzig and push into the city unhindered. That must be prevented at all costs."

"I'll leave at once, *Herr Leutnant;* hopefully I'll get through."

"You must, Bix. You must reach the estate before midnight and destroy the enemy tanks by dawn, or at least prevent them from breaking through toward Danzig."

It was already getting dark. As if that were not enough, it also began to snow as Bix penciled in the march route on his map. Looking at his map he saw that it was fifteen kilometers to the Death's Head. In the darkness and blowing snow he would have to drive slowly to avoid getting lost.

"Igel, Schwafferts to me!" He called the two tank commanders over and gave them a precise briefing on the situation. Closing the briefing he said, "We will be met by two guides from the *Volksgrenadiers* about two kilometers from the estate. We will halt them at first and I will go ahead on foot, contact the commander of the grenadiers, and have him fill me in on the situation. Then I'll come back and the dance can begin. Now to your tanks and mount up!"

The Jagdpanthers drove into the blowing snow. Their progress was slowed by the columns of refugees heading west. They came toward them in dense clusters. More than once Bix had to leave the road to get past the masses of people fleeing the Russians. Finally he couldn't wait any longer. He drove through the columns and the refugees' vehicles had to pull off into the ditch to let the tank pass.

The refugees cursed Bix. They simply didn't understand that this man and his three tanks were there to save them, too. If he and his comrades failed to halt the Soviets and save the *Volksgrenadier* battalion, then the Russians would break through and none of the refugees would have a chance.

Despite everything they arrived on time at the place where the guides were to meet them. The fact that they had made it despite the darkness left them in an optimistic mood.

"All right, comrades, wait here until I come back, understood?" With these words the *Oberfeldwebel* took his leave of the others.

"We'll wait for you, *Herr Oberfeld!*" Igel shouted after him, then the three figures were swallowed up by the darkness.

The three walked in single file through a park. All around the Russians were firing into the farmhouse. Finally they reached a long, flat building and climbed in through a cellar window. It was the main room of the distillery and there Bix saw a mass of haggard, tired soldiers sitting on the floor. The major stood up and came toward the panzer commander.

"This is my fighting force, *Oberfeldwebel.* Early in the morning I will go into battle with these men and you are to help me. How many tanks have you?"

"Three Jagdpanthers, *Herr* Major," replied Bix.

"That is not many, but at least it's something. Pay attention and I will explain the situation and describe the terrain as best I can."

Tersely the major briefed the *Oberfeldwebel* on the situation. He showed him the general situation on the map. A sketch of the estate was used to show the positions of the enemy tanks. The commander of the grenadiers indicated to Bix where the tanks had been when darkness fell. When he had finished, Bix nodded to the veteran officer.

"Yes, we can do it, *Herr* Major. Where can I swing wide and get close to the enemy tanks during the night and where will I have a good target when it gets light?"

The major unfolded the map again. "Here, *Oberfeldwebel,* this hill called 'the Skull.' One of our quadruple-flak is still in position on the hill. I haven't heard anything from them since the previous afternoon."

"Hmm, that would be about 1,200 to 1,500 meters from the Russian tank position, exactly the right range from which to open fire," commented Bix. "I'll try to get my tanks up there tonight, *Herr* Major."

"Good, and how can I assist you?"

"It would be best if your grenadiers stay here in the cellar until they don't hear any more tank gunfire. I wouldn't want them to walk into my line of fire during the battle," explained Bix. "When the tank fire dies down you and your grenadiers attack the Russian infantry."

"Good, Bix! I hope for all our sakes that you and your three tanks do it."

They parted with a handshake, and the major knew that he could depend on this man.

Bix returned to his tanks, where he was met with relief. Briefly and factually he explained the situation to the two commanders and three crews. Everyone had to know what was at stake here.

"All right, into the tanks and after me toward 'the Skull.' "

They climbed aboard and drove off. The tanks rolled along the edge of a wood and up a path that led up to the Skull that was quite passable. It was already starting to get light. The shapes of the estate buildings were emerging slowly from the darkness, when they were hailed just below the hill.

It was a sentry from the light flak, which was in fact still in position on top of the hill. A *Leutnant* explained the situation to Bix as he saw it. The *Oberfeldwebel* now learned how many tanks were in the farmhouse garden and received precise information on his targets.

"Drivers, gunners, and commanders, dismount and gather around," Bix called to his men. He then assigned each commander a position. They could now make out the whole outline of the farmhouse, and each commander received a sector to keep under observation.

Then Bix ordered, "Back to the tanks and roll up to the crest so that your cannon project slightly beyond it."

He and his tank were now at the foot of the Skull and completely screened to the right. To the left and ahead he had a good field of view. When it had become somewhat lighter, he tried to scan the area of the garden through his field glasses. In the morning twilight he spotted groups of white figures which could only be the turret numbers of Russian tanks. Then he saw several Russian tanks driving toward the estate from the right at high speed.

"Igel," called Bix to his left tank, "do you see the Russians?"

"I see them. The approaching tanks must be bringing supplies to the Ivans because their wheeled vehicles aren't close enough, *Herr Oberfeld*."

"Yes, that could be."

As it grew lighter more enemy tanks were spotted in the estate garden.

"Do you have them all in sight?" asked Bix.

"All ready, *Herr Oberfeld,*" answered his two comrades.

"Then open fire!"

Gunner Rollmann had targeted the white numbers on one of the tank turrets. The first shot smashed into the enemy tank, which immediately began to burn. The other two tank destroyers likewise opened fire. Panic broke out on the estate. The Russians had been taken completely by surprise. The shouts and commands of the Russians could be heard as far as the positions of the three Jagdpanthers.

Just as Rollmann was about to fire for the second time, another spurt of flame shot up from behind the burning Russian tank. A second tank, standing close behind the first, had also caught fire.

"We've scored a double!" shouted the gunner excitedly. He had every reason to be excited as such a feat was extremely rare. The Russians now had to get their remaining tanks out of cover if they were not to be engulfed by the flames, too. Tanks drove in all directions in a wild mixup.

Schwafferts and Igel each knocked out a Russian tank. The two had just turned and were traversing their guns in the direction of the incoming fire.

Four T-34s rolled out of the garden and into the open. They were now completely without cover. Rollmann destroyed three, one after another. The crews jumped clear and ran across the snow-covered fields, their forms clearly visible.

"We're firing on the approach road!" reported Igel and Schwafferts. A little later Bix saw sheets of flame and dark smoke clouds from that direction, marking the locations of burning tanks.

In the meantime it had become bright as day. The milling Soviet tanks rammed trees in the park, knocking them down. Bix now had an even better view.

A few T-34s and KV-Is attempted to escape down the back slope, but Rollmann had the range. He hit one of the T-34s in the rear. The enemy tank began to smoke, but it nevertheless reached the slope and disappeared.

Rollmann began to say that the enemy tank had got away,

when a twenty-meter-high spurt of flame shot up from the far side of the slope where the T-34 had disappeared and there was the crash of an explosion. The T-34 had blown up.

Igel reported four Soviet tanks destroyed, Schwafferts at first three, then another.

Bix scanned the area of the garden through his binoculars. Suddenly he saw an antenna moving behind a barn. That could only be a tank.

"A tank behind the barn with the windows, Rollmann. He is moving directly toward the right corner."

"Target in sight, I'm aiming at the next window!" shouted the gunner. He moved the gun slightly to the right.

Rollmann targeted the window frame. The enemy tank must appear there. There he was! Rollmann adjusted his aim a little higher. The white number appeared in the window and there was a crash as the "eighty-eight" fired. The shell smashed into the turret of the Soviet tank with a mighty crash. It halted and smoke billowed from the hatches.

Soon there were no enemy tanks to be seen that were not burning or smoldering. The three Jagdpanthers ceased fire.

Jubilantly the grenadiers came storming out of the cellar. They had witnessed the surprise attack by their three tanks from their holes in the cellar and from windows. They had heard the explosions and seen the fires. The release from fear and the certainty that they had been saved moved the high-spirited young soldiers to throw their helmets into the air. Then they came running up to the three tanks, led by the major. When they reached Bix's tank, he was standing in his turret hatch scanning the terrain.

"Oberfeldwebel, I thank you!" shouted the major. He reached for his Iron Cross, First Class, and was about to remove it from his service coat.

"I would like to decorate one of your commanders with this, Bix," he said, seeing the questioning look in the *Oberfeldwebel's* face.

"They're well provided for in that respect, *Herr* Major," replied Bix, smiling.

They counted nineteen knocked-out enemy tanks. In *Oberfeldwebel* Bix's field of fire were eleven destroyed T-34s and KV-Is. The rest had been accounted for by Igel and Schwafferts.

The men took a break. They climbed down from their steel crates and lit cigarettes, some turning their thoughts to the destruction they had wrought on the Russians and the enemy soldiers sitting burned and shattered in the destroyed tanks.

In the following days the German forces were forced to withdraw to Danzig. After the city fell, the tanks of the 4th Panzer Division fought on on the Frische Nehrung.

Hermann Bix awoke on the morning of 22 March 1945 and washed. As he was about to leave the small, shell-battered house, the door opened and *Leutnant* Tautorus walked in.

"Good morning, Bix!"

"Good morning, *Herr Leutnant!* Is something special up?" asked the *Oberfeldwebel,* as he could think of no other explanation for Tautorus's appearance.

"Actually no, Bix. I'm just bringing an order from *Hauptmann* Kästner that you're to rest today and remain at the company command post."

"Then can I stand down my entire crew?" Bix asked at once.

"Certainly. They're not going anywhere without their commander, Bix."

Long weeks of great stress lay behind the *Oberfeldwebel*. In the past weeks he had destroyed seventy-five enemy tanks and received the Third Grade of the Panzer Assault Badge, a decoration usually awarded only for taking part in one hundred actions.

Danzig had fallen, but the grenadiers and tank crews were still holding out at the edge of the city. What did this order mean? Bix couldn't explain it. Perhaps the battalion commander had a special assignment for him.

The day passed. It was evening before *Hauptmann* Kästner arrived with the battalion adjutant, *Oberleutnant* Grigat, and *Leutnant* Pintelmann, the battalion executive officer. *Leutnant* Tautorus reported to the chief.

A little later the men sat together in a small room. Several noncommissioned officers who had destroyed enemy tanks were also there. A round of cognac was passed out, but Bix still didn't know what they were celebrating. Then Major Kästner stood up.

"Comrades, we have not gathered here without a special reason. I have the great joy and honor to present to one of our most experienced panzer commanders the Knight's Cross, which has just been awarded him. *Oberfeldwebel* Bix, I hereby present you with the Knight's Cross in the name of the Führer!"

Leutnant Pintelmann had taken the box from his briefcase and the battalion commander now placed the high decoration around the *Oberfeldwebel*'s neck.

For Hermann Bix the surprise was complete. He had no idea this was to happen. Certainly he had often been named and praised in the front-line newspaper as a "tank-cracker," but he had not expected this.

The *Oberfeldwebel* from the small village in Silesia was now wearing Germany's highest decoration for bravery. What would his mother say when she heard the news? What about his teacher, his comrades? But his mother had already begun the trek toward the west.

Then Bix thought about his comrades who had always stood by him in the many, many actions. The faces came and went. Several were buried somewhere in the vastness of Russia, others had been wounded and evacuated.

They were bitter thoughts that moved him in this hour.

The war was moving toward its end. The troops fighting on the split of land called the Frische Nehrung were squeezed together more and more. Only Nickelswalde and Schiefenhorst were still in German hands. Feverish efforts were under way there to evacuate women and children to the west by boat. Wherever the tanks went there were civilians, tattered and exhausted, a cargo of misery and tears.

The soldiers who no longer had weapons built loading ramps and helped the civilians. But there were still 180,000 people on the Frische Nehrung and it would take a long time to get them all away.

It was the job of Hermann Bix and his panzers to enable this giant escape action to succeed by defending the surrounding area. There, where the Russians were trying to break through, were the tanks of the 4th Panzer Division; on the beach along the bay, in the dunes of the Danzig Bight.

One of the Jagdpanthers was commanded by *Oberfeldwebel* Bix, who, on 20 April 1945, had been named *Fahnenjunker-Oberfeldwebel* (officer cadet).

Ten defensive positions were planned. On 4 May, Bix was in Position 9. Bix was given the job of fighting delaying actions back to Position 6 with the company's last four tanks, providing cover until the last civilians and soldiers had evacuated the Frische Nehrung via Hela.

This was to last until 12 May. The last tank crews were then to blow up their Jagdpanthers and be picked up by a motor launch that was to take them to a U-boat on the high seas. A light cruiser of the *Kriegsmarine* was still in the Danzig Bight and was to provide covering fire during the critical final minutes.

The Russians were pressing hard. They attempted to push into Nickelswalde, but all of their leading tanks were knocked out. The enemy now moved his heaviest tanks forward. In Position 7 the four German tanks were outflanked by Russian infantry; nevertheless, they succeeded in beating back the Soviets.

It had just become light on the morning of 6 May, when *Oberfeldwebel* Bix saw through his binoculars that the Russians were felling trees for a barricade.

"What are they planning now?" he asked Schwafferts.

"Surely they don't intend to dig in now," replied Schwafferts.

Suddenly they heard engine noise. Then a cloud of blue smoke rose into the air behind the barricade. A pair of Russians appeared and pulled the branches of the fallen trees to the side, and Bix saw the muzzle of a giant gun with a muzzle brake.

"That can't be a tank," he observed. "Load armor-piercing. Range four hundred!"

His gunner had the target in sight. Bix checked his sight once more to ensure it was adjusted properly. Then he gave the order to fire. As it fired, the area around the Jagdpanther, which had gone into cover behind some fir trees, was shrouded in fumes and smoke. Needles showered down on the tank, blocking the crew's view of the target. Also, there was no spurt of flame that would have indicated a direct hit.

When Bix could see again, he saw that the enemy was still there. They fired a second and a third time, but the enemy gun showed no ill effects. The Soviets now opened fire. The first shot struck the ground about three meters in front of the Jagdpanther. Smoke and flames were forced into the fighting compartment.

The second shot from the enemy's giant cannon raced past a

few meters above the roof of the tank destroyer, but the third was on target. Bix noticed that the recoil guard of his own cannon rose backward and felt the blow of the impacting shell. The fearful crash of the impact left him deaf. Thus he did not hear the gunner report that he could no longer see, as the optics port had been shattered.

Bix tried to open the cannon's breech in order to peer down the barrel and aim in that way. But he found that the recoil guard was up at the edge of the turret on the inner armor. Now he knew that the gun mantlet had been sprung from its trunnions and that the end was near for them.

"Back up!" he ordered the driver, and the tank roared to life and began to move.

"Chief to Hofknecht," called Bix to the *Feldwebel* commanding the second tank in the dunes. He had heard the order and likewise began to back up.

Bix then called battalion. *Leutnant* Pintelmann, who had been at the bay, came roaring up just in time to see Bix backing away.

"Careful, careful!" Bix warned the *Leutnant*. But it was already too late.

The mighty cannon again spat a tongue of flame. The *Leutnant*'s tank was also hit on the gun mantlet and disabled. He was forced to give the order to withdraw.

Feldwebel Hofknecht reached a side road and saw that the "battering ram," as they had named the heavy assault gun, had begun to roll forward slowly. When he had the entire broadside of the newest and heaviest Russian assault gun in his sight, he fired two armor-piercing rounds into its flank. The crew climbed out and surrendered to the *Feldwebel*.

Feldwebel Hofknecht saw that the three shots from Bix's cannon had struck the center of the bow of the assault gun and had penetrated about ten centimeters. They had been unable, however, to pierce the twenty-centimeter-thick, sloped frontal armor.

Oberfeldwebel Bix had finished second-best this day. Two days later he received orders from the battalion commander to withdraw toward Nickelswalde with his crew. On the way he heard from civilians that Germany had already surrendered.

During the night they sailed for Hela aboard a *Kriegsmarine* vessel. Just before reaching their destination they were picked up by two minesweepers, which was fortunate, as otherwise they would never have escaped from Hela.

On 14 May they reached Kiel and entered British captivity. The war was over. . . .

Hermann Bix

10 October 1914:	Born in Silesia.
1 October 1941:	Promoted to *Feldwebel*.
20 October 1941:	Awarded the Iron Cross, First Class, for single-handedly destroying a Russian motorized battalion.
1 August 1942:	Promoted to *Oberfeldwebel*.
22 August 1942:	Wounded by mine. Evacuated to Germany, and after convalescing is sent to NCO school.
5 November 1942:	Awarded the German Cross in Gold.
Spring 1944:	Returns to Eastern Front, Army Group Center.
22 June 1944:	Soviet offensive against Army Group Center begins.
August 1944:	Unit transferred to Army Group North.
18 August 1944:	Wounded again, awarded the Wound Badge in Silver and Panzer Assault Badge, Second Class.
27 October 1944:	First Battle of the Courland begins.
December 1944:	4th Panzer Division transferred from Courland to Danzig.
Early 1945:	Platoon is equipped with Jagdpanther tank destroyers. Bix destroys seventy-five enemy tanks in three weeks, including sixteen in one day.
22 March 1945:	Awarded the Knight's Cross.
May 1945:	Evacuated from Frische Nehrung by sea. Surrenders to British forces in Kiel.

3

Rudolf von Ribbentrop

In Action with the *Leibstandarte*
and *Hitlerjugend* Divisions:
The Battle of Kharkov

In January 1943 the SS-Panzer Division *Leibstandarte* was transferred from France to Russia. On 14 January 1943 a Soviet offensive had ripped open a breach 350 kilometers wide in the front held by the Germans and their allies.

The German 2nd Army had been badly battered. The Hungarian 2nd Army had been virtually destroyed. The German army corps deployed in its sector of the front was conducting a fighting withdrawal toward Oskol. The remains of the Alpini Corps and the XXIV Panzer Corps were no longer fit for operations.

Like Army Group Center, which was holding a line Belgorod-Graiworon-Lebedin, Army Group South was in danger of being overrun or outflanked.

Attacking west, the Soviet army groups that were designated Southern Front and Southwestern Front and the southern wing of the Voronezh Front had taken Kursk and Slavyansk. Their objective was the Dniepr River.

During those dramatic January days the only forces holding the German front were the 320th Infantry Division east of Oskol near Svatovo, the battered 298th Infantry Division, which had assembled near Kupyansk, and elements of the Panzer Grenadier Division *Grossdeutschland* west of Valuiki.

Between the divisions there was only open space, and it was just a matter of time until the Soviet forces broke through.

It was in this critical situation that Hitler ordered the OKH to send the newly formed II SS-Panzer Corps from France to Russia. It was the end of January before elements of the 1st

SS-Panzer Division *LSSAH* and the 2nd SS-Panzer Division *Das Reich* arrived in the Kharkov area.

The massed counterattack planned by the OKH did not materialize, however, because of the Red Army's advance deep into German-held territory. Elements of both divisions were thrown into battle as they arrived in an effort to prop up the German defenses.

The *Leibstandarte* Division assembled on the Donets. *Das Reich,* on the other hand, was sent forward across the Donets toward Valuiki by the commanding general of II SS-Panzer Corps, *Obergruppenführer* Hausser.

On 28 January 1943 command of Army Group A, which had been formed with the arrival of the two SS divisions, was assumed by Hubert Lanz, who had been promoted to the rank of *General der Gebirgstruppen* the same day. Kharkov was to be held at all costs.

On 1 February the Soviets resumed their offensive on a broad front. The Soviet 3rd Tank Army advanced toward Valuiki, cutting off the 298th and 320th Infantry Divisions belonging to Army Group A.

March to the East

Second Battalion, 1st SS-Panzer Regiment paused for several days on its journey to Russia, stopping at Burg, near Magdeburg, to collect tanks from the army vehicle park there. These additional panzers were to bring the unit up to its authorized strength before it went into action.

The leader of 6th Company's 1st Platoon was *Untersturmführer* Rudolf von Ribbentrop. Ribbentrop described the journey to Russia and the conditions under which it took place:

> It was clear and cold the night we entrained. We traveled through Pomerania and East Prussia, then straight across Russia to Kharkov, where we detrained one night in early February 1943.
>
> Our unit possessed a healthy self-confidence. We trusted our commanders blindly, as we had known them all for a long time; likewise our men, who were prepared to go through thick and thin with us.

As we detrained we had a feeling that it was probably going to be more thick than thin. We encountered depressed railway officials and bewildered stragglers from many divisions. Wild rumors were circulating that night as we unloaded our heavy tanks from the special rail cars and drove on several kilometers into a village with the name of Merefa. We found shelter in peasant cottages in the village.

Because of the bitter cold, teams of two men had to take turns starting the engines with the hand cranks, so as not to put too great a strain on the batteries.

The next morning *Untersturmführer* Janke and I went outside and stood in front of our cottage. The smoke rising from the chimneys of the cottages reminded Janke of Dwinger's books about his experience as a prisoner in Siberia.

It was a deeply peaceful scene. However, a report soon arrived that the Red Army had launched a tremendous offensive aimed at advancing from Kharkov to the Dniepr and on to the Black Sea, in order to surround all of Army Group South and prepare for it a similar fate to that which had just befallen Stalingrad.

This ends Ribbentrop's description. What follows is a summary of the overall situation that II SS-Panzer Corps found itself faced with.

At the beginning of February the corps was facing encirclement in and around Kharkov. It had received a Führer order to "defend Kharkov to the last round." Even as the order arrived, enemy forces were already in the process of encircling Kharkov.

Obergruppenführer Hausser was faced with a difficult decision: launch an immediate attack against the Red Army forces that were completing the encirclement of the city to the south—and thus abandon the city—or concentrate his forces for an all-round defense of Kharkov. The latter decision would of course lead to encirclement and destruction of II SS-Panzer Corps.

Obergruppenführer Hausser therefore decided to strike south with three battle groups, smash the threat to the right flank, and avert the encirclement of Kharkov.

Assembling the attack forces in the deep snow proved to be very difficult. The battle group commanded by *Obersturmbann-führer* Meyer received instructions to advance toward Alexeyevka, which meant an advance through seventy kilometers of enemy-occupied territory. The battle group assembled south of Merefa. Meyer wrote in his book, *Grenadiers:*

There was no movement to be seen. To the right behind the village a wood stretched along the road. There, too, there were no signs of life. Standing next to me was the commander of the spearhead, *Obersturmführer* Schulz, who had been with me during the advance on Rostov. Commanding the first tank was *Untersturmführer* von Ribbentrop.

The deep snow made maneuvers in open terrain almost impossible and a time-consuming business. Schulz had been ordered to drive through the village under the protection of the tanks of von Ribbentrop's platoon and wait for the battalion in the small wood that lay on the other side. Under no circumstances was he to halt in the village itself and accept combat. I wanted to confuse the enemy with the breakthrough by the spearhead and lead the battle group quickly toward the south.

The Attack Begins

The first action was an attack against the enemy's armored spearhead by 7th Company, 1st Panzer Regiment. This attack became bogged down in a marshy area. 6th Company drove forward to free the "Seventh" and cover its withdrawal. The company found the bogged-down panzers and watched over the recovery operation. A number of enemy antitank guns and light tanks, as well as several sleighs, were destroyed with accurate gunfire.

During the action, Rudolf von Ribbentrop heard the voice of *Untersturmführer* Alt, the company commander's radio operator. Alt, who had been seriously wounded the day before when his tank was hit, calmly reported that the company commander's tank had been knocked out and that the leader of 1st Platoon was to assume command of the company.

Von Ribbentrop's Panzer IV received a minor hit on its right side. Fortunately, the shell bounced off, but it did destroy the vehicle's antenna, cutting it off from further radio communication.

The light Soviet forces were thrown back. By evening the panzers of 2nd Battalion were back in Merefa.

Next morning the commander of 6th Company, *Obersturm-führer* Astegger—one of the old hands of Kurt Meyer's reconnaissance battalion—informed his platoon leaders that the company had been attached to Meyer's reconnaissance battalion and was to take part in its attack against the Russians, which was intended to create some breathing room for the corps.

The next morning the company assembled among the last houses of Merefa. It was a cold, sunny winter day.

"We were called out into the open. There we found ourselves face to face with *Obergruppenführer* Paul Hausser. I was at the head of my platoon, which was drawn up in front of the house, when the old General stepped into the open. Standing in my turret, I saluted. He raised his hand informally in thanks and called up to me: 'Good luck!'

"We in our tanks had no idea that the commanding general had just reached a decision which was to save his corps and its two proven panzer divisions, *Leibstandarte* and *Das Reich*."

Hausser's move would save the divisions for the counterattack he was already planning. On the other hand, the decision to disobey a *Führerbefehl* might result in his facing a firing squad. What he had done was no less than the refusal to obey an order.

The *Leibstandarte*'s reconnaissance battalion under *SS-Obersturmbannführer* Meyer had orders to smash through the weakest part of the Soviet encircling ring near Novaya Vololaga. It was to break through the positions held by the Soviet 6th Guards Cavalry Corps, advance as far as Alexeyevka-East, and establish contact there with the northern battle group under *SS-Standartenführer* Fritz Witt, the core of which was made up of the 1st SS-Panzer Grenadier Regiment of the *Leibstandarte* Division.

The 2nd Platoon of 6th Company, 1st Panzer Regiment under *Untersturmführer* Eckardt was assigned the lead position, followed by the company's remaining platoons.

The leader of the reconnaissance battalion's lead platoon became involved in a brief firefight with enemy forces among the houses in the village, in which he was killed. Eckardt's tank was also hit. While his platoon was still moving up, *Untersturmführer* von Ribbentrop received orders to take over the lead. He placed himself at the head of the company and drove on at high speed. The panzers rolled past Soviet units, which scattered in all directions. Several light tanks were shot up and three antitank guns silenced without significantly slowing the advance.

This surprise advance brought Battle Group Meyer to a position about forty kilometers behind the Soviet spearhead.

Riding in his heavy Horch Kübelwagen, Meyer stayed close behind von Ribbentrop's tank. Since his car was faster than von Ribbentrop's Panzer IV, even in the snow, it appeared that "Panzermeyer" was giving the tanks a chance to show what they could do. The company was already advancing at maximum speed.

Whenever the tanks halted on a hill to scan for the enemy, Meyer immediately stood up in his car and raised his fist, which meant: "Move on! Faster!"

So we raced across the snow-covered plain south of Kharkov, now and then spotting Russian columns on the horizon to the left and right, but meeting very little real opposition.

The main effort of the Red Army's offensive was farther to the north and south. We had obviously advanced into a gap, and the intuition of "Papa Hausser" had found the exact place where the corps could escape the Russian encirclement.

As darkness fell we reached the village of Yefremovka, not far from Alexeyevka, which was our objective for the day. Here "Panzermeyer" halted the battle group, as the situation was totally unclear.

Sturmbannführer Meyer ordered me to secure the far side of the extended village with my platoon and explained with a laugh:

"We are already surrounded!"

He had deduced this from the fact that the supply train had not got through and that everything seemed to be closed off behind us.

I led my four tanks along the main street to the exit from the village, without encountering any opposition. There I assigned positions to my tanks, with two to the left and two to the right. They could scarcely be seen in the evening twilight, as they had been painted white and their outlines merged with the village houses.

After briefing my commanders, I looked again in the direction of the enemy, scanning the white, snow-covered, slightly undulating terrain. I noticed a dark spot on the road, which grew quickly and turned out to be a horse-drawn vehicle. It was moving toward our village from the direction of Alexeyevka at a trot.

I thought it might merely be a farmer, who had perhaps been in a neighboring village and was now returning home.

I sauntered slowly toward the vehicle, intending to stop it and bring its occupant to the commander to report on the situation in Alexeyevka.

I grasped the reins and shouted *"stoy!"* At the same instant I realized that the sleigh was occupied by about ten Russians, all armed to the teeth. I wasn't even carrying a pistol, as it hindered me in getting in and out of the tank quickly.

Instinctively, I struck the driver in the face as hard as I could and began to beat the Russian, who was as shocked as I, with my bare fists. I did this only because I believed that the Russians would have no time to shoot at me in the confusion.

While the Russians were trying to escape from the tangle of arms and legs and get clear, I dove away from the milling throng to avoid being hit by my own tanks, which had meanwhile opened fire on the Russians. I fell into the snow.

One of the Russians stopped and fired two bursts from his submachine gun. I felt a heavy blow in the small of my back, which completely knocked the wind out of me.

Then the Russian ran off. Wounded, I lay in the snow, together with two soldiers from the 320th Infantry Division, who had been taken prisoner by the Russians and who had been freed in this unusual manner.

At the dressing station they discovered a bullet wound in Ribbentrop's right shoulder blade and another in his left shoulder. The doctor deduced from this that there were two bullets in the wounded man's chest. When the shock wore off and his breathing returned to normal, the doctor said to him: "You've been lucky, because lung wounds are usually either fatal or minor. Since you're still alive, you will probably survive."

The *Obersturmführer* lay in a farmer's cottage with another wounded man, a young soldier from Meyer's reconnaissance battalion. During the night *Obersturmführer* von Ribbentrop developed a fever.

Obersturmführer Schulz had been killed in the attack on 11 February 1943. Beginning at daybreak the next day,

Battle Group Meyer fought on through the raging snowstorm. Russian and German forces passed each other unawares. At 1400 the advance detachment assembled at a rail crossing near Oktyabrsky, about seven kilometers west of Alexeyevka.

It was on this day that Hausser's corps received Hitler's order to hold Kharkov at all costs. Paul Hausser nevertheless broke out and gave the order for his forces to fall back to avoid being surrounded and destroyed. On the evening of the fourteenth the commander of the army once again described the desperate situation in an effort to extract an order from Hitler to abandon Kharkov, but in vain.

During the night of 14/15 February the Red Army drove into the northwestern and southern sections of Kharkov behind the German forces. In the northwest, a panzer battalion of the *Das Reich* Division inflicted heavy losses on the Soviets, temporarily halting their advance.

Once again the corps reported the difficult situation, but by midday on 15 February there had been no response from the army.

At 1230, *Obergruppenführer* Hausser ordered the *Das Reich* Division to leave its positions, withdraw to the Udy River, and occupy new positions there.

With support from the panzers, the one and a half divisions of the II SS-Panzer Corps were able to withdraw through Kharkov and then toward the southeast. When, at 1630, a new order from the army arrived ordering the defenders to hold on "at all costs," Hausser replied: "The matter has been settled: Kharkov has been evacuated!"

"The importance of this decision lay in the fact that the freeing of the main body of the SS-Panzer Corps was necessary for the continuation of the attack south to link up with Army Group South, to which *Armeeabteilung* A was attached."

At noon that day, after he had been delivered to the peasant cottage serving as the reconnaissance battalion's dressing station, the unit medical officer came to von Ribbentrop to tell him that a Fieseler *Storch* had landed with fuel. He was to be flown out aboard the aircraft.

Von Ribbentrop objected, stating that, as an officer, he should not be the first to be flown out, rather that the young soldier should be the first in line.

The medical officer, in charge of all wounded no matter what their rank, declared that he alone would decide who was the more seriously wounded and therefore who would be flown out first.

The doctor then ordered von Ribbentrop to get aboard the aircraft at once. Von Ribbentrop explained calmly, but firmly, that in this case he would have to disobey.

Finally the medical officer was forced to authorize the evacuation of the young soldier, because the "stubborn ox" von Ribbentrop wanted it that way.

Unfortunately, Battle Group Meyer's situation worsened in the days that followed, and the *Storch* did not return. Von Ribbentrop was forced to remain with the unit.

"Panzermeyer" prepared to break out on foot. The wounded, whose numbers had meanwhile grown considerably, were each given a pistol to prevent their falling into the hands of the Russians alive. However, a daring relief operation by 1st Battalion, 1st SS-Panzer Regiment changed the situation completely. The tanks rolled through the Soviet positions and made a wide circle around the village, scattering the surrounding enemy forces. The battalion then drove to the dressing station, where all of the wounded were loaded aboard the tanks. That evening the battle group set out back through the Soviet lines.

The last-minute relief effort had been a success, and just in time. Low on ammunition, Battle Group Meyer could have held out for several more hours at most.

Several months later Rudolf von Ribbentrop overheard a conversation between the commander of a Luftwaffe short-range reconnaissance unit, Major Rinke (who was later to become his father-in-law), and his division's Ia, *Sturmbannführer* Lehmann. Rinke asked: "How is he?"

Von Ribbentrop realized they were talking about him and became all ears. He learned that the Fieseler *Storch* had been sent expressly to fly him out in order to prevent the son of the Reich foreign minister from falling into Soviet hands, which would have been a great propaganda coup for the Soviets.

Von Ribbentrop: "Suddenly wide awake, I stood up, and in a most unmilitary tone and style reproached the Ia for placing me in such a situation. One can imagine the reputation I would have obtained if I had accepted the offer.

"Lehmann listened to my reproach politely and replied affably:

" 'Don't get excited, Ribbentrop. You are one of our own, and as far as I was concerned, it had nothing to with your father's position.' "

The attempt by Battle Group Meyer, which had driven into Alexandrovka, to establish contact with the northward-attacking Battle Group Witt had failed. The Soviets pressed toward the village from all sides in an attempt to eject the Germans. Rudolf von Ribbentrop found himself in the middle of this situation. Further complicating his position was the fact that all of the clothing had been cut away from his upper body at the dressing station, and all they had to give him was a large driver's coat. Von Ribbentrop had himself driven to the battalion command post so he could keep abreast of the situation.

His own tank was no longer serviceable, as it had been hit by enemy fire, which had jammed its turret. Only the bow machine gun, manned by the radio operator, was still functional.

We positioned my tank so that at least the machine gun could be used if the Russians neared the command post.

Soviet troops tried to enter the village from every side. Battle Group Meyer's situation became critical. My tank's machine gun had to be used several times to help repel the Russians advancing on the command post.

After three or four days Panzermeyer prepared everything for a breakout. This would have to be done on foot, as our fuel was gone. Meyer gave pistols to the wounded who were unable to walk, and bade them farewell with the words:

"Better to put a bullet in your head than be massacred by the Russians!"

The battle group commander had decided to break out through the deep snow with the survivors and try to reach our troops. The chances of crossing the thirty to forty kilometers successfully were slim.

During the late morning, on the fifth day of the encirclement, Kurt Meyer spoke by radio with the commander of our panzer regiment's 1st Battalion, *Sturmbannführer* Max Wünsche, and described the situation. Wünsche declared himself ready to try and break through the Russian front to save us.

Meyer implored him: "Be quick, Max, the battalion is at stake!"

As a listener, it was clear to me that our fate hung by a silken thread.

Everyone waited anxiously for Wünsche. Early in the afternoon the first of Wünsche's panzers appeared, much to the joy of the soldiers of Battle Group Meyer. They rolled around the village in a wide circle and blasted the Russians off the hills, where they were massing for an assault on Alexandrovka.

We saw flames and smoke, burning tanks and wagons, saw the fleeing Russians and knew: Wünsche was going to get us out.

Rudolf von Ribbentrop took part in the engagement in his only partially serviceable panzer. He joined Wünsche's tanks and opened fire with his bow machine gun as the Red Army soldiers tried to return to their foxholes behind Wünsche's tanks. Thus he played his part in opening a lane of escape for the surrounded battle group.

The following night the Germans left the village along the main road. Alexandrovka had almost proved the end of Battle Group Meyer. The wounded were taken along, and even the dead—except for those who had already been buried—were not left behind.

During the night Meyer's forces reached the German lines. In the following days these were subjected to almost uninterrupted Soviet attacks. East of Novaya Vodolaga, Ribbentrop attacked a strong group of enemy forces attempting to overpower a smaller German force occupying a hill. Through his field glasses von Ribbentrop could see that the Soviets were assembling for their final assault.

"Maximum speed!—Everyone follow me!"

"Everyone" was two panzers that had joined the platoon leader, whose tank was already rolling toward the main body of the enemy. "Spread out and open fire at your discretion!" ordered von Ribbentrop.

High-explosive shells smashed the largest group of enemy troops. The Russians turned to flee, but this brought them in front of the machine guns of the three panzers, which opened fire. The enemy force was completely wiped out and the situation saved; the small battle group on the hill was able to withdraw and rejoin its unit.

Small battles like this one were commonplace. The attackers were worn down by the stubborn German defense. With insufficient forces to force a decisive breakthrough, the Soviets were repeatedly forced back.

Two days after von Ribbentrop's rescue mission the Soviets made another attempt to break through, this time with stronger forces. The spearhead of the attack ran into the 1st Panzer Regiment's 7th Company, which met the attack with all the tanks at its disposal. Despite bitter and desperate resistance, the Red Army surged through.

Untersturmführer Alt, who had taken over 7th Company, was killed in battle. The 6th Company rolled out of its readiness positions and threw itself against the enemy. The attackers had meanwhile reached a deep ravine, which they apparently considered a secure position.

At high speed the panzers rolled through the ravine and along both edges. The Soviets threw themselves into the snow and played dead. Bursts of machine gun fire forced them to abandon this ploy, and soon the Soviet unit had been all but wiped out.

Several small groups of Soviets escaped the ravine, but they then ran into a scratch German force of drivers, cooks, and other rear-echelon personnel and were overpowered.

The Soviets had advanced several kilometers on either side of the stubbornly defended village of Novaya Vodolaga, however, and the defenders were forced to withdraw. The village had already been under enemy artillery fire for many hours. Once the first houses caught fire, it wasn't long before the entire village was shrouded in flames.

The withdrawal proved to be very difficult in the bitter cold. Three or four of 2nd Battalion's small number of panzers slid off the icy side road they had been forced to take, when they strayed from the narrow path. What was more, the smoke from the burning village and dense fog combined to reduce visibility.

It took the efforts of three tanks to extract each one that slid off the road. The fog and smoke also made these recovery efforts much more difficult. Had the Soviets attacked in this situation, the battle group could have been wiped out. However, the feared attack did not materialize.

The next morning the men and their tanks arrived in the selected area where they were to prepare for further operations.

On 17 February 1943 the corps headquarters of II SS-Panzer Corps released the following order of the day:

> In alternating battles of offense and defense since 30 January 1943, the SS-Corps has halted the onslaught of three Russian armies and inflicted heavy losses on the enemy. A cavalry corps has been almost completely destroyed.
>
> For the first time the *Leibstandarte* and *Das Reich* Divisions, which are soon to be joined by the *Totenkopf* Panzer Grenadier Division, have been able to fight shoulder to shoulder. All elements have given their best during these arduous weeks, and despite the mixing of units, which made the job of command much more difficult, have achieved a decisive defensive success.
>
> Side by side with the old battle-tested regiments and battalions, the newly formed units, in particular the panzer regiments and rifle battalions, have undergone their baptism of fire in the most difficult terrain conditions. Once again the panzer grenadiers have borne the brunt of the battle.
>
> Fighting in the ranks of the Waffen-SS, elements of the 213th and 298th Infantry Divisions have also played a role in the success.
>
> In one ten-day period the 320th Infantry Division, recently attached to the corps, brought decisive relief to the corps' southern flank by fighting its way through under extremely difficult conditions.
>
> To the commanders and troops of all attached units, I express my full recognition for your achievements and conduct in these difficult weeks.—signed Hausser, *Obergruppenführer*.

With 7th Company during the Attack on Kharkov

On 1 March 1943, Rudolf von Ribbentrop became the successor to the fallen *Untersturmführer* Alt as commander of the 1st SS-Panzer Regiment's 7th Company.

Now began the counterattack which *Obergruppenführer* Paul Hausser had been planning since he ignored a *Führerbefehl* and withdrew his two divisions from the pocket around Kharkov.

The following description of the battle is from the personal diary of Rudolf von Ribbentrop:

> My two company officers were *Untersturmführer* Stollmeier and *Untersturmführer* Sternebeck. Both were outstanding soldiers and experienced officers whom I knew well, as I had been leader of the company's 1st Platoon since the formation of the unit.
>
> On the first day we were assigned to be the spearhead company. We advanced northward rapidly in the direction of Walki. The village was attacked simultaneously from the west by our regiment's 1st Battalion.
>
> We reached the area above Walki, which was located in a valley. As we rounded a curve—I was driving in the lead position at that moment—the valley appeared far below us. It was dotted with withdrawing Russian infantry.
>
> "Open fire on the enemy!" I ordered. All tanks opened fire in an effort to prevent the enemy from withdrawing into Walki and establishing himself there, which would have been especially dangerous for 1st Battalion.
>
> For me it was important to observe the generally limited effect of several machine guns firing from ranges of two hundred to four hundred meters against the widely separated infantry advancing at a run in open formation across flat terrain.
>
> To be sure the Russians suffered considerable losses, but the larger part of the enemy infantry reached the safety of Walki in spite of our dense fire. We could not tell whether the Russians had been engaged by 1st Battalion, which had already entered the village, or if they had managed to find cover in the houses and mount resistance from there.

One thing was certain, however, as acknowledged by the men of 1st Battalion. As a result of its speedy intervention, the 7th Company had prevented a larger contingent of enemy infantry from entering the village and making things more difficult for them.

The attack was resumed early the next day. The panzers advanced along the Walki-Lubotin road. An antitank position was spotted and von Ribbentrop ordered his tanks to attack. The panzers advanced widely separated, making individual firing halts, and silenced the antitank front. Nevertheless, the Soviets succeeded in halting the advance until the afternoon. Not until then could the advance be resumed, once again with 7th Company leading the way.

At the entrance to Lubotin the "Seventh" encountered another antitank front. This, too, was silenced by concentrated fire from the panzers, which again suffered no losses to the antitank guns.

At this time there was no radio communications with battalion—probably because of the unfavorable terrain. Once again Rudolf von Ribbentrop takes up the narrative:

Before me I observed the large, extended village of Lubotin. Through my field glasses I could see Russian troops everywhere. The entire village seemed to be crammed with Russians. All of them were moving toward the northeast, and were therefore engaged in evacuating Lubotin.

While I was deliberating whether to drive into Lubotin with my three panzers without waiting for orders, which was not without risk as we had already expended all of our high-explosive ammunition, *Untersturmführer* Stollmeier, who was driving directly behind me, alerted me by radio that *Oberführer* Witt, the commander of the 1st SS-Panzer-Grenadier Regiment, was outside my tank. (On 1 March 1943, Fritz Witt had been decorated with the Oak Leaves and promoted from *Standartenführer* to *Oberführer.)*

Witt, an extremely brave soldier, had driven forward in his car, and when I looked out of the hatch, he said:

"Ribbentrop, we must have Lubotin!"

"We have no more high-explosive shells, *Oberführer!*" I remarked, and he replied drily:

"That may be, but we must have Lubotin!"

Very well then, I thought to myself, if we must have Lubotin then we'll drive in. I passed on the order and thus set in motion a wild chase which took us into the midst of the Russians. Our only chance of avoiding destruction at the hands of Russian tank killing specialists in the village was our speed, an advantage we intended to exploit.

From somewhere an *Oberscharführer* of the pionier platoon had jumped onto the back of my tank. With him on board we careered through the kilometer-long village of Lubotin, firing wildly. As we had no more high-explosive shells, our guns were loaded with armor-piercing, which would have little effect against antitank guns.

We drove around a curve and suddenly found ourselves thirty meters from an antitank gun that was ready to fire.

"The last thing you see is a bright fireball, because a hit from this range by a heavy Russian antitank gun—the *Ratschbum*—would blow us to pieces."

It was the *Oberscharführer* who jumped down from the tank and attacked the antitank gun with hand grenades. After the first blast the surviving gunners abandoned their gun and ran to a house, seeking cover.

This brave man, whose name I never knew, had saved our lives.

We raced on through Lubotin. Everywhere Russians fled left and right before our tank. Rounding another turn, this time near the exit from the village, we drove into a withdrawing Russian column. When I stopped to allow my machine gun to open fire, Stollmeier drove past me into the column. He was standing in his turret, firing his pistol, and shouting *"rucki werch!"*

The Russians raised their hands or ran away. One, however, charged toward Stollmeier's tank, weapon at the ready. Stollmeier threw his now empty pistol into the Russian's face, causing him to turn away. Suddenly, a hand grenade exploded in front of the tank, and Stollmeier was struck in the cheek by a fragment.

Orders came by radio for us to halt, although in the falling darkness we could hear the Russians, who were recovering one of their abandoned tanks several hundred meters in front of us.

A little later the supply column arrived. We refueled and took on a fresh supply of ammunition. Afterward we were given a new assignment. We were to drive in a wide arc to the north around Kharkov and reach the village of Dergatchi.

We set off. In the meantime it had begun to snow. Without adequate maps the night march became a nightmare. But we had to succeed in order to be in position the following morning for the next attack.

Orientation during the night march was a catastrophe. It was pitch black and snowing. Once again we were the spearhead company, which was an honor, but a great burden. I will never forget the thoughts that went through me during this drive. My radio operator sat quite comfortably inside the fighting compartment, reading and drinking coffee, while I, soaked to the skin and completely frozen, stood in the open turret hatch and tried desperately to find the right way. It was clear that I bore a great responsibility—the rest of the battalion was behind me and relying upon me. It didn't bear thinking about what would happen the next morning if we weren't on hand. This was just one of the things that was expected of every subordinate commander, and especially of every tank commander.

During the course of the night we reached Dergatchi and made contact with the battalion's infantry under *Sturmbannführer* Max Hansen [2nd Battalion, 1st SS-Panzer-Grenadier Regiment of the *Leibstandarte* Division].

At first light, 2nd Battalion, 1st SS-Panzer Regiment was ready to attack. As it was not possible to send rations forward, we all had to fall back on the rations chest: a large box fitted behind the turret of every tank that contained rations for just such an emergency.

The next morning I was a witness to a disagreement between our battalion commander and the leader of the grenadier battalion that was to attack Dergatchi. The two disagreed on how to conduct the attack. Our commander ended the discussion by ordering me to drive into the village along the road. I was to drive through the village to the far end, and there join in the assault on the village with the grenadiers.

I recall that we still had three or four panzers at that time. In one was Stollmeier, in the second Sternebeck; the third was commanded by *Unterscharführer* Killat.

We rolled into the village along an unusually narrow village road. Fences flitted past to the left and right. Through gaps in the fences we could see Russian infantry, who threw hand grenades and fired rifles. Now and then we could hear the crack of an antitank rifle.

Suddenly the approximately eight-centimeter-thick armor glass block in front of my vision slit shattered. A projectile from an antitank rifle had scored a direct hit on the turret cupola.

The vision block was quickly changed. However, without the grenadiers we were quite helpless against the Russian infantry. Now and then we fired high-explosive shells into the fences. This had little visible effect and was done more for reasons of morale.

All of a sudden there was a hard, shattering crack. We had been hit. In view of the many Russians about, abandoning the tank would be certain death. However, the motor continued to run normally and the turret still turned. I called Stollmeier, who was driving behind me, by radio and asked what had happened.

The latter answered dryly: "I knocked a Russian off your tank with a high-explosive round. He was about to set you on fire with a Molotov cocktail."

"You could have done that with the machine gun!" was my reply.

"It was jammed and I had to hurry, so I fired a high-explosive shell," he replied.

I decided to drive through the village at maximum speed, because the Russian infantry—if they had been supplied with tank-killing weapons—were a deadly enemy to tanks without supporting infantry.

My next orders were: "Ahead maximum speed! Stay close together! Each tank protect the others!"

On reaching the far end of the village we drove straight into a column of withdrawing Russians. The enemy soldiers fired a few bursts in our direction, then fled in all directions.

As fast as we could go, we drove out of the village into an open field, so as to block the retreat of the Russians still in the village and prevent them from reaching their own lines. We had just reached a small hill, when suddenly a platoon from our reconnaissance battalion, recognizable by their wide-tired Schwimmwagen vehicles, appeared from the right, driving across the plain at full speed. They approached and then roared past in the direction of the Kharkov-Belgorod road. We later learned that the platoon was on a reconnaissance mission. From it we learned more about the situation of our 1st Battalion. I immediately passed on the information to our commanding officer by radio.

We set out again. The next objective was called Cherkasskoye, which was overrun quickly. The enemy troops there were blasted out of the village. Panic-stricken, the enemy fled.

Soon after, we reached the Kharkov-Belgorod road, which we cut. Then we turned south and destroyed several enemy tanks fleeing toward Kharkov. [According to statements from the accompanying tank commanders, two were destroyed by von Ribbentrop.] We then reached Kharkov airfield, where we spent the night in our tanks. We were startled by a group of enemy tanks, which appeared from nowhere, blasted away in all directions, and then disappeared again.

The next morning followed the 1st Panzer Grenadier Regiment's attack on Kharkov. Our company was to provide support. We drove along the road behind the advancing grenadiers.

The advance came to a temporary halt when the grenadiers reported dug-in T-34s in the blocks of houses directly in front of them.

Meanwhile, our artillery had gone into action. However, we were under no illusions as to the likely effects of the artillery fire on the T-34s. To silence a dug-in tank would require a direct hit from above.

Suddenly one of the first Tiger tanks to reach the Eastern Front appeared on the road behind us. It had been given the job of eliminating the T-34s that were holding up the advance.

The mighty tank with its long gun rolled past at high speed. It halted about two hundred meters in front of us and fired. The mighty crash of the discharge almost merged with the thunderclap of the impact. The Tiger rolled on a short distance, halted once more, and fired. Again the sounds of its gun firing and the impacting shell were almost one. This maneuver was repeated a dozen times.

Then the Tiger rolled back in reverse, its giant cannon pointing to the side. When abeam our position, its commander, obviously wounded, called to us that a hit on the gun mantlet had disabled his main gun and that he was forced to withdraw.

This unlucky hit on the Tiger killed the tank's gunner and inflicted serious leg injuries on its commander.

We were standing beside the road, when suddenly *Oberführer* Witt—jumping from hole to hole amid the artillery fire—approached from the direction of the front line with his operations officer, an older *Obersturmführer.* Laughing, and without his belt and cap, he called to us that the Russians had done a good job of making him find his legs. He had gone to the front lines to see the state of the attack for himself. To the men of his regiment who were under fire this meant a great deal.

Witt was an outstanding infantry commander possessed of extraordinary personal bravery, calm, and circumspection. Every one of his soldiers knew that all of his orders were carefully considered and that he took no unnecessary risks. This distinguished the success of Witt the man and his panzer grenadier regiment.

By late afternoon the attack by the unit on our right, the 1st Panzer-Grenadier Regiment's 2nd Battalion, commanded by *Sturmbannführer* Hansen, began to make itself felt. The Russian fire diminished, and late in the afternoon the panzer grenadiers entered the first blocks of houses. We received orders to follow up and escort the panzer grenadiers as far as Red Square.

Once again we drove into the city at high speed. Suddenly a barricade appeared ahead. The Russians had blocked the thoroughfare with an abandoned KV-I, the heaviest of the Russian tanks.

The panzer grenadiers advanced past the barricade, while my crew and I—with the exception of the driver—climbed out and attached the tow cable to the KV-I in order to pull it out of the way and allow my three tanks to follow the panzer grenadiers.

As we had pulled the KV-I out of the thoroughfare, Stollmeier, who was commanding the second panzer, was already on the move. He called to me that he was going to escort the panzer grenadiers; I agreed and called back to him:

"Be careful!"

Stollmeier set off down the narrow street. There was little sign of activity, but on the other hand danger might be lurking at the other end which he, without infantry support, might not be able to cope with.

Stollmeier had proved to be a daredevil. His cheek was still badly swollen where it had been hit by the grenade fragment, but he had refused to leave his unit for treatment.

As we were climbing into our tank after stowing the tow cable, a shell from an antitank gun suddenly whistled past overhead. Stollmeier had apparently run into an antitank gun, which had opened fire on him.

As we drove around the next curve we saw his tank enveloped in flames. A little later his driver and radio operator appeared and reported to us that Stollmeier had come upon another barricade, this one containing a T-34. Stollmeier had fired immediately, and was just calling to his gunner to lower his aim when the fatal hit smashed into the turret, killing all those inside.

The tank burned out completely. The next day, after Red Square had been cleared, we found the charred remains of Stollmeier, identifiable by the remains of his headset.

We spent the night in the houses at the north end of Red Square with the panzer grenadiers. It was a cold night, too cold to sleep. We grieved for our fallen comrade and tried to get some rest, because the battle would go on the next day.

The next morning we supported the panzer grenadiers as they cleared the blocks of houses, silencing the nests of resistance that soon appeared. The battle against the Russians barricaded in the upper floors of the houses was brought to a successful conclusion, and I issued strict orders for the crews to remain inside their tanks. Not long before, *Unterscharführer* Killat had been wounded in the arm by grenade fragments as he looked outside his tank.

By evening the Russian resistance had lessened. The capture of Kharkov was complete. However, for us this was not the end of the battle, because the next morning we received orders to go with a platoon of grenadiers to clear a giant collective farm east of the city. There was little we could do, but we did suffer further casualties to Russian snipers firing from well-concealed positions in apartment buildings, houses, stables, and silos. Another gunner was killed when he opened his hatch and looked out to say something to the grenadiers.

This extract from von Ribbentrop's diary graphically illustrates the types of operations the tanks were engaged in during the recapture of Kharkov. It is obvious from the detailed account that even the limited number of tanks available made a decisive contribution to the operation, providing valuable support to the infantry forces.

These operations were far different than those envisaged by *Generaloberst* Heinz Guderian and the other creators of the panzer arm, namely independent raids deep into enemy territory. The tactics described by von Ribbentrop were in response to the situation at hand, and demonstrated that tanks could provide vital support in roles other than that for which they had been designed.

Leibstandarte's View

The results of the attack were described thus in the order of the day issued by the *Leibstandarte* Division:

(1) The enemy has been taken completely by surprise by the *Leibstandarte*'s rapid advance and has been driven back.

(2) On 11 March the SS-Panzer Corps will take Kharkov, with its eastern flank on the Merefa screened by elements of the SS-Division *Das Reich,* and its northern and north-

western flanks in a line Russkoye-Dergatchi-Festki-
Olchany by the SS-*Totenkopf* Division.
(3) Attacks will take place as follows: SS-Division *Das Reich*
with a strong regimental group from the west, *Leibstandarte* with two regimental groups from the north.
(4) Assignments:
  (a) Reinforced 2nd Panzer-Grenadier Regiment with at-
    tached 1st Battalion, 55th Rocket Regiment, assault
    gun battalion less one battery, an 8.8cm flak battery,
    1st and 2nd Battalions of the Artillery Regiment, as
    well as the 5th Company of the Flak Battalion, will at-
    tack the northern edge of Kharkov along the west
    road, advance to the boundary with the *Das Reich* Di-
    vision and clear that section of the city of the enemy.
  (b) Reinforced Panzer Grenadier Regiment (Battle Group
    Meyer, Corps *Nebelwerfer* Battalion, otherwise as be-
    fore) will send its battle group along the east road into
    the northeast part of Kharkov, as far as Rogan at the
    southern exit from the city, clear the city core of the
    enemy, and send security forces to the east and north-
    east.

During the night of 12/13 March, the *Leibstandarte* Division
headquarters was transferred to Dergatchi. There *Obergruppenführer* Sepp Dietrich received a call from Hitler, who had traveled to *Generalfeldmarschall* von Mantein's headquarters
(Army Group South) in Zaporozhye. Hitler asked Dietrich about
the state of his troops, and ended this memorable conversation
with the words, "If my *Leibstandarte* attacks with its usual
verve, we must succeed in wresting Kharkov back from the
enemy."

On 17 March, Battle Group Peiper, the 3rd (Armored)
Battalion, 2nd Panzer-Grenadier Regiment, resumed the attack toward the north in the direction of Belgorod. Sent to
support the attack was 7th Company, 1st SS-Panzer Regiment
under *Obersturmführer* von Ribbentrop. Because of the very
poor road conditions, the battle group did not reach the bend
in the road southwest of Nekotayevka until darkness was
falling. Just south of the bend the battle group ran into a Soviet
antitank front. Peiper's battalion broke through the Soviet position, supported by the tanks of von Ribbentrop's 7th Company.

The line that had been reached, where Peiper's forces were joined by the reinforced 2nd Battalion, 2nd Panzer-Grenadier Regiment, was secured for the night. The next objective for the *Leibstandarte* was Belgorod. The city was to be captured in a joint operation with the Panzer Grenadier Division *Grossdeutschland*.

The battle group received the following assignment for 19 March: "Secure the area north of Belgorod." On the twentieth the 1st Panzer Grenadier Regiment of the *Leibstandarte* was ordered to send a battalion to the 2nd Panzer Grenadier Regiment near Mikoyanovka.

On the afternoon of 19 March, the 2nd Panzer Grenadier Regiment's 3rd (Armored) Battalion set out with von Ribbentrop's 7th Company and two Tigers. Near Streletskoye there was an engagement with Soviet tanks. Seven were destroyed, against the loss of one armored personnel carrier, which was destroyed by a direct hit. Von Ribbentrop's company suffered no losses.

The bridge in Streletskoye had been destroyed by Soviet forces. The battalion withdrew to the eastern section of the town for the night.

Following the withdrawal, Peiper ordered *Obersturmführer* von Ribbentrop, who had volunteered for the job, to drive to the location of the destroyed half-track to see if there were any wounded there. Unfortunately, all that von Ribbentrop was able to bring back was several pay books and identity disks. None of the half-track's crew had survived.

The following is von Ribbentrop's description of this part of the battle:

Following the capture of Kharkov we were sent north in the direction of Belgorod to support our division's 2nd Panzer Grenadier Regiment as it attempted to break through the Russian positions. We carried out a picture-perfect attack with the armored personnel carriers of the Peiper Battalion (3rd Armored Battalion, 2nd SS-Panzer Grenadier Regiment). As we crossed a rise, beyond which the terrain fell away toward a village, we ran into an antitank front that the Russians had set up at the edge of the village.

They immediately opened fire. The armored personnel carriers rolled forward on a zigzag course. Smoke shells were fired in an attempt to escape the fire of the enemy guns, which were only several hundred meters away. This was the procedure Peiper's panzer grenadiers followed in their operations without tanks, and it had often saved them from heavy losses; in this case, however, it made accurate firing by my panzers difficult. This did not prevent them from putting the antitank front out of action within a few minutes though. They simply drove through the swaths of smoke and opened fire as soon as the enemy came into sight.

The company commander's tank also played a role in silencing the antitank front, although he was loath to take credit for it. For von Ribbentrop, his company was a homogeneous unit, and successes were credited to the entire company rather than to an individual. It is known that he commonly attributed only a small role to himself in such difficult victories, such as the overpowering of the antitank front.

Enemy antitank guns, especially the heavy Soviet guns, which often waited in well-camouflaged positions to ambush German armor, were a more dangerous opponent than enemy tanks. As a result, successes against these Soviet weapons were rated highly in the German armed forces.

The surviving Soviet gunners ran back into the village. The commander of the panzer grenadier company called out, "After them, Ribbentrop!"

A panzer grenadier officer commented, "It is always a very reassuring feeling in such situations to hear the firing of our tanks, which are eliminating the deadly antitank front for us."

Von Ribbentrop resumes his narrative:

Although hindered by a deeply eroded streambed in the valley, we quickly reached our objective for the day, followed closely by the panzer grenadiers. Once again we had to spend the night inside our tanks. Compared to our grenadiers, who were forced to pass the night in hastily built snow shelters, this was quite comfortable.

The next morning we set out under clear skies with the Peiper Battalion to break through to Belgorod. Escorted by three Bf-110 close-support aircraft, which now and then fired smoke signals to indicate the position of the enemy, we drove north along the main road against negligible opposition. After about twenty kilometers we passed through a village. A number of T-34s sat empty and abandoned at the edge of the village. It had obviously been the site of a Russian repair facility, which had been engaged in repairing battle-damaged tanks.

As the lead tank I rolled into the village. The first enemy tank to appear before our guns received a direct hit and burst into flames. The shadowy forms of Russian soldiers scurried away to avoid being overrun. My loader had already laid the next round. I called out the next target:

"Half right, 250 ahead!"

My gunner already had the target in his sight. The crash of gunfire and the thunderous impact merged almost into one. The empty shell casing clattered into the canvas bag. The tank lurched forward. One or two projectiles from an antitank rifle whizzed past, while another struck the turret at an angle and was deflected off to the side.

We rolled on. Behind us we could hear the other panzers firing as they came upon the Russian tanks. We spent no more time dealing with them, as our objective was Belgorod.

Apparently the panzer grenadiers had not succeeded in eliminating all of the Russian tanks. After Belgorod was in the division's hands, we learned that shortly after we had passed through there had been a wild shootout on the main road. The following units had encountered the T-34s and had to put them out of action before they could continue.

We continued on at a high tempo. The armored personnel carriers of the legendary Jochen Peiper, who was later to lead the *Leibstandarte*'s panzer regiment, stayed right with us.

There was little danger of a Russian ambush, as the terrain was open and snow-covered; as well, the three Bf-110s were still overhead, and would have reported any assembly of enemy forces.

When we reached Belgorod we found that the enemy had already "left town." The only Russian we saw was a second lieutenant, whose departure had obviously been delayed. His truck rolled straight in front of the machine guns of the armored personnel carriers.

From the heights above the Donets we could see endless Russian columns on the far side, all withdrawing toward the north. We fired a few high-explosive shells at them, but they had little effect, as the distance was too great. Nevertheless, we did accelerate the Red Army's departure.

In the afternoon we were assigned to carry out a relief attack for the *Grossdeutschland* Panzer Grenadier Division. *Untersturmführer* Ekkehard destroyed three T-34s that had been deployed as flanking cover for the Russians withdrawing toward the north. The tanks had been expertly camouflaged in haystacks, and the glare from the evening sun added to the effectiveness of their cover. However, Ekkehard spotted steam from their exhausts, which was visible above the haystacks in the cold winter air.

He rolled toward them at high speed and made a timely firing halt. His gunner destroyed all three Russian tanks with three quick shots. Three blood-red torches marked the scene of this brief and violent encounter.

These were the men in our tanks, each and every one a soldier through and through and all completely fearless.

The next morning Peiper's armored group was sent north from Belgorod. The armored personnel carriers and another panzer company formed the spearhead. After advancing several kilometers the spearhead came under heavy artillery fire. One armored personnel carrier was hit and within seconds was blazing furiously.

"Withdraw! Back to the back side of the slope!" ordered Peiper. Turning to the panzer battalion commander, he continued, "There's nothing to be gained here!"

Anyone who knew Jochen Peiper knew that he would want to find out with certainty what had happened to the crew of the armored personnel carrier, but he did not want to send one of the lightly armored half-tracks back into the artillery fire.

Peiper, who had worn the Knight's Cross since 9 March of that year, looked around in surprise when Rudolf von Ribbentrop reported to him.

"Sturmbannführer, I would like to go back out to see if there are any wounded to be found, or if perhaps I can find something else."

Peiper responded gratefully to this unsolicited offer: "Thank you, Ribbentrop, but be careful."

I later learned that the commander of the half-track was one of the battalion's veteran NCOs, whose death or wounding and capture by the Russians would have struck close to Peiper.

My tank rolled toward the half-track, which was still smoldering. I placed my trusted gunner Borgsmüller in charge in the turret, while I climbed out to inspect the site. Luck was with me. The enemy seemed not to have noticed us, and the artillery fire I was expecting did not start.

My search for survivors was unsuccessful. All that I found were pieces of uniforms, pay books and several identity disks, which had not been consumed by the flames.

I climbed back into my tank and headed toward the position on the rear side of the hill at top speed to report to Peiper what I had seen.

Even though there were no survivors, Peiper was pleased to hear that at least none of his comrades had been left lying there.

Jochen Peiper never forgot me for this incident.

This brought our winter operations to a close. To my great surprise, shortly after our return to Kharkov I was transferred to the panzer regiment as adjutant. I had gone through so much with the 7th Company that I was loath to leave it. What was more, in the past weeks I had been acting as company commander and had been quite successful. This was due to the exemplary readiness for action and spirit of sacrifice of the tank crews, who were always ready to take part in and lead the attack.

The fact that the transfer to the position of regimental adjutant entailed a certain degree of recognition did nothing to change my attitude, my disappointment was great. I asked the commanding officer to abandon the plan and let me stay with the company, whose leader I had become. But our commanding officer would not change his mind, in fact he was somewhat annoyed by my request.

For his actions during the fighting in the Kharkov area, von Ribbentrop was awarded the Iron Cross, First Class and the Wound Badge in Silver (this was the third time he had been wounded).

The *Führerbefehl* of 19 March 1943:

ORDER OF THE DAY!
Soldiers of Army Groups South and Center, *Luftflotte* 4 and the *Luftwaffe* Eastern Command!
Weeks ago during one of the most serious crises of the war I was forced to turn to you with the request that you defend bitterly every meter of ground, so as to give me time to send new units and new weapons to the front, which were necessary to decisively break the Soviet onslaught.

Through the sacrificial actions of countless officers and soldiers and thanks to superior leadership, these conditions have been met.

It became ever more difficult for the Soviets to advance. The empty spaces were steadily filled with improvised units or new German divisions.

As a result, the enemy encountered ever-stiffening resistance. Finally, the days of holding on were past and those of the counterattack had arrived.

The battle-tested soldiers of the Army and *Waffen-SS* in the East were joined by new divisions from the Army and *Waffen-SS*.

At the front's vital points the Russians succumbed to your determined, violent attack and the ongoing heroic actions of the *Luftwaffe*.

Kharkov is again in our hands!—Signed Adolf Hitler.

In his book *Die Ritterkreuzträger der Waffen-SS,* Ernst-Günther Krätschmer lauded this great victory by the II SS-Panzer Corps: "The last major German victory of the Russian Campaign was a result of the outstanding tactical leadership of *General der Waffen-SS* Paul Hausser.

"This success was only possible because Hausser, as Commanding General of the SS-Panzer Corps, refused to carry out Hitler's repeated orders to hold Kharkov at all costs, assuming great personal responsibility. Instead, he evacuated the city, which had been surrounded by the enemy, and prevented the certain destruction of his corps. As a result he preserved three of the best German divisions, and with these decisively smashed the Soviets in the battle between the Donets and the Dniepr and returned the city of Kharkov to German hands."

Only after this success was *Generalfeldmarschall* von Manstein able to put his great operations plan into action.

The Battle of Kursk

Von Ribbentrop between the Battles

As the regimental adjutant of the *Leibstandarte* Division's panzer regiment, Rudolf von Ribbentrop gained a deeper insight into the command of a large armored unit. He soon became acclimatized to his new surroundings and took part in many discussions with the commanders of the panzer battalions, the commanding officer of the regiment, and the commanding general, *Obergruppenführer* Paul Hausser.

He learned that the SS-Panzer Corps' losses during its brief period of action in Russia had been shockingly high. These totaled 615 officers and 11,154 NCOs and men.

He soon learned, too, of new German plans for a major offensive. The salient around Kursk was to be cut off and destroyed in a gigantic pincer movement from the north and south. If this great coup succeeded, the Red Army would probably suffer losses that would decide the war.

Precisely one month after beginning his service at the panzer regiment headquarters, Rudolf von Ribbentrop was named to command a training company. The majority of the replacements reaching the panzer corps at that time had received little or no training. In this case the new men being assigned to the panzer regiment were former members of the *Luftwaffe*.

The *Obersturmführer* approached this new assignment with great enthusiasm. He knew from his own experience that "sweat helped spare blood." On 15 June, on completion of this task, the young officer took over the panzer regiment's 6th Company. Now he had a command which was more to his taste; within a few days he was well known by all of the new soldiers joining the "Sixth." Von Ribbentrop knew that a new attack was being prepared, and the soldiers of the *Waffen-SS* agreed that something big was in the offing.

The operations plan for Operation *Zitadelle* had been submitted to the OKH on 12 April 1943. Hitler had decided to launch the new offensive as the first great blow of 1943. The attack's objective was a rapid advance by two armies, one from the Belgorod area in the south, and another from south of Orel in the north, which would surround and destroy the Soviet forces in the Kursk area.

The attack was scheduled to begin on 2 May, but was put off several times. On 4 May, *Generalfeldmarschall* von Manstein, *Generaloberst* Model, *Generalfeldmarschall* von Kluge, *Generaloberst* Guderian, and the chief of the *Luftwaffe* general staff Jeschonnek attended a meeting with Hitler.

Generaloberst Model pointed out that the enemy had built a deep net of fortifications opposite his 9th Army and requested an appropriate reinforcement of his assault forces.

Hitler assured his commanders that by 10 June large numbers of the latest Tiger and Panther tanks would be on hand, and that one or perhaps two battalions of the superheavy Ferdinand tank destroyers as well as larger numbers of assault guns would be sent. Hitler promised a doubling of the number of panzers.

The two field marshals, von Manstein and von Kluge, were against any further postponements, because the increase in German tank strength was being more than equaled by the enemy. Erich von Manstein emphasized that Soviet tank production was running at 1,500 (!) per month. Above all, he feared that further delays might see the enemy take the offensive on the Donets and Mius Rivers.

Hitler dismissed his commanders in chief without giving them his decision. Not until 11 May did he issue the order postponing Operation *Zitadelle* until mid-July.

The Soviet high command had recognized the strategic importance of the Kursk salient early on. Stavka, the headquarters of the Red Army, issued the commanders in chief of the Bryansk and Voronezh Fronts the following instructions for the defense of the salient: "During the defensive battle inflict maximum losses on the enemy assault groups from the north and south, wipe out their forces and then begin the counteroffensive" (W. G. Posnyak, *The Battle near Kursk*).

In addition, Stalin and the Stavka decreed: "With the beginning of the enemy's attack, the Central Front and the Voronezh Front are to go over to the defensive, wear down the enemy in defensive battles, and then open a counteroffensive as soon as the enemy forces have been bled to death. The Western Front and the Bryansk Front are to prepare an offensive in the direction of Orel" (Ilya Ivanovich Markin, *The Battle of Kursk*).

By the end of June the Soviets had established defensive zones, built antitank strong points and an in-depth system of obstacles, and laid belts of mines in the main defensive area around the Kursk salient. Altogether they laid 434,667 antitank mines and built 604 powerful antitank barriers.

To counter the air forces of *Luftflotte* 4 (the 1st, 4th, and 8th *Fliegerkorps* with a total of 2,000 aircraft of all types) the Soviet high command deployed the 2nd, 16th, and 17th Air Armies with a total of 3,500 aircraft. In addition, the Kursk salient boasted the greatest concentration of antiaircraft artillery ever seen on the Eastern Front.

Thanks to the respite granted the Red Army, by the end of

June 1943 it was well equipped to face and defeat the German offensive.

The Attack

On 4 July 1943, following a preparatory artillery bombardment and air strikes, the divisions of the 4th Panzer Army attacked the system of hills between Belgorod in the east and Rakitnoye in the west in order to gain the necessary observation positions for the main attack, which was to take place the next day.

When the attack began, Army Group South, under the command of *Generalfeldmarschall* von Manstein, had available 1,081 tanks and 376 assault guns. With the 11th Panzer Division on the right, and the Panzer-Grenadier Division *Grossdeutschland* on the left, von Manstein's forces stormed toward Butovo.

Setting out on the right flank were the three assault groups of the II SS-Panzer Corps under *Obergruppenführer* Paul Hausser. Their objectives were the hills near Jochontov and Streletskoye, which were taken.

The main attack began simultaneously on the northern and southern fronts early on the morning of 5 July. The 7th Panzer Division (III Panzer Corps) crossed the Donets west of Dorogobushino and fought its way through dense field positions as far as Rasumnoye. It was there that the first Soviet counterattack took place, in which a number of Soviet tanks were destroyed.

At about 1800 the 7th Panzer Division's 25th Panzer Regiment crossed over a *Pionier* bridge to the east bank of the Donets. On 6 July the regiment drove into a Soviet tank assembly area. The attack was led by *Oberstleutnant* Adalbert Schulz. Schulz had worn the Knight's Cross since the end of December 1941, and after this attack he was awarded the Swords.

As usual, Schulz was in the first wave. His regiment destroyed thirty-four Soviet T-34s. *Hauptmann* Fortun, commander of 1st Battalion, was killed. He was awarded a posthumous Knight's Cross on 7 August.

The 7th Panzer Division continued its advance on 7 July. By 9 July, Schulz's armored group had reached the high ground south of Scheino. By the evening of the eleventh the entire III Panzer Corps had followed into the area north of Scheino. The main body of the 4th Panzer Army battered its way through the in-depth system of enemy positions. Its divisions reached the area of Prokhorovka. II SS-Panzer Corps, one of the army's flanking corps, also broke through into the Prokhorovka area, arriving on the evening of 11 July.

By 12 July the Red Army units in the southern sector of the offensive had lost 24,000 men captured, 1,800 tanks, 267 guns, and 1,080 antitank guns. The battle had reached its climax. *Generalfeldmarschall* von Manstein was confident that his forces could punch through the Soviet defenses and achieve victory.

But what was the state of the northern pincer?

The 9th Army under *Generaloberst* Model, which had been formed to take part in *Zitadelle,* possessed eight panzer divisions with a total of 478 tanks, including Tigers of the 505th Heavy Panzer Battalion. As well, 348 assault guns were on hand to support the infantry units.

The spearhead of the attack, the XXXXVII Panzer Corps, was to smash the first breach in the enemy positions. The second wave was then to drive through the gap deep into enemy territory. If necessary this would be followed by a third wave.

Generaloberst Model had placed one panzer division, the 20th, in the first attack wave. In the opinion of the panzer expert *General der Panzertruppe* Nehring this was too little. General Nehring told the author:

"Of the six fast divisions five (!) were held in reserve. That was too many! It would have been appropriate to assign two panzer divisions to the direct support of the infantry units. This method would have been effective against a dug-in and fortified defender, as both arms could provide mutual support and protection."

Walther K. Nehring likewise pointed out the vital importance of the 653rd and 654th Heavy Tank Destroyer Battalions. Employed in concentration under the 21st Panzer Brigade, these two units with their ninety Ferdinands and the forty-five superheavy 15cm self-propelled howitzers of the 216th Armored Assault Battalion could have rolled up any enemy defensive position. All that the units required was protection for their flanks.

The suggestions of the armor experts were ignored, however, and none of this was done. As a result the attack by the northern pincer on 5 July was a failure. On the following day the second wave, the XXXXVII Panzer Corps with the 2nd and 9th Panzer Divisions, was committed. On the evening of the sixth, Model demanded the release of the 4th Panzer Division, in order to, as he put it, "be able to continue the advance toward Kursk without delay."

The 21st Panzer Brigade, which had not been sent the Ferdinands, captured a hill south of Teploye with the 2nd and 4th Panzer Divisions. However, on this day the advance by the 9th Army as a whole had already been halted.

The attack was resumed on 10 July but made no progress. Losses had been heavy and could not be made good from the reserves. On 12 July, Walter Model ordered only limited attacks, and thus on the northern front any chance of a quick strategic decision had been relinquished.

On 12 July, Field Marshals von Kluge and von Manstein were ordered to Führer headquarters. There Hitler explained that the situation in Sicily, where the Western Allies had landed on 10 July, was very serious. Hitler was certain that they would cross over from there to the mainland. The Eastern Front would have to release panzer divisions to defend this position and, therefore, *Zitadelle* could not be continued.

Generalfeldmarschall von Manstein explained imploringly that the battle in the southern sector had reached a decisive point. The enemy had thrown almost all of his reserves into the battle and been stopped. "The time has now come to smash him in the southern sector. If we break off the battle at this stage we will be throwing away victory!"

Hitler's decision was, *"Zitadelle* is called off!"

The II SS-Panzer Corps on the Attack

On 12 July the III Panzer Corps and the II SS-Panzer Corps of the southern pincer reached the Prokhorovka area. The Red Army was preparing to throw several motorized and tank brigades and the 5th Mechanized Guards Tank Corps at the two powerful panzer units in an effort to halt their advance and drive them back. General Rotmistrov, the Soviet commander, had assembled 850 tanks.

Generaloberst Hoth, commander in chief of the 4th Panzer

Army, had more than 600 tanks in the II SS-Panzer Corps and over 360 in the III Panzer Corps.

The three SS panzer divisions rolled from the southwest toward the northeast. On the left flank was the *Totenkopf* Division. In the center was the *Leibstandarte,* and on the right flank, making straight for the 2nd Soviet Tank Corps, was the *Das Reich* Division.

A Soviet flanking attack was smashed by *Luftwaffe* close-support aircraft under *Hauptmann* Meyer (4./SG 9) and Major Druschel (1./SG 1). The 3cm cannon of the recently introduced Hs-129 proved lethal to the Soviet armor. The close-support pilots destroyed fifty T-34s within sixty minutes, eliminating the threat to the corps' flank.

Obergruppenführer Hausser sent his corps forward. The *Totenkopf* Division crossed the Psyol River near Vesely. The other two divisions pushed through across the land bridge between the Psyol and the rail line to Prokhorovka and engaged the Red Army's 18th and 29th Tank Corps.

The next morning, 2nd Battalion of the LAH's 1st Panzer Regiment under *Sturmbannführer* Martin Gross encountered enemy armored forces. The tanks met in an area 500 meters wide and 1,000 meters deep. The tank battle lasted three hours. When it was over, ninety Soviet tanks lay burning on the battlefield.

On the left flank the Tigers of the 1st SS-Panzer Regiment's 13th (heavy) Company suddenly found themselves facing a wave of sixty Soviet tanks. The battle began at ranges of from 600 to 1,000 meters.

The first enemy tank was knocked out by *SS-Untersturmführer* Michael Wittmann's Tiger. Wittmann's tank was hit twice, but the guns of the T-34s could not penetrate the Tiger's frontal armor at this range.

SS-Hauptsturmführer Heinrich Kling, Wittmann's company commander, warned him of the approach of another Soviet armored unit with about one hundred tanks.

Wittmann opened fire on the new enemy from 1,800 meters. The other two Tigers under his command joined in. The Red Army tanks were halted. One of the soldiers who had played a decisive role in this success was *Obersturmführer* Rudolf von Ribbentrop. This was to be his most successful day of the entire war.

"Born Again—Near Prokhorovka"

The morning of 12 July 1943 had dawned. The sun hung blood-red over the horizon and was bathing the land in its glowing rays when *Obersturmführer* von Ribbentrop was awakened harshly. Exhausted after seven days on the attack, he had slept soundly.

"*Obersturmführer— Obersturmführer!*" The persistent calls dragged von Ribbentrop from his stupor. He sat up quickly and banged his head on the underside of his tank. He and his men had been sleeping in a trench under the tank. He had instructed all of his crews to do the same in order to avoid unnecessary casualties in the event of a nocturnal bombing raid or artillery bombardment.

The sound of the DKW motorcycle penetrated his consciousness. That was a sign that he had been ordered to battalion. The motorcycle belonged to the company messenger attached to the battalion.

"*Obersturmführer* to the commanding officer!"

Von Ribbentrop got up at once. During the short trip to the battalion commander's command vehicle he could see that the front was restive.

Sturmbannführer Gross stuck his head out of the command vehicle, a converted radio truck, when he heard the motorcycle.

"Listen, Ribbentrop. Reports from the infantry indicate that the Russian tanks are assembling. We have no details. Make contact with the infantry and be ready to intervene if necessary."

In his account of this day, Von Ribbentrop stated:

> The tone of the battalion commander's voice suggested that it should not come as a great surprise that the offensive, which had developed into one great tank battle, should encounter further tanks, and that it actually seemed superfluous to point this out.
>
> I was initially a little cross as a result of this vague and unconventional order, because the evening before Gross had decreed that my company was to become the reserve company. Now came this assignment, rudely interrupting a much needed rest period.
>
> I rode back to my company on the passenger seat of the mo-

torcycle, and ordered my men to come to battle readiness and warm up the engines of the tanks. The weapons were uncovered and made ready for action. Then I ordered the leader of my company's headquarters personnel, *Oberscharführer* Gebauer, to report to me with a motorcycle-sidecar combination, as I wanted to drive up to the infantry positions myself to assess the situation and, if need be, to be in a position to take appropriate measures at once.

My 6th Company's losses so far had been heavy. Of the twenty-two tanks with which we had started on 5 July, only seven were still available for action on the evening of 11 July. Fortunately, not all of these had been total losses, and a steady stream of repaired Panzer IVs was returning to the company.

The previous day we had fought our way across a Russian antitank ditch. Our battalion's other two companies were now in position there, while we at the moment were in the rear as reserve company.

The antitank ditch, which naturally ran across the front, had a single crossing, over which ran the road to Prokhorovka. The bridge there had not been destroyed, or had already been rebuilt.

The antitank ditch lay in a valley. From there an approximately four-hundred-meter-wide slope extended in the direction of Prokhorovka. On the right the slope was bordered by the road to Prokhorovka. Beyond it was an overgrown railway embankment, which could be considered tank proof.

At the embankment the front bent back behind the antitank ditch, and then ran east again to the boundary with the neighboring *Das Reich* Division.

A battalion of our panzer grenadiers had occupied the embankment, while a second battalion had gone into position at right angles, up above on the previously mentioned slope.

Our left flank was open and we had no contact with friendly forces there. I drove along the road at the railway embankment until I came to the command post of the battalion commander, which was located in a passage beneath the embankment. The commander was just about to interrogate a captured Russian lieutenant. The latter was very German looking—tall, blond, and blue-eyed. He was very composed and answered few questions; then, after being given some cigarettes, he declared:

"Russian soldier poor rations, good morale. German soldier good rations, bad morale." I learned little from the panzer grenadier commander. He, too, had received reports of tank noises, but beyond that he had heard nothing more.

I left my company NCO with the motorcycle at the battalion command post, so that he could report to me at once if something concrete happened and bring me appropriate instructions.

I walked back to my tanks, which were visible several hundred meters away at the antitank ditch in the valley below. Scattered across the slope were the men and vehicles of the armored group, which consisted of the division's self-propelled battalion and the battalion of armored personnel carriers under Jochen Peiper. There was so much equipment scattered across the slope, which was out of sight of the Russians, that it appeared to be dotted with vehicles and weapons of every kind.

All of the units were enjoying a rest. The day before, our attack on Prokhorovka, which had been tantalizingly near, had been broken off because the *Das Reich* Division on our right and the *Totenkopf* Division on our left—with which we had no contact—had been unable to keep pace, as they had been attacked by strong Russian forces.

As a result of this situation, our forces formed a wedge that jutted deep into enemy territory, with a secure right flank at the railway embankment, and a completely open left flank on the Psyol.

Since, without contact with our two neighboring divisions, it appeared that the attack on Prokhorovka was impractical, our men slept the sleep of the exhausted. In any case, seven of the hardest days of fighting of the entire Russian campaign lay behind us.

Personally, I always considered lack of sleep to be the greatest deprivation in war, outweighing hunger and thirst and the cold, rain and dampness.

As I walked back it was obvious that the front was unsettled. Artillery fired here and there. Bursts of machine gun fire echoed over us, and the sky was full of aircraft.

When von Ribbentrop arrived at his company, he was welcomed by the unit's senior NCO with a hot coffee. His tank's loader opened the rations box and got the company commander some bread. The company officer, a brave and cheerful man, reported 6th Company at battle readiness. The men enjoyed the fresh coolness of the morning. The 6th Company had six tanks available that morning. In the past few days it had suffered several losses while taking part in an attack against a dangerous Soviet antitank front with the Peiper battalion. The company had been making a "horizon crawl" with the objective of destroying the Soviet tanks and antitank guns caught between the German attack groups, when it came upon the antitank front.

As he and his men were rolling toward the enemy position, von Ribbentrop received a counterorder from his battalion commander. Von Ribbentrop could not understand the order. To turn away now meant leaving the Peiper battalion to attack the powerful enemy position alone. Peiper's half-tracks were very vulnerable to the fire of the Soviet antitank guns.

"I knew only one thing; this was out of the question, and I took part in the attack despite the battalion commander's angry objections over the radio.

"When we assembled after destroying the antitank front and blowing up the last of the antitank guns, I received from Peiper the highest praise spoken to me in the whole course of the war, when he said to me: 'I would gladly take you and your company into our bunch!'

"Back at battalion I managed to convince the irritated battalion commander that it would have been impossible to break off the attack and leave the armored personnel carriers to face the fire of the antitank guns without tank support."

As von Ribbentrop was sipping the hot coffee that had been handed him, he turned casually toward the front. The sight that confronted him made him think he was hallucinating. A purple wall of smoke rose into the air, produced by smoke shells. It meant: "Tank warning!"

The same signals were to be seen all along the crest of the slope. The threatening violet danger signals also appeared farther to the right at the railway embankment.

Everything immediately became clear: beyond the hill, still out of sight of those in the valley, a major Soviet armored attack was under way.

Von Ribbentrop dropped his mess kit and shouted: "Start up!—Follow me!"

Then he called to company officer Malchow, "We're going to drive in a line up the slope. You and your platoon to the left;

I and the other three tanks in the center and to the right. Bend the left flank back a bit in case we're outflanked. We'll move into hull-down positions on the slope and engage the Russians from there!"

Once again von Ribbentrop takes up the narrative:

At the same moment I spotted the leader of the company headquarters personnel, whom I had left at the infantry battalion's command post. Shrouded in a gigantic cloud of dust, he was racing down the slope on his motorcycle, all the while extending his fist into the air, which meant:

"Move out at once!"

With this the company set itself in motion, and deployed on the slope as if on the exercise field, with a precision that made my twenty-two-year-old heart beat faster. It was an especially uplifting feeling for me to lead these young but experienced soldiers into battle.

On reaching the crest of the slope we saw another low rise about two hundred meters away on the other side of a small valley, on which our infantry positions were obviously located.

By radio I ordered my company to drive into position on the slope ahead of us and take up the battle from there.

The small valley extended to our left, and as we drove down the forward slope we spotted the first T-34s, which were apparently attempting to outflank us from the left.

We halted on the slope and opened fire, hitting several of the enemy. A number of Russian tanks were left burning. For a good gunner eight hundred meters was the ideal range.

As we waited to see if further enemy tanks were going to appear, I looked all around, as was my habit. What I saw left me speechless. From beyond the shallow rise about one hundred fifty to two hundred meters in front of me appeared fifteen, then thirty, then forty tanks. Finally there were too many to count. The T-34s were rolling toward us at high speed, carrying mounted infantry.

My driver Schüle called over the intercom: *"Obersturmführer,* right, right! They're coming! Do you see them?"

I saw them only too well. At that second I said to myself: "It's all over now!" *(Nun ist es aus!)* My driver thought I had said "Get out!" *(Raus!),* and began to open his hatch. I grabbed him rather roughly and hauled him back into the tank. Meanwhile, I had poked the gunner in the right side with my foot. This was the signal for him to traverse right.

Soon the first shell was on its way and with the impact the T-34 began to burn. It was only fifty to seventy meters from us. At the same instant the tank next to me took a direct hit and went up in flames. I saw *Unterscharführer* Papke jump clear, but that was the last we ever saw of him. His neighbor to the right was also hit, and soon it, too, was in flames.

The avalanche of enemy tanks rolled straight toward us: tank after tank! Wave after wave! It was a simply unimaginable assembly, and it was moving at very high speed.

We had no time to take up defensive positions. All we could do was fire. From this range every shot was a hit, but when would a direct hit end it for us? Somewhere in my subconscious I realized that there was no chance of escape. As always in such hopeless situations, all we could do was take care of what was at hand. So we knocked out a third, then a fourth T-34, from distances of less than thirty meters.

The Panzer IV we were using carried about eighteen to twenty rounds of ammunition within immediate reach of the loader, of which the larger number were high-explosive and the rest armor-piercing.

Soon my loader shouted: "No armor-piercing left!"

All of our immediately available armor-piercing ammunition had been expended. Further ammunition had to be passed to the loader by the gunner, radio operator and driver. At this point remaining stationary was the surest means of being spotted and destroyed by the Russian tanks. Our only hope was to get back behind the slope again, even though the Russians had already crossed it, because our chances of escaping there were better than in our present exposed position.

We turned in the midst of a mass of Russian tanks, rolled back about fifty meters and reached the back slope of the first rise. There we turned to face the enemy again, now in somewhat better cover.

Just then a T-34 halted about thirty meters diagonally to our right. I saw the tank rock slightly on its suspension and traverse its turret in our direction. I was looking right down the muzzle of its gun. We were unable to fire immediately, as the gunner had just passed the loader a fresh round.

"Panzer forward, move!" I shouted into the microphone. In my driver Schüler I had the best driver in the battalion. He had already put the tank in gear, and the lumbering Panzer IV set it-self in motion. We drove past the T-34 at a distance of about five meters. The Russian tried to turn his turret to follow us, but was unable to do so. We halted ten meters behind the stationary T-34 and turned. My gunner scored a direct hit on the Russian's tur-ret. The T-34 exploded, and its turret flew about three meters through the air, almost striking my tank's gun. While all of this was going on, other T-34s with mounted infantry were rolling past us.

In the meantime, I tried to pull in the Swastika flag which was lying across the box on the rear of the tank. The flag's purpose was to let our pilots know where we were. I only half succeeded in this, with the result that the flag now fluttered in the wind. One of the Russian commanders or gunners would have to no-tice it sometime. It was only a question of time until we received the fatal hit.

We had only one slim chance: we must remain constantly in motion. A stationary tank would be immediately recognized by the foe as an enemy and fired upon, because all the Russian tanks were rolling at high speed across the terrain.

We now faced the additional danger of being destroyed by one of our own tanks, which were sitting below at the antitank ditch by the railway embankment in a wide line and which had begun firing at the approaching enemy tanks. On the smoke- and dust-shrouded battlefield, looking into the sun, it would be impossible for our crews to distinguish us from a Russian tank.

I repeatedly broadcast our code-name: "Kunibert here! We are in the midst of the Russian tanks! Don't fire at us!"

I received no answer. In the meantime, the Russians had set several vehicles on fire as they rolled through Peiper's APC bat-talion and our artillery battalion. But now the fire of our two re-maining panzer companies was beginning to have an effect.

The artillery's battalion of self-propelled guns and Peiper's panzer grenadiers—the latter with close-range weapons—were also taking a toll on the Russian tanks and pinning down the Russian infantry, which had jumped down from the T-34s and were attempting to advance on foot.

The entire battlefield lay under a thick pall of smoke and dust; out of this inferno continued to roll fresh groups of Russ-ian tanks, which were knocked out on the long slope by our panzers.

It was an indescribable jumble of wrecked tanks and vehicles. This undoubtedly contributed to our salvation, in that we were not recognized by the Russians.

Suddenly, ahead of us I saw a dense mass of Russian infantry and called to the driver: "Turn slightly to the left!"

Seconds later he spotted them. Machine guns firing, we rolled through the mass of troops from behind, who did not realize that they were being overtaken by a German tank.

Our chance now lay in orienting ourselves to the left, or toward the road. There we must meet our own infantry and lose the Russian tanks.

In the meantime, the rest of the crew—driver, radio operator, gunner—scoured the tank for additional armor-piercing rounds. As soon as one was found, we knocked out another of the T-34s, which overtook us when we halted. It was unbelievable that we had still not been fired upon. All of the experts are certain that this was because none of the Russian tanks yet had dedicated commanders. It was still the gunner who commanded the tank, and he could only see in the direction his cannon was pointing. Had it been otherwise, we would not have survived.

To our displeasure, the Russians were now also heading left toward the road in order to cross the antitank ditch there. We could not understand why the attack had been made in an area guarded by an antitank ditch, even though the Russians must have known it was there. After advancing one thousand meters at most, the impetus of their attack must be broken by this obstacle.

The Russians therefore turned left in an attempt to reach the road and cross the bridge over the antitank ditch. There, however, a simply unbelievable scene was played out.

At the repaired bridge over the antitank ditch our tanks and antitank guns fired at the onrushing enemy. I had managed to roll into cover behind a knocked-out T-34. From there we took part in the battle against the enemy tanks, which were storming toward the bridge from every direction. This made it easier for us and our battalion to find our targets.

Burning T-34s drove into and over one another. It was a total inferno of fire and smoke, and impacting shells and explosions. T-34s blazed, while the wounded tried to crawl away to the sides.

The entire slope was soon littered with burning enemy tanks. We remained behind the smoldering wreck. Just then I heard my loader report: "No more armor-piercing available!"

We had expended our entire supply of armor-piercing ammunition. Now all we had left on board were high-explosive shells, which were ineffective against the heavily-armored T-34s.

From now on we busied ourselves with the destruction of the Soviet infantry forces. This had become more difficult, as these had also overrun our own lines, and we ran the danger of hitting one of our self-propelled guns or the armored personnel carriers of Peiper's battalion.

Initially I held my fire. Then I heard my gunner cry out. I heard him blurt out, "My eye! My eye!!"

We had taken an unlucky hit on the turret precisely at the tiny opening for the gunner's sight. The shell had not penetrated all the way through, but far enough to drive the sight backward with terrific force. My gunner, who had been peering through the sight, suffered a serious head injury as a result.

Our tank was no longer able to continue the fight, so I decided to take it out of the battle and drive across the bridge over the antitank ditch to the rear, in order to try and reassemble any of my company's tanks that had managed to save themselves from the chaos.

We rolled toward the rear. I directed the tank to the back slope of a low rise, where we could remove the gunner and have his injuries seen to.

At that moment my company's maintenance sergeant arrived with a repaired Panzer IV, so that my crew and I needed only to climb aboard in order to rejoin the battle again, fully armed.

For the tank's crew—with the exception of the gunner, whom we needed—it was a bitter pill to have to climb out and hand over their tank to my crew. However, as company commander one needed an experienced crew in view of the numerous tasks that had to be carried out simultaneously. The company commander had to maintain contact with battalion by radio, lead his company and direct his own tank. In addition, it was important to provide fire direction for the gunner.

We rolled across the bridge in our new tank. The force of the Russian attack had been broken in the meantime. The field was strewn with T-34s, all of them burning. From one of my battalion's operations officers, who came over to the tank on foot, I learned that the battalion commander intended to launch a counterattack to regain the high ground. We rolled quickly up the slope. Only a short time before we had driven down it among the Russians. By shortly before midday the high ground was back in our hands.

The losses suffered by my company were astonishingly low. The only two total losses were those I witnessed at the beginning of the attack. The other two companies had suffered no total losses. The artillery battalion and the armored personnel carrier battalion likewise escaped with minimal losses.

Statements from prisoners revealed that the enemy had a third wave of tanks ready; however, this was not committed. Within our main line of resistance there were over one hundred knocked-out Russian tanks [fourteen of those had been destroyed by von Ribbentrop and his crew].

The commanding general, *Obergruppenführer* Hausser, came to the scene of the battle that afternoon, to confirm for himself that the reports of this stunning success were true. It was later reported that he had marked the knocked-out tanks with a piece of chalk and counted them in disbelief.

We had played a part in this defensive success, because we had not been caught napping by the completely unexpected mass attack by the Russian tanks, and were able to engage the enemy from the top of the hill and knock out a number of T-34s straight away, sowing confusion among the enemy.

Furthermore, the noise of battle and the fires from the enemy—and sadly from two of our own—tanks had alerted the Peiper Battalion and the artillery battalion in time.

The courageously fighting grenadiers had kept their nerve in the face of the onrushing mass of enemy tanks and stopped and wiped out the advancing enemy infantry.

The Russian attack had been carried out with great mass and unbelievable stubbornness. Obviously the Russian command intended to master with brute force the threat posed by our forces. With better leadership and by exploiting the element of surprise, this numerically far-superior enemy should have been able to drive back the Peiper armored group, and possibly destroy it completely.

The Russian command must have realized from the outset, that the attack would be decisively hindered by their own anti-tank ditch.

This great defensive success did nothing to change the fact that the tank battle near Prokhorovka, which had seen both sides suffer heavy losses, had ended Operation *Zitadelle*.

The battle near Prokhorovka saw the greatest concentration of tanks assembled during the entire war. Soviet general Rotmistrov, who was known as the "Lion of Prokhorovka," said at the end of the battle: "In view of the situation and the heavy losses, our troops cannot actively carry out any further combat operations."

On 20 July 1943, Rudolf von Ribbentrop was decorated with the Knight's Cross of the Iron Cross. At the time he remarked: "Every one of the men in my tank has earned this decoration. I wear it for my crew."

Eight days later *Obergruppenführer* Paul Hausser became the 261st German soldier to be awarded the Oak Leaves to the Knight's Cross.

On 1 August 1943, Rudolf von Ribbentrop was transferred to participate in the formation of the *Hitlerjugend* SS-Panzer Division.

A Soldier's Path

From Recruit to Participant in the Western Campaign

When war began on 1 September 1939, Rudolf von Ribbentrop enlisted as a recruit in the replacement battalion of the SS-Infantry Regiment *Deutschland* in Munich. The unit's commanding officer was *Standartenführer* Felix Steiner. Steiner was one of the officers within the *Waffen-SS* who had long since realized that a successful unit must be highly mobile. Such mobility would provide an element of surprise in attacking and breaking through an enemy position, and ensure a rapid pursuit of the retreating enemy and the maximum territorial gain. As a result, the regiment's leaders ensured that the unit was motorized to the greatest possible extent.

In October 1939, von Ribbentrop was transferred to the field regiment, which was located in the Protectorate, where he joined 11th Company. At the beginning of April, 11th Company won a regimental field march competition. As a member of the winning company, von Ribbentrop was granted a day's special leave. He requested permission to use the leave to go to Berlin on 30 April for the birthday of his father, Germany's foreign minister, Joachim von Ribbentrop. The request was denied, as the regiment's commanders wished to avoid anything that might be construed as favoritism. The day's special leave was supposed to be used within a radius of three hundred kilometers, and Berlin was significantly farther away.

Von Ribbentrop assumed that his leave had been authorized and approved by Himmler's headquarters and that he could go nevertheless.

On this occasion he was taken aside by a major with the regiment, whom he had got to know. The latter advised him that such an intervention—even if I were not involved—would be damaging to me. I was able to assure him that I knew absolutely nothing about the matter. He believed me, but asked that I be more careful in future, in order to avoid something similar being repeated.

I drove to Berlin and there had two noteworthy experiences. I spent half an hour close to Hitler, when he, as was his custom on the birthdays of his ministers, appeared a half hour before the meal to personally congratulate my father.

It was 30 April, and throughout the Führer's visit I sat at the next table and followed the conversation between Hitler and my father attentively.

Hitler spoke of the European transportation situation and was of the view that after the war the European railroads would have to be converted to the wider Russian gauge, because this would enable the rational transportation of bulk goods. There was not the least anti-Russian sentiment in his words. On the contrary! Hitler spoke approvingly of the self-reliance of the Russian government to have gone to a wider track gauge in the previous century.

In reference to the success of Operation *Weserœbung* in Denmark and Norway (fighting was still going on at Narvik, where General Dietl was hanging on desperately), Hitler spoke of building bridges to link Scandinavia with the mainland, as Europe was going to grow closer out of necessity.

Finally, he spoke with surprising openness about the chances of an offensive in the west. He had concluded that the size of the British Expeditionary Force had been greatly overestimated. From his words it was quite apparent that he intended to attack in the west in the near future.

I myself hoped that the attack would begin soon, as I had heard from my friend Wedel, who was serving in our regiment's 2nd Company, that all suitable leadership candidates were being sent on the next course at the officer candidate school in Braunschweig.

We both hoped that we would nevertheless be able to take part in a campaign in the West, because it was not our intention to go to an officers candidate course without front-line experience and then have to command men who had such experience.

Officer candidate training began with the regiment's 3rd Battalion in Ahlen, Westphalia, on 9 May. When the selected soldiers reported to the instructional officer, they were advised that the training would have to be canceled, as the instructor had been assigned operational duties.

That day von Ribbentrop and his comrades witnessed an extraordinary amount of activity in front of the hotel housing the regimental headquarters. Staff vehicles came and went, and messengers hurried here and there, indicating that some special event must have taken place. What else could it be, but the opening act of the western offensive?

The young soldiers questioned a friend serving with the regimental headquarters and learned that the unit had been placed on the highest level of alert. The pair went to their company, where everyone had likewise been placed at alert readiness. This time it must be serious, and for von Ribbentrop this meant that he was to go to the front and not on an officer candidate course.

The 11th Company was ready to depart at 1400 on 9 May. The vehicles were loaded and each soldier had been issued live ammunition. Nevertheless, the order to move out had not yet been given. The men remained in their quarters, indicating that departure would not begin until after dark.

The alert was given at 0100 on 10 May. The unit departed soon after and von Ribbentrop learned that the officer candidates would be going to the officer candidate school in Braunschweig.

On the occasion of my father's birthday I had summoned the courage to speak to the *Reichsführer-SS*, Heinrich Himmler, who had come to offer his congratulations. I brought up the rumor that I was to be sent to the officer candidate school without first having an opportunity to prove myself in action. I suggested that this would diminish me and my officer school comrades in the eyes of the soldiers with front-line experience and make it difficult for us to exert our authority.

Himmler clapped me on the shoulder and declared dryly: "You will do as you are ordered."

On the evening of 9 May I was so furious that I requested a priority call in order to speak with my father. In spite of all that was going on, my father accepted the call and explained to me sympathetically that he had nothing to say about what went on in the SS and therefore could do little directly. He did say that he would speak to Himmler about the matter at the earliest opportunity, because he understood my argument.

Ribbentrop now recalled a conversation he had had in a *Gasthaus* a few days earlier with the regimental adjutant, *Hauptsturmführer* Reichel, and decided to go to the Hotel Gretenkort and ask for him at the regimental headquarters there. It was 0200 when he met *Hauptsturmführer* Reichel in the hotel. Von Ribbentrop asked him for permission to go along with his unit for the western campaign. Reichel spoke with the regiment's commanding officer, and when he returned explained, "The CO is willing to take you along, but he would like to have your father's consent, in case anything happens to you during the campaign."

Von Ribbentrop declared to him that his father was obviously in complete agreement. *Hauptsturmführer* Reichel laughed and observed: "The regimental commander would like to hear that for himself."

Rudolf von Ribbentrop gave him his father's telephone number and ran back to his quarters to fetch his things. Reichel had indicated that he could go along with the regiment's train units, as 3rd Battalion had already left.

Ribbentrop hurried back to the regimental headquarters with his luggage, arriving just as the CO was leaving the hotel. The latter informed him that his father was not in agreement, and that he would therefore have to decline to take him along.

Felix Steiner slapped the young soldier on the back and said, "Believe me son, you will have plenty of time to get into this war. When you are an officer, come back and see me, because I will probably be forming a new division." Steiner then went to his car and set off in the direction of France.

Rudolf von Ribbentrop attempted to reach his father, but the secretaries would not put him through. So he called his mother and explained that the word would now spread through the regiment that he had been excused because he was the son of a government minister. This disgrace would be disastrous for him and the family. Suddenly, he heard his mother say:

"Speak with him yourself!"

His father took the phone and declared that it was quite fine with him if he participated in the campaign. "I am in complete agreement with you. I cannot order it, but I will speak to Himmler when I get the chance."

It turned out that Steiner's discussion had been with an adjutant of the Reich foreign minister, and that he had informed the young soldier's commanding officer that the Reich minister could not order the SS. This was interpreted to mean that the senior von Ribbentrop was "not in agreement."

Von Ribbentrop had his answer at 0300. The landlord at his quarters fetched him a taxi, and in this the young soldier drove off after his regiment. Traveling by side roads—the main roads were reserved for the movement of troops toward the west—Ribbentrop finally reached Lüdinghausen, where he caught up with the march column of the regiment's antiaircraft battalion. The taxi drove along until it came upon several figures standing beside the lead vehicle of another column.

One of the men was the CO of Ribbentrop's regiment. Von Ribbentrop reported himself present and Felix Steiner observed, "Since you're already here, you might as well stay."

During the drive to the regiment in the car of the regimental medical officer, Dr. Braun, the men saw hundreds of Ju-52 transports overhead. These were carrying German paratroops to their objectives within Fortress Holland.

Ribbentrop received a noisy welcome from his comrades. His company commander, company officer, and senior NCO grinned and joked that the young soldier would probably be ordered back before action began. This was not to be the case.

On the morning of 11 May the *Deutschland* Regiment crossed the Rhine near Rees and marched into Kalkar. That afternoon the German frontier was crossed near Mook. The advance road was lined with smiling and waving Dutchmen. The advance continued toward Hertogenbosch. From there a whole day was spent on a high-speed drive through Holland. The regiment's 10th Company led the way, while 11th Company drove behind the advance battery. When resistance was met at a blown bridge, the advance battery moved forward and into firing position. The battery provided supporting fire as the platoons jumped down from their vehicles and attacked without first pausing to make preparations.

The *Pioniers* had soon repaired the bridge. After they had passed over it, the troops saw the first dead of the campaign lying at the sides of the road. They were French troops.

The next morning 11th Company took over the lead position. The troops were ordered to dismount south of Breda. The platoon to which von Ribbentrop belonged, which was under the command of *Obersturmführer* Koop, was sent ahead along a country road.

"To the right of us lay an open field, to the left a grove of pines. Suddenly, through the barely fifty-meter-wide wood, we saw a French patrol of approximately twenty men, marching in the same direction as we. *Obersturmführer* Koop held his index finger to his lips. On his signal we turned left and moved silently through the grove, until we were about thirty meters from the Frenchmen. As I watched, one of the French soldiers suddenly spotted us. I stared for a few seconds as if frozen. Then I raised my rifle and fired, but hit nothing. At that moment—we had meanwhile fixed bayonets—we fell upon the Frenchmen, shouting loudly, and no more shots were fired. The French surrendered.

"As the only French-speaker, I conducted the initial interrogation of the French troops. These correctly refused to identify their unit and were sent to the rear."

Thus ended von Ribbentrop's first contact with the enemy. The following day the regiment advanced as far as Bergen op Zoom, which lay on the coast. At the edge of the city the regiment's troops came upon some Dutch soldiers who were in the process of pulling out.

"As I had been assigned to the role of messenger, and was thus somewhat more independent than my comrades, I entered a farmhouse that was full of Dutch soldiers. I suddenly found myself facing a lieutenant. From a distance of only a few meters I shouted to him: 'Hands up!' He answered my bluff in fluent German, and informed me that he was the representative of a German firm. He ordered his men to lay down their weapons."

Here von Ribbentrop "found" a 350cc DKW motorcycle in the hands of a Dutch soldier. As a messenger in a motorized unit, the motorcycle suited his needs very well. His platoon leader ordered him to drive west and establish contact with 2nd Battalion, which was on his battalion's left.

I drove in the direction of the 2nd Beveland Peninsula and spotted a sentry on a dike. I overtook *Unterscharführer* Seiler, who suggested it must be one of 2nd Battalion's sentries.

I drove toward the sentry at top speed. When I had approached to thirty meters, I realized, for one thing, that the man was not wearing a camouflage uniform and for another that he was an unarmed Dutchman. He took me for a French soldier, and waved me closer. I waved back, spun the machine around, laid myself across the fuel tank and roared back. Fortunately, the bursts of machine gun fire fired at me by the enemy all missed.

When I again met Seiler, who had meanwhile procured bicycles for himself and his men, we decided to take out the sentry position. We worked our way up to the position in the cover of an intersecting dike and threw a hand grenade over. Then our party—about five men strong—jumped over the dike. We saw the Dutch troops about one hundred meters away, already on the retreat. All we saw of them were their backs.

We then came under fire from a bunker and took cover on the other side of the dike. In the meantime the battalion had arrived. While we lay behind the dike, the Dutch bunker line was taken under covering fire from all weapons.

In the meantime, we had found bicycles for ourselves and began pedaling like crazy toward the west. Our platoon leader, who had in the meantime taken over the company, kept his three platoon messengers with him. We three drove after the motorcycle troops, which we spotted a few kilometers later on a country road. To the left and right the entire area had been flooded by the Dutch by opening the dikes. Just as we came to the position of the motorcycles, a large number of machine guns opened fire from a line of bunkers.

We immediately jumped to the left. Right away we came under fire from that direction and changed position to the other side of the road. Once again we were met by a long burst of machine gun fire. We then jumped down from the road and took cover behind a low mound of gravel in a depression. Hartmann lay in front of me, and my other comrade, whose name I have forgotten, behind me. My head was directly in line with a motorcycle whose driver had been hit. The engine was still running at full speed and within a few moments I was stone-deaf.

When I cautiously raised my head, I saw a bunker ahead, which was firing at us with all weapons. Bursts of machine gun fire slammed into the motorcycle's sidecar. Our chances of survival looked slim. An hour passed, then two. Suddenly, the legs of the regimental adjutant appeared beside the still-running motorcycle, followed by the entire man. He was "armed" with a white flag and walked over toward the bunker. The fire ceased. I jumped up and reported myself present, only to be berated loudly for having placed myself at risk. I therefore set off toward the rear. Behind a bend in the dike, where I had wanted to withdraw to earlier but which had appeared too dangerous, I found the entire company.

The regiment had received news that the Dutch army under General Winkelman had surrendered. Here, too, the Dutch were pulling back.

Obersturmführer Koop sent me to the dressing station, as I had a fragment in my shoulder, which had originated from a bullet which shattered on striking the gravel. My two comrades, who had been pinned down with me by the motorcycle, had both been killed. Sadly I stood before them. They had been killed to my left and right. Fate had spared me.

Moving through the undefended village of Krabbendijk, the regiment quickly reached Verseke, which was likewise free of enemy troops. The canal was to be crossed the next day. *Pioniers* appeared early in the morning and made preparations to cross by inflatable boat. The initial crossing was to be made by three-man boats. The men of the first wave were to establish a bridgehead on the far bank.

In the shelter of the dike *Obersturmführer* Koop called, "Volunteers to me!" He continued, "There are better places ahead. Secure one of them!" Volunteer Ribbentrop was assigned to the first wave, together with one of his comrades and a *Pionier.* The German artillery laid down a brief bombardment. The three men jumped up on a whistle signal, crossed the crest of the dike, and ran down toward the canal. They then jumped into the inflatable boat and paddled for the other side under enemy machine gun fire. Soon they were out of the enemy fire zone. The three soldiers worked their way toward the crest of the dike. They were immediately reinforced by other sections from the company and opened fire on the withdrawing French troops. Staying on the heels of the retreating enemy, the regiment pushed on to Kapelle. There the men were able to procure bicycles and pedaled on in the direction of Goes. As they rounded a corner, they saw two companies of French troops, which were obviously ready to lay down their weapons.

"We walked toward them with one of our section leaders and a *Leutnant* from our platoon. We were met by an older captain who saluted and then surrendered the two units. I spoke with him and asked him to give me the pair of large binoculars hanging around his neck. He wanted to keep them, however, and explained that they were his personal property. I allowed him to keep them, even though such binoculars were military equipment and we were under orders to relieve prisoners of all such equipment immediately.

"A Bavarian corporal was not so impressed by the French captain's protestations, and relieved him of the binoculars. The French prisoners were then sent to the rear."

The *Deutschland* Regiment moved on quickly, and the absence of motor vehicles was keenly felt. The crossing from the Beveland Peninsula to Walcheren was reached. It was a narrow embankment, over which led the road to the island. To the left and right of the embankment the countryside had been flooded. Pedaling along the embankment, the men of 11th Company came upon some French pickets. On account of their camouflage uniforms—another invention of Felix Steiner—the French took the Germans to be British troops.

"We were quite close to the French machine gun position when the enemy realized his mistake and opened fire. The advancing troops leapt into the ditches to the left and right and worked their way back to better cover, sometimes up to their waists in water, intending to rejoin the company, which was now approaching.

"Suddenly an armored car of the regiment's reconnaissance platoon appeared. It roared past at high speed, firing its 2cm cannon in an effort to drive the French from the far end of the embankment to Walcheren and clear an assembly area for the attack on the following morning. The armored car was hit by an enemy antitank gun and pulled back. Nevertheless, the French abandoned their positions and pulled back to the far side of the flooded area."

The *SS-Verfügungsdivision,* which included the main body of the *Deutschland* Regiment, was sent across Belgium through Huy into the corridor that was forming at the coast. Motor transport was now available, alleviating the need for a difficult three-day foot march. The trucks had finally arrived following the capture of Vlissingen.

First, however, the regiment's 3rd Battalion had to reach the embankment leading to Walcheren Island. The battalion met bitter resistance from the French and the attack bogged down. The next morning three He-111 bombers, directed by the air liaison officer, arrived on the scene and bombed the enemy-held end of the embankment. The French defenders wavered and 9th Company stormed forward, capturing the far end of the embankment. Eleventh Company was sent in immediately. As the men of the "Eleventh" advanced, they saw the bodies of their comrades of 9th Company, lying where they had fallen on the slopes of the embankment.

When the *Deutschland* Regiment's 3rd Battalion reached the island, French troops emerged from the surrounding farm buildings and bushes and surrendered. When the commander of a 3.7cm Pak trained his gun on a group of French troops assembled some distance away, *Hauptsturmführer* Gesecke jumped up and smacked his fist against the gun commander's helmet and shouted at him, "We're not gypsies!"

The gun commander protested that this was only a precautionary measure and that he had no intention of firing.

Under the protection of the lone antitank gun, 3rd Battalion pedaled to Vlissingen. On reaching the harbor the men saw the last French ship leaving. It was fired on by the antitank gun but managed to escape.

Rudolf von Ribbentrop wrote in his diary:

> In a house at the harbor we found a table obviously set for a French headquarters staff. We were all very hungry, as regular rations had not reached us for the past several days due to the speed of our advance. After we had eaten our fill we all fell into a deep sleep of exhaustion.
>
> We were awakened early the next morning and set out by truck toward the east. Near Krabbendijk we stopped for a prayer

at the graves of my two messenger comrades who had fallen there. Somewhere in southern Holland we stopped to rest. While we were still washing and shaving we suddenly heard the command: "Fall in!"

Reichsführer-SS Himmler stepped out of a large, three-axled car. I slipped back into the third row to stay out of sight. At the end, however, Himmler's adjutant, *Gruppenführer* Wolf, who was later to become quite well known, called to me.

"Ribbentrop, how's it going?"

Himmler turned abruptly, called me to him and said in a sweet-and-sour voice: "So, you managed to get your own way after all." He then gave me permission to remain with the regiment until 31 May. Just before he left, Himmler said, "But then see to it that you go to Braunschweig!"

After he left we climbed aboard our trucks and resumed our journey into the corridor along the coast. We drove and drove, always heading northwestward. Suddenly a messenger came from up front and called up to me:

"Ribbentrop, your father is up ahead!"

Soon after, I was standing in the farm which was being used by the regimental headquarters staff, facing my father. He had managed to sneak away from Führer headquarters and had driven to the front with his OKW liaison officer, the charming *Oberst* von Geldern.

It was a wonderful day. I was permitted to stay for supper, and afterward we sat in the open and enjoyed the lovely evening. The orders for the next day had been issued, and my father said to me:

"It's going to start again tomorrow!"

As we parted he said to me, "Keep a stiff upper lip!"

How often during the war he was to say that to me when we parted. The last time he spoke those words was at Nuremberg through the screen that separated us during the brief visit I was allowed as a prisoner. Following his sentencing, further visits by me—I was interned in the Dachau camp—were denied.

On my return to the company, I crawled beneath a truck, where we spent the night in a constant state of alert.

An early departure had been ordered for the next morning, but we were kept waiting for some time in our vehicles, ready to move out as soon as the word was given. Then the order came down to dismount, which meant back to waiting again.

The next day we were driven to a point east of Merville, where we got down from our vehicles and attacked toward the north. This time we were up against a British unit with tank support. We had no tanks; *Waffen-SS* units were not to receive these until 1942. There was little chance of winning any prizes with our 3.7cm antitank guns, the so-called "army door-knockers." One of our antitank guns took a direct hit, which killed or wounded the entire crew.

The men raced to their aid. One seriously wounded man, with one arm shattered and many fragment wounds in his body, called to them: "Fight on, comrades!"

This impressed me deeply. We were hardly veteran warriors; I had just turned nineteen a few days earlier.

The commander of 14th Company, who had led his antitank guns forward, appeared in his Kübelwagen. Ignoring the enemy fire, he evacuated the wounded in his own vehicle and then raced over to the nearest antitank gun to direct fire from there. He did this so skillfully that the British tanks withdrew. The battalion worked its way up to the canal and crossed in inflatable boats. In the face of resistance it fought its way past Merville as far as the road leading into the town from the east and blocked it. During the night the battalion's machine guns shot up a large number of British vehicles attempting to escape Merville.

The next day we set out once more and crossed the road in the face of light resistance. The road itself was a scene of desolation. Shot-up vehicles were everywhere, and fallen British soldiers lay at the sides of the road and in the ditches.

When it became evening we dug in along a hedgerow. Here we found an old German steel helmet from the First World War. We were fighting in Flanders, whose soil contained many such finds. In the distance was the notorious Kemmelberg, several times the scene of heavy fighting, where so many French and German soldiers had been killed.

The next morning *Unterscharführer* Kratochwil took a patrol to scout in the direction of an abandoned village. I was one of those who volunteered for this mission. Kratochwil led the patrol coolly and skillfully, so that we were able to reach the village without incident, where it was determined that the British had withdrawn.

As we made our way back, we were significantly more light-hearted than we had been on the way in. Along the way we encountered some army riflemen who had approached the village from the other side. We were amazed that the German side was not pressing harder and stronger after the enemy. The British Expeditionary Corps was on the retreat, and the faster it was pursued, the more British would be captured and prevented from returning to their island. This would have to be a decided advantage in a planned landing in England, which was already being talked of.

The company had taken several prisoners, and I received orders to convey them to the rear. At the same time I learned that my stay with the regiment was coming to an end. The thirty-first of May was the day I was to go to Braunschweig. Contrary to my hopes, the date had not been forgotten. I later learned that in a difficult argument with Himmler, my father had been forced to promise to allow me to be recalled.

I set off with my twelve to fifteen prisoners and deliberated as to what I could do if they simply ran away or decided to make me their prisoner.

I had them march in a double line and walked along behind them. They marched in good order and I arrived with my column at the regimental command post. There I reported to the adjutant and learned from him that, unfortunately, there was no transport available and that I would have to stay with my company. In the hope of being "forgotten" I marched back to my company, but the next morning I was fetched by a car from the motor pool.

I arrived at the Junkerschule in Braunschweig as a *Sturmmann* decorated with the Iron Cross, Second Class and the Wound Badge in Black. At the end of the campaign against Holland eight men from my company had been promoted to this rank for bravery in the face of the enemy. It was, as I remember, the most satisfying promotion of my career. One of the *Sturmmänner* spontaneously took the chevron from his uniform and gave it to me, so that I could sew it on straight away.

Rudolf von Ribbentrop arrived at the Junkerschule in Braunschweig three weeks late.

"I had done it. No one could say of me that I had been transferred to the Junkerschule instead of seeing action because I was the son of a minister.

"The problem of 'kinship liability,' as I called it, began not after 1945, but was always there, and had to be met with skill and—on occasion—with stolidity."

From the Junkerschule to the Far North

Rudolf von Ribbentrop passed through the platoon leader course in Braunschweig with enthusiasm, demonstrating his suitability for the role of platoon leader. The course, which began on 1 September 1940, was run in a peacetime fashion. In February 1941, von Ribbentrop was promoted to *Standartenoberjunker.* This was followed, on 20 April, by his promotion to *Untersturmführer.* At the same time he was named a platoon leader in the 1st Company of Reconnaissance Battalion *Nord.* This battalion was part of *SS-Kampfgruppe Nord,* which was formed in March 1941 and later evolved into the 6th *Gebirgsdivision Nord.*

The battle group was initially under the command of the headquarters for the Salla sector. It was later sent to *Gebirgskorps Norwegen* (Mountain Corps Norway) under Gen. Eduard Dietl. Its transfer into the command of *Gebirgskorps Norwegen* was mentioned in the corps headquarters' activity report of May 1941, with special reference to the fact that the battle group's 10th Company was to be the only unit to make the trip overland, requiring three days to make the 125-kilometer journey from Lakselv to Ifjord.

When the eastern campaign began early on the morning of 22 June 1941, *Gebirgskorps Norwegen* moved into the Petsamo area. Not until after 25 June, when Soviet aircraft raided Helsinki, Turku, Joensuu, Heinola, and other cities in inner Finland, did the Finnish high command move into its new headquarters in Mikkeli, from where Field Marshal von Mannerheim had commanded the Finnish forces in the First war of Liberation and the recent "winter war" against the Soviet Union.

On 26 June, Finnish president Ryti broadcast to the Finnish people. He explained that following the treacherous bombardment of Finnish cities, a state of war existed between Finland and the USSR. Thus Finnish and German soldiers had once more become brothers in arms. In an order of the day to Finland's armed forces, Field Marshal von Mannerheim said: "We are now allied with Germany and as comrades in arms are launching a crusade against our enemy, in order to create a secure future for Finland."

Young von Ribbentrop proved himself as a platoon leader in action in the far north and was awarded the Finnish Freedom Cross, Fourth Class. He was wounded once again on 2 September, when a bullet fractured a bone in his left forearm. Von Ribbentrop was hospitalized in Hohenlynchen until February 1942. He was granted a short home leave, after which he was to report to the panzer battalion of the SS-Division *Leibstandarte,* which was just being formed.

As a result of this move the young soldier finally found his true home. Initially, however, he served as leader of the battalion's motorcycle reconnaissance platoon. Later he became the leader of the 3rd Company's 1st Platoon, before serving with regimental headquarters as operations officer in order to gain an insight into staff work. Finally he reached his ultimate position as 1st Platoon Leader in the panzer battalion's 6th Company. This was the position he held when the division was sent into the Kharkov area on the Eastern Front in February 1943.

His actions and the success he achieved have been described in the opening chapters of this account. We will now turn to the final part of his biography, which describes von Ribbentrop's subsequent career.

Formation and Training of the 12th SS-Panzer Division *Hitlerjugend*

Following his transfer to the 12th SS-Panzer Division, which had been formed as a panzer grenadier division in the summer of 1943, and which in the fall was being reorganized into a panzer division, Rudolf von Ribbentrop was reunited with many of his old comrades in Mailly-le-Camp, near Châlons-sur-Marne.

The men were NCOs, junior officers, and cadre personnel from his old division, the *Leibstandarte*. However, the majority of the arriving soldiers were young men who had just completed their basic training with the Panzer Training and Replacement Regiment in Bitsch, Lothringen.

The new division's panzer regiment was commanded by *SS-Obersturmführer* Max Wünsche. The division's commanding officer was *SS-Brigadeführer* Fritz Witt, who until now had commanded one of the two panzer grenadier regiments of the *Leibstandarte* Division.

The panzer regiment's 1st Battalion was under the command of *Hauptsturmführer* Arnold Jürgensen. He, too, had come from the *Leibstandarte* and shortly after his arrival was promoted to the rank of *Sturmbannführer.*

Following his arrival, *Obersturmführer* Ribbentrop conducted two junior officer training courses before taking over the panzer regiment's 3rd Company on 1 December 1943. Von Ribbentrop said of this period:

> During the formation of the 12th Panzer Regiment *Hitlerjugend* all the commanders and company commanders were keenly aware that the only way to avoid difficulties was through the maintenance of strict discipline.
>
> We were certain, and this was confirmed with the arrival of the first soldiers, that we would be dealing with enthusiastic volunteers. We therefore tried to use entirely new methods.
>
> The training was intensive. The underlying theme, toward which everyone strived, was:
>
> "What you fail to learn in training will cost blood in the real thing!"
>
> We succeeded in instilling a sportive spirit into the training, where the greatest emphasis was placed on weapons training and combat under the most difficult conditions.
>
> The solid officer and NCO corps in my company (likewise in all the others) had a great deal to do with the enthusiasm of the soldiers. The need for good comradeship was obvious.

As there were only limited numbers of Panzer III, IV, and Panther tanks available at first, the training of tank crews was difficult. Each company was allocated a few hours at a time in the available tanks.

On 10 December, Reich Youth Leader Artur Axmann, who had assumed the role of the division's patron, arrived in Mailly-le-Camp for an inspection of the 12th SS-Panzer Regiment. The 3rd Company took part in the march-past.

Another visitor was the inspector general of panzer troops, Heinz Guderian, who came to witness a demonstration of the new Goliath remote-control tank.

In January 1944 followed the transfer of the 12th SS-Panzer

Regiment to the Beverloo training grounds in Leopoldsburg, Belgium. There, on 17 January, the regiment's 3rd Company reached its authorized strength.

The men of the training company, which was likewise commanded by von Ribbentrop, were from Dondangen in Latvia. Before January ended the company was moved to Winterslag, while the regiment was housed in Hasselt. A training exercise on 6 February with loaned Panzer IVs raised questions as to what type of equipment the regiment's 1st Battalion was to receive. A review board was established, which included Inspector General of Panzer Troops Guderian, the commanding general of I SS-Panzer Corps, *Obergruppenführer* Sepp Dietrich, the division commander, and all available battalion commanders. Its findings were: "1st Battalion will be equipped with the Panzer V Panther." *Generaloberst* Guderian ordered the delivery of twenty Panthers, ten of which were taken on strength by 3rd Company.

The battalion was now in a position to push ahead with its tank training. The training program included maintenance, range practice, and cross-country exercises. In addition, there was special training for commanders, drivers, gunners, loaders, and radio operators.

Division maneuvers were held on 15 March, the highlight of which was an armored attack with live ammunition. Observing the maneuvers were the Reich youth leader and the inspector general of panzer troops. Sepp Dietrich also took advantage of this opportunity to see one of his divisions in action.

To France—Wounded Again

On 7 April 1944 the *Hitlerjugend* Division received its marching orders. The following day 3rd Company entrained in Houthalen. The company was going to Normandy. During a stop at the Belgian border the company commander's German shepherd "Bodo" went missing. Like the troops, he had been stretching his legs, and when the train suddenly pulled out he had failed to return. A search was initiated.

At the next station *Unterscharführer* Hermani was ordered to go back and told not to return without the dog. Hermani returned fourteen days later without the dog. He was greeted not only by the company commander, but by "Bodo" as well, who had found his own way back to his master.

Following this minor episode the company was billeted in the village of Harcourt, near Le Neubourg. The mayor of the village was the First World War general Chretienne. He made a plea to the local population: "Treat the German soldier with the respect he deserves. Their company commander is the son of the German foreign minister von Ribbentrop and a wearer of the highest German decoration for bravery, the Knight's Cross. Treat him also with the respect and deference he deserves."

This appeal achieved the desired results. At no time were there any incidents or reprisals in Harcourt.

In May the "Third" received the rest of its tanks and tracked and wheeled vehicles. Instead of the planned four platoons, each with four tanks, three platoons were formed with five tanks each. In addition there were the tanks of the company commander and leader of the company headquarters personnel, so that the 3rd Company, like the regiment's other companies, had seventeen tanks on strength.

On 3 June, *Obersturmführer* von Ribbentrop was traveling between Le Neubourg and Évreux when his car was attacked by low-flying aircraft. Von Ribbentrop described the incident:

On 3 June the division held a radio communications exercise. As I had been assigned to 2nd Battalion as an umpire, I set out to drive to the battalion. The exercise began in the evening and lasted throughout the night.

The exercise ended late in the afternoon the next day. I drove home from Évreux along the Route National. As I was dead tired, I placed my driver Schulz behind the wheel and settled in next to him in the small Volkswagen to take a nap.

I sat up suddenly when I heard the unmistakable crack of machine gun fire. I turned around. A Spitfire raced toward us, all guns firing. He was out to get us! Instinctively I ducked down as far as possible and shouted to Schulz:

"Stop!—It's a fighter-bomber!"

Just then I felt a light blow in my back, and from that moment on I could feel nothing below my shoulder blades. Immediately I realized that I must have suffered a spinal injury, resulting in partial paralysis. The fighter flew past and began to turn for another attack to finish us off.

I called to Schulz: "Pull me into the ditch!"

But before he could do so, the fighter was on us again. It was not only most impressive to lay on the asphalt road and see and hear the enemy's machine gun fire pass about a meter from my head and spatter into the car and the road, but it was also a helpless feeling to face the attack while totally defenseless.

Fortunately we were not hit again. The Volkswagen had been riddled but did not catch fire. The Spitfire turned to make a third attack. Schulz summoned all his strength and managed to drag me into the ditch just in time, and we survived the fighter's third pass.

I was bleeding from a gaping wound in my upper torso. As a hunter, I knew that I had suffered a lung wound and thought to myself: "Now it's all over!" With my entire body paralyzed and a lung wound besides, there was probably little that could be done.

After some time, however, I began to feel a prickling sensation in my toes, and after a few more minutes of suspense full feeling and movement returned to my limbs. These were typical symptoms of a wound where the spinal column is only grazed, paralyzing the nerves for a time.

When the fighter had disappeared, we drove as fast as we could in the riddled Volkswagen to the dressing station in Le Neubourg.

When Ernst Schulz returned to his unit, the story of the wounding of the company commander spread like wildfire. The entire company was in shock.

After preliminary treatment, Rudolf von Ribbentrop was taken to Bernay hospital for further attention. There he was assured by Dr. Daniel that his back wound was not fatal. The next day von Ribbentrop, who was already feeling much better, learned that the invasion was expected to begin the following day.

Ribbentrop wrote: "The night of 5/6 June was a bad one and I slept poorly. There was a great deal of activity in the air, which I had not noticed the night before. At 0500 in the morning the sister came into my room and said: 'The invasion has begun!' "

The Invasion—The *Hitlerjugend* Division on the Attack and in Defense

Early on the morning of 6 June the *Hitlerjugend* Division received the order "Class 1 Alert!" The panzer regiment's marching orders did not arrive until 1130, however. 1st Battalion assembled in Le Neubourg before setting out through Thibouville and Bernay to Orbec. Massive numbers of enemy fighter-bombers appeared, attacking anything that moved. To continue would have meant heavy losses, so the companies took cover in fruit groves and behind heavily wooded hills. The 3rd Company pulled back into the Chateau de Launey near Orbec. That evening part of the combat echelon drove through St. Pierre-sur-Dives, past Falaise, then crossed the Orne near Thury-Harcourt and took cover in a defile near Maizet. On the evening of the 7th and the morning of the 8th the tanks that had participated in division maneuvers on 4 and 5 June turned up. Now the company was complete. The combat echelon, led by *Hauptmann* Lüdemann, moved forward to take up its position in the regiment. A German armored force, comprising the 12th SS-Panzer Regiment and the 22nd Panzer Regiment of the 21st Panzer Division, was preparing to attack. However, orders for the attack were not forthcoming. Each unit was now to attack independently.

On 9 June the 12th SS-Panzer Regiment's 3rd Company reached a valley near Le-Bourg-Rots. An attack was to be launched from this assembly point at noon.

Here there was a happy reunion between *Obersturmführer* von Ribbentrop and his company. Ribbentrop had taken advantage of his transfer from Bernay to Germany to drop in on his unit at the front. When he learned of the attack plan, he warned that the company's right flank was too weakly protected. Nevertheless, the attack was so ordered by *Hauptmann* Lüdemann, an experienced panzer company commander.

The company drove to Norrey, its right flank protected by the Caen-Cherbourg railway embankment. When the lead platoon under *Untersturmführer* Stagge left the protection of the embankment it was badly shot up by well-concealed antitank guns. All five of the platoon's tanks were lost as well as the panzers of *Untersturmführer* Alban and Krahl. Almost all of the tanks burned out. The advance by the "Third" was halted. After the loss of seven tanks, *Hauptmann* Lüdemann was forced to break off the attack. One member of the "Third" distinguished himself that day: *Medic Rottenführer* Siegfried Goose, who drove back and forth along the advance road in a motorcycle-sidecar combination driven by *Unterscharführer* Harting under enemy artillery fire until all the wounded had been recovered. Sadly, Goose was killed by a burst of machine gun fire after completing his incredible rescue mission. The cost of this day's fighting was seven tanks lost and eighteen men killed.

Rudolf von Ribbentrop was forced to watch the attack helplessly. As he stood beside the company commander's tank, which was driven by driver Bunke, the vehicle was hit by an antitank round. The shell did not penetrate, but the tank began to burn. (The Panther was very prone to catching fire, the cause being its hydraulic steering fluid.)

In spite of his serious wounds and orders to return to Germany, von Ribbentrop assumed command of the company from *Hauptmann* Lüdemann, who had suffered a nervous breakdown.

The 3rd Company moved into the village of Fontenay-les-Pesnel. All of the company's tanks suffered mechanical breakdowns and the unit was transferred back to Harcourt. There the men of the company erected a memorial to their fallen comrades.

By 1 July the company was again fully operational. *Obersturmführer* von Ribbentrop reported to the battalion command post in Esquay, near Maltot. From there on 5 July the 3rd Company rolled back into action, and on the evening of the sixth was in positions near the Ardenne Monastery, not far from Caen. The following evening several hundred enemy bombers attacked the city of Caen, reducing it to a pile of smoking rubble. In addition to heavy high-explosive bombs, the bombers also dropped phosphorous canisters. The next day the 3rd Company's train was caught by a surprise artillery bombardment. During the night of 7/8 July the combat echelon moved into a security position west of the monastery in the direction of Authi-Franqueville. Here the 3rd Company and its commander, who had recovered completely from his wounds, struck the enemy a hard blow. But first the overall situation as seen by the division commander and the commander of the 25th SS-Panzer Grenadier Regiment, whose command post was in the Ardenne Monastery.

The commander of the 25th SS-Panzer Grenadier Regiment was *Standartenführer* Milius. From his command post in the Ardenne Monastery, which was under heavy artillery fire, Milius, who was already wounded, spoke by radio with the commander of his 3rd Battalion. The latter pleaded for assistance, as the village of Buron, which his battalion was defending, had been surrounded by the enemy and the first Canadian tanks were about to roll into the village. Just then the division commander arrived, followed soon after by General Eberbach, commander in chief of the 5th Panzer Army. Kurt Meyer recalled:

"All available tanks were sent toward Buron. The attack failed to get through. From the monastery church tower I watched the tank battle as it surged back and forth. Both sides suffered heavy losses. Then, suddenly, enemy tanks appeared from Authi, heading straight for Ardenne.

"The von Ribbentrop company with its fifteen Panthers was deployed against this mass of enemy tanks. The Panthers shot up the enemy armor and halted its advance. Von Ribbentrop had saved the command post. The last enemy tank was destroyed only one hundred meters west of Ardenne."

The following is a description of the action by von Ribbentrop himself:

Our attack began the morning after the enemy air attack on Caen. After several hours of fighting Canadian troops entered the village of Buron. My company was moved forward from the Ardenne Monastery for a counterattack with the APC battalion. Our objective was to relieve the panzer grenadiers under *Hauptmann* Steger fighting near, and particularly in Buron, and regain possession of the village.

At the same time we received orders to send a platoon to engage enemy tanks which had appeared to the left of Buron.

We were unable to establish radio contact with the armored personnel carriers. Consequently, the company set out alone, with one platoon on the left and two platoons on the right. The village limits of Buron were reached in two quick dashes, with one platoon providing cover in each case. There we destroyed several enemy tanks, and were then faced with the problem of entering the village, which was surrounded by thick hedgerows.

The commander of the armored personnel carriers appeared beside my tank. Since radio communications were impossible, I stood up in my turret hatch and shouted to him, asking where his armored personnel carriers were.

The infantry and the protection they provided against enemy tank-killing squads in the close quarters of the village were an absolute necessity before our tanks entered Buron.

The APC commander, an Army *Hauptmann,* shrugged his

shoulders. Obviously he, too, had no radio communications with his battalion.

Just then a well-camouflaged Canadian antitank gun must have opened fire, because two or three tanks to my right went up in flames one after another. There was nothing left to do but pull back to our starting position and support the hard-pressed infantry from there.

The company's remaining tanks spent the rest of the day under heavy artillery fire around the monastery. Several duels with enemy tanks took place, which prevented the enemy from advancing any farther and enabled the monastery to be held until it had to be abandoned soon afterward.

This ends von Ribbentrop's report, which made little mention of the company's major achievement and its total of enemy tanks destroyed. *Unterscharführer* Freiberg of the "Third" provided a somewhat more dramatic description of the events that day:

We crossed the open field to the wall around the village of Buron at high speed. As we drove by an opening in the wall there were suddenly two explosions, and Sepp Trattnick's and another tank burst into flames. We immediately opened fire with both machine guns on the opening in the wall. I saw some movement there and then a flash from the muzzle of an antitank gun. The shell struck our gun mantlet and the solid projectile ended up in the fighting compartment. Our gunsight was smashed and the gunner was wounded in the face. I received several fragments in my left arm.

The turret crew bailed out at once, and, because of the heavy machine gun fire, took cover behind the Panther. My radio operator and driver had not bailed out, and were still calmly sitting in the tank, whose engine was still running.

I therefore jumped back up onto the tank and grasped the throat microphone, which was dangling over the side of the turret. I called to my driver: "Back up."

We backed up in the direction of Ardenne. After a few meters the antenna mount, on which I had braced myself with one foot, was shot away, as was my boot heel. After driving five hundred meters we reached our infantry and found my gunner and loader already there. When we reached the Ardenne Monastery we were attacked by fighter-bombers with rockets and machine guns.

Despite its losses, the 8th of July had been a successful day for 3rd Company. It had destroyed twenty-seven enemy tanks as well as eight Bren gun carriers and four antitank guns. *Untersturmführer* von Ribbentrop contributed to this total by knocking out several enemy tanks. During the night of 9/10 July the "Third" pulled back across the Orne River with the remaining panzer grenadiers of the *Hitlerjugend* Division. The 12th SS-Division had been unable to prevent the fall of Caen; however, it made sure that the enemy's hopes of capturing the city on X-day plus one were foiled. As a result of the efforts of the *Hitlerjugend* and *Panzer-Lehr* Divisions, the battle for Caen lasted over a month.

At the end of July, Rudolf von Ribbentrop was forced to enter the hospital in Bernay with jaundice. His accomplishments in the Normandy combat zone were acknowledged with the award of the German Cross in Gold. In addition, he received the Panzer Assault Badge for having participated in at least twenty-five tank attacks, which he had earned some time before.

On 1 September, von Ribbentrop returned to his regiment, where he assumed the position of regimental adjutant.

The Ardennes Offensive and the End in Austria

When the Ardennes offensive began, *Obersturmführer* von Ribbentrop was regimental adjutant. On 20 December he was wounded in the mouth by a shell fragment. As this was his fifth wound, he was awarded the Wound Badge in Gold. He returned to the division at the beginning of 1945. On 2 January the American 6th Armored Division, reinforced by the 69th Tank Battalion, launched an attack near Bastogne with its 68th Tank Battalion. The attack was beaten off by *Nebelwerfer* rocket launchers and assault guns near Arlencourt. Eight American tanks were knocked out and the rest withdrew under cover of smoke.

On the left, the men of the American 50th Infantry Battalion had set out at 0925 and captured the village of Obourcy. There they came under fire from German field guns and *Nebelwerfers* from the Bouncy area. Not until 1500 did the Americans break through the positions held by the 78th *Volksgrenadier* Regiment (of the 26th *Volksgrenadier* Division) to Michamps. The tanks of the First Battalion, 12th SS-Panzer Regiment *Hitlerju-*

gend, led by *Obersturmführer* Rudolf von Ribbentrop, together with the Division Escort Company, were sent to counterattack and restore the situation. For the first time since Normandy, Rudolf von Ribbentrop again led his tanks against the enemy. The panzers rolled into Michamps and Obourcy and drove the enemy back. By evening both villages were firmly in the hands of von Ribbentrop's battle group. His tanks had destroyed nine enemy tanks and several antitank guns as well as other weapons.

During the night the Division Escort Company sent out patrols to the west, south, and east.

An enemy attack against Arloncourt and Wardin was repulsed and fifteen tanks of the American 15th Tank Battalion were destroyed.

On 2 January 1945, headquarters I SS-Panzer Corps took command of a sector in XXXXVII Panzer Corps area which had been selected for an attack ordered by *Generalfeldmarschall* Model. The 340th *Volksgrenadier* Division and the 12th-SS Panzer Division *Hitlerjugend* were to attack east of the Noville-Bastogne road, exploiting the extended wooded areas between the Longchamps-Bastogne and Noville-Bastogne roads. The 340th *Volksgrenadier* Division was attacked by the American 501st Parachute Regiment while it was still making preparations near Bois Jacques. The Americans penetrated into the forest, but their attack was halted by a German counterattack.

The 12th SS-Panzer Division was to attack from the area south and southwest of Bourcy, with its right wing following the Bourcy-Bastogne rail line. Its objective was the northeast entrance to Bastogne, the city that the *Panzer-Lehr* Division had come within a hair of taking shortly after the beginning of Operation *Wintergewitter* (as the Ardennes offensive was named). However, Allied troops had dug in there and turned back every attack.

The division's formation for the attack was as follows: on the right the 26th Panzer Grenadier Regiment with attached 12th Antitank Battalion, and on the left the 25th Panzer Grenadier Regiment. The 12th Panzer Regiment had been instructed to assist both attack groups.

The 12th Panzer Regiment's 1st Battalion was now led by *Obersturmführer* Rudolf von Ribbentrop, who had succeeded the fallen *Sturmbannführer* Jürgensen. Jürgensen had been awarded the Knight's Cross on 16 October 1944 for his actions during the Allied invasion.

The *Hitlerjugend* Division began moving into its assembly area on 1 January. By 3 January all of the units had assembled at their jumping-off positions.

The attack began at 1400 but made little progress. A resumption of the attack was ordered for 4 January. Once again the attack forces gained little ground.

Another attempt on 5 January so exhausted the strength of I SS-Panzer Corps, especially of the 1st SS-Panzer Division *Leibstandarte,* that it was no longer able to attack on a broad front. Von Ribbentrop and his battalion had tried several times to achieve a decisive breakthrough that would open the way for the panzer grenadiers. However, in the face of the enemy's overpowering superiority in numbers and weapons, it was impossible to expand minor successes into breakthroughs because the enemy always moved fresh forces into the gap and sealed it off.

Neither the bravery of the panzer crews nor the bravado with which they carried out their attacks—in spite of the limited numbers of tanks available—could change the outcome of the Ardennes offensive. The German forces had suffered heavy losses that could no longer be made good.

The commander in chief west's daily report from 8 January 1945 stated, "Following initial success our attack east of Bastogne failed to progress any farther."

This brought to an end the operations by the 12th SS-Panzer Division in the Ardennes. The division was pulled out of the line and assembled in Dyfeld, fifteen kilometers southwest of St. Vith. Soon afterward it was sent to Cologne. The division was now part of the 6th SS-Panzer Army, and together with the *Leibstandarte* Division formed the I SS-Panzer Corps. The panzer army also included the II SS-Panzer Corps, which included the 2nd SS-Panzer Division *Das Reich* and the 9th SS-Panzer Division *Hohenstaufen.*

Commander in chief of the 6th SS-Panzer Army, which was now to be employed in Hungary, was *SS-Oberstgruppenführer* Sepp Dietrich.

Commanding the 12th SS-Panzer Regiment was *Obersturmbannführer* Gross. The official commander of the 1st (Mixed) Panzer Battalion was *Obersturmführer* von Ribbentrop. This battalion was now exchanged for 2nd Battalion, which was commanded by *Hauptsturmführer* Hans Siegel. Siegel had won the Knight's Cross on 23 August 1944 as the commander of 8th Company.

It was a heavy blow for von Ribbentrop to learn that the 2nd, 4th, 7th, and 8th Companies, which had been brought up to strength at the troop training grounds and had not participated in the Ardennes campaign, were to take over his battalion's remaining Panthers and Panzer IVs. Von Ribbentrop and the 1st, 3rd, 5th, and 6th Companies, and Headquarters, 1st Battalion, which had fought in the Ardennes, were sent to Fallingbostel to be rested and brought back up to strength. As a result, only the regiment's 2nd Battalion saw action in Hungary. On 10 February 1945 it had at its disposal forty-four Panthers and thirty-eight Panzer IVs, of which fourteen had been taken over from 1st Battalion.

The Final Weeks of the War—The End

The tankless crews of 1st Battalion, 12th SS-Panzer Regiment under the command of Rudolf von Ribbentrop, who had by now been promoted to *Hauptsturmführer,* had already been sent to Hungary with 5th Company under the command of *Obersturmführer* Gasch. There they participated in the battles north of Lake Balaton. The 6th Company, commanded by *Hauptsturmführer* Götz, followed somewhat later. Traveling via Vienna by truck, the company reached the area around Laaben on 12 April and was placed under the command of Battle Group von Reitzenstein.

An attack by the battle group recaptured the main line of resistance formerly held by the 560th Heavy Antitank Battalion and it dug in on a line from Pamet to Höfer (two kilometers northeast of Höfer).

Headquarters, 1st Battalion, 12th SS-Panzer Regiment under von Ribbentrop and the battalion's 1st and 3rd Companies entrained at Fallingbostel on 1 April 1945. On 8 April they arrived in Wilhelmsburg, eleven kilometers south of St. Pölten. After detraining, the panzer companies, which were without tanks, were converted to infantry companies. The train units were issued Hungarian horse-drawn wagons. The entire battalion had only a few MG42 machine guns, as well as a few MG34s, which were the tank version with central supports. The rest of the men were armed with long-model Karabiner 98 rifles. The platoon leaders and some section leaders still had their submachine guns.

During the night of 12/13 April the battalion was loaded aboard trucks and driven to Laaben. There it relieved 3rd Company, which was stationed near Forsthof. This company, which was commanded by *Hauptsturmführer* Minow, was composed of ethnic Germans. The Headquarters Company was led by *Untersturmführer* Jauch, while *Untersturmführer* Schulz commanded 1st Company.

During the night *Hauptsturmführer* von Ribbentrop took command of the entire Forsthof-Audorf sector. In addition to his own units, von Ribbentrop had under his command a flak battle group near Hinterholz and several smaller units.

The panzer crews fought well in their new infantry role, repelling a series of enemy breakthrough attempts. Rudolf von Ribbentrop was constantly at the front with his men. On 21 April, Battle Group Gross launched an attack to capture a ridge. The attack bogged down in the face of an enemy antitank front. Several more of von Ribbentrop's longtime comrades were killed here. Von Ribbentrop and his men took over a line of security extending from Schreiberhof, only five hundred meters south of the ridge, through Lower Götzhof and Upper Götzhof as far as Kuminerer, 2.6 kilometers southwest of the disputed ridge.

After Battle Group Gross had pulled back to its starting positions, von Ribbentrop's forces were ordered by *Gruppenführer* Hermann Priess to recapture Kaumburg, which had likewise been lost, and close the gap between the division and Battle Group Gross. As the bridge near Gerichtsberg had been blown, the tanks that had been sent from the west for Battle Group Gross were unable to reach the unit. The commanding general held *Obersturmführer* Gross responsible and ordered him replaced.

Command of the entire battle group was now passed to *Hauptsturmführer* von Ribbentrop. *Hauptsturmführer* Minow took over 1st Battalion in his place.

On 25 April, the 25th Grenadier Regiment, under the command of Battle Group Reitzenstein, and Battle Group von Ribbentrop were ordered to hold the northward-facing line of security. The Soviets attacked several times with tank support and each time were driven back. In crisis situations, even on foot, von Ribbentrop's tankers refused to give an inch.

On 27 and 28 April the *Hitlerjugend* Division battle group moved into a new area of operations via Kalte Kuchel, Hohenberg, Schrambach, and Tragidist. On 29 April the division relieved *Oberst* Trettner's 10th Parachute Division. It was there, on 2 May, that the men of the division heard the news of Hitler's death and the proclamation by *Grossadmiral* Dönitz, his successor. The *Hitlerjugend* received orders to assemble in the Kilb area and there place itself at the disposal of the 6th SS-Panzer Army. The von Ribbentrop battalion—*Untersturmführer* Gross had once again taken command of the regiment, as it had been proved that he had been completely guiltless in the destruction of the bridge—was the only unit to remain in its old positions, providing the rearguard for the division's withdrawal which began early on the morning of 3 May. When all of the other units had withdrawn, the battalion carried out a fighting withdrawal. This brought to an end operations by the 12th SS-Panzer Division *Hitlerjugend*. In the period 10 February to 8 May the division lost 4,376 men killed or wounded. Thirty-two Panzer IVs and thirty-five Panthers had been lost trying to hold off the avalanche of Soviet armor. On the last day of the war the division's operational tank strength was six Panzer IVs and nine Panthers.

On 7 May the division, less the von Ribbentrop battalion, which again stayed behind as rearguard, moved into the Steinkirchen area. There the division's leaders learned from the chief of staff of the panzer army, *Gruppenführer* Fritz Kraemer, that *Generaloberst* Jodl had signed the document of surrender in U.S. Army headquarters in Reims, and that hostilities would cease at 2400 on 9 May.

Brigadeführer Hugo Kraas, the last commander of the 12th SS-Panzer Division, thanked the men of the division for their loyalty and readiness for action and asked them to continue to conduct themselves with honor in memory of their fallen and imprisoned comrades, and to help in the reconstruction of their battered and bleeding Fatherland. He concluded with the words: "We begin the bitterest walk of our lives as soldiers with heads held high. We march toward our destiny with tranquillity. We have fought bravely and honorably in every theater of the war. Nevertheless, the war has been lost.

"Long live Germany!"

The following is the final impressive experience described in von Ribbentrop's writings: "My order to the companies of the battalion on the night of 8 May was: 'Force march to the village of Texing, get aboard the remaining train vehicles and cross the demarcation zone to the Americans at the Enns.'

"It was *Untersturmführer* Post's job to remove all unnecessary ballast from the train vehicles.

"At 0000 on 8 May my companies moved out and crossed the point of departure on a small road. I waited for them there. When they had all passed through I waited for the security teams. When these passed by I was left alone under the clear night sky with my driver and messenger. We were all lost in thoughts of what lay ahead of us. In any case I had sent the last of my men ahead of me."

A Final Word from Rudolf von Ribbentrop

The greatest test for the morale of a soldier is at the moment of defeat. This company (3rd Company, 12th SS-Panzer Division *Hitlerjugend),* like all the veteran units of the *Waffen-SS,* entered captivity with the dignity, calmness and self-confidence of an elite unit.

We can say with pride, that at no moment during the war years or in those that awaited us afterward, did we surrender our dignity.

The following words have been true for us and our dead comrades right up to the present day: They can treat us like dogs, but they cannot degrade us.

Comradeship is a simple, but at the same time, a great word. It was tested and proved countless times during the war. Our mutual comradeship was something which developed from hard work and effort.

At this point I wish to express my thanks for the comradeship shown me by all the soldiers of my 3rd Company, which it was my honor to form and command for a year.

Thanks also to all my other comrades in the various units in which I was allowed to serve and fight.

Military Career

1 September 1939:	Recruit with the replacement battalion of the SS-Regiment *Deutschland* in Munich-Freimann.
October 1939:	Transfer to the field regiment in the Protectorate. 11th Company.
10–30 May 1940:	Participation in western campaign in Holland and France. Promotion to *Sturmmann* for bravery in the face of the enemy.
	Wounded for the first time: fragment in right upper arm. Award of Iron Cross, Second Class. Infantry Assault Badge. Wound Badge in Bronze.
1 June 1940:	Transfer to Platoon Leader Course at Junkerschule in Braunschweig. Demonstrates suitability for platoon leader.
From about 1 September 1940:	Peacetime course at Leader School, Braunschweig. Named *Standartenoberjunker* (graduate from Junkerschule) in February 1941.
20 April 1941:	Promoted to *Untersturmführer*. Platoon leader in 1st Company, Reconnaissance Battalion *Nord*.
2 September 1941:	Wounded; bullet wound left forearm.
Until February 1942:	Hohenlychen hospital. Finnish Freedom Cross, Fourth Class. Posted to the *Leibstandarte* Division's new panzer battalion. Commander of motorcycle reconnaissance platoon. 1st Platoon leader in 3rd Company. Operations officer in regimental headquarters. Moved to 6th Company as 1st Platoon leader.

From 5 February 1943:	In action in the Kharkov area. Third wound: Shot in the back. Iron Cross, First Class and Wound Badge in Silver.
From 1 March 1943:	Commander of 7th Company. Counterattack toward Kharkov and Belgorod.
1 April 1943:	Regimental adjutant.
From 1 May 1943:	Commander of training company for members of the *Luftwaffe* sent to the unit.
From 15 June 1943:	Commander of 6th Company, Operation *Zitadelle*.
20 July 1943:	Knight's Cross.
1 August 1943:	Transfer to newly formed *Hitlerjugend* Division. Commander of two junior officer courses.
1 December 1943:	Commander of 3rd Company.
3 June 1944:	Fourth wound: wounded in back by strafing enemy fighter-bomber. Operations in Caen area.
End of July 1944:	Enters hospital in Bernay suffering from jaundice. German Cross in Gold, Panzer Assault Badge "25."
From 1 September 1944:	Regimental adjutant.
From 16 December 1944:	Ardennes offensive.
20 December 1944:	Wounded for fifth time: Shell fragment in mouth. Wound Badge in Gold.
From January 1945:	Commander of 1st Battalion, 12th SS-Panzer Regiment, *Hitlerjugend* Division.
8 May 1945:	Taken prisoner by the Americans.

4

Hans Bölter

Russian Offensive in the North

On 12 January 1943, the Soviets opened the Second Battle of Lake Ladoga with a tremendous bombardment from 4,500 guns. A rain of artillery fire lasting 140 minutes fell on both sectors forming the German corridor south of Schlüsselburg.

When the artillery fire stopped, the divisions of the 2nd Soviet Shock Army under Lt. Gen. W. S. Romanovski attacked from the east. At the same time the five rifle divisions and the tank brigade of the 67th Soviet Army under General Dukanov stormed forward from the west.

The Soviets hoped to smash the narrow German-held corridor with this great pincer movement and reestablish a ground link to Leningrad. Once this had been accomplished the attack would continue south toward the Kirov railway line.

General Dukanov's divisions stormed toward the meager strong points held by the 170th Infantry Division. The Soviet 86th Rifle Division tried to storm across the frozen Neva River and roll up Schlüsselburg from the flank, but the attack failed in the face of concentrated fire from the German defenders. The ice was littered with the bodies of fallen Russian soldiers. The waves of attacking Soviet regiments were decimated by the defenders' rapid-firing MG42 machine guns. The attack had to be called off.

The 45th Guards Rifle Division under General Krasnov tried to break through at the southern perimeter road. Defending there was the 399th Grenadier Regiment under *Oberst* Griesbach. (As a major, Griesbach was awarded the Knight's Cross on 14 March 1942. As an *Oberst* he became the 242nd German soldier to receive the Oak Leaves. On 6 March 1944 he was awarded the Swords while commanding the 170th Infantry Division.)

The Russian Guards were halted in front of the battered German trenches. Those who had managed to penetrate the German positions were driven out in close-quarters fighting.

Only near Marino did the Russians achieve a penetration. The first four waves of attackers were shattered, losing three thousand dead, but the fifth wave got through. Combat engineers led T-34s across the treacherous Neva ice, and the tanks drove into the German positions firing high-explosive shells and machine guns, expanding the gap they had smashed in the German line. *Oberstleutnant* Kleinhenz, commander of the 401st Grenadier Regiment, tried in vain to seal off the penetration. He and his adjutant were severely wounded in the attempt. The Russian rifle divisions stalled near Schlüsselburg were now turned around and sent toward Marino.

Should the Soviet 67th Army also break through with a flanking attack near Dubrovka and Gorodok, then the way would be open across the frozen marshes and over the Sinyavino Heights to the southern part of the German "bottleneck" along the Kirov railway line.

The outcome of the Second Battle of Lake Ladoga hung in the balance. *Generaloberst* Lindemann, commander in chief of the 18th Army, recognized the significance of this Russian penetration. On the evening of 12 January 1943 the situation reports revealed that there were four enemy rifle divisions and a tank brigade near Marino trying to push through to the "bottleneck" before linking up somewhere in the middle with the shock divisions from the east and veering southward.

"We'll have to send in the 'Watzmänner,' " he said.

The "Watzmänner" were the 96th Infantry Division under *Generalmajor* Noeldechen. The division and what was left of its three Grenadier Regiments were in the Sinyavino area. At this point the division was at about half its authorized strength.

On the evening of 12 January, the 96th Infantry Division received orders to attack from its assembly area toward the northwest and throw the enemy back across the Neva.

Generalmajor Noeldechen had only five grenadier battalions at his disposal. Supporting his grenadiers was a battalion of the 36th Flak Regiment with its 8.8cm guns and four Tiger tanks of the 1st Company of the 502nd Heavy Tank Battalion under *Oberleutnant* von Gerdtell accompanied by eight Panzer IIIs.

The battle could begin.

Swearing and grumbling, the grenadiers fought their way through the chest-deep snow. Their exhalations hung over the advancing groups of soldiers like a cloud of fog as they struggled forward through the ice-cold night.

"Shit!" said *Feldwebel* Grüninger grimly. They had entered the forest, and contact with any of the young fir trees resulted in an instant avalanche of snow.

"Where are our famous Tigers?" asked Lutschky.

"Can't you hear? They're farting around somewhere behind, while we have to look after ourselves to get ahead."

"I wonder if the Russians are waiting in the Scheidies Forest?" asked one of the men, breathing heavily as he leaned against a tree in an effort to catch his breath.

"Shit forest would be more like it!" murmured Bösebeck, who was carrying the machine gun.

"Don't do it in your pants! The Russians are waiting for us up ahead, and then you can shit if you want to!"

The order was given to shoulder weapons and move on.

The grenadiers moved off. From ahead they could hear the sound of firing by Soviet *Ratschbums* (Russian 7.62cm multipurpose guns). Machine guns rattled, and now and then salvoes from a Stalin organ howled in their direction. Instinctively the men ducked at the terrific din of the incoming rockets and explosions. They gripped their weapons and ammunition canisters a little tighter and moved on.

Suddenly, fire flashed through the night. In at least a dozen places machine guns hacked and Russian fast-firing guns roared. Antitank guns barked and tracers flitted among the trees.

"Attack! Forward!"

The grenadiers shouted as they attacked. The sounds of their voices provided encouragement.

Feldwebel Grüninger saw the muzzle flashes from a Maxim machine gun. He turned. Hearing his platoon follow, Grüninger threw himself to the ground and crawled onward. He saw that Bösebeck was providing covering fire. All of this took place, as usual, without a word.

Lutschky followed him with his submachine gun. He was an experienced soldier and knew what to do. Lutschky cut down a Russian who was sneaking through the undergrowth to Grüninger's right. Grüninger now saw the muzzle flashes from the Maxim about ten meters to his right. He crawled behind a snowdrift, pulled three hand grenades from his belt, screwed down the caps, and pulled them off. One after another he threw the grenades into the enemy position.

The three grenades exploded almost as one. Grüninger jumped to his feet. The men of his platoon saw him run forward. They reached the Russian position and broke in. The grenadiers took the forward Soviet bastion in hand-to-hand fighting, often sinking to their armpits in the snow. They were joined by their comrades from the left and right. The perimeter road had been reached.

Suddenly a shout went through the ranks: "Tanks from in front!"

It was now morning and the Russian tanks were advancing across the snow-covered fields toward the edge of the forest. Flames spurted from the muzzles of twenty-four tank cannon. The shells shaved off the tops of the young trees. Snow-covered branches crashed down.

"They're turning toward us, *Herr Feldwebel!*" shouted *Gefreiter* Gudehus.

"Give covering fire!"

Leutnant Eichstädt had moved in from the left. He carried two concentrated charges and several demolition charges, which he had bound together with wire.

"Give me one, *Herr Leutnant!*" said Gudehus. Eichstädt nodded.

"On the following infantry!"

From two sides the MG42s opened fire on the Russian infantry following the tanks. The *Leutnant* looked around.

"Ready, Gudehus?"

"Ready, *Herr Leutnant!*"

"Then let's go! You take the right, I'll take the left!"

The two jumped up, ran forward, and threw themselves to the ground as a machine gun opened up on them. They crawled on and reached a narrow ravine. When they reached its upper edge they were already abeam the T-34s advancing on their company. The tanks rocked as they fired their guns.

"Let's go, Gudehus!"

The pair reached one of the tanks and from behind threw their charges under the overhanging turret.

"Fuses lit!" shouted the *Leutnant* through the din, as the two threw themselves into cover.

The mighty double explosion of the three-kilo charges shook the tank. The blasts dislodged the T-34's turret, effectively putting it out of action.

"Calling Gerdtell!" crackled over the radio. "Enemy tanks have reached our main line of resistance and are overrunning our men. Tigers attack!"

Oberleutnant Gerdtell cleared his throat before calling his company: "Gerdtell to everyone: follow me at maximum speed!"

The four Tigers rolled off, crushing the trees in their path into the snow. The *Oberleutnant* could already hear the enemy tanks firing. He veered to the left slightly.

"Join up on my right. Open fire only on my command!"

The four Tigers spread out until they had formed a wide wedge. The first Soviets appeared. Then *Oberleutnant* Gerdtell gave the command:

"Open fire!"

The gunners had already selected their targets. At once there was a series of crashes as the "eighty-eights" opened up.

Two T-34s were burning after the first volley from the four Tigers. The tanks' gunners and loaders formed precisely functioning teams. Everything happened quickly. Before the Russian tankers could turn to face the new threat, the Tigers fired their second salvo. Two more T-34s caught fire.

"Forward to the depression!"

Gerdtell's driver stepped on the gas. The Tiger rolled into the depression and drove up the far side. The company commander had a clear view of the area from the shallow rise. Von Gerdtell watched as a T-34 maneuvered through the undergrowth and trained its gun on the farthest Tiger to the right.

"*Achtung,* Schneider! Enemy to your right!"

The gunner already had the enemy in his sight. There was a sharp crack as the "eighty-eight" fired echoed across the fields.

Two seconds later there was a flash as the armor-piercing shot struck the right flank of the T-34. As if raised by a ghost hand the turret flew into the air and crashed down into the snow.

"A hit! Keep firing!"

The gunner peered through his telescopic sight. The next T-34 had just come into view when a tremendous crash reverberated through the fighting compartment. Steel on steel.

"Ahead and to the left! That came from those trees. Move forward!"

But before the commander's tank could maneuver it was hit again. The shell pierced the steel of the gun mantlet. A long, jagged splinter struck the gunner in the chest, mortally wounding him.

His comrades removed the gunner from the stricken Tiger and carried him back to an infantry position. *Oberleutnant* Gerdtell took his identity disks.

The remaining Tigers continued to fire. When the last T-34 disappeared, twelve Soviet tanks lay burning and smoldering in the moor.

The Tiger had demonstrated its lethal capabilities for the first time. Gerdtell's disabled Tiger was recovered.

As evening fell the Soviets tried once again to break into the Scheidies Forest. Once again the call went out from the grenadiers:

"Enemy tanks approaching! Tigers forward!"

"Bölter, move out with your platoon. We must rearm first. Call us if things become ticklish."

Oberleutnant von Gerdtell raised his hand.

Hans Bölter nodded. His narrow face wore a serious and reflective impression. He stood in the open turret hatch and waved back to his company commander. Then he gave the order to move out.

The two steel giants drove through the snow in trail. The outlines of the white-painted Tigers merged with their surroundings in the half light of the evening twilight.

Oberfeldwebel Bölter saw a flash as an enemy antitank gun suddenly opened fire. He immediately ducked into the turret and shut the hatch cover. The armor-piercing round hissed past overhead.

Herbert Hölzl, Bölter's driver, steered the tank to the side.

Rumbling, the Tiger laid over on one track as it drove through a shellhole.

"Fire, Gröschl!" shouted Bölter.

Gunner Gröschl aimed at the muzzle flash as the antitank gun fired its second shot, which passed a few meters to the right of the Tiger. He made a slight correction as the tank halted. There was a crash as he fired, and the Tiger rocked backward from the recoil.

The shell smashed into the midst of the Russian antitank position, detonating the ammunition stockpiled there. The antitank gun was no longer a threat.

"Well done, Bastian!"

In the meantime it had become dark. There was nothing to be seen of the other Tiger, which was supposed to be maintaining position several hundred meters to the side. Bölter was unconcerned, because *Oberfeldwebel* Schütze, commander of the second Tiger, was an experienced tank commander and would be in position when required.

Suddenly, shadowy figures appeared in front of the tank as Bölter peered through his vision slit.

"Bow and turret machine guns open fire!"

Both guns opened up, and when he opened the turret hatch slightly to have a better look around, Bölter saw a flash to his right as the second Tiger opened fire.

An armor-piercing round howled past the right flank of the Tiger barely a meter away. Bölter saw a muzzle flash not six hundred meters ahead.

"Target in sight!" called Gröschl as he took aim at the new enemy.

The driver halted immediately. Gröschl made a slight correction and pressed the firing button.

The Tiger jerked from the recoil, and before the movement had subsided the commander, gunner, and driver saw a bright column of flame shoot up from the position of the Russian tank.

"Direct hit!" shouted Bölter with relief. He had expected the T-34 to fire again at any second.

Victory went to the quicker in such engagements. Being faster ensured survival in this pitiless struggle with an enemy whose harshness was well known.

Fountains of snow sprayed upward like geysers to the left and right of the *Oberfeldwebel*'s Tiger. A harsh glare flooded the fighting compartment as a shell detonated close beside the tank, showering the Tiger with steel splinters and chunks of frozen earth.

"There's more!" shouted Hölzl, as he suddenly saw a white shadow roll across a patch of open ground.

"To the right, Hölzl! We must get out of the light from the burning tank!"

Hölzl gripped the steering wheel and shifted into the next gear. With a jerk the Tiger accelerated and turned to one side.

As the Tiger was driving for the cover of darkness, Gröschl spotted the next T-34. It was heading straight for them.

"Stop!" he shouted. A slight foot pressure by Gröschl and the turret swung around, until the enemy tank, which had likewise halted, was in the crosshairs of his sight.

He pressed the firing button. The "eighty-eight" roared. The shot struck the sloping side of the T-34's turret and bounced off.

Then there was a flash from the T-34's gun. The shot whizzed past just overhead.

Before the T-34 could reload, the Tiger fired again. This shot struck the Soviet tank precisely between its turret and hull. The force of the impact tore the T-34's turret from the turret ring. The entire turret tumbled backward and crashed into the snow a few meters behind the tank.

Flames spurted from the shattered T-34. Seconds later its ammunition exploded, turning the tank into a blazing steel coffin.

The German listening post in Sinyavino heard the Russian tank commanders call:

Tigrii!—Tigrii!—Tigrii!—Pajechli, Pajechli—suda priott!

"Tigers coming!" Words that showed the respect the enemy had for the new German tank.

Things were still looking bad for *Oberfeldwebel* Bölter, however. He saw three or four Soviet tanks swing out to the right. More tanks appeared to his left.

"They're trying to catch us between them!" he explained to his crew. "Keep your nerve. Everything depends on it!"

The Tiger veered to the left. Gunner and loader were ready. They knew one another well and their movements were sure. A shell slid into the chamber and the breech mechanism snapped shut. Seconds later the gunner fired.

Constantly changing positions, the Tiger was able to evade the fire from the Soviet tanks. It was as if Hölzl had a sixth sense. He seemed to know when it was time to turn, when to change direction before a T-34 fired.

Emerging from a depression, Bölter suddenly found himself facing another enemy tank not two hundred meters away. Both tanks fired simultaneously. The T-34 missed its target by barely a meter. The shot from the "eighty-eight" was on target, however. It pierced the T-34's armor and turned it into a smoking, smoldering wreck.

Then a shell struck the Tiger's frontal armor with tremendous force. It bounced off and rocketed into the sky like a comet. The impact threw Bölter backward. He felt a blow against his back as if he had been struck by a fist.

"Turn! Maximum speed!"

The Tiger got through. Bölter and his crew had long since passed their own front lines when they destroyed the next T-34 with a shot from the flank.

A group of Russian soldiers sprang toward the Tiger. Standing in the turret cupola, Bölter loosed off a burst in their direction. The Tiger rumbled over the frozen ground, its tracks rattling.

The night was filled with the roar of tank cannon and the hectic rattle of machine gun fire. Grenades exploded and bursts of Russian machine gun fire sprayed the grenadiers who were struggling to recover their former positions. They were able to drive back the Soviet troops, who had been robbed of their covering armor.

Suddenly three more T-34s appeared. Three hits in rapid succession shook the Tiger. None penetrated, however.

Richter rammed the next round into the chamber of the "eighty-eight." Gröschl fired, and a direct hit smashed the closest enemy tank. The others turned away and fled at high speed.

"After them, Hölzl!" ordered Bölter.

He would have to eliminate the Russian tanks to prevent them from returning during the night and overrunning the positions held by the grenadiers.

The Tiger raced along at maximum speed, its 700-horse-power engine roaring. The big tank disappeared into a depression, and as it rumbled up the far side Bölter saw the back end of one of the T-34s not four hundred meters ahead.

Gröschl shouted something that the driver could not understand. But he knew what to do, and brought the Tiger to a halt.

The gunner aimed carefully. Bölter was about to shout that he didn't have all day, when the Tiger's gun roared.

A jet of flame shot from the rear of the T-34. Its fuel tanks went up and the T-34 was left burning on the snow-covered field in front of the forest.

"The second one turned to the right and disappeared into the forest!" said Gröschl.

"After him! Step on it!"

The driver shifted gears. The Tiger picked up speed. Bölter instructed his driver to roll past the edge of the forest to the right. When they reached the far end of the woods, Bölter saw the enemy tank about two hundred meters ahead.

The Tiger jerked to a halt. Gröschl fired and the shot smashed one of the T-34's tracks.

The damaged Russian tank turned. Flames spurted from its gun as it fired. But the hastily aimed shot missed.

The T-34 began to burn after Gröschl's second shot. The armored duel was over. Bölter had destroyed seven enemy tanks in this one action.

"Turn around!" he ordered, his voice calmer now.

The Tiger turned, leaving its tracks in the hard frozen snow, and rolled back toward the German lines.

"Bach, call Schütze and find out where he is!"

Josef Bach, Bölter's radio operator, called the second Tiger, but received no answer. The set was no longer functioning.

"Radio equipment damaged, *Herr Oberfeld!*"

Bölter was about to answer when a heavy blow shook the Tiger.

"Hit in the engine!" shouted Bach.

"Damn!" Bölter was considering what to do next, when the enemy decided for him.

A second hit smashed into the Tiger. Suddenly the tank was filled with the smell of gasoline. Then flames spurted from the rear of the tank.

"We're on fire!" shouted Hölzl.

"Get out!" croaked the *Oberfeldwebel.* "Quick! Out! Get out!"

The men jumped out. Bölter pulled his pistol from its holster and swung himself out of the turret. For a few seconds he stood on the Tiger's engine decking and then jumped down—right onto the back of a Russian soldier.

Bölter acted instinctively. He thrust his pistol into the chest of the enemy soldier, who was in the act of raising his own weapon, and pulled the trigger.

Nothing happened.

The Russian shouted something Bölter could not understand. Then he jumped up and disappeared into the darkness.

Bölter worked his way through the Russian soldiers, who had evidently pulled back to this position to await the next attack by their tanks.

The *Oberfeldwebel* tried to orient himself. Where was the second Tiger? Where were the Panzer IIIs that were supposed to be supporting them? Where were his comrades?

The Russians began to recover from the panic caused by the two Tigers, which had probably been enhanced by the sight of the seven burning tank wrecks. The *Oberfeldwebel* looked around. There, behind those young fir trees, that must be where *Oberfeldwebel* Schütze's Tiger was. Hopefully!

Bölter stood up and ran forward a few steps. Several Russian soldiers approached and shouted something to him.

Bölter gestured ahead and turned his face away. When the Russians had gone Bölter threw himself to the ground and crawled away to the side. Finding himself relatively alone, he breathed a sigh of relief.

Suddenly he heard the roar of an engine from the direction where the German tanks should be. Meter by meter he worked his way through the enemy skirmishing lines.

Bölter was freezing. The cold bit through his winter things. Once a Russian officer called to him and pointed toward the German lines. Bölter produced some unintelligible sounds and tagged along with the group of Russians for a while before sneaking away once more.

The darkness was his salvation. Had it been light the Russians would have realized who he was and probably shot him.

All of a sudden the second Tiger loomed up out of the darkness. There was a flash as it fired its main gun. Off to Bölter's right the high-explosive shell hammered into the ground. Both machine guns began to fire. The *Oberfeldwebel* ducked into a hole in the snow so as not to be shot by his countrymen.

What should he do to identify himself? Carefully he crawled farther to the right, and when the Tiger reached his little hill he jumped onto the rear mudguard and crawled cautiously forward to the radio operator's hatch. As he was about to call out to his comrade, the latter shouted, "Russian on the tank!"

Weakly, but clearly enough, Bölter heard the call, and he knew what was going to happen next.

A burst from a Russian machine gun had just hissed over his head, when the turret hatch opened and the face of the tank's commander appeared. Bölter noticed that he had his "zero-eight" pistol in his right hand.

"It's me, Schütze!" he called hastily. The *Oberfeldwebel* recognized his platoon leader. Bölter climbed inside.

His first words were, "My crew must be somewhere nearby!"

The other four men were in fact nearby, and soon they, too, were on board Schütze's tank. The Tiger turned for home and it was only then that Bölter realized that he had received three fragment wounds when his tank was hit.

"That will get you home, Hans," said the battalion medical officer. But *Oberfeldwebel* Bölter didn't want to go home, because he knew how desperately every tank commander was needed just then.

He was sent to a field hospital just behind the front. Eight days later he returned to his battalion. He had simply walked out of the hospital.

When he reported to *Hauptmann* Wollschläger at the battalion command post, he learned that his company commander, *Oberleutnant* Bodo von Gerdtell, had been killed on the night of 16 January. *Oberleutnant* Diehls was now in command of the company. Major Marker, the battalion CO, had also been wounded, and *Hauptmann* Wollschläger was acting in his place.

The heaviest losses had been suffered by the crews in the battalion's lightly armored Panzer IIIs. These tanks were hopelessly inferior to those of the Soviets. *Leutnant* Petz had been killed. *Oberleutnant* Ebert had been badly wounded and lost a leg. Seventeen men from the Panzer III crews had been killed.

Bölter was badly shaken by further bad news. While *Oberst* Pohlmann was at the front with the 284th Grenadier Regiment directing the defense against a Russian attack, a heavy air attack struck the regiment's command post. Twenty-three officers and men of the wheeled platoon stationed there were killed in one blow.

Despite the heavy losses they inflicted on the defenders, the Russians failed to reach their objective, the Kirov railway line. Even so, Leningrad radio reported the breaking of the German blockade on the evening of 18 January 1943. The recapture of Schlüsselburg and other territory allowed the Soviets to build a thirty-six-kilometer temporary railroad along the southern shore of Lake Ladoga from Polgami to Schlüsselburg. From Schlüsselburg the track crossed a makeshift bridge and linked up with the main line to Leningrad. Because this line could be severed at any time by a German counterattack, the Soviet command continued its strenuous efforts in the Leningrad area in hopes of breaking the blockade of the city once and for all.

As before, the objective was the Kirov railway line and the important junction at Mga.

The second and third phases of the Second Battle of Lake Ladoga began.

One day after his return, Bölter again climbed into a Tiger. His first mission with his old crew was a local reconnaissance, which was conducted without incident.

The next day the Tigers encountered Russian KV-I tanks. Two of these were destroyed and the rest turned and fled into the forest. With this success Bölter had raised his total of enemy tanks destroyed to thirty-four.

On 31 January 1943 the *Wehrmacht* communiqué declared: "Between Lake Ilmen and the Gulf of Finland the Soviets have been able to gain more ground despite local defensive successes by our forces. The defensive battles in this area are continuing with undiminished intensity.

"*Unteroffizier* Herbert Müller, a member of a heavy tank battalion, destroyed twenty-five Soviet tanks in his Tiger during these battles."

General von Leyser, commanding general of XXVI Army

Corps, acknowledged the efforts of the 502nd Heavy Panzer Battalion in an order of the day:

> The 502nd Heavy Panzer Battalion has been one of the corps' most effective weapons in the defensive battles since 21 January, whether in leading a successful counterattack or helping the hard-pressed infantry against overwhelming numbers of enemy tanks.
>
> The 55 enemy tanks destroyed in the corps area is good proof of this.
>
> The battalion has demonstrated its willingness for action through the death of a company commander, the wounding of the battalion commander and other heavy casualties.
>
> I express my special recognition to all officers and tank crews, but also to the tireless technical personnel.
>
> Corps Command Post, 18. 1. 1943 signed: von Leyser

Tigers to the Front

It was 4 February 1943. Hans Bölter was sitting in his billet when the report came that the battalion's last Panzer III had been destroyed by the Russians. The tank's commander, an *Unteroffizier,* had been killed.

With this setback the morale of the tank crews fell to zero. In spite of the great success of the Tigers it could not be overlooked that the battalion, which had been forced to employ numbers of Panzer III tanks to make up for the shortage of Tigers, had suffered heavy losses.

"If the 2nd Company under *Hauptmann* Lange had come with us, Hans," said *Oberfeldwebel* Schütze, "then things would have looked much better!"

"The 2nd has been placed under the command of Army Group Don, nothing is going to change that. We'll never see them again!"

"If at least some new Tigers would arrive as replacements," interjected Hölzl.

"It shouldn't take much longer. *Hauptmann* Wollschläger told me that we're supposed to receive three new tanks in the next few days."

"Sounds like a latrine rumor, doesn't it," said *Leutnant* Meyer, joining the conversation.

"We'll soon know if it's true. But now we must get ready, men."

Soon afterward *Oberleutnant* Bölter's Tiger rolled off in the direction of Hill 343 to take over a security sector. Its mission was to engage enemy tanks and antitank guns.

Finding no targets, they shot up a few earth bunkers and then turned back toward their billets, frozen to the bone.

The next morning the rumors were proved correct. Three new Tigers drove into the battalion vehicle park. That afternoon the crews began the job of carrying out adjusting fire with the Tigers' 8.8cm guns.

At 0600 the following morning two of the Tigers carried out an attack on Soviet-held positions directly in front of Hill 343.

Hauptmann Wollschläger, who had temporarily taken command of the battalion following the wounding of Major Marker, climbed into the command tank.

Major Scultetus, a recovery specialist and the designer of special recovery equipment for the Tiger, who had been attached to the battalion, went along in the second Tiger.

The two steel giants drove through the snow up to Hill 343. Their mission was to engage enemy bunkers and infantry positions with direct fire.

Both Tigers began to shell the enemy positions. The bunkers were eliminated one after another. The exploding shells tore away camouflage material, and beams and sheet metal whirled high into the air. Exploding ammunition tore up the ground. Soviet soldiers ran for their lives and disappeared into foxholes and trenches in an effort to escape the deadly fire of the German tanks. The barrage resulted in total confusion on the Russian side.

The Tigers were almost out of ammunition when Russian artillery began to answer. Shells of every caliber began to fall on the hill. Chunks of frozen earth showered down on the two Tigers. Shell fragments smacked against the tank's armored sides.

"We're heading back!" ordered *Hauptmann* Wollschläger.

The two Tigers turned and began to withdraw, pursued by bursting shells and showered with dirt and ice.

The grenadiers in their positions suddenly saw the command tank brake harshly. In the midst of the artillery fire the hatches flew open. Smoke billowed out, but none of the five crew members emerged.

Luckily, the snow that had begun to fall in the meantime now intensified and the Russian artillery fell silent. Major Scultetus ordered his driver to move on a bit farther and then halt.

"Radio operator, gunner, and loader stay in the tank! Driver come with me!"

The major jumped down from the tank and called over a pair of grenadiers. They hurried on skis over to the stationary Tiger. When they reached the tank they were met by a grisly scene. All five crew members had been badly wounded.

Oberfunkmeister Orth was recovered first. He had lost both eyes. *Oberfähnrich* Sepp Schmeisser's injuries were so severe that he died the next day. *Hauptmann* Wollschläger, who had managed to swing himself out of the Tiger, lay in the snow with serious head injuries.

Summoned by radio, the battalion medical officer, *Stabsarzt* Dr. Blatt, hurried to the scene and directed the evacuation of the seriously wounded men.

What had happened? An inspection might show what had caused the explosion within the tank. Or had the Tiger been hit by the Russian artillery? Statements by the grenadiers did not suggest the latter.

"We'll recover the tank after darkness falls and inspect it in the workshop," said Major Scultetus. It was later discovered that one of the Tiger's own high-explosive rounds had detonated in the ammunition rack.

The morning of 10 February 1943 dawned. It was still not yet light when Russian artillery fire began to fall on the German positions near Krasny Bor and north of Smerdyna.

At the same time the Soviets launched a pincer attack from the area south of the Pogostye pocket in the east and the Kolpino-Krasny Bor area in the west in an effort to capture Mga and the Kirov rail line. Guns of every caliber, as well as multiple rocket launchers and heavy mortars poured fire onto the German positions.

On the west side, in the area held by the 4th SS Police Division and the Spanish 250th "Blue" Division, 33,000 Soviet troops attacked, with sixty T-34s leading the way.

The Russians penetrated three kilometers into the German lines. They captured Krasny Bor, but were halted at the Ishora.

It was there that the Spanish grenadier Antonio Ponte fought his dramatic battle against seven T-34s. Ponte was killed in the action, but his bravery was acknowledged by the posthumous award of Spain's highest decoration, the Laureda San Fernando.

The "Blue" Division's Fusilier Battalion lost 90 percent of its effectives. Nevertheless it held on until a counterattack by the 212th Infantry Division under *Generalmajor* Reymann threw back the Soviet forces.

On 11 February 1943 the 1st Company of the 502nd Heavy Panzer Battalion launched a counterattack with the Flanders Legion.

"Watch out, Hans! Antitank guns in the trees ahead and to the right!"

The warning call from *Leutnant* Meyer reached Bölter's Tiger just in time.

Hölzl immediately brought the tank to a halt. Then there was a flash as a Russian antitank gun opened fire from behind a snow-covered hillock. The shell flitted past in front of the Tiger.

The crash of the Tiger's gun echoed through the morning stillness. There was an explosion at the site of the antitank gun, and camouflage material, wood, and snow flew through the air. When the smoke cleared, the barrel of the deadly antitank gun was pointing toward the sky.

"Chief to everyone: move on! Not too fast, or the infantry won't be able to keep up!"

The small force of Tigers, whose mission was to drive the Soviets out of the former positions of the "Blue" Division, moved off again.

Suddenly enemy tanks appeared. Within a few seconds Bölter counted ten, approaching from a snow-covered wood to the right.

There was a roar as Meyer's gunner opened fire, and soon the first T-34 was burning.

"Six hundred, eleven o'clock!"

"Target in sight!"

Again there was a crash as the "eighty-eight" fired. However, the shot missed, as the enemy tank had pulled back from its original position.

Hölzl turned the steering wheel. Its tracks grinding, the Tiger swung around. Gröschl quickly rotated the turret and adjusted his aim.

The T-34, which had just stopped, rotated its turret to bring its gun to bear on the Tiger. Peering through the driver's vision port, Hölzl recognized the deadly danger.

"Quick, Bastian!" he shouted.

Gröschl pressed the electric firing button. The crash of the gun firing was followed almost immediately by the sound of the impact. The shot pierced the armor of the enemy tank. Its turret hatch flipped up and a jet of flame shot into the morning sky.

The shells fired by the Tigers smashed into the wave of attacking Soviet tanks in rapid succession. *Leutnant* Meyer had a particularly successful day. His tank was hit several times by rounds from Soviet antitank rifles, but none penetrated. Meyer himself destroyed at least ten T-34s.

Schütze and *Unteroffizier* Krennmayer also took part in the fighting. Then, suddenly, it happened. Krennmayer's Tiger took a direct hit from a concealed antitank gun. *Unteroffizier* Krennmayer was killed.

Several times Bölter and his crew also found themselves in difficult situations from which there appeared to be no way out. But each time something happened to save them. Either it was timely evasive action, accurate firing, or a comrade knocking out an enemy tank that was maneuvering into position for a lethal shot at the Tiger.

The battle lasted for hours. Russian troops charged the Tigers and were driven off by the escorting infantry. The Flemish Legion stormed after the tanks, reached the former main line of resistance, and drove out the Russians in close quarters fighting.

New orders came in: "Continue to advance! Enemy in the former main line of resistance has been destroyed!"

Once again the Tigers rolled forward. Bölter directed his vehicle into a ravine that led off to the left. The Tiger drove down through the snow at high speed and then headed up the ravine about one thousand meters. There it turned into a branching valley and a little later stopped behind a clump of snow-covered fir trees.

"There, *Herr Oberfeld!*"

The gunner gestured ahead excitedly. A quick look and Bölter realized that *Leutnant* Meyer had got himself into a difficult situation.

"Fire, Gröschl!"

The gunner was already swinging the turret around to the three o'clock position. Then he adjusted his aim. Gröschl fired just as flame spurted from the muzzle of the T-34 that was behind the Tiger and to the right.

The Russian missed, but Gröschl's shot struck the front of the T-34, putting it out of action.

Suddenly there was a crash against the left flank of Bölter's Tiger. The din inside the tank was terrible, but the shell, fired by a light field piece, did not penetrate the Tiger's armor.

The huge tank swung around like an angry giant until its tormentor came into view. The first high-explosive round smashed the gun and its crew and blasted what was left into a ravine.

"Four armor-piercing rounds left, *Herr Oberfeld!*" called Josef Richter. The loader's face was streaming with sweat.

"We'll head back slowly," replied Bölter.

The Tiger rattled back down into the ravine. As the tank turned into the main valley, the crew saw the rear end of a T-34 about one hundred meters away.

The first shot turned the T-34 into a wall of flame. Then its ammunition went up, sending pieces of wreckage flying past the Tiger.

"Up to the right!" ordered Bölter.

The nose of the Tiger rose alarmingly. Would it tip over? No, it drove up the slope and rolled back toward the German lines.

Before returning, however, Bölter spotted two more Soviet antitank guns, which he eliminated with the last two rounds of 8.8cm ammunition.

Bölter arrived at the battalion command post together with *Leutnant* Meyer and *Oberfeldwebel* Schütze.

"Refuel and rearm immediately!" he ordered upon climbing out of the Tiger.

The crews climbed out and leaned against the sides of their tanks, limbs trembling from the tension of the just-completed

Oberst Dr. Franz Bäke (center) with his adjutants, *Hauptmann* Lappe (left) and *Hauptmann* Herbert (right).

Franz Bäke: Knight's Cross on 11 January 1943; 262nd recipient of the Oak Leaves on 1 August 1943; 49th recipient of the Swords on February 1944.

Hermann von Oppeln-Bronikowski, Bäke's regimental commander, led the way in many battles. The dressage champion at the 1936 Olympics in Berlin, following the war he headed the Canadian Olympic Equestrian Team.

Near Prokhorovka on 12 July 1943: XXXXVIII Panzer Corps is ready to attack.

Tigers of the 503rd Heavy Panzer Battalion prepare for action near Bagdukhov.

A disabled Tiger burns near Prokhorovka.

Hermann Bix received the Knight's Cross on 22 March 1945. At that time he was an *Oberfeldwebel* and platoon leader in 3rd Company, 35th Panzer Regiment, 4th Panzer Division.

In the Panther, Bix found the tank in which he would achieve his greatest success.

This heavily armored Russian KV 1 was hit dozens of times by Bix's panzer, before a precision shot through its gun barrel finally rendered it harmless.

Oberst Heinrich Eberbach, commander of the 35th Panzer Regiment. Born in 1895 and a World War I officer, Eberbach was a steadying influence on his young tank soldiers. He won the Oak Leaves, receiving the decoration as commander of the 5th Panzer Brigade outside of Moscow.

After an action: exhausted, but alive.

In the autumn of 1944, 1st Battalion, 35th Panzer Regiment was led by *Hauptmann* Walter Grohe. On 22 October he was awarded the Knight's Cross; three days later he was killed trying to halt a wave of Russian tanks.

Summer 1942: Parade in Paris, Rudolf von Ribbentrop, commander of a Panzer IV.

13 March 1943: Street fighting in Kharkov. Here is a tank of the *Das Reich* Division.

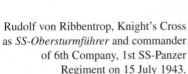

Rudolf von Ribbentrop, Knight's Cross as *SS-Obersturmführer* and commander of 6th Company, 1st SS-Panzer Regiment on 15 July 1943.

A T-34/76B knocked out near Prokhorovka.

In Kharkov, summer 1943.

Paul Hausser ordered the evacuation of Kharkov, saving his forces, which later played the leading role in the recapture of the city. He won the Oak Leaves and was later awarded the Swords as an *Oberstgruppenführer* and commander in chief of the 7th Army.

A Panzer IV G on the firing range. Beside the tank is *Sturmbannführer* Jürgensen, commander of 1st Battalion, 12th SS-Panzer Regiment.

Caen after four weeks of fighting. The Allied invasion plan had called for the city to fall on D Day plus 1, or 7 June.

A Panther of 3rd Company, 12th SS-Panzer Regiment.

The 12th SS-Panzer Division *Hitlerjugend* waits in camouflaged positions for orders to depart for the Normandy Invasion front in June 1944.

Rudolf von Ribbentrop returns to his unit in spite of his wounds. On the right, at the controls of his motorcycle, is Regimental Commander Wünsche, who was also wounded.

Sturmbannführer Jochen Peiper, commander of 3rd (Armored) Battalion, 2nd SS-Panzer Grenadier Regiment, fought hand-in-hand with his division's Panzers. Winner of the Knight's Cross and Oak Leaves as commander of 1st SS-Panzer Regiment, Peiper was later murdered in France on 14 July 1976.

Hans Bölter, Knight's Cross on 16 April 1944; 581st recipient of the Oak Leaves on 10 September 1944, as *Leutnant* and commander of 1/502 Heavy Panzer *Abteilung* (Tiger).

The business end of a Tiger's "88," April 1944. There is still time for humor in spite of the difficult operations.

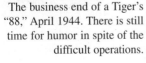

A Tiger 1 of 2./sPzAbt. 502 in the northern sector of the Eastern Front.

Bölter received the German Cross in Gold on 29 March 1943 while serving as an *Oberfeldwebel* in 1st Company, 502nd Heavy Panzer Battalion.

Tiger 133, commanded by *Unteroffizier* Knapp, broke through a bridge near Pustoshka on 23 November 1943. Knapp was killed in the mishap.

Oberleutnant Otto Carius, Tiger commander and winner of the Knight's Cross with Oak Leaves, fought with Hans Bölter in the northern sector of the Eastern Front and with Albert Ernst in the Ruhr Pocket.

Michael Wittmann was the most successful tank commander of World War II. He was awarded the Knight's Cross on 14 January 1944 as an *Untersturmführer* with the 1st SS-Panzer Regiment of the *Leibstandarte*. Sixteen days later, following an unparalleled run of success against enemy tanks, he was awarded the Oak Leaves. On 22 June 1944 he was awarded the Swords. His unequaled series of victories came to an end with his death on 8 August 1944.

Obergruppenführer Sepp Dietrich was Wittmann's commanding officer. He led the 1st SS-Panzer Division *Liebstandarte Adolf Hitler*. In Normandy he was the commanding general of 1st SS-Panzer Corps.

Michael Wittmann (left) with his successful crew in January 1944. Beside him is gunner Balthasar "Bobby" Woll, who received the Knight's Cross on 16 January 1944 after participating in the destruction of eighty enemy tanks.

Two Tigers near Villers Bocage. Tiger number 231 is Wittmann's. It has been disabled by fire from an enemy antitank gun.

Seventeen shot-up British vehicles, destroyed by Wittmann near Villers Bocage.

A Cromwell tank of the British 7th Armored Division, the famous "Desert Rats," knocked out by Wittmann, together with other vehicles destroyed by him.

A knocked-out Sherman tank in front of a church in Lingevres.

Villers Bocage: Wittmann's greatest day. There he stopped the main body of a British armored regiment. Here is a Panzer IV of 6th Company, 130th *Panzer-Lehr* Regiment, *Panzer-Lehr* Division.

Albert Ernst received the Knight's Cross on 22 January 1944 as a *Leutnant* and platoon leader in the 519th Heavy Tank Destroyer Battalion's 1st Company. As a result of his exploits Ernst was known as "the Tiger of Vitebsk."

Albert Ernst's Nashorn Büffel is congratulated following a major victory near Vitebsk.

Preparing for action: Tigers were also employed in the defense of the Vitebsk area in the winter of 1943/44.

Three armored commanders. From left: *General der Panzertruppe* Hasso von Manteuffel, *Generalleutnant* Wolfgang Thomale, and *Generalfeldmarschall* Walter Model in the Ardennes.

Hans-Georg Reinhardt received his tank training at Kasan (code name "Kama"), Russia. He led the 4th Panzer Division in Poland and the XXXXI Panzer Corps in France and during the opening stages of the eastern campaign, following which he was given command of the 3rd Panzer Army. One of the outstanding personalities of the armored forces, he received the Knight's Cross, Oak Leaves, and the Swords.

As commander in chief of the 1st Panzer Army on the Eastern Front, *General der Panzergruppen* Hans Hube was involved in the thick of the fighting and on 20 April 1944 received the then highest decoration, the Diamonds. At the same time Hube was promoted to the rank of *Generaloberst*.

Generalfeldmarschall Walter Model led the 3rd Panzer Division as commander and the XXXXI Panzer Corps as commanding general. He was commander in chief of the Ninth Army and later Army Group Center.

General der Panzergruppe Hasso von Manteuffel was involved with armored forces from the beginning. In 1939 he was commander of the instructional staff of *Panzertruppenschule* 2 in Krampnitz. As commander of the 7th Panzer Division and the *Grossdeutschland* Panzer Grenadier Division he was able to put all of his knowledge and experience to practical use.

Generaloberst Hermann Hoth assumed command of the 18th Infantry Division on 1 October 1935. In April 1942 he became commander in chief of the 4th Panzer Army.

mission. Cigarettes were lit and slowly life returned to normal. They had been lucky again!

The German main line of resistance had been recaptured from the Russians. Now it would have to be held against the counterattacks that must come soon.

The rearming had just been completed when the commanding general arrived at the command post and presented *Leutnant* Meyer with both Iron Crosses, First and Second Class.

That night Bölter and his men slept the sleep of exhaustion. The *Oberfeldwebel* woke them an hour before the start of their next mission. Following a meager breakfast they walked over to their Tigers.

Major Scultetus, who was planning to go along on the mission, was already waiting for them.

Even before they reached the battlefield the men in the tanks could hear the sound of the Flemish heavy antitank guns firing. Also audible was the characteristic crack of Russian tank guns.

"It's started again already, Hans!" called Meyer.

"So I see! Be careful!" replied Bölter.

They reached the front and spotted the T-34s, which had approached to within several hundred meters of the German lines. Two tanks were burning in the background of the winter landscape. Black smoke curled upward from their open hatches.

The Tigers joined the battle five minutes later. When the Soviets pulled back they left eleven burning tanks behind them.

The Flemish troops held the position until 17 February, when they were relieved by a battalion from the 5th *Gebirgsdivision*. By then, however, there was little left of the Flemish Legion. Forty-five exhausted, filthy soldiers crawled out of their trenches. They were all that was left of the original five hundred Flemish volunteers.

The few available Tigers were soon in action again. They found themselves facing superior numbers of Soviet T-34s, which tried to surround the German tanks. The battle began. The Tigers commanded by *Oberfeldwebel* Bölter and *Leutnant* Meyer opened fire.

In the first hour, six enemy tanks were destroyed. The situation then became critical for the two Tigers. The Soviets employed tanks, antitank guns, and even artillery in an attempt to knock out the pair.

"Damn, here come three at once, *Herr Oberfeld!*" swore Hölzl as the silhouettes of T-34s appeared over a hill about two thousand meters away.

"Go, Gröschl! Let's see what your gun can do!" called radio operator Richard Bach.

Gröschl lined up on the T-34s on the hill. He trained his sight on one of them, made a slight correction, and pressed the firing button.

The armor-piercing shell raced toward its target. A few seconds later there was a bright flash as it struck the middle Russian tank.

"Hit!" reported the *Oberfeldwebel.* "Bravo, Gröschl!"

The two surviving T-34s rolled down the hill. There was a flash from the muzzle of Meyer's gun. A little later his Tiger turned to the right and rattled down into a ravine.

"We'll draw them toward us to give Meyer a clear shot!" ordered Bölter. Suddenly, the Russian tanks reappeared about four hundred meters away.

Gröschl fired three times, but failed to hit the dodging enemy tanks.

Bölter's Tiger roared backward about sixty meters and disappeared into a stand of small trees.

Through his cupola vision slit Bölter watched as the two T-34s gave chase and approached at high speed.

"Ahead a few meters!" ordered the *Oberfeldwebel.*

The Tiger moved forward until it reached the T-34s' field of view, then halted.

The Russians halted as well. The Tiger pulled back again as the Russians opened fire. Bölter's ruse had worked. The two T-34s were now stationary targets for the second Tiger.

There was a flash as Meyer's Tiger, concealed behind some bushes, opened fire. The selected T-34 began to burn.

The second T-34 swung its turret about to face the new threat, but before it could take aim at Meyer's tank, Gröschl fired again.

The impact of the armor-piercing shell caused the T-34 to slew about and its shot went wide of the target. Seconds later Meyer fired again. A direct hit blew off the T-34's turret.

"We got them both, Hans!" called Meyer.

The two heavy tanks drove back a distance and then halted on a hill to the right when they saw Russian infantry advancing.

"Load high-explosive!"

Suddenly Meyer's voice crackled in Bölter's headset: "*Achtung,* Hans! Behind you!"

"Turn to the left!" ordered Bölter at once.

The Tiger swung around. In the next instant there was a crash as an antitank gun fired. This gun had been positioned somewhat farther forward than the rest and had been silent until now.

The armor-piercing shot struck the Tiger at a sharp angle as it turned, and ricocheted skywards. Inside the tank there was a sharp ringing sound.

"We've been lucky again," called Bölter as the tank was still turning. Then he saw a flash as the antitank gun fired again. The second shot whizzed past the Tiger's turret.

"I have him!" shouted Gröschl. There was a crash as the "eighty-eight" fired. The high-explosive round detonated against the antitank gun's protective shield, killing the gun crew.

The Tiger turned again, rejoined its companion, and opened fire on Russian machine gun units. These had hauled their machine guns into position on sleds and were providing covering flanking fire for their infantry from the many shell holes.

Some time later five more enemy tanks appeared. Bölter and Meyer immediately engaged the new enemy.

Bölter's gunner and loader performed like robots. Between crashes from the main gun could be heard the hammering of the radio operator's machine gun. Bach was firing at the Russian infantry, trying to keep them at a distance.

Suddenly Hölzl spotted a group of Russians carrying demolition charges not fifty meters in front of the tank. The Russians jumped up and ran toward the Tiger. Hölzl immediately gunned the engine and drove straight for them.

The terrifying sight of the Tiger bearing down on them caused the Russians to abandon their plans. They scattered and fled.

Both German tanks were now running low on ammunition. The T-34s that survived the attack had already turned for home.

The two Tigers turned and drove toward the rear. Between them they had destroyed a total of twelve Soviet tanks.

* * *

The next morning the crews were awakened by the sound of gunfire. They jumped out of bed and ran outside.

"Damn!" said Bölter. "I think the Russians have spotted our withdrawal and are firing on our people."

"Look at that!" shouted Meyer, who had just arrived.

"That's where the train is," remarked Richter.

Artillery fire was falling on the area where the train was quartered. Flames leapt high into the air.

"I wanted to say goodbye!" said Meyer, explaining his early arrival. *"Leutnant* Popp has just arrived and is relieving me."

"Good luck, Meyer!"

The two men shook hands and *Leutnant* Meyer, Bölter's comrade in so many defensive battles, left. For good? No one knew.

On 22 February 1943, at Novo Lissino, Major Marker assumed command of the battalion.

The next day Soviet artillery again fired on the German billeting areas. The Second Battle of Lake Ladoga was not yet over.

The remaining elements of the battalion were moved by wooden sleigh to Tosno and Szablino.

Bölter and his men and the entire 1st Company now moved into quarters that were worse than anything they had seen so far in the war. There was a "major action" every night, but it was not fought against Russian tanks or infantry, rather against lice and bedbugs.

A period of warmer weather set in. Soon all the roads had been transformed into muddy tracks.

On 1 March 1943 the Headquarters Company transferred to Wyritza. *Oberleutnant* Grix, the battalion's popular adjutant, was also relieved. One old comrade after another was leaving the unit. The few left behind were not looking forward to the immediate future with optimism.

Rumors of an impending move by the battalion were borne out on 10 March. The battalion headquarters and the Headquarters Company drove to Tosno on the night of 11 March. From there they left for Germany early on the morning of 13 March.

On 13 March those elements that had been left behind, 1st Company and the train units, were no longer a trials battalion, but rather the 502nd Heavy Panzer Battalion, of which 1st Company was the backbone.

The unit was placed on alert readiness.

While the transport aircraft carrying Major Richter, Major Scultetus, *Hauptmann* Heck, *Oberleutnants* Heiss, Lent, Frey, and Hergarden, *Leutnant* Burk, and *Stabsarzt* Dr. Blatt had already arrived in Paderborn, the Tigers that had been left behind at the front were assembled at the railroad bridge near Nikolskoye.

An enemy attack was expected. Before the attack began, *Leutnant* Meyer, who had returned to the company much to the joy of his former comrades, took part in a mission against enemy bunkers opposite the German main line of resistance.

The company was led by *Oberleutnant* Diehls. The unit's tank commanders, including *Leutnant* Meyer, *Oberfeldwebel* Bölter, and *Oberfeldwebel* Schütze, were all experienced men.

The Soviets attacked on 19 March. Their massive thrust struck the positions of the *SS-Polizeidivision* and the Flanders Legion.

A new and difficult period of operations for the Tigers began. It was a period that demanded the utmost of the small number of crews and brought every man to the verge of total exhaustion.

The Third Phase of the Battle

At the beginning of March the fighting around Leningrad died down and it appeared that the Second Battle of Lake Ladoga had ended. However, on 19 March the fighting flared up again as the battle entered its third phase.

This time the Soviets directed their main thrust straight at Mga.

The Soviets launched one pincer toward Karbussel from the area south of Voronovo. It consisted of ten divisions, two brigades, and seven armored brigades.

The other pincer attacked from the area around Krasny Bor. It consisted of six divisions, two brigades, and five armored brigades.

If the attack succeeded, the Soviets would be in possession

of the Kirov rail line and be able to supply Leningrad. Then the entire combat zone around the Sinyavino Heights and Sinyavino itself would be like ripe fruit for the picking.

What could the Germans do to counter these efforts, and which divisions were available to defend against this third phase of the Soviet attack?

Holding the Leningrad front were the divisions of L Army Corps, namely the SS-Police Division, the 24th Division, elements of the 215th Division *(Gruppe Heun)*, the 250th (Spanish) Division, and the 215th Infantry Division. Securing the coast were coastal batteries, alert units, and Latvian volunteers.

The Oranienbaum bridgehead was being held by the divisions of III *Luftwaffe* Field Corps, namely the 9th and 10th *Luftwaffe* Field Divisions.

The army had four divisions in reserve: the 21st, 69th, and 121st Infantry Divisions, and the 5th *Gebirgsdivision* (mountain infantry division).

In Badayev the men of the Tiger crews could hear the dull thump of gunfire in the distance. The Tigers had been assembled there in preparation for the anticipated Soviet attack. It was still dark when the first call for help arrived.

Combat orders were issued. "Let's go, men!" shouted Bölter.

They ran from the hut across to their tank. To the right Schütze and his crew were doing likewise, and to the left Meyer, who had just returned to the company.

The terrain alternated between mud and snow-covered frozen ground. The nearer the tanks came to the scene of the enemy penetration, the heavier became the artillery fire.

Oberleutnant Diehl's voice crackled over the radio. "Combat readiness!" All hatches were closed.

"Weapons loaded and secured!" reported Gröschl.

The Tiger rumbled through a shallow ditch. Its wide tracks tore up huge chunks of earth and sent them spinning high into the air.

Two minutes later Bölter could see the inferno of the battle through his scissors telescope. Mortar rounds were falling all about, showering the tanks with shrapnel and mud.

An infantry officer waved to the tank; he immediately disappeared from view again as a Russian heavy machine gun began to rattle.

"Open fire!"

Both of the Tiger's machine guns opened up.

The Tiger halted near the officer's foxhole. Bölter opened his hatch slightly.

"What's going on?"

"Over there, six hundred meters ahead, enemy two-level bunkers, with at least ten machine guns. They are supporting the attacking troops."

Bölter heard a burst of gunfire and ducked. The hatch cover clanged shut.

"Ahead six hundred, Gröschl. Enemy bunker with many machine guns!"

A moment later the gunner spotted several bursts of tracer coming from the bunker and reported, "Target in sight!"

The first armor-piercing round smashed into the bunker. A fountain of dirt shot up, but several machine guns continued to fire.

Six shells hammered into the enemy position before it exploded in a cascade of flame.

The Tigers were still at least three hundred meters behind the front line when a dense wave of Russian infantry attacked.

"High-explosive!" ordered *Oberleutnant* Diehls.

The shells smashed into the wave of infantry. The results were terrible. In two minutes the first wave had been stopped. Russian artillery began to range in on the Tigers, which were in widely separated firing positions.

Shells burst all around Bölter's Tiger. Steel fragments whistled overhead and bounced off the sides of the tank. Then a shell burst close by, illuminating the interior of the tank with a harsh glare, followed seconds later by another.

The tremendous impact of the heavy shell was enough to shake even the heavy Panzer VI.

"Change position! Forward one hundred meters!"

The tank rumbled forward. "Damn, we've jumped out of the frying pan into the fire!"

"We must pull back, *Herr Oberfeld!*"

Mortar rounds exploded all around the Tiger without letup. Several 5cm shells exploded against the turret and the rear of the tank. Mud spattered against the vision ports.

"Back! Back up, Hölzl!"

The Tiger jolted backward, crushing a birch tree into the ground. Soon it reached a shallow depression and halted.

* * *

"Tanks! Tanks!"

The warning call made its way from the front to the rear. A little later the men inside the tanks heard the order from their company commander: "All Tigers to the front!"

The Tigers immediately left their camouflaged readiness positions and drove to the front lines, where they charged toward the second wave of Russian infantry.

Richter fired his machine gun. A group of enemy tanks appeared in echelon formation. Pairs of tanks halted and fired, then rolled onward while others stopped and fired.

"Halt! Begin from the left. Range eight hundred. Ten o'clock!"

Gröschl took aim. The turret turned smoothly and quickly. A slight correction and the first shell was on its way.

The armor-piercing shot raced past the T-34's turret and disappeared into no-man's-land, leaving behind a thin smoke trail.

Now the Russian tank fired; its target was *Oberfeldwebel* Schütze's Tiger. The shot ricocheted off the tank's bow armor and rocketed almost vertically upward.

Gröschl now had the T-34 squarely in his sights. The second shot from the deadly "eighty-eight" sliced through the T-34's armor plate. At the same time Schütze scored a lethal hit on another T-34. A third and a fourth were destroyed in rapid succession. The rest disappeared into a small valley.

Bölter saw that the Legionnaires were driving back the enemy infantry. He watched the battle unfold: men standing and fighting shoulder to shoulder, others running, then being caught by machine gun fire and thrown to the ground. Once he saw a severely wounded Russian being hauled to his feet by a comrade not one hundred meters in front of his Tiger. All of this unfolded before his eyes in a matter of minutes.

This was war as it really was: pitiless, bloody, and filled with deadly danger. This thought was driven home when a shell raced past the turret, missing by a hair's breadth. Bölter ducked his head instinctively.

"Where did that come from?" he asked.

"From that depression on the right!" shouted the driver.

Gröschl stepped on the rocker plate and swung the turret in that direction. Peering through his sight, the gunner suddenly saw the upper edge of a tank turret. It was emerging from a clump of bushes and lowering the barrel of its long gun.

"Look out!" he warned.

Hölzl stepped on the gas and the tank shot forward. It had moved about four meters when the T-34 fired again.

The Tiger halted. Gröschl adjusted his aim. He selected a point about a hand's width below the enemy tank's turret and pressed the firing button.

The impact blasted the turret right off the T-34. It seemed to spin through the air in slow motion before crashing into the shallow ravine in a cloud of snow.

Several Russians clambered out of the shattered tank. The Tiger's machine guns began to rattle. The tank crew disappeared. A moment later Schütze's cannon hammered through the morning. He, too, had encountered and destroyed one of the fleeing Russian tanks.

"Aircraft!" shouted Diehls. Russian close-support aircraft were approaching at treetop height. There were at least twenty machines. They dropped fifty-kilo bombs, aiming at the German tanks. One bomb passed barely two meters above the turret of Bölter's Tiger and crashed into the earth about a dozen meters behind the tank.

The aircraft strafed the tanks with their 2cm cannon. Shells smacked against the turret and hull of Bölter's Tiger. The tank shook and the crew's ears hurt from the frightful noise. The aircraft roared past, then turned in a wide arc and came around for another pass.

A pair of Flemish antiaircraft guns opened up on the attackers. One of the Russian aircraft was hit. It dove steeply toward the earth, passed over the Tigers, and crashed into the ground just short of the front lines.

A ball of fire rose into the air above the crash site, first red, then white from the aircraft's fuel. Engines sailed through the air and the aircraft's wings fluttered to earth like giant leaves.

The tanks returned to their support base at Badayev just as it was getting dark, completely out of ammunition. Bölter and his men had no idea how they had managed to survive the hours of heavy enemy fire. But even now they got no rest.

"Refuel, rearm, and see to the transmission!"

The members of the crew worked with the men of the supply train and then the field workshop until the Tiger was ready for action again.

Dead tired, Bölter collapsed onto his bunk. His nerves were still on edge from the strain of the day's fighting. Once again the few available Tigers had saved the front from collapse, destroying ten enemy tanks in the process.

At first light on 20 March they were all ready for action once more. *Oberfeldwebel* Schütze came over to Bölter.

"I have a feeling that it's going to be another hot day, Hans!" he offered with characteristic coolness, which Bölter was always forced to admire.

He nodded and said, "If we know the Russians, they'll try everything to reach their objective."

Oberleutnant Diehls came over to his men. They saluted. "All ready?" he asked.

"Everything is in order!" replied *Leutnant* Meyer.

"We can move out then. Same as yesterday: support the Flanders Legion and the policemen."

Ten minutes later the tanks moved out. Standing in his turret, Bölter watched as the waving men of the supply train disappeared in the distance. Then he glanced at the other three Tigers as they left the support base to face the overwhelming mass of Soviet armor.

The sounds of battle intensified. Bölter ducked involuntarily when he heard the sound of an incoming salvo from a Stalin organ.

Then he heard the voice of *Oberleutnant* Diehls:

"Combat readiness!"

Bölter slid down onto his seat. The turret hatch was locked. The gunner reported all weapons loaded and secured.

The tanks were driving through shallow shell holes, nosing down into them and crawling up the other side, their engines roaring.

Grenadiers waved to the tanks. To Bölter their faces looked like those of old men. They had become exhausted, dirt encrusted, and haggard from the constant strain.

It was the grenadiers who were accomplishing the unimaginable, crouching in their holes, waiting for the enemy tanks, and then springing at them in an attempt to destroy them with little more than their bare hands.

There were three loud crashes as three shells fell close in front of the Tiger.

For a few seconds there was nothing to be seen through the vision ports except fountains of dirt and bright flashes. Shell fragments rang off the tank's steel sides.

"Across to the hills, Hölzl!"

The driver turned his steering wheel slightly. The caterpillar tracks ground up the earth and the Tiger rolled forward, its roadwheels squeaking.

The tank reached the hill on the right, which was still two hundred meters behind the main line of resistance. After reaching the relative cover of a cluster of bushes, Bölter opened the turret hatch.

He peered toward the northwest through his binoculars and saw dense waves of earth-brown figures advancing across a shallow depression. Farther to the rear, trucks were arriving with further battalions of Russian soldiers.

The Russians emerged onto the shell-torn plain. The forward German outposts, which were in shell holes in front of the main line of resistance, opened fire.

The MG42s began to bark. Long bursts of fire raked the advancing waves. Then Bölter saw the men in the forward outposts pull back, and shortly afterward all hell broke loose again.

The main body of Soviet infantry reached the plain, which within minutes was littered with a tangle of human bodies.

At that moment rockets began to roar over the front lines. The German heavy rocket launchers fired their large rockets six at a time. Trailing fiery tails, they fell on the waves of attacking Russians, leaving black, scorched circles in the snow where they fell.

"*Achtung!* Chief to everyone: tanks from the direction of Hill 67.9. Let them approach until they are abeam our position. Then fire into their flanks!"

Seconds later Bölter caught sight of the steel phalanx of T-34s and KV-Is. Their job was to get the attack moving again by blasting a path into the German positions for the infantry.

It was a breathtaking sight to watch the tanks drive through the depression, leaving their tracks far behind on the far slope.

"All ready, Gröschl?"

The gunner nodded.

Loader Richter was already holding the next round.

The excitement within the tank grew. Not until *Oberleutnant* Diehl's voice came over the radio again did it slowly begin to subside.

"From now on fire at will!"

Farther forward there was a crack as *Oberfeldwebel* Schütze's Tiger fired the first shot. Bölter saw the flash of the impact.

"The T-34 which is just coming out of the depression!" he ordered.

"Target in sight!"

Gröschl fired and the shot struck the bottom of the T-34's hull between the tracks. For a second it looked as if the tank might tip over backward from its sloping position. But instead its nose dropped forward and the tank remained motionless. A pair of crewmen leapt out and fled, pursued by machine gun fire.

From then on there was constant firing. A veritable firestorm raged over the land.

The Soviet tanks spread out and advanced in a wide line-abreast formation, firing at any muzzle flashes they saw.

After the fourth shot, three or four T-34s began to concentrate their fire on Bölter's Tiger, which was on the ridge.

A shot smacked into the ground a few meters below the Tiger. The next landed three meters in front of the tank. A thick bush was thrown onto the tank in front of the driver's visor, blinding Hölzl.

But Gröschl could still see. He fired, and another T-34 went up in flames.

"Back down the hill!"

The Tiger backed up. Two shells whistled past overhead, and then the tank was behind the crest of the slope and safe for the time being.

The driver opened his hatch and removed the bush, which was still blocking his vision. The Tiger drove around the small hill and came upon a gully which crossed its path. The driver turned the tank into the gully and drove on straight toward the plain. A group of about ten Red Army soldiers appeared not thirty meters ahead at a bend in the gully. Bölter, who had stuck his head out of the turret hatch for a better view, ducked as a burst of submachine gun fire whipped by overhead. Bach fired a burst from his machine gun, forcing the Russians to take cover.

"Turn left, up the side of the ravine!"

Hölzl hauled the wheel around to the left. The big tank crawled up the forty degree incline. The engine roared as the Tiger climbed meter by meter in first gear. A shot rang out from somewhere as the muzzle of the Tiger's gun appeared over the top of the slope.

The shell struck the turret at an angle and jolted the Tiger to one side. The men inside the tank were deafened for a few seconds by the noise.

The Tiger's nose dropped with a crash as the tank cleared the top of the slope.

Hölzl stepped on the gas and the Tiger shot forward, which was fortunate, because just then the next shell flitted past the rear of the tank. Hölzl swung the Tiger around on the spot, its tracks ripping deep furrows in the ground.

Again there was a flash. This time the commander, driver, and gunner all saw the muzzle flash. The quick turn caused the enemy to miss again.

Gröschl fired, but his aim was hurried and the shell struck the ground in front of the T-34, throwing up a fountain of dirt.

The T-34 fired again and for the third time the crew of the Tiger was fortunate because the shell, fired from a range of at most one hundred meters, bounced off and howled away to one side.

Gröschl's next shot was on target. The armor-piercing round bored through the T-34's armor. The force of the blast within the tank caused all of its hatches to fly open. Flames spurted out; the T-34 was finished.

The Tiger rolled forward about fifty meters and Bölter saw that Schütze was engaged in a duel with a T-34.

"There!" shouted Hölzl suddenly. He had spotted a KV-II emerging from the bushes behind Schütze's tank. The heavy turret rotated slowly. The 12.2cm gun swung toward Schütze's Tiger. If one of its shells struck home, Schütze and his crew would be doomed.

Gröschl stepped on the rocker plate which controlled the

power traverse and at the same time adjusted the elevation handwheel.

There was a crash and a spurt of fire from the KV-II's gun. Bölter and his men watched the smoking trail left by the Russian shell. It struck one of the tracks of Schütze's Tiger, rendering it immobile.

Gröschl made a slight correction. Now he had time to aim precisely. When he was satisfied that he could not miss, he pressed the electric firing button. The armor-piercing shot raced toward the KV-II.

The shell struck the Russian tank with a bright flash and a shower of sparks. The huge turret tipped forward and the long gun pointed earthward. A hatch flipped open at the front of the tank. Several Russians appeared for an instant, then disappeared. The rest of the crew died in the flames that enveloped the tank.

"Your rear is clear, Schütze!" called Bölter to his comrade.

"Position yourself in front of me, I'll repair the track!"

Only the loader and gunner remained behind in the Tiger. Even though their vehicle was disabled and immobilized, they managed to destroy another T-34.

The Soviet tanks veered away from this armored barricade but still managed to reach the forward trenches of the Flanders Legion.

Antitank guns knocked out several T-34s, but the remainder drove through the trenches, collapsing them with their tracks. They then fired high-explosive shells into the surviving positions, killing all who were there.

Three men who approached one of the T-34s were killed by a long burst of machine gun fire.

Oberleutnant Diehls called the other Tigers. He was alone against the flood of at least twenty T-34s that had reached the forward German positions. Behind them were Russian shock troops.

"There's one left, *Herr Leutnant!*" called Bölter.

"Very well, you deal with it, I'll turn and join the chief."

Leutnant Meyer ordered his driver to turn the Tiger around and head for the scene of the battle at top speed. When he saw the enemy tanks rolling over the infantry's trenches, he clenched his fists.

"Fire!" he shouted excitedly. "Fire!"

The first shot struck a T-34 and left it immobilized in a trench. Two grenadiers appeared near the tank's tracks. They jumped onto the T-34, threw hand grenades into the hatches, and disappeared again.

The *Leutnant* veered around the T-34 and found himself facing two more. A shell crashed against the side of the Tiger, but failed to penetrate.

The Tiger swung about like an angry giant. There was a flash from its gun and another T-34 was put out of action. The rest turned away and rolled along the front lines toward the south and southeast.

The fleeing tanks were intercepted by *Oberleutnant* Diehls. This caused them to turn once again, however, and the three men who had just completed repairs to the track suddenly found themselves facing a hail of fire from six or seven T-34s.

The driver hauled the Tiger around and the gun crew joined in the concentrated barrage from the other two German tanks.

Four of the seven Soviet tanks split up and fled in different directions. Hits from the rear and sides caused several of them to catch fire within a few minutes. Their blazing, smoking hulks lay at the edge of the German front line.

One Soviet tank escaped, however. It rolled southeast, crossed the front lines, and drove into Badayev. The T-34 fired high-explosive shells into the houses occupied by the supply train, wreaking havoc in the village.

A member of the supply train shouted a warning to *Oberleutnant* Diehls: *"Achtung,* he's going for our fuel dump!"

Diehls grabbed a Teller mine and ran across the street at a crouch. A shell whistled past overhead. The shock wave forced the *Oberleutnant* to the ground, but this saved him from a rain of machine gun bullets that perforated the street.

A short time later he reached the street the T-34 would have to use if it were to attack the fuel depot.

Diehls threw the Teller mine to the ground and dove to one side as the enemy machine gun fired another burst.

"There, he's seen the fuel tanks!"

The T-34 turned. Then it halted and trained its gun on the fuel dump.

"He has to move closer!" shouted an *Unteroffizier,* reaching for an antitank rifle.

He fired into the flank of the Soviet tank. The shot did not penetrate, but the T-34 moved forward without firing.

Two meters to go, one meter . . .

The T-34 drove over the mine!

There was a brilliant flash and the nose of the T-34 was lifted at least a half meter into the air. The force of the blast must have torn out the bottom of the tank, as fuel now came streaming out. The fuel ignited with a dull thump, and suddenly the tank's crew emerged from the flames enveloping the T-34. Their clothes on fire, they ran screaming to the side of the street where they threw themselves into the snow. A short time later they were captured by members of the supply train, who saw to their injuries.

Throughout 21 March the entire area around the main road was filled with the sounds of tank-versus-tank duels. The German tactics alternated between rapid advances and changes of position, and concealment and ambush.

Bölter felt himself being overcome by exhaustion. He was forced to resort to stimulants to stay awake. It was a dangerous game, but they had to remain alert if they were to stay alive. There was no other choice.

The men frequently nodded off during pauses in the fighting. During trips to the rear for ammunition they sought shelter behind a pile of fuel drums, smoked a cigarette, and went to sleep until Bölter called for them. Then they climbed stiff-legged into their tanks and set out once again for the front, where they were soon in combat with Soviet tanks and assault guns once more.

By midday on 21 March another ten knocked-out Soviet tanks lay along the German front line and on both sides of the main road.

At about 1450 that day Bölter and his crew returned to the front after rearming their Tiger. Suddenly they were caught in a hail of rocket projectiles. The first salvo passed overhead and crashed to earth behind the tank. A high-pitched howling noise announced the approach of a second salvo, and all of a sudden there were explosions and crashes directly ahead, coming nearer and nearer.

All of this happened in seconds, but it seemed to Bölter to be taking place in slow motion.

The fighting compartment was lit by a bright flash, and the

men inside were deafened by the terrific din. It was as if the ground beneath the tank were shaking. The tank felt like a ship being tossed by a heavy sea.

Then it was over, and everyone was amazed that they had survived and the tank was still in one piece.

Bölter saw the next wave of Soviet tanks approaching. On his orders the gunner opened fire from a range of more than two thousand meters. It was as if they were on the practice range. Then Soviet artillery began to zero in on the Tiger. Bölter moved to a different position, evading the artillery fire, and resumed the engagement.

One of the Tigers failed to get through. It was ambushed by a Soviet assault gun firing from a well-camouflaged position. The first 12.2cm round was a direct hit. Bölter watched the duel through his scissors telescope and saw the entire cupola blown off the Tiger.

"Watch out, Gröschl! Assault gun behind the bushes. Range eight hundred at exactly twelve o'clock!"

"Target in sight!"

Gröschl had the assault gun in his sights before it could fire a second shot. He pressed the firing button, and the armor-piercing shell flashed toward the Soviet assault gun. A jet of flame ten meters high shot upward as the shot struck home.

"A hit!"

Bölter's Tiger covered the four crew members as they pulled their severely wounded commander from the tank and carried him to safety.

"Up behind! Quickly!"

With the five men from the knocked-out Tiger aboard, Bölter headed back across the front lines and delivered the severely wounded man to the dressing station.

Afterward he headed back to the front, arriving just in time to take part in the last engagement between the two Tigers still there and the approaching T-34s.

Bölter had a good view of the battlefield through his cupola vision slits. He spotted two T-34s trying to slip past the Tigers and ordered his driver to turn the tank around.

Oberfeldwebel Bölter's Tiger sustained another hit during the battle with the two enemy tanks, without, however, impairing its effectiveness.

Once again Bölter flipped open the cupola hatch cover

and emerged from the turret. A good view was important, perhaps the most important thing in an encounter with enemy tanks, which might approach from low ground or wooded areas.

This time, however, there was nothing to be seen but burning, smoking wrecks.

The battle was over. The Soviets had failed to break through the German main line of resistance. This failure in spite of the Soviet numerical superiority was due in large measure to the efforts of the handful of Tiger tanks. During the fighting of 21 March they had destroyed eighteen Soviet tanks.

It was obvious that the German armored forces now had a tank that was superior to all others.

German engineers went forward to destroy a damaged Tiger that could not be recovered. It had been hit twice by antitank guns and was beyond repair.

The Soviets had lost forty tanks within three days in the area around Krasny Bor. The majority had fallen victim to the small number of Tiger tanks. It appeared that the Soviets had exhausted their armored resources. They now changed tactics, employing infantry covered by heavy antitank guns—which were moved forward under cover of darkness and installed in camouflaged positions—in an effort to turn the tide in their favor. These tactics resulted in the loss of two more Tigers.

In the period between the twenty-second and thirtieth of March, Bölter came under fire from the concealed antitank guns many times. It is a mystery even to him how he managed to evade all of the shells aimed at his tank and destroy some of the Soviet antitank guns.

Every day Bölter and his Tiger came under fire from at least one concealed antitank gun. Twice he had to endure hours of Soviet artillery fire, and for a third time he and his crew were forced to abandon their Tiger and escape on foot.

That night he led a party into no-man's-land to recover the Tiger. Bölter and his group exchanged fire with a Russian patrol while a repair crew worked on the tank.

The operation was a success. They drove the Tiger back to the support base and worked through the night to have it ready for action the next morning.

Bölter and his men made repeated sorties to the front, freeing surrounded positions or eliminating heavy machine guns that the Soviets had moved up during the night.

The stress on every man was great. They slept while at readiness in forward positions and were often awakened by enemy fire.

The Tigers played a major role in the battles against the Soviet antitank guns, tanks, and massed infantry around Krasny Bor, and it was largely due to their efforts that the German front was able to withstand the attacks by the numerically superior Soviet forces.

On 1 April the battle was over, and everyone was assembled in front of the battalion command post. Major Marker presented *Oberleutnant* Diehls with the Iron Cross, First Class. Then he announced the promotion of *Oberfeldwebel* Schütze to the rank of *Leutnant.* In conclusion he called the name of *Oberfeldwebel* Bölter.

"*Oberfeldwebel* Bölter, for your bravery in the past weeks the Führer has awarded you the German Cross in Gold. It is my great honor to be allowed to present it to you today."

He motioned for the adjutant to come forward, took the German Cross from its case, and pinned it onto the right breast of the *Oberfeldwebel*'s tunic.

Then he saluted and offered Bölter his hand.

Operations resumed on 11 April. An attack was scheduled to win back the lost sections of the main road. The attack failed, however.

The next morning three Tigers drove forward to halt probing Soviet forces. Commanding one of the tanks was *Stabsfeldwebel* Sanderring, one of the "old hands" of the German panzer arm.

This attack provided a demonstration of the damage a lucky hit from a Russian antitank rifle could inflict on a Tiger tank.

A well-concealed Soviet soldier took aim at the *Stabsfeldwebel*'s tank as the Tigers approached. He fired his antitank rifle from a range of fifty meters. The shot penetrated the armor-glass of one of the cupola vision slits. *Stabsfeldwebel*

Sanderring was killed instantly. The Tiger withdrew. A single Soviet soldier had accomplished what several T-34s were often unable to do: put a Tiger out of action.

The Second Battle of Lake Ladoga ended on 6 April. But what had the Soviets achieved?

They had recovered the Gorodok electrical generating plant on 17 February. The Germans pulled back their main line of resistance four kilometers to the south, where it ran along the so-called "Burma Road," which led from the Neva through Sinyavino to the Wengler Block.

However, the efforts of the German grenadiers and panzer grenadiers, combat engineers and artillerymen, and above all the panzer crews, prevented the Soviets from reaching their main objective, the Kirov rail line.

A handful of German divisions had held out against an assault by forty-eight Soviet rifle divisions, nineteen rifle brigades, a mechanized shock division, nineteen armored brigades and regiments, and ten independent armored battalions.

The Soviets had suffered heavy losses. Four kilometers of ground had been gained at a cost of 270,000 dead and wounded. A total of 847 tanks had been destroyed or put out of action, and 693 aircraft were lost over the front.

For their efforts during the battle, two German soldiers were awarded the Oak Leaves to the Knight's Cross, and thirty-four more the Knight's Cross.

During its three and a half months of action south of Leningrad, the 502nd Heavy Panzer Battalion, with its single company, had destroyed one hundred sixty three enemy tanks and at least fifty antitank guns as well as a large number of bunkers and field positions.

One result of this success in the northern sector of the Eastern Front was the creation of the "Tiger legend," which reached its high point following a demonstration by the 500th Panzer Replacement and Training Battalion in Paderborn.

At the invitation of the public relations offices of the Reich government and the Reich minister of armaments and munitions, Albert Speer, hundreds of reporters came to Camp Senne to see the new wonder panzer.

The magazine *Angriff* was the first to publish an article on the new tank, the results of which were more harmful than beneficial to the Tiger crews. The great publicity given the Tiger was one of the factors that led the Soviet command to look more closely at designs for more powerful tanks for the Red Army.

The first tangible evidence of this was the appearance of an improved T-34 with a five-man crew and an 8.5cm gun. The new tank was designated the T-34/85 and its new 8.5cm gun was capable of inflicting somewhat more serious damage to Tiger tanks than the "dents and scratches" that the reporters had described in their fanciful magazine articles.

The Soviets also hurried new and more dangerous antitank guns into service. Another new design that appeared at the front somewhat later was the Stalin tank, armed with a 12.2cm gun.

The most harmful aspect of the overblown publicity surrounding the Tiger, however, was the effect it had on senior German commanders, who tended to overestimate the tank's capabilities. Division commanders believed that with the Tiger they held the ultimate weapon in their hands, which could solve all their problems.

As a result the Tigers were often sent into action in unsuitable terrain without the necessary supporting forces, in spite of objections from the tank commanders themselves. Frequently the result was the loss of a number of the tanks involved. Operating on their own, they were picked off by enemy antitank guns and usually had to be destroyed to prevent them from falling into enemy hands.

The fact that only thirty Tigers were written off as total losses for every thousand enemy tanks destroyed is a tribute to the tireless efforts of the tank commanders, officers, rear echelon personnel, and repair services.

Generaloberst Guderian made the following observations concerning the use of the Tiger: "Whenever a Tiger unit has been employed in concentration under the strict command of a competent leader, it has been an outstanding success. The main effect of the Tiger lies in the successful destruction of enemy tanks.

"Close cooperation with other arms is necessary to completely exploit the potential of a Tiger unit.

"In addition, due to its limited short range self-defense capabilities, all other arms have a special duty to work closely with and protect the Tiger tanks."

It became summer. On 7 June, Japanese general Oshima visited the 502nd Tiger Battalion to see the new tank for himself.

Oberleutnant Diehls led the battalion in a live firing display. Plans were already being made to ship a Tiger to Japan in a large submarine. These plans were not realized, however.

While the 1st Company was undergoing inspection in the Siverskaya area, the remainder of the battalion was being assembled in Paderborn. The 2nd and 3rd Companies were formed using experienced tankers as well as young volunteers.

Training involved battle exercises in small and large formations and range practice as well as general training. All training was done at a high tempo.

Otto Carius, author of *Tiger im Schlamm,* who at that time was converting to the Tiger from another type, characterized the training as follows: "The way into the Tiger was marked by sweat and hard work. Today the recruits from those days add that they often cried tears of rage. If they complained, they often heard the words: 'What do you think is awaiting you all in Russia? This is a kindergarten by comparison! Anyone who doesn't like it can report to the infantry at once!' " It is significant that no one did so.

While the two new companies were undergoing training in France, the 1st Company enjoyed a period of rest in Tosno. The only disturbances were the nightly Soviet air raids. This was followed by a period during which the Tigers carried out local patrols and occasionally shelled Soviet bunkers facing the German front line. But there were signs that a new Soviet offensive was not far off.

The two new Tiger companies entrained in France on Corpus Christi Day 1943. The fast trains rolled straight across Germany bound for the Leningrad area. A major Soviet offensive was expected at any time.

The first Tigers were unloaded in the vicinity of Gatchina. There were no loading ramps available, and one of the Tigers tipped forward onto its nose while leaving its flatcar.

On 21 July 1943 the Tigers were sent on by rail in the direction of Mga, the key point of the entire front in northern Russia. The tanks were unloaded at a small station called Snigri, once again without the aid of loading ramps. Soviet artillery fire fell near to the station as the unloading was taking place.

The men of the "Second" learned that the Tigers of 3rd Company had already detrained at the same station. The company had been thrown into the battle immediately after disembarking, and two of its officers, *Hauptmann* Oehme and *Leutnant* Grünewald, had been killed already.

At 0300 on 22 July 1943 the Soviets began a tremendous artillery bombardment of the German positions in the northern sector of the Eastern Front. They directed the greatest weight of fire on the eastern and northern sides of the salient around Mga.

The German infantry parried the first assault while the artillery laid down carpet fire on the approaches to Mga. *Nebelwerfer* brigades fired salvoes of rockets into the Soviet assembly areas.

The Soviets achieved their first penetrations north of Mga and east of the Neva. They threw in additional forces with strong armor support in an attempt to force a decisive breakthrough.

It was then that the call went out:

"Tigers to the front!"

The Knight's Cross for *Leutnant* Bölter

The Third Battle of Lake Ladoga began on 22 July 1943. The battle was timed to coincide with the Soviet offensive on the central sector of the Eastern Front.

Artillery fire rained down on the German lines. The Soviet Air Force launched heavy raids in an effort to smash the German artillery positions before the attack began.

Finally, the divisions of the Soviet 67th Army attacked. Five divisions of the 30th Guards Rifle Corps also took part in the offensive. The Soviet 8th Army attacked from the east.

The 30th Guards Rifle Corps managed two local penetrations. One was at the triangle of railroad tracks near Posselok 6, west of the Sinyavino Heights, the other at Rangun Station, extending as far as the bank of the Neva. Although they fought bravely, the two German divisions involved—the 11th East Prussian and the 23rd Brandenburg—were unable to halt the

Soviet advance. Over the following two days the Soviets tried to force a decision at these two locations.

The German 18th Army committed its reserves: the 121st Infantry Division on the eastern front and the 28th *Jäger* Division on the northern front, west of the Sinyavino Heights.

The 11th Infantry Division held out for twenty days against attacks by seven Soviet divisions. During that time the division's artillery fired 95,000 rounds.

In the first days of August the Soviets shifted their main effort to the eastern front between Voronovo and the Kirov rail line. Twenty-nine infantry battalions attacked there from the 2nd to the 4th of August in the direction of Mga, in a flanking assault intended to unhinge the Sinyavino defenses.

Neither this offensive nor a subsequent attack by Soviet tanks was able to break through the positions held by the 5th Mountain Division and the 1st Infantry Division. The failure of the Soviet armored attack was largely due to the efforts of the 502nd Battalion's Tiger tanks.

Taking part in the action were the battalion's 1st Company, which had been in the Leningrad area since the summer of 1942, and the 2nd and 3rd Companies, which had arrived from France on 22 July.

The Tigers operated from the Snigri support base, and Bölter was almost always involved. These missions included duels with Soviet tanks, nighttime attacks on dug-in Soviet infantry, local patrols, and counterattacks with supporting infantry.

Oberleutnant Diehls continued to lead 1st Company. His commanders included *Leutnant* Schütze, *Leutnant* Heer, and *Unteroffizier* Lötsch. Lötsch survived a very difficult mission on 30 July, and the next day returned to the front with *Unteroffizier* Federizzi and *Unteroffizier* Hornung to drive back a group of Soviet forces that had penetrated the German lines. Several bunkers occupied by the Soviets were destroyed by direct fire.

The Tigers were frequently hit by return fire and there was much feverish work in the repair shops. Repair crews took advantage of the hours of darkness to go up to the front and repair Tigers disabled with track damage.

The fighting spirit of the infantry was at its highest when the Tigers were there to lend their support, whether at the bunker complex known as *Bunkerdorf* or at Strongpoint Balzerweg.

The Third Battle of Lake Ladoga raged on until the end of August, when the fighting began to die down. Soviet casualties had once again been heavy, with 100,000 men lost, and the German defenders destroyed 344 Soviet armored vehicles and 307 aircraft. Again the Soviets had failed to reach their objective.

While the 502nd Battalion was still engaged in repairing and overhauling its tanks and other vehicles, the Soviets struck again. This time they chose the right wing of the northern front near Nevel. The 502nd Battalion was immediately ordered to Nevel.

In the meantime the battalion had received a new commanding officer, Maj. Willy Jähde. On 8 October the tanks set out by rail from Tosno.

The Soviets had taken Nevel two days earlier in a surprise attack by sixty tanks followed by trucks carrying infantry.

The German 58th Infantry Division and the 502nd Battalion were given the job of retaking the city. The 58th Division intercepted the advancing enemy forces and stopped them north of Nevel in the area of Aluntovo and Medvedko.

Four battles raged around the city. It was there that part of 1st Company, which had been sent into battle straight from the loading ramps, was surrounded on the main road by the Soviets. The platoon led by *Leutnant* Meyer was completely wiped out. The *Leutnant,* one of the bravest of the German tank commanders, shot himself rather than be taken prisoner by the Soviets.

A few days later Gatchina had to be abandoned. German forces withdrew along the Gatchina-Volosovo-Narva road. Whenever the situation became threatening Major Jähde and his Tigers were there.

Near Volosovo it was the major and the battalion adjutant who went out in the last two fully-armed Tigers to face the onrushing Soviet armor. After destroying nine enemy tanks, Jähde's Tiger was hit. Although wounded, he remained with his unit. During the action Jähde's adjutant, commanding the second Tiger, destroyed six Soviet tanks.

On 19 January 1944 the battalion was transferred from the Pustoshka area back to the Ladoga Front, where heavy fighting had erupted once more. Firing trials were carried out before leaving to ensure that all was in order.

* * *

The Soviets had captured Krasnoye Selo on the night of 19/20 January and were now advancing on Kipen.

Major Jähde received orders from the commanding general of the L Army Corps to form a battle group and hold the positions near Voronovo-Syas-Kelevo.

"Your position is the most important pillar of the defensive front north of Gatchina," declared the general emphatically.

On their first day in action—22 January—the Tigers destroyed twelve enemy tanks. Nevertheless, the German troops were forced to withdraw on 26 January.

Two Tiger companies were temporarily detached to the III Germanic Panzer Corps following a Soviet breakthrough.

The Tigers' success against the onrushing Soviet forces created some breathing room for the hard-pressed German infantry divisions. They forced the Soviet armored divisions to halt, even if only temporarily.

Just as the Tigers were entraining for Narva, Bölter, who was now a *Leutnant* (since 1 May 1943), received news that his friend, the commander of 1st Company and exemplary comrade *Oberleutnant* Diehls, had been fatally wounded while riding in his Kübelwagen.

In the new area of operations, the battalion was once again split up and did not see action as a unit. While 2nd Company was engaged in defensive fighting near Narva, 1st and 3rd Companies carried out counterattacks south of Pskov and near Idritsa.

Generalfeldmarschall von Küchler, commander in chief of Army Group North, congratulated the battalion on its success.

Bölter and his crew spent the evening before Good Friday in their tank, which had been deployed to guard the command post of an infantry regiment.

The five men dozed off now and then. Rumbling noises could be heard in the distance. Soviet armor was assembling for an attack.

Dawn came slowly.

"I'm going into the command post to see what they have planned for us," said Bölter to his comrades.

He swung himself out of the tank. The rumbling from the Russian lines grew louder as he walked over to the command post, his legs stiff and sore.

Inside, Bölter had a brief conversation with the regiment's commanding officer.

"Is there somewhere I can lie down, *Herr Oberstleutnant?*" he asked.

"You can sleep over there, Bölter."

But before he could stretch out, there was a tremendous crash as shells began to burst nearby. A glance at his watch showed that it was just six o'clock.

The Soviets opened their new offensive with an artillery bombardment from hundreds of guns. These were joined by numerous batteries of Stalin organ multiple rocket launchers, which directed their fire at the German main line of resistance, softening it up for the attack.

Shells smashed into the ground all around. The command post swayed and shook. Thousands of artillery shells were falling in the regiment's sector, a sign that this was where the Soviets would be seeking to break through the German lines. The main line of resistance extended between the villages of Vadrino and Bol Usy.

The Battle of Pskov approached its climax. The artillery barrage lasted two hours, then the Soviet infantry attacked the positions of the 8th Infantry Division.

Waves of Red Army soldiers stormed forward. Stuka dive-bombers plunged down on them, dropping dozens of small antipersonnel bombs and strafing with cannon and machine guns.

The enemy infantry halted. The Soviets then attempted a flanking attack with thirty tanks. They found a weak spot in the German defenses where there were no heavy weapons.

The thirty tanks broke through.

Bölter knew nothing of this as he directed his Tiger nearer to the command post so that if need be he and his crew could jump in and drive away quickly.

A wounded messenger arrived at the command post.

"Enemy tank attack, *Herr Oberstleutnant!* The tanks have penetrated the main line of resistance and are overrunning the infantry!"

"Bölter, this is a job for you!" said the regimental commander. "Head over there and . . ."

Bölter raced out of the bunker. At the same moment four shells fell nearby. The shock wave threw the *Leutnant* back into the bunker. He felt as if he had been struck by a giant fist. Dazed, he got to his feet.

The commander of the infantry regiment looked at him beseechingly.

"Bölter, you must go out and repulse the tank attack! If the Russians reach here the front is finished. There's no other way, you must try!"

Bölter was gripped by fear, but he could also see the outline of his Tiger. Never before had the infantry waited for him in vain, and it was not going to happen now.

He tensed himself, and after the next group of shells fell he hurried out of the bunker and began to run. Bölter hadn't gone ten steps when he heard the terrible howling sound of an approaching salvo from a Stalin organ. Acting quickly, he threw himself into a shell hole. There was a terrific din as rockets burst all around him.

The thick cloud of cordite smoke and dust made it difficult to breathe. Fist-size clumps of earth rained down on him. Then more artillery and mortar rounds began to fall nearby. Bölter crawled back toward the command post. Along the way he was grazed three times by shrapnel. Finally he made it back to the command post bunker, completely out of breath.

Bölter saw the look of resignation on the infantry commander's face: "I'm going, *Herr Oberstleutnant!* I'm going!"

Bölter knew that he would have to do what the messenger had done.

After the next salvo he raced outside. Bölter knew very well that he was running for his life. Blast waves from the exploding shells threw him to the ground, but he was on his feet again before the smoke cleared. Lungs burning, he finally reached his Tiger. Gunner Gröschl had already opened the turret hatch. Bölter placed his right foot on the track, then his left on the mudguard and jumped up onto the turret before hopping inside and closing the hatch cover. Shells fell all around, spraying the steel sides of the tank with shrapnel.

"Here, *Herr Leutnant!*"

Gröschl, who sat ahead of and somewhat lower than the

commander, passed a lit cigarette over his shoulder. Bölter in-
haled the smoke deeply.

Hölzl began to drive in the direction of the front lines. There
was little need for orders. They were a close, tightly-knit crew.
Each knew what to expect of the others in any situation.

The Tiger rolled through a gully and reached an area of
sparsely treed, undulating terrain. A little later Bölter spotted a
mass of enemy tanks as they rolled out of the forest at the far
side of no-man's-land. He watched as the heavy assault guns,
which were driving on the flanks of the Soviet armored formation, halted now and then and fired their 12.2 and 15.2cm shells
into the German positions.

"They're forming up for an attack, *Herr Leutnant!*" shouted
Hölzl who, now that the tank had cleared the trees, had an excellent view through his driver's visor.

The range was about a thousand meters when Gröschl
opened fire. Gunner and loader worked quickly and in a few
minutes four T-34s lay burning on the open field. The sudden
appearance of this deadly foe appeared to have paralyzed the
Soviets.

A warning cry crackled over the Soviet frequency: *"Tigrii!—
Tigrii!—Tigrii!"*

The T-34s, KV-Is, and assault guns spread out and opened
fire on the German Tiger.

Shells flashed past over the turret. Bölter could see them flitting by his vision slits, and hear them as well.

Gröschl shouted a warning. But the driver had just halted to
allow him to fire, and it was already too late to react.

A shell howled toward the Tiger. A bright flash lit the
fighting compartment and there was a murderous crash. The
Tiger shuddered under the impact of the shell, which had struck
the tank's forward plates. Dense smoke shrouded the tank for
a few seconds, but it had survived the blow without serious damage. In any other tank the crew would have been finished.

With a roar of its engine the Tiger turned to the right and
drove into some bushes in a shallow depression. Only the commander and gunner could still see the enemy tanks. An assault
gun wandered in front of the Tiger and halted. Fire spewed
from the muzzle of its huge gun.

Gröschl had it in his sights and pressed the firing button.

They were too close to miss, and the armor-piercing round smashed through the armor plate and turned the Soviet assault gun into a smoldering wreck.

Gröschl immediately stepped on the rocker plate controlling the power traverse, which could rotate the turret through 360 degrees in one minute.

A T-34 grew in his sight. Gröschl followed the Soviet tank as it rolled closer and then halted. A slight correction, and fire! The hit apparently detonated a shell in the chamber of the T-34's gun. Flames spewed from the doomed T-34. To the left and right fast Soviet tanks rolled past the Tiger about a kilometer away.

"They're trying to outflank us!" reported Bölter to his comrades. His voice was noticeably calm. This apparent confidence was passed on to his crew.

Crash!

Another hit, this time low on the left side. There was a clattering noise from the left track.

If only the track hasn't been damaged! thought Bölter. "Forward thirty meters!" he ordered.

The track had not been damaged. The Tiger responded to the driver as before. Behind a low rise it temporarily found cover.

"We need reinforcements! How does it look, do you have radio contact, Bach?"

"Help is coming, *Herr Leutnant; Oberleutnant* Göring and *Unteroffizier* Sperling are on their way to us."

"Hopefully they'll get through the barrage fire."

For the first time Bölter realized that the Soviets had shifted their artillery fire farther to the rear so as not to endanger their attack units.

Suddenly there was a crash from the left flank.

"It's Göring, *Herr Leutnant!* He says that he is attacking T-34s approaching from the flank."

Seconds later there was also firing from far to the left of the *Leutnant's* Tiger.

"That must be Sperling," declared Bölter, relieved and full of confidence again.

The two Tigers had raced toward the front. They had rolled through the enemy barrage and were now attacking the flanking elements of the Soviet armored brigade.

Oberleutnant Göring destroyed four T-34s in rapid succession. The rest turned away and fled into nearby gullies and ravines.

Unteroffizier Sperling encountered the Soviet heavy assault guns. An experienced tank commander, highly decorated and cool under fire, he waited until one of the assault guns fired, then drove to within six hundred meters, where he could not miss. He had more than a minute, because it took that long for the assault guns to reload. The ammunition for the heavy 12.2 and 15.2cm guns was loaded in two parts, shell and charge. This took time, and it was this interval that Sperling used to his advantage. He knocked out two assault guns that were in his way and damaged a third so severely that it turned away smoking and disappeared into the forest.

In the meantime the Soviets tried to break through in the center past *Leutnant* Bölter's Tiger. The battle had been going on for two hours now, but things were still happening quickly for the men inside the Tiger. Within a space of two minutes they destroyed three more T-34s. Then Bölter ordered a change of position. The Tiger turned left and drove through shell holes and several shallow depressions until it came to a dense, narrow stand of trees. Bölter instructed the driver to push on, and as they reached the far side he found himself looking straight at several T-34s whose crews were apparently deliberating as to the best way of dealing with these Tigers.

Gröschl fired three times before the surprised Soviets could reply. Two of the T-34s would fire no more, because they were already shrouded in flames at the far side of the small wood.

Shells whistled into the trees to the right and left of Bölter's Tiger. One grazed the turret, making a hellish sound.

"Back up, thirty meters.—Stop! Turn right and through the woods."

The Tiger crashed through the trees as shells burst in its wake. After about three hundred meters Bölter turned back toward the clearing. Hölzl raced the Tiger out of the trees, then turned to face the Soviet tanks. Gröschl again opened fire.

The Tiger fired five times. That was too much for the Soviets. The T-34s that had survived the ambush drove straight into the woods seeking cover.

Bölter and his crew drove in a wide arc back to their former position. There they again took up the battle against the advancing Soviet armor. Gröschl knocked out a T-34 from a range of more than a thousand meters.

The battle raged back and forth for three hours. The Soviet armored brigade had already lost more than twenty tanks. Göring and Sperling were now in position on either side of Bölter's Tiger, allowing the three tanks to provide mutual support and call out their targets.

Oberfeldwebel Göring reported his fifth and sixth kills. There was no need to announce the seventh. Peering through a vision slit, Bölter saw it explode in a tremendous display of fireworks.

Suddenly a Soviet tank began to fire on Sperling's Tiger.

Bölter called a warning: *"Achtung,* Sperling! Assault gun to your left! I'll take the T-34!"

Two rounds smashed into the T-34 that was firing on Sperling. The tank burst into flames.

Just then the Soviet assault gun, which Sperling's first shot had failed to disable, opened fire. The 15.2cm shell struck the Tiger's front armor plate and cracked open the weld seam. Fortunately it did not penetrate, but Sperling was forced to leave the battlefield.

"Must withdraw, nose torn open!" reported the *Unteroffizier* after the dust settled. Bölter, who had feared the worst, breathed a sigh of relief.

"Good, Sperling, get going!"

The *Unteroffizier* laughed, and Bölter watched as the damaged, but still mobile Tiger withdrew.

A shell from *Oberfeldwebel* Göring's Tiger caused the Soviet assault gun to turn quickly and disappear.

Sperling had destroyed four tanks and assault guns, while Göring was up to seven. Bölter had destroyed fifteen tanks. But now Gröschl called him.

"We can't go on, *Herr Leutnant.* Our gun is recoiling to the red marking."

"We'll have to withdraw."

"The Russians have given up anyway!" shouted Hölzl.

"That's right! No more to be seen!" seconded Gröschl.

The Soviets had in fact given up. Their losses at the hands of the three Tigers had been too high. The threatened armored breakthrough, which would undoubtedly have been a disaster for the entire sector, had been foiled by Bölter's small force.

The rest of the battalion's Tigers, including those commanded by *Leutnant* Ruppel, *Leutnant* Schürer, *Feldwebel* Böckelmann, and *Feldwebel* Laube, fought on in other sectors of the front. They were constantly in action against the masses of Soviet armored vehicles.

The Soviets continued to try their luck until 9 April 1944. Then it was over. The Soviets had lost their great breakthrough battle. Seven of their rifle divisions had been beaten back while suffering bloody losses. Seventy-two Soviet tanks had been destroyed, the majority by the·502nd Heavy Panzer Battalion.

The fighting died down. The men of the battalion moved into quarters in the village of Robinyaty. On the morning of 25 April, in front of the assembled battalion, *Leutnant* Hans Bölter was presented with the Knight's Cross he had been awarded on 16 April.

The Oak Leaves for *Leutnant* Hans Bölter

On returning from a brief leave, *Leutnant* Bölter took over temporary command of the battalion's 3rd Company in its rest quarters in Robinyaty. Bölter had received his commission in the field and had therefore received no officer training. Nevertheless, he.commanded the company as well as any other officer.

The weather was fine and warm during what was to be the last quiet interlude of the war. It lasted seven weeks. During this time the battalion, under its new commanding officer, Major Schwaner, reached the highest combat strength since its formation.

The 2nd Company was billeted in several villages behind Robinyaty, while the Headquarters Company had been transferred to Iborska in Estonia.

An unfortunate incident occurred during Bölter's period as CO of 3rd Company. One day, while cleaning his flare pistol, an *Unteroffizier* accidentally fired a flare that landed on the straw roof of a hut, setting it on fire. Soon almost every building in the village was burning. The "eighty-eight" ammunition, which was stored in one of the huts, went up.

Luckily, *Hauptmann* Leonhardt returned soon afterward and was able to smooth over the whole affair.

Since mid-July a front-line theater troop had been entertaining the soldiers several kilometers to the rear of Robinyaty. On the evening of 22 June 1944, Bölter and the last platoon were enjoying a violin solo. At about 2000 the Soviets began a tremendous bombardment northwest of Ostrov.

A messenger arrived and informed Bölter that the battalion had been placed on alert. The men drove at once back to their company.

From their readiness positions the tankers could hear the dull rumble of artillery fire.

Only a week before Hans Bölter had been awarded the Panzer Assault Badge, Second Grade, and it seemed likely that he would see further action very soon.

The Soviet artillery bombardment concentrated initially on the two-kilometer-wide sector northeast of Ostrov held by the 121st Infantry Division. More than three hundred guns and fifty Stalin organs poured fire into the German lines in an effort to soften them up for the Soviet offensive.

Two hours later the Soviet rifle divisions stormed forward. They broke through the shattered German lines and reached the high ground near Suyevo, the so-called "Jew's nose." The villages of Shapkov, Bayevo, and Vankovo fell into their hands, and by the evening of 23 June, Soviet tanks and mounted infantry were advancing along the Suyevo-Judino ridge toward the Pskov-Ostrov rail line.

If the Soviets broke through here they could be in Ostrov in an hour.

On the evening of 23 June the tanks of the 3rd Company left Robinyaty and assembled at the main road. There were fourteen Tigers. They drove forward, the commanders standing in their turrets, and crossed the road.

Bölter saw horse-drawn wagons streaming toward the rear with their cargoes of wounded. He saw terror and bitterness in their faces. "Why didn't you come sooner?" one of the wounded men called up to him.

Bölter clenched his teeth. There were too many "whys" and he had no answers.

That night ten Tigers of the "Second" and eleven of the "Third" reached the combat zone after a drive of thirty kilometers.

Oberst Löhr, commander of the 121st Infantry Division, gave the company commanders and the battalion CO their combat assignment: "Attack at X-Hour on 24. 6. 44. from the assembly areas. Third Company from Pyljai, 2nd Company four kilometers to the northwest, due west of the village of Seshtkino. Counterattack with the newly arrived GR 94 along the route Kirovo State Farm—Shapkovo, and recapture the high ground near Suyevo."

As the attack began, 2nd Company drove forward with the 94th Grenadier Regiment. Heavy artillery fire began to fall among the Tigers. The grenadiers were halted at the edge of a forest behind the state farm.

Inside the tanks the radio operators, drivers, and commanders could see the flashes of exploding artillery shells and rockets. The Tigers reached their objective, but without the infantry, and as darkness approached they were forced to withdraw.

Since the attack by the neighboring infantry unit on the right, the 121st *Pionier* Battalion, was making better progress, 3rd Company was sent there to lend its support.

The eleven Tigers raced toward the scene of the fighting with Bölter leading the first group. They reached the enemy-held territory in front of the "Jew's nose," and at about midday Bölter's Tigers, followed closely by several other armored vehicles, rolled up the high ground in front of Suyevo. But the Soviets had occupied the former German bunkers and trench system. Soviet antitank rifles fired from every trench, aiming for the tanks' vision slits and periscopes.

Gröschl kept up a steady fire on recognized enemy positions. Antitank rifle projectiles smacked into the Tiger's flanks and gun mantlet.

One by one the enemy-held bunkers, mortar positions, and machine gun nests were put out of action by direct fire from the approaching tanks.

Several Soviet tanks that attempted to intervene were destroyed. Nevertheless, the German infantry forces suffered high losses. The company repeatedly sent single tanks back to assist pinned down groups of infantry and silence Soviet mortar and machine gun positions.

Three Soviet counterattacks were repulsed in the course of the afternoon and seven more tanks destroyed.

In spite of this the day ended in tragedy. The Tiger commanded by *Leutnant* Carius was in an exposed position atop the heights. It was hit between the hull machine gun ball mount and turret. The shot had been fired by Carius's own company commander, who mistook the Tiger for a Soviet tank.

Nevertheless Carius, who had received the Knight's Cross on 4 May 1944, carried on. He called a warning to *Leutnant* Naumann of 3rd Company as he was about to drive over a hill. Naumann apparently did not receive the warning, however. He continued over the crest of the hill where he was ambushed by several Soviet heavy assault guns. Naumann's Tiger was hit and burst into flames. The crew got out but remain listed as missing to this day.

Obergefreiter Egon Kleine, radio operator in the Tiger of *Unteroffizier* Loewe of 3rd Company, heard Carius's warning call:

"Achtung, Ivan! *Achtung,* Ivan!"

He also heard other commands in German, but these were part of the Russian plan to lure the Tigers into an ambush. The commands were:

"Drive forward! Over the hill!"

It was later discovered that the false orders had been issued by renegade Germans of the Soviet-sponsored "Free Germany" Committee.

The Tiger commanded by *Feldwebel* Wesely also suffered major damage after being hit by a Soviet assault gun. Thus the left battle group, commanded by *Leutnant* Carius, had already suffered two losses.

Several tanks of the right battle group, formed from 3rd Company, had also been hit. The Tiger of *Unteroffizier* Loewe was struck in the right running gear by a shell fired by an anti-tank gun. Loewe managed to bring the Tiger back under its own power. On the way he was able to pick up the crew of

Riehl's Tiger, which had been forced to abandon its tank. Both Tiger companies were pulled back from the ridge at about 2200.

Leutnant Bölter drove back to Pyljai with the other operational Tigers. There they were refueled and rearmed. A little later part of 2nd Company also arrived in Pyljai. One of its platoons had been left behind in Shapkovo with the infantry.

Most of the Tigers remained in Pyljai on 25 June, although *Leutnant* Carius led a platoon from 2nd Company to Shapkovo to support the 1st Battalion of the 94th Grenadier Regiment. Several Soviet counterattacks were repulsed.

On 25 June the Tigers, led by *Hauptmann* Leonhardt, successfully turned back a Soviet attack with tank support, destroying three KV-Is. The battle for the "Jew's nose" raged on.

In the period to 30 June the battalion's Tigers destroyed three assault guns, twenty-five tanks (T-34s and KV-Is), eighteen antitank guns, and several artillery pieces.

On several occasions groups of grenadiers and panzer grenadiers were cut off and surrounded by the Soviets. Each time the message went out:

"Hold on! Tigers on their way from the west!"

News that the tanks were on the way heartened the decimated companies and battle groups, giving them the inspiration to fight on until the Tigers could come to their rescue.

On 3 July the battalion was placed under the command of II Army Corps. Only 1st Company, this time under the command of *Leutnant* Bölter, remained in the Idritsa area with X Army Corps.

On 12 July, Bölter received orders for his company and its sixteen Tigers to transfer by rail to Dünaburg (Daugavpils).

On his arrival, Bölter reported to the battalion commander, who was most pleased to receive this substantial reinforcement as well as once again have the entire battalion under his command. Unknown to him, however, plans already existed to remove 1st Company from II Corps. On the evening of 12 July the corps' commanding general, *Generalleutnant* Wilhelm Hasse, ordered 1st Company split into two formations. Five Tigers were dispatched to back up 3rd Company with the 225th

Infantry Division in Vensavai. The remaining five were sent to the Vazsaliena Estate, twenty kilometers east of Dünaburg, to help relieve the pressure on the 81st Infantry Division.

Leutnant Bölter led half of 1st Company to the 225th Infantry Division, joining 3rd Company. On the afternoon of 14 July he was given command of a battle group comprising 3rd Company and his half company.

"Drive to the command post of 2nd Battalion, 377th Grenadier Regiment and discuss a counterattack with the battalion commander."

Leutnant Bölter drove off. At the battalion command post in Gaideliai it was decided that the Tigers should drive over Hill 175 and recapture the village of Stosjunai which lay on the other side.

The Tigers started out at 1915. Soviet antitank guns opened fire before the tanks reached the hill. One shell struck Bölter's Tiger, but fortunately bounced off.

Gröschl and Richter worked swiftly and surely. Before the antitank gun could fire a second time it took a direct hit that put it out of action. The gun crew fled.

Projectiles from Soviet antitank rifles hailed down on the tanks. Bölter could see flashes all around as he peered through his periscope.

"Hold on!" shouted Hölzl, as the tank came upon a trench.

The Tiger's nose dropped sharply. The engine roared as Hölzl steered the Tiger through the trench at full throttle.

Soviet soldiers appeared in front of the tank. Bach opened up with his machine gun and they hastily took cover. The Tigers crashed through the Soviet positions; the infantry of 2nd Battalion followed in their tracks, clearing the foxholes and trenches of enemy soldiers. The battle for the approaches to Hill 175 was brief, but bitter.

The tanks now headed up the steep slope. Bölter was the first to reach the crest. Bright muzzle flashes revealed the presence of Soviet antitank guns.

"Watch out everyone: antitank guns on the hill!"

The lead Tiger drove into the guns' field of fire and raced across the plateau. An antitank gun appeared right in front of the tank. It fired. The shell struck the Tiger's sloped bow plate and shot straight up into the evening sky. The blow seemed to jolt the Tiger to a halt.

"Forward!"

The tank rumbled on. It was right on top of the cleverly situated antitank gun. There was a terrible crunching and grinding noise as the Tiger rolled over the Soviet gun. Hölzl caught a glimpse of the terrified face of a Russian soldier. As he tried to get out of the way he slipped and fell beneath the left track.

The heavy Tiger crushed the antitank gun into the ground. The tank leaned dangerously, then it was past the obstacle.

All of the Tigers were now on the hill. Their guns crashed. Machine gun fire swept the hill, forcing the Soviets to fall back. High-explosive rounds smashed into enemy bunkers.

"Radio message to regiment: 'We have reached and taken the hill.' "

Exactly one minute after the message was sent, artillery fire began to fall on the hill. Bölter watched as the bursting shells crept closer and closer toward the Tigers.

Shells were now falling a mere ten meters from his tank, their harsh flashes blinding the crew. Bölter gave the only possible order: "Change position!"

The Tigers rolled across the top of the hill, evading the Soviet artillery fire.

"They have an observer somewhere, *Herr Leutnant!*" suggested *Feldwebel* Böckelmann of 3rd Company.

Bölter scanned the terrain. His gaze fell on a hill south of Swentoji Brook.

"It must be coming from there!"

The tanks opened fire on the visible Soviet positions in front of the hill. Their high-explosive shells destroyed bunkers, machine gun positions, and antitank guns.

"Two tanks go to the right to the end of the plateau. I'll drive directly to the edge with Laube."

The four Tigers set themselves in motion. They reached the far edge of the hill, and there *Feldwebel* Karl Laube was the first to discover the Soviet tanks on the back slope.

"Enemy tanks on the back slope. Range twenty-five hundred meters!" he reported.

Leutnant Bölter raised his head through the turret hatch and peered through his binoculars. He, too, saw the enemy tanks, KV-Is and T-34s. If they made a move things could get difficult for the infantry, which was about to resume its advance to the left and right of the hill. The men would walk into the enemy fire.

"Open fire!"

The Tigers' heavy guns opened fire from a range of two and a half kilometers.

The shells struck the ground in front of the camouflaged Soviet tanks. After ten rounds Bölter called a halt.

"We're just wasting ammunition at this range!"

"*Herr Leutnant.* Two thousand, in front, in the ravine!"

"It looks like a Stalin organ moving into position.—Gröschl, you'll have to take care of it!"

A multiple rocket launcher was in fact moving into firing position in the ravine. It was followed by two trucks carrying ammunition and one with personnel. Gröschl fired. The shell fell to the right of the rocket launcher. The third hit one of the munitions trucks and its load of rocket projectiles exploded in a ball of fire. Then the *katyusha* launcher was hit and destroyed.

All of a sudden there were flashes from below and from the opposite hill. Shells whizzed past overhead.

"Enemy antitank guns! Everyone open fire!"

The Tigers had moved forward to the edge of the hill. They opened fire, destroying six antitank guns one after another. However, the German infantry, without cover and at the mercy of the Soviet artillery fire, was unable to hold the captured territory.

When Bölter went to see the battalion commander to receive directions for the night he was told: "We'll have to give up the ground we've won, Bölter. The regiment agrees that we should pull back to the next valley and wait there."

"Very well, Herr Major. My tanks will pull back and establish a blocking position."

"The battalion command post is in the shot-up cottage in the valley. Assemble there at 2200 for new orders."

It had also been a day of heavy fighting for the Carius group. *Feldwebel* Kerscher had enjoyed an especially successful day. He had pushed far beyond Hill 173.3, destroying every enemy position as far as the shore of Lake Ricu and forcing large numbers of Soviet infantry to fall back.

The half of 1st Company commanded by *Leutnant* Baumann remained in the 132nd Infantry Division's assembly area, about eight kilometers to the east, near the Solonja Estate.

The next day was uneventful. Bölter inspected his Tigers and exchanged opinions with the other commanders as to whether the Soviets were going to attack again.

On 16 July the Baumann force was moved forward to lead an attack by the 132nd Infantry Division. It was to spearhead an advance southward along the Babascki-Borony road and eliminate any pockets of resistance. The results were to be quite different, however. *Leutnant* Baumann set off at 1600 as ordered. The initial charge overran the forward Soviet outposts, but as the tanks approached the village of Dubinovo they suddenly were fired on by no less than eight antitank guns.

"Fire! Fire!" shouted the *Leutnant*.

A duel began between the tanks and antitank guns. The antitank guns had the advantage of well-camouflaged positions. The first Tiger was hit, and its crew forced to abandon the tank. A second was disabled before the first antitank gun was destroyed by a direct hit.

Then the three remaining Tigers went into action. They changed positions frequently in an attempt to outmaneuver the antitank guns. Nevertheless, three minutes later a third Tiger was hit and burst into flames. The crew bailed out and was picked up by another Tiger.

Leutnant Baumann was forced to break off the battle as darkness fell, when he learned that the infantry had not started out. Three Tigers had been knocked out in the bitter fighting. The Soviets lost six heavy and four medium antitank guns, but this was little compensation for the loss of the greater part of the Baumann group's fighting strength.

Late in the evening of 16 July, *Leutnant* Bölter received orders to lead his Tigers, including those of the half-company from the 1st Company, which had been merged with 3rd Company, out of the 225th Infantry Division's area of operations. He was to make an eighty-kilometer march through Dünaburg and the Vaschalina Estate to the 81st Infantry Division. This would require a risky high-speed drive under the burning summer sun. The move was justified to Bölter as follows:

"The 81st Infantry Division is involved in heavy fighting, and if you and your Tigers aren't there by tomorrow morning the whole front might collapse."

Bölter understood what was at stake. He explained the situation to his men. The Tigers reached the 81st Division's combat zone without suffering a single breakdown, and Bölter was immediately deployed with three other Tigers to secure the village of Silene. The division command was expecting an attack there, as the Soviets had sent probes toward the village from the wooded area east of Silene on the morning of the seventeenth.

The Soviets did not come that night, however. Overwhelmed by exhaustion, Bölter came close to dozing off several times. He left his Tiger and went over to the other vehicles to make sure everyone was awake.

When the sun came up on 18 July everyone breathed a sigh of relief. Soon they would be able to pull back to the rear and rest. These hopes were soon to be dashed, however.

Bölter had just stretched out in his improvised quarters when a messenger burst in.

"Leutnant Bölter, you are to proceed immediately to the command post of the 189th Grenadier Regiment for a briefing. I will take you there, *Herr Leutnant!"*

Bölter splashed some water on his face and then he was ready.

Oberst Konstantin Meyer greeted the *Leutnant* with a handshake.

"Good that you could come, Bölter. You are the last. We can begin now."

Bölter saluted a *Hauptmann* from the assault guns, nodded to the others, and sat down.

"Comrades," began Meyer, "the enemy has broken off his attack southeast of Silene and has withdrawn to the south. We intend to launch a counterattack with all motorized weapons and mounted infantry. The objective of the counterattack is to win back our former main line of resistance between Ricu and Lake Suadi. We have at our disposal fifteen assault guns, two centimeter and 'eighty-eight' flak, and your tanks."

He nodded to Bölter.

"At 1400 we will set out from Silene toward the southwest

and advance directly toward Plauskiety. From there we will continue on in the direction of Urbany."

Leutnant Bölter looked around him as he stood in the open turret hatch of his Tiger. Behind him he saw the faces of his loyal comrades. Farther to the right the grenadiers were climbing aboard the ten assault guns assigned to them. Somewhat further to the rear the men of the Latvian Grenadier Battalion climbed into the trucks that were to carry them into battle.

"Panzers—forward!"

Bölter raised his arm. The idling tank engines roared to life. The Tigers moved off and reached the road that led south. Dense, gray-brown dust clouds rose behind the tanks and soon shrouded the entire assault force. Peering through his binoculars, Bölter watched as Soviet pickets and rearguards broke and ran.

Two trucks emerged from a small wood and drove toward the road. Gröschl opened fire. The first shell blasted the rear truck right off the road. The second blew the remaining Soviet truck to pieces.

"Faster!" ordered the *Oberst,* who had driven forward in his armored half-track and halted beside Bölter's Tiger. Plauskiety appeared ahead and still there was no sign of resistance.

The assault gun commander called over the radio, "I don't like this, Bölter!"

The vehicles had advanced about another kilometer when suddenly antitank guns opened fire from wooded areas and ditches on the flanks.

"Assault guns veer off into the woods. The Tigers continue straight ahead!"

While the five assault guns without infantry turned off into the woods to eliminate the antitank guns firing from the flank, Bölter led his Tigers forward at high speed.

Soon they sighted antitank guns directly in front of them. Shells whistled past the tanks. When he was certain they could not miss, Hölzl made a quick halt.

There was a crash as the "eighty-eight" fired, followed by a ten-meter-high spurt of flame from the Soviet position. The tanks drove through and destroyed five heavy antitank guns. They reached the village of Urbany, two kilometers southeast of Plauskiety, at 1730.

The commander of the Tiger driving at the rear called, "Damn, the infantry isn't following, *Herr Leutnant!*"

Bölter emerged from his turret. He could hear the sounds of light weapons firing and the slow rattle of Soviet heavy machine guns.

"That's coming from the two strips of woods.—That's Russian infantry behind us!"

"Turn, load high-explosive!"

Soviet troops had moved out of the forest and barred the advance road. Tracks rattling, the Tigers swung about. They blasted the Russians out of their positions on the road. Suddenly there was a crash from the right flank.

"Watch out! Antitank rifles!"

Projectiles smacked against the Tiger's armored sides. They were no threat unless they hit a vision block or under the gun mantlet. All five Tigers fired. High-explosive shells burst at the edge of the wood and the tanks' machine guns opened up on any Soviet soldiers who came in sight.

The Tigers drove down from the road to the left and right, seeking cover. The flanking fire from the west grew ever heavier, as did the Soviet artillery fire. *Leutnant* Bölter reported that ammunition was running low. At 2000, *Oberst* Meyer ordered the armored spearhead to withdraw from Urbany to Silene to rearm.

The Tigers rolled back slowly, collected the infantry that had gone to ground, and provided cover as the grenadiers withdrew and dug in on a line from the south shore of Lake Ulacz to Domini, about four kilometers southeast of Silene. Not until the infantry had completed digging in did the tanks drive back to Silene.

The Baumann group received one of the damaged Tigers back following repairs and was deployed to support the 436th Grenadier Regiment (132nd Infantry Division) with a total of three Tigers and two assault guns. It, too, launched a counterattack and won back several kilometers of ground. However, the attack had to be called off abeam Dzierku. Seven antitank guns were destroyed. One Tiger sustained running gear damage.

On 19 July the enemy suspended his attack along the entire width of the corps' sector. The battalion's 1st Company was forced to make another eighty kilometer overland drive to Sarasai, where it became the corps reserve.

An hour past midnight on 22 July 1944, the II Army Corps chief of staff telephoned and placed the 502nd Battalion on alert. The previous evening powerful Soviet armored forces had broken through the 290th Infantry Division on the north bank of the Düna (Dvina) and penetrated as far as Kraslau. The Soviet armored battle group had reached the Kazanova Estate at 1900, passed the Kombuli Estate shortly afterward, and then advanced toward Izvalta, which lay only twenty-eight kilometers east of Dünaburg.

The 290th Infantry Division fell back. It had been placed under the command of II Army Corps and had received orders to set up a blocking position near Izvalta.

The 502nd Heavy Panzer Battalion was to proceed there with all available tanks and fend off the expected Soviet attempt to break through toward Dünaburg.

In the battalion command post near Gorki, two and a half kilometers southwest of the rail line to Dünaburg, *Leutnant* Eichhorn received orders to lead four Tigers out of Pestki. He was to reach the road to Izvalta by 0500 and establish contact with the command post of the 290th Infantry Division. *Leutnant* Bölter was to follow with his six Tigers at 0600.

The 2nd Company, led by *Leutnant* Carius, which could not be at the battalion command post until about 0800, was ordered to accompany 1st Company.

Major Schwaner was given complete freedom of action. When *Leutnant* Bölter and 1st Company arrived an hour later, Major Schwaner sent them against Leikumi and Lielie-Truli.

Leutnant Eichhorn and two Tigers were sent back along the Izvalta-Dünaburg road. Eichhorn was instructed to scout toward the north from Naujene Station, fifteen kilometers from Dünaburg, and determine and report the whereabouts of fifteen enemy tanks sighted near Barsuki.

In the meantime, Bölter and his Tigers had set off in the direction of Leikumi. Five hundred meters southwest of the village they suddenly came under fire. The Soviets had established themselves there with eight tanks and several antitank guns.

"Attack!" ordered Bölter. "Spread out and then converge

from both flanks. Only my tank and that on my right will attack frontally!"

The Tigers were facing a new foe: the T-34/85, a considerably improved version of their old enemy the T-34.

It took three shots for Gröschl to knock out the first T-34/85. The Tiger was hit once, but the shot bounced off when Hölzl had swerved the tank just in time.

The six Tigers maintained a high rate of fire. Soon five Soviet tanks were burning. A sixth was disabled, and after two further hits the T-34/85 blew up in a ball of fire.

"The truck with the limbered antitank gun!" shouted Hölzl, as he saw an antitank gun being moved into position.

The Tiger halted. Gröschl fired and the shell smashed into the truck's cab. Russians jumped down and ran for their lives, pursued by fire from both the Tigers' machine guns. The next shot struck a munitions truck, which went up with a tremendous explosion, sending pieces of metal flying through the air.

Two of the Tigers were hit and disabled with track damage. The remaining four pushed onward. They fought their way to Leikumi and barricaded the Russian supply road.

A Soviet supply column was caught by the tanks just outside the town and wiped out. The raid had been a complete success.

At about 1300 the 2nd Company, which had followed two hours behind 1st Company, came upon twenty Soviet heavy tanks near Malinava.

Leutnant Carius, who had spotted the Soviet movements, drove ahead in a Kübelwagen with *Leutnant* Kerscher to reconnoiter. When they reached the Dünaburg-Rositten road they were confronted by a mass of fleeing trucks and other vehicles. They learned from an NCO that Soviet tanks were not far behind. Soon after they learned from an *Oberleutnant* that an assault gun battalion had been shot up by the Soviet tanks on the other side of Krivani.

Kerscher and Carius drove back to their tanks. They led 2nd Company into an intercept position and engaged the Soviet armor. The enemy unit was the 1st Tank Brigade *Josef Stalin.* In the bitter fighting that ensued, seventeen Stalin tanks and five T-34s were destroyed. The Soviet armored spearhead had been smashed and a serious threat to the German front eliminated.

For this action *Leutnant* Carius was awarded the Oak Leaves on 27 July 1944. His efforts had saved the 290th Infantry Division and enabled it to establish a new defensive line. Other commanders who participated in the destruction of the Soviet tank brigade were *Leutnant* Nienstedt, *Leutnant* Eichhorn, *Oberfeldwebel* Kerscher, and *Oberfeldwebel* Göring.

The very hot month of July 1944 saw the Tigers in action with various units all along the front, where they were employed as a mobile "fire brigade," intervening wherever the situation became threatening.

The month of August began with the loss of a Tiger. Near Birsen one of the tanks drove over a mine, which seriously damaged its running gear and ripped open the hull. A second became bogged down in marshy ground. Ten Soviet antitank guns were destroyed.

Hans Bölter was in action again on 4 August, leading five Tigers of 1st Company. His mission was to drive south from Kirkelai through Kalai and free the 390th Grenadier Regiment. The Tigers smashed through the Soviet front, destroying eight antitank guns and several companies of infantry that stood in their way.

During the night of 6/7 August, Bölter's armored force, which had grown to seven Tigers, drove forward to secure the Schöneberg-Birsen road near Pauperiai. Unknown to *Leutnant* Bölter, a Soviet unit of thirty-five tanks and forty trucks shielded by antitank guns had assembled in a small wood only three kilometers to the south.

It was later learned that the Soviet unit consisted of elements of the 6th Guards Tank Army, an elite formation with well-trained, experienced personnel.

Hauptmann Leonhardt, commanding the battle group formed from 1st and 2nd Companies, received a reconnaissance report on the threatening Soviet armor concentration. He immediately committed a Tiger platoon under the command of *Leutnant* Bölter. The four German tanks drove right into the assembled armor, taking the Soviets completely by surprise.

The four tanks fired high-explosive shells into the fully loaded supply trucks. Explosions echoed through the forest as ammunition and other supplies went up in flames. Several antitank guns, which were limbered behind the trucks, were destroyed as well.

The Soviet tanks, which were behind the trucks, did not attack north in the direction of Schöneberg as expected, but turned away to the east.

Afterward Bölter received the following orders:

"Bölter, two more Tigers under *Leutnant* Eichhorn are on their way to you. *Leutnant* Plassmann and four tanks will take over your former blocking position. You are to drive south through Schöneberg along the Schöneberg-Birsen road, and launch a flanking attack on the enemy tanks heading east."

Soon after, the 81st Infantry Division ordered this attack broken off and instructed the Tigers to proceed to Jasiskiai to guard against an expected tank attack there.

Since no tanks appeared there and *Hauptmann* Leonhardt still suspected that the enemy was along the Schöneberg-Birsen road, he suggested that the Tigers return to the road. This request was approved. As he established contact with the infantry at the road, *Leutnant* Eichhorn came upon enemy antitank guns. He managed to put these out of action in a brief firefight and drove on to free a surrounded artillery battalion.

The entire 502nd Battalion was moved several times that day but did not make contact with enemy armored forces.

The next day a Soviet armored attack was reported near Suostas. Bölter led an attack by six Tigers at 1200. On the way to a wooded area twelve hundred meters north of Suostas, he met retreating German infantry.

A *Feldwebel* shouted to him, "Tanks and antitank guns in the village!"

"We'll drive on! Open fire as soon as the enemy is in sight!" Bölter instructed his tank commanders.

The Tigers drove ahead in wedge formation. They advanced six hundred meters before coming under fire from antitank guns and tanks. The Tigers returned the Soviet fire.

Bölter called *Hauptmann* Leonhardt: "Concentrated defensive fire from Suostas!"

"I'll send the remaining Tigers with the infantry for an enveloping attack from the west. Move on the village as soon as you hear us!"

When Bölter heard the sound of gunfire from the west he ordered his panzers forward. The Tigers fired on the move, destroying several Soviet tanks, and pressed into the village. The Soviet tanks regrouped and attacked from the south, but they were spotted by the Tigers and four were destroyed.

The rest turned away from the village. "After them!" ordered Bölter. The Tigers gave chase and destroyed two Soviet antitank guns. One of them was a captured German 8.8cm Pak 43, with which the Soviets had already put two Tigers out of action.

On 9 August, *Oberleutnant* Schürer, now in command of 2nd Company, drove back Soviet forces that had penetrated the German lines on the Memele River, destroying two heavy assault guns, a T-34, and a KV-85.

On 11 August the battalion was again alerted and placed under the command of the 81st Infantry Division, which was engaged in heavy fighting.

Leutnant Bölter immediately set out with nine Tigers of the 1st and 3rd Companies. *Hauptmann* Leonhardt and *Leutnant* Bölter went ahead by Kübelwagen for a briefing. They received orders to launch a counterattack at 1200 and recapture the former main line of resistance. Infantry support was to be provided by the 189th Grenadier Regiment and 3rd Company, 226th Grenadier Regiment.

The attack began on time. The Memele was reached at 1430. The Tigers were forced to go around a marshy area and ended up far from their objective, the village of Breiline. They swung north and ended up driving into heavy defensive fire from the Soviets. The accompanying infantry were left a thousand meters behind. Bölter and his panzers worked their way forward, knocking out antitank guns and shooting up machine gun nests in houses at the edge of the village.

Soviet tank-killing squads pressed toward the Tigers from all sides. The panzer crews managed to save their skins, holding off the Soviets with machine gun fire and desperate maneuvers, even driving straight into the infantry formations on occasion.

"We must abandon the edge of the village, *Herr Leutnant,* or the Russians will surround us!"

Hans Bölter thought for a few seconds. There was no other choice, as they had no covering infantry.

"We'll pull back six hundred meters!"

The Tigers turned and withdrew.

* * *

The next day Bölter's Tigers drove forward again and established contact with the 174th and 501st Grenadier Regiments. They then led the way for this battle group and reached a well-developed trench system about a thousand meters north of Anes-Memele. From a wooded area Soviet defensive fire whipped toward the German infantry.

Bölter called his tank commanders: "Advance across the trenches!" As the tanks approached the meter-and-a-half-wide trenches, Bölter realized that they were being used as an assembly point by a Soviet infantry unit. The trenches were heavily manned. He saw Mongolian faces as he peered through his periscope.

"Across! All weapons fire!"

Despite the threat of Soviet tank-killing squads, Bölter led his Tigers forward with all guns blazing. The Soviets made no attempt to escape. The tank attack had taken them completely by surprise. The Tigers rolled over the trenches, collapsing their walls and burying mortar crews trying to bring their weapons into firing position. The broad tracks ground two mortars into the dirt. All around were frantic cries and shots.

For a moment Hölzl felt pity for the cornered Soviet soldiers, but he gripped the steering wheel hard. These Russians had shot up the following German infantry without pity. Now it was they who faced death and screamed because they could not escape.

Two trucks loaded with fuel and ammunition were hit by Bölter's Tigers and blew up. The chaos was complete.

The Tigers then found themselves facing an extended antitank front. Enemy tanks fired from hull-down positions. The Germans had driven into the midst of a Soviet assembly area. If this force had entered the battle earlier, things would have looked bad for the Germans.

The leading Tiger was hit frontally by an armor-piercing round, which penetrated its armor. Bölter watched as the tank began to burn. A second Tiger drove into a marshy area and became bogged down. The Tigers kept firing, however, destroying seven antitank guns and four tanks.

Soviet heavy artillery began to fire on the German tanks. A 17.5cm shell struck a Tiger not twenty meters in front of Bölter. Flames gushed from its engine compartment.

"Get out!" called Bölter.

The crew of the stricken Tiger scrambled out of the burning tank. They were caught in the next flurry of bursting shells. Another Tiger was knocked out of action, its radiator holed by an exploding artillery shell.

"Attack!" ordered Bölter.

They had to take advantage of this opportunity. The Tigers had crossed the trenches and the antitank barrier and now they were only two hundred meters from Anes-Memele. However, the Soviets had set up another barrier of antitank guns in a small wood in front of the river and placed heavy assault guns in ambush positions.

Concentric fire hammered down on the Tigers. They returned fire but the odds were against them.

"Withdraw to the back slope!"

The three Tigers reached the comparative safety of the back side of a small hill. Bölter left his tank to assess the situation. He saw that the Soviet infantry had launched a counterattack and was moving in on the Tiger that had bogged down. This was the critical point of the battle. He had to make the correct decision.

"Counterattack into the Russian attack!"

The Tigers rumbled forward again. Their high-explosive shells smashed into the advancing Soviet infantry. Six machine guns fired long bursts into the enemy formations. The Soviet advance halted as their troops frantically sought cover.

"One Tiger will tow our comrades away. We'll drive ahead and cover you!"

The third Tiger turned toward the marshy area and two men jumped out to attach the tow cables.

The Soviet artillery fire intensified. While Bölter and the other Tiger continued to fire, he could hear shells bursting behind them and then a terrific crash. Bölter looked behind. Then he heard a call from the second Tiger:

"Have been hit! Turret armor has been penetrated! We're bailing out!"

The radio operator of the doomed tank was killed by an artillery shell as he tried to scramble clear. The surviving members of the crew were picked up by the other two Tigers.

Bölter was forced to once again pull back to the safety of the back slope of the hill.

At about 1900, Bölter's group was instructed to provide supporting fire for an infantry attack on the wood northeast of Anes-Memele, and after its successful capture move on the village itself. In the meantime two Tigers had returned from the repair shops and rejoined the battle group.

The Tigers moved out at 2000. Two were knocked out by massed Soviet defensive fire. Bölter sent the remaining tanks to recover the two damaged Tigers while he engaged the Soviet infantry. Under his covering fire the two Tigers were towed to safety.

13 August dawned. Bölter was sent two Tigers repaired during the night and the five from 2nd Company. *Hauptmann* Leonhardt, now the battalion commander, took over the entire battle group and led an attack against the Soviet bridgehead in Anes-Memele.

Leonhardt described his plan during the preattack briefing: "You will swing out and attack the enemy from the flank!"

13 August was a Sunday. At about 0400, Bölter's Tiger set out for the front. The clear sky indicated they were in for a hot summer day, and it was already getting warm in the tank's fighting compartment.

"Into that small wood, Hölzl!" ordered Bölter. "That's where the assembly area is."

Hölzl turned, and moments later the Tiger stopped in the protection of the wood.

"Herr Leutnant, radio message from one of the other Tigers. He has battery trouble and needs a push, as he's taking harassing fire."

"Thank you, Bach!" replied the *Leutnant.*

"All right Hölzl, move toward him!"

The Tiger left its ideal cover beside a shed and moved onto an open field before setting out at high speed in the direction of the stranded tank.

Driver Hölzl described what happened next:

As we were driving along we heard firing from our flank at about the ten-thirty position. Before we got to the other Tiger we were hit. A shell penetrated the hull cleanly behind the driver's position. The Tiger caught fire and someone shouted, "Bail out!"

Our gunner, Sebastian Gröschl, was dead. Loader Josef

Richter was also killed. The shell had cut him in half. Our radio operator, Richard Bach, was caught by a burst of machine gun fire as he tried to escape and was also killed. *Leutnant* Bölter received serious burns to his face and hands. With the last of his strength he managed to leave the tank and get a few meters away.

I tried to open the hatch cover, but unfortunately the gun was directly over the driver's hatch. In spite of the heat from the flames I crawled back into the tank to the revolving platform, and using the gun laying controls turned the gun to one side. Unfortunately, in my excitement I forgot to take off my headset and throat microphone. As I leapt clear the wires ripped the skin from my neck and I suffered third-degree burns as a result.

After an adventurous flight in a Ju-52, I ended up in Troppau hospital.

That ends Hölzl's account, but what had become of *Leutnant* Bölter?

The *Leutnant,* who had been recommended for the Oak Leaves some time earlier, was sent to Troppau hospital aboard the same Ju-52. He was fortunate there to receive care from an outstanding skin specialist, who operated on him immediately. It is thanks to this doctor that Bölter later showed little scarring from his terrible injuries. Also worthy of mention is Helmut Scheffer, a radio operator in an accompanying armored personnel carrier. He heard Bölter's distress call and immediately drove to the scene, where the wounded men were recovered.

Unteroffizier Gröschl, *Oberschütze* Josef Richter, and *Gefreiter* Richard Bach were buried in the military cemetery just behind the front.

By smashing the assembly area of the Soviet 6th Guards Tank Army, Bölter had prevented a planned enemy breakthrough. On 10 September 1944, in recognition of this accomplishment and his earlier successes, he was awarded the Oak Leaves to the Knight's Cross, becoming the 581st German soldier to receive the decoration.

The 502nd Heavy Panzer Battalion fought on. Bölter was promoted to the rank of *Oberleutnant* with an effective date of 1 July 1944. He had earlier received the Wound Badge in Gold on 3 August 1944.

The War Comes to an End

By the end of October, Bölter was well enough to travel to Salzburg to receive the Oak Leaves. *Reichsführer-SS* Himmler had by now taken over this ceremonial duty from Hitler. After the award ceremony, Himmler confided to Bölter:

"The situation isn't very rosy, Bölter. We are short twenty fully equipped mechanized divisions. But with a little luck we'll master the situation in spite of the difficulties caused by the enemy air attacks."

Bölter could not agree with Himmler's assessment of Germany's prospects. Otto Carius, who received the Oak Leaves from Himmler a day later, felt the same way and told Himmler so.

After his wounds had completely healed, Bölter was posted to the 500th Panzer Replacement and Training Battalion in Paderborn. There he passed on the lessons of his experiences in the east and west to the young recruits.

One day in Paderborn there was an air raid alert just as lunch was being served. The first bombs began to fall on the barracks grounds while the sirens were still wailing. Everyone left the table and ran for the shelters. Bölter realized that there was little chance of reaching the shelter in time, so he remained seated and calmly ate his soup. By the time the others returned he was eating dessert.

Some time later Major Jähde summoned Bölter to join him at the NCO school in Eisenach.

In the meantime the war was fast approaching its conclusion. In mid-1944 the training tanks in Eisenach, which included Tigers and *Königstigers,* were assembled into an improvised battle group and sent to Kassel. Together with the men and vehicles of the 500th Panzer Replacement and Training Battalion from Paderborn, the battle group was sent into action against the Americans.

Bölter, who had held the rank of *Hauptmann* since 1 January 1945, once again found himself in command of an armored battle group. The panzers detrained in the middle of a bombing raid. Bölter climbed into a Tiger and drove to the entrance to the city of Kassel, where the American tanks and antitank guns were.

The first battle began. A Sherman tank was blown apart. Kassel was abandoned to avoid unnecessary civilian casualties. Bölter's battle group pulled back into the Harz Mountains and at the end of March was fighting in the Braunlage area.

One day in April, Bölter was standing guard on a wooded ridge when twelve Sherman tanks approached along a defile. Bölter cold-bloodedly knocked out the first and last tanks in the enemy column, trapping the rest.

The American advance was halted, allowing the German forces to withdraw. Bölter could have inflicted a real bloodbath on the Americans, but with the end of the war so near, he wanted only to do what was necessary to ensure the safety of the troops under his command.

The battle group withdrew into the area of Brockens. Near Stecklenbach, Bölter requested new orders by radio. Just as he was sitting down to a meal in a *Gasthaus* a report arrived of approaching tanks.

"We want to try and withdraw without fighting," Bölter advised his adjutant. But as they reached their tank the Americans opened fire. Bölter's Tiger was the last remaining operational tank, and the *Hauptmann* accepted battle. Within a few minutes three knocked-out Sherman tanks lay burning near the village.

During the battle, Bölter's Tiger took a direct hit in the turret. His gunner Kraus was killed instantly. The rest of the crew bailed out.

Under fire from the Americans, the surviving members of Bölter's crew reached the safety of the forest. There he released his men to find their way home.

About twenty-five soldiers, stragglers from dispersed units, joined up with him in the next hour. By day they hid in barns and haystacks and traveled only by night. It was May, and soon Bölter found himself alone again as the others dropped out as they reached their homes.

Not far from Erfurt, where Bölter's wife and children were living, he ran into a pair of American sentries. Still in his black panzer uniform he was spotted straight away. Bölter disappeared into some bushes. The Americans ordered him out. When he failed to do so they fired their machine guns into the bushes.

Bölter kept running and finally reached Gispersleben. There

he hid in his mother-in-law's garden, in which there was a summer house. By chance his wife and mother-in-law came the next day to tend the garden.

Bölter hid in the summer house for five days. His wife brought him a suit of clothes and, dressed as a civilian, he walked from Gispersleben to Erfurt, where he went to his wife's apartment.

A few weeks after the war ended he turned himself in and received identification papers. The Russians reached Erfurt, but Bölter stayed in the city, as his wife and child were ill.

Even though Bölter had fought merely as a soldier, he was arrested by the Soviets in early 1949 and imprisoned. However, the Soviets were unable to prove that he had been involved in any war crimes.

After getting his two children through to the west, Bölter and his wife escaped to West Germany on a motorcycle in mid-June 1950. They made their way to Mülheim-Ruhr where Bölter found employment with a major manufacturing firm.

Hans Bölter

Johann Bölter was born on 19 February 1915 in Mülheim-Ruhr, the son of a machinist. Bölter's ambition was to become a career soldier, and on 1 March 1933 he enlisted in the army, joining the 3rd Squadron of the 10th Cavalry Regiment in Züllichau.

A year later he went to the 4th Motorized Reconnaissance Battalion in Leipzig, where he was trained on the first German armored cars. The following year he joined the 8th Company of the 1st Panzer Division's 1st Panzer Regiment. Bölter was thus one of the earliest members of the new German armored forces. His company commander at that time was *Hauptmann* Hochbaum.

By then a *Feldwebel,* he and his company, now under the command of *Hauptmann* von Köckeritz, participated in the campaign against Poland.

Even though he was only an NCO, *Feldwebel* Bölter commanded a heavy tank platoon equipped with the Panzer IV. He experienced the Polish cavalry attacks near Pomorska and Petrikau, which saw the Polish horsemen mount a charge against the German tanks before being blown away like chaff.

Feldwebel Bölter destroyed four enemy tanks in Poland and engaged Polish artillery and antitank guns. During the advance deep into Poland he spotted an enemy battery in position eight hundred meters from the road. Without waiting for orders he veered off the road and put the Polish battery out of action. In recognition he was awarded the Iron Cross, Second Class, by Major Dittmann a few days later.

In the western campaign *Feldwebel* Bölter took part in the 1st Panzer Division's famous dash across France. Near Sedan the division's grenadier regiment was held up by a bunker in a valley that the French had camouflaged as a farmhouse. Bölter drove up to the bunker and put it out of action by putting several well-aimed shots through its embrasures. For this feat he was awarded the Iron Cross, First Class, becoming the first noncommissioned officer to receive the decoration. The award document also mentioned the seven French tanks he had destroyed during a tank battle south of Orleans.

Soon afterward, as part of a scouting party, he destroyed two tanks and an antitank gun at a French roadblock. On 26 July 1940 he received the Panzer Assault Badge in Silver. Earlier, on 2 July 1940, he had been presented the Wound Badge in Black.

With the beginning of the Russian campaign, Bölter, an *Oberfeldwebel* since 1 October 1940, took part in all of his division's early actions in his Panzer IV. The German advance took him to the gates of Leningrad. He destroyed ten Soviet tanks before his tank was hit by Soviet fire. He and his crew escaped without injury. In early October he was wounded while outside his tank and sent to a hospital in Germany. Following his recovery, Bölter was sent to the 1st Panzer Regiment's replacement battalion in Erfurt. There he became an instructor of officer cadets.

In late autumn 1942 he reported back to the front. *Hauptmann* von Schlieffen suggested that a transfer to another division might result in an earlier promotion to the officer ranks.

So in January 1943, following a Christmas leave at home,

Bölter was sent to the Leningrad front to join the 1st Company of the 502nd Heavy Panzer (Trials) Battalion. Initially he saw action in a Panzer III, but just before the beginning of the Second Battle of Lake Ladoga he received a Tiger. His actions while commanding a Tiger form the main part of this narrative.

By the end of the war Hans Bölter had destroyed 139 enemy tanks, making him the second most successful tank commander of the Second World War after *SS-Obersturmführer* Michael Wittmann.

Military Career

19 February 1915:	Born in Mülheim in the Ruhr.
1 March 1933:	Enlists in the German army and joins 3rd Squadron, 10th Cavalry Regiment.
1935:	Joins 8th Company, 1st Panzer Regiment, 1st Panzer Division.
September 1939:	Participates in the Polish campaign with the rank of *Feldwebel,* wins Iron Cross, Second Class.
May 1940:	Participates in French campaign, wins Iron Cross, First Class.
2 July 1940:	Awarded the Wound Badge in Black.
26 July 1940:	Awarded the Panzer Assault Badge in Silver.
1 October 1940:	Promoted to *Oberfeldwebel.*
22 June 1941:	Beginning of campaign against Russia.
Early October 1941:	Wounded in action, evacuated to Germany.
January 1943:	Posted to Leningrad front to join 1st Company, 502nd Heavy Panzer Battalion.
12 January–1 April 1943:	Participates in Second Battle of Lake Ladoga as Tiger commander.
1 April 1943:	Awarded the German Cross in Gold.
1 May 1943:	Promoted to *Leutnant.*

22 July–31 August:	Third Battle of Lake Ladoga.
16 April 1944:	Awarded the Knight's Cross.
15 June 1944:	Awarded the Panzer Assault Badge, Second Grade.
August 1944:	Wound Badge in Gold. Promoted to *Oberleutnant,* effective date 1 July. Posted to 500th Panzer Training and Replacement Battalion in Paderborn.
10 September 1944:	Awarded Knight's Cross with Oak Leaves (581st recipient).
1 January 1945:	Promoted to *Hauptmann.*
8 May 1945:	End of war in Europe.
Early 1949:	Arrested by Soviets, then released.
June 1950:	Escapes to West Germany with wife.

5

Michael Wittmann

The sun rose above the horizon. Within a few minutes the long, dark shadows had withdrawn and it was almost completely light.

Michael Wittmann shielded his eyes with one hand and gazed toward the east. There, in the forest that extended off to the north, the motorcycle troops of the advance detachment were moving ahead.

"How does it look, *Unterscharführer?*" asked *Rottenführer* Klinck.

"Nothing to be seen. We'll stay as ordered and wait. There's nothing happening here!"

Seconds after these hastily spoken words, several antitank guns opened up in the woods. The crash of bursting shells was followed by the sawing sound of machine gun fire and finally the hard crack of tank cannon.

"Now they've got Meyer after them!" observed Koldenhoff, the assault gun's driver. Wittmann's assault gun was armed with the short 7.5cm gun, known to the troops as the "stump."

Wittmann thought back to the briefing that had been held two hours past midnight at *Sturmbannführer* Meyer's command post. He had received orders to secure this southern position at the forest's edge in order to protect the advance detachment from being outflanked by the enemy.

The *Leibstandarte* Brigade's reconnaissance battalion had to fight its way through the forest to establish contact with the 25th Motorcycle Battalion of the 25th Motorized Infantry Division. The few available assault guns were scattered along a ten-kilometer front.

"*Adler* ["Eagle"] calling *Bussard!*—Come in!"

Wittmann ducked involuntarily as he quite unexpectedly heard the voice of his company commander.

"Bussard to *Adler.*—I hear you!"

"Advance to the stream near Point 56.9 and secure the area. The reconnaissance battalion reports enemy tanks."

"We're advancing. Out!"

The assault gun rolled on until it reached the back slope of Hill 56.9, then halted.

At that moment Michael Wittmann heard the rattling and roaring of tanks. Several backfires reverberated amid the gunfire from the northern section of the wood.

"There they are!" said *Rottenführer* Klinck, who was crouching behind the "seventy-five."

Wittmann issued his instructions to the driver: "We'll move up onto the hill. Eleven o'clock into that line of bushes. Drive in far enough to allow me to observe. No farther, or we'll be in the open."

"As if I didn't know that!" mumbled Koldenhoff, slightly offended. He stepped on the gas pedal; cautiously, meter by meter, the assault gun pushed its way up the hill. It reached the line of bushes on the crest and stopped. Wittmann peered through his binoculars, trying to see something.

"Another two meters!" he ordered.

The assault gun moved forward. Just then Wittmann caught sight of the Soviet tanks. He didn't need his binoculars because they were already rolling along the depression from the northeast. Wittmann felt his heart pound as he counted twelve enemy tanks.

What should he do? How could he stop such a large force without sacrificing his assault gun and crew?

While he was still considering what to do, six more Soviet tanks broke out of the forest about four hundred meters to the left and turned toward the south. They joined the main body of enemy tanks, which would probably reach the top of the hill in about two minutes.

"How many, *Unterscharführer?*" asked loader Petersen. The other members of the crew called him the "quiet one," but the noise made by the many engines and the rattle of tank tracks had shaken him from his reserve.

"Eighteen!" answered the assault gun commander.

"That's all?" asked *Sturmmann* Zehmann, Wittmann's seventeen-year-old radio operator.

"That's all!" replied Wittmann. Then he bent down slightly.

"Back up, Koldenhoff! Then left around the hill."

The assault gun backed up, turned, and rolled about twelve meters down and around the hill.

"As soon as we have a clear field of fire, approach at full speed to two hundred meters—and straight toward them so that Klinck won't have to make any major adjustments."

The assault gun rolled around the hill. The enemy tanks came into view. Wittmann saw that the closest was about three hundred meters away and had already crossed the lower third of the hill.

The engine roared as the assault gun leapt forward. It crossed the remaining one hundred meters and came to an abrupt halt. Klinck needed to make only a slight correction.

"Fire!"

The "seventy-five" roared and the shell smashed into the side of the enemy tank, setting it ablaze. Seconds later there was a mighty explosion as the tank's reserve ammunition went up.

Without waiting for further orders, Koldenhoff moved the assault gun forward, turned slightly, and braked. In the meantime, loader Petersen had rammed the next round into the chamber. The breech snapped shut and Klinck fired again. The assault gun was still rocking from the recoil when the empty shell casing clanged against the rail of the shell-catcher and tumbled into the canvas bag below. Petersen had already placed the next round in the chamber. Koldenhoff turned the assault gun sharply toward the east. In doing so he avoided the flitting projectile from the nearest enemy tank, which had turned on one track after the first hit and opened fire.

The second enemy tank was now burning.

The assault gun rolled down the hill at high speed and headed toward the wood from which the six Soviet tanks had emerged. It crashed into the forest as shells whipped into the trees all around, shearing off branches that showered down on the assault gun. Then it was completely hidden by the forest.

After half a kilometer Wittmann instructed his driver to turn south. They drove two kilometers in the new direction before turning west again. About one minute later the assault gun reached the edge of the forest.

"Stop!" ordered Wittmann. The hatch cover flipped open. He leapt onto the assault gun and jumped down to the ground from the fender. Using the cover of the bushes he worked his way to the edge of the wood. From there he had a good view of the plain, the depression, and the eastern slope of Hill 56.9. He saw three Soviet tanks, which had rolled on unhindered and were now standing on the crest of the hill. Looking to his right, he spied the main body of enemy tanks, which had turned toward the forest again.

A moment later another tank appeared a few hundred meters to the right of the forest's edge and drove straight toward Wittmann.

With long strides Wittmann ran back to his assault gun, its engine idling. Swinging himself up onto the vehicle, Wittmann took his place in the commander's seat.

"Aim at the gap, Klinck! Watch out, they'll be coming any minute!"

Klinck pressed his forehead against the rubber pad of the gunsight. The clearing appeared in his telescopic sight. Then he saw the gun barrel of a KV-I, followed by the bow of the tank and finally the mighty turret.

He hesitated slightly, making a minor correction. Then Klinck pressed the firing button.

The crash of the shot and the shattering blow of the impact merged almost into one sound. The shell struck the KV-I at the junction between its hull and turret, blowing the armored turret right off the tank. As the heavy turret crashed to the ground, the muzzle of the long gun barrel buried itself in the soft earth.

A few moments later two surviving crew members bailed out. A machine gun opened fire from somewhere. The tankers disappeared from view. The remains of the KV-I were soon shrouded in flames.

The assault gun set itself in motion again. It rolled several hundred meters south along the edge of the forest. Suddenly all hell broke loose as ten Soviet tanks began firing into the wood. Branches of trees and leaves showered down on the assault gun and shell fragments clattered against its steel sides. One shell struck the ground only a few meters in front of Wittmann's vehicle. A bright flash lit the interior of the assault gun. For a few seconds Wittmann thought it was all over. Deafened by the noise, he gave Koldenhoff a hand signal.

The assault gun moved off. After a short distance it turned

west again and rattled across the open field. Three Soviet tanks were still on the crest of the hill, apparently waiting for their companions. The tanks were silhouetted clearly against the sky. A small stream appeared ahead. Turning on one track, the assault gun quickly came to the stream, which was merely a shallow rill running over the stony ground. Wittmann's assault gun crossed the stream and reached the back slope unseen, then drove up the southwest side of the hill.

Wittmann was approaching the enemy tanks from the flank. Soon he was within four hundred meters. One of the Soviet tanks showed him its rear.

The armor-piercing shot bored into the enemy tank's engine compartment. Whitish gasoline flames spurted out. The tank was soon enveloped in flames. The others turned and approached.

"Fire, Klinck!" shouted Wittmann.

The next shot struck the frontal armor of one of the Soviet tanks. Wittmann saw the shell strike home, but apparently with no effect.

Petersen gasped. He worked like mad, bending to pick up the next round, holding it ready until the empty shell casing flew out and clattered into the shell-catcher's canvas bag, then placing it in the chamber. Klinck fired at the leading enemy tank at least four times before disabling it. The following Soviet tank turned away. It rolled down the hill and disappeared into the wood, into which the other Soviet tanks had gone.

The disabled Soviet tank kept on fighting, however. Its next shot struck the assault gun's sloping bow plates and ricocheted almost vertically into the air.

Then, before the enemy tank fired a possibly fatal shot, Klinck scored a direct hit on its turret ring. Now it was finished. Flames shot into the sky and the tank's hatch covers flipped open. Several men leapt out, their uniforms on fire. The Russians threw themselves to the ground in an effort to smother the flames. It was a terrible sight!

Wittmann reported his success: "Enemy flanking attempt with eighteen tanks halted. Six enemy tanks destroyed!"

"Repeat please! Confirm eighteen!"

"Eighteen enemy tanks tried to reach Hill 56.9. They were turned back. Six enemy tanks destroyed!" explained Wittmann once again. "Send an ambulance, we have three wounded Russians here!"

The Soviets did not repeat their attempt to break through with tanks at this location.

In the meantime, *Obersturmführer* Gerhard Bremer and the 1st Motorcycle Company of the reconnaissance battalion had pushed through the northern wood and thrown back the enemy with the assistance of the main body of the assault gun company. The objective had been reached.

When Wittmann rejoined his company that evening, he was ordered to division headquarters.

"Man, wash up, Michael!" said his old friend, *Untersturmführer* Kling. "Sepp will tear your head off!"

Ten minutes later Michael Wittmann was standing before the division commander. *Obergruppenführer* Dietrich looked at him with a smile.

"Wittmann, you and your assault gun prevented the reconnaissance battalion from being outflanked by a Soviet tank unit. I hereby present you with the Iron Cross, First Class." With these words the division commander placed the decoration on the assault gun commander's tunic.

"Do you have a special request, Wittmann?"

"I would like to see the three wounded Russians on Hill 56.9 looked after, *Obergruppenführer*."

Sepp Dietrich, a *Leutnant* in the First World War and one of the Imperial Army's first tank commanders, nodded.

"I will see to it, Wittmann!"

The battle went on. The *Leibstandarte* Brigade advanced toward Kiev as part of Army Group South *(Feldmarschall* von Rundstedt). Coming from Greece, it had crossed the Soviet border near Usciług on 30 June 1941. The brigade drove to Luck along the north road, and there, on 2 July 1941, received orders to advance through Klevan toward Rovno and establish contact with *General der Kavallerie* von Mackensen's III Army Corps.

Third Army Corps had advanced too far too quickly, and its panzer divisions had been virtually surrounded by the enemy east of Rovno. The leader of the brigade's advance detachment outlined the situation as follows:

"As of today the enemy is everywhere!"

The description by *Sturmbannführer* Kurt Meyer had hit the nail right on the head.

The action by Wittmann and the reconnaissance battalion of the "LAH" *(Leibstandarte Adolf Hitler)* averted the threat to III Army Corps.

Together with *Panzergruppe* 1, the *Leibstandarte* Motorized Brigade stormed through the Stalin Line near Lyubar. The army group headquarters issued new orders, the essence of which was: ". . . take possession of a deep bridgehead east of the Dniepr near Kiev as the basis for a continuation of the attack east of the river."

As a result of this order the *Leibstandarte* found itself fighting two hundred kilometers ahead of the infantry divisions, which were incapable of keeping up with the fast armored thrust.

At the same time, the Red Army was trying to turn Kiev into an impregnable fortress. Militia units—a sort of people's guard—were raised from among the local populace. Battalions of women and young people built bunkers and field positions. The "Kiev Group" threw itself against the 14th Panzer Division. The Soviet 206th Rifle Division tried to halt the 13th Panzer Division approaching from the southwest. The Soviet 3rd Airborne Corps was transferred to Kiev. Soviet Marshal Budenny ordered the tank divisions of the 5th and 6th Soviet Armies to move against *Generaloberst* Ewald von Kleist's *Panzergruppe* 1 and halt its advance.

During the last weeks of July the *Leibstandarte* secured Irpen, its front facing east and north. However, the attempts to take Kiev in early August failed. On 9 August, Army Group South ordered:

"Halt the attack from Kiev to Korosten and go over to the defensive!"

The great battle of encirclement near Uman came to an end. On 9 August a special bulletin announced the capture of 103,000 Soviet prisoners, among them the commanders in chief of the Soviet 6th and 12th Armies. While the battle was going on, III Army Corps, which included the *Leibstandarte,* had covered the German rear.

Now, however, the brigade rolled east, and soon reached

Nikolayevka. There the brigade veered southeast to attack Kherson. Michael Wittmann and his assault gun were part of the advance detachment. On 18 August the advancing German forces reached the mouth of the Dniepr. Kherson was the next objective.

On the following day the brigade's forces drove into Kherson. The entire Dniepr bend from Dniepropetrovsk (which had been taken by the 14th Panzer Division and the 5th SS-Division *Wiking)* to Kherson was in German hands. However, Kiev had not yet fallen. After *Panzergruppe* 1 veered off, the Soviets had turned Kiev into a virtually impregnable fortress. Nevertheless, the city fell to the attacking German forces.

Until 26 September 1941, when Kiev fell, marking the end of the battle of encirclement, the *Leibstandarte* was in the southern sector of the Eastern Front with the 11th Army. The 11th Army had been given the double task of capturing the Crimean Peninsula and advancing along the northern shore of the Sea of Azov toward Rostov with the bulk of its divisions.

Since 12 September the 11th Army's commander in chief had been *General der Infanterie* von Manstein. The army's previous commander in chief, Ritter von Schobert, had been killed when his Fieseler *Storch* aircraft landed in a minefield. The aircraft blew up on landing, along with its pilot and the general.

With the capture of the Crimea and Rostov, the 11th Army would create a base from which *Feldmarschall* von Rundstedt could overrun the Donets Basin and subsequently advance to Stalingrad and Astrakhan.

Early on the morning of 12 September 1941, three spearheads stormed toward the Soviet defensive positions on the Isthmus of Perekop. Among the units was the reconnaissance battalion of the *Leibstandarte* under *Sturmbannführer* Kurt Meyer. It was accompanied by the vehicles of the assault gun company.

"Comrades, at General Bieler's command post (CO of the 73rd Infantry Division) I received orders to break through to the Isthmus of Perekop with my advance detachment."

Sturmbannführer Meyer paused briefly. He saw his company commanders staring at him. One was bewildered, the other surprised.

"We won't be attacking alone, men! Taking part in the attack with us will be Major Stiefvater, who fought with us in Greece. *Untersturmführer* Montag will be commanding the lead platoon."

"Get ready!" The voice of *Hauptsturmführer* Fischer rang through the headsets of the assault gun commanders. Michael Wittmann looked ahead. Far to the east the sky was growing lighter. The company commander raised his arm three times.

"Forward!"

The engines went from idle to full throttle. The unit set itself in motion and rolled toward the assembly area, arriving there at 0445. There it met the advance detachment commanded by Major Stiefvater. After a brief pause the vehicles moved on. The sun tinged the sky with red, and the steppe glowed with color.

The vehicles drove toward the isthmus and the Tartar trenches. Riders appeared on the horizon from the direction of Preobrashenko, but disappeared immediately. Other than the noise of his own assault groups, Wittmann heard nothing. The closest huts in the village became visible as the German troops approached.

"Look at that!" called driver Koldenhoff in surprise, pointing toward a herd of sheep that had emerged from a stand of young trees. The animals trotted toward the village. Standing in the open hatch, Wittmann gazed at the peaceful scene.

Suddenly the stillness was shattered by a thunderous explosion. This was followed by more explosions along the entire width of the herd. The fiery blasts sent pieces of sheep and clumps of earth flying into the air. The surviving animals ran deeper into the minefield until they, too, detonated mines and were killed.

"Damn, damn!" murmured Klinck. "If we'd driven into that . . . !"

He didn't say what would have happened, but there was no need. Every man knew what that would have meant for Meyer's advance detachment.

A few seconds after the last mine went off, the Soviets opened fire. Shells smashed into Stiefvater's forces, knocking motorcyclists from their seats and setting the machines on fire.

Suddenly a long, dark object appeared on the right flank and halted. What seemed like a hundred guns opened fire.

"Armored train!" roared the company commander, flabbergasted.

The assault guns opened fire. Two loud crashes from the right caused Wittmann to turn and look in that direction. Smoke was pouring from one of the nearby assault guns, and another sat immobilized with a shattered track.

"Pull back. Turn around!" came the order from the *Sturmbannführer.*

As Wittmann's assault gun turned he could hear the bursting shells and the clanging of shrapnel against the vehicle's armored sides. Finally they reached safety.

The armored cars laid smoke to cover the motorcycle troops' withdrawal. A 3.7cm Pak tried to pick off a tank mounted on the train, but just as Wittmann reached the antitank gun it took a direct hit and was blown to pieces.

Artillery fire began to fall, forcing the German troops to take cover. The armored train steamed off and disappeared in the direction of Perekop. The withdrawing German units halted four kilometers west of Preobrashenko and reassembled.

"We'll have to wait for the arrival of the infantry divisions!" said Major Stiefvater. His face looked tense and tired. A half hour later *Generalleutnant* Bieler received a radio message from *Sturmbannführer* Meyer:

"Surprise capture of Perekop impossible. Complete combat report to follow."

That evening the *Leibstandarte* Reconnaissance Battalion was relieved by a regiment of the 73rd Infantry Division in preparation for a new mission. Sepp Dietrich now sent his brigade against the center of the isthmus near Sjalkov. The brigade crossed the isthmus and pushed on to Genitchesk. The next objective was Melitopol.

"Straight toward the city. If we attack at night, we can take it in a coup de main."

This time the assault gun *"Bussard"* escorted the spearhead group. Ahead of him in the failing light Wittmann could see the commander's vehicle. To his right was a group of motorcycles, their sidecar-mounted machine guns at the ready, and to the left, somewhat farther away, the group's two antitank guns. The vehicles reached the small wood that had been penciled in on the Russian map and halted to allow the main body to catch up.

Untersturmführer Stolle set out with a patrol to scout the area ahead. Ten minutes later several antitank guns roared to life from the direction in which he had disappeared.

"We'll go and get him! 1st Company on the left! Bremer to me!"

The commander of the 1st Motorcycle Company appeared from out of the darkness. Meyer briefed him on the plan.

They drove off, over an initially good road. The road soon became little better than a path, which led across a field dotted with evergreens. The sound of fighting helped the rescue force find its way. When the vehicles were abeam the scene of the fighting and about to turn toward it, several Soviet antitank guns opened up on them. A motorcycle was hit and blasted off the road.

"Attack!" ordered Meyer.

Standing in the open commander's hatch, Wittmann issued directions to his driver. Bursts of machine gun fire hissed past. In the harsh light of the muzzle flashes, Wittmann saw that the commander's vehicle had veered off.

"Three o'clock!" he shouted, as he saw a bright muzzle flash from a Soviet gun.

Koldenhoff swerved the assault gun around. Klinck adjusted his aim and fired. The shell struck the gun's ammunition supply. Seconds later a fireball lit the darkness and the crew heard the sound of the explosion.

The assault gun rattled on and struck a stump that Wittmann had failed to notice. The vehicle came under fire and turned away to the right. Immediately afterward it turned back toward the commander's vehicle, which had been chosen as a target by several Soviet antitank guns.

"Drive over them! Maximum speed!"

The assault gun drove toward the antitank guns from the left. Several figures ran for cover. Wittmann ducked as a burst of fire from a submachine gun zipped past his head. Then they were on top of the Soviet guns. The assault gun rocked, nearly tipping over, and crushed the first antitank gun into the ground. Ten meters farther Koldenhoff brought the assault gun to a halt. Klinck fired again and the second antitank gun was silenced.

"Enemy from behind!"

The warning call came from Wittmann's platoon leader. The

assault gun turned to the right and crashed through a small stand of trees. At the other end of the wood Wittmann found the CO's vehicle and halted beside it.

There was no doubt: they were cut off. The battle had shifted to the west and northwest.

"We're in the sack, Wittmann," said Meyer's adjutant.

"We'll get through," replied the taciturn assault gun commander.

For the next hour they drove back and forth across the countryside. Again and again the Germans ran into the enemy, were fired on, escaped, and turned again, only to run into more enemy troops.

The race through alien territory lasted until early morning. At first light—out of ammunition—the vehicles broke through to the west, pursued by fire from half a dozen enemy guns.

Unterscharführer Koldenhoff drove across the landscape like a drunken man, swerving left and right to evade the enemy fire. Finally, Wittmann's assault gun reached the German positions and safety.

Melitopol was too strongly defended to be taken by such a surprise attack. There were no special forces available to assist the *Leibstandarte,* as the infantry divisions of XXX Army Corps, to which the brigade was attached, were still three hundred kilometers behind.

On 21 September 1941 the *Leibstandarte* received orders to break contact with the enemy in preparation for a move to the Crimean Peninsula.

On 26 September the regiments of the 73rd Infantry Division broke through the Soviet positions, crossed the Tartar trenches, and took Perekop by storm. Before *Leibstandarte* saw any further action, Soviet forces broke through farther to the north. The die was cast. The *Leibstandarte* did not go to the Crimea.

Instead it went to Mariupol. Taganrog was taken ten days later, and on 22 October the leading elements of the "LAH" entered Rostov. Soviet counterattacks soon forced the abandonment of the city, however. Michael Wittmann was wounded for a second time and sent back to Germany.

Later he was sent to the Junkerschule (officer candidate school) in Bad Tölz, where he attended an officer training course. Wittmann returned to his unit as an *Untersturm-führer.*

Michael Wittmann was born on 22 April 1914 in Vogelthal, near Beilngries in the Upper Pfalz. He hoped to become a farmer and one day own his own farm.

After high school he began a program of agricultural studies. At the age of twenty-three he was a qualified farmer and went to work on a small holding. Then, however, he decided to become a soldier and joined the *Leibstandarte* Regiment.

In Berlin-Lichterfelde, Wittmann frequently saw duty in ceremonial guards and watches. In the city he also had a chance to get to know some of the men he was later to lead into action.

Following the outbreak of war his unit was placed at the disposal of the Army High Command (OKH), where it was subject to military laws and ordinances. In this way a clear line was drawn between Michael Wittmann's unit and the *Allgemeine SS* and police units.

In carrying out its new duties the *Leibstandarte* saw action in Poland as a reinforced motorized infantry regiment.

Michael Wittmann became the commander of an armored car and was promoted to *Unterscharführer.* He advanced to Lodz with the regiment's advance detachment and participated in the fighting near Warsaw.

Wittmann remained with the regiment's armored reconnaissance unit during the 1940 campaign in the west, advancing through Holland with the 18th Army. The *Leibstandarte* Brigade first saw action west of Osnabrück. On 10 May 1940 it marched south of Lake Ijssel as far as Zwolle, and from there through Barneveld-Arnhem and Herztogenbosch to Moerdyjk. Afterward, the regiment took Rotterdam together with the paratroops and subsequently advanced as far as Amsterdam–Den Haag.

Sent through Maas and Valenciennes to the 6th Army, and finally to *Panzergruppe* von Kleist, the brigade drove through Arras and Boulogne, reaching the sea on 22 May. Then, attached to Panzer Corps Guderian, it attacked eastward in the direction of Dunkirk, took Watten, and fought its way into the enemy bridgehead at Esquelbek-Warmhout.

During the second phase of the war against France, the *Leib-*

standarte fought as one of the units of the 6th Army at the Somme in the Ham-La Fére-Laon area, crossed the Marne and advanced as far as the area southwest of Lyons.

Following the end of the war in the west, the brigade received its first assault guns. Michael Wittmann tried everything to become the commander of such a machine. The brigade received only six vehicles, and Wittmann was given command of one of them.

Wittmann took his assault gun to Greece. Moving out of the Küstendil area, the *Leibstandarte,* together with the 73rd Infantry Division and the 5th and 9th Panzer Divisions, fought its way through southern Serbia. Prilep was reached. Near Skopje the *Leibstandarte* took the lead. With the unit's armored reconnaissance battalion under *Sturmbannführer* Meyer, Wittmann took part in the capture of Bitolj. On 10 April contact was established with Italian forces on the northern Greek frontier.

During the drive through the Klidi Pass, Wittmann and his assault gun destroyed several flanking gun positions and machine gun nests belonging to a New Zealand division. For this action Wittmann was awarded the Iron Cross, Second Class.

Wittmann again distinguished himself in the storming of the Klissura Heights. In pouring rain he took his assault gun up Hill 800 and helped his comrades push back the enemy forces there (elements of the Greek 13th Division and 1st Cavalry Division). Twelve thousand prisoners were taken.

The young man from the Upper Pfalz was no young daredevil, rather he was a cool, deliberate type, the antithesis of the stereotyped hero. He was one of those who let his deeds do his talking. Wittmann did not come from any particular group; he was simply one of the millions of young Germans who believed that they were fighting for a just cause.

What he did possess was an inner strength and a compulsion to protect his comrades from danger. Even in the most dangerous situations his primary concerns were his crew, then his platoon and his company. Throughout he remained a friend to his soldiers, even when his fame reached great heights. There were no shadows along this soldier's path. He was one of those who fought, suffered, and died for his German Fatherland.

By the time *Untersturmführer* Wittmann rejoined his division it had been transferred to France, following the difficult defensive battles on the Mius River that had lasted into June 1942.

There, at the large troop training grounds in northern France, the *Leibstandarte* was reorganized and reequipped as a panzer division. The 1st Panzer Regiment became part of the division, which also added a 13th "Heavy" Company. This was to be equipped with the first of the new Tiger heavy tanks, which began to arrive at the training grounds in ones and twos.

After seeing this new giant and its 8.8cm gun, Wittmann knew at once that he had to have one. He called on the regimental commander.

"Obersturmbannführer," he began, "I must command one of these tanks!"

Obersturmführer Georg Schönberger, who had formed the regiment, nodded to the tall young man.

"Wittmann, I believe it would be a good weapon for you. You will be a platoon leader in the 'Thirteenth.' "

In France the *Leibstandarte* Division completed its reorganization and carried out unit exercises. On 6 November 1942 it was assembled at the demarcation line which marked the border with unoccupied France. On the twenty-first it moved out to take part in the occupation of the rest of France. On 26 November the division occupied Toulon. While all of this was going on, Wittmann was at the Ploermel training grounds, becoming familiar with his new Tiger.

Instructors arrived from the 500th Replacement and Training Battalion in Paderborn, which was standard procedure for all new Tiger units. The instructors were all veteran tank men with experience in Russia. Wittmann also met his new crew, which consisted of gunner *Rottenführer* Balthasar Woll, loader Kurt Berges, driver Gustl Kirschner, and radio operator Herbert Pollmann.

Following his first drive in the Tiger, Kirschner shouted, "It drives like a Volkswagen! I can engage seven-hundred horses with two fingers!"

Kirschner had good reason to be impressed with the fifty-five-ton giant. It was responsive, and could travel at fifty-five kph on roads and twenty kph cross-country.

The crew quickly learned that the Tiger used 535 liters of fuel per 100 kilometers. Engine and transmission, reduction gears, turret, and ventilator drives consumed 82 liters of oil. The engine had a displacement of 220 liters.

What impressed *Rottenführer* Woll, however, was the turret's hydraulically-activated power traverse system. The gunner's foot rested on a rocker plate. When he pressed forward, the turret rotated clockwise. If he exerted reverse pressure, the turret moved counterclockwise. The farther he depressed the plate, the higher the speed of rotation. At maximum rotation it took sixty seconds for the turret to turn through 360 degrees. Once, Woll experimented to see how long it would take to rotate the turret using minimum depression. It took a full hour for the turret to rotate through 360 degrees.

It was Christmas 1942. Wittmann was given leave to go home and visit his wife. He knew that soon he would be returning to Russia, and he and his entire division knew Russia.

In November 1942 the Soviets had begun their winter offensive in the great bend of the Don. They planned to break through across the Don near Sefiramovich and at Krasnoarmeysk, south of Stalingrad; launch an attack with the two army groups assembled north and west of Stalingrad; and advance on both sides of the Don by Army Group Southern Front toward Rostov and the Donets Basin.

From Stalingrad to Orel the Soviet offensive proceeded according to plan. A five-hundred-kilometer gap was torn in the front held by the Italian 8th and Hungarian 2nd Armies, and the German 6th Army was surrounded in Stalingrad. Stalin announced his next objective: On to the Dniepr.

The I *Waffen-SS* Panzer Corps, which consisted of the divisions *Leibstandarte, Das Reich,* and *Totenkopf,* was placed on alert. By the time it was sent into the threatened area on 9 January 1943, it seemed as if the situation were beyond saving.

The I SS-Panzer Corps arrived in the Kharkov area at the end of January. By then the Soviets had reached the Donets on a line Voroshilovgrad-Starobjelsk-Valuki-Stary Oskol.

The SS-panzer divisions disembarked east of Kharkov. Among the units was the heavy panzer company of the *Leibstandarte* under *Hauptsturmführer* Kling.

"This place is called Merefa. Behind us is Kharkov. The Russians will attack here and then try to encircle Kharkov."

"Nonsense, 'Panzergeneral!' " shouted *Hauptscharführer* Höflinger, a section leader in Wittmann's unit.

Oberscharführer Georg Lötzsch, known to all as the "Panzergeneral," because he knew everything about the Tiger tank, shook his head. Born in Dresden, he was the oldest member of the company at twenty-nine.

"We are too few, comrades. We must have escorting infantry and . . ."

"Get ready, *Hauptsturmführer!*" the executive officer called from the company commander's Tiger.

"All right, comrades, everyone stays where they are and halts the enemy. Meyer and his motorcycle troops are up ahead. If we take off, then he's had it!"

Michael Wittmann went over to his Tiger, climbed up, and slid into the turret. He put on his headset and pushed it back slightly so he could hear his comrades inside the tank as well.

"What's up, Michael?" asked Gustl Kirschner.

"We're going to drive into an assembly area and wait there until Meyer and the reconnaissance battalion return from the Donets."

The tanks moved off. Höflinger's section formed up on Wittmann's right. Wittmann watched the individual Tigers of his platoon as they rolled through a snow-covered depression. Meter by meter the Tiger climbed up the far side until it reached the level plain.

"Everyone halt! Position yourselves so that we can see the Russians at once if they come out of the village over there!"

The Tigers rolled into the assembly area, which had been scouted an hour earlier. After the engines fell silent, the men inside could hear the rumble of battle from the direction of the river.

"I'm going forward to reconnoiter. Pollmann, come with me!"

Wittmann reached for his submachine gun. Radio operator Pollmann did the same.

The fields and bushes at the edge of the stream were covered with a deep layer of snow, so the two walked up to the road that led into the village. Suddenly Pollmann shouted a warning. He stood stock still as if rooted to that spot. Slowly, he sank to his knees.

"There, *Untersturmführer!*" whispered Pollmann.

Wittmann recognized the positions of two emplaced antitank guns, which had been overlooked by the scouting party an hour ago.

The pair returned to their tank without being spotted. Wittmann reported his discovery to the company commander, who assigned targets to his commanders. *Unterscharführer* Kurt Kleber was to engage the Soviet observation post. The "Panzergeneral" was to attack the antitank gun to the left of the road, and Wittmann the one to the right.

Moments later Wittmann was again standing in his turret. He gave the signal to attack, and the heavy tanks moved off along the snow-covered road toward the village.

As Wittmann closed the turret hatch, there were flashes on both sides of the road ahead. The first shot from the antitank gun passed high over the Tiger's turret. The tank jerked to a halt. Woll had already taken aim and needed only to make a slight correction.

There was a mighty crash, and the Tiger rocked from the recoil of the "eighty-eight." The high-explosive shell whizzed toward its target. There was a bright flash and a cascade of flame from the position of the antitank gun.

"A hit!" shouted Woll, while Berges slid the next round into the chamber.

All five Tigers were firing; then they raced toward the village. Peering through his scissors telescope, Wittmann saw men running in every direction. Then he saw flashes from the windows of the houses in the village, and steel smacked against the Tiger's frontal armor.

"Antitank rifles!" shouted Woll.

The "Panzergeneral" destroyed the second antitank gun as the tanks reached the entrance to the village.

Wittmann let out a surprised whistle, because just then a long column of Soviet vehicles, including self-propelled guns and tanks, was rolling into the other end of the village. Behind the vehicles came infantry on foot.

"Attack! Attack!"

The others came at full speed and rolled behind the houses along the village street. A T-34 halted and trained its gun on Warmbrunn's Tiger.

Gunner Woll aimed and fired more quickly than the Russian. The armor-piercing round blew the turret off the T-34.

The other Tigers now opened fire. Soviet tanks exploded and munitions trucks blew up. Soldiers ran across the village street. The Tigers' machine guns rattled.

The five Tigers maintained a high rate of fire. The Soviet column got no farther. Several vehicles tried to reach open ground, but they became bogged down in the deep snow and were destroyed one by one.

In the days that followed, Wittmann took part in the battle to hold Kharkov, the city Hitler had ordered defended to the last round.

He thought of Stalingrad. Several days earlier he had learned that the entire 6th Army had been lost as a result of a similar *Führerbefehl.*

The next morning the units of the *Waffen-SS* attacked southward. Three assault groups rolled out of Merefa through the deep snow. Leading the battle group was the 1st Panzer Regiment's 6th Company, under the command of *Obersturmführer* Rudolf von Ribbentrop. The Tigers were held in reserve.

Michael Wittmann and his platoon drove into a wild snowstorm. The big tanks plowed through the falling snow, which hung before them like a thick, twinkling wall.

The battle group reached Alexeyevka, where the troops set up for all-round defense. *Obersturmführer* von Ribbentrop was wounded while on a patrol. He was supposed to be flown out in a Fieseler *Storch,* but declined. "I'll wait until the last grenadier has been flown out," he said.

Strong Soviet forces attacked. They drove around Kharkov and surrounded the city. During the night of 12/13 February, Soviet forces broke into the tiny village where Wittmann's platoon had stopped for the night. Fortunately, the sentries spotted the Soviets in time and fired warning shots.

Wittmann, who had been sleeping fully dressed, ran outside

followed closely by his crew. They leapt into their Tiger and rolled into the attacking Red Army troops, firing high-explosive shells.

The remaining panzer crews and a small number of grenadiers from an advance patrol, which had taken shelter in the houses, defended the village while Wittmann kept the road under fire and forced the main body of enemy troops to turn away. A half hour later the danger had passed. The men returned to their billets. Wittmann went back to his bed of straw and was soon asleep once more.

The Battle of Kharkov was nearing its conclusion. Poltava, the German supply base west of Kharkov, had been overrun by the Red Army. On the afternoon of 14 February the Soviets entered the northwestern section of the city. Hitler's latest order, to hold "at all costs!" arrived. Nevertheless, on 15 February 1943, General Hausser gave the order to withdraw to the Udy.

The 13th Heavy Company formed part of the rearguard. Firing at long range, they kept the masses of Soviet tanks at bay. Once again gunner Woll demonstrated his unbelievable accuracy. The German forces carried out a successful fighting withdrawal from Kharkov.

The following weeks saw the *Leibstandarte* in action in the area north of Krasnograd. The battle between the Donets and Dniepr ended on 4 March 1943. Then Hausser gave the order everyone had been waiting for:

"We're going to retake Kharkov!"

"Achtung! Chief to everyone: enemy tanks ahead!"

They saw the tanks emerge from their hiding places behind the houses. Wittmann waited for the Russians to fire before halting. Then the ten Tigers opened fire. Armor-piercing shells smashed into steel armor plate.

"Forward!" called *Hauptsturmführer* Kling over the radio. "Everyone follow me!"

The German armor rolled into Kharkov. Leading the way were Jochen Peiper's half-tracks. The Tigers followed, destroying the enemy's antitank positions. Soon they reached Red Square, and Kharkov was again in German hands.

Hausser's courageous action in defying Hitler's order had

prevented the destruction of his entire panzer corps and made possible the recapture of the city.

The Soviet forces were spent, the front stabilized. Both sides prepared for the next round. On the German side this was Operation *Zitadelle,* which was to become known as the Battle of Kursk. There, the war in the east was to be decided.

Stalin's failure to force a decision between the Don and Donets, largely as a result of *Feldmarschall* von Manstein's inspired command, presented the German high command with an opportunity to regain the initiative in the east by taking advantage of the enemy's momentary weakness.

But Hitler wanted more. He wanted to change the entire course of the war with a new offensive and achieve final victory.

Thus the war in the east approached its climax, a battle the official Soviet history of the war categorized as "the most significant battle of the entire war."

The attack was planned as a gigantic pincer movement, the tactic that had proved so successful in Russia before. The northern pincer consisted of the 9th Army under *Generaloberst* Model. Attacking from the area south of Orel, its three panzer corps were to advance southeast toward Kursk.

The southern pincer, the 4th Panzer Army under *Generaloberst* Hermann Hoth, was to attack toward Kursk from the area north of Kharkov, due west of Belgorod. The meeting of the two pincers in Kursk would seal off the great salient and inflict a defeat on the Red Army from which it would never recover.

The southern German pincer possessed 1,000 tanks and about 400 assault guns. The northern pincer was of similar strength.

I SS-Panzer Corps, which was part of *Armeeabteilung* Kempf, was grouped west of Belgorod. Its alignment from east to west was 3rd, 2nd, 1st SS-Panzer Divisions. To the *Leibstandarte*'s left was the 167th Infantry Division. The initial objective of the two divisions was Streletskoye, then Olkovka.

July 4 neared. The units were in their starting positions. The attack could begin.

"How much longer, *Untersturmführer?*" asked Woll.

Michael Wittmann looked at his watch. The illuminated dial showed that it was only 0200.

·"Another hour!" he said, and went over his plan in his mind once again.

Together with Wittmann and his platoon, the 230,000 German soldiers of the southern pincer waited for the order to attack.

The German artillery bombardment began at 0330. Now they could move, the divisions of the SS-Panzer Corps, of which Lieutenant General Chistyakov, commander in chief of the Soviet 6th Army, had said:

"Be careful, gentlemen! Before you stands Hitler's guard. We must expect one of the main efforts of the German offensive in this sector."

The corps' 300 tanks and 120 assault guns rolled forward.

For Wittmann this was to be a battle unlike any he had ever dreamt of. It was a battle that would demand the utmost of him and his men.

The panzers drove across the field in wedge formation. Suddenly antitank fire whipped toward them.

"Attack! Attack!" shouted Wittmann over the radio.

The tanks raced forward. To his right Wittmann saw a Tiger grind to a halt with a shot-up track.

Suddenly, not one hundred meters ahead, there was a flash as an antitank gun fired. Almost at once there was a shattering blow, a crash, and flames, but Woll had targeted the enemy gun. He fired, and the shell smashed into the antitank gun. Kirschner closed up and the advance resumed.

They reached a line of bunker positions that had been attacked by Stukas a half hour before. Not a shot came from the bunkers. Instead, tanks appeared.

The 13th Company attacked. *Hauptsturmführer* Kling barked out an order. The Wendorff platoon veered off toward the northwest. One of the Tigers was struck in the flank by a shell. The crew scrambled clear.

Wittmann directed the movements of his five tanks. They concentrated their fire on the approaching phalanx of enemy tanks.

Moving quickly, Wittmann's Tigers reached the bunker line. A Soviet tank appeared from behind a tall bunker. A jet of flame spurted from its gun. It seemed to Wittmann as if the shell was aimed directly at him. The shot struck the Tiger's sloped bow plate. There was a mighty crash and the shell howled vertically into the sky.

Woll fired back. The T-34's turret was blown clear of the rest of the vehicle and flames enveloped the wreck.

The Tigers pushed on, passing two groups of Soviet tanks waiting in a ravine. These now left their hiding place and moved forward.

There was a loud crash as a shell struck the side armor of Wittmann's Tiger, without, however, inflicting any major damage. A village appeared ahead.

"*Achtung!* Chief to everyone: antitank guns ahead!"

The Soviets had set up an antitank front. Once again Wittmann decided on a rapid advance. The Tigers raced ahead at full throttle in eighth gear. Armor-piercing shot from the antitank guns bounced off their thick armor.

A concealed antitank gun suddenly opened fire, and Wendorff's Tiger slewed to a stop. Wittmann's Tiger rattled toward the gun. The enormous weight of the tank crushed the antitank gun into the ground. The Tiger leaned dangerously, then righted itself. Berges howled in pain and anger. A shell had fallen on his hand, but he labored on. Blood ran down his fingers and sweat over his face. There was no time to pause, death was waiting outside.

The Tiger halted, and Woll fired. As the tank began to move again he took aim at the next target. The Tiger halted again and seconds later Woll fired once more.

After about an hour the tanks had broken through the Soviet position. The panzer grenadiers took advantage of the panzers' success and moved up through the gap behind the tanks. They rounded up a number of prisoners, secured the area, and then decided to press onward. After a brief rest the Tigers also moved off.

"Michael, I'm back!" reported Wendorff. His track repairs had been completed and he had rejoined his comrades. "If we can continue like this, we'll be able to do it!"

"I hope so!" called Wittmann. "As long as we break through quickly and don't let ourselves become engaged in firefights, but rather charge in and overrun the enemy."

The attack continued. *Brigadeführer* Theodor Wisch appeared beside the Tigers.

Wittmann heard Warmbrunn call, "Lunch in Kursk!" He had to smile. If only you would look at the map! he thought, and imagined Warmbrunn studying the map. An hour later the Tigers came upon another antitank front.

Once again Wittmann's platoon led the way, and once again his fast charge caught the enemy by surprise. Shells hammered into the ground to the left and right. Several projectiles from Soviet antitank rifles cracked against the tank's steel sides. In seconds the Tigers were in a favorable firing position. As one, the Tigers halted, fired, and moved off again. Soon they had reached the intermediate Soviet position.

Wittmann spotted a Soviet tank-killing squad appear in front of his tank. He threw back the hatch cover and opened fire on the Russian soldiers with his submachine gun. Wittmann ducked as a burst of machine gun fire whistled past his ears. Before he could close the hatch cover he heard a terrible scream. The tank rumbled over something. Then the danger was past.

Wittmann clenched his teeth. There was a faint taste of blood on his tongue. He felt sick at the thought of what had just happened outside.

Wittmann forced himself to concentrate on the job at hand. He had five tanks and twenty-five men to worry about. It was his job to get them out of this difficult situation in one piece.

Eventually the Tigers fought their way through the enemy position. During a second rest stop, Wittmann heard Wendorff's voice on the radio, calling for help.

"Warmbrunn and Kleber stay here! Lötzsch and Höflinger follow me!" ordered Wittmann.

The Tigers turned and drove toward a small wood. From the far side of the wood could be heard the sound of gunfire: the hard crack of the Tigers' "eighty-eights," the bark of Soviet antitank guns, and the crash of the 7.62cm guns of T-34s.

The big tanks crashed through the woods, snapping off tree trunks and crushing them into the ground. Wittmann spotted the Soviet tanks in a hollow. They had knocked out one of Wendorff's Tigers, which was burning, and were now concentrating their fire on the platoon leader's tank.

"Lötzsch, Höflinger, take the antitank guns!"

Wittmann charged out of the trees at full speed. He drove on until he was in a position from which he could fire at the T-34s without endangering Wendorff's Tiger.

"We're here, Helmut!" he called.

The Tiger stopped. Woll's first shot struck the rear of one of the T-34s. The tank blew up. He hit the second one exactly fifteen seconds later. The third Soviet tank escaped destruction by backing up quickly, causing Woll's shot to pass wide.

The T-34 turned amazingly quickly on one track, and Woll missed again. Then the Soviet gunner fired and hit one of the Tiger's tracks. Driver Kirschner screamed in pain.

Woll now had the enemy square in his sights. His next shot pierced the T-34's frontal armor. Seconds passed before the T-34's hatch cover flipped open. Flames shot out. The Russian driver tried to get out, his clothing on fire. He was half out of the driver's hatch when the tank was blasted apart by a terrific explosion. It was a terrible scene, one that was to be replayed many times in this battle—on both sides.

Meanwhile, the two antitank guns at the edge of the wood had been destroyed by Lötzsch and Höflinger. Quiet settled over the wood.

Together with his radio operator, Michael Wittmann lifted their injured driver from his seat. They laid him on the ground, where Woll had spread out a tent square.

"Is it all over for me, *Untersturmführer?*" murmured Kirschner.

Wittmann stared at the wound, which had been covered with four packet dressings. Blood was seeping through the bandages. He shook his head.

"You'll make it, Kirschner!" and then he said to the others, "Get started repairing the track!"

Untersturmführer Wendorff provided cover while the crewmen carried out repairs to their tank's damaged track. Pollmann called for an ambulance. Before the tanks left, a medic arrived with the ambulance and placed Kirschner inside.

"Unterscharführer Möller!" reported a driver from one of the disabled tanks of Wendorff's platoon. "I would like to take your driver's place."

"Glad to have you with us, Möller! Climb aboard!"

Dusk had begun to fall. It had been a successful day; Wittmann and his Tiger had destroyed eight enemy tanks and seven antitank guns.

Hauptsturmführer Kling reported to the commander of the panzer regiment: *"Untersturmführer* Wittmann and his Tiger platoon provided support vital to the regiment's advance."

By the evening of the first day of the great Battle of Kursk the I *Waffen-SS* Panzer Corps had broken through the antitank barriers and artillery positions of the Soviet 52nd Guards Rifle Division. The *Leibstandarte* Division had overcome well-camouflaged field positions, dug-in T-34 tanks, and antitank fronts.

The German tanks had penetrated twenty kilometers into the Soviet defensive positions. That evening Wittmann learned who had led the Stukas in their attacks on the Soviet positions: it was an officer who would one day wear Germany's highest decoration for bravery, Hans-Ulrich Rudel.

The advance by the southern pincer that first day demolished the Soviet barrier in front of the Belgorod-Kursk road. The offensive was going well.

During the early morning hours of 6 July 1943 the Tiger tanks of the 13th (Heavy) Company of the *Leibstandarte* were refueled and rearmed.

The attack continued. Once again Wittmann was at the head of the armored wedge. The panzers advanced northwest, toward the bend in the Psyol River. Near Lutski I the leading tanks came under enemy fire. Soviet 15cm batteries poured fire onto the advance road.

"Wittmann, veer off and put that battery out of action!" came the order.

Wittmann obeyed. His five Tigers turned left and rolled toward a wood. They reached the wood undetected, and once inside turned in the direction of the enemy battery.

Two hours later they were there. The Tigers drove out of the wood onto the open plain in line abreast. They saw the first battery, which was in the process of releasing a salvo.

All five Tigers fired simultaneously. Flames leapt from the enemy position. The Soviet radio station was destroyed by a direct hit. An ammunition dump went up. The enemy fled. The Tigers raced onward, reached the second artillery position and put it out of action as well.

In the village of Lutski I the panzers came under fire from antitank guns. Kleber's Tiger was hit. Wittmann and Warmbrunn positioned themselves in front of the disabled Tiger and destroyed four antitank guns in quick succession. In the meantime Kleber was able to repair the damage.

All resistance was broken and the advance continued. The 3rd Platoon took over the lead. The unit encountered another antitank front at the eastern edge of Lutski II. A dug-in KV-I knocked out the leading Tiger from a range of six hundred meters. The crew scrambled clear of the burning tank but were caught by a burst of Russian machine gun fire and killed.

A hail of shells rained down on the panzers. Wittmann's Tiger was hit, but the shell bounced off.

"Fire high-explosive, aim in front of the two dug-in KV-Is!" ordered Wittmann.

Wittmann and Warmbrunn fired on the enemy position. The bursting shells raised great clouds of smoke and dust, blinding the Soviet gunners.

"Forward, follow me!"

The other Tigers rumbled after the platoon leader's tank, as they had done so often in the past two days. The enemy was now firing blind. Shells flashed past high over the Tigers.

"Halt!" ordered Wittmann.

The Tigers halted five hundred meters apart. The gunners took aim at the muzzle flashes that pierced the clouds of dust, and waited. As the dust settled, the turret of the first KV-I became visible. Woll made a slight correction and fired. Barely a second later the KV-I disappeared in a mighty explosion as its reserve ammunition went up.

To the left and right the other Tigers opened fire. The enemy position was eliminated, and the unit drove on toward the north. As evening fell on the second day of fighting, the Tigers turned west toward Hill 260.8, which lay between Werchnopenje and Gresnoye.

Gresnoye was the objective of the *Totenkopf* Division, while *Das Reich* veered northeast toward Tetrovino.

The battle was nearing its climax. The tank crews had had no rest in forty-eight hours. When the tanks and trucks stopped for the night, the exhausted crews dropped to the ground beside their vehicles and slept.

Wittmann left his platoon, which was down to four tanks. One of the Tigers had broken down along the way with transmission damage; of all people it belonged to the "Panzergeneral," *Oberscharführer* Georg Lötzsch.

As he walked along, Wittmann came upon *Rottenführer* Pötter of Höflinger's crew, sound asleep. He shook the young man awake. Pötter froze.

"Please, *Untersturmführer,* don't bring me before a court martial. I hope to attend the Junkerschule!" pleaded Pötter, a volunteer on his first combat mission.

"If you carry on like this you'll be dead before you get to the Junkerschule. That would be your own affair if it weren't for the fact that the whole platoon would suffer!"

Pötter was scared to death. He knew how strict Wittmann was, and he was aware of what a serious matter falling asleep on watch was. The seconds passed slowly as Wittmann considered what to do. Then he spoke.

"Go and get some sleep, Pötter. I'll take over your watch."

"Thank you, *Untersturmführer!*"

The young man disappeared. An hour later Wittmann woke his relief. The man was not a little surprised to see his platoon leader instead of Pötter.

Wittmann walked over to his Tiger. He looked up at the twinkling stars. Then he, too, went to sleep.

Wittmann was awakened by Balthasar Woll.

"Michael, the chief wants to see you!" The gunner passed him a steaming cup of coffee. Wittmann drank the coffee, then washed quickly and pulled on his boots. He hurried over to the regimental command post, joined along the way by Wendorff and Kling.

Sturmbannführer Max Wünsche, commander of 1st Battalion, and *Sturmbannführer* Gross, commander of 2nd Battalion, waved to their comrades to move faster. The men gathered in an open circle and *Obersturmbannführer* Georg Schönberger began:

"Comrades, the decisive breakthrough is to be made today. The *Grossdeutschland* Division has taken Dubrova. A breakthrough toward Oboyan is within our reach. We have just intercepted and decoded a Russian signal. It is signed by a general called Vatutin and his war council named Khrushchev and reads: 'Under no circumstances are the Germans to be permitted to break through toward Oboyan!' "

"But that's in the sector of our neighbor to the left, the 4th Panzer Army, *Obersturmbannführer!*" interjected Max Wünsche. The officer, who wore the Knight's Cross at his throat, pointed to the map fixed to the wall of a farm cottage.

"That's correct!" replied the regimental commander. "But we'll be advancing parallel to the Panzer Grenadier Division *Grossdeutschland* and the 11th Panzer Division."

Sturmbannführer Gross now joined the discussion. "We must move quickly to prevent the Russian 6th Army from plugging the gap that we've torn open. Before us lies Tetrovino, and air reconnaissance reports powerful tank forces massing there."

Martin Gross was soon to learn how accurate that report was.

Half an hour later Michael Wittmann's Tigers were preparing to go into action again. Tired but alert, Wittmann was standing in his open turret hatch when a formation of Henschel close-support aircraft roared over the *Leibstandarte*'s panzers.

"The new close-support aircraft, Wittmann!" called Kling over the radio.

They were Hs-129s, flying antitank guns armed with a 3cm cannon. Over the battlefield between Kursk and Belgorod the new aircraft was seeing action for the first time. Flying at low altitude, the tank-destroyers came upon a group of Soviet tanks and attacked at once. The 3cm cannon shells penetrated the thinner armor at the rear and on top of the Soviet tanks. Soon, one tank after another was bursting into flames.

All of a sudden a group of Fw-190 fighter-bombers appeared, led by Major Druschel. It was the same Druschel who had helped the *Leibstandarte* near Kharkov earlier in the year while leading a *Gruppe* of *Schlachtgeschwader* 1. On 20 February 1943 he had become the twenty-fourth German soldier to receive the Swords to the Knight's Cross. Druschel and his pilots attacked the Soviet infantry positions facing the *Leibstan-*

darte. They strafed the enemy positions with cannon and machine guns and dropped fragmentation bombs. The Soviet infantry scattered.

"Panzers, forward!"

The attack got under way. The tanks advanced until they came upon a Soviet defensive position with concealed antitank guns, well dug-in tanks, and infantry positions with concrete cupolas.

The battle raged back and forth. Four Tigers were disabled. Not destroyed but out of action, they were a job for the recovery crews, who would recover them from the battlefield during the evening and night.

Once again Wittmann was in the thick of things. His Tiger curved and dodged at high speed. Driver Möller had caught on quickly to his new commander's fighting style. Seven more Soviet tanks fell victim to Wittmann's Tiger. The number of antitank guns destroyed climbed to nineteen.

All afternoon the Tigers, Panthers, and Panzer IVs stormed the positions of the Soviet 29th Antitank Brigade. Wittmann could not help but admire the enemy gunners. They fought with great courage, trying to cover the withdrawal by the 6th Guards Army and the battered 21st Tank Corps. The Soviet antitank gunners knew that if they failed, the front would collapse.

However, *Hauptsturmführer* Alfred Lex and his 3rd Motorcycle Company managed to get through a gap that one of the Tigers had blasted in the Soviet defenses. The motorcycle troops raced a kilometer into the enemy rear and reached the Soviet command post. The commanding general, his officers, and entire command staff were taken prisoner.

Wittmann heard of the success that evening before falling asleep, totally exhausted, in a hastily-erected camp.

The ninth and tenth of July passed. For Wittmann both days were a blur. Never before had he faced such a test of endurance.

The Soviet defenses were wearing the attackers down. Concealed antitank fronts inflicted heavy losses. The lighter escort tanks and the motorcycle troops suffered heavily at the hands of the Soviet artillery and close-support aircraft.

By the evening of 10 July the German forces had fought their way to the bend in the Psyol River. During the night the troops of the *Leibstandarte* Division, which was in the middle of I SS-Panzer Corps, battled its way into the area due southeast of Bo-gorodiskoye. On the left flank, the *Totenkopf* Division was preparing to force a crossing of the Psyol near Krasny Oktyabr with the 6th Panzer Grenadier Regiment, while on the right the *Das Reich* Division had veered toward the line of fortifications south of Prokhorovka.

Late on the evening of 10 July, *Obersturmbannführer* Karl Ullrich led his unit across the Psyol and established a bridge-head.

Early on the morning of the eleventh the *Leibstandarte* stormed forward between the rail line and the Psyol, which turned northward here, toward the area due north of Prok-horovka.

Following a rapid advance the division came upon the positions of the 18th and 29th Soviet Tank Corps. A battle began, the likes of which the Russian theater had never seen.

The fighting died down somewhat during the night. The occasional flash of gunfire was the only reminder that the front was just up ahead. The two sides waited for the dawn. Finally the sky began to brighten and General Hausser gave the order for his forces to attack.

The two tank corps of the Soviet 5th Guards Tank Army, which had been rushed in from the Steppe Front, drove out to meet the German panzer armada. The two corps were commanded by Soviet General Rotmistrov.

The battle began. The first unit to engage the enemy was 2nd Battalion of the 1st Panzer Regiment under *Sturmbannführer* Martin Gross. The two armored forces met in an area five hundred meters wide and a kilometer deep. In a tough three-hour battle, Gross and his panzer companies destroyed ninety Soviet tanks. The battlefield, measuring half a square kilometer, had been transformed into a tank graveyard. (For this action *Sturmbannführer* Gross was awarded the Knight's Cross on 22 July 1943.)

The Tigers of 13th Company began an advance on the left flank, but the panzer grenadiers failed to get through. The big tanks rolled through thickets and behind hedgerows. Suddenly a wave of sixty enemy tanks burst forth from a wood. The Soviet tanks broke through the German advance detachment and swept on toward the Tigers, approaching to one hundred, fifty, even thirty meters. The Germans fought bitterly. Four panzers were knocked out. Wittmann's tank was hit twice. Radio operator Pollmann was wounded in the upper arm. His blood dripped down onto his comrades. Ammunition exploded. Fuel tanks blew up in flashes of white flame.

"Three o'clock, three hundred!" shouted Wittmann, spotting a T-34 as it rolled out of a group of bushes. The Soviet tank stopped. The 7.62cm gun turned toward the Tiger.

Woll reacted quickly and fired before the Soviet tank could get the Tiger in its sights. A direct hit blew off the T-34's turret. The Tiger drove on, halted again, and fired, then turned on the spot to help a comrade in trouble. The temperature inside the tank was sixty degrees centigrade; the air was heavy with the smell of powder smoke, sweat, and blood. The five men in the Tiger knew that one second of inattention or a momentary lapse would cost them their lives.

Wittmann's calm was an example to his men and helped them hang on. He rapped out a staccato of orders, overcoming crisis situations and saving comrades from apparently hopeless situations. He seemed to be everywhere. This time there was no breaking off the engagement and returning to the starting point. Here the fight was to the bitter end.

From close range the T-34's 7.62cm gun was lethal, even against the heavily-armored Tiger as well as the other German tanks, the Panther and Panzer IV. All over the battlefield tanks were torn to pieces as their ammunition blew up; turrets spun through the air like giant toys. Everywhere there was smoke, flames, and screaming, burning men staggering about, their clothing on fire.

In this situation there was only one alternative: You or me!

Suddenly, help for the German side appeared in the sky above the battlefield in the shape of Major Rudel and his Stukas. The dive-bombers plunged down on their targets, cannon flashing. Soviet tanks exploded under the deadly hail of fire from above. Then Soviet fighters appeared and set upon the cumbersome Stukas, shooting down nearly a dozen. Finally, German fighters arrived on the scene and a wild dogfight began.

The Battle of Kursk had reached its climax. Death could come in many forms. There was no longer any thought of victory on either side; the men in the tanks were fighting for survival. Soon the entire battlefield was shrouded in a dense cloud of powder smoke, dust, and oily black smoke.

The tank commanders heard *Obersturmbannführer* Schönberger's voice crackle over the radio: "Continue the attack along the riverbank! Break through at high speed!" Shortly afterward came an order from *Hauptsturmführer* Kling.

"Wittmann, you and your platoon screen the forward right flank and stop any attacks from the northeast!"

Wittmann acknowledged. He assembled his three surviving Tigers. The other two were somewhere behind him on the battlefield. He had heard the distress calls from Warmbrunn and Kleber and hoped that they and their crews had managed to get out of their tanks.

The three Tigers rumbled forward in line astern, their turrets trained to two o'clock, until they reached a position at the head of the German armored force. Then they set out again, keeping pace with the main body. Some time later they rolled through a cornfield and then along an extended *balka* (ravine). The tanks halted on a low rise. The silver band of a stream appeared through Wittmann's vision slit.

Prokhorovka already lay behind them. Wittmann hoped to veer toward the village, which was still shrouded in the smoke and flames of battle, and hurry to the aid of his comrades. If they could attack the enemy from behind, they would turn the tide of battle in their favor. But then he heard a warning call from his company commander, followed soon after by the voice of *Hauptsturmführer* Kling.

"Achtung! Strong force of enemy tanks approaching from ahead! Many tanks!"

Moments later Wittmann, too, saw them. There were at least a hundred enemy tanks of all types, and they were approaching quickly.

"Fire from the halt! Begin firing at eighteen hundred meters!"

Each gunner selected a target. The mass of Soviet tanks rushed toward the Germans, disappeared into a depression, and reappeared again a good thousand meters away.

"Aim well, Woll!" gasped Wittmann.

The long-ranging guns of the Tigers opened fire. The first

gaps were smashed in the advancing phalanx of enemy tanks. There were explosions and fires. Pillars of smoke rose into the sky. But the main body of enemy tanks—the 181st Brigade of the Soviet 18th Tank Corps—continued to come.

The Soviets were trying to close the range as quickly as possible, because they knew that they had to get to within eight hundred meters to pose a threat to the heavily armored Tigers.

The Soviet tanks raced on, not stopping to help their disabled comrades; to stop now would mean their own certain destruction. The enemy tankers stormed forward with an elan that filled Wittmann with admiration and at the same time consternation.

His crew and those of Lötzsch and Höflinger maintained a high rate of fire. By the time the Soviet tanks were within a thousand meters, every shot was a direct hit. The enemy now began to reply. They fired on the move and were therefore unable to aim precisely. Nevertheless, a Panther was soon burning and one of the Tigers was hit and disabled.

One group of about fifteen tanks rushed in from the flank. They rolled directly toward Wittmann's three Tigers.

"The lead tank, Woll!" shouted Wittmann.

Gunner Woll aimed and fired. They all saw how the shell pierced the side of the T-34.

"Hit!" roared *Unterscharführer* Möller. But the enemy tank merely halted briefly, then rejoined its comrades.

Woll fired again. Another hit. The T-34 halted again. From inside the Tiger they watched—Woll through his gunsight, Wittmann through his scissors telescope, and Möller through his driver's visor—as two Russians pulled their wounded commander out of the tank and dragged him to cover in a shell hole.

As Wittmann watched, the burning T-34 suddenly began to move toward Lötzsch's Tiger. He called a warning to the "Panzergeneral": "Look out! He's coming!"

"Damn! Damn!" cursed *Oberscharführer* Lötzsch. "Move forward, or he'll blind us with his smoke."

Lötzsch's driver steered the Tiger straight toward the enemy tank, then braked sharply. The gunner took aim at the approaching T-34 and fired. The shell smashed into the rounded edge of the Soviet tank's turret and ricocheted howling into the sky.

The blazing ball of fire rolled onward. Seconds later the T-34 rammed the Tiger. Flames covered the German tank. It seemed as if the Tiger crew had lost its nerve.

"Lötzsch, back up! Back up!" implored Wittmann.

Suddenly the Tiger began to back up, separating itself from the ball of fire; one meter, two meters, five meters!

At that moment the T-34's reserve ammunition exploded. After the dust settled, the Tiger returned to its original position. It had escaped destruction at the last second.

The Soviet armored phalanx had been halted. The battlefield was saturated with burning and disabled tanks. Some of the stricken tanks continued to fire on the Tigers, until they, too, were hit again and destroyed.

General Rotmistrov's forces had not broken through the German armored wedge, but they had taken the impetus from the SS-Panzer Corps' attack.

The fighting died down for several hours. In the afternoon *Generaloberst* Hoth appeared at the command post of the *Das Reich* Division's *Der Führer* Panzer Grenadier Regiment. The general viewed the battlefield through a scissors telescope. What he saw was still-smoldering tank wrecks and a chaotic jumble of caterpillar tracks, turrets, motorcycles, and armored cars. That same hour Soviet tanks tried to smash their way through the German front lines, but were repulsed.

The battle was at a standstill. The I *Waffen-SS* Panzer Corps had been forced from the offensive to the defensive. Finally, the report arrived that the *Das Reich* Division—on the corps' right flank—was being attacked by tanks of the 2nd Soviet Tank Corps. The enemy had pushed through the gap that had appeared between the *Waffen-SS* Panzer Corps and *General der Panzertruppe* Breith's III Panzer Corps, which had been held up by the Soviet 3rd Guards Mechanized Corps.

Near Rshvets on the northern Donets were the three panzer divisions of the II Panzer Corps (the 6th, 7th, and 19th Panzer Divisions). They were only twenty kilometers from the main battlefield and the crews could hear the sounds of the battle near Prokhorovka.

Oberst von Oppeln-Bronikowski, commander of the 11th Panzer Regiment, sent Maj. Franz Bäke and his battalion together with a battalion of armored personnel carriers to seize a crossing over the river. Bäke and his tanks rolled past the Soviet positions. The Soviets believed them to be one of their own units, as the force was being led by a captured T-34. Its markings had been painted over, and instead it wore a *Balkenkreuz,* "a very small one," as Bäke later put it.

The German tanks passed a Soviet unit of twenty-two T-34s, apparently without being recognized. But then seven of the T-34s turned around. Bäke faced them in his command panzer. It was a Panzer III with a dummy gun made of wood.

The Soviet tanks didn't fire, however. Their commanders seemed unsure of what to do. They smelled a rat, but were uncertain.

Taking advantage of the enemy's indecision, Major Bäke and his executive officer, *Oberleutnant* Zumpel, leapt from the tank. A hollow charge in each hand, Bäke ran over to the nearest stationary T-34. He passed one of the charges to Zumpel. The two men placed the charges and then dove for cover, landing in chest-deep water. Two explosions followed.

Suddenly all hell broke loose. Tracers flitted through the darkness. The German tanks raced toward the bridge. Just before they got to it, the bridge was blown up by the Russians. Nevertheless, *Pioneers* crossed followed closely by grenadiers. The bridgehead was established, and the next morning Bäke's men were on the north bank of the Donets. (Major Bäke was awarded the Oak Leaves for this action.)

The 6th Panzer Division had successfully taken the first step. The bridge was quickly repaired and General Breith's panzers rolled across. However, on 12 July, as they were preparing to advance toward Prokhorovka and tip the scales of battle in favor of the SS divisions fighting there, the tanks were recalled. They crossed back over the Donets and were sent in great haste to Alexandrovka, where the 6th Panzer Division's 4th Panzer Grenadier Regiment was under heavy attack and facing destruction. The forces attacking near Alexandrovka saved the battle for the Soviets. (This brief overview clearly shows how near the southern pincer was to achieving a decisive success, and the imponderables that led to its failure.)

During the early morning of 13 July the *Waffen-SS* divisions and the other divisions of the southern wing continued their desperate efforts to force a decisive breakthrough.

* * *

While Wittmann was destroying four Soviet tanks and silencing an enemy battery that morning, and while every man of the 13th Tiger Company was giving his all in an effort to turn the tide of battle, in the Führer headquarters in East Prussia the commanders in chief of the eastern front were facing Hitler.

They were *Feldmarschall* von Manstein, who earlier in the year had halted the Soviet avalanche on the southern part of the Eastern Front, and *Feldmarschall* von Kluge. Twelve days earlier Hitler had given the order to begin the attack. Today he must tell them something they already knew.

"The Allies attacked Sicily on 10 July and have landed on the island. The Italian defense has collapsed. Only the three German divisions on the island are still putting up a fight.

"Thanks to the Italians' miserable conduct of the war, the loss of Sicily is as good as certain. Perhaps the Allies will land on the Italian mainland tomorrow, or in the Balkans.

"Since, following the transfer of the 1st Panzer Division from France to the Peloponnes, I can move no further divisions from anywhere else, they will have to come from the Kursk Front. I am therefore forced to call off *Zitadelle.*"

Feldmarschall von Manstein, who was responsible for the southern pincer, was appalled. So far his forces had taken 24,000 prisoners and destroyed or captured 1,800 tanks, 267 guns, and 1,080 antitank guns in the southern sector alone. The battle was approaching its climax, the decision whether it was to be victory or defeat was at hand. Even if the 9th Army of the northern pincer had been forced to call off its attack, even if the enemy had forced the 2nd Panzer Army onto the defensive, he—*Feldmarschall* von Manstein—did not want to break off the battle now, "perhaps just before the decisive success."

Feldmarschall von Manstein still had one ace left to play: XXIV Panzer Corps, with the 17th Panzer Division and the battle-tested 5th SS-Panzer Division *Wiking* under *Gruppenführer* Gille. The panzer corps was waiting west of Kharkov. Hitler had removed it from the command of the army group and named it OKH Reserve.

Feldmarschall von Kluge reported that the 9th Army could

advance no farther and had suffered twenty thousand casualties. Von Manstein then explained:

Victory is almost within our grasp, following the defensive successes of the past few days when the enemy threw in nearly his entire strategic reserve. To break off the battle now would probably mean throwing away victory.

If the 9th Army can at least tie down the enemy forces facing it, and perhaps resume the attack at a later date, we will try to smash the enemy forces engaging our armies.

As soon as this happens, Army Group South—as reported to the OKH on 12 July 1943—will once again set out toward the north, send two panzer corps across the Psyol east of Oboyan and, swinging west, force the enemy forces in the western part of the Kursk salient into battle. In order to screen this operation to the north and east, however, the XXIV Panzer Corps must be sent immediately to *Armeeabteilung* Kempf.

Manstein had explained the situation clearly. Hitler, however, replied that Army Group South should continue its efforts to smash the enemy in the field, but only to allow a subsequent withdrawal of forces from the *Zitadelle* front.

Michael Wittmann and his crews, together with the divisions of the southern pincer, fought on until 17 July. When the Tigers of 13th Company disengaged from the enemy on the evening of the seventeenth, every man knew that they could have done it, because, with the exception of one panzer division, all of the German divisions were still largely intact.

Zitadelle was over, and the initiative on the Eastern Front had passed to the Soviets for good.

The battle had lasted ten days and nights. For the first time in that period, Wittmann was able to leave his tank knowing that he would be able to sleep through the night. In the past ten days he had destroyed thirty enemy tanks and twenty-eight antitank guns, and put out of action two heavy batteries with a total of eight guns.

Sturmbannführer Martin Gross, whose battalion destroyed ninety enemy tanks during the heavy fighting on 12 July, was awarded the Knight's Cross on 22 July 1943.

Soon after, Wittmann was given a well-earned leave in Germany. He was accompanied by Woll and many others. They had survived yet another difficult test. The men went home, perhaps for the last time.

Untersturmführer Wittmann was soon back with his unit. The *Leibstandarte* Division was being withdrawn from the front for transport by rail to Italy.

On the evening of 6 September 1943 the Italians terminated their alliance with Germany. The *Leibstandarte* was being sent to Army Group Rommel, which had been active since 17 August 1943 in northern Italy securing rear echelon services and disarming Italian units. All of this was carried out without bloodshed.

"How long is this loafing about going to last, Michael?" asked *Untersturmführer* Wendorff as the two sat together in Wittmann's quarters late on the evening of 4 November 1943.

"I think our days here are numbered," replied Wittmann. "What do you think, Heinz?"

Hauptsturmführer Kling nodded. He glanced at his watch and then tuned in armed forces radio. It was one minute before ten. The announcer read the evening news:

"Following a heavy artillery bombardment, and supported by large numbers of close-support aircraft, the Soviets have gone to the attack north of Kiev. Heavy defensive fighting is in progress . . ."

"Men, this means that it will soon be our turn, like our comrades in the *Das Reich, Totenkopf* and *Wiking* Divisions."

Heinz Kling had said what they were all thinking. They had now been renamed the II SS-Panzer Corps. The I SS-Panzer Corps had just been created in Berlin and was being established in Brussels and Meran. The new commanding general was Sepp Dietrich.

The day before, on 3 November 1943, 2,000 Soviet guns and 500 Stalin organs had poured destructive fire on the German positions in the area around Lyutesh for forty minutes.

The three Soviet generals in charge of the offensive had received one, brief order: "Kiev must fall on the anniversary of the October Revolution!"

The man who gave Stalin's order to the three army commanders in the schoolhouse basement in the village of Petrovtsy was called Nikita Khrushchev.

General Vatutin, commander of the 1st Ukrainian Front, had summoned General Rybalko (3rd Guards Tank Army) and General Moskalenko (38th Soviet Army). Also present was General Kraftshenko, commanding general of the 5th Guards Tank Corps.

The generals received their orders and put them into action.

The massed Soviet tank divisions threw themselves against *Generalmajor* Hasso von Manteuffel's 7th Panzer Division. Manteuffel was unable to prevent the Soviets from crossing the Irpen eight kilometers west of Kiev and advancing toward Zhitomir.

On 5 November, *Generaloberst* Hoth learned that the *Das Reich* battle group had been forced back and that only the 88th Infantry Division was still holding out in Kiev.

As midnight struck on 6 November 1943, the anniversary of the Russian Revolution, General Kraftshenko's tanks were already rolling into the city along the Krastchatik, Kiev's main boulevard. Infantrymen of the Soviet 4th Reconnaissance Company worked their way under fire to the party headquarters at Red Square and hoisted the Soviet flag. Dressed in his general's uniform, Nikita Khrushchev entered Kiev in triumph.

The tank units under the command of General Rybalko, the actual conqueror of Kiev, pressed on toward the south. There they encountered the 10th Panzer Grenadier Division and were thrown back. Rybalko's forces quickly regrouped. Veering southwest, they drove through a gap in the German front and on 7 November captured Fastov. This placed Rybalko's forces in the rear of Army Group South.

Feldmarschall von Manstein flew to Führer headquarters. He pleaded with Hitler to release to him three panzer divisions earmarked for the defensive front on the lower Dniepr. Hitler refused, and von Manstein replied, "If this goes wrong, *mein Führer,* then the fate of Army Group South is sealed."

Hitler gave von Manstein permission to employ the 1st Panzer Division and the 1st SS-Division *Leibstandarte* on the Kiev front rather than on the lower Dniepr.

However, the *Leibstandarte* Division, which had been placed on alert and entrained early on the morning of 5 November, was still on its way to Russia. The Russian front again. For the third time in his career Michael Wittmann was bound for the east and another hellish winter battle.

* * *

"Panzers forward!"

The Tiger company set itself in motion. Driving at high speed, the tanks reached the Kamenka River by midday on 13 November and crossed near Potshniki. To the left were the tanks of the 1st Panzer Division.

The appearance of German units took the Soviets completely by surprise. The panzers first met the massed enemy forces in the bottomland south of Unova. The Panther battalion attacked, driving straight toward the wave of enemy tanks, which pulled back toward Moknatshka.

When the Tigers arrived, the enemy was already on the move. The Soviets withdrew toward the north before the 1st Panzer Division and the *Leibstandarte*. By 20 November the latter unit had reached the area northeast of Chomutes, where it was able to shield the flank of the XXXXVIII Panzer Corps toward the east.

The Tiger company moved out with the rest of the division north-northwest toward Brusilov.

Wittmann stood in the turret cupola. Before him appeared a wood, extending toward the southeast in the direction of Brusilov.

The tanks had approached to within eight hundred meters of the wood when an antitank gun opened fire. Seconds later the morning quiet was shattered as countless guns began to fire.

The first shell landed dangerously close to the Tiger. Wittmann ordered a halt. The five panzers stopped. Seconds later there was a crash of gunfire, and lances of flame whipped from the long gun barrels. The first enemy tanks began to burn.

The Tigers rolled through the sparse wood in wedge formation, firing as soon as targets became visible, jinking to avoid enemy fire. They arced around in a semicircle and came to a large clearing, where they found themselves facing about thirty parked enemy tanks.

The Tigers halted. A hail of shells smashed into the assembled Soviet tanks. The Tigers had surprised the enemy unit as it was breaking camp. The Soviet tanks tried to flee, but they only got in each other's way. T-34s collided as they tried to escape, then backed up into other of their comrades.

Lötzsch's Tiger was hit. Driver Pötter was killed instantly while radio operator Aberhardt lost an arm.

Wittmann heard the call for help from his comrade, who was being attacked by three enemy tanks, and turned at once. He approached the T-34s from behind and within a minute Woll had destroyed two. The third turned and approached Wittmann's Tiger. The T-34 fired. The shell just missed the Tiger's turret, but tore off the light metal storage bin on the back. Then Woll fired. The impact of the shell striking home dislodged the T-34's turret, but the tank kept moving. Several figures jumped clear and ran toward the Tiger.

Wittmann emerged from the turret and opened fire with his submachine gun. The burst of fire struck the Soviet tankers and knocked them to the ground.

A rifle bullet creased one of Wittmann's knees. He quickly ducked back inside the turret and slammed the hatch cover closed.

By midday Wittmann and his crew had destroyed ten enemy tanks and five antitank guns. The Tigers rolled back to refuel and rearm. The exhausted crew snatched a few moments' sleep as their tanks were serviced. Wittmann was everywhere at once, encouraging his comrades, studying the maps, and trying to form a picture of the situation. While the panzer crews slept, Wittmann led a patrol into enemy territory and discovered a camouflaged antitank gun as well as several tanks.

Wittmann gave his men a quick briefing. One after another they climbed into their tanks. The Tigers drove slowly through the woods in single file, crossed a stream, then headed down a forest lane. Moments later they came upon the concealed antitank gun, which was positioned at the edge of a clearing. At the same time the enemy tanks came into view. There were eleven.

Wittmann's voice crackled over the radio: "Open fire!"

Four "eighty-eights" roared. Four detonations followed. The antitank gun, which was Woll's target, was flipped over by the blast. Three T-34s were burning. One turned away, trailing smoke. Woll fired again. The shell pierced the side of the T-34, which exploded. The surviving Soviet tanks opened fire.

Just then Wendorff roared onto the scene and joined the battle. The sudden arrival of more German tanks confused the Russians. All eleven Soviet tanks were destroyed. Nevertheless, the attempted German breakthrough failed. The Soviets regrouped just outside Brusilov and halted the *Leibstandarte*'s advance.

Evening fell; the exhausted tankers collapsed onto their straw-filled mattresses in the village of Khomutets and fell asleep. By day's end Wittmann and his crew had destroyed ten enemy tanks and seven heavy antitank guns.

The next day the Germans threw all their available forces against Brusilov. This time the 1st Panzer Division was also on hand. The 19th Panzer Division had moved up on the right flank and took part in this bitter action. On 20 November *Obersturmbannführer* Schönberger was killed by a direct hit. Max Wünsche took over command of the *Leibstandarte* Panzer Regiment. The 1st Panzer Regiment stormed toward Brusilov from the northwest. Kocherovo fell. By the twenty-fourth the division had taken Brusilov.

On the evening of 5 December 1943 the 1st Panzer Division reached the Kamenka-Fedorovka area, north of Zhitomir. To the north was the 7th Panzer Division, which had earlier captured the city. The *Leibstandarte* had assembled to the south, due north of Zhitomir. On the division's right, the 68th Infantry Division, the 2nd Parachute Division under General Ramcke, and the *Das Reich* Division were sent to the attack toward Radomyshl.

"Lousy cold!" complained *Untersturmführer* Wendorff as the crews walked to their Tigers at first light on 6 December.

"You're right!" Wittmann shouted back. The cold was biting and he felt it even through his thick winter clothing.

The tanks moved off. Once again Wittmann's company was in the first wave. Its assignment was to break through the enemy antitank front that aerial reconnaissance had discovered near the Soviet airfield between Kortyky and Styrty.

Unterscharführer Möller steered around a deep shell hole and then turned back onto his original course. The other tanks kept pace to the left and right. One platoon was echeloned to the right, covering the company's rear. The rattle of tank tracks drowned out the thump of artillery fire. The Soviets were firing into the German assembly area. Kortyky appeared ahead and to the right.

"Achtung, Wittmann! Cover the flank toward the village. Don't allow yourself to be held up!"

There were numerous flashes from the houses at the northern edge of the village and from behind bushes as ten antitank guns opened fire, blinding Wittmann.

"Forward! Maximum speed!"

The Tigers rumbled toward the enemy antitank guns at forty kilometers per hour. Several shells struck home, but were deflected by the thick armor of the Tigers. Flames and smoke seeped into the fighting compartment of Wittmann's tank. Everywhere gunner Woll looked there were muzzle flashes from Soviet antitank and field guns.

The tanks opened fire. Shells smashed into the Soviet antitank positions. The Panther battalion rolled through a gap that had been smashed in the line and drove toward Styrty.

Suddenly a gigantic vehicle opened fire from a group of bushes. Its gun was at least eight meters long. The huge, low-slung form emerged from the bushes, halted, and turned on one track.

"Assault gun, *Untersturmführer!*" shouted Möller.

The giant lowered its gun.

"Watch out, Möller!"

Möller turned sharply, and the Tiger leaned dangerously. He drove ahead two hundred meters and then turned to the right, accelerating toward the enemy vehicle. The Tiger was now facing the enemy's vulnerable flank. The driver of the Soviet assault gun tried to turn with the German tank, but he was not quick enough. Woll traversed the turret to the nine o'clock position. The Tiger halted. Seconds later there was a roar as Woll pressed the firing button.

The armor-piercing shot penetrated the flank of the Soviet assault gun. There was a mighty explosion as its ammunition exploded, and the huge assault gun was blown to pieces.

Wittmann saw Warmbrunn engage two antitank guns and watched as one of the guns scored a direct hit, disabling the Tiger. The other antitank gun was about to finish off the German tank. Möller quickly brought the platoon leader's Tiger into firing position. Once again, Woll's aim was sure, and the threat to Warmbrunn was averted.

Kling and the Wendorff platoon emerged from the village. Wittmann and his remaining tanks joined them at the southern

exit. House-to-house fighting had broken out. The panzer
grenadiers worked their way through the village, flushing out
pockets of Soviet troops until all resistance had been eliminated.

The tanks drove toward a distant fruit farm. A T-34 appeared
from behind a barn and was fired on. The enemy tank was left
disabled and on fire.

Suddenly, Möller let out a cry and gestured ahead excitedly.
"Through the window!" he shouted.

Wittmann saw the long gun barrel of a Soviet tank appear in
the right corner of a window, followed by the front of the tank
and then the turret. The rear of the house had been blown away
and the tank had taken refuge inside. Woll aimed carefully, and
fired. The shell whizzed through the window and blew the turret off the T-34.

Silence fell over the battlefield. Above the crackle of flames
the tank crew suddenly heard an unusual dull roar, which in a
matter of seconds intensified into a wild howling and whistling.
A salvo of rocket projectiles was on its way.

The men slammed shut the hatches they had just opened and
ducked instinctively. It seemed as if the portals of hell had
opened up all around them. The air was filled with smoke and
flames and the ground shook. Stones and earth rained down on
the tanks.

Wittmann's Tiger shuddered and shook as if being shaken in
the fist of a giant. Flames lit the inside of the tank and the air
was filled with an acrid smell. Finally the barrage, which had
lasted five minutes, ended.

Five minutes later the tanks halted at the northeast end of
Golovin and the commanders climbed down. "If the panzer-
grenadiers had been here, that would have been the end of
them," said *Untersturmführer* Wendorff.

Obersturmbannführer Wünsche, who had taken temporary
command of the regiment on 20 November, came driving up.
He was bleeding from a scratch on the left side of his face.

"I have just heard that you have now destroyed sixty tanks
and almost as many antitank guns, Michael. Your gunner has
destroyed his fifty-fourth tank. I think that will mean the
Knight's Cross for you."

"Thank you, *Obersturmbannführer!*" replied Wittmann. "But

I think that Woll is the man who deserves the decoration. He was the gunner who destroyed fifty-four of my sixty enemy tanks."

The days passed. On 11 December the *Leibstandarte* reached the Weprin-Wyrwa area, due south of the rail line to Kiev. On 24 December an urgent SOS from the 4th Panzer Army reached "Corps Balck." XXXXVIII Panzer Corps and its three panzer divisions, including the *Leibstandarte,* had to be withdrawn from the Melini sector and rushed south to close a gap the Soviets had smashed in the front in the area of Berdichev.

Michael Wittmann and his platoon rolled south with the rest of the company. His thoughts were the same as those of many of his comrades: Kiev has not been retaken!

The first day of Christmas found the *Leibstandarte* on the march south in the bitter cold, across a snow-covered landscape. The division set up a provisional main line of resistance at the northern limits of Berdichev. The 1st Panzer Division moved into position at the eastern edge of the city and to the south. Soviet ski troops attacked from the west and northwest.

In the meantime, Wittmann had destroyed his sixty-sixth enemy tank, and on 13 January he received the Knight's Cross.

On the evening of 13 January 1944 the Tiger company was placed on alert. Early the next morning the Tigers and Panthers of the *Leibstandarte* counterattacked. A dramatic battle ensued, which saw the Soviets halted with the loss of over one hundred tanks and assault guns.

A day later, Balthasar Woll, Wittmann's gunner, who had taken part in eighty of his commander's kills, received the Knight's Cross from the hand of the division commander.

On the evening of 19 January 1944 the exhausted *Leibstandarte* panzer crews fell exhausted into the straw beds of their billets in the village of Kostovetska. *Hauptscharführer* Höflinger switched on the radio to listen to the daily *Wehrmacht* communiqué. The announcer's voice came through clearly: "On 13 January 1944, *SS-Untersturmführer* Michael Wittmann, a platoon leader in a panzer regiment of the SS-Panzer Division *Leibstandarte,* who was mentioned in the *Wehrmacht* communiqué of 13 January 1944, was awarded the Knight's Cross for his outstanding accomplishments. From

July 1943 to January 1944, Wittmann destroyed fifty-six enemy tanks in his Tiger, among them Soviet T-34s and superheavy assault guns as well as American and British tanks. On 8 and 9 January 1944, he and his platoon halted a penetration by a Soviet tank brigade, during which he destroyed ten enemy tanks. In the fighting on 13 January 1944, Wittmann engaged a powerful enemy armored force, destroying nineteen T-34s as well as three superheavy assault guns. This raised Wittmann's total to eighty-eight enemy tanks and assault guns destroyed. . . ."

On 20 January 1944, Michael Wittmann was promoted to the rank of *Obersturmführer* for bravery in the face of the enemy. Following the departure of *Hauptsturmführer* Kling, who had been selected to become battalion commander, Wittmann took over the 13th (Heavy) Company.

The battle went on. During a heavy snowstorm several days later, Wittmann destroyed five T-34s. The enemy tanks were picked off one at a time as they appeared like ghosts out of the dancing clouds of snowflakes. Dense masses of enemy tanks stormed toward the German main line of resistance. Day after day, Wittmann, Wendorff, Kling, and all the other Tiger commanders went out to face an enemy who possessed seemingly inexhaustible resources in men and machines.

On 28 January the Soviets attacked again. Once again it was the heavy Tiger company that formed the backbone of the German defense.

The accomplishments of the men in the tanks bordered on the unbelievable. They rolled into the attacking waves of enemy tanks, halting briefly, firing, then moving off to the flank before attacking the main body again. Wherever they went, the Tigers left a trail of shattered enemy tanks, flames, and pillars of black smoke. For those unlucky crews forced to abandon their tanks, the battlefield, snow-swept and cold, was a hellish place.

Gradually the impetus went out of the Soviet attack, and the divisions of the panzer corps were regrouped to act as a mobile "fire brigade."

In the Cherkassy area the 2nd Ukrainian Front (General Konev) and elements of the 1st Ukrainian Front had surrounded the German *Korpsabteilung* B—the XXXXII and XI

Army Corps with a total of six and a half divisions. Among these units were the *Waffen-SS* Division *Wiking* and the *Wallonien* Brigade under Leon Degrelle.

The *Leibstandarte,* together with the 1st Panzer Division, prepared to advance toward Shenderovka-Lysyansk and open the pocket.

On the evening of 31 January, in the midst of the preparations, a report arrived that Michael Wittmann had become the 380th German soldier to be awarded the Oak Leaves to the Knight's Cross.

On 1 February 1944 the *Leibstandarte* Division left the Zhitomir-Berdichev area to hurry to the aid of the surrounded German divisions.

Inching their way along the main road, the vehicles of the *Leibstandarte* drove toward the Cherkassy Pocket. The great column of vehicles also included those of the 1st, 6th, and 16th Panzer Divisions. The desire of all involved was to help their surrounded comrades avoid the fate suffered by the 6th Army at Stalingrad. Wittmann and his platoon led the way.

The Soviets were trying desperately to reduce the pocket. They thought they had the entire German 8th Army (General Wöhler) in the bag. On 3 February 1944, General Konev, commander in chief of the 2nd Ukrainian Front, said, "This time it is done! I have the Germans cornered and I'm not going to let them get away."

But Konev was deceiving himself. The trapped German force was not the entire 8th Army, but only *Korpsabteilung* B. With two army groups at his command, General Konev intended to create another Stalingrad.

General Stemmermann, who was commanding in the pocket, tried to maintain a cohesive force and hold the center of the pocket, the village of Korsun and its vital airfield. Under his command were fifty-six thousand soldiers.

German divisions were on the way to relieve their trapped comrades. Among them were some of the most powerful panzer divisions in the German arsenal, each a match for a Soviet tank corps. One such unit was the *Leibstandarte* Division. As had often been the case before, it was to be right in the thick of things.

General Nikolaus von Vormann was to lead one of the "hammers" of the relief effort. Among the units of the XXXXVII Panzer Corps was the 24th Panzer Division under General von Edelsheim. However, on 3 February it was diverted on Hitler's orders, as Russian forces had broken into the rear of the new 6th Army *(Generaloberst* Schörner).

Thus plans for a combined attack by the XXXXVII Panzer Corps and the III Panzer Corps under General Breith, commander of the second "hammer," came to nothing.

On 4 February, General Breith committed the 16th and 17th Panzer Divisions and Battle Group Bäke. This first thrust ran into elements of the 1st Ukrainian Front just as the leading elements of the *Leibstandarte* Division arrived on the spearhead's right flank. Four Soviet tank corps and the *rasputitsa* (the mud produced by the first thaw), brought on by a period of warm weather since 2 February, stopped the first attempt to open the pocket.

"The first objective is the Gniloy Tikich!"

This was the key sentence in the commanders', briefing held early on the morning of 6 February 1944. A half hour later the Tigers of 13th Company were crawling northeast through the mud. They had barely covered half a kilometer when Soviet tanks and assault guns appeared on the flank.

Wittmann ordered an attack. Employing his standard tactic, his plan was to drive quickly into the enemy, take advantage of the resulting confusion, and smash him. The Tigers stormed toward a battalion of T-34s of the Soviet 5th Guards Tank Corps.

Wittmann destroyed nine enemy tanks in this action. The other members of the company scored as well. Two Tigers were knocked out. The crews were picked up by other tanks.

The battle resumed the next day. By the evening of 8 February the *Leibstandarte* Division had fought its way to the bank of the river that was to play such a fateful role in the escape from the pocket, the Gniloy Tikich. To the SS-Division's right, the 1st Panzer Division had also reached the river. A member of the division, *Oberfeldwebel* Hans Strippel, distinguished himself in action there.

In action since the beginning of the war, Strippel had by now destroyed more than seventy enemy tanks. He had received the Knight's Cross a year earlier, on 26 January 1943. For his actions in this battle, the breakout from the Cherkassy Pocket, he was to become the 485th German soldier to be awarded the Oak Leaves to the Knight's Cross (presented 4 June 1944).

The struggle to open the pocket became more dramatic day by day. The Soviets fired everything they had at the German tanks in an effort to foil the relief attempt. The panzers rolled against a wall of antitank guns, assault guns, and tanks.

Unterscharführer Franz Staudegger, who had proved one of the most successful Tiger commanders in Operation *Zitadelle,* distinguished himself once again during the battles for the Cherkassy Pocket. During *Zitadelle* he had been a member of the Wendorff platoon. A crisis arose, and his was the last available Tiger. Staudegger took charge of the situation and saved the entire panzer regiment, for which he was awarded the Knight's Cross on 10 July 1943.

And now, on 10 February 1944, something similar happened. Eighteen enemy tanks and assault guns approached the Wittmann platoon from the flank and the rear. Staudegger had been left behind to repair a minor problem with the tank's gearshift. As he drove to rejoin his unit, he suddenly saw the enemy tanks rolling through a depression in the Wittmann company's rear.

"Wittmann! Watch out!" he shouted over the radio. "Behind you! I'm coming!"

Wittmann recognized Staudegger's unmistakable Carinthian accent. "Turn around to the left and open fire!" he ordered.

The six Tigers swung around. Fire flashed from the muzzles of the Soviet assault guns. Just then Staudegger hit one of the assault guns from behind. The Soviet vehicle burst into flames. In the ensuing melee all but two of the enemy armored vehicles were destroyed. Staudegger accounted for five.

The Tigers drove on together and smashed into an antitank front, which they put out of action. This created some breathing room for *Sturmbannführer* Herbert Kuhlmann, who had taken command of 1st Battalion following *Obersturmbannführer* Wünsche's departure.

The Tigers and Panzer IVs formed up behind Kuhlmann, who intended to break into the pocket at any cost.

Soon afterward the Tigers and Panthers of the Bäke Regiment joined the attack. The relief forces reached a position a short distance from Dzhurzhentsy before the enemy once again stopped them, this time by attacking from the north against their open left flank.

In the days that followed, more and more enemy tanks emerged from the forests. The number of white victory rings on the gun barrel of Wittmann's Tiger increased steadily. Already there were ten broad rings and seven narrow ones, indicating 107 enemy tanks destroyed. Each day brought fresh successes.

The division's panzer grenadiers had to bear the burden of holding onto the ground that had been won. The regiment's numbers melted away like snow in the spring sun. Hill 239 claimed hundreds of victims. And still the surrounded soldiers waited inside the pocket. They had turned their front and were preparing to break out.

Fords were discovered across the river. The first tanks drove through, often up to their fenders in water. Engineers built a north and an east bridge. Lysyanka, the important village, was firmly in German hands as the morning of 16 February 1944 dawned.

Ju-52 transports flew over the pocket at low altitude and dropped two-hundred-liter containers of fuel at designated locations.

The weather now turned cold again. The 503rd Heavy Panzer Battalion under *Hauptmann* Scherf joined the fight. Oktyabr was taken from the Soviets. Still twenty-five kilometers from the edge of the pocket, on 17 February 1944 the entire III Panzer Corps became bogged down.

A message was radioed into the pocket: "Break out toward us!"

After a fearful battle and under continual Soviet tank and rocket fire, 35,000 men reached the safety of the relief force's positions. Every gun and every tank was in action twenty-four hours a day. Each man gave his all. One man whose actions were representative was *Feldwebel* Wohler. Three times he swam the Gniloy Tikich to retrieve wounded nonswimmers.

Sadly, 18,800 German soldiers were left dead or dying in the pocket. It was due to the efforts of *Obersturmführer* Michael Wittmann and the other members of the relief force that the figure was not higher.

Hauptsturmführer Kling had been promoted to the rank of *Sturmbannführer.* When he was wounded, Wittmann took over the heavy company. In the next few weeks he led his men through a true hell. They faced Marshal Zhukov's 1st Ukrainian Front (General Vatutin, the front's previous commander, had been shot by Ukrainian guerrillas), which had broken through on the left wing of Army Group South. The *Leibstandarte* threw itself against the storm of enemy armor, resulting in further dramatic battles. Wendorff, who had received the Knight's Cross on 15 February, was wounded when his Tiger was knocked out. The German forces were unable to halt the Soviet advance.

The *Leibstandarte* Division fought in the ice and mud along the main road east of Ternopol. Together with the 1st Panzer Division, the unit was surrounded in the Kamenets-Podolsk area at the beginning of March 1944. Several days later, however, the division fought its way out to freedom.

The *Leibstandarte* Division's strength was now spent. The survivors were withdrawn from the front and sent to Belgium, where it was planned to reorganize the division.

Wittmann was ordered to Führer headquarters to receive the Oak Leaves. He met Hitler, received his decoration, then went home to his family.

Wittmann's leave was brief, and he soon received orders to go to Belgium, where he was to take over the 2nd Company of the 501st SS-Panzer Battalion. The battalion, whose 1st Company was commanded by *Hauptsturmführer* Möbius, was a new formation and under the direct command of the I SS-Panzer Corps *Leibstandarte,* which included the 1st SS-Panzer Division *Leibstandarte* and the 12th SS-Panzer Division *Hitlerjugend.*

On 6 June 1944 the Allies landed in Normandy. The tanks of I SS-Panzer Corps rolled in the direction of the Calvados Coast. The 501st Battalion's destination was Caen.

The Allied invasion of France had begun. On the morning of 6 June the mightiest naval armada the world had ever seen appeared off the French coast between the Cotentin Peninsula and St. Mère-Église while swarms of Allied aircraft filled the air over the invasion area. For Michael Wittmann it was the start of a very different war.

When the invasion began, the *Leibstandarte* Division and other corps units of I SS-Panzer Corps were in Belgium. The 12th SS-Panzer Division *Hitlerjugend* had been designated OKW reserve and was in the Lisieux area. With it, although still east of Paris, was the 501st SS-Heavy Panzer Battalion, which had been assigned the role of mobile "fire brigade."

Bayeux was captured by Allied landing forces on 7 June. By then they had already lost eleven thousand men.

The *Hitlerjugend* and *Panzer-Lehr* Divisions waited for orders to go into action. Both divisions had been ready to move since 0400 on 6 June. The 12th SS Panzer Division was not given permission to attack until 7 June. *Gruppenführer* Witt gave the order.

"Together with the 21st Panzer Division's 22nd Panzer Regiment, the division is to attack enemy landing forces and throw them back into the sea."

Max Wünsche led the 12th SS-Panzer Regiment, *Oberst* von Oppeln-Bronikowski the 22nd Panzer Regiment. The panzer grenadiers of the *Hitlerjugend* under Kurt "Panzer" Meyer attacked. Following initial success the attack bogged down. Decimated by Allied air attacks, the *Panzer-Lehr* Division was unable to join the battle until the next day.

The following two days saw various counterattacks by German forces, all of which failed to break through to the sea. Three panzer divisions had driven from west to east into position around Caen and along the Caen-Bayeux-Carentan coastal road.

The battle raged back and forth. On 12 June the 501st Tiger Battalion reached the combat zone. The Wittmann company assembled in a sparse wood east-northeast of the village of Villers Bocage. The 1st Company under *Hauptsturmführer* Möbius drove into the assembly area on Wittmann's right.

Statements from prisoners had revealed that the British 7th Armored Division was advancing on the open left flank of the *Panzer-Lehr* Division, which was engaged in the battle for Tilly. While the British 50th Infantry Division launched a frontal attack on Tilly, the "Desert Rats" attempted to slip around into the rear of the *Panzer-Lehr*.

Wittmann's Tigers, which had begun their march from Beauvais through Paris to the invasion front on 7 June, were attacked by Allied aircraft near Versailles on the morning of the 8th. Several Tigers were put out of action and had to be towed away for repairs.

The surviving Tigers reached the area of Villers Bocage early on the morning of 12 June. The next day Wittmann carried out a local reconnaissance.

"Damn, Michael, I have the feeling that something's happened!" said *Oberscharführer* Woll, the only member of Wittmann's old crew still with him.

"Possibly, Balty," replied Wittmann.

Wittmann ordered a halt. The Tiger was on the crest of a small hill, still in cover. Wittmann had a good view of the open plain below. The tank's engine fell silent. As Wittmann scanned the horizon he spotted movement to the north near Sermentot.

"Enemy tanks on the road to Villers Bocage and on the way to Hill 213. Woll, come to battle readiness!"

Wittmann directed the Tiger around the hill and into a small wood. He halted about ten meters from the edge of the wood.

Wittmann peered through his scissors telescope.

"An entire armored unit, men. They're rolling into Villers Bocage and will probably turn onto the Caen road.—Message to 2nd Company: Operational Tigers come to readiness and drive in the direction of Hill 213! Further orders to follow!"

The weather was hazy late on the morning of 13 June 1944 and there were no fighter-bombers in the air.

The enemy tanks and armored personnel carriers rolled onward. There was no screening force. These were the leading elements of the British 7th Armored Division, the 22nd Armored Brigade, and units of the 1st Infantry Brigade. Also present were two companies of the famous 8th Hussars and elements of the 1st Armored Regiment.

Wittmann was aware of the threat these forces represented. If the 7th Armored Division reached the rear of the German front, the battle in this sector would be over.

The enemy tanks came nearer. The closest was two hundred meters away. Gunner Woll already had it in his sights.

The tanks approached another hundred meters.

"Go!" ordered Wittmann.

The Tiger's engine roared and the tank began to move. It left the wood, reached the road, and halted.

Woll opened fire. The first shot blew the turret off the leading British tank. Flames shot from the shattered tank's hatches. The next round was already in place. The second British tank blew apart. Slowly the Tiger rolled forward. The enemy column halted. From this range every shot was a direct hit.

The Tiger rolled down the column past tanks, trucks, motorcycles, half-tracks, and armored personnel carriers, blasting everything in its path. The first barrage lasted two minutes. When it was over the front of the enemy column had been destroyed.

A Cromwell tank pulled out of the column and fired. The shot struck the Tiger's bow plate and bounced off.

Woll swung the "eighty-eight" in the direction of the Cromwell that had fired. The first shot pierced the British tank's armor and left it in flames.

The Tiger rolled on, firing high-explosive and armor-piercing shells. It destroyed the British unit that was to have forced the decision near Tilly, and which probably would have, had this lone German panzer not been in position. Then a voice crackled in Wittmann's headset: "Stamm to chief: have reached Hill 213. Engaging reconnaissance tanks!"

"Move forward, Stamm!" replied Wittmann.

Within a few seconds the four Tigers that had survived the march to the front added the weight of their fire to that of the company commander.

Untersturmführer Stamm led the four Tigers against the 8th Hussars. Soon the surviving enemy tanks were turning away. They rolled into Villers Bocage, into which the main body of the British force had withdrawn.

Finally the battle was over. Twenty-five tanks and armored vehicles were in flames or had been knocked out as well as a large number of other vehicles. Suddenly Wittmann heard the voice of *Hauptsturmführer* Möbius.

"Coming with eight Tigers. Directions please!"

"Enemy has pulled back to Villers Bocage. We are about to attack the village from the direction of Hill 213. Come in from the south!"

Wittmann drove to Hill 213. When he arrived there he found his four Tigers. Stamm reported. The Tigers attacked and rolled into Villers Bocage. British antitank guns opened fire.

A British antitank battalion under Major French "tried to stop the mighty elephants," as he later put it. Thirteen Tigers attacked Villers Bocage from three sides and pushed into the town. Wittmann directed his Tiger into a side street. He heard the sound of antitank guns firing and the hammering sound of impacting shells from the main street. Berger pulled back a few meters. They turned and saw an antitank gun fire on a German tank and set it on fire.

Woll traversed the turret. He targeted the antitank gun as it was preparing to fire a second time. The 8.8cm shell smashed into the enemy gun, but the German tank had been destroyed as well. It was the Tiger of *Untersturmführer* Stamm. None of the five men inside managed to escape from the blazing steel coffin.

Three minutes later the Tiger of *Oberscharführer* Ernst Krieg went up in flames. Once again none of the crew escaped. In spite of these losses the surviving tanks smashed through the antitank barrier.

Wittmann and his Tiger were far ahead of the rest. He saw that the town was occupied by British infantry. The Tiger turned onto the main road, when suddenly there was a flash from the side. A shell struck the Tiger's forward right roadwheel with an earsplitting crash. The impacting shell smashed the Tiger's right track.

"Tank is disabled, *Obersturmführer!*" shouted Berger desperately.

"Take all weapons and bail out!"

The crew leapt out of the hatches only to be greeted by machine gun fire. They ran for their lives and finally reached a low wall in front of a house, behind which they took cover.

"Everyone here?" asked Wittmann.

"Everyone, *Obersturmführer,*" confirmed *Hauptscharführer* Berger.

The five crawled into the house, climbed out the back side and crept through the garden in the rear. Soon they reached the exit from the village. One of the company's Tigers approached and took them on board.

Corps had already heard of Wittmann's feat. An hour later Sepp Dietrich came to the battalion command post. He had Wittmann describe the action. Then he said, "You have done well, Wittmann. You decided the battle.—What would you like?"

"I would like my Tiger recovered, *Oberstgruppenführer*," answered Wittmann with a sideways glance at Woll, who nodded in agreement.

"I think I can promise you that, because a quarter of an hour ago the 2nd Panzer Division and a battle group from the *Panzer-Lehr* began their attack on Villers Bocage. The repair party will set out as soon as the town is in our possession."

"Thank you, *Oberstgruppenführer!*"

That evening the report arrived that the enemy had abandoned Villers Bocage. Wittmann and Woll went with the repair party into the town. They found the Tiger where they had abandoned it. Nothing had been removed by the enemy. The repair party went to work, and shortly before midnight the *Hauptscharführer* said, *"Obersturmführer, you can climb aboard!"*

The British called this engagement "The Battle near Villers Bocage." The British 7th Armored Division suffered its heaviest losses of the entire invasion campaign here. The entire division headquarters and Tank Company A, with twenty-seven tanks, were lost, as well as all the wheeled and tracked vehicles of the 22nd Armored Brigade.

The commander of the 22nd Armored Brigade, Brigadier W. R. N. Hinde, was desperate. He had lost fifteen officers and 176 men. The 1st Infantry Brigade lost its commander, three officers, and sixty men.

Operation *Perch*, planned and executed by Field Marshal Montgomery, had failed. Caen, the objective of the enveloping attack, would now have to be stormed frontally. Montgomery attacked in an effort to create the conditions necessary for a breakthrough. Defending the Tilly-Caen area were the *Panzer-Lehr* and *Hitlerjugend* Divisions.

During this period Wittmann was heavily involved, leading attacks, counterattacks, and reconnaissance missions. On 22 June 1944 he became the seventy-first German soldier to receive the Swords to the Knight's Cross. By now he had destroyed 138 enemy tanks and assault guns as well as 132 antitank guns, making him by far the most successful tank commander in the German armed forces. For demonstrated bravery in the face of the enemy Wittmann was promoted to the rank of *Hauptsturmführer.*

Wittmann continued to lead his company in his Tiger. His next action took place in the Falaise area. Montgomery had ordered the 1st Canadian Army to attack the town. Lieutenant General Simonds, commanding Operation *Totalize*, had at his disposal two armored divisions, two armored brigades, and three divisions of infantry.

The attack force assembled south of Caen on the evening of 7 August 1944. Six-hundred (!) tanks in six groups formed the spearhead of the attack. Their orders were to advance east and west of the major road leading to Falaise and capture the town by midday. One thousand heavy bombers were to blast open a ten-kilometer-wide breach for the tanks.

The attack began. By evening the enemy had penetrated five kilometers into the German positions. If the assembled tanks of the 4th Canadian and 1st Polish Armored Divisions advanced now, there would only be two battle groups of the 12th SS-Panzer Division with a total of fifty tanks to meet the threat. However, "Panzermeyer" had a recipe to deal with this.

"Defend the front with center point Cintheaux and an enveloping attack by our panzers!"

Oberführer Meyer turned to the tall Tiger commander and said, "Wittmann, drive north and take possession of Cintheaux and halt there. Your Tigers are to secure the flank against an enemy tank attack!"

Wittmann and his battalion (he had since been given command of the battalion) rolled north. They reached Cintheaux, where they destroyed a number of enemy tanks attacking panzer grenadiers holding out in the ruins of the village. Then the Tiger commanders saw the enemy tanks: six hundred of them, approaching in several waves.

Wittmann's Tigers had driven behind a long hedgerow when *Oberführer* Meyer arrived and issued further orders.

Wittmann climbed into his tank. The two panzer companies moved out and headed north, accompanied by the panzer grenadiers. Enemy artillery fire began to fall among the tanks. The others heard Wittmann's voice over the radio.

"Ahead at maximum speed. Through, through, through!"

The tank commanders saw Wittmann, in the lead as always, roll into the wall of enemy fire. This was a tactic that had never failed him. The tanks burst through and the panzer grenadiers followed into the hellish enemy fire.

Suddenly all of the men in the rear German positions who had witnessed Wittmann's heroic charge began shouting and pointing skyward. There they came: 1,900 bombers and 1,800 fighters and fighter-bombers (as learned later from Allied war records)!

"Forward! Into the open!" ordered Meyer.

The bombers released their loads over several French villages. One village after another was leveled, and some of the bombs even fell among some Canadian positions. The commander of the 3rd Canadian Infantry Division, Major General Keller, was wounded and had to be evacuated. Many of his soldiers were killed or wounded. The carpet of bombs plowed up a ten-kilometer-wide section of French countryside.

Following the aerial bombardment, Wittmann's Tigers stormed the flank of the Polish armored division, opening fire from a range of eighteen hundred meters. Wittmann's attack halted the wave of Shermans, which was rolling toward Cintheaux. The battle raged for hours. Several Tiger commanders reported that Wittmann had destroyed two, then three enemy tanks. The successful German counterattack ended Operation *Totalize.*

When evening fell the commander's tank was missing. *Oberführer* Meyer sent search parties to look for Wittmann. He interrogated all the tank commanders who had been in the vicinity of the *Hauptsturmführer.* Soon Meyer pieced together what had happened.

Leading his Tigers, Wittmann had charged into the heaviest fighting and engaged a group of Sherman tanks east of Cintheaux. He destroyed two of the Shermans and damaged another so that it could not move, before leading his battle group on toward the north. Driving into a superior force of enemy tanks, his Tiger was showered with shells. Finally, Wittmann's Tiger was cornered by three to five Shermans. Under fire from three sides, the Tiger was overwhelmed.

Flames licked from the hatches of the Tiger and none of the

crew managed to escape. All had probably been killed earlier by the impacting shells.

Thus died Michael Wittmann near Caen on 8 August 1944.

Editor's note: The manner in which Michael Wittmann and his crew met their end has been the subject of much controversy. The generally accepted version, that he was killed in combat with Sherman tanks, has been challenged in recent years. Later versions of the events of 8 August 1944 give the credit for the destruction of Wittmann's Tiger to British artillery fire or rocket-firing Typhoon fighter-bombers. The remains of Wittmann and his crew were found and identified in the summer of 1983. They are now buried at La Cambe Military Cemetery along with many of their comrades who fell during the fighting in Normandy in 1944.

Military Career

22 April 1914:	Born in Vogelthal, Upper Pfalz.
1937:	Joins LAH SS-Regiment.
September 1939:	Participates in Polish campaign as commander of an armored car. Promoted to *Untersturmführer.*
May 1940:	Takes part in invasion of France as a member of LAH Armored Reconnaissance Battalion.
April 1941:	Participates in the invasion of Yugoslavia as commander of an assault gun. Awarded Iron Cross, Second Class for actions at Klidi Pass.
June 1942:	Rejoins LAH SS-Panzer Division in France.
November 1942:	Begins training on Tiger heavy tank.
January 1943:	Accompanies I SS-Panzer Corps to the Eastern Front; takes part in subsequent fighting for Kharkov.
July 1943:	Battle of Kursk.
July/August 1943:	LAH Division transferred to Italy.
November 1943:	LAH sent back to Eastern Front.
13 January 1944:	Awarded the Knight's Cross.

20 January 1944:	Promoted to *Obersturmführer.*
31 January 1944:	Awarded the Knight's Cross with Oak Leaves.
Spring 1944:	Transferred to Belgium, given command of 2nd Company, 501st SS-Panzer Battalion.
6 June 1944:	Allied invasion of France.
13 June 1944:	Single-handedly halts a breakthrough by British armored forces near Villers Bocage.
22 June 1944:	Promoted to *Hauptsturmführer* for bravery in the face of the enemy, awarded the Swords (total at that time: 138 enemy tanks, 132 antitank guns destroyed).
8 August 1944:	Killed in action east of Cintheaux.

6

Albert Ernst

Eight Enemy Tanks Destroyed

"Herr Leutnant, all hell's broken loose over there!"

With these words *Unteroffizier* Kötter, driver of the platoon leader's tank destroyer *Falke,* passed comment on the hellish noise of the Russian artillery.

It was early on the morning of 19 December 1943, and the Russian offensive was in its seventh day. The army's 519th Heavy Tank Destroyer Battalion had driven in a forced march to the front, where it was to be employed as a mobile "fire brigade."

"It will soon be time," observed *Unteroffizier* Herbert Colany, sucking on his tongue.

Leutnant Albert Ernst, leader of the *Hornisse* Platoon of 1st Company, puffed on a cigarette. He was excited. He was taking the big tank destroyer into combat for the first time. Everything had certainly gone well in training. It was a great opportunity to be selected for the *Hornisse* ("Hornet") tank destroyers with their much-feared "eighty-eight" guns.

"Someone's coming," shouted *Gefreiter* Bretschneider from the entrance to the hut. Seconds later a motorcycle-sidecar combination pulled up and the door burst open. It was *Hauptmann* Strehler, commander of 1st Company.

"Ernst, get ready! You and your three wagons have to leave in three minutes. Direction Surash."

"All of us?" asked the *Leutnant. Hauptmann* Strehler nodded.

"The platoons will be distributed along the entire width of the Russian assembly area. Corset-stays for the grenadiers, so to speak, Ernst."

The *Hauptmann* drove on to the 2nd Platoon. There was

much activity in the low-roofed peasant hut. The three *Hornisse* crews billeted there were standing by their vehicles a few minutes later. The tank destroyer was a Panzer IV chassis with a fixed superstructure housing the 8.8cm gun, the long barrel of which gave it the appearance of a giant, prehistoric elephant.

Leutnant Ernst took his place and heard that *Feldwebel* Neigl and his platoon were already under way.

"Move out!" he ordered.

The big engine revved up and the three tank destroyers moved out in wedge formation toward the roaring sound of the impacting artillery shells. The crew stood in the fighting compartment, which was open on top. Albert Ernst looked at them for a moment. They were all men he could depend on.

The artillery fire came nearer and nearer. In front of them earth sprayed up in tall geysers. Frozen clumps of earth whizzed through the air.

"Straight toward the shell bursts, Kötter!" Ernst ordered his driver. The excitement that had gripped him earlier gradually fell away. His face tensed and became narrower. His eyes also grew narrower, staring at the approaching inferno.

It was close to midday when they reached the town that lay in the center of the artillery fire. Flames billowed from the village and the sharp, biting east wind drove black-yellow clouds of smoke and flames toward the three tank destroyers. *Leutnant* Ernst scouted ahead. Then they came to a battalion command post.

"How does it look?" Ernst asked the executive officer. "Are the Russians coming?"

"For sure! Yesterday they probed our lines and ranged in their guns. They'll be here soon.—Cigarette?"

Leutnant Ernst took another cigarette. Later, in battle, there would be no time, and afterward he didn't want any. He smoked hastily.

"They've been trying at this spot for a week," continued the executive officer, surreptitiously eyeing the *Leutnant* in the black panzer uniform. He noticed his decorations: both Iron Crosses, the Silver Wound Badge, and the high Bulgarian decoration at his throat. He must be a good man, this *Leutnant*.

Leutnant Ernst accompanied the infantry officer into the

command post. He was shown where the most favorable ambush position was and then walked back into the open. Hollmann and Fressonke, the commanders of the other two tank destroyers, came over to him.

"What's the war doing, *Herr Leutnant?*"

"The Russians are throwing fresh divisions into the battle. They want to take Vitebsk and remove the thorn in the side of their front."

"Poor swine over there," said Fressonke, gesturing in the direction of the raging inferno of shell bursts.

"We're going to drive as far as that line of hills and go into hull-down positions on the back slope," said Ernst. "The attack waves will probably be on the move as soon as the barrage lifts."

They drove off, reached the line of hills, and rolled upward until the superstructures of the tank destroyers just protruded above the crest of the rise, giving them a clear field of fire on the flat plain below. The *Hornissen* were spaced laterally about one hundred meters apart. Engines were switched off. The thunder and crash of the artillery barrage became even louder.

Unteroffizier Georg Kötter had opened the driver's hatch and was staring at the inferno before them. The days were short in December; it was early afternoon and twilight was already falling.

Before them the firestorm of artillery fire and bursting shells became higher and wider. It seemed to blot out almost the entire sky.

"Shit!" said *Obergefreiter* Sötte as he wiped the optical sight clean for the tenth time.

"Falke to everyone! Are you ready?" asked *Leutnant* Ernst. One after another the commanders reported ready for battle.

All of a sudden the artillery fire grew to a new intensity. That was the sign! Albert Ernst knew this from the winter of 1941/42 before Moscow and the period that had followed, when he and his tank destroyer had been attached to the 3rd Motorcycle Battalion of the 3rd Panzer Division: the Russians were about to attack!

Only a few shells fell near the tank destroyers, smashing into the frozen earth, causing it to tremble. Steel from a thousand guns hammered the German positions. Under this hellish fire were the grenadiers of the 14th Infantry Division.

They were forced to endure thirty minutes of massed fire. On the line of hills shells were falling nearer. One burst about thirty meters in front of *Falke*. The men ducked low; thick clumps of earth smacked against the frontal armor.

"The bastards!" roared Bretschneider as a lump of earth struck him in the small of the back.

Imperturbable as ever, Colany said, "Keep your complaints to yourself," and went back to sucking his tongue.

Suddenly the enemy fire ceased. Ernst raised his binoculars. In the distance, in front of the enemy-occupied village of Surash, he saw dense masses of Red Army soldiers and, between them, dark, compact points. They were . . . yes, they were Russian T-34 and KV-I tanks!

"They're coming. Get ready!"

The first shell lay in the breech. *Unteroffizier* Colany took a rough aim in the direction of the advancing Soviets.

"Don't fire yet!" ordered the *Leutnant*. "Not until we're sure that we'll hit one with every shot. Then we'll let them have it."

Standing on the platform to the left and behind, the *Leutnant* had the best view but was exposed to machine gun and artillery fire. With a look to the left and right he saw that *Bussard* and *Adler* were ready to fire. Meanwhile, the Soviet tanks had disappeared into a shell-torn wood. When they appeared again they would be in range of the *Hornissen*. The men waiting in the tank destroyers could already hear the rumbling and roaring of the approaching tanks. They must soon be in the vicinity of the German main line of resistance where the grenadiers waited behind their machine guns in icy foxholes.

Russian mortars fired into the German lines. Again and again there was the sharp, tearing sound of bursting mortar rounds. The first armor-piercing shells began to fall around the three tank destroyers, then mortar salvoes began to fall on the hills.

Earphones pressed tightly over his ears, the radio set at a high volume so he could hear above the crash of the exploding mortar rounds, *Leutnant* Ernst stood behind the telescopic sight. Now he took the cigarette from his mouth and let it fall to the floor, and, without taking his eyes from the sight for a second, ground the glowing butt with the toe of his boot. It was a routine he had followed often enough.

Suddenly he knew: this is our moment!

Tanks appeared from the end of the shattered strip of forest: ten, fifteen, twenty. More followed.

"*Falke.* to everyone. Range eighteen-hundred!"

Aim, check, and adjust the aim.

"Fire!"

Unteroffizier Colany pressed the firing button. The first shell left the long barrel of the "eighty-eight." The tank destroyer rocked from the recoil. For the first time after many long weeks of practice they were firing at an enemy. Now they must prove themselves—or go under.

"He's burning!" roared loader Sötte, a bull of a young man, as he cradled the next round in his arm and pushed it into the breech. Flames erupted from the stricken T-34. Abruptly the entire phalanx of attacking tanks stopped. *Bussard* fired. A second later, almost merging with the crash of the other gun, followed the first shot from *Adler.*

Aim again. Colany worked quickly and surely.

"Sixteen hundred, eleven o'clock!"

Another correction, target in the sight and—fire!

Another hit, this time in the hull. The tank burned. The three tank destroyers fired faster and faster. Hit! Hit! Hit!

The enemy tanks returned the fire and began to take evasive action, trying to escape this hell.

The three *Hornissen* with their long-barreled "eighty-eights" continued to pour fire into the attacking Soviet tanks. More and more of them lay stricken and burning or turned and drove back into the protective darkness of the forest.

Suddenly shells began to rain down on the high ground. Obviously the enemy artillery had just been given a new target. Shells fell close to the three vehicles. Around them all hell broke loose. Everywhere flames leapt high, steel crashed against steel, and wounded cried out. Mortars joined in. The "potatoes" fell like hail but did little damage, because the fragments from the 5cm mortar rounds either passed harmlessly over the tank destroyers or crashed ineffectively against the steel of the superstructure.

Loader Rudolf Sötte reloaded. The "eighty-eight" roared,

and the empty shell casing rumbled through the iron spring-action door of the shell casing ejector and clattered onto the floor.

There was a spurt of flame from the enemy tank as its ammunition went up, turning it into a steel coffin.

Leutnant Ernst had forgotten everything else around him. His concentration was directed at destroying every tank that had reached the German main line of resistance and was attempting to collapse the frozen trenches or run over the foxholes.

The battle went on. Ernst's orders were brief and sure, driving any uncertainty from the men. There was no doubt that they would stop this armored assault.

One after another the last enemy tanks disappeared into the falling darkness. They left behind eight of their fellows—shot-up, torn apart, unusable. Six had been destroyed by *Falke* and one each by the other two crews.

The Russian infantry had also pulled back. Several groups stayed put in no-man's-land in front of the German lines, possibly waiting for the next attack.

Many fires burned throughout the night. Up front several houses were burning. Two of the enemy tanks were still glowing. Thick clouds of smoke hung over them like black memorials to their destruction.

The Soviet troops regrouped in Surash. New assault groups moved forward. *Leutnant* Ernst pulled out a front-line newspaper and read out the latest *Wehrmacht* communiqué to his crew.

"The heavy fighting in the Nevel area places the other battles on the Eastern Front in the background."

"Good Lord, they started out near Nevel, *Herr Leutnant.*"

"That was fourteen days ago north of here," replied the *Leutnant.* "Now they want to smash the northern wing of our 3rd Panzer Army as well."

"But the Russians haven't had much luck," interjected *Feldwebel* Hollmann, who had come over to them. "They've been attacking in vain since 13 December. It's already the nineteenth. They'll be finished soon."

"I fear that they'll hold out longer than that, and that this was just the beginning," said the *Leutnant.* "The Russians probably want to create a starting base here for a push into the Baltic states. To achieve their objective they must bring about the collapse of the northern wing of our panzer army."

"If only the grenadiers can hold; otherwise the Russians will smoke us out of the *Hornissen* with their close-range weapons," offered Hollmann.

"*Generalmajor* Flörke (commander of the division, decorated with the Knight's Cross four days earlier) is staying here and spends most of his time up front in the trenches with the grenadiers," interjected the *Leutnant.*

"Enough of that rubbish!" complained *Unteroffizier* Fressonke.

"Should we speak of fried eggs and roast potatoes?" asked Hollmann.

"Damn!" shouted Fressonke furiously, "*Herr Leutnant,* forbid him to talk about food."

Albert Ernst grinned.

"Do you remember, Fressonke, near Borna in the 'Wilden Sau.' Roast potatoes and Mettwürstchen with . . ."

"*Herr Leutnant,* are you trying to kill me?" asked Fressonke accusingly.

They ate cold rations. The tea, which they had brought along in their canteens, was warmed up on the engine cover plates.

Soon it was midnight. The three tank destroyers moved to new positions on the hill near the grenadiers.

"Man, if hadn't been for you," said a bearded *Obergefreiter* wearing the German Cross in Gold, "they would have simply run right over us."

"Just take care that the Russians don't jump us, we'll take care of everything else," called Fressonke.

"Don't shout so!" said Ernst, smiling in spite of himself. This youngster from eastern Germany was a special sort and very dependable.

It was five minutes past midnight. "Do you hear something, *Herr Leutnant?*" asked *Feldwebel* Hollmann, who had moved the farthest to the northeast. "It sounds like tanks!"

Seconds later they all heard the rattling and rumbling, and then they saw the flames from the exhausts of an enemy tank flickering in the darkness.

Leutnant Ernst scanned the terrain. There they were! No doubt: tanks driving forward! And the dense masses behind them and farther to the rear were the infantry forces of a new attack.

"Herr Leutnant, don't let any of them through!" called one of the grenadiers, who had come over to the tank destroyer. He looked up at Ernst. In the pale light of the full moon the *Leutnant* recognized a narrow, young face. The eyes were large and fixed on him almost beseechingly.

"We won't leave you alone," replied Ernst.

"Achtung! Bussard, take the one on the right and *Adler* the one on the left flank. Do you have them?"

"Target in sight!" reported both commanders almost simultaneously.

"Don't fire until we're certain!"

They waited. Farther ahead the first MG42 opened up. The battle was under way between the grenadiers and the Russian infantry. Then the main body of enemy tanks halted. Flames spurted from their 7.6cm guns.

"Achtung! Fire!"

The three "eighty-eights" fired as one. The shells howled toward the enemy, smashed into the steel armor, and left three tanks disabled with one blow. Two of them were still firing, even though immobilized.

"They're storming the cemetery hill, *Herr Leutnant!"*

"We'll stop them!"

They opened fire when the first T-34 appeared on the upper chain of hills. Again the roaring blasts of the cannon, the clang of shell casing ejectors, the crash of armor-piercing shot striking steel. Then there was a hammerlike blow on the right. Fire spurted upward. Dirt showered the men. A lump of earth, fortunately a soft one, struck Sötte, the powerful loader from Leipzig, right in the face. He swore and spat and went back to work.

A T-34 rolled through a depression straight toward them. The first shot passed right over its turret. The turret traversed, the long gun swung around. Then there was a flash from its muzzle and two seconds later the nearby *Adler* took a direct hit.

Ernst heard the voice of *Unteroffizier* Fressonke over the radio. *"Herr Leutnant,* we are . . ." Then the words broke off with a long, gurgling groan. The *Leutnant* turned his head. He saw the men from *Adler* lying on the ground.

"Fire!" he shouted.

This time Colany was on target. The shot struck the turret of the T-34. Blown clean off the hull of the tank, it fell to the ground ten meters behind the T-34.

Bussard knocked out another T-34. With that the enemy tank attack collapsed. The Russians had lost six more tanks. That made a total of fourteen to the credit of the tank destroyers. Eight of these had been accounted for by *Leutnant* Ernst.

The grenadiers cleared the terrain of enemy infantry. They pulled back two hundred meters near the cemetery hill.

Just as *Unteroffizier* Kötter was lighting the first cigarette, *Obergefreiter* Jolassen, *Adler*'s loader, came over to them.

"*Herr Leutnant,* the crew has been evacuated. *Unteroffizier* Fressonke is dead. But I don't want to go back, I want to stay with you."

For a few seconds Ernst was speechless. Then he collected himself for a reply.

"What shape are you in?"

"A piece of metal in my left elbow, *Herr Leutnant.*"

"With a wound like that you belong in the dressing station at once, Jolassen. You can't stay here."

"But, *Herr Leutnant,* it's quite harmless. Surely you can still use me. I don't want to go back, *Herr Leutnant.* Please let me stay."

Leutnant Ernst looked at the *Obergefreiter.* He saw the determined look on the young man's face. But still he hesitated.

"*Herr Leutnant,*" offered the *Obergefreiter* anew, "look at this!" He tried to extend his arm. It made a terrible crunching sound and the young man grimaced with pain.

"Jolassen, you must . . ."

"I must stay here, *Herr Leutnant.* There's only a handful of grenadiers. I can get a submachine gun and at least cover you. Perhaps they can use me on a patrol. I'm good enough for that. I only need one hand to shoot with."

He reached down with his right hand and pulled his "zero-eight" (8mm pistol) from its holster. With that the *Leutnant* gave up. He knew that it was useless, and he really could use him. He nodded silently. For a second a smile crossed his face, which even now—after the battle—had lost none of its grim attentiveness. He would never leave these men in a jam. They stayed with him. That's the way it was.

An hour later *Leutnant* Ernst summoned the *Obergefreiter.*

"Jolassen, we're both going on patrol."

"Fine, *Herr Leutnant*," said the young man.

They left at once, moving at a crouch deep into no-man's-land. They found no Russians. It didn't look as if there would be any more attacks that night.

In the next hour Jolassen twice went forward as a messenger.

"We're going to pull back. Rearm, refuel, and then a few hours' rest. Gather our wounded men together—the dead too!" ordered Ernst.

In the next half hour they also picked up many wounded from the 14th Infantry Division and laid them in the fighting compartment. The second *Hornisse* also had a full load. The less seriously wounded men climbed up behind onto the motor cover plates.

"Watch out," called the driver, "that your rear ends don't melt from the heat."

They drove back slowly. *Unteroffizier* Kötter carefully steered his terrible cargo to the main dressing station. There *Leutnant* Ernst ran into the battalion medical officer, *Oberstabsarzt* Dr. Brunz.

"Have Fressonke brought to the cemetery, *Herr Oberstabsarzt*. We want to bury him in the morning."

"It will be done, Ernst," said the doctor, and offered his hand to the thirty-year-old *Leutnant*.

Shortly before they were to return to the front *Obergefreiter* Jolassen appeared.

"*Herr Leutnant,* I can't stay here. Take me with you!"

"You're completely mad, Jolassen," answered Ernst. "You simply can't come back with us! Be reasonable!"

Leutnant Ernst gave the man a proper dressing down. The *Obergefreiter* stared at him for a long time, imploringly and silently. For the second time the *Leutnant* weakened. He motioned Jolassen over to the tank destroyer.

"Thanks, *Herr Leutnant!*" called Jolassen and, as if fearing that the *Leutnant* might change his mind, ran over to the vehicle, swung himself on board, and held on tight.

The night passed. Both *Hornissen* were made ready for action again. Ernst and his men learned that the entire battalion, together with the Tiger company (of the 501st Heavy Panzer Battalion, which had been sent in by *Generalmajor* Flörke), had destroyed sixty enemy tanks. Of these, *Leutnant* Ernst's three *Hornissen* had alone destroyed fourteen.

The men then drove to their billets, threw themselves down on the straw, and were soon fast asleep.

Leutnant Ernst woke early on the afternoon of 21 December. The dull growling sound of artillery fire came into the room through the open window. He got up and washed in the basin that stood waiting for him filled with fresh water.

"Are you coming with me, Boghut?"

Feldwebel Willi Boghut nodded. They left the hut containing their comrades, some of whom were still sleeping, and stepped out into the open. The *Hornissen* had been driven up to the west side of the hut and camouflaged with straw. Looking like small extensions to the building, they were almost invisible from the air.

"How did last night go with you, Willi?" Ernst asked his friend.

"Nothing!" answered Boghut, a little exasperated. "It almost seems as if when I'm out with my platoon the Russians never come. And always when you are out they appear en masse."

It began to snow. The snow was driven toward the village in billowing clouds by the sharp east wind. It splashed against the tank destroyers and had already covered the platoon's unprotected motorcycle-sidecar. One of the company sentries, his feet in thick, fur-lined boots, came around the corner. He was bent low against the snow. When he saw the two men he began to straighten up to salute, but Albert Ernst waved him on. The two went inside again.

"Shouldn't the mail come from the assembly point today, *Herr Leutnant?*" asked Hollmann, who had just finished washing and had now begun to shave.

"Could be that it will come at noon with the rations.—Hey, Uncle Sasha, what are you doing?"

The aged Russian, who served as everyone's factotum, straightened his bent frame and showed the *papyrossi* (cigarette) he was rolling.

"Here, *Pan Leutnant!* Good tobacco!" he said, and held up one of the cigarettes.

"Hmm, that smells like sunflowers and peppermint, we'd

better leave it," said Ernst, and he laughed. The old man grinned and lit one of the cigarettes. Then he stood up and shuffled off into his shed.

Ernst looked around. There on the flatbed was where they had laid Fressonke. Now he lay at the cemetery, and tomorrow they would bury him.

"The field kitchen is coming!" said one of the men, who had all awakened in the meantime. They ran to the door and threw it open. The battle had subsided. The war was catching its breath for the next round.

The field kitchen set up behind the company commander's hut. The men came into the open. There was one man from every crew, each carrying five mess kits. The handles were entwined together so that they could carry all five in one hand. The other was for the box with the cold rations.

Colany and Hollmann ran over to the accompanying truck.

"Where's the mail, Schaarschmitt?" they asked the First's orderly room *Feldwebel*. He blinked through his thick eyeglasses and gestured behind him.

Hollmann grabbed the mailbag and ran back to the huts. When Bretschneider arrived with the food, the mail had been neatly separated and the pouch sent on to 2nd Platoon.

They ate quickly. Albert Ernst, too, caught himself wanting to leave his food and tear open the letters, two of which bore the handwriting of his young wife. But he forced himself to wait and spooned up the hot pea soup.

Almost simultaneously they opened the envelopes. Afterward, it was so unusually still that Uncle Sasha knew what was going on.

"Your wife?" he asked the *Leutnant*. Ernst nodded.

"Is she well?"

"Yes, she is well," said Ernst. The words contained in the letter, written by the hand of his beloved wife, turned his thoughts to a journey over several thousand kilometers.

Everything else was forgotten. All that he saw was the handwritten lines and the knowledge that far away someone was praying for him and worrying about him.

Noisy exuberance broke the stillness. Relief, joy, and confidence filled the room until *Feldwebel* Hollmann brought the platoon leader three letters. They were for *Unteroffizier* Fressonke, one from his parents in Leipzig and two from his bride in Borna.

This was the reverse side. Fressonke was dead. While those at home still hoped for the best, he had met a soldier's fate. He had died as he had lived: inconspicuously. He was a comrade they would never forget.

Ernst, as his platoon leader, would have to write to his parents. Perhaps his words would bring them the comfort they needed. Reassurance and the certainty that he had not suffered. That would not change the fact that he was dead, but it might ease their pain.

The Counterattack

The telephone jangled. The morning of 22 December came early. Albert Ernst saw that the *Gefreiter* was motioning him to the telephone. He jumped up quickly and took the receiver.

"1st Platoon, *Leutnant* Ernst."

The sonorous voice of Maj. Wolf-Horst Hoppes rang from the wire.

"Ernst, you are to drive immediately with one tank in the direction of Surash. Russian infantry attack. The grenadiers need support."

"I'll leave at once, Herr Major!"

"Has it started again, *Herr Leutnant?*" asked Hollmann.

"You stay here. *Falke*'s crew get ready!"

Three minutes later they left the hut. An icy snowstorm blew in their faces. The snow was nearly ice, but fortunately not too dense. After they had taken their places and warmed up the engine, the snow abated somewhat.

"Forward, Kötter! In the direction of the cemetery!"

The *Hornisse* began to move. The powerful engine roared. The tank destroyer took the hollow rapidly, rolled over the crest in a spray of snow, and then headed down into the next valley.

A group of *Pioniers* pointed the way. They rolled in the direction indicated, skirting the Teller mines that had been laid as a defense against enemy tanks, and finally reached the assembly area of the grenadiers. An unfamiliar major ran over to them.

"How does it look? Have you enough high-explosive shells, *Leutnant?*" he asked.

Albert Ernst nodded.

"Where is the main push?" he asked.

"Follow me, I'll take you there. A machine gun position over there is holding us up!"

They rattled along behind the major. When a burst of machine gun fire forced him to take cover, the tank destroyer rolled past him. Ernst leaned over the side of the *Hornisse.*

"We've made out the target, Herr Major. Attack signal?"

"One green fired obliquely forward! Don't drive too fast!"

"Tell your men not to bunch up behind the tank, otherwise they'll be in great danger."

The major nodded. Then they were past and reached a group of small fir trees. At that moment four lances of flame erupted from the hill.

"Take out the machine gun!" ordered Ernst.

Unteroffizier Colany targeted the position. He aimed so that the shell would strike a half meter below the muzzle flashes. It was a high-explosive round.

There was a crash as he fired and the recoil drove the *Hornisse* back a step.

"A hit!" shouted one of the grenadiers, who lay to the left and right in their foxholes. The second and third shots totally devastated the machine gun position.

"The signal, *Herr Leutnant!*"

Albert Ernst had already seen it.

"Forward! At a walking pace!"

The tank destroyer rolled forward. The next high-explosive shell lay in the breech. Colany didn't fire; he was waiting for a sure target. The grenadiers walked along not ten meters behind the tank destroyer. When a couple of mortars coughed to life they went into cover.

Leutnant Ernst peered through the telescopic sight. He saw the earth-brown shapes of Russian soldiers in the hollow. At that moment the *Hornisse* was standing on the crest of a hill. The view from there was excellent.

"Six hundred. Twelve o'clock!"

"Target recognized!" reported the gunner a few seconds later.

"Fire!"

The big gun roared. The shell-casing ejector rattled. The empty casing clattered to the floor. Sötte had already rammed the next shell into the chamber. The breech mechanism snapped shut.

The shell fell in the midst of a group of Red Army soldiers assembling in the hollow for a new attack. The German attack had beat them to it.

"Forward, forward!" roared the major, who had appeared next to the *Hornisse*. He raised his arm and pointed toward the hollow. The grenadiers jumped up and began to run. *Unteroffizier* Kötter steered the tank destroyer after them, its engine roaring.

Leutnant Ernst saw that *Obergefreiter* Jolassen was assisting the loader. The young soldier's face was chalk white. As long as he doesn't pass out, thought Ernst. Just then Jolassen collapsed. With the last of his strength he crawled to the side so as not to get in Sötte's way. Ernst promised himself that if they got out of this he would personally carry Jolassen to the dressing station.

The attack gained ground rapidly. They reached the forward Russian positions. High-explosive shells smashed into nests of resistance. The Russians began to run.

"Tanks, *Herr Leutnant!*" shouted *Unteroffizier* Kötter. He had suddenly spotted a T-34 through his driver's vision port as it emerged from the right out of a ravine. Three, four, then five other tanks followed.

The last high-explosive shell roared from the tank destroyer's gun. The loader shoved an armor-piercing round into the breech. Russian shells crashed into the frozen ground to the left and right. A lump of earth frozen hard as stone struck Colany in the forehead. Noiselessly the gunner slid to the floor.

"Pick him up!" shouted the *Leutnant*. He and Sötte lifted their unconscious comrade to the side. *Gefreiter* Bretschneider immediately began to care for him. Ernst scanned through the gunner's sight. The first T-34 came into view. It was held in the crosshairs. A slight correction, then he pressed the firing button. With a whipping blow the armor-piercing shot left the barrel and struck the T-34, ripping its turret from the turret ring.

"A hit, *Herr Leutnant!*" roared Sötte.

Leutnant Ernst saw the sweat-covered face of the massive *Obergefreiter* as he handled the shells as if they were matchsticks. He knew that this was a man he could count on.

"Watch out, Sötte!" he warned, as the big man's hand got too close to the ejector. Many loaders had had hands crushed by the barrel recoil, but Sötte was already aware of the danger.

"Herr Leutnant, Colany is coming to," called Bretschneider, relieved.

Ernst didn't hear a word he said. He saw a muzzle flash and then watched as the shell passed close by over the tank destroyer and smacked into ground far behind them.

"Three o'clock!" he ordered. Kötter swung the vehicle around and then made a minor correction. This shot from the "eighty-eight" tore the forward right roadwheel from the T-34, which was just preparing to fire a second time. The force of the blow spun the tank around; its second shot went wide.

Suddenly the *Hornisse* came under fire from half-left from a range of three hundred meters.

"Zigzag, full gas!" shouted Ernst.

The tank destroyer swerved like a tottering giant, then turned directly toward the T-34, whose cannon once again spit flame as it fired.

"Haaalt!—Haaalt!"

The *Hornisse* stopped with a jerk and Ernst fired. It was a shot "from the hip" with an 8.8cm gun. The armor-piercing shot struck the bow armor of the T-34 and pierced it.

For a few seconds it looked as if nothing had happened. Then the turret hatch was thrown open. The tank commander and his gunner, both in flames, jumped out. They ran to the side and threw themselves to the ground to smother the flames. The head of a third crewman appeared in the hatch. When his body was half out of the hatch, two explosions ripped the T-34, killing him and the fourth member of the crew.

The *Hornisse* rolled forward a short distance, stopped in a hollow, then rattled to the side and rumbled up the slope at full speed to reach a new firing position.

It was a battle for life or death. If the Russian tanks succeeded in destroying them, then the grenadiers, who had been forced to take cover in the open field, would be overrun and cut down.

Again they drove toward the enemy. The fifth Soviet tank

blew apart under the hammer blows of the "eighty-eight." Then they knocked out a sixth. The gap in the enemy assembly area was now so large that the enemy preparations were as good as smashed.

When it had become quiet and they had driven back to their initial starting position, Colany asked, "How many did you knock out, *Herr Leutnant?*"

"Six, old boy!"

"Then you did well on my behalf!" answered Colany.

Ernst went over to *Obergefreiter* Jolassen, who was being cared for by the radio operator. He lay on a blanket and two more were spread over him. Jolassen was still unconscious.

They reached their own main line of resistance. The grenadiers had pulled back to this position. The major expressed his thanks to *Leutnant* Ernst.

"If it hadn't been for you, we would have walked into the middle of the Russian assembly area. You can imagine what would have happened then."

"We did what we could, Herr Major," answered Ernst and reached over the side to grasp the hand offered him by the major. Then the tank destroyer's motor roared to life again.

"To the main dressing station," said Ernst after they had reached the village. Kötter drove on. The men carried their comrade inside. When they were certain Jolassen was being well looked after they drove on to the supply train to rearm and refuel.

On their return to the village the crew received a report that the Russians were attacking the infantry.

"All of the other vehicles are in action, *Herr Leutnant!*" said *Feldwebel* Boghut.

"All right then, we'll drive in again and get them out!"

Ernst and his crew rolled into action for the second time that day. Before the infantry's positions they saw that the enemy was this time attacking on a broad front in depth.

Through his telescopic sight Ernst could see the dense ranks of Red Army soldiers lying in front of the main line of resistance. There were dead just beyond the wire. It was a terrifying scene. The earth-brown coats of the dead Russians stood out clearly against the snow. There may have been hundreds. But over and over again fresh waves attacked and were driven to ground by the hammering machine guns. More waves followed and disintegrated. Individual soldiers came closer, dug into the snow and disappeared from sight.

Suddenly the Russian artillery opened up with a heavy barrage. With high, singing whistles and howls, countless shells rushed in, smashing into the most forward German lines. Some also fell short, landing among the leading Russian attack formations. A little later the barrage shifted onto the German rear. The air was filled with the sound of bursting shells, the whistle of projectiles, and the shrill chirping of glowing shell fragments.

"There's another tank, *Herr Leutnant!*" shouted Kötter. Again he had been the first to spot the approaching enemy.

Now *Leutnant* Ernst saw it too. At least two thousand meters away the T-34 rumbled around between the densely packed waves of the fourth attack formation like a monstrous giant.

"Range two thousand, Colany!"

The *Hornisse* halted. The *Unteroffizier* aimed carefully and fired. The first shot was a direct hit that destroyed the T-34.

A German mortar platoon they had just passed began lobbing 8cm shells into the attacking Russian formations. Machine guns rattled and two quadruple-flak hammered away in a rapid staccato.

The dense formations of Soviet soldiers went to ground. Companies disintegrated. Wounded men crawled back toward their own lines, others dug themselves in. The inferno seemed to have no end. A short while later German artillery began laying down barrage fire on no-man's-land, over which the fourth wave was advancing.

"Isn't it ever going to stop, *Herr Leutnant?*" moaned Kötter, as he saw the fifth wave appear far to the rear. Ernst shook his head. It probably wouldn't stop until all of the attack troops had been driven to their deaths. The Russians were apparently willing to sacrifice everything to force a decision.

The storm of death came from the depths of Russia. The Red Army troops charged the German positions, trying to break through and envelop everything in a whirlwind of destruction. The *Leutnant* believed he knew why the Russians were attacking so bitterly. Behind the assault troops were blocking battalions, which intercepted any fleeing soldiers and chased them back into the battle. That was usually so.

"High-explosive!" he ordered.

The next fifteen minutes were filled with the hammering of impacting shells, the smacking of machine gun bullets against the armor of the *Hornisse*, and frequent explosions as enemy personnel carriers were hit and caught fire. All the while high-explosive shells burst amid the waves of human bodies.

"The last two high-explosive rounds, *Herr Leutnant!*" reported Sötte.

"Fire! Then we'll go back and reload. We'll save the few armor-piercing rounds we have left in reserve just in case." They fired the last two shells, then reported by radio that they were pulling back and rolled to the rear. When they reached the village of Plissovo, which lay between the front line and their quarters, they were stopped by a group of grenadiers. Almost all of the men were wounded. *Leutnant* Ernst saw the horror reflected in the faces of the soldiers.

Leaning far over the side he asked, "What's happened?"

"Russian tanks have broken through due north of here!"

"Where exactly?"

"Right there up that rutted road. Then you'll see them, *Herr Leutnant!*"

"Turn, Kötter!"

Without waiting to hear any more, Sötte rammed an armor-piercing round into the breech. They reached the northeastern end of the village and halted. Through his binoculars Ernst saw a tank that stood out like a small point on the open plain.

"At least four kilometers, Colany. Can we get him?"

"Certainly we can get him, *Herr Leutnant!*" replied the gunner. He took aim at the enemy tank.

The first shot flashed from the barrel; fifteen seconds later the second. A cloud of snow was thrown up directly in front of the T-34 by the third shot. The fourth was a direct hit. A dark banner of smoke rose from the stricken Soviet tank, becoming larger and thicker. Flames licked higher and higher through the smoke. A relieved smile crossed Ernst's face. Then four explosions. The tank was finished. He was pleased that he had been able to help his comrades in the infantry. For the first time he noticed how cold his hands were. He stuck them into the pockets of his camouflage uniform.

The men smoked as Kötter turned the tank destroyer back in

the direction of the supply train. The motor roared at high speed. Wind whipped past the *Hornisse*.

They were on their way back, heading for their warm billets. When they had rearmed *Falke* and parked it out of the wind behind the cottage, *Feldwebel* Schaarschmitt came out the door and shuffled toward them. He grinned. His eyes twinkled behind the thick lenses of his glasses.

"The chief is inside, Ernst," he said.

"All right," replied the *Leutnant*. He went inside and reported.

"Ernst platoon reporting back from action. Seven T-34s destroyed. Russian attack repelled."

"Terrific, Ernst! After this day I expect you'll soon be due for the Knight's Cross. Yesterday the army high command mentioned your success of 21 December in the army order of the day."

"Thank you, Herr Major!"

Ernst grasped the hand offered by his battalion commander. He was a unit leader of his own style. The tall officer had been awarded the German Cross in Gold. He had seen action in Spain in the battalion commanded by *Oberstleutnant* Ritter von Thoma and wore the Spanish Cross in Silver as well as the Spanish Tank Assault Badge.

"You have learned to handle the *Hornisse* well, Ernst. Remember how it was during conversion training in Spremberg? When you couldn't find your jacket and reported barechested?"

The major grinned at his platoon leader. The two men understood each other well. The *Leutnant* thought back to their early days with the army's 519th Tank Destroyer Battalion.

He saw himself once again at work with a *Hornisse* crew. It was summer 1943, the sun was hot. He had taken off his jacket and was working in the tank destroyer wearing only his pants. As an officer he wanted to know every control, because he knew that someday his life might depend upon it. They were installing a new chamber when it was reported that the major had arrived. Ernst immediately crawled out of the fighting compartment and was about to pull on his jacket—but couldn't find it.

He even recalled the thoughts that had gone through his

mind then. But he had overcome them and presented his crew to Hoppe shirtless.

"What's this then?" the major had asked.

"Leutnant Ernst, Second Platoon in training, Herr Major. I have to know how everything works."

The major thought for a few seconds. Then he turned to the *Leutnant* again.

"I'll go with you and have a look!" he said at last, and walked over to the *Hornisse* with the *Leutnant*. Afterward he observed how well Ernst worked with his men and how quickly everything happened.

A little later he called the officers of the battalion together and said to them, "Gentlemen, I expect you to arrive in overalls tomorrow morning just like your men. The officer is the first member of the gun's crew. He must know everything. And when I say *everything* I mean just that, understood?"

From then on Albert Ernst was not too popular with the other officers. But it was not long before that changed.

"You were thinking of Spremberg, Ernst?" asked the major, looking inquiringly at the officer.

"Yes I was, Herr Major," answered the *Leutnant*.

"A lovely time, especially the sendoff in Oldenbrück with the guests from the OKH (army high command) and OKW (armed forces high command) when we paraded our *Hornissen*."

"And the party afterward, Herr Major."

"Yes, the next day I couldn't get any of you out of bed."

The major smiled and handed out the cigarettes he had brought with him as well as the usual sweets.

"Take care, men! Every wagon is important and every man equally so!"

He left the cottage. The men lay down on the piles of straw. Another day of fighting had come to an end. This time they had suffered no casualties and were thankful to have a roof over their heads and a chance for a few hours' sleep in a warm place.

It was not long before they were asleep.

The old Russian laid a stack of bricks at the chimney and the large oven, which was in need of repairs. He worked quietly, as if he knew how much these men needed their few hours of rest. *Leutnant* Ernst had placed his hands under his head. His gaze fell on the heavy, sooty beams in the room. With a quick movement he swatted away a bedbug before it ran under the covers.

Then he looked at Bretschneider, who was sitting against the other wall of the cottage on an overturned crate, writing a letter. He was using the map board to write on.

What was he writing to his sweetheart? Telling her that they were living in a magnificent hotel, taking their ease. Bretschneider was something of a poet and it was amazing how he could find something good to say about most situations.

A few moments later Ernst, too, was asleep.

Nighttime Reconnaissance

It had become evening and Uncle Sasha covered the windows of the 1st Platoon's cottage. A pair of Hindenburg lights (small candles) flickered in the breeze blowing through the open window. *Feldwebel* Hollmann was playing skat with two members of his crew. They threw the trumps on the table, banging it with their fists. They laughed when they won or cursed when they lost in spite of having good cards.

Albert Ernst had stripped down his submachine gun and was cleaning it. Everything would depend on the weapon if the Soviets ever managed to board *Falke*.

He had just reassembled the weapon when the field telephone rang. The *Leutnant* jumped up and ran over to the set.

"Ernst platoon!"

"Ernst, it looks as if the Russians are planning to attack again tonight. Check out the area. See what's going on, and if there's trouble, drive up to the front lines and support the grenadiers."

"Understood, Herr Major! Out!

"Bernlöhr, get ready for a reconnaissance patrol."

The *Obergefreiter,* a virtuoso on a motorcycle, stood up. He got into his fur-lined leather jacket, pulled his fur cap down over his ears, and put on his large driver's goggles. Then he picked up his submachine gun, slung it over his shoulder, and reported ready.

"Good, I'm all set. Go get the motorcycle and bring it around!" said the *Leutnant.*

Ernst also took his submachine gun. Soon afterward he

stepped out of the cottage. The sound of artillery, which before had been heard only in the distance, was now perceptibly louder.

The motorcycle rumbled out of the shed. Friedhelm Bernlöhr brought it to a stop before the door. The passenger's seat had been wiped clean and dry.

"Everything ready, Bernlöhr? Is the tank full?"

"We could drive to Moscow, *Herr Leutnant.*"

"We don't want to go that far," replied the *Leutnant,* and he swung himself into place behind the driver.

The motor roared. The motorcycle drove off and they took the old, familiar route. They climbed the icy slope after a running start, rolled through a ravine, and came down hard in a pothole. Bernlöhr heaved the motorcycle out again and skidded onward.

Finally the pair reached the huts near the forward positions. They were met by an *Oberleutnant.* He gave them directions and the pair drove on a distance into no-man's-land.

Just before reaching the enemy-occupied village, the two men heard the sound of tanks.

"They're not driving, but just idling to keep their engines warm, *Herr Leutnant,*" suggested Bernlöhr.

"You're right! And that means a new attack!!"

At that moment the Russian artillery suddenly opened up. From one second to the next the sky was filled with howling, screaming shells that burst all around in a hellish display of noise and light.

"Let's go back, Bernlöhr!" ordered Ernst.

"Through this thick shit, *Herr Leutnant?* Shouldn't we wait until they shift their fire to the rear?"

"Then it would be too late. That's when their infantry will move out; get going."

The two of them made it. A little later they heard the noise of the attack behind them. When they reached the top of a hill and looked back they could see dense, barely perceptible groups of advancing infantry. Among the infantry could be seen the red flames from the exhausts of the escorting tanks.

"That's an attack on our sector," said Ernst. "We must get to our vehicles and warn the grenadiers."

Shells fell close by. The shock wave from a nearby blast

threw the men from the motorcycle. The *Leutnant* fell headfirst into a snowbank; his driver landed a few steps beyond, spraining his right hand. Cursing, they shook themselves off, righted the still-running motorcycle, and drove on. Pursued by shells, they came to the infantry positions.

"Russian attack with tanks! Get ready! I'll come back with my three tank destroyers!" Ernst shouted to an officer.

The motorcycle rattled away toward the area where the tank destroyers were parked. Once there, Ernst sent Bernlöhr back to the aid station.

"Get ready! Russian night attack with tanks from the forward Russian village. They must be there already. Everyone ready? You too, Störtz?"

Feldwebel Störtz, who had taken over Fressonke's tank destroyer *Adler,* reported ready.

"Then move out! Everyone after me, don't lag behind!" ordered Ernst.

Falke assumed the lead. Artillery shells hammered down, throwing up stones and frozen earth, showering the vehicles with snow. They rolled through a shell hole, the men hanging on tight to the handgrips so as not to be flung against the walls.

A little later the icy slope appeared before them. They took it in second gear and roared on. Before them the terrain in the path of the Russian attack had been torn up by bursting artillery shells. That's where the grenadiers had been. If they had stayed put, there would probably be none of them left alive. Fortunately the major had pulled them back three hundred meters. They cowered in hastily dug foxholes and stared into the thunder of the impacting shells.

"How does it look ahead of us to the left and right, Herr Major?" Ernst asked the battalion commander, who had just made his way to the tank destroyer.

"No idea, telephone communications are dead. But we have to drive the Russians out of the village, or else they'll assemble there and finish us for good."

"Are there tanks in the village, too?" asked the *Leutnant.*

"Four for certain, possibly more, Ernst!" replied the battalion commander.

"That's a real dangerous hornet's nest," observed Ernst. "We must do something about it at once."

"If you and your three *Hornissen* join in, we can launch an immediate counterattack, Ernst."

"All right then! We can form three spearheads so that the enemy will have three targets and be forced to divide his fire."

The two officers discussed the most important details of the operation. Then Ernst gave the order.

"Wedge formation! Two hundred meters lateral spacing. Störtz right, Hollmann left; I'll drive in the center. Not too fast, so the grenadiers can keep up."

The three spearheads, each with a *Hornisse* and about a company of infantry, moved forward. They moved toward the village from which tank noises were coming, betraying the enemy's position.

"Look out, there comes one!"

Kötter abruptly brought *Falke* to a halt. The grenadiers took cover. A tank emerged from the dark wall of shadows. It rolled at right angles to the spearhead, showing *Falke* its broadside. At that moment the Russian tank commander apparently spotted the enemy, because the tank turned and its gun began to swing around.

"Open fire!"

Colany had already taken aim at the enemy tank, and a split second after the order was given the shell was on its way to the target. The armor-piercing round struck the T-34 below the turret, pierced its side armor, and flew out the other side. The shell had sliced through both sides of the T-34.

The Russian tank halted and its crew jumped clear, pursued by automatic weapons fire.

"Into the village all at once!" ordered Ernst.

"In with sack and flute!" roared Störtz, who had not yet become used to the strict radio discipline practiced in the Ernst platoon.

Ernst wanted to reprimand him straight away, but hesitated because he knew the deleterious effects of such a dressing down on the battlefield. Later he would bring the matter up between the two of them. The vehicles rolled faster and faster. In the final stretch the three tank destroyers left the grenadiers behind. Then they were at the entrance to the village. Russian soldiers scattered as the tank destroyers opened fire with HE rounds.

Cautiously they worked their way forward. The *Leutnant* assigned targets as groups of enemy soldiers appeared. The crew displayed excellent teamwork, everyone working swiftly and without error.

"Where are the tanks, *Herr Leutnant?*" asked Störtz.

"None to be seen. But watch out!" Ernst called back.

They pulled around a corner and were met by a hail of machine gun fire. Bullets spattered against the steel of the frontal armor, bouncing off and whistling away into the night.

"Attention! Chief to everyone: fire on the machine gun nest!"

There was a triple blast as the three "eighty-eights" fired. The barricade, which would have cost the blood of many grenadiers, had been eliminated.

The motors raced again. A group of Russians burst from a garden and ran toward Ernst's vehicle. Instinctively he grabbed for his submachine gun. The Russians were upon them. One raised his arm to throw a Molotov cocktail (a gasoline-filled bottle with burning wick). The *Leutnant* pulled the trigger. The burst struck the Russian and knocked him to the ground. The spilled gasoline flared up and enveloped the dead man in a wall of flame.

Gefreiter Bretschneider, the radio operator, operated the machine gun, firing from his seat. The first burst sprayed the onrushing enemy. Only a few escaped with their lives. The attack on the *Hornisse* was beaten off practically at the last second.

Bussard rumbled in from the right. *Feldwebel* Hollmann fired on a group of Soviet soldiers running across the road with a mortar. Then he drove on, ramming the wall of a house as he turned, bringing it down on the tank destroyer with a crash.

The grenadiers had meanwhile caught up to the tank destroyers and were involved in a street battle with Soviet infantry. Their rifles and submachine guns cracked. Hand grenades exploded. The soldiers leapt from one position to another. Cries filled the night—death cries. *Leutnant* Ernst heard them, too. Shuddering, he looked into the shadowy darkness. All of a sudden he saw an antitank gun directly in front of him. It was being pulled down a side street toward the village square by a group of soldiers.

"Kötter, back up!"

The driver engaged reverse gear and the *Hornisse* rattled

back to the side street. Then it turned on the spot and opened fire just as the Russians had set up their antitank gun.

The shell smashed against the gun's steel shield, spraying countless numbers of steel fragments. The gun crew never had a chance to fire.

"Herr Leutnant, a report from the major: a group of Russians with four machine guns is holding a position ahead!"

The soldier who had brought the report was gasping for breath after his run.

"Jump on behind, show me the way!"

The man jumped onto the *Hornisse* and they drove off. As they reached the position they saw flashes from the Russian guns. Colany aimed carefully.

The first shot silenced two of the four machine guns. A slight correction and a loud report, followed almost at once by the sound of the impact. All four machine guns were destroyed.

Groups of grenadiers ran past the *Hornisse* and stormed toward the house and the wall, throwing hand grenades and firing on the run.

Feldwebel Hollmann radioed a warning to Ernst: "Attention, enemy artillery!"

Seconds later Ernst and his crew felt its presence. Shells from the Russian guns smashed into the village. The Soviets were determined to hold onto the village as a springboard for a new offensive.

The Russians held, fighting to the last breath and dying by shell or bullet. Nevertheless, the survivors kept advancing for fresh attacks.

"Only five high-explosive rounds left, *Herr Leutnant!*" reported loader Rudolf Sötte.

"We'll fire those and drive the last Russians out and then . . ."

The *Leutnant* stopped. He heard a wild howling and in the seconds before the impact knew that this shell was meant for them.

"Take cover!" he shouted to the others.

In that instant the shell hammered into the frozen earth in front of the tank destroyer. A tremendous blast of air struck the *Hornisse,* swung it around, and threw the crew to the floor.

Leutnant Ernst held on for dear life. Then he felt a painful blow on his left shoulder. This is it, he thought.

He heard a cry, which came from Sötte's lips. When he looked to the side he saw that the left sleeve of the gunner's camouflage uniform was bloodstained.

"What is it, Sötte?"

"Shrapnel, *Herr Leutnant!*" moaned the *Obergefreiter.*

In spite of the unsteady light from the many muzzle flashes and fires, Ernst could see that the face of the twenty-two-year-old was pale. His sallow skin showed through the dust and powder residue.

"We can't go any farther, the *Falke* has had it, *Herr Leutnant!*" cried a member of the crew.

"Get out!" croaked Ernst.

He jumped over to Sötte. Together with Colany he picked up the wounded man. The two men lifted him out of the vehicle.

Unteroffizier Kötter left the driver's position. He had scarcely jumped over the side when a Maxim machine gun opened up. The burst caught him and drove him back a few steps. Slowly he fell to the ground.

Meanwhile, *Leutnant* Ernst and Colany had reached the ditch with the wounded loader.

Gefreiter Bretschneider, who had run over to Kötter, shouted something to them through the din of battle, but they couldn't understand.

A pair of Russians came running toward the lone *Gefreiter.* He squeezed the trigger of the machine gun and expended the entire clip of ammunition. He had been seized by a wild desperation over the death of his friend.

"Don't go away," moaned Sötte as the *Leutnant* began to stand up.

"I'm staying, Sötte," replied Ernst.

"I'm very sorry, *Herr Leutnant!*" gasped the wounded man. "I'll probably have to leave."

"Don't worry, Sötte. You'll come back when your wound has healed."

They placed an emergency dressing on their comrade's wound. Bretschneider came running over to them.

"Herr Leutnant, Kötter is dead!"

Ernst nodded. He couldn't find any words. Someone shouted

to him, "The enemy is pressing, *Herr Leutnant.* The grenadiers are pulling back!"

"The equipment must be recovered!" remembered Colany.

"Cover me! I'll get it," said Ernst.

He bounded across the road, reached the vehicle, and jumped inside. Ernst tore out the important instruments. When he stood up he realized how critical the situation had become. A Russian assault group had worked its way close to the stranded men. But then *Adler* came roaring toward them at high speed. *Feldwebel* Störtz jumped down.

"Herr Leutnant, three men down with shrapnel wounds!" he shouted over the noise of battle.

"Very well, we can use you. We'll form a new crew. From now on you will be gunner, Colany will load!"

They jumped onto the tank destroyer after putting their dead comrades and *Falke*'s wounded gunner aboard. A little later they rolled in the direction of the enemy. *Adler* shot up several nests of resistance.

Then they were down to their last shell. It was used to silence a machine gun nest. *Adler* turned and rolled back toward the German lines, where a new defensive front had been established. By smashing the Soviet assembly area in the village, the tank destroyers and grenadiers had given their comrades of the infantry time to regroup.

The tank destroyer drove to the dressing station. After leaving Sötte in good hands, the crew was left the sad job of taking the two dead men—one from *Bussard* and *Unteroffizier* Kötter from *Falke*—to the cemetery.

After refueling and rearming, they drove their *Hornisse* back to their billeting area. Everyone was depressed and exhausted.

Three hours had passed since their return. *Leutnant* Ernst sat on an ammunition crate, deep in thought. His thoughts were on the *Falke*. The vehicle lay about five hundred meters beyond the German lines in enemy territory. It was always possible that another tank destroyer or ammunition for the "eighty-eight" might have fallen into Russian hands, which would allow the Russians to use the *Falke* against its former owners.

"It has to go!" said the *Leutnant* softly.

"What has to go?" asked Willi Boghut.

"The *Falke!*" replied Ernst.

"And how do you plan to do that? It's in enemy territory. Perhaps the Ivans are already inside."

"I don't think so. Willi!"

Major Hoppe came in. He didn't ask for a report because he already knew what had happened. Wordlessly he sat down next to Albert Ernst. His broad face showed respect and concern.

The major lit a cigarette, then said, "We must destroy the wagon before the enemy can recover it and use it against us, Ernst."

Ernst nodded.

"I think, Herr Major, that we can do it with a small assault team. I will lead the team."

"Good, Ernst. Do it! But take only volunteers."

When Ernst asked for volunteers, everyone wanted to go.

Ernst concluded his address. "The major has meanwhile called the grenadier battalion commander. He is providing a detachment to cover us."

"And what will we use to blow it up, *Herr Leutnant?*"

"We have four Teller mines and three concentrated charges. I think that two Teller mines and two charges should be enough."

The men who were to make up the assault team got ready. They still had a few hours to kill. Suddenly a fir tree appeared as if by magic. It had been decorated, and Herbert Colany sucked on his tongue harder than ever as he lit a pair of small candles.

"Christmas Eve, men," he said.

"We'll celebrate when we come back, Colany," replied the *Leutnant.*

Soon it was time. Wordlessly they shook hands with those who were staying behind.

"Good luck!" said Bretschneider, and softly, so that scarcely anyone could hear, he added, "And God be with you!"

He could say that without remorse because the others were not on their way to kill men. They only wanted to destroy the vehicle stranded in enemy territory.

The night was inky black as they set off. The men had pulled on light snow capes captured from the Russians and wore Soviet fur caps in case they were spotted by the enemy.

There were four of them. *Leutnant* Ernst led the way, followed closely by Colany, *Feldwebel* Hollmann, and *Feldwebel* Boghut. The latter was an officer cadet and wasn't about to see his close friend Hollmann go on such a dangerous mission without him.

Each man carried an explosive charge and a submachine gun. Boghut had a Russian submachine gun with a seventy-two-round magazine.

Initially they made good progress. Soon the four met up with the grenadiers led by *Oberleutnant* Peltz.

"I'm leading the escort group, Ernst," said the *Oberleutnant*. "This is a risky game, you know."

"We're after the *Falke, Herr Oberleutnant*," replied Ernst. "Good luck then. And be careful! We will secure to the left and hold off any pursuers, clear?"

"Clear, and thanks in advance."

The team moved on. Soon they had left the escort group behind. Moving slowly, bent low, they continued on their way, making not a sound. The three men kept their eyes on the back of the *Leutnant* at the front.

Minutes passed. Each one seemed an eternity. The men perspired heavily from the unaccustomed struggling through the snow; their backs ached from their crouched posture and the Teller mines pressed on them. But if the *Leutnant* could carry one and say nothing, then Hollmann, who was carrying the second, was determined to do the same.

Occasionally the four paused to shift their loads. They took cover whenever a flare rose into the sky and threw its harsh light over the torn, snow-covered landscape, cowering in shell holes and trenches. Then the first Red Army soldiers appeared. From now on they would have to proceed with extra caution.

By now the Teller mines seemed to weigh a hundred kilograms, but they needed them and couldn't leave any behind.

The first houses of the village came into sight, their outlines clearly visible. Suddenly *Leutnant* Ernst heard voices. They were Russians, talking among themselves. The sentries!

The farther they went, the more sentries there were. There were now Soviet soldiers all around them.

They stopped behind a thick hedge, breathing heavily. Their limbs shook from the strain and exertion. But they were not yet at their objective. They still had some distance to go.

"We'll have to be faster," groaned the *Leutnant*. They got up and ran along the hedge. After a few dozen meters the men were soaked in sweat.

The sound of their footsteps crunching in the snow was drowned out by the noise of the cannonade. The artillery of both sides was engaged in a duel. Now and then the sixteen fire-trailing rockets of a *katyusha* salvo roared overhead toward the German lines and impacted with a tremendous crash.

"There it is!" said Colany, as they recognized the vehicle at the side of the road.

"No Russians to be seen," answered Boghut.

Ernst could see plainly the name *Falke* on the side of the tank destroyer. He read it several times, as if taking his leave of the steel giant in which he had come through so many battles.

The small party ran past the snow-covered bushes to the right of the road. *Feldwebel* Hollmann climbed into the tank destroyer's fighting compartment. The others passed him the explosive charges. Boghut tore open the motor compartment access panel and Colany opened the driver's hatch. The charges were put in place and the fuses set, while the others covered their comrades with submachine guns at the ready. Soon the job was done. *Leutnant* Ernst checked the charges once more.

"Well done!" he said on rejoining the others. "Now let's get out of here or the pieces will be flying around our ears!"

They crawled to the rear as quickly as possible and made it back to the bushes. Then they stood up and ran toward a house. In its shadow they hurried on a ways farther, took a quick look around, and then reached the exit from the village. There they were again: Russian voices, laughter, and an occasional command.

"Take cover! As soon as it goes up the way will be open," whispered Ernst.

They pressed themselves into the snow, huddled together in a large shell hole and waited. A glance at the illuminated dial of his watch showed Ernst that it was almost time.

The last few seconds of waiting for the explosion that would signal the success of their mission seemed endless, but then a bright tongue of flame shot up from the location of the tank destroyer *Falke*. At the same time a thunderous fourfold explosion shook the night. All hell broke loose in the village.

There were cries, orders, shouts, the clatter of footsteps, and then the sound of tank engines being fired up.

"There they are!" whispered Boghut, pointing toward the Russian sentries who were now running in a group in the direction of the explosion.

Other Russian soldiers appeared, also running toward the scene of the explosion. Suddenly the Russian artillery fire intensified, and was matched by return fire from German batteries.

Not far away, perhaps two hundred meters to the right, a Maxim machine gun began to rattle. In the shell hole all eyes were on the *Leutnant.* He stood up.

"Let's go, follow me quickly!"

The others got up, ran from the shell hole, fell, and got up again. They raced toward their own lines, their lungs burning. A burst of machine gun fire was directed their way and they flung themselves to the ground, their snow capes merging into the snow. During brief pauses in the firing they crawled forward, often centimeters at a time, until it was again possible to jump up and run.

Ernst felt the burning in his chest caused by the cold air he was sucking deeply into his lungs. There was a roaring noise in his ears. He heard the bursts of machine gun fire chasing him and dove for cover. Then he was up again and running.

Completely out of breath, they reached the covering group, whose machine guns had pinned down the pursuers. A few rifle shots still whistled in their direction. Then they were in a German communications trench. Their mission had been successful.

The *Falke* existed no more. It had been blown to pieces by the four explosions.

Fourteen Tanks Destroyed with Twenty-one Shells

That Christmas Eve, Albert Ernst was unable to sleep. On returning from their mission he and his men had lit the candles on the Christmas tree Colany had decorated earlier that day. The Christmas celebration was to take place that evening. The school had been decorated for the entire battalion.

Ernst turned to his new driver. "Heinrichs, go warm up *Büffel.* I have a feeling that something's up."

"Before the Christmas celebration, *Herr Leutnant?*" interjected Bernlöhr.

"I don't think the Russians will give that any consideration."

Leutnant Ernst hastily smoked a cigarette. As he tossed the butt into the stove and immediately lit another cigarette, Colany nudged his new loader, Gustav Götte, in the side.

"The old man is nervous! He smells something again."

They all knew this. When the *Leutnant* smoked like this the air was thick, and not just with cigarette smoke. Albert Ernst only smoked when he became restless or when going into action. During battle he had no time to smoke and afterward it was no longer necessary.

Obergefreiter Heinrichs pulled on his lined jacket. Together with Bretschneider he left the simple hut, through whose broken window panes the dull sounds of battle were clearly audible.

Ernst had been a soldier for twelve years. In November 1930, when just eighteen, he had enlisted with the 2nd Company of *Kraftfahrerregiment* 4 in Magdeburg. The young man from Wolfsburg, an enthusiastic and successful athlete, was prominent in many competitions. He was one of the few applicants to be accepted into Germany's 100,000-man army.

Ernst was first sent to the training regiment in Halberstadt. It was the 12th Infantry Regiment. Later he joined the 2nd Prussian Rifle Company in Magdeburg.

It was there that he underwent various types of training. Soon he was familiar with the motorcycle, the armored car, and finally the tank. At that time the tanks were simulated, made of cardboard. Ernst passed through NCO school, sports school, and various courses. Albert Ernst wanted to get ahead in the *Reichswehr,* and that was damned difficult.

Finally he came to the 24th Infantry Division's 24th Panzer Battalion in Borna, near Leipzig. In the meantime he had passed through the army technical school and later the school for administration and economics. During special examinations in Leipzig, in which he led the class, his maturity was commended. He received free study time and was allowed to work toward a position as an army instructor, a career that demanded a great deal of preparation.

The outbreak of war interrupted the young man's ambitious plans. He became a reserve officer candidate.

In Poland, Ernst destroyed his first tank with a 3.7cm anti-tank gun. He distinguished himself in a battle near Kutno and received the Iron Cross, Second Class from *Generalleutnant* Friedrich Olbricht.

On 27 October 1939, General Olbricht became one of the first German soldiers to receive the Knight's Cross. Olbricht was, *Oberfeldwebel* Ernst felt, a man of high quality. He was a soldier who placed fairness above everything else, a man who loved his country and who dared to revolt against the despots. As a result *General der Infanterie* Olbricht ended his life on the gallows on 20 July 1944.

Albert Ernst shook himself from his reminiscing. He went to the window and looked outside. It had become dark. The tank destroyer stood before the door like a wide, mighty shadow.

The tank destroyer's crew was ready. Ernst grinned involuntarily. The men knew him well and they were aware that he was waiting for something. Earlier he had waited for a posting after recovering from minor wounds. He was transferred from the replacement battalion to the 294th Infantry Division.

It was with this unit that Ernst experienced the French campaign. Later he went to Bulgaria. Rumors suggested a campaign against Yugoslavia and Greece.

From Bulgaria the tank-hunters drove into Yugoslavia as an advance detachment. Once again, as in France, they drove far ahead of the division. All of a sudden they found themselves in the midst of a Yugoslavian position. The Ernst platoon was suddenly alone.

Oberfeldwebel Ernst requested the Yugoslavian colonel there to surrender. He explained to him that if he didn't surrender the Stukas would come in half an hour and bomb everything flat.

The Yugoslavians laid down their weapons. Four hundred

men surrendered to the Ernst platoon. Albert Ernst received a high Bulgarian decoration for this coup.

Following the Yugoslavian campaign the 294th Infantry Division was transferred back to central Germany. It had already been earmarked for the offensive against Russia, where it was to follow behind the panzers as Army Group Center's OKW reserve.

The 294th Infantry Division drove in the direction of Kiev. The tank-hunters suffered heavy losses near Kharkov while serving as an advance detachment. With his antitank platoon, which was still equipped with peacetime vehicles—Krupp six-wheeled trucks—but with the new 5cm antitank guns, *Oberfeldwebel* Ernst took part in both battles for Kharkov.

Afterward the tank-hunters were sent to the 3rd Panzer Division, which had suffered heavy losses in the winter battle. Ernst was sent to the 3rd Motorcycle Battalion, which was under the command of Maj. Günther Pape.

At the beginning of February 1942, Major Pape established a ski platoon. Bitter fighting developed in the Werchne-Olchowatoje area. A *Waffen-SS* infantry battalion and several tanks were placed under Ernst's command.

Ernst was with the leading group during the capture of Solojewka. His tank-hunters destroyed several enemy machine guns, overran a Russian mortar position, reached the positions of the 32nd Soviet Cavalry Division, and destroyed it.

The Russian division commander was taken prisoner. With the last of their fuel, Ernst and his tank-hunters and several tanks drove after the fleeing Russians and reached Nikolskoye.

Subsequently Ernst and his men assembled in Solojewka and Rudino. Novo-Danilovka was taken in the first rush. A half hour later Ernst and his tank-hunters entered Moskwinka, and at eleven o'clock, after a five-hour drive and four hours of fighting, Stakanovo was taken. They had carried out the first successful attack in the east following the winter retreat.

On 10 February 1942, Major Pape received the Knight's Cross for successfully commanding the battle group. Later, on 15 September 1943, as an *Oberst* and commander of the 394th Panzer Grenadier Regiment, Pape became the 301st German soldier to receive the Oak Leaves to the Knight's Cross.

Albert Ernst was decorated with the Iron Cross, First Class. *Hauptmann* Kirsch, commander of the antitank company, recommended him for preferential promotion to officer for bravery in the face of the enemy. Ernst knew nothing of this, however, because a few days later he was seriously wounded during another attack and sent to a hospital in Germany.

"Herr Leutnant, Herr Leutnant! Report from battalion command post. Tank alert! Soviet armored brigade on the move toward the village of Xanino."

Ernst was at once brought back to reality. He clapped on his steel helmet and reached for his submachine gun. His binoculars already hung from his neck.

"Ready?" he asked.

"Ready!" replied the two tank destroyer commanders.

"You stay behind in reserve, Hollmann," said Ernst. "I'll attack with two tank destroyers."

"Thank you, *Herr Leutnant,*" said Störtz.

"What for, Störtz?"

"For not holding my breaking radio silence against me."

"It's forgotten, Störtz; and now let's go. Position yourself behind me. Stay close, don't lose contact!"

One after another they left the hut. Outside they were struck by the wind; the cold bit through their winter things. The men climbed aboard their tank destroyers. *Obergefreiter* Heinrichs looked around.

"Let's go, Heinrichs!" ordered the *Leutnant,* flicking his half-smoked cigarette over the side.

With a dull roar the engine accelerated from idle as first gear was engaged. The new tank destroyer *Büffel* began to move. Shifting gears quickly, Heinrichs brought it up to speed. Following close behind was *Adler.* The two tank destroyers rolled along a track toward the area of operations.

"Toward that hill ahead, Heinrichs!—Listen, Störtz, toward the hill! From there we'll have a good field of fire against the attacking enemy tanks."

"Clear, *Herr Leutnant!*" answered the *Feldwebel.*

"If we get there in time we can take the attackers from the flank."

The two tank destroyers increased speed. Their tracks rattled and threw up dense swaths of snow behind them. The two drove ever faster. They passed the positions of the infantry on the left flank. The grenadiers had dug in and were awaiting the onrushing armada of enemy tanks.

"Still faster, Heinrichs!" shouted Ernst, because he knew that they must reach their objective in time. Only thus could they protect their comrades here on the crest and in the last German-occupied village in front of the hill.

"Damn, we're in a swamp, *Herr Leutnant!*" called Heinrichs.

"Haaalt!"

Ernst unfolded his map. Somewhere there must be a way around the swamp and up the hill. Somewhere! But where? For a second he considered simply driving straight on. But if they became stuck in the swamp they would be sitting ducks and certainly be destroyed if the Russian tanks reached the hill in front of them.

Seconds passed. Ernst considered the situation carefully. He must do something. Suddenly he had it. His voice betrayed none of the uncertainty that he still felt.

"Move out! Straight toward the hill with the four pines.— Accompanying destroyer follow at a distance of five hundred meters. If we bog down, turn at once and look for another way around."

The two tank destroyers began to move again. Just then a *Hauptmann* with the Knight's Cross at his throat jumped in front of them, waving his arms wildly. They stopped. The officer stood where he was and took a couple of deep breaths.

"A Russian tank at the edge of the village. T-34 type. You have to destroy it before it drives into the village!"

"Where is he, *Herr Hauptmann?*" asked Ernst.

"If you drive to that cottage there, you'll be able to see him. Range approximately two thousand meters."

They rumbled forward about ten meters and stopped close by the hut. Ernst saw the black outline of the T-34.

"Twelve o'clock!—Range two thousand!"

"Have him, *Herr Leutnant!*" called Colany, adjusting his aim slightly.

"Fire!"

The tank destroyer rocked from the recoil of the "eighty-eight." The flat flight path of the shell could be seen clearly. Then a bright yellow rosette of flame flared up in the position of the T-34. The crash of the hit rang across to them. They drove on.

"Thanks!" roared the voice of the *Hauptmann* through the hectic rattle of beginning machine gun fire.

"Driver, go! And gas, gas!"

Albert Ernst knew what a burning tank looked like, and his crew knew as well. For them there was no time to watch their victim, because they still faced the problem of overcoming the swamp and reaching the hill. Perhaps if the swamp had frozen enough they could drive across. But only perhaps!

The two tank destroyers rolled at top speed toward the hill with the four pines. The *Adler* veered off a bit and waited until the specified interval had been achieved behind *Büffel*. Then it drove on slowly.

Feldwebel Störtz watched the platoon leader's machine. Had he already bogged down? No, he drove on.

Damn, he thought, the old man had done it again. He had gone ahead, running the risk of being stuck in the middle of the swamp and becoming an easy target. He hadn't ordered someone else to do it. Hats off to him! Störtz ceased his reflections.

Some grenadiers appeared and followed *Büffel* through the swamp toward the hill. Their orders were to deal with the escorting Russian infantry, and they had an interest in doing so, because these two tank destroyers were going to keep the Russian T-34s at bay.

They were now at the swamp proper. Heinrichs involuntarily halted the tank destroyer when he felt it sink deeper.

"Check the way ahead, *Herr Leutnant?*" he asked.

Albert Ernst thought for a second, but already he could hear the dull roar of tank engines and the whirring of caterpillar tracks on the frozen ground beyond the hill. Time was precious. Time meant life or death for the grenadiers, and that decided the issue.

"Onward, Heinrichs! Move! Straight through toward the hill. And not too slowly or we'll sink.—Move out!"

The tank destroyer moved off. The men stood at their battle stations and listened to the sound of the roaring engine. The tracks bit into the swampy ground. They sank somewhat deeper, ten, twenty centimeters, but the sagging upper surface held, having been frozen hard by the cold.

The swamp bore their weight. The tracks slid over its surface. Hopefully they would continue to do so.

Suddenly the rear end of the tank destroyer sagged alarmingly.

As one voice they all shouted, "Gas! Gas!"

There was a hard jolt and the tracks clattered. The tank destroyer was again on a firm subsurface, which rose gradually.

They had passed the marshy area and now rolled up the hill. The motor continued to sing, and everyone aboard could have sang along with it from relief.

"Hull-down position, Heinrichs!"

The *Leutnant* needed to say no more. They all knew what it meant. They were to drive forward until only the superstructure and gun extended over the crest of the hill. In such a position they offered a poor target and would be difficult to spot if they changed positions after firing.

Finally they were in position. It was very cold. Nevertheless, *Leutnant* Ernst had to wipe the sweat from his brow.

He turned and watched the progress of the accompanying *Adler*.

The mighty tank destroyer seemed to roll across the swamp without difficulty. It, too, drove at high speed so as not to sink into the marshy ground.

Adler made it across and drove up the slope. The *Leutnant* jumped down and directed the tank destroyer into position about two hundred meters to the left.

"When we make a change of position, you fire, and then I will fire when you move to the left, Störtz!"

"Understood, *Herr Leutnant!*"

Afterward the two tank destroyers crawled forward. Slowly the long barrels of the 8.8cm guns emerged over the highest point of the hill. They were now on the highest row of an amphitheater. Below them they saw the dark but easily recognizable Soviet tanks as they neared the German positions.

"There, ahead! Range twelve hundred meters, *Herr Leutnant!*" shouted Heinrichs.

Albert Ernst, who had been scanning far into the forefield,

lowered his glasses somewhat. He, too, saw two T-34s which, as the spearhead of the Soviet tank brigade, were about to attack the German positions from the flank.

"Do you have him, Colany?"

"In my sights."

"Open fire!"

Colany fired. Seconds later there was the sound of the impact.

The first T-34 was on fire. Heinrichs turned the tank destroyer thirty or forty degrees. Colany took aim. Gustav Götte, the new loader, had fed a fresh round into the breech and closed it.

Fire!

Recoil. The tank destroyer vibrated, as did the nerves of the crew. They had done it! The second shot had also been a direct hit; the T-34 was in flames. Nevertheless, it turned and swung its gun toward its attacker. But before Colany could fire again, the colossus blew apart with a mighty explosion.

That had been the start of the engagement. The second vehicle was also in position to fire, and both tank destroyers now began to fire on the enemy tanks as they emerged from the night.

The experienced crews maintained a steady rate of fire, aiming at the enemy's flanks. A hit there by an 8.8cm shell spelled the end for any enemy tank.

The tank destroyers increased their rate of fire. The Russian tanks answered, but all of their shells passed over the German vehicles and fell behind them. This was the night of "peace on earth."

The open field over which the enemy tanks were driving was dotted with blazing hulks. Eight Russian tanks were burning, and the others—still far outnumbering their opponents—concentrated their fire on the second tank destroyer. Below *Büffel,* shells smacked into the frozen ground of the hillside. Earth and stones showered the men inside.

Götte jammed his thumb. He continued to work even though he was in great pain. He had to continue to load fresh rounds, as the *Leutnant* was assigning new targets quickly and precisely. These instructions had to be followed quickly, because seconds meant the difference between life and death.

All of a sudden there was an explosion to the left, in the position of the second tank destroyer. Ernst turned his head and saw flames and figures trying to extinguish the fire.

"Have been hit. Everyone wounded!" came the quivering voice of *Feldwebel* Störtz.

"Pull back, Störtz! Take care of the wounded."

Adler pulled back. Ernst watched until the two exhaust flames had disappeared behind the flank of the hill.

"They're trying to approach from our blind side, *Herr Leutnant,*" called Colany.

Ernst stood up and peered over the hill. No doubt! The enemy was trying to slip past and attack from the flank. There was only one answer: after them!

"Up the hill at top speed and then turn to the right, so we can get them in our sights. Stand ready to fire, Colany!"

The men tensed. They knew what it meant to drive into the open on top of the hill, a target for twelve enemy tanks!

Heinrichs pushed the gearshift lever forward. The engine roared and the tank destroyer began to move. It reached the crest of the hill, moving faster and faster. Firing began from all sides. Shells struck the frozen earth, bounced up like great fleas, and howled skyward.

The T-34s in the valley had worked their way into favorable firing range. It was fortunate for the tank destroyer's crew that the enemy's vision was hampered by the glare from the blazing tanks. All of the shells aimed at them missed.

Suddenly they saw an enemy tank driving up the hillside.

"Firing halt!" roared the *Leutnant*. It took three seconds for Colany to press the firing button.

"A hit. He's burning!" shouted Bretschneider.

They continued to fire. The four Russian tanks in the valley were destroyed. *Büffel* once again turned its attention to the approaching wave of enemy tanks. The crew continued to fire and more shells fell nearby. Ernst's orders came faster. The men worked feverishly. Fractions of a second decided life or death: for the tank destroyer on the hill, and finally for the grenadiers who were fighting desperately against the Russian infantry that was flooding into the valley behind the tanks. The rattle of machine gun fire mixed with the crash of tank cannon and the roaring and whistling of the flames.

The only chance was to demoralize the enemy before he could use his tenfold superiority to break through. Ernst's force of will must decide the outcome. He would have to force the enemy to fight his fight and prevent him from taking advantage of his superior numbers.

Ernst saw that Götte could no longer carry on alone. "Bretschneider, lend a hand!"

Bretschneider slid down and laid the shells that were farther away within Götte's reach.

Ernst counted thirteen knocked-out enemy tanks. Suddenly he also saw a muzzle flash in the dense smoke. An enemy tank, and it was in the ravine that ran across the battlefield.

"Ten meters to the right and turn," he ordered.

Büffel turned and moved into the new position.

"Twelve o'clock, in the ravine, range one thousand!"

"I don't see it, *Herr Leutnant!* I've . . ."

The second muzzle flash showed Colany the position of the last still-intact enemy tank. He took aim. The shell from the Russian tank smacked into the ground about ten meters to the side, shaking the tank destroyer. The crash deafened the crew for several seconds. Then they felt *Büffel* rock backward and knew that Colany had fired.

The five men shouted with relief. But their joy was premature. The T-34 had not been hit. The shell had struck the ground in front of it.

Suddenly the Russian tank rolled forward. Its turret pushed higher out of the crevice. Through his binoculars, Ernst watched as its gun swung around toward them.

"Next shot!"

The gunner had the enemy precisely in his sight. The next round was in the breech. He pressed the firing button.

Misfire!

"Damn!" shouted Ernst. The Russian must fire any time. Then it would be too late for a third shot.

"Main firing mechanism defect, *Herr Leutnant!*" reported Colany.

"Engage emergency firing mechanism!"

A shot from the T-34 flitted toward them. It howled past overhead and crashed into the frozen earth somewhere behind them.

The men worked feverishly. They simply tore out the cable for the main firing mechanism and engaged the emergency mechanism. Colany had already adjusted his aim.

Ernst saw another flash from the T-34's gun. "Watch out!" he shouted.

The shell landed directly in front of *Büffel*. The force of the explosion threw the men from their feet. A tall fountain of ice, muck, and steel showered down on them.

Leutnant Ernst got to his feet and targeted the T-34. He would have to be faster, because the next shot from the T-34 would probably be a direct hit.

Don't panic, he ordered himself. Aim well. A little higher. Then: fire!

The shell covered the thousand meters in seconds. Ernst followed its path through his sight and waited for the impact.

"A hit!" they shouted together, and this time they were right. There was a flash of flame from the enemy tank. The shell had struck the turret ring of the T-34 and raised the turret from its track.

"That was the last, *Herr Leutnant!*" shouted the driver, opening his hatch. Stiff all over, he forced his upper body into the open.

Leutnant Ernst also straightened up and stretched his stiff limbs. It had suddenly become quiet. The only sounds of battle, the crack of tank cannon and the long "eighty-eights" of German tank destroyers, came from far to the southeast. The battle there was also going in favor of the Germans under the command of Major Hoppe. During the fighting there *Feldwebel* Ludwig Neigl destroyed four T-34s.

Leutnant Ernst counted the visible tank wrecks. The total came to fourteen! They had destroyed fourteen enemy tanks in the dramatic and brief thirty-minute battle. When the armor-piercing rounds were counted, it was discovered that they had destroyed the fourteen tanks with only twenty-one shells! There was only one armor-piercing round left in the fighting compartment.

Gefreiter Bretschneider pulled a crumpled pack of cigarettes from his pocket and offered one to *Leutnant* Ernst. Ernst nodded gratefully. The battle was over. He was no longer nervous but still a little excited.

The members of the crew puffed on their cigarettes. Then

they received orders by radio to return to their billets. The enemy had ceased his attack.

"We'll make it to our Christmas celebration after all, *Herr Leutnant,*" observed Colany.

"Of course, old man, what did you think?" asked Ernst. "I knew it all the time."

He said this with conviction, even though he had been anything but certain that they would get out in one piece, especially when the last T-34 had them in its sights.

Outside their billets they heard from Schaarschmitt, the orderly room *Feldwebel,* that Maj. Erich Loewe was missing. He was commander of the 501st Heavy Panzer Battalion, which had been in action with the 14th Infantry Division to their right. Nothing more was ever heard of Major Loewe. On 8 February 1944 he became the 385th German soldier to be awarded the Oak Leaves to the Knight's Cross.

Later the large bridge over the Düna near Beshenkovichi was named the "Major Loewe Bridge" in his honor.

"Get ready for the Christmas celebration!"

The men washed and put on clean uniforms. Then they went through the village to the school.

Leutnant Ernst was the first to enter the large room. The news of his great defensive success had preceded him. He saw two men from his company, who were members of the train, hide a half-meter Knight's Cross.

The *Leutnant* had to grin as he watched them trying to conceal the thing. Did they think he was suffering from the famous "sore throat" (desire for the Knight's Cross)? Or was it meant to be an allusion that today he had once again placed everything on one card? Obviously their consciences were smiting them, because they knew very well that as platoon leader he always drove in the lead and that he immediately and without hesitation took on any assignment that required only one vehicle. Several times already it had been *Falke* that had rescued comrades from dangerous situations. Never had he abandoned a comrade, even when it meant that he had to drive into what appeared to be his own certain undoing.

Now Ernst was surrounded by his men. *Hauptmann* Strehler came toward him with his hand outstretched.

"Congratulations, Ernst. This probably means the Knight's Cross for you!" he said.

"I don't know, *Herr Hauptmann*," answered Ernst.

They chatted and sang old Christmas carols, and soon they felt that the war was a thousand miles away. Nothing brought them closer together and closer to those at home than these hours of reflection and the thoughts of those who were also sitting around Christmas trees thousands of kilometers away—and thinking of them at the front.

A little later the major arrived. He, too, congratulated the *Leutnant* and his platoon on their great success.

"The 1st Company has knocked out thirty enemy tanks within twenty-four hours. With your fourteen you have accounted for the lion's share. I am proud of you and your men, Ernst!"

"How do things look in general, Herr Major? Do we stand a good chance?"

"I think so, Ernst! At this moment the *Feldherrnhalle* Panzer Grenadier Division is moving into the 246th Infantry Division's sector. At five o'clock it will attack northwards east of Krynki in order to recapture the former main line of resistance."

"And the planned withdrawal of the northeast front? That affects us, Herr Major. What is up with it?"

"Hitler's decision arrived early this afternoon. He has approved *Generaloberst* Reinhardt's request. At this moment the 14th Infantry Division, the 3rd and 4th *Luftwaffe* Field Divisions, and the 129th Infantry Divisions are moving back into the Losvida blocking position."

Leutnant Ernst breathed a sigh of relief.

"Then perhaps we will be able to do it, Herr Major! That would make things a great deal easier for the grenadiers and for all of us as well."

"Go ahead and celebrate. Hopefully we won't have to go out again during Christmas, because outside it's snowing quite hard."

An hour later they went back to their billets, mellow and in a relaxed mood. It was snowing so hard they could scarcely see anything.

"The Russians are going to come for sure, *Herr Leutnant!*" offered Bretschneider. Albert Ernst nodded.

"Yes, this is the kind of weather for the Russians! They sneak through the snow and no one notices anything until they're suddenly there. And then it's often already too late!"

"Poor swine!" replied the *Gefreiter,* and they all thought of the grenadiers who had to face the snowstorm while they went back to their warm billets.

The Award of the Knight's Cross

During the final days of 1943 the Russians had concentrated thirty-seven rifle and three cavalry divisions in the Vitebsk area as well as fifteen armored units and four mechanized brigades.

However, despite numerous attempts, they had been unable to gain any further ground.

Since 19 December, the day that the 519th Heavy *Panzerjäger* Battalion entered the fray, the Soviets had lost 355 tanks. The defensive battles at various points along the front grew tremendously in intensity. To the Russians, the light frost coupled with the heavy snowfall seemed just right for a new attack.

The Vitebsk area had become the hot spot of the Eastern Front. *Feldmarschall* Busch, commander of Army Group Center, appealed to the other three armies of his army group to voluntarily send whatever forces they could spare to the threatened 3rd Panzer Army. Only thus could a disaster be averted.

The 4th Army, which was itself engaged in heavy fighting, was the first to answer the call, sending a strong blocking force into the sector held by the IV Army Corps.

During the last three days of 1943 the Soviets tried to force a breakthrough southeast of Vitebsk. They managed to penetrate as far west as the Vitebsk-Orsha road.

This important road was reopened by an immediate German counterattack, in which several *Hornissen* took part. Fifteen enemy tanks were destroyed.

The fighting died down in the 14th Infantry Division's sector, and the crews of the tank destroyers got several days of rest. On one of those days *Generaloberst* Hans-Georg Reinhardt suddenly arrived at the recently formed "fire brigade company," commanded by *Leutnant* Albert Ernst.

Reinhardt shook hands with every *Hornisse* crewman. This commander in chief, who came from the tank arm and had won the Knight's Cross in Poland as a *Generalleutnant* and commander of the 4th Panzer Division, knew what it was like to fight as a member of a tank crew. He knew the responsibility and self-discipline required. He was one of them.

The two had a long talk, and *Leutnant* Ernst openly informed the commander in chief of some things he wanted for his men. The *Generaloberst* promised to obtain the requested games, books, and records.

"I'll be back, Ernst, and I hope to see you in good health again."

The *Generaloberst*, who really had plenty of other concerns on his mind, did in fact return to the front and visit the men of the tank destroyers again.

Nineteen forty-four began with a period of intense cold. This was to be a fateful and decisive year on the Eastern Front. No one suspected the fate that would befall not only 3rd Panzer Army, now at Vitebsk, but the entire Army Group Center only seven months later.

It was later written that by the beginning of 1944 the German soldier had lost his will to fight and that it was the generals alone who were prolonging the war. Such nonsense was soon to be proved false by the sacrificial efforts of the 3rd Panzer Army. In January 1944 every soldier in the east was convinced that the war could still be decided in Germany's favor.

At the beginning of January 1944 the Soviets brought further reinforcements to Vitebsk. They threw everything they had into the battle: five Russian armies with fifty-two rifle divisions, five rifle brigades, three cavalry divisions, and twenty-two armored units. Punishment battalions and entire punishment camps were incorporated into the front.

Heavy snowstorms and cold temperatures marked the first days of fighting in the new year. Attacks alternated with counterattacks. It seemed as if the Soviets were exhausted, because the striking power of their armies was decreasing.

On 5 January 1944, however, the Soviets resumed—quite by surprise—their offensive all along the front. A day later the battle reached an intensity never seen before. Tremendous swarms of close-support aircraft accompanied the Soviet assault while their artillery maintained hours-long barrages in support. The battles in all the sectors around Vitebsk were fought in regiment strength. The Soviets employed massed rocket-launcher batteries. The hundreds of howling rocket projectiles caused the grenadiers to crawl deeper into their foxholes.

Southeast of Vitebsk the Red Army introduced a new army, the Soviet 5th Army.

At the headquarters of IX Army Corps on 7 January 1944 *Generalfeldmarschall* Busch outlined the instructions that had arrived from Führer headquarters. Afterward *Generaloberst* Reinhardt suggested:

The objective of the Soviets, who are attacking Vitebsk with two armies each from the east and northwest, is undoubtedly— for strategic as well as prestige reasons—the cutting off of the city. There are still no indications of any further strategic intentions. On the contrary: the enemy was still concentrating exclusively on Vitebsk.

A new enemy army is approaching from the east. It also appears that a further army is moving into this battle zone from the north.

The clear task of the 3rd Panzer Army is to hold the cornerstone of Vitebsk within the framework of the entire front. This task is not only under pressure from the superior enemy, but also from signs of the ever decreasing fighting strength of our own forces. The fresh Soviet forces that are steadily arriving are facing German troops who have been fighting for months without a rest.

Recently the troops have not even been able to rest at night, because the enemy now attacks mainly by night.

The *Generaloberst* suggested shortening the front. He concluded with the words, "I therefore consider it necessary that the Panzer Army direct its efforts to holding Vitebsk at all costs. In order to do so it must be free to shorten its lines wherever the situation begins to become threatening."

The winter battle of Vitebsk went on. The battle was to see no more quiet periods—and no more pity. On 8 January all of the *Hornissen* were placed on alert. They drove to the front by platoons to help the overtaxed grenadiers.

* * *

"Russian attack repelled. Assembly areas spotted for a night attack on the sector held by the *Feldherrnhalle* Division and the left wing of the 14th Infantry Division. All *Hornissen* are to accompany the grenadiers and help destroy the assembly area."

Major Hoppe had called his platoon leaders to his command post, where he issued his orders briefly, factually, and precisely. A final salute, and then the officers and NCOs drove back to their platoons by motorcycle.

Five minutes later the tank destroyers drove forward, reached the positions of the grenadiers, halted, and were briefed on the situation.

Leutnant Ernst bade farewell to the two vehicles of his platoon, which had been assigned to the two neighboring infantry companies. "Good luck, men!"

"Thanks, *Herr Leutnant!* Good luck to you, too!"

The two tank destroyers disappeared into the dark, cloudy night.

"Don't drive too fast, Ernst," said Major Kleffmann when they were ready to advance. "The grenadiers won't be able to keep up in the fresh-fallen snow."

"Understood, Herr Major!"

The tank destroyers drove off. The grenadiers began to move. They didn't follow too close behind, as they knew that's where the shells would fall.

To his right Ernst saw the tank destroyer *Adler*. He called and *Feldwebel* Störtz answered at once.

Then he tried to reach *Büssard,* which was out of sight. Hollmann also answered at once.

"Call if anyone gets in trouble!" said Ernst.

They drove on, knowing that they could depend on one another and knowing that they would fight until the job was done.

Now and then the heavy vehicle dropped into a snow-covered shell hole and roared out the other side in first gear. The attack force stalked nearer and nearer to the Soviet assembly area.

"There's the village!" said Ernst. They had stopped and the *Oberleutnant* leading the infantry company caught up.

"Only an outline, difficult to see. And it appears to be empty."

Leutnant Ernst shook his head, however.

"They're there and . . . What's that? Sounds like tank tracks and a large column of vehicles."

"There they are, *Herr Leutnant*. On the road in front of the village!"

Ernst scanned the road and made out four dark shadows that he could not yet identify.

"It could be tanks or possibly horse-drawn vehicles!" he said cautiously.

"Call your tank destroyers to move forward and join us."

The grenadier company deployed.

After calling his two tank destroyers and assigning them positions, Ernst said, "I'm going on ahead to scout the target."

"If necessary, Colany, you take over my wagon."

"Understood, *Herr Leutnant!*"

Together with the *Oberleutnant* and the company headquarters personnel, Ernst worked his way up close to the road.

Widely separated, the grenadiers had crossed half the distance to the road and then halted as ordered.

"Damn, they are tanks! Their engines are running."

The *Oberleutnant* spoke excitedly. Ernst nodded. He saw the Russian tank crews smoking cigarettes. Their voices were clearly audible from the distance of only 250 meters.

"What should we do, Ernst?" asked the *Oberleutnant*. "Do we move in?"

"We may not get this chance again. We'll have to be quick: fire before the crews finish their break and get back in their tanks. If they attack first with their T-34s and KV-Is, things will look bad."

"Good. When you open fire, I'll fire two green flares and attack simultaneously."

Leutnant Ernst raced back to his men. He had to be quick, quicker than ever before.

He reached the position and leapt aboard his tank destroyer. Ernst called the other two vehicles, which had meanwhile moved closer.

"We're going to attack the tanks on the road. *Büssard* will take over the right flank, *Adler* the left. Fire from the ends of the column toward the center to block their line of retreat. I'll come from the center."

Both commanders acknowledged the orders. Then the *Leutnant* took aim. He sat behind the sight, scanning the entire column, then positioned the illuminated spoke over the middle tank. It was squarely in his sight.

"Achtung!—Fire!"

There was a crash as the "eighty-eight" fired, and even before the shell impacted, two green signal flares hissed into the night sky.

The shell struck home. Flames spewed from the engine compartment of the stricken Russian tank.

At the same time, perhaps a half second later, the other two tank destroyers opened fire. It was the signal that began an unparalleled inferno.

Through his binoculars Ernst watched Russian tank crewmen running about left and right. Some tried to get into their tanks, but they were soon cut down by machine gun fire from the grenadiers.

The cries of the Russian tankers reached the grenadiers through the noise of battle.

Several crews managed to reach their tanks. Ernst saw several of the Soviet tanks begin to move and turn to face their attackers in order to offer a smaller target and reach firing positions.

Meanwhile the tank destroyers continued to fire. Armor-piercing shot struck steel armor plate and blasted out fountains of snow from the earth that were blown away by the wind.

Fires blazed and thick clouds of smoke rose into the sky over the knocked-out enemy tanks. Five T-34s and a KV-I escaped into the night. Some of the crews who had managed to reach their tanks were incinerated in their steel coffins.

With loud shouts the grenadiers stormed forward and reached the enemy tanks. Several wounded Red Army soldiers surrendered. Tank crewmen came out of their holes with hands raised, completely stunned by this unexpected firestorm.

The new main line of resistance was established along the road. The grenadiers now had a chance for an elastic defense when the next attack came, able to withdraw to their own lines if necessary and meet the attack there.

It began to snow heavily again as the men around Ernst

drove back to their billets in the pale early light of 9 January. They were happy that they could crawl into their huts again after refueling and rearming their vehicles.

The mechanics immediately set to work repairing the reported damage to the tank destroyers so they would be ready for action again when called upon.

On 9 January 1944 the army's order of the day reported the destruction of sixty enemy tanks as well as twenty-seven others damaged and recovered by German forces for their own use.

The report concluded, "Once again the *Hornissen* of the 519th Heavy *Panzerjäger* Battalion played an outstanding part in the success."

On 7 February 1944, *Leutnant* Ernst was called into the battalion command post. When he arrived he saw the staff car of the *Generaloberst,* recognizable by its pennant and driver.

The battalion was drawn up behind the building.

"Ernst, man, where is your helmet?" asked *Hauptmann* Strehler when he saw the young *Leutnant.*

"Why do I need my helmet?" Ernst asked back.

"You're supposed to present yourself before the company and the entire battalion in your best service uniform. What do you think that means, Ernst?"

Suddenly the light came on for the *Leutnant.* His first thought was that he was being transferred. Then Schaarschmitt came running toward him.

"Take my helmet, Albert, it will do!"

Ernst placed the helmet on his head and took his place at the head of his company.

The commander in chief of the army stepped into the open. *Hauptmann* Strehler reported to the battalion commander. Then he turned to the *Generaloberst* and reported to Reinhardt.

"519th Heavy *Panzerjäger* Battalion assembled, *Herr Generaloberst!*"

"Thank you, Hoppe."

The *Generaloberst* shouted a greeting, which was returned by two hundred voices.

Leutnant Albert Ernst stepped forward. *Generaloberst* Reinhardt extended his hand.

"Leutnant Albert Ernst, you have become the most success-

ful tank destroyer of the great winter battle of Vitebsk. For the destruction of twenty-five enemy tanks and several anti-tank guns the Führer has awarded you the Knight's Cross of the Iron Cross. It is my honor to present it to you today in person."

He picked up the medal and its black, white, and red ribbon, which was resting in the open case held by his adjutant. Major Hoppe had stepped behind Ernst and now fastened the medal ribbon.

Then the major, the *Leutnant,* and the *Generaloberst* marched along the row of assembled men.

When they reached his company Ernst stopped, turned, and saluted.

"Kötter!" he said softly. The reference to their fallen comrade was also meant for all those who had died.

For a long time afterward, *Generaloberst* Reinhardt spoke of the "Vitebsk fire brigade" and the "Tiger of Vitebsk." He expressed to all of them—down to the last mechanic—the appreciation of the grenadiers who had been saved many times by the efforts of the tank destroyers. Albert Ernst later said of this moment, "It was my greatest day, I still remember it with pride. But I also know that it was made possible only by the efforts of all the other men of my crew and the crews of the other two vehicles of my platoon."

The Destruction of a Russian Armored Brigade

By the end of the first winter battle of Vitebsk the Russians had lost 40,000 men, and 1,203 tanks lay shattered on the broad battlefield. The efforts of the antitank units were described in a *Wehrmacht* communiqué:

"In addition to the brave and determined fighting grenadiers and panzer grenadiers, the artillery, tanks and antitank units, as well as the assault artillery and the *Luftwaffe* played an especially decisive role."

It was during the two subsequent weeks of quiet that Albert Ernst was awarded the Knight's Cross.

Hoppe had recommended the young *Leutnant* and submitted the necessary documentation. He wished to see the man decorated who had seen more action than any of the others in his unit and who several times had influenced the course of the battle.

The period of warm weather in mid-January had left all roads nothing better than bottomless morasses. The Second Winter Battle of Vitebsk began on 3 February 1944. Powerful Soviet forces attacked once more, especially northwest of Vitebsk between Lake Loswida and Lake Saronovskoye.

A short time later the Soviets also attacked the southeast of the Vitebsk front. The same day that *Leutnant* Ernst received the Knight's Cross, Soviet regiments stormed the Noviki bridgehead. Major Ludwig Schütte, commander of the 131st Division Fusilier Battalion, and his men repelled a total of twenty-one enemy attacks. Schütte was awarded the Knight's Cross for his efforts.

Then it was the turn of the tank destroyers. Attack orders arrived. In this first action, Albert Ernst accounted for two T-34s destroyed during a brief engagement.

That evening Ernst reported to Major Hoppe: "It appears as if the enemy has developed a tremendous respect for us. He no longer employs his tanks en masse as before, rather in ones and twos."

"That will make it more difficult for us to destroy them, Ernst. But the enemy attacks will not have the same striking power as before. The grenadiers will be thankful for that." The next day the tank destroyers were again called forward. A Russian armor assembly area had been spotted opposite the positions of the grenadiers and was to be taken out.

While they were driving forward, the crews heard the hammering of tank cannon as the Russians opened fire on German machine gun positions with high-explosive shells.

"Forward at maximum speed! Heinrichs, step on the gas!"

The tank destroyer *Büffel* picked up speed. The two accompanying vehicles hung back on the left and right in case the enemy appeared from the shattered woods in an effort to attack the tank destroyers from the flank.

Suddenly there was a roar in the sky behind them. *Büffel* stopped. The crew turned to scan the sky.

"Stukas!" shouted Colany. "Stukas are attacking!"

The German ground forces had dubbed the cannon-armed Stukas the "artillery of the air."

The dive-bombers plunged toward the wood containing the

Russian armor assembly area. Everyone followed the progress of the howling Stukas. Bright flames spat from their underwing cannon. Just as it seemed that the machines must clip the treetops, they pulled up and climbed away steeply. A short time later they turned and passed directly over the waiting tank destroyers.

Again the Stukas dove toward the wood, and this time the tank destroyer crews had a better view of the attack. They could see the muzzle flashes from the Stukas' cannon and the smoke trails left by their armor-piercing shells. All of a sudden *Feldwebel* Hollmann shouted a warning: *"Achtung!* Open fire!"

Eight enemy tanks were approaching. All three tank destroyers fired. Hollmann was the first to score a direct hit. Then *Büffel* was successful with its second shot. The Russian tank blew up.

The battle had begun. Like hunting dogs the Stukas had driven the eight Russian tanks out of the woods straight into the guns of the tank destroyers. They fired as if on the practice range. The Soviets returned their fire. A shell struck one of *Adler's* tracks. Störtz, who had also reported the destruction of an enemy tank, now set about changing the track under fire with his crew.

"Hollmann, give covering fire for *Adler!*"

Feldwebel Hollmann knocked out the enemy tank that had disabled *Adler.*

The Russians were taken completely by surprise. Obviously their plan had been foiled.

Ernst's second and third victims were shrouded in bright flames. The last of the eight Russian tanks turned and disappeared into a gully that extended into the forest.

"After him! To the gully next to the bushes!"

At full speed the tank destroyer rumbled through shell holes and over lumps of earth. Once it came perilously close to tipping over on its side. However, it came through, engine roaring, and reached the designated position at the edge of the ravine, which threatened to crumble. The tank destroyer pulled back several meters. Then the T-34 appeared around a slight bend in the ravine; he was in their sights.

"Let him come until we can see his rear!" shouted Ernst.

They waited. From a range of five hundred meters the T-34 showed them its rear.

"Fire!"

There was a crash from the "eighty-eight." The ground under the tank destroyer began to give way. Heinrichs quickly engaged reverse gear and pulled back a few meters.

A column of flame spurted from the engine compartment of the T-34 and within seconds the tank was shrouded in flame. The tank's four-man crew was not able to get out.

This brought Ernst's total of enemy tanks destroyed to thirty-two. His latest victory was the three-hundredth enemy tank destroyed by the battalion.

The battle went on. The Russian efforts diminished, major attacks became less frequent. But they had plenty of tanks left and *Leutnant* Ernst and his tank destroyers were constantly in action.

Tank after tank was added to Ernst's balance. His list of successes grew and grew. Virtually the entire length of the long barrel of his tank destroyer's "eighty-eight" was covered with victory rings.

When the Soviets called off the Second Winter Battle of Vitebsk on 17 February 1944, *Leutnant* Ernst's men breathed a sigh of relief. They had been in constant action from the eighth of February until the seventeenth and had survived many close calls. They were at the end of their endurance.

The strain of the battle was reflected in the faces of the men. Together with the grenadiers they had endured all its worries and hardship. Two major battles lay behind them. Their reward: they could sleep properly again. The long-overdue letters home were written and mailed off.

Their main concern during the period of quiet was to bring their weapons, the *Hornisse* tank destroyers, back up to peak fighting condition, because the enemy might attack at any time, day or night.

Conversation with a Field Marshal

At the end of February 1944 the Russian assault divisions attacked again. This time, however, they attacked not en masse, as before, but at most in regiment strength with six to eight tanks assigned to each assault unit.

The tank destroyer *Büffel* had become a common sight at the front. *Leutnant* Ernst and his men carried out one mission after another. At the end of February, Jolassen returned from the field hospital. He was supposed to go to Germany, but instead slipped away and returned to the front.

After reporting his return to *Leutnant* Ernst, he grinned and said, "You won't send me away, *Herr Leutnant*." This was followed by an outburst of laughter, because Jolassen had made such a painful expression.

"Fine then! You can go back to *Adler* as loader again and carry shells."

In the following weeks the tank destroyers were everywhere. Major Hoppe had established a "fire brigade company" led by Ernst.

The company drove to the Noviki bridgehead and freed the 197th and 299th Infantry Divisions. Then it was ordered to the west bank of the Luchesa to reinforce the Wolosso blocking position.

There was bitter fighting. The sector changed hands six times in one night. The Soviets believed they could break through here to the west. The "fire brigade company" was sent to this sector again on 4 March 1944.

"Be careful! I'll drive ahead. Everyone else wait and see what happens! Step on it. Heinrichs!" Ernst called to the driver of the *Hornisse*.

The men were at their battle stations. At any second Russian tanks could appear from behind the slope where their mortars were firing.

The *Hornisse* rolled up the hill, crushing the bushes beneath its tracks. All at once *Büffel* came to an abrupt stop.

Leutnant Ernst didn't need his binoculars to see the Russian tank assembly area. Engines running, they were poised for the next attack. In the failing light Ernst could see the dense masses of soldiers behind the tanks.

"Everyone after me, up the hill!—Range six hundred—enemy tanks!"

Colany waited for the order to fire. He had already targeted the tank on the right flank and knew that at this range a hit from the "eighty-eight" would be deadly.

Still the enemy took no notice of the approaching danger. The noise of their own engines must have drowned out the noise of the *Hornissen* climbing the slope.

At the last second, as the other seven vehicles of the German battle group approached, the Russians woke up. Albert Ernst watched as the first Russian tank began to move.

"Fire!" came his order.

The crash of gunfire and the impact of the shot merged into one. With a mighty crash the armor-piercing round from the "eighty-eight" smashed through the armor plate of a T-34 and set it ablaze.

Load—fire! Load—fire!

The remaining tank destroyers had meanwhile reached the crest of the hill and joined the battle. Soon three, four, then ten T-34s were rolling toward them. At the bottom of the hill they were in the tank destroyers' blind spot, as they could not depress their guns far enough to engage the Russian tanks.

A *Feldwebel* appeared with an assault squad.

"Herr Leutnant, we'll take care of them!" he shouted, gesturing toward the tanks that had already started up the hill.

Ernst nodded. He saw the satchel charges and Teller mines in the hands of the men.

Ernst's tank destroyers fired until the enemy tanks turned away and disappeared into a belt of forest. Then there was an explosion from about two hundred meters below. Teller mines and satchel charges went off, and the resulting shock waves traveled up the side of the hill, uprooting bushes.

From the top of the hill Ernst and his men could see three disabled tanks below. One had escaped destruction, however, and was now only sixty meters below.

"Go, Heinrichs! Straight down!"

The *Hornisse* began to move. It rolled about fifty meters down the hill and turned. Ernst saw the T-34 at about the same elevation. It was stationary and had just fired its main gun.

The T-34 showed them its right flank. Colany didn't wait for the order to fire. As soon as he had the T-34 in his sight he pressed the firing button.

There was a mighty double crash. Pierced by the shot from the "eighty-eight," the T-34 was finished.

The spearhead of the Soviet attack had been blunted. A gap had been smashed in the steel phalanx. The following infantry attack was rebuffed by the grenadiers without difficulty.

Leutnant Ernst had now destroyed forty-nine tanks. He was at the top of the victory list, but there was no end in sight as the skirmishes and Russian attacks continued unabated.

During one enemy attack the tank destroyers did not arrive in time. On this occasion, however, the *Luftwaffe* was in a position to intervene. Ninety Bf-110s and Ju-87s swept over the front. They destroyed the enemy tanks and strafed the Russian infantry.

The days were filled with heavy snow showers and above zero temperatures. The March nights were still cold, with temperatures sometimes falling to ten below zero. The early-year storms raged and the roads became bottomless once more. With their caterpillar tracks the heavy *Hornissen* dragged themselves through the meter-deep mud.

During the defense of the Luchesa front, nine German battalions were forced to hold off nine enemy rifle divisions, a rifle brigade, and two tank brigades. They were able to hold thanks to the efforts of the *Hornissen,* the Tiger battalions, and the six assault gun brigades assembled on the Vitebsk front.

On 28 March, Ernst led his tank destroyers into an enemy artillery barrage. German signals intelligence had pinpointed 110 Soviet batteries with 404 guns. These were raining down a tremendous barrage on the German positions.

Büffel managed to drive under the artillery fire and reach a Russian observation post, which was destroyed with four high-explosive shells.

Russian infantry attacked the tank destroyer. *Büffel*'s crew fought back with hand grenades and machine guns. The crew breathed a sigh of relief when they saw *Bussard* coming to their rescue.

For five days the Russians tried to force a breakthrough. Then, however, they halted their assault following fifty attacks. The fifty attacks had mostly been carried out in regiment or division strength. A further eighty actions had been conducted by the Russians in battalion and company strength. Four thousand dead and forty-nine knocked-out tanks littered the ground in front of the German main line of resistance.

The battlefield fell silent. On 20 April a report reached the units at the front that *General der Infanterie* Hans Jordan, commanding general of VI Army Corps, had become the 464th member of the German armed forces to receive the Knight's Cross with Oak Leaves.

Generaloberst Reinhardt visited Albert Ernst several times. Soon the troops at the front were saying, "The defense of Vitebsk—that's Reinhardt!"

On 26 May 1944 the *Generaloberst* became the sixty-eighth German soldier to receive the Swords and Oak Leaves. Of this he said, "I am happy and proud to put on this decoration in the knowledge that this Oak Leaves with Swords decorates my entire Third Panzer Army for its victory in the difficult winter battles during the siege of Vitebsk."

The next day *Leutnant* Albert Ernst was invited to the headquarters of Army Group Center. *Generalfeldmarschall* Ernst Busch had invited the most highly decorated and soon-to-be-decorated soldiers of the army group to Minsk.

Leutnant Ernst drove to the airfield. Those who escorted him there knew what was in store for him. *Feldwebel* Schaarschmitt, in particular, had already been speculating on the subject. Their *Leutnant* was about to receive the Oak Leaves.

Feldwebel Hollmann, who had meanwhile been awarded the German Cross in Gold, was taking all bets that their "old man" would return from Minsk with the Oak Leaves in his pocket.

Several of his friends took him up on the bet, and Hollmann—lost, for the following reasons.

They sat at a large table in the dining room of the army group headquarters. The officers chatted amongst themselves. Looking around, Ernst saw many highly decorated officers. Nervously, he came forward and sat down opposite the commander in chief. While they were smoking after supper, the *Feldmarschall* asked him, "How is it that you haven't been promoted yet, Ernst? You've been a company commander for some time."

Leutnant Ernst swallowed before answering, *"Herr Generalfeldmarschall,* we men in the *Hornissen* don't think about promotions. It's our job every day to destroy enemy tanks—

and there's a chance every day that we will be destroyed ourselves."

"That doesn't answer the question. I mean, why aren't you an *Oberleutnant?*"

"I was told, *Herr Generalfeldmarschall,* that I would have to serve several years as a *Leutnant* before I could become an *Oberleutnant.*"

Generalfeldmarschall Busch turned to the army group's Ia.

"Groeben, what do you say? Is what Ernst here says true?"

"*Leutnant* Ernst is correct. He cannot be promoted to *Oberleutnant* just because he wears the Knight's Cross. He must wait a while."

Albert Ernst had already been made an officer for bravery in the face of the enemy. Even then his promotion had been held up for long months, and it looked as if Ernst would be remaining a *Leutnant* for some time.

But then *Feldmarschall* Busch turned to the *Leutnant.*

"What, dear Ernst, would you rather have, the Oak Leaves for the destruction of your fifty-fifth tank or a promotion to *Oberleutnant?*"

Everyone stared at the *Leutnant,* and Ernst suspected what most of them were thinking: the Oak Leaves would bring him much more fame, and human vanity would lead him to select the decoration.

His thoughts, however, were in another direction. He was married with two children. His *Leutnant*'s pay was less than that he had received as an *Oberfeldwebel* with twelve years' experience.

"If the *Herr Generalfeldmarschall* is leaving it up to me, then I would like to take the promotion to *Oberleutnant.*"

For a few seconds one could have heard a pin drop. Many questions were directed his way, which Ernst answered by stating that he needed more money for himself, and above all for his family, rather than a decoration.

As a result, Albert Ernst was promoted to the rank of *Oberleutnant* for bravery in the face of the enemy. For a simple soldier of the *Reichswehr* he had taken a tremendous step forward.

A few weeks later Ernst was called away from the 519th Heavy *Panzerjäger* Battalion. He was finally to attend a commanders course since he had never taken officer training and had been selected to command a new *Panzerjäger* battalion. *Oberleutnant* Ernst was forced to bid his comrades farewell.

"If you get a new command and it's possible for you to bring us, then do it, Albert," said Boghut. The others made the same request.

The *Oberleutnant* was deeply moved, because he had led these men into many difficult and dangerous actions.

In the Mielau Panzertruppenschule, Ernst passed his commanders course with distinction. At the end of the course he found out that he was to serve under Major Noack, who had won the Knight's Cross with the 46th *Panzerjäger* Battalion in France. On 17 January 1942, outside Moscow, Noack had become the sixty-third German soldier to receive the Oak Leaves.

The new battalion was to be equipped with the potent new Jagdpanther tank destroyer.

This command did not materialize, however. Ernst could have learned a great deal from Major Noack, who commanded the 654th Heavy *Panzerjäger* Battalion equipped with Ferdinand tank destroyers during the Battle of Kursk.

Ernst had instead been chosen to take part in the formation of the 1299th *Panzerjäger* Battalion.

He now had the opportunity to bring his former comrades home from Russia. As chief of the newly created battalion, he was allowed to select the personnel he wanted.

So Ernst's comrades came home from Russia. Not all of them were there, however. During the great summer offensive by the Soviets against Army Group Center the battalion had been employed with the 299th Infantry Division and suffered heavy casualties.

Leutnant Boghut, *Oberfeldwebel* Tarlach, and *Leutnant* Rondorf were there, together with Colany and Bretschneider from Ernst's old crew. The rest were dead.

During this period Ernst had several opportunities to visit his family in Leipzig. These were weeks of relaxation and happiness. For the first time he experienced the comfort of civilian life.

That summer was a beautiful one. Finally, however, the time came to take the new tank destroyer battalion (initially consisting of one company) into action. The unit was sent to the Eastern Front into the area southwest of Leningrad, where the Red

Army had launched a new offensive. Once again Albert Ernst
came under the command of the 3rd Panzer Army.

The Soviets had reached the Njemen near Olita. The 4th and
7th Panzer Divisions were to launch an attack from the
Babriskis area ten kilometers north of Orany to destroy these
forces. *Oberleutnant* Ernst and his Jagdpanther tank destroyers
were assigned to participate in the pincer attack. One group was
formed from elements of the 25th Panzer Regiment and the attached 6th Panzer Grenadier Regiment. Its assignment was to
attack on the left flank along the road to Olita.

On the right flank was the Ernst tank destroyer company
with fourteen brand-new vehicles and an attached infantry battalion.

It was early on the morning of 11 July. Albert Ernst, now in
command of a battalion, raised his arm and the tank destroyers
began to move.

"Onward, men! We can't get bogged down in this swamp or
we'll be hammered by the Russians!"

The Jagdpanther tank destroyers rattled onward.

These new antitank weapons, of which only about two hundred were built, were armed with the 8.8cm Pak L/71 gun, one
of the most powerful and accurate guns of its time.

Here near Olita the Jagdpanther was to receive its baptism of
fire.

The voice of platoon leader *Leutnant* Rondorf, who had gone
on ahead, crackled through Ernst's headset: "Enemy antitank
gun, *Herr Oberleutnant!*"

"Everyone after me! Attack!"

The big tank destroyers picked up speed, leaving the infantry
and panzer grenadiers far behind.

Flames spewed from among the bushes. Shells struck the
forward armor of Ernst's tank destroyer and bounced off. Inside
the noise was such that he thought he would be deafened.

Colany opened fire. The selected antitank gun was torn from
its emplacement and whirled through the air.

"Forward!"

Feldwebel Zellmann, Ernst's driver, shifted into sixth gear.
The tank destroyers came upon a Soviet rocket-launcher section, whose four launchers were firing on the German infantry.

The heavy vehicles rolled straight through the position

toward the antitank guns. When they reached the position the Russian gunners leapt up and tried to run away. They didn't have a chance. The noise was terrible as the tank destroyers ran over the antitank guns, crushing them into the ground. A short distance farther they came upon the main Russian defensive positions and saw the road to Olita ahead.

Machine gun fire and the salvoes from a rocket-launcher brigade turned the battlefield into a raging inferno. Caught in the open the panzer grenadiers were mowed down. The wounded cried in pain, and the survivors dug into the soft summer earth with their hands and spades.

"The attack has bogged down, *Herr Oberleutnant!*" reported *Feldwebel* Unterschmitt.

Rondorf's voice once again came over the radio. "Enemy column on the road, *Herr Oberleutnant!*"

"Everyone remain here in a wide semicircle and give covering fire! Destroy every recognized enemy position immediately—Boghut and Rondorf come with me!"

Oberleutnant Ernst intended to employ the tactics that he had so often used successfully as the "Tiger of Vitebsk": break through in a sudden rush, destroy the enemy vehicles, and intimidate the enemy. If the enemy gave way, he would follow through with his entire unit and open the way to the objective for the panzer grenadiers.

Boghut's vehicle came rolling up. From ahead to the right Rondorf drove out of the thicket where he had been hiding. Ernst watched the two Jagdpanthers approach. The sloping front, the long gun with the small cradle, and the sidemounted armor skirts gave the tank destroyer a compact, solid appearance.

"We'll attack spaced fifty meters apart. Everyone select a target on the road. Work your way from the left and right toward the center of the column!"

Engines howling, the tank destroyers rolled forward until they reached a favorable firing position with a good field of view.

"Fire at will!"

Flames spewed from the muzzles of all three guns. Shells smashed into the Russian tank, truck, and armored personnel carrier columns. Vehicles exploded in flames while others were blasted off the road.

Rondorf reported his first successes, then Boghut's voice also came crackling over the radio.

"Have destroyed three, Albert!"

The three vehicles rolled forward, halting only to fire. Shells whistled past overhead. Only the forward surfaces of the tank destroyers were facing the enemy, and these were steeply sloped and heavily armored. It seemed as if nothing could stop them.

"Boghut, stay here. Rondorf and I will go on ahead. Remain in touch with the others!"

Feldwebel Zellmann steered the Jagdpanther toward the enemy at forty kilometers per hour. The bow machine gun, operated by Bretschneider, fired at the Red Army soldiers who came in sight.

"They're starting to run, Albert!" called Rondorf.

The Russians had lost thirty vehicles and several tanks. The surprise thrust by the three fast and powerful tank destroyers had thrown them into confusion. They fled, and the flight became ever more panic-stricken.

The road was littered with burning trucks. Several antitank guns that had rolled down from the road in an attempt to move into firing position were run over.

"Keep firing!" shouted Ernst.

The two 8.8cm guns continued their work of destruction, while the two machine guns rattled without pause. Panic had broken out among the enemy troops.

Suddenly there was a flash from about three hundred meters ahead. Then a shattering blow and the Jagdpanther ground to a stop.

"We can't go any farther, roadwheels shot away, *Herr Oberleutnant!*" reported the driver.

"Be careful, Rondorf, we've been hit!"

"I saw it. Am ready to pick you up. Boghut radioes that he is also standing by."

"Tell him to remain where he is!" ordered Ernst. If another tank approached, the antitank gun, whose location was still unknown, would certainly knock it out as well.

"Achtung, the Russians are attacking!"

The Russian soldiers—who had regained their composure and assembled into attack groups—came running toward Ernst's tank destroyer.

"All round defense! Break out the hand grenades!"

They had brought along two crates of hand grenades, which proved to be a wise move. The Russians approached the Jagdpanther. Hand grenades were thrown from every hatch. Peering through the vision ports, the crew saw Russian soldiers fall. Wounded dragged themselves away from the fighting. But other Russian troops followed up. They threw Molotov cocktails, that fell short, showering their own wounded with blazing gasoline.

Ernst threw grenades from the opened commander's hatch. The bow machine gun fired an entire belt in an effort to halt the main body of Russians, which was approaching from the front. The five men in the tank destroyer heard the screams and the cracking of bursts of machine gun fire and saw the bright flames.

Ernst, who as commander was responsible for defending the turret area, stood up in his hatch. Several Russians had jumped onto the mudguards. Ernst fired his pistol at them and then ducked into cover to load a fresh clip.

It was a battle of life and death. *Leutnant* Rondorf fired high-explosive shells into the main group of attackers trying to overwhelm the disabled tank destroyer.

Oberleutnant Ernst loaded his last clip of ammunition. He stood up in the turret hatch again and fired four times, then ducked down as a burst of machine gun fire hissed overhead.

Ernst stood up again. Then he was looking into the face of a Russian officer not a meter away. Ernst raised his pistol. He was a split second faster than the Russian—but the "zero-eight" misfired. Instead there was a crack as the Russian officer fired his Nagan pistol. Albert Ernst felt a sharp blow on his forehead. The bullet entered his head just below his headset and exited behind.

The *Oberleutnant* must have grabbed the turret hatch cover instinctively, because when he fell back into the vehicle the hatch cover clanged shut. Bretschneider locked it tight.

"They're all around us, we'll have to fight our way back to our comrades, *Herr Leutnant,*" called *Unteroffizier* Feige, the gunner in Rondorf's tank destroyer.

"Open fire, high explosive!" ordered the *Leutnant.* Shells

burst all around the company commander's vehicle. The men inside endured the hell. Only the commander was unaware of what was taking place, because he was unconscious.

Bretschneider put on Ernst's blood-soaked headset.

"Achtung! The chief has been badly wounded. You must get us out or he'll die."

They bandaged the *Oberleutnant,* winding a pair of dressings around his head and pressing on the entry and exit wounds with a thick pad.

"Forward, four more shots, and then move in! Nössgen, ready the shackle and hand it up to me."

"I'll throw it to you, *Herr Leutnant!*" replied driver Herbert Nössgen.

"Good, that's fine!"

The last round was fired and the tank destroyer began to move forward. It pressed on through a group of Russian soldiers that had gone into cover and reached the rear of the company commander's vehicle. Nössgen appeared in the driver's hatch and threw a steel shackle across. His aim was good and the shackle hooked immediately.

Leutnant Rondorf fired his submachine gun at some enemy soldiers who were taking aim at his driver. Then the tank destroyer jerked backward and pulled the disabled Jagdpanther along with it.

Boghut had come forward with the third vehicle, firing almost without pause. Rondorf also fired a shot now and then whenever a pursuing tank came in sight.

The Jagdpanthers withdrew meter by meter. Finally they had left the enemy concentration behind and stopped. They were now under the protection of the remaining tank destroyers; little could go wrong now.

"We must get the chief back as quickly as possible. We'll have to move him!" said one of the men.

The still unconscious *Oberleutnant* was put in another tank destroyer, which drove carefully to the main dressing station. On the way Ernst regained consciousness and realized that they were heading west. In spite of his wound he felt relieved. They were taking him back and soon he would be safe. He heard the rattle of tracks, saw the faces of the others above him, and tried to smile, but he couldn't.

Blood was still seeping through the bandages. His olive

green jacket was crusted with blood. Even his Knight's Cross looked as if it had been dipped in blood.

Ernst lost consciousness again from loss of blood. When he again regained consciousness he noticed that he was being carried by two comrades through a potato field in a tent square.

They reached an infantry command post. Confusion reigned as the officers of the tank destroyer battalion had hurried there as well. They were engaged in an argument with the regimental commander over who should lead the unit. Ernst heard all of this before slipping back into unconsciousness.

Suddenly *Leutnant* Boghut, the giant Upper Silesian, stormed into the command post. He had been following and had also broken through the Soviet antitank barrier. He went over to his friend and leaned over him. Then he stood up and thundered, turning to the officers, "I'm leading our unit from here on! This has cost us enough losses already! No one has anything more to say about it. Not any of you!"

"What's got into you?" asked the *Oberst* with consternation.

Just then Ernst sat up.

"Boghut can do it, no one else!" he murmured, barely audible. Then he slipped back into unconsciousness.

Leutnant Boghut took command of the unit. Ernst was driven to the main dressing station by *Stabsfeldwebel* Wippermann, his senior NCO, and two others. The Soviets were still pressing and it was only a matter of time until they broke through again. An hour later Ernst was lying in a small hut, a medical officer leaning over him.

"Doctor," said Ernst thickly, "just put a bandage on it and everything will be alright."

"A bandage?" replied the doctor. "This is something that requires treatment in Germany!"

These were the last words Ernst heard before sinking into oblivion. He was operated on immediately. When he awoke the next day he was again in a peasant cottage, in which there were about two dozen severely wounded soldiers. He heard moaning and cries of pain and smelled the stench of infected wounds. Suddenly he saw a familiar face before him. It was Wippermann.

"What—are—you—doing—here?" he asked hesitantly.

"I'm keeping an eye on you, *Herr Leutnant,* and I'm going

to stay with you until I see you safely aboard the hospital train for home."

Wippermann did in fact remain with his company commander, because the Russian volunteers who were acting as orderlies *(Hiwis)* were not too particular. If one of the wounded stopped moving and his breathing became shallow, they picked him up—in the belief he was dead—and carted him outside and placed him with the bodies of the dead.

Wippermann was there to see to it that nothing of the sort happened. Not until Ernst was safely aboard the makeshift hospital train—a freight train with straw beds and pillows for the wounded—did he return to his unit. On one occasion, unknown to Ernst, Wippermann had brandished his pistol at several *Hiwis* who were about to carry off the *Oberleutnant.*

When Ernst later heard of this, tears came to his eyes for the first time in a long while. He had been hardened by the tempering fires of battle, but this display of loyalty and comradeship softened him momentarily.

Oberleutnant Ernst was named in the Honor Roll of the German Army and received the Honor Roll Clasp, a decoration seldom awarded. In a hospital in Karlsdorf, near Dresden, he received the Wound Badge in Gold.

His wife and children were permitted to visit him there. The doctor told Ernst that for him the war was over. Ernst didn't want to believe it; things couldn't be that bad.

Several weeks of rest and relaxation followed, although he still suffered pain from his head wound. Otherwise he felt quite well.

When he recovered, Ernst was posted to Berlin. "Albert," his wife said to him, "don't push too hard. Fate has been kind once. It is a wonderful gift that you are still alive and here with me and the children. One shouldn't ask more of God."

He promised his wife, because he loved her and the children, and hoped to return to a normal life when it was all over.

On his arrival in Berlin, Ernst was summoned immediately to see General Bolbrinker. In army headquarters the general told him that he had been chosen for a special mission. Because of his knowledge of English and French he was to join *Sonderverband* Skorzeny.

Oberleutnant Ernst knew of Skorzeny, the *Waffen-SS Hauptsturmführer.* His picture had been in all the newspapers following the rescue of Mussolini by his paratroops. He was a giant of a man with many scars on his face.

So Albert Ernst became one of the few army officers to join *Sonderverband* Skorzeny. The unit's mission was a critical and dangerous one. Employing American uniforms and captured vehicles, it was to drive through enemy lines and create confusion and chaos in the rear as part of the planned Ardennes offensive.

Albert Ernst became a U.S. "captain" commanding the 405th Armored Battalion, which consisted of German soldiers.

During training Ernst had several opportunities to speak with Otto Skorzeny. He described the V-3, which he indicated was soon to enter service. This was not the case, however.

Once one of the members of the unit offended Ernst. He grabbed his Knight's Cross and said, "What did you do for this piece of tin?"

Ernst reacted. This was an insult to him and his men, many of whom had been killed. He himself had been wounded six times.

He leapt to his feet and knocked the man down. But many hounds are the death of the hare and Ernst soon found himself in a cell again, but he was soon freed by Skorzeny.

Skorzeny acted fairly, punishing the man who had offended Ernst's honor. Ernst himself got off. Nevertheless he was in an awkward position and tried to get out of the unit. This he was unable to do.

The operation was not a 100 percent success, but Operation *Greif* did sow suspicion in the U.S. command. American sentries arrested their own officers, thinking them members of the *Sonderkommando*.

Following the operation, Ernst flew back to Cologne-Wahn. There he managed to wangle a transfer to the replacement battalion in Borna together with his longtime comrades *Oberleutnant* Boghut and *Leutnant* Rondorf, who had joined the *Sonderkommando* with him.

Once again Ernst was able to spend time with his family. Fourteen days later he was posted to the 500th Replacement (Tiger) Battalion in Paderborn. There he trained on the Tiger tank and was sent to take part in the creation of the 512th Tiger Battalion under *Hauptmann* Scherf.

The battalion was equipped with the new *Jagdtiger* tank destroyer, which was built at the Hindenburg factory in St. Valentin near Linz, Austria. Ernst was impressed by the giant vehicle and its 12.8cm gun, whose barrel was more than eight meters long.

Following firing trials in the Döllersheim area, on 10 March 1945 the new tank destroyers were thrown into action against the American bridgehead across the Rhine at Remagen. For crews experienced in conventional tanks, fighting in the *Jagdtiger* held some novelties. Before entering combat the gun's travel lock and barrel support had to be disengaged. Aiming required pointing the entire vehicle, as the 12.8cm gun was housed in a fixed superstructure. For Ernst and others with experience in tank destroyers, conversion to the *Jagdtiger* posed few problems.

The German assault on the Remagen bridgehead failed mainly because the attack forces were committed piecemeal. *Generalleutnant* Bayerlein, commanding general of the German LIII Army Corps, suggested that the attack not begin until all three designated divisions and their heavy weapons were in place. This idea was rejected, however, and he was forced to attack on 10 March. Hitler had given orders to attack "immediately with every available unit."

The attack, in which the Ernst company took part, was unsuccessful. Guderian's maxim, to strike hard and not disperse one's forces, had been disregarded.

Following the failure of the attack, Ernst and his *Jagdtigers* were given the job of covering the German withdrawal. The tank destroyers moved into position and knocked out pursuing American tanks from a range of two kilometers, demonstrating the outstanding accuracy of the *Jagdtiger*'s 12.8cm gun. Ernst and his unit then fell back through Niedernepfen and Obernepfen to Siegen. A German attack was planned from there to open the Ruhr pocket.

Surrounded in the Ruhr Pocket

In Siegen a situation briefing was given by *Generaloberst* Harpe. Albert Ernst, now a *Hauptmann* and commanding an armored battle group, was in attendance.

"Gentlemen, we have been given the task of covering the

rear of the retreating army. Ernst, you and your battle group will form the rearguard."

"Who will be the escorting infantry?" asked Ernst.

"You will be accompanied by the *Freikorps Sauerland!*"

"Herr Generaloberst, I have never heard of that unit," replied the *Hauptmann* in the black panzer uniform.

Just then a large figure stood up and cleared his throat.

"Freikorpsführer Echterkamp!" he said smartly. *"Freikorps Sauerland* is under my orders, and it will fight where it stands!"

Hauptmann Ernst almost felt like apologizing for his skeptical tone. The *Freikorpsführer* was obviously convinced that he was in command of a first-class unit.

When the *Jagdtigers* carried out their first attack, the men of the *Freikorps* followed close behind them. A single enemy shell would be enough to simply blow away several dozen.

Hauptmann Ernst leaned out of the cupola.

"People," he shouted, "spread out more. Don't bunch up. One shell could kill you all!"

Ernst's words fell on deaf ears. All of a sudden *Feldwebel* Zellmann spotted the first Sherman tank.

"Firing halt!" ordered Ernst.

The *Jagdtiger* halted. The crew released the gun lock in preparation for firing. *Feldwebel* Colany fired the first shot. The mighty "twelve-eight" crashed. The shell struck the Sherman and blew it apart.

The new ammunition left a great deal of smoke, and the Tiger was completely obscured. Suddenly one of the *Freikorps* men shouted, "The Tiger has been hit!"

As if a signal had been given, the men of the *Volkssturm,* from which the *Freikorps* had been recruited, ran away. They fled through the forest until they reached their homes in Iserlohn and the surrounding cities.

Major Scherf was detached to serve on the staff of LIII Army Corps. Each of the *Jagdtiger* companies was assigned an area of operations, the Carius company being assigned the defense of Unna, for example. Ernst's company was beefed up by the addition of an assault gun platoon, several Panzer IVs, and an antiaircraft platoon with four self-propelled 3.7cm flak. The resulting battle group possessed considerable firepower and its effectiveness was further enhanced by the experience of its personnel and strict leadership of its commander. Several members of Ernst's old unit served under him in the new formation. Sepp Tarlach, an *Oberfeldwebel* and officer candidate, joined Boghut and Rondorf. Boghut, who had meanwhile been promoted to *Oberleutnant,* took over the position of operations officer, while Rondorf, now also an *Oberleutnant,* commanded the *Jagdtiger* company.

The unit moved through Siegen, Meinerzhagen, Kalte Eiche, Brüggen, and Lüdenscheid. Arriving in Altena on 8 April, Ernst received orders to entrain for Iserlohn. There were still several intact airfields in Deilighofen, and it was these that Ernst's unit was to defend.

Several assault guns and tanks drove to Iserlohn while the elements shipped by rail detrained in Menden. Ernst led his *Jagdtigers* through Hagen. The town had been bombed heavily and the armored vehicles had to work their way through rubble-filled streets. Ernst drove ahead in his light armored command vehicle. He was stopped by military police at the Hohenlimburger Bridge. The major in command refused to allow them to go any farther.

"I've told you what we're doing here," said Ernst to the major. "You can hold us here, but it's on your head!—Come on, boys!" said Ernst, turning to his men. "This a good opportunity for us to get some sleep."

Ernst and his men stretched out in a cafe and went to sleep. Five hours later the police major came and woke them.

"Excuse me, *Herr Hauptmann,* for stopping you. Everything you said checked out. Of course you can drive on immediately."

The vehicles continued their journey and stopped in a forest near Bührenbruch-Ergste. There Ernst was given the job of relieving Unna, which had fallen to Allied forces on 9 April. It was at Unna that the Americans closed the Ruhr Pocket. Ernst and his battle group were to open it again.

The next morning while it was still dark the tanks and assault guns set out toward the north along Bundesstrasse 233. They crossed the Ruhr near Langschede. Following Ernst's armored battle group were several battalions of panzer grenadiers and grenadiers.

Oberleutnant Rondorf was the first to hear the report from the commander of an armored car positioned on Bismarck Tower Hill.

"American tanks approaching!"

"That can't be right!" responded the *Hauptmann* on receiving the report. "I'm going there to see for myself!"

Ernst's command vehicle climbed the steep hill. When he reached the position of the scout car he looked down and saw in the distance a long column of tanks, trucks, and artillery moving along the B 1 in the direction of Dortmund. As he watched, a group of vehicles turned onto the B 233 and headed straight toward them.

"Everyone into position on the hill!" ordered *Hauptmann* Ernst by radio. The *Jagdtigers,* tanks, and assault guns moved into hull-down positions on the crest of the hill. Four *Jagdtigers,* four assault guns, and three Panzer IVs were lined up facing north. The 3.7cm flak were moved into position farther to the sides.

Someone reported: "They're coming straight toward us, *Herr Hauptmann!*"

"That's good. All of our weapons will have an equally good field of fire!" answered Ernst. And then, "Don't fire until I give the order. We can't afford to give them a chance to fight back. We'll all fire at once."

The American battle group rolled toward the hill on a wide front. Apparently the Americans were planning to drive straight into the heart of the Ruhr Pocket from the north.

Looking in the direction of the highway through his scissors telescope, Ernst saw a group of disarmed German soldiers marching back along the road into captivity.

Ernst cleared his voice before giving the decisive order. His throat was unusually dry.

"All weapons open fire!"

All of the German armored vehicles opened fire simultaneously. Smoke trails marked the paths of their shells as they whistled toward the American tanks and other vehicles.

"Hit! Hit! Hit!" shouted the men. Below on the plain, vehicles were shrouded in flames. Two Sherman tanks leading the American column were knocked out.

The two *Jagdtigers* fired more slowly than the tanks and assault guns. Their targets were the enemy tanks farthest away, and they scored hits from a range of four kilometers.

The scene on the plain below was like a disturbed beehive. In their panic to escape, American vehicles left the road and became stuck in the ditches and fields, where they fell prey to the quadruple-flak.

So far not a single American shell had fallen on the hill. The 12.8cm guns of the *Jagdtigers* withstood their baptism of fire well. A single hit was sufficient to blast a Sherman to pieces. But what was the sense of it all now?

Peering through his binoculars, Ernst assigned targets. The tanks continued to fire, aiming for areas where there were no houses. Any American vehicle that managed to reach the cover of a house was safe.

The battle group was on its own, fighting a hopeless battle, but no one bothered to think of that now. The American advance had been halted.

At last the Americans began to answer, but the Germans had selected their position so well that none of the shells reached its target. The American tanks withdrew. The tanks and tank destroyers continued to fire, however, destroying large numbers of trucks and armored cars.

Finally all of the American vehicles had withdrawn out of range of the German guns.

"We've done it, *Herr Hauptmann!*" called one of the assault gun commanders, as he leaned out of his hatch and scanned the terrain below.

"Yes, they won't come back today," replied Ernst. He knew the fighting style of the Americans well enough to know that they would send their air force in next.

Leutnant Kubelka, in charge of the *Jagdtiger* platoon, came running over. He was grinning from ear to ear.

"We knocked out four Shermans, *Herr Leutnant!*" he reported breathlessly.

"I saw it. But be careful, damned careful, when the fighter-bombers come. When they do, get under your vehicle!"

"Will do, *Herr Hauptmann!*"

The *Leutnant* walked back to his vehicle. Scarcely had he climbed into his *Jagdtiger* when the air was filled with the roar of aircraft engines.

"Aircraft alarm!" Two flares were fired, the agreed-upon signal for an air attack. The four quadruple-flak pointed their barrels toward the north and northwest. Then the fighter-bombers appeared. They were at an altitude of no more than five hundred meters and appeared to be searching for the German position.

"Let them come!—Now!—Open fire!"

The four antiaircraft guns opened fire. Sixteen smoke trails flitted toward the attacking machines. The leading aircraft took a direct hit and blew apart in a flash of fire. Pieces of wreckage whirled through the air. A severed wing fluttered over the heads of the flak crews and chopped off the top of a tree.

A second fighter-bomber was hit. It stood on its nose, howled toward the hill, and roared overhead before crashing into the bushes a hundred meters behind the German position.

The remaining Thunderbolts disappeared from view to the southwest, but ten seconds later they reappeared from the northwest. This time they approached very low at an unfavorable angle for the antiaircraft guns. Four aircraft fired 50kg rockets, which exploded against the slope.

A fifth, however, dove on the antiaircraft gun on the left flank, machine guns blazing, and dropped a bomb. The American pilot's aim was good, and the bomb fell in the middle of the flak position, killing the entire crew. The gun's reserve ammunition went up, enveloping the immediate vicinity in smoke and flames.

The three remaining guns continued the battle. Half an hour later Ernst received a shocking report. "Guns two, three, and four out of ammunition!"

Seconds later another formation of fighter-bombers appeared. The tanks opened fire with machine guns, damaging one of the enemy aircraft. The rest flew on and dove on their targets. Bombs whistled down. One of the *Jagdtigers* was hit. The bomb went straight through the hatch on the upper deck and exploded, killing *Leutnant* Kubelka and his crew. A second *Jagdtiger* was hit, but its crew escaped with various injuries. *Leutnant* Kubelka and the members of his crew were buried in Schwerte.

It was clear to *Hauptmann* Ernst that they would have to abandon their position on the hill, because without ammunition for the antiaircraft guns the tanks and other vehicles had no way of fighting off attacks from the air.

The order was passed around the hill: "We will withdraw slowly. Rondorf, Boghut, and I will form the rearguard."

The battle group began its withdrawal. *Hauptmann* Ernst scanned the roads from his hilltop position, but the enemy land forces had obviously received a severe shock and were not about to pursue. The losses to the American spearhead had been fifty vehicles, including eleven Shermans.

The German breakthrough attempt had to be called off, however, as the enemy forces had proved to be too strong.

The next morning Ernst received orders from LIII *Fliegerkorps* to hold Deilinghofen airfield for twenty-four hours. The same day, 12 April 1945, he led an advance party into Hemer and saw the "golden pheasants" and party bigwigs making their way to Deilinghofen and the airfield. The rats were leaving the sinking ship and leaving the soldiers to face the bitter music.

Hauptmann Ernst set up his command post in a house in Hemer. The panzers, tank destroyers, and antiaircraft guns—which again had some ammunition, thanks to the efforts of the officer in charge—established a defensive position around Deilinghofen airfield.

On Hill 300, near the Stockschlade forester's house, were an assault gun and a Panzer IV. A *Jagdtiger* had been positioned at the rope factory near Bilveringsen. Further groups stood ready on the four-hundred-meter-high Hemerberge. Several groups of grenadiers that Ernst had commandeered were employed to secure the airfield, as were the airfield's antiaircraft guns, which were now a part of Battle Group Ernst.

Ernst was especially concerned about the nearby prisoner of war camp, which housed about thirty thousand Russians. He could imagine what would happen if the Americans simply released the Russians.

On the evening of 12 April the Americans began feeling their way forward. The *Jagdtigers* destroyed two Shermans from a range of four thousand meters. Ernst was summoned by the mayor of Hemer and invited into his office. He had a long discussion with Herr Pelzing, which was interrupted several times by the roar of heavy aircraft passing overhead. Pelzing informed Ernst that Hemer was a hospital city and that there were many German wounded there.

Finally, the mayor asked, "What do you intend to do, Herr Ernst? Do you plan to fight on or not?"

"If I am ordered to put an end to it here, then I will put an end to it, *Herr Bürgermeister,* and will do what I am required to do. But I am not responsible for the decision. That is a matter for gentlemen of higher rank."

The thirteenth of April began quietly, but incoming reports indicated to *Hauptmann* Ernst that the end was near. Menden, a few kilometers north of Hemer on Bundesstrasse 7, had fallen. Soon there was firing close by, and the *Jagdtigers* on the Stockschlade opened fire on advancing enemy forces. These hurriedly withdrew after losing two tanks.

Shells began to fall near Hemer. It appeared as if the Americans were ranging in for a general attack. A *Stabsarzt* (medical captain) from the hospital in Hemer came to see Ernst.

"Herr Hauptmann, are you willing to cease fighting here?"

Ernst looked at the officer in amazement.

"You should know that that's the job of a general and not a lowly *Hauptmann,*" he replied. "I must have orders to do so."

"But there's no one left here, *Herr Hauptmann.* I have the impression that yours is the only intact unit in the area. All the rest have left. You are the only one who can avoid a disaster here. If the enemy artillery fire comes closer the wounded, who are confined in a small area, will be killed. The hospital, the wounded soldiers . . ."

The medical officer's voice trailed off.

"All right then," said Ernst, knowing he was sticking his neck out, "considering the circumstances, I have decided to act. But you, as medical officer, must drive to the *Amis* [Americans] and fetch a *parlementaire* with whom I can speak."

"I'll leave immediately."

"Good. I'll try to find a headquarters so a general can handle the surrender negotiations."

The *Stabsarzt* drove off at once. *Hauptmann* Ernst had a message sent to the Americans by radio that an emissary was coming under a white flag. He wanted to ensure that nothing happened to this brave man.

Ernst and his two longtime compatriots, Tarlach and Boghut, scoured the area by car. Many unit headquarters had already disappeared. Those still there were hesitant to act. There was much debate about how and when the negotiations were to take place. Finally, Ernst asked the question:

"Can you at least take part if I handle the negotiations?"

Almost all of the officers agreed. The Americans accepted the proposed cease-fire. All of the units of Battle Group Ernst remained at their posts.

Finally an American major and several staff officers arrived. The major was Boyd H. McCune of the 99th Infantry Division, adjutant to Lieutenant Colonel Kriz, who commanded the division's 394th Infantry Regiment.

The negotiations took place near the house in Hemer. In the midst of the negotiations the report arrived from one of the units of Battle Group Ernst that the situation in Hemer was deteriorating. Many foreigners were running about the town and the Russian prisoners had been freed. They had already attacked several women. There were reports of shooting. Albert Ernst turned to McCune.

"Herr Major, I handed the city over to you in good order. What are you going to do about this situation?"

Major McCune stood up.

"Give the order to all your men: All civilians bearing arms are to be shot. I will issue the same order to my troops. This is the only way we can ensure order and security and the peace that is to return here."

Major McCune had the American tanks circle the POW camp, as the German militia was unable to handle the Russian prisoners. Groups of Russians nevertheless managed to break out. They wanted to be there, they wanted to be free at last. And some wanted more.

The American tanks opened fire and returned the prisoners to the camp.

Hauptmann Ernst drove into Hemer with Major McCune. Both wanted to see the state of the city for themselves. When they reached the center of Hemer they were approached by an armed group of foreigners. They saw the German officer in his black panzer uniform and shouted, "There is one of the German swine! Kill him!"

They made as if they were about to rush the command car. The U.S. major pulled out his submachine gun and fired a burst over the heads of the approaching throng. Startled, the men split up and fled down a side street.

The American major made very unfriendly remarks about the behavior of his allies.

Ernst later said, "If the Americans had not acted quickly and decisively, then the 3,000 escaped men would have overrun everything. It would have led to murder, violence, and rape." Several local residents echoed this sentiment.

The German units remained in their positions. The Americans wanted to move in and gradually take over these positions. All German units were to go into captivity except one: Battle Group Ernst. It was to withdraw with all of its weapons.

In the meantime, Ernst asked one of the American staff officers to drive to the flak barracks in Iserlohn, where the headquarters and the fortress commandant, General Büchs, were. The area around Iserlohn fell within Büchs's fortress zone.

Oberleutnant Boghut blindfolded the envoy and drove him to Iserlohn. The envoy's mission was to negotiate the surrender of the Ruhr Pocket. But the officers in the protection of the flak barracks said no, and the American was forced to return empty-handed.

Battle Group Ernst left Hemer and pulled back toward Iserlohn along Bundesstrasse 7. Above on the Hardt was the demarcation line where it was to go into position again. Ernst was at the back of the column in the major's jeep. Behind them in a Kübelwagen were two men from the staff of his battle group. Suddenly the jeep stopped. Major McCune turned to Ernst and said, "Captain, the time of the cease-fire has run out. I can now open fire on any of you, but I'll give you another twenty minutes. Make sure you reach your unit by then.—Wait another moment."

The American got on the radio and ordered his forces to hold their fire for another twenty minutes. Then he turned to the German *Hauptmann* with the Knight's Cross.

"Herr Ernst," he said, "I would like to ask you: Please stay with us."

"I can't do that! I have my orders, just as you do. I have surrendered a city to you that I was not supposed to surrender. We have a new law of family punishment, which states: 'Whoever surrenders a city or fortified place will pay for this decision with his life and the lives of his family.' I ask you again, please do not mention my name. Don't say that I surrendered Hemer. My family lives in Leipzig. Nothing has happened there yet. It would be a terrible thing if I were to lose my wife and children because I tried to save the lives of civilians and Russian prisoners here."

"Herr Ernst, I ask you to consider again. Do you want to be killed so near the end of the war?"

"Herr Major," replied the German, "millions have fallen before me, including many comrades and friends; I am not afraid to become the last."

Wordlessly the major gave the German officer his hand. At that moment they ceased to be enemies.

Ernst drove back to his *Jagdtiger*. Iserlohn was already burning in several places where artillery shells had fallen. He reported to General Bayerlein in a small house in Iserlohner Heide.

"Herr General, I have surrendered Hemer to the enemy!" he reported. The general nodded reflectively.

"I understand what you have done, Ernst. But you may later have to accept the responsibility for it. Then you will have to present justification for your actions."

He took his glass, placed one before *Hauptmann* Ernst, and filled them with champagne. Then he toasted the *Hauptmann*. Ernst knew that he had the general's unspoken approval. Bayerlein could say no more than he already had.

Finally, General Bayerlein ordered Ernst to report to General Büchs in Iserlohn. In the meantime the heavy weapons of Battle Group Ernst had taken up position on the Hardt, in Iserlohn, and near Hohenlimburg.

Ernst received a radio message from Ergste that *Oberleutnant* Carius's company had arrived there. When *Hauptmann* Ernst reported to General Büchs, he received orders to send out patrols to discover where the front was and what operational forces were still available.

When he reported that he had handed Hemer over to the enemy, the staff officers and generals were furious as were the senior party officials there.

"Reconnoiter in the direction of Hemer, Altena, and Letmathe, Ernst, and report to me immediately!"

Hauptmann Ernst set out at once in an armored car. He passed the *Jagdtigers* and assault guns guarding the arterial roads and reached the underpass of the rail line to Hagen, where his battle group headquarters and major radio station were located.

Ernst's patrol revealed the same picture everywhere: several groups still defending fanatically and others that had streamed into the open areas seeking refuge. Among the latter groups were deserters and criminals who saw an opportunity to loot and steal.

The night of 14/15 April passed relatively quietly. On the fifteenth, American tanks began feeling their way toward Iserlohn from several directions. A number were destroyed by the *Jagdtigers, Oberleutnant* Rondorf accounting for three Shermans that day.

The determined and effective defense put up by Battle Group Ernst created the conditions for further negotiations, which had to begin soon if Iserlohn, into which two hundred thousand refugees had fled, was to avoid destruction.

Hauptmann Ernst was determined to spare Iserlohn the terrible fate of "scorched earth." The battle group received a stream of new orders. Twice during the night and early morning of 15 April, Ernst came within a hair of having his vehicle knocked out. During the day American artillery fired isolated rounds into Iserlohn. There was little time left.

Furious that nothing had been done, Ernst drove back to General Büch's headquarters in the flak barracks.

"Herr General," he said to the old, gray-haired general, who was in no way equal to the situation, "I can go on making report after report on what is going on, and no one is concerned. You up here have no idea what's taking place and simply bury your heads in the sand. You, Herr General, only know the troops from your maps. Go and see their situation out there for yourself!—In this situation I can offer you only one piece of advice: Go to the city! Prevent unnecessary casualties among the civilian population!"

Hauptmann Ernst had placed his head on the block, because to talk of surrender, even in this hopeless situation, was playing with his own life.

The large conference room was abuzz with whispers. General Büchs turned to the *Hauptmann* and said, "I will hold a discussion now."

"Hopefully I can take part," interjected Ernst, "because I alone know the overall situation and can give you important information and . . ."

"No more from you!" roared General Büchs suddenly. Then

he turned to a *Hauptmann* and a major of his staff. "Take charge of *Hauptmann* Ernst! Take him to the next room. He is not to leave that room! You are responsible to me with your heads!"

Now they've got you! thought Ernst. Either they'll have you shot right after the conference or they'll lock you up. You must find a way out of this situation.

In front of the mess was an armored car. If he could reach it he would be safe, because his men would not leave him in a jam.

The sound of excited arguments drifted over from the conference room. Gradually the mood became quieter and Ernst realized that he had not much time left. The major, who was sitting opposite him, looked very unhappy, while the *Hauptmann,* who was beside him, did not look overly energetic either. Only a good and quick bluff could save him.

Ernst, still in his camouflage uniform, stood up. He came to attention, gave the "German salute," and said, "Herr Major, tell the general that I will be back in two hours!"

"You're not allowed to leave! Stay here or else . . ."

"Tell the general!" shouted Ernst, and then marched resolutely toward the door. Any moment he expected to hear a shot and feel a bullet striking him in the back. But he reached the door, tore it open, and then slammed it shut behind him.

With rapid steps he walked through the hall, reached the terrace, and ran down the steps to where the armored car was parked. Ernst swung himself in.

"Drive to the radio station," he shouted. *Feldwebel* Zellmann let in the clutch and the armored car moved off. Ernst informed his comrades of what had happened. All begged him not to return to the flak barracks. But Ernst wanted to go back to report the results of his patrol, which were crushing. To be on the safe side he took the reserve platoon—two *Jagdtigers* and an assault gun—with him.

When they reached the flak barracks, Ernst had the drivers shut off the engines of their vehicles.

"Stay alert," he said, "I'm going into the officers mess now. If you hear a shot, open up with the 'twelve-eight' and move in."

Hauptmann Ernst believed the surprise of his return would prevent them from shooting. He climbed out and walked through the hall into the mess. When he saw the two figures sitting there, he knew at once what had happened. Here too the rats had abandoned the sinking ship.

"Where is General Büchs?" he asked.

"The general has gone into the city. He is looking for you, *Herr Hauptmann,*" said a young *Leutnant.*

"I saw no general. Do you think he's run off and left you in the shit?"

"I don't believe that," said the *Leutnant,* close to tears.

"I will take command," said an old *Oberst,* a veteran of the First World War. Ernst turned to face the gray-haired officer.

"Herr Oberst, I have the unit behind me, therefore I will also take command here!"

"Do what you think is right, Ernst!"

"Fine, stay here and I'll be back."

With these words *Hauptmann* Ernst left the command post. On seeing him emerge, obviously in one piece, his men breathed a sigh of relief.

"We must look for General Büchs," said Ernst to his comrades in the armored car. "He's supposed to be in the city."

Ernst and his men scoured Iserlohn but the general was nowhere to be found and had not turned up at any of the other headquarters.

"Herr Hauptmann, General Büchs has taken off!" offered Bretschneider, just back from home leave.

At the headquarters Ernst was told, "Ernst, you speak English. You have a powerful unit in your hands that you can depend on and you know the situation. Put an end to this nonsense!"

Afterward, Ernst drove back once more to the flak barracks and declared to the officers there, "Gentlemen, I am in command of Iserlohn! My headquarters is located in the railway underpass. If anything happens, you are to check with me first! Is that clear?"

It was midnight when Ernst returned to the "front." He handed a message he had personally signed to one of the radio operators. It read:

"Situation in Iserlohn hopeless—awaiting further orders—will try to hold out until morning."

The message had to be sent in the blind, as no other stations were answering. The operator transmitted for a good twenty minutes with no response. The only answer to his broadcast came by messenger from an ominous headquarters:

"Iserlohn is to be defended to the last stone!"

Ernst tore up the message. The Americans were firing into Iserlohn more frequently now. Obviously they were closing in. Early in the morning Ernst called his battle group together. He said to his men, "Comrades, I am the new commander in Iserlohn. Things look bad. Nearly three hundred thousand people are crammed into a small area. We cannot and should not fight on if it will place the lives of these civilians in danger.

"Comrades, we have fought for years to protect our people. Fighting on here can only result in their destruction.

"I firmly intend to make contact with the Americans and surrender the city of Iserlohn. I will go over myself in the armored car. The vehicle will be covered by a white bedsheet and fly a white flag of truce. I intend to implement this plan as soon as the sun comes up.

"Comrades! Since I am speaking of surrender, according to the rules of war you have the right to take me prisoner and assume command yourselves. You are not obliged to follow my orders."

The men gave the commander of their battle group three cheers.

The officers talked, and moments later *Oberleutnant* Rondorf, one of the most experienced and successful tank destroyer commanders, went over to *Hauptmann* Ernst.

"Albert, you have led us this far, we want you to lead to the end. We are firmly convinced that you are doing the right thing."

"Thanks, Rondorf!" said Ernst, moved.

Early on that morning of 16 April 1945 two men of Battle Group Ernst were killed by an artillery shell. They were the last of Ernst's men to be killed in action during the Second World War.

When the sun came up, Ernst drove off in the direction of the Seilersee. He encountered the first Americans at the end of the Hindenburgstrasse and asked to be taken to their commanding officer. The commander of the American regiment was not interested in receiving a *parlementaire* and made arrangements for *Hauptmann* Ernst to be made a prisoner.

Ernst answered the captain:

"Can you justify taking prisoner an emissary who is offering an honorable surrender? Can you justify the further shedding of blood? My battle group will fight on if I do not return."

Silence reigned for a few moments. Then the American captain asked, "Are you by any chance *Hauptmann* Ernst?"

"Yes, I am *Hauptmann* Ernst," replied the panzer commander.

"Good, the colonel will give you a cease-fire."

The colonel arrived a few moments later and the two spoke. Afterward the cease-fire was announced by radio and loudspeaker. Ernst contacted his radio station, which spread word of the cease-fire on the German side.

It was one o'clock in the afternoon. The *Hauptmann* asked for medics and medicines. These were provided without delay and Ernst sent them to care for his own and enemy wounded.

The colonel closed the discussion. "We wish to complete the surrender by 1400."

Ernst promised to obtain a general as the German partner in the surrender. All firing had ceased when he drove by armored car to Bayerlein's headquarters in the Rothehausstrasse. The general was there.

"Herr General," began Ernst, "I request that you drive back with me and surrender the city of Iserlohn."

"Ernst, I am a captive general and am no longer able to do that."

In this way Albert Ernst learned that *Oberst* von Hauser had surrendered the twenty-six hundred men of the *Panzer-Lehr* Division on 15 April and that the soldiers of the LIII Army Corps in the corps headquarters in Rafflingen had also surrendered. And they were going to have him shot the same day for using the word "surrender!"

"What should I do, Herr General?" asked Ernst.

"I can no longer give you orders!" answered Bayerlein.

"Then I will surrender Iserlohn to the Americans myself, Herr General."

"Yes, do that. That would be best" was the general's answer. Ernst drove away. He made contact with his people in Hohenlimburg, as well as the Jagdtiger crews in Letmathe, before driving on to Iserlohn. He contacted Rondorf, who was already in the city, by radio and informed him what was taking place.

By the time Ernst arrived, Rondorf had made all the necessary preparations and made contact with every unit he could still reach.

Ernst drove to the city hall, escorted by three *Jagdtigers*. They drove into the square and Ernst walked into the police station.

Inside were three unarmed policemen. Father Dietze of the Catholic parish of Iserlohn was also there, as well as a physician, Dr. Möcke, and a man who was said to have been a former mayor of the city.

Ernst saw a police major standing stiffly at attention. When he extended his hand to greet the major, Ernst saw that the man had already removed his decorations and badges of rank. Ernst turned around abruptly and left the man standing.

Then he sat down at the negotiating table. His American counterpart was Lieutenant Colonel Kriz, an officer of the 99th Division. During the negotiations Ernst succeeded in clarifying all significant issues. The surrender was to take place at the Schillerplatz in the presence of the entire Battle Group Ernst.

Ernst left the city hall, satisfied that he had spared hundreds of thousands a terrible fate. Just then a civilian came up and said, "There have never been such cowards as you!" and spit.

Oberleutnant Rondorf wanted to hit the man, but Ernst held him back. Ernst turned away so that the others could not see that he was weeping.

Then it was over. The Jagdtigers were driven onto the Schillerstrasse. Civilians streamed into the square, which was soon filled with people.

The crews climbed down and stood in front of their vehicles. Albert Ernst assembled his men, then turned to the American commander.

"The last fighters of the pocket, the fighters of Iserlohn, surrender in the face of a hopeless situation and request honorable treatment!"

Ernst reached for his pistol and handed it to Lieutenant Colonel Kriz. The American commander saluted and took the weapon.

Albert Ernst turned to his men, told them to lay down their arms, and dismissed them. The American commander again directed his words to *Hauptmann* Ernst.

"We have made an honorable arrangement. All of your soldiers may keep their personal weapons." Then he turned directly to Ernst.

"Don't go into captivity, Captain. Come to my headquarters, we have plenty for you to do!"

"That won't do, I'm staying with my soldiers. We have fought together for years, and now, in our darkest hour, I can't abandon them."

"Then at least take your own freedom, Captain," offered the lieutenant colonel.

"Unfortunately, I must refuse that offer as well, unless you can offer freedom to my men as well."

Just then the division adjutant, who had just arrived in a jeep with the division's commanding officer, General Lauer, came over to Ernst.

"General Lauer asks that you take your freedom in any case."

"Only if you give all of my men their release papers" was Ernst's final word. General Lauer sent a staff car to drive Ernst into captivity. But Ernst even refused this offer. He walked into captivity with his men.

The war was over. Research later revealed that Iserlohn was the only city in the Ruhr Pocket to be surrendered to the enemy.

The later colonel and head of the Kriz-Davis Wholesale Electric Company of Grand Island, USA wrote:

"It is difficult today to describe the indelible impression and respect I gained of *Hauptmann* Ernst. With him we negotiated an open and official hand-over, the only one I ever experienced. My impressions of the entire period of fighting involving the city of Iserlohn are based on my memories of this courageous German unit."

And Colonel Kriz wrote to Ernst:

Dear Albert, The city of Iserlohn owes you a great debt. You had no chance of winning in the final phase of the fighting in the Ruhr Pocket. When I drove through the German lines to discuss surrender with you I had the air force and many batteries of artillery at my disposal. But I wanted to spare as many of my men as possible, so I went. If something had happened, if, for example, one of your men had fired, or one of us had fired, if you had not surrendered with your brave soldiers: the city of Iserlohn would have had to bear the consequences.

I still have your pistol. I examined it yesterday, it bears the serial number 5921. You, Albert, are welcome any time at our home in the Midwest.

Beginning with Rommel's desert battle to the invasion of Europe, you, as a German officer played the greatest role.

God protect you!

Your Bob

Albert Ernst took up residence in Iserlohn, the city he had saved from destruction. He remained the same modest man he always was. His friends are always welcome in his home. And he still embodies the best traditions of the German soldier, and a bearing which is respectfully acknowledged by his former enemies.

Albert Ernst

15 November 1912:	Born in Wolfsburg, Germany.
1 February 1942:	Awarded the Iron Cross, First Class.
7 February 1944:	Awarded the Knight's Cross.
1944:	Received the Wound Badge in Gold.
7 January 1945:	Awarded the Honor Roll Clasp of the German army.
Ultimate rank:	*Hauptmann.*

7

The German Panzer Arm of World War II

Principles of Its Strategic, Tactical, and Technical Development

With the appearance of his book *Taschenbuch der Tanks (Pocket Book of Tanks),* retired major and technical doctor Fritz Heigl became the first author to depict the history and future employment of the then young weapon. Heigl was born in Pragerhof in Southern Styria. He saw action during the First World War, first as an officer candidate and platoon leader in the Imperial Army's 73rd Infantry Regiment.

After recovering from wounds suffered in action, Heigl returned to his regiment, which had meanwhile been moved to South Tirol. Later, as a *Leutnant,* he saw action on the plateaus of the Sette Communi (known to the Austrians as the Sieben Gemeinden) during the great Austro-Hungarian offensive. On 21 May 1916, Heigl was again badly wounded.

Heigl subsequently took part in the battles at Isonzo and the advance along the Piave as a *Leutnant* with *Feldkanonenregiment* 9. On 15 June 1918, near San Giovanni on the Piave, Heigl was once again wounded. In spite of his wounds he continued to direct the firefight from a stretcher until he finally lost consciousness. Not until 11 December was the highly decorated officer released from the hospital. By then the Austro-Hungarian Army had collapsed and the Hapsburg monarchy had disappeared.

After the war he entered the Technischen Hochschule in Vienna, and following graduation became a scientific assistant.

In this capacity he worked exclusively in the field of defense research. Following some initial work with artillery, he turned to the new field of armored fighting vehicles, or tanks.

In 1924 and 1925 he produced four "Tank Instructional Tables" through the military publisher R. Eisenschmidt of Berlin, which dealt with Italian, French, and British tanks. Appearing from the same publisher in 1925 was his book *Die schweren französischen Tanks—die italienischen Tanks mit einem Überblick über das Entstehen der italienischen und französischen Panzerwaffe (The Heavy French Tanks—The Italian Tanks with a Summary of the Development of the French and Italian Tank Arms).*

In 1926, Heigl began work on *Das Taschenbuch der Tanks,* which went on to become a standard reference work for all the soldiers who later became the creators of the German tank arm. These men added their own concepts of armored warfare, contributing to a process which was to make the German armored forces the best and most advanced in the world.

In June 1928, Heigl ended his activities at the Technischen Hochschule and attempted to enlist in the Austrian *Bundesheer* (Federal Army), which had just been created. He hoped to become an official in the military research branch, a position for which he was ideally qualified. However, the Federal Ministry of the Army rejected his application "in view of the reduced numbers of officers" in the new army.

In 1929 engineer Fritz Heigl opened an engineering consulting office in his Vienna apartment.

Heigl had earlier been promoted to major on 15 May 1925. The promotion was awarded him by the Austrian chancellor J. Schober on behalf of the federal president.

Retired major Fritz Heigl died on 11 December 1930 at the age of thirty-seven as a result of liver disease. On 11 October 1930, just before his death, he was named to the Technischen Hochschule in Vienna as a lecturer.

Fritz Heigl did not live to write the definitive work on the employment of tanks; nevertheless, his *Taschenbuch der Tanks* had served as an "eye-opener." His successor continued his work, releasing revised editions of volumes I and II and adding a new volume III, which not only described the various types of tanks, but also how they were to be used on the battlefield and their role in larger operations. Heinz Guderian stated that the book "answered a vital need."

By then a *Generalleutnant* and commanding general of XVI

Army Corps, Guderian wrote of the new edition which appeared in 1938:

"It is essential to produce in a brief and factual format a collection of all the lessons so far learned in war, which on the one hand can serve as a reference work, and on the other a history from which may be derived the principles for the strategic, tactical, technical and wartime economic development of the panzer arm.

"May this book fulfill this purpose in the spirit of its late creator Heigl, a man of Greater Germany, in service to the united German nation."

It was with this goal in mind that *Hauptmann* G. P. von Zeschwitz, an officer of the 25th Panzer Regiment, created volume III of the pocket book series. His own experiences of tank warfare allowed von Zeschwitz to recognize the potential of the new weapon and see the opportunity presented German panzer officers to create a new and revolutionary fighting force. Zeschwitz wrote:

The tank battle is a new element in conducting a land war. Its mastery demands a departure from compromises with the past. Its tools are the fighting spirit and marksmanship of the infantryman, the dash and flair of the cavalryman, and the technical knowledge and reasoning of the artilleryman.

This is the formula by which German tank officers will have to be shaped and trained.

Borne out by the increased defensive strength of the infantry, the tank arm is growing to become a vital new part of the army. The force of its attack will be met by the antitank defenses of every type of unit as well as by specialized antitank units.

In the future no decisive battle will be possible without tanks, and no armored attack without an antitank defense. The tank battle will therefore decide the fate of the armored attack. Eliminating the enemy's antitank defenses without losing one's own attacking strength will lead to victory through the armored attack.

The presence of a superior, unbreakable antitank defense at the decisive moment will seal the fate of an armored attack.

With these few sentences the author of the third volume of the *Pocket Book of Tanks* had laid down two of the fundamental rules of armored warfare, without however moving on to the essential point of the German panzer arm, whose development had already made great progress at the time the book was written.

The third ground rule was vital to an armored force if it was to be equal to the tasks allotted to it: "Its nature rules out tying it to cavalry or even foot troops. The state which allows this to take place, consciously or unconsciously, relinquishes the advances already achieved, in that it adjusts the speed and mobility of the new weapon to the tactical and strategic tachometer of previous armies.

"In its mobile and freewheeling form, however, an armored force is the great weapon of decision in the hands of the generals and commanders."

These findings originated not from the studies and experiments of the head of the armored force, but from one of its instructors and officers. Von Zeschwitz also performed a great service by infusing this spirit into the officers and men of the panzer arm. In doing so he made the tactical and technical rules of the past and their practical, strategic, and economic value transparent.

During the First World War the English general Fuller had been involved in the first large-scale tank operations. He worked tirelessly to prevent the tanks from being used in pointless positional warfare, urging instead that they be used in such a way as to exploit their potential. His motto was:

"The more mechanization progresses, the less we should mechanize the spirit."

In England it was Fuller who fought vehemently against the greatest sin "contrary to the spirit of the armored weapon": tying them down to infantry units. When he was unsuccessful in this he took his leave and was decried by his superiors right up to the minister of war as being "tank crazy."

It was not until 1936—far too late—that Fuller's concepts were adopted by the British army.

In the United States it was Col. Robert J. Icks who tried to revolutionize the U.S. armored forces after the end of the First World War. All of his efforts to join the tank corps during the war failed. Not so his later efforts to place the American tank forces on a better footing. In 1933 he and two other officers produced the book *Fighting Tanks since 1916*. This was the first book on armored fighting vehicles to appear in the United States.

During the Second World War, Icks, by now a captain, was involved in the testing of armored vehicles at the Aberdeen Proving Grounds in Maryland. There he advanced to the rank of colonel and became the acting director of development and production for the American Armored Vehicle Department in Detroit. In recognition of his efforts he was awarded the Army Commendation Ribbon and the Legion of Merit.

Icks's book *Tanks and Armored Vehicles,* which appeared during the final phase of the war in the Pacific, had been ready to go to the printers before war broke out, but its publication was held up by the wartime paper shortage. A revised version of this work appeared in 1970.

This paper shortage had significant negative effects on the training of officers and men for America's armored forces.

France Takes the Wrong Path

During the crisis at Verdun it had been Colonel Doumenec who organized the truck shuttle service on the "Holy Road." The resulting rapid transport of weapons, munitions, and men averted a seemingly imminent German victory at Verdun, which might have cost France the war.

A few years later Doumenec summed up his theories in a speech at the Centre des Hautes Études Militaires—the war college:

"Initial mobilization will take place at 0000 on X-Day. At X-Day plus six hours the tank corps, which is based in the Bordeaux area, is at the Seine; at X plus ten hours it is at France's eastern frontier.—There, gentlemen, you have a view of tomorrow."

Doumenec's prophetic call for change was ignored by the commanders of the French army. The army operations manual, which appeared in 1930 under the title *Instruction sur l'emploi des Chars de combat (Instructions on the Employment of Battle Tanks),* did not subscribe to the theory of concentration as espoused by Doumenec and some other French officers, like generals Estienne and Maistre. What then did the new "combat manual" propose?

"Battle tanks are escort weapons for the infantry, which are attached as special units or detachments (tank companies, tank battalions, or even tank regiments) to certain large units as required. In battle, tank units or detachments fight within the scope of infantry units."

The authors went on to define this concept in the key sentence of the manual's first chapter: "Battle tanks are support weapons only, which are to be detached to the infantry for a limited period of time. They add considerable strength to the infantry's attack, but do not replace the infantry as the main weapon of attack."

However, the final straw was contained in the second paragraph of chapter 2. Referring to the operation of tanks and their value to the army, the authors wrote: "Battle tanks can neither replace the infantry nor increase its fighting value as their performance in battle is too limited. They are effective only in concert with the infantry. It is the attack tempo of the latter and its occupation of the general objective alone which are decisive."

As well as the French general staff and the army high command, *every* institution which studied the use of armored forces in war reached the same mistaken conclusions. The German victory in France, achieved through the effective use of armored forces, was largely the result of this mistaken interpretation.

Tying tanks to the infantry, with its maximum speed of five kilometers per hour, robbed them of their breakthrough potential. France was forced to pay a bitter price for this terrible error in judgment.

Former colonel Charles de Gaulle, an enthusiastic pupil of General Estienne, was the only French tank proponent to demonstrate the potential of armored forces to act as a counter to German developments in the field of armored warfare. It was de Gaulle who requested the formation of large tank units which could meet the German panzer divisions on equal terms. The proposals put forward by de Gaulle, who had kept abreast of current technical advances and reached the correct conclusions concerning tank construction and strategy, were disregarded by the leaders of the French Republic.

When, in autumn 1938, France nevertheless began to push ahead with the formation of independent armored divisions, it was in recognition of the correctness of the German strategy, which had been worked out in various armed forces maneuvers during 1937 and 1938.

By the time the "Sitzkrieg" or "Phony War" on the French frontier ended, France had created three such large units, but had not had time to conduct large-scale combat exercises.

The Evolution of Tank Design, Strategy, and Tactics

From General Radlmeier to Heinz Guderian

When the future General von Radlmeier saw a demonstration of the SHE tractor at the 1927 DLG exhibition in Dortmund, he proposed the construction of a military wheeled-tracked vehicle based on this example. The first prototype was built at the Esslingen Machine Factory and sent to the German army's tank testing grounds at Kama, near Kasan in the Soviet Union, for trials.

Dr. Otto Merker, technical director of the Magirus Werke in Ulm, was responsible for much of the early work in German tank construction. Two men who had been working for years toward the creation of a German armored force were the former Major Lutz and General Staff *Hauptmann* Heinz Guderian.

Major Oswald Lutz was the commander of the 7th (Bavarian) Motor Transport Battalion. Lutz made great efforts to provide Guderian with an insight into the new service. Guderian soon acquired a reputation as an expert in the use of motorized units. The war games held during the winter of 1923–24 saw motorized units used in conjunction with aircraft. Guderian, suitably prepared through his study of the first chapter of the *Pocket Book of Tanks,* was appointed by *Oberstleutnant* von Brauchitsch (who later became commander in chief of the army) to command the "armored and motorized group."

By the autumn of 1934, when Guderian was ordered to Stettin to join the staff of the 2nd Division, he had already directed a series of map exercises and training maneuvers, which had explored the use of armored vehicles.

The *Reichswehr*'s initial formative period ended with the retirement of *Generaloberst* von Seeckt from the position of chief of the army command. The new chief, Wilhelm Heye, pushed for a further expansion of the "mechanized combat units." Under the command of *Oberst* Alfred von Vollard-Bockelberg, who had succeeded *Generalmajor* von Natzmer in October 1926, becoming the third inspector of motorized troops *(In* 6), further findings concerning motorization, and in particular tanks, were translated into fact. On 1 April 1929, Vollard-Bockelberg was promoted to *Generalleutnant* and became head of the *Heereswaffenamt* (Army Ordnance Office). He gave his successor as *In* 6, *Generalmajor* von Stülpnagel, a free hand. *Generalmajor* von Vollard-Bockelberg pushed for the adoption of the latest technical concepts, and thus the motorization of the German army, and therefore must be considered one of the leading figures in the creation of the *Panzertruppe*. It was under his management that the Panzers I and II appeared, even though Germany was still forbidden to build tanks under the Treaty of Versailles. One of his coworkers in the *Heereswaffenamt* was the then major Johannes Streich, who was later to command a panzer division in North Africa.

The staff of the Inspectorate of Motorized Troops was as follows:

Inspector:	*Generalmajor* von Stülpnagel
Chief of Staff:	*Oberst* Oswald Lutz
Department Heads:	Maj. Ludwig Ritter von Radlmeier, Maj. Werner Kempf, *Hauptmann* Josef Harpe, and General Staff *Hauptmann* Hans Baehsler.

In 1930, *Hauptmann* Friedrich, *Hauptmann* Kühn, and *Hauptmann* Irmisch joined the inspectorate. Early in 1929, Maj. Ritter von Radlmeier had assumed command of the Tank Testing and Training Station at Kama in the Soviet Union. *Oberleutnant* Charles de Beaulieu also joined this staff of experts, replacing *Hauptmann* Baehsler.

One of the driving forces behind the development of the *Panzertruppe* was Maj. Werner Kempf. He was responsible for the development of the heavy six-wheeled scout car and the light scout car.

In 1929 orders were issued for the reorganization of *Kraftfahrabteilung* 6 *(Kf* 6) based at Münster. In its new form the unit was to have a motorcycle company, a scout car company (with mock-ups), and a tank company, also equipped with mock-ups. The latter company had already been formed in 1927 under *Hauptmann* Fritz Kühn.

Under the overall command of *Oberstleutnant* Erler, the battalion's companies were commanded by:

1./Kf 6:	*Hauptmann* Walther K. Nehring
2./Kf 6:	*Hauptmann* Hero Breusing
3./Kf 6:	*Hauptmann* Johannes Nedtwig

In autumn 1928 the head of the motor transport instructional staff, *Oberst* Stottmeier, approached Major Guderian and asked him to provide his students with instruction in tank tactics. Guderian's superiors in the *Truppenamt* approved, and once again he became officially involved with armored vehicles.

Guderian, who had never sat in a tank, not even in a mock-up, now set about assembling everything written on the subject so far. He also obtained several motorized mock-ups, which he used in training exercises. During these experiments he came to know some of the young officers who, many years later, were to become his closest colleagues. One such officer was Walter Wenck, adjutant of the 9th Infantry Regiment's 3rd Battalion. Wenck and Guderian studied the use of tanks as individual vehicles as well as in platoon, company, and battalion formations.

Gradually, as a result of their experiments, Guderian and the other officers developed a concept for the employment of tanks in a future conflict.

In 1929, Guderian was sent to Sweden as an observer. There he became familiar with actual tanks and the principles behind their operation. Guderian was invited to be the guest of the Strijdsvagn Battalion, the second battalion of the Götz Guard. There he came to know Colonel Burén, who proved most helpful, and developed a close friendship with Captain Klingspor, one of the company commanders to whom he was assigned.

This was the final, decisive breakthrough, and that year Guderian proposed the idea of a strategic tank force, a concept which had not been advanced before. It is obvious that Guderian's earlier work from the period beginning 1 October 1927 had contributed to his concepts, because while with the *Truppenamt,* the predecessor to the general staff, he had written a manual entitled *Troop Transport in Motor Vehicles,* in which he acknowledged the advantages of motor transport over horse-drawn vehicles and rail transport. Guderian then went on to acquire further experience with the motor transport instructional staff. During his four-week stay in Sweden, Guderian became familiar with the Lk II, one of the last tanks developed by Germany during the First World War.

By now Guderian was convinced that tanks could never achieve their full potential operating alone or tied down to the infantry. He formulated his ideas on the subject as follows: "The study of military history, the exercises in England (Guderian visited England in 1927 and 1928) and my own experience with mock-ups convinced me that tanks would only be capable of their optimum performance when the speed and cross-country capabilities of the other weapons on which they depended were raised to a similar level. Tanks would have to play the leading role in this unit, which combined all arms, and the others would have to act in harmony with the tanks. Tanks were not to be used in infantry divisions, rather panzer divisions were to be formed which included all the weapons necessary to allow the tanks to fight effectively" (see Guderian, Heinz: *Errinerungen eines Soldaten).*

On 1 February 1930, Heinz Guderian received orders from the chief of staff of the Inspectorate of Motor Transport Troops, *Oberst* Lutz, to take command of the 3rd (Prussian) Motor Transport Battalion at Berlin-Lankwitz. With support from *Oberst* Lutz, Major Guderian reequipped and reorganized the battalion, which now took the following form:

1st Company: newly equipped with scout cars
2nd Company: panzer company with mock-ups
3rd Company: antitank company with wooden guns
4th Company: equipped as motor-transport (truck) company

When the inspector, Gen. Otto von Stülpnagel, retired in early 1930, he said to Guderian: "You are too impetuous. Believe me, you will never live to see the day when German tanks roll!"

Not just General Stülpnagel, but all the entire senior command staffs as well, suffered from this misconception.

The New 1st General Staff Officer
under General von Bockelberg

When the general staff officer of the *Infanterieführer* II at Schwerin, Mecklenburg, Maj. Werner Kempf, was detached to Motor Transport Battalion 1 for technical training in early 1926, it began a process which was to see him become one of the most ardent supporters of army motorization. With his appointment to the position of first general staff officer in the Inspectorate of Motor Transport Troops on 1 October 1928, he took the final step in a developmental process similar to that involving Heinz Guderian. His task with the inspectorate was to generally advance the significance of the tank and the process of motorization. Of this he said: "It was clear to us that a modern army must possess tanks, but tanks had been forbidden us by the Versailles Treaty. Did it make sense to equip the *Reichswehr* with mock-ups and in this way train the troops to fight with and against tanks? This question was hotly debated, but we emphatically said yes. This led to the acquisition of tank mock-ups to be mounted on automobile chassis."

Kempf worked faithfully under his first chief, General von Bockelberg, and his successor, General von Stülpnagel, and was on the closest terms with the inspectorate's chief of staff, *Oberst* (later *Generalmajor)* Lutz.

Oswald Lutz became the first German general to hold the new rank of *General der Panzertruppe,* which was created in 1935. He was one of the few officers to have commanded an army motor transport unit during the First World War, and, as a technical specialist, was ideally suited to play a role in the development of this new branch of the service. A short time later he became the inspector of motor transport troops and brought in Heinz Guderian as chief of staff, as previously related.

Oberstleutnant Kempf became CO of the 7th (Bavarian) Motor Transport Battalion stationed at Munich. There he gained experience which was later to be of great significance. As anticipated, on 1 July 1934 he succeeded Guderian as chief of staff of the Inspectorate of Motor Transport Troops and was thus placed in a position from which he could exert a great deal of influence on the motorization of the army. The idea of creat-

ing motorized combat units from the motor transport units originated with General Bockelberg.

"The battle in the *Reichswehr* Ministry," wrote *General der Panzertruppe* Kempf, "was mainly over two concepts which had already been put forward by General Lutz and Guderian:

1. The tank is not a support weapon for the infantry, but the main weapon of an independent, fully motorized armored division.
2. The process of general motorization must be pursued at a much greater tempo. The engine is far superior to the horse. The motor vehicle's cross-country capabilities are adequate.

At that time no one could have imagined that when the Anglo-Americans landed in Normandy in 1944 they would not bring a single horse with them.

An important contemporary witness, the later *General der Panzertruppe* Kempf, said of General Lutz: "The contributions made to the motorization of the army by General Lutz were extremely great. His calmness was an excellent balance to the temperament of Guderian, who easily antagonized the influential men in the ministry.

"Nevertheless, Guderian was the driving force. In particular he realized early on the significance of tanks in any future war, and later he was one of the leading proponents of fully-motorized panzer divisions."

The First Panzer Divisions:
The Founding of the Panzer Arm

On 1 April 1931, Gen. Oswald Lutz was promoted to the rank of *Generalmajor* and named inspector of motor transport troops. On 1 October he received *Oberstleutnant* Guderian as his chief of staff. While Lutz oversaw the motorization of the army, it was Guderian, continuing his earlier work, who was the creator of Germany's armored forces.

Assisting these two officers from January 1932 were General Staff Major Walther K. Nehring as first general staff officer and

Hauptmann Charles de Beaulieu as second general staff officer. In autumn 1933, de Beaulieu was succeeded by General Staff *Hauptmann* Walther von Hünersdorff. *Hauptmann* Hermann Breith and *Hauptmann* Ritter von Hauenschild later joined the inspectorate as department heads for tanks and armored cars. *Hauptmann* Werner was in charge of personnel, and *Hauptmann* Irmisch automotive mechanics.

It is understandable that many officers refused to acknowledge the opinions of this *Oberstleutnant* Guderian as "the last word" on the subject. High-ranking cavalry officers and some in the General Staff—especially in the *Truppenamt* under the later *Generaloberst* Beck—had quite different ideas. These men adhered to the concepts adopted by the British and French, namely the "coupling of panzer units to the infantry." Guderian's ideas, which were shared by Colonel de Gaulle and General Fuller, were not accepted by the members of the General Staff, and these polarized against him. Guderian fired back, suggesting that "the cavalry is nothing more than a giant supply train with inadequate protection."

Guderian soon realized that he had once again put his foot in it. Nevertheless, his work went on and he soon found capable officers who were willing to work with him toward the goal of a "practical organization for the future employment of tanks." Their organizational goal was initially the formation of a panzer division, followed by a panzer corps. This was an indication that they were striving to create not just an armored unit to be employed tactically in support of an infantry attack, but a strategically capable and therefore decisive weapon that would be capable of functioning independently.

Retired *General der Panzertruppe* Walther K. Nehring recalled that "it was very difficult to interest the Chief of Army Operations and the representatives of the other established arms in this idea." Nehring went on to add that "the older Generals were hesitant to quickly develop and form such tank units, as they did not understand the principles of the tank war of the future and felt uncertain about wielding such a new and fast means of combat."

It was recognized that the experimental tanks under test at Kama failed to meet the tactical and technical standards required to cope with the latest foreign tanks. New models would have to be developed.

The Panzers of the Development Years

During the initial stages of efforts to create a German armored force the officers responsible had relied on a British manual written in 1927, the *Provisional Combat Manual for Tanks and Armored Vehicles*. Before long the Germans were working feverishly to produce their own manuals. The decisive breakthrough was made by *General der Artillerie* Ritter von Eimannsberger. Eimannsberger studied the available tank manuals and read all the relevant technical and tactical studies before releasing his book, *Der Kampfwagenkrieg (The Tank War)*, in 1934. The book contained all the technical and tactical theories of the German "experts." *Der Kampfwagenkrieg* soon became an indispensable component of every motorized unit. Guderian said of the book: "Our tank personnel learned a great deal from it."

In 1938, General von Eimannsberger gave a speech to the Defense Science Society in Berlin, titled "The Tank Crisis," in which he declared: "Half measures, such as an attack by inadequately trained or numerically weak tank forces, or inadequate cooperation between weapons must today, as always, lead to defeat."

What was required, then, was the construction of tanks possessing the proper balance between armament, armor, and speed.

Initially the *Heereswaffenamt* ordered two medium types and three light types from various firms. Two examples of each were built. These ten tanks possessed maximum speeds of 20 kph in open country and 35 to 40 kph on roads.

The officer responsible for the construction of the first tanks, *Hauptmann* Pirner, endeavored to take into account the latest technical requirements, such as a good wading capability, heavy armor, a rotating turret with 7.5cm gun for the medium type and good maneuverability.

The experts recommended equipping the first panzer divisions with a light tank armed with a high-velocity gun and turret and bow machine guns, and a medium tank with a large-caliber gun and two machine guns. While the light type was to serve with the panzer battalion's three light companies, the medium tanks were to be assigned to a heavy company.

The standard panzer crew consisted of five men: the tank commander, gunner, loader, driver, and radio operator. The crew used throat-type microphones for communications inside the tank, while radio ensured fast and reliable communications between tanks.

Guderian succeeded in having the size of the Panzer III's turret ring increased, which later allowed the tank to be fitted with a 5cm gun.

It was clear to all involved that it would be some years before the two advanced types (Panzer III and IV) entered frontline service. These delays in production forced General Lutz to accept an interim solution, namely the MAN firm's Panzer II, armed with a 2cm gun and one machine gun.

With the naming of Adolf Hitler as Reich chancellor by Reich president Hindenburg on 30 January 1933, and the appointments of General von Blomberg as Reich defense minister and General von Reichenau as head of the ministry soon afterward, the way was open for a rapid expansion of the *Panzertruppe.* During a display of new weapons staged at Kummersdorf by the *Heereswaffenamt,* Guderian had an opportunity to show Hitler a motorized unit in action.

Hitler watched demonstrations by a motorcycle platoon, an antitank platoon, and a platoon of Panzer I tanks. Amazed by the speed with which the motorized units carried out their orders, Hitler said to Guderian: "I can make use of that! That's what I want to have!"

Thus the rapid expansion of the *Panzertruppe* was assured in 1933.

In the autumn of 1933, Gen. Freiherr von Fritsch became head of the army GHQ. Fritsch was a man who had the trust of the entire German officer corps. As head of the *Truppenamt*'s 1. *Abteilung,* he had shown interest in questions of motorization and tank development. Fritsch had devoted much time to studying the operation of a panzer division and had an open mind where tank development was concerned.

In contrast, his new chief of staff, General Beck, voiced his opposition to plans for the development of an armored force at every opportunity. Like the leading French and British generals, Beck wanted to see the tank used as an infantry support weapon, and he pleaded for the establishment of the panzer brigade as the largest armored formation.

It was thanks to Guderian, an *Oberst* since 1 October 1933, that Beck finally agreed to the formation of two panzer divisions. Guderian wanted three, and accordingly painted a bright picture of the tank's effectiveness for his superiors. Beck's response was: "No, I don't want you! You are too fast for me!"

The "Third Modification Order for the Expansion of the Army" was issued on Whitsunday 1934. It provided for the expansion of the army to twenty-one peacetime divisions and other army units and resulted in accelerated growth from 1 November 1934. The expansion of the army also provided for the formation of the first three panzer divisions. For some time the army command had been throwing up a brick wall in front of such a move, but now the orders came from the highest authority.

On 1 June 1934 the former inspectorate *In 6* was renamed the *Kommando der Kraftfahrtruppen* (Mechanized Troops Command) and was given a free hand to set up its own organization. As an independent command it had to carry out all necessary measures. On 27 September 1935 it was designated *Kommando der Panzertruppe* (Armored Troops Command).

The new weapons inspectorate *In 6* was now established as the Inspectorate for Army Motorization and Armored Troops. *Oberstleutnant* Kempf became the inspectorate's chief of staff. Both inspectorates were under the overall command of *Generalleutnant* Lutz.

At that time there existed seven mechanized battalions, each with 14 officers and 454 NCOs and men. In addition there was the Motor Transport Training *Kommando Zossen,* which had been formed on 1 November 1933 following the abandoning of the camp at Kama in the Soviet Union. On 1 April 1934 the *Kommando*'s headquarters were transferred from Berlin-Moabit to Zossen.

The *Kommando* was organized as follows:

Commander:	Major Harpe
Adjutant:	*Oberleutnant* Martin
Staff *Hauptmann:*	*Hauptmann* Baumgart
CO 1st Company:	*Hauptmann* Conze
Officers:	*Hauptmann* Thomale, *Oberleutnant* Kühn, *Oberleutnant* Ebert, *Oberleutnant* Hennig, *Oberleutnant* Mildebrath

On 1 March 1934, the *Kommando* was expanded to three companies. On 16 April of that year it was again expanded, this time to four companies, and a signals platoon was added. The *Kommando*'s 2nd Company was led by *Hauptmann* Köppen and the 3rd by *Hauptmann* Thomale.

On 1 August 1934 the *Kommando*'s 2nd Battalion was formed under the command of Major Breith. The 3rd and 8th Cavalry Regiments and the 3rd, 5th, and 6th Mechanized Battalions all had to release personnel for the formation of the new battalion. *Oberleutnante* Mildebrath and Hennig left the *Kommando*'s cadre company to join 2nd Battalion. A *Kommando* headquarters was established to provide the two battalions with a unified command. The command personnel of this predecessor of the later regimental headquarters were:

Kommando Headquarters:	*Oberstleutnant* Zuckertort
1st Battalion:	Major Streich
2nd Battalion:	Major Breith

The consolidation of the *Kommando* into *Kampfwagenregiment* 1 took place on 1 October 1934. The regiment's command personnel were:

Commanding Officer:	*Oberstleutnant* Ritter von Radlmeier
1st Battalion:	*Oberstleutnant* Friedrich Kühn
Adjutant:	*Oberleutnant* Klingspor
2nd Battalion:	Maj. Ritter von Thoma
CO 1st Instructional Unit:	*Hauptmann* Materne
CO 2nd Instructional Unit:	*Hauptmann* von Drabich-Wächter
CO 3rd Instructional Unit:	*Hauptmann* Stephan
CO 7th Instructional Unit:	*Hauptmann* Hochbaum

In command of the two training *Kommandos* was the Mechanized Training Headquarters Berlin under *Generalmajor* Fessmann. This training headquarters was roughly equivalent to a panzer brigade headquarters.

During 1934 and 1935 each company had available only a single LaS, a Panzer I light tank chassis without turret. These vehicles were camouflaged as farm tractors. The first Panzer I tanks arrived at the end of 1935, allowing driver training to be added to the program of instruction.

In May 1935 the 4th Cavalry Regiment (Potsdam), the 7th Cavalry Regiment (Breslau), and the 12th Cavalry Regiment (Dresden) were disbanded. Together with the two Mechanized Training *Kommandos* they were used to form the six panzer regiments needed for the first three panzer divisions. At first the new units had neither troops nor tanks.

The Birth of the *Panzertruppe*

The 15 October 1935 was not only the day of birth of the famous 5th Panzer Regiment, but of the first three panzer divisions as well.

1st Panzer Division
  Commanding Officer: *Generalleutnant* Maximilian von Weichs
  Ia: General Staff Major Hans Baehsler
  Garrison: Weimar
2nd Panzer Division
  Commanding Officer: *Oberst* Heinz Guderian
  Ia: General Staff *Hauptmann* Charles de Beaulieu
  Garrison: Würzburg
3rd Panzer Division
  Commanding Officer: *Generalmajor* Ernst Fessmann
  Ia: General Staff *Hauptmann* Hans Röttiger
  Garrison: Berlin

1 November saw *Generalleutnant* Oswald Lutz, the "father of army motorization," become the first *General der Panzertruppe,* and at the same time the first commanding general of the first German panzer corps.

The founding detachment of the *Panzertruppe* was renamed the 5th Panzer Regiment and was moved into the new barracks at Zehrensdorf-Wünsdorf, the first built for the soldiers of a panzer unit. The regiment's command structure was as follows:

5th Panzer Regiment
Commanding Officer:	*Oberst* Zuckertort
Adjutant:	*Oberleutnant* Kühlein
Signals Officer:	*Oberleutnant* Voss
1st Battalion:	Major Streich
Adjutant:	*Oberleutnant* Reidel
Signals Officer:	*Oberleutnant* von Stünzer
1st Company:	*Hauptmann* Kühn
2nd Company:	*Hauptmann* Thomale
3rd Company:	*Hauptmann* Linke
4th Company:	*Hauptmann* Wendenburg
2nd Battalion:	*Oberstleutnant* Breith
Adjutant:	*Oberleutnant* Kühlein
(from 15.10.36)	*Leutnant* von Oertzen
Signals Officer:	*Oberleutnant* Weiss
(from 15.10.36)	*Leutnant* Hofmann
5th Company:	*Hauptmann* Volckheim
6th Company:	*Hauptmann* Schenk
7th Company:	*Hauptmann* Ilgen
8th Company:	*Hauptmann* Wagner

At the time of their formation the first panzer companies had about eight tanks each, but by 1936 this number had risen to about twenty-two. The first Panzer IIs were not introduced until the summer of 1937. With a turret-mounted armament of one 2cm cannon and an MG34 machine gun, it represented a considerable improvement over the Panzer I with its weak armament of two MG08/15 machine guns.

In autumn 1938, Hitler created the new position of "chief of fast troops" and named Heinz Guderian to the post, at the same time promoting him to the rank of *General der Panzertruppe*. Under his command were all armored units, as well as antitank, motorized, and cavalry units. The new command's chief of staff was General Staff Major von le Suire, and its first general staff officer was General Staff *Hauptmann* Röttiger.

More large armored formations—panzer divisions and brigades—were created on 10 November 1938:

> 4th Panzer Division at Würzburg
> 5th Panzer Division at Oppeln

> 4th Panzer Brigade at Stuttgart
> 5th Panzer Brigade at Bamberg
> 6th Panzer Brigade at Würzburg
> 8th Panzer Brigade at Sagan

The newly created panzer regiments were:

> 23rd Panzer Regiment (1st Bn. only) at Mannheim-Schwetzingen
> 31st Panzer Regiment at Königsbrück and Gross-Born
> 35th Panzer Regiment at Bamberg
> 36th Panzer Regiment at Schweinfurt

Also formed were several panzer battalions for the light divisions, which would later be transformed into panzer divisions:

> 65th Panzer Battalion at Sennelager, later Iserlohn
> 66th Panzer Battalion at Eisenach, later Gera
> 67th Panzer Battalion at Gross-Glienicke, later Spremberg

On 1 March 1939 the personnel complement of the *Panzertruppe* was:
In the Field Army:

> 961 officers, 174 civilian officials, 5,444 NCOs, and 16,988 men.

In the Replacement Army:

> 246 officers, 130 civilian officials, 1,608 NCOs, and 9,038 men.

It is clear from these numbers that the panzer divisions, brigades, regiments, and battalions at first existed only on paper or were skeleton formations. The *Panzertruppe*'s 26,000 men was barely enough for two full panzer divisions. Deliveries of tanks, especially the more advanced Panzer III and IV types, were also slow in coming. On 10 May 1940, when the shooting war against Britain and France began, the tank strength of the panzer divisions was:

Panzer I:	1,026—at the front:	523
Panzer 35(t):	143—at the front:	106
Panzer II:	1,079—at the front:	955
Panzer III:	349—at the front:	349
Panzer 38(t):	228—at the front:	228
Panzer IV:	280—at the front:	278
Command panzers:	243—at the front:	135

The German army went to war against France with only 2,574 tanks. When the attack began early on the morning of 10 May 1940, the panzers led the way. A special bulletin released that morning read: "This morning at dawn the German Western Army has launched an attack across Germany's western frontier on a broad front."

The first major tank battle of the Second World War took place three days later between Orp-le-Grand and Hannut. The high rate of fire and fire discipline displayed by the German armored forces decided the battle in their favor.

The next section will discuss the strategic and tactical concepts employed by the *Panzertruppe* during the Second World War and the planning that went into its operations.

Panzer Strategy and Tactics

Armored Strategy and Operational Command

"Will we tie down the panzers to close cooperation with the infantry or will we employ them in open country in a strategic sense to outflank and encircle?

"Will we try to decide a defensive war quickly through the large-scale, concentrated use of the main offensive land weapon—the tank—or will we thoroughly tie down this offensive asset to the slower pace of the infantry and artillery war, ignoring its innate capability for fast, wide-ranging movement, and thus give away in advance any chance of deciding the battle and the war?"

Generaloberst Heinz Guderian, the great tank strategist, had long since decided in favor of the fast solution, the tank. He categorically rejected frittering away the *Panzertruppe*'s strength by assigning small groups of tanks to infantry units.

It was Guderian, supported by his circle of officers, who developed the principles for the operational conduct of an armored war: independent operation, uniform standards of command and training, concentration of forces to break through the enemy's defenses, and flanking attacks aimed at encircling and destroying the enemy's forces.

The strategy developed for this revolutionary new weapon, the command of units over large areas, was described in detail in the army's operational planning for employment of the *Panzertruppe*. This strategy described it as an independent branch of the army which, by carrying out independent operations suited to its unique qualities, was the key to victory in future wars.

Strategic and operational planning merged in Hitler's directive for the conduct of the war. In it he specified that the *Panzertruppe* was to be employed as the main weapon of attack, and not as a "protective shield" or stationary fire front. As the most powerful weapon of attack on land, the *Panzertruppe* was *always* to be used at the focal point of a battle. It was the panzer units that would achieve the decisive breakthrough and open the way for the infantry.

The tank, the most innovative offensive weapon of the First World War, had contributed to Germany's defeat. Now, used in an entirely new way, it was to bring victory for Germany. The next war was to be fought as an armored war. This not only fit the wishes of Germany's leaders, but those of every officer in the newest branch of the armed forces as well. The new panzer divisions, large mechanized units combining all arms, were to be the "heart and soul" of the battle. Their success or failure would decide victory or defeat of the whole. As a result, the panzer units were the decisive land weapon throughout the Second World War. What Germany's planners and strategists had in mind was blitzkrieg, or "lightning war."

The synthesis of German tank strategy was accurately summed up by Guderian in four words: *"Nicht kleckern, sondern klotzen!"*

Literally, this meant "Don't disperse your forces, rather strike hard and quickly!" The Soviets later adopted this strategy, as did the western Allies.

As Germany's strategic planning evolved, the *Panzertruppe* came to be thought of as a weapon of surprise. The speed of the large mechanized units allowed the strategists to base their plans on this element. They were fully aware of the effectiveness of the new weapon conferred by the power of its engine and its armament, range, and cross-country capabilities. What the strategists had in mind was a rapid breakthrough, followed by a drive deep into the enemy's rear, the encirclement of enemy forces, and a resumption of the advance.

To the following masses of infantry would be left the job of clearing any remaining pockets of resistance as well as guarding the flanks and securing supply lines. Assault guns would provide direct fire support to the infantry.

While the infantry was engaged in occupying and securing the area which had been overrun, the tanks would advance to the left and right of the enemy's route of retreat, overtaking and engaging the enemy and destroying or capturing his rear-echelon units. In doing so they would deprive the enemy forces of their supply installations, supply troops, and the supplies themselves.

The commanders of panzer units, from divisions through panzer corps *(Panzerkorps)* and panzer groups *(Panzergruppen),* and later panzer armies, had to adhere to the principles of their great strategist, Guderian. The central thought in the strategy of armored warfare was: "Mobility is the key to victory!"

This was the concept that motivated the men who had enthusiastically embraced the strategy of armored warfare and were now trying to translate it into action. Mobility brought the troops to the enemy. In previous conflicts, when movement was stopped by defensive fire the enemy had to be totally defeated before movement could resume. A lightning strike by massed armored forces and the achieving of surprise—a precondition for success—was an entirely different concept.

During the Second World War, armored attacks relied on movement. Once the first line of defense had been broken, the speed of the advance prevented the enemy from forming second and third lines of defense. The attacking thrust was carried deep into enemy territory. Movement was the key to success of the armored attack and was maintained after penetration and breakthrough of the enemy front had been achieved. The German tank troops and their commanders were firmly determined to exploit and maintain the lead Germany had gained in the field of armored strategy and tactics. They saw the *Panzertruppe* as the "weapon of decision."

The German concept of armored warfare was: assemble and employ armored forces in mass where the decision is to be sought and where the nature of the terrain makes success possible. Victory was to be achieved by rapidly bringing all weapons to bear on the enemy. A decisive success required the defeat of large bodies of enemy forces and their capture (thus preventing their retreat and participation in later battles), and thus required the massed use of armored forces.

The results of such strategic considerations were reflected in the war directives issued by Hitler. The following is an extract from the directive issued before the Polish campaign: "Drive through the enemy center by strong armored forces from Silesia in the direction of the middle Vistula, followed closely by infantry units. Attacks on the Polish wings, one from Slovakia, the other in the 'Polish Corridor,' breakthrough of same, advance into the enemy hinterland, joining of forces from north and south and encirclement of major part of the Polish forces."

The plan of operations was devised by the head of the army high command, *Generaloberst* von Brauchitsch, and his chief of staff, *General der Artillerie* Halder, with no involvement by Hitler. It was based on earlier studies and planning, but also drew heavily on the new strategy of armored warfare.

The plan of operations for the western campaign originated from the chief of staff of Army Group A, *Generalleutnant* Erich von Manstein. Following discussions with leading tank authorities, he formulated Operation *Sichelschnitt* (Sickle Cut). Von Manstein's plan was as follows: "Penetration of a tank-proof forest by nearly all our panzer units with initial objective Amiens-Abbéville. Fastest possible advance by the panzer units in an arc to the coast and the splitting of the Allied forces into two. Subsequent destruction of these two elements in separate actions."

Hitler, who had so far kept himself in the "strategic-political" background, was about to step into the "operational foreground," even though he lacked the necessary knowledge and background.

The Balkan campaign was carried out along lines similar to the Polish and French operations. The plan of operations was devised by *Generaloberst* Halder. "Attack, envelopment and breakthrough. The skilfull employment of fast units will ensure surprise and speed."

The plan of operations for the campaign against Russia was based on express directives from Hitler. He anticipated a breakthrough by three powerful armored spearheads. In the south *Panzergruppe* von Kleist would advance on Kiev. Army Group Center, whose objective was Moscow, was given two *Panzergruppen,* making it the strongest spearhead. Army Group North was assigned *Panzergruppe* Hoeppner. Numerically the weakest spearhead, its objective was Leningrad.

Had the French command recognized in time the significance of the tank in a war of movement, then the French armored forces with their 4,800 tanks—twice the number available to Germany—would have been a much more serious adversary. However, France lacked the strategists, and therefore the strategy, of armored warfare. French tanks were parceled out to the infantry divisions, where they were overrun and eliminated. The German side, on the other hand, planned and carried out a concentrated surprise strike through Sedan toward Amiens and the sea.

In the eyes of the armored strategists, Hitler's halting of the panzer units before Dunkirk, which gave the British Expeditionary Force the chance to escape to England and later return to the European battlefield in 1944, gave away the victory in France and the entire war.

Tactics—New Conclusions and New Measures

The previous section on armored strategy and operations illustrated how strategy, operational considerations, and tactical requirements were bound closely together.

The tactical requirements for the tanks of the *Panzertruppe* can be summed up as follows:

The most important elements were firepower and mobility. Secondary considerations were the effectiveness of the tank's armor and the lowest possible placement of its main armament in the turret, so as to present the lowest possible silhouette.

Technical demands of various kinds followed during the Second World War, resulting in ever more powerful types which eventually replaced the tanks of the early war years. In Hitler's *Memoir and Guidelines on the Conduct of the War in the West* he described the success of the *Panzertruppe* and the *Luftwaffe* in Poland:

> As weapons of attack the *Panzertruppe* and *Luftwaffe* have now reached a level unattained by any other state, and not just in the area of technology. Thanks to their organization and unified command, their operational effectiveness is better assured than in any other state.
>
> In its actions in Poland the *Panzertruppe* has far exceeded the highest expectations. The attack is therefore to be preferred over the defensive as a method of deciding the war.
>
> The *Panzertruppe* must be used in actions for which it is best suited and which hold the greatest promise of success. It is therefore necessary that the strategic forward movement of the army be maintained through the massed breakthrough of weak positions, in order to avoid the development of a stationary front.
>
> It will be the duty of panzer units which have broken through to come to each other's aid.
>
> Since the attack (against France) is to be scheduled for this fall if at all possible, it is absolutely imperative that the putting in order of the panzer and motorized units be pursued with the utmost energy.

Thus did Hitler adopt all of the concepts developed by Guderian and his fellows as his own.

The tank was the most potent weapon in land warfare and

was by its very nature an offensive weapon. Development of specialized tactics for use by the armored forces was therefore of vital importance. One of the primary threats to armored units was the enemy's antitank weapons. It was vital to eliminate these weapons, and it was expected that the *Luftwaffe* would play a major role in this.

One of the most important operational principles for a commander of armored forces was not to commit his most effective weapon prematurely in a support role, or reduce its value by dividing his forces. Only the employment of armored forces en masse, operating independently and taking advantage of their mobility, could determine the time and place of the decisive battle.

It was obvious that this fast, mobile style of warfare and the quick and full exploitation of available firepower required firm and flexible command, if possible from up front with the troops. "Thinking, the issuing of orders and acting all had to match the speed of the engine, otherwise the advantage of the tank's speed would have been lost" (see Munzel, Oskar: *Die deutschen gepanzerten Truppen bis 1945*).

The greatest revolution in command and control came with the advent of radio, which made it possible for unit commanders to issue orders to individual tank commanders through the platoon leaders and unit commanders. By accompanying their units in armored command vehicles, unit commanders were able to recognize changing situations and respond immediately. Senior German panzer commanders, right up to the commanders in chief of army groups, were able to participate directly in an ongoing battle through the use of radio and telephone. Commanders such as *Generaloberst* Guderian and *Generalleutnant* Model paid frequent visits to their front-line troops and became well known to them.

Every tactical move by the commanders of armored forces was intended to bring as many weapons as possible into action at the right place, under favorable conditions, and at the right time.

Good weapons and ammunition together with excellent weapons training allowed German panzer crews to maintain the upper hand over less well trained and equipped opponents.

The success of any tank depended on accurate shooting. The firing process had been so simplified that tanks could quickly suppress enemy fire, thus preserving their own offensive capability. Firing positions were selected which provided the best possible cover, so that the enemy was usually unaware of the tank's presence until it had opened fire.

Rapid, accurate shooting and the successful engagement of tanks and dug-in antitank weapons depended on clear target designation and good fire control. It was the commander's responsibility to provide accurate target information and assign target priority. The commander also selected the type of ammunition to be used, and it was his decision to change targets or cease firing. Poor fire control or slow and imprecise execution could render good tactical leadership worthless.

The tactics of modern armored warfare depended as much on supply and technology as on thorough training. Without fuel, ammunition, and spare parts the best tactics in the world would have been useless. Without timely deliveries of fuel, the fastest tank was helpless. Fuel and ammunition had to be transported close to the battlefield so that tanks could refuel and rearm during pauses in the fighting. Spare parts were a particularly difficult problem, because it was impossible to predict when a component would fail or how quickly it would wear out. This was particularly acute in Russia, where tanks often covered one hundred kilometers or more per day.

Factors such as these illustrate the importance of an efficient supply organization to the success of an armored unit. Repairs were carried out by regimental workshop companies or battalion maintenance units.

Other rear-echelon units provided equipment and clothing as well as rations and medical services, all of which were necessary elements of a successful unit.

Tactical Reconnaissance and Security

The principles of tactical reconnaissance by armored units were initially similar to those of every other unit. Reconnaissance was under the direct control of the unit's tactical leader.

The most important type was battlefield reconnaissance, which was carried out by the light reconnaissance platoons. Associated with this type of reconnaissance was the evaluation of terrain, the resulting information being used by the units in planning their operations.

As the threat of enemy air attack grew, panzer units assumed an increasing responsibility for their own antiaircraft defense, which culminated in the deployment of specialized antiaircraft tanks.

A number of measures were employed to enhance security while the tanks were on the move, such as the use of an advance platoon; support for the lead tank, which was most vulnerable; maintenance of constant radio contact with the advance platoon, so as to relay immediately any important occurrences; and the posting of security forces in the direction of the advance during rest stops. All the while commanders had to bear in mind the old axiom concerning security: "Secure, but don't secure too much! Total forces against the total objective!"

What the German *Panzertruppe* of World War II represented is perhaps best described in the opening sentences of a tank manual produced before the war:

1. A leader is one who makes followers of his troops through his ability, conduct and character.

2. Willingness to accept responsibility is the most outstanding leadership quality. This must not be allowed, however, to lead to arbitrary decisions made without regard for the whole. Priggishness must not be allowed to take the place of obedience, or independence permitted to become arbitrariness.

3. In addition to physical and military training, it is moral and emotional strength which determines a soldier's worth in combat. Increasing this worth is the task of a soldierly education.

4. Comradeship is the tie which binds the troops together in any situation. Each man is responsible not only for himself, but for his comrades as well. Those who are more able or capable must assist and guide the inexperienced and weak. From such a basis grows a feeling of close comradeship, which is as important between leader and soldier as it is between the men of the unit.

5. Battle demands fighters who can think and act independently and who are able to cope with any situation delib-

erately, decisively and coolly, indoctrinated in the belief that success depends on everyone. Every man, from the youngest soldier up, must be expected to employ all his mental and physical strength at all times.

6. The objective must always be to seize the initiative from the enemy. Special training is required in flexibility of command, mobility and speed of the troops, marching ability even in difficult terrain, clever use of camouflage, use of terrain and darkness, and surprise and deception of the enemy.

7. Decisive action remains the first requirement in war. Everyone, the most senior commander as well as the youngest soldier, must always be aware that neglect and errors of omission are a greater burden than a mistake in the choice of means.

Panzers in Action

The foundations on which the success of the German panzer arm was based were a clear and firm command, efficient training, and a core of experienced crews. Additional factors in its success were the tempering of commanders and crews in battle and the application of lessons learned in action.

In order to ensure success, every armored attack required thorough preparation. Briefings and exchanges of views with all participants had to be held and arrangements made with the other arms which were to provide support. All reconnaissance and intelligence information was evaluated prior to the attack.

Variations in the method of attack, flexible command in battle, deception and confusion of the enemy, the element of surprise: all were basic requirements for success. Other measures employed by armor commanders were diversionary attacks, assaults against the enemy's flanks and rear, and the use of smoke.

Attacks against enemy tanks and antitank defenses called for the cunning of a hunter and the efficient use of terrain in their planning and execution.

Precise concentration of the panzer unit was a necessary requirement, especially when smaller or weaker units were involved. The employment of individual tanks was avoided, even on security duties, where a minimum of two vehicles was recommended. Operations at less than company strength generally led to heavy losses that were in no way comparable to the results achieved.

The timing of an armored attack was usually planned to begin as night was giving way to day, and not the reverse. Similarly, attacks were planned not to face into the sun.

Even when forced onto the defensive, tanks were to be used in an offensive manner. In this type of situation the normal assembly procedure was dispensed with, as this only presented the enemy with an opportunity to bring the assembly area under massed artillery fire.

Great pains were taken to identify mistakes made by panzer units and implement measures to avoid similar errors in the future. Two of the most common mistakes were the employment of individual tanks at the front as mobile "bunkers," and the use of tanks as support weapons for the infantry in the role of escorts for combat patrols or as armored weapons carriers for reconnaissance purposes.

Any operation begun without a thorough scouting of the terrain and the necessary preparation carried a high risk of failure.

The independent operation of a panzer company without infantry support was generally avoided. Attacks against a prepared enemy without artillery support were usually fatal. Bunching up of the infantry behind the tanks was to be avoided, and it was vital that the infantry exploit any success by the tanks.

Another vital consideration was ensuring the availability of supply and repair facilities, so as to keep breakdowns to a minimum.

With the introduction of the Tiger heavy tank, several guidelines were added which applied only to this vehicle. Initial experience with the Tiger showed that it was no more suitable to the role of a mobile "bunker" than other tanks. Neither was it suited to strengthening the "backbone" of the infantry in the main line of resistance. The most suitable role for the Tiger was as a mobile reserve. Ideally they were held in concentration just behind the front, near the location of a likely enemy penetration. From there they launched counterattacks against penetrations by enemy forces together with grenadiers and assault guns and in close cooperation with the positional infantry and artillery.

Thanks to its outstanding weapon, the Tiger was able to engage the enemy from a great distance. Commanders who employed Tigers in situations where they could not make use of their long-ranging weapons were robbing them of their greatest advantage.

Employing its much-feared "eighty-eight," the Tiger could pin down the enemy and provide decisive relief to the infantry. The infantry, on the other hand, kept enemy tank-killing squads away from the Tigers and provided cover during the repair of minor battle damage in the field. *Pioniers* cleared lanes through minefields, thus assuring a rapid advance.

The assignment of Tigers to rearguard duties was not recommended. It was always difficult, if not impossible, to recover damaged or broken-down machines under pressure from the enemy. Whenever possible, Tigers were to be transported to the front by rail. In doing so they arrived at the front fully fueled and armed, ready to be used as a mobile reserve.

The previously mentioned rules concerning preparation were even more vital when a Tiger unit was concerned. Due to the vehicle's great weight, thorough scouting of the terrain was vital. As with other tanks, swamps and streams were impassable obstacles. The commander of a Tiger unit had to brief his subordinates and tank commanders thoroughly. Any overhasty operation might lead to the loss or partial destruction of one or more of the heavy tanks, which were always in short supply and therefore especially valuable.

Tiger commanders were trained to withdraw or turn away immediately upon encountering a minefield, antitank ditch, or other obstacle. Remaining stationary only presented the tanks as "sitting ducks" and served no useful purpose.

The Panzer Battalion as a Combat Unit

For tactical purposes the basic panzer unit was the battalion, and success depended on its efficient deployment.

The standard battalion consisted of three or four companies.

Initially one company was designated as a medium company, equipped with tanks armed with a 7.5cm gun. Its task was to support the light companies in battle. Not until later in the war, when tank-versus-tank fighting became the rule and maximum firepower was necessary, were the battalions equipped with the same type of tank. Due to fluctuating production figures, panzer regiments had one battalion equipped with Panzer IVs and another with Panthers or even assault guns.

The panzer company's normal strength of twenty-two vehicles was later reduced to seventeen, and for Tiger companies to only fourteen. Late in the war, battalion headquarters consisted of only two or three four-wheel-drive vehicles and a few motorcycle messengers.

The "command group" was part of the battalion headquarters and organizationally was subordinate to the headquarters company. It consisted of two command panzers for the commander as well as the adjutant and signals officer. One of these officers manned the commander's vehicle when he was away from the unit. Also part of the "command group" was the battalion medical officer.

Each panzer battalion included a reconnaissance and a combat engineer *(Pionier)* platoon. These fulfilled the roles of traffic control, scouting, and reconnaissance. The engineer sections were motorized, initially in trucks and later in armored half-tracks. Within the battalion the engineers proved extremely versatile and were a valuable asset.

The role of the flak platoon was the protection of the supply units, but also of the combat echelon if required. When the unit was at rest or in quarters, the platoon assumed the antiaircraft defense role for the entire unit.

In battle the battalion commander could exercise his command through verbal orders or radio. The battalion adjutant, who usually accompanied the commanding officer, assisted as a sort of tactical aide. The signals officer and operations officer provided expert advice in the areas of communications and supply matters. The battalion medical officer and battalion engineer completed the small circle responsible for the men and weapons of the battalion.

The company commander led his unit by radio. In cases where his unit consisted of only a few vehicles or where vehicles were committed individually, he issued individual orders to each tank. Normally he led his company into battle until it had deployed. When battle was joined he moved to a position that offered the best view or to where his presence was required. His attitude and personal example were decisive factors in the results achieved by his commanders and crews. As the war went on his example and those of the platoon leaders became ever more important.

The platoon leader was responsible for the combat readiness of his unit, assisted by his section leaders.

The tank commander was responsible for his vehicle. It was his job to weigh all the tactical and technical considerations before acting. This meant, for example, that he had to use care in selecting a favorable position for his tank from which he could engage the target.

The commander had to remain alert to the needs of his driver, providing him with information on other tanks and obstacles. As well, he had to provide the driver with precise target information and order necessary course changes. In battle, however, experienced drivers often acted without waiting for orders when the vehicle came under fire from enemy tanks or antitank guns.

Close cooperation within the tank was a matter of life and death. Actions had to be swift and sure, and each man had to be able to carry out his function "in his sleep." Every member of the crew was expected—where possible—to help scan the battlefield and assist the tank's commander.

Tank crews formed close fighting teams. The unnecessary removal of any member of the crew was to be avoided. It was these close-knit fighting teams that allowed the German panzer arm to survive in conditions of frequent enemy numerical superiority during the course of World War II.

The success of the German panzer arm was largely based on its adoption of the latest strategic and tactical concepts, and the thorough tactical and operational preparation of its leaders, who developed their concept of armored warfare based on the principles laid down by the great experts.

The panzer units fought with great bravery to the very end; nevertheless, they were unable to alter the eventual outcome.

In conclusion, the words of *Generaloberst* Heinz Guderian from 1944: "The tank is a weapon of attack. They must be led with vigor and their thrust carried deep into the heart of the enemy positions.

"I am certain that the panzer officer corps will always remember its proud conduct during the past four years of the war and will act similarly in the future."—Guderian.

Appendix

I. Panzer Army Headquarters (AOK)

Panzer AOK 1: (formed from Headquarters, XXII Panzer Corps).

Panzer AOK 2: (from Headquarters, XIX Panzer Corps).

Panzer AOK 3: (from Headquarters, XV Panzer Corps).

Panzer AOK 4: (from Headquarters, XVI Panzer Corps).

Panzer AOK 5: (from Headquarters, XC Panzer Corps, Tunisia).

SS-AOK 6: (from Headquarters, LXVII Panzer Corps, I and II SS-Panzer Corps).

Panzer AOK 11: (formed from various units on 28 January 1945).

Panzer AOK 12: (formed on 6 April 1945 on orders from Hitler. From Headquarters, XXXIX Panzer Corps and XXXXI Panzer Corps. Also Headquarters, XXXXVIII Panzer Corps).

II. German Tank Construction 1939–45

The actual production of tanks never equaled the requested totals and production targets set by the OKW.

Although the requested production figure was 600 tanks per month (including assault guns), actual production remained less than 200 per month.

The "Speer Report" broke down tank production year by year as follows:

1940:   2,154 tanks and assault guns.

1942:   9,287 tanks and assault guns.

1944: 27,340 tanks and assault guns.

These figures included all armored vehicles; self-propelled antitank guns, armored cars, and heavy infantry guns on tank chassis.

Losses of armored vehicles of all types were:

1/12/1943–30/6/1944:	3,631 vehicles.
30/6/1944–31/7/1944:	4,674 vehicles.
31/7/1944–30/9/1944:	5,569 vehicles.
30/9/1944–31/10/1944:	5,463 vehicles.
Total:	24,963 vehicles.

III. U.S. Production of Armored Vehicles

1939–45:	88,000 tanks of all types.
Of these:	57,027 were medium tanks.
Of these:	49,234 were M4 Sherman tanks.

Total production of armored vehicles in 1944: 90,000.

IV. Armored Units of the Red Army (on 1 April 1945)

25 tank corps with 5,000 tanks.
13 mechanized corps with 2,600 tanks.
60 tank brigades with 4,140 tanks.

There were as many as 160 independent tank regiments with 6,400 tanks.

The official figures for annual Soviet tank production is 30,000 tanks of all types. German tank experts are dubious about this figure.

Index